Darwin-Inspired Learning

NEW DIRECTIONS IN MATHEMATICS AND SCIENCE EDUCATION

Volume 28

Series Editors

Wolff-Michael Roth, *University of Victoria, Canada*
Lieven Verschaffel, *University of Leuven, Belgium*

Editorial Board

Angie Calabrese-Barton, *Teachers College, New York, USA*
Pauline Chinn, *University of Hawaii, USA*
Brian Greer, *Portland State University, USA*
Lyn English, *Queensland University of Technology*
Terezinha Nunes, *University of Oxford, UK*
Peter Taylor, *Curtin University, Perth, Australia*
Dina Tirosh, *Tel Aviv University, Israel*
Manuela Welzel, *University of Education, Heidelberg, Germany*

Scope

Mathematics and science education are in a state of change. Received models of teaching, curriculum, and researching in the two fields are adopting and developing new ways of thinking about how people of all ages know, learn, and develop. The recent literature in both fields includes contributions focusing on issues and using theoretical frames that were unthinkable a decade ago. For example, we see an increase in the use of conceptual and methodological tools from anthropology and semiotics to understand how different forms of knowledge are interconnected, how students learn, how textbooks are written, etcetera. Science and mathematics educators also have turned to issues such as identity and emotion as salient to the way in which people of all ages display and develop knowledge and skills. And they use dialectical or phenomenological approaches to answer ever arising questions about learning and development in science and mathematics.

The purpose of this series is to encourage the publication of books that are close to the cutting edge of both fields. The series aims at becoming a leader in providing refreshing and bold new work—rather than out-of-date reproductions of past states of the art—shaping both fields more than reproducing them, thereby closing the traditional gap that exists between journal articles and books in terms of their salience about what is new. The series is intended not only to foster books concerned with knowing, learning, and teaching in school but also with doing and learning mathematics and science across the whole lifespan (e.g., science in kindergarten; mathematics at work); and it is to be a vehicle for publishing books that fall between the two domains—such as when scientists learn about graphs and graphing as part of their work.

Darwin-Inspired Learning

Edited by

Carolyn J. Boulter
University of London, Institute of Education, UK

Michael J. Reiss
University of London, Institute of Education, UK

and

Dawn L. Sanders
Department of Pedagogical, Curricular and Professional Studies, University of Gothenburg, Sweden

SENSE PUBLISHERS
ROTTERDAM/BOSTON/TAIPEI

A C.I.P. record for this book is available from the Library of Congress.

ISBN: 978-94-6209-831-2 (paperback)
ISBN: 978-94-6209-832-9 (hardback)
ISBN: 978-94-6209-833-6 (e-book)

Published by: Sense Publishers,
P.O. Box 21858,
3001 AW Rotterdam,
The Netherlands
https://www.sensepublishers.com/

Cover picture: 'Going for a thinking walk' – students on Charles Darwin's Sandwalk at Down House. © IntoUniversity

Printed on acid-free paper

All Rights Reserved © 2015 Sense Publishers

No part of this work may be reproduced, stored in a retrieval system, or transmitted in any form or by any means, electronic, mechanical, photocopying, microfilming, recording or otherwise, without written permission from the Publisher, with the exception of any material supplied specifically for the purpose of being entered and executed on a computer system, for exclusive use by the purchaser of the work.

TABLE OF CONTENTS

Foreword   ix
Rosemary & Peter Grant

Acknowledgements   xi

Open Window   xiii
Ruth Padel

Introduction: Darwin-Inspired Learning   1
Michael J. Reiss, Carolyn J. Boulter & Dawn L. Sanders

Darwin's Heritage

1. Entering Darwin's Life   15
   Randal Keynes

2. The World of Downe: Charles Darwin's Living Laboratory   25
   Dawn L. Sanders

3. 'Pester Them with Letters': Using Darwin's Correspondence in the Classroom: The Darwin Correspondence Project   35
   Sally Stafford

Developing a Sense of Place

4. Learning in Cultivated Gardens and Other Outdoor Landscapes   47
   Paul Davies, Dawn L. Sanders & Ruth Amos

5. Learning to Read Nature to Understand the Natural World and How It Works   59
   Ola Magntorn

6. Walking with Darwin in Rio de Janeiro: Learning about Cultural and Historical Values   73
   Sandra Escovedo Selles

7. Getting the Kids Involved – Darwin's Paternal Example   89
   James Moore

TABLE OF CONTENTS

   8. Using Collections of Darwiniana in Darwin-Inspired Learning   107
      Ruth Barlow

The Importance of Active Hands-on Enquiry

   9. Object Lessons in Evidence-Based Learning   117
      Mike Corbishley

  10. Sailing the Backyard *Beagle*: Darwin-Inspired Voyages of
      Discovery in Backyard and Schoolyard   131
      James T. Costa

  11. Naming the Living World: From the Infant's Perception of
      Animacy to a Child's Species Concept   147
      Stephen P. Tomkins & Sue Dale Tunnicliffe

  12. Scientific Enquiry: Searching for and Interpreting
      Evidence to Construct Arguments   165
      Shirley Simon

  13. Using Darwin to Teach Earth Science: The Development of the
      Darwin Workshop Methodology   177
      Peter Kennett & Chris King

Critical Thinking about What and How We Know

  14. Darwin the Scientist: Working Scientifically   199
      James D. Williams

  15. Teaching Evolution in Schools: A Matter of Controversy?   211
      Ralph Levinson

  16. The 'Attentive and Reflective Observer': Darwin-Inspired
      Learning and the Teaching of Evolution   221
      Neil Ingram

  17. Darwinian Case Studies Within a Post-16 Programme
      for the History and Philosophy of Science: The Perspectives on
      Science Course   237
      John L. Taylor

  18. They Really do Eat Insects: Learning from Charles Darwin's
      Experiments with Carnivorous Plants   243
      Aaron M. Ellison

19. DNA Barcoding Darwin's Meadow: A Twenty-first-century
    Botanical Inventory at Historic Down House   257
    Karen E. James

Interdisciplinary Studies

20. Darwin's Barnacles: Learning from Collections   273
    Miranda Lowe & Carolyn J. Boulter

21. Darwin-Inspired Drama: Towards One Culture in
    Teaching and Learning Science   285
    Martin Braund

22. Evolutionary Narratives: Darwin's Botany and US
    Periodical Literature   299
    Tina Gianquitto

23. Darwin in Natural Science School Textbooks
    in the Nineteenth Century in England and Spain   311
    Margarita Hernández-Laille

Developing Work with Learners

24. Writing and Representing to Learn in Science   327
    Vaughan Prain

25. Routes to Conceptual Change in
    Teaching and Learning about Evolution: Experiences with
    Students Aged between 11 and 16 Years   339
    Emma Newall

26. Developing a Model for Post-16 Teaching and Learning 353
    Carolyn J. Boulter & Emma Newall

27. Transformation of the School
    Grounds for Darwin-Inspired Learning   367
    Susan Johnson

28. Transition: Darwin-Inspired Learning Approaches at
    Crucial Junctures in Science Education   383
    Susan Johnson

29. Staging Darwin's Science through Biographical Narratives 399
    Dawn L. Sanders

TABLE OF CONTENTS

Epilogue: Transforming the Ordinary 411
Dawn L. Sanders, Carolyn J. Boulter & Michael J. Reiss

About the Contributors 425

Index 431

ROSEMARY & PETER GRANT

FOREWORD

Through the introduction of Darwin's inspirational writings, this important book, *Darwin-Inspired Learning* will create an atmosphere among students in which scientific and creative imagination flourishes. Students will be encouraged to pose their own questions and be allowed to discover their own answers through the formation of their own hypotheses and experiments. There can be no better guide to the success of this approach than an in-depth examination of Darwin's writings, his books, notebooks, and letters. Even today his writings are a pleasure to read, his descriptive passages poetic in their elegance, and his acute scientific observations and analytical logic exciting. They reveal his intense desire for a full and accurate understanding of a phenomenon by raising questions and posing explanations (hypotheses). Darwin, the writer, talks to the reader, but in fact he is talking to himself, out loud, in print.

Darwin was an exceptionally talented and acute observer, whether it was describing in detail the anatomy of a marine invertebrate, the reproductive parts of a plant, the ecology and behaviour of a bird or mammal, or an unusual rock formation. A characteristic of all his writings and particularly prevalent in his notebooks is his analytical approach when confronting a problem. Evidence is considered from all angles: the geographical location, geological formation, climatic variation, the flora and fauna, in other words the complete context of the problem. His hypotheses, always subjected to a lengthy process of deliberation and contemplation, were often followed by experiments. When experiments were not available he tried to check his ideas for consistency with other facts. And being intensely aware of the dangers of being led astray by a favoured hypothesis, he constantly questioned the implications of his findings. In his notebooks, he sometimes uses the Spanish *cuidado*, careful, as a warning when in danger of being carried away by his enthusiasm.

Another striking feature is the immaculate organisation of his field notes, especially remarkable for a man suffering constant sickness at sea, subjecting himself to long hikes over hot lava in the Galapagos and climbs up to 3700 metres in the Andes. The date and location head each page and there is a margin for afterthoughts, comments and additions.

FOREWORD

This book comes at a propitious time. Today we face immense global challenges, both environmentally and socially. To come up with imaginative solutions to our problems we need to foster the magic of curiosity-driven research in both arts and science in our students, children and grandchildren. There is no better source of inspiration than the writings of Charles Darwin.

Rosemary & Peter Grant
Princeton University
USA

ACKNOWLEDGEMENTS

The editors are very grateful to Karen Goldie-Morrison who kindly volunteered to copyedit the entire manuscript and did so wonderfully, to Stephen Keynes for his leadership of the Charles Darwin Trust and to the many others who have supported the Trust and helped bring this book to fruition.

RUTH PADEL

OPEN WINDOW

He's glad that she is glad. He has not publicly
rejected the idea of a Creator.

Frederick Temple, soon to be
Archbishop of Canterbury,

says you can square evolution with God.
God operates through the slow work

of natural cause. 'Even better
than making the world,' says a letter

from Charles Kingsley, novelist,
'God makes the world make itself.'

He watches her open a window, for air,
and smile at Lenny. Religion. A burned heart

in its thorns. A basket of molten glass.
A rock face shot with quartz

on which the sun shines
as it rises, lighting the rock to fire.

Down House, Kent 1860

MICHAEL J. REISS, CAROLYN J. BOULTER & DAWN L. SANDERS

INTRODUCTION

Darwin-Inspired Learning

This book is both a celebration and a clarion call. It is a celebration of all that has been done by the Charles Darwin Trust and others to enhance education by drawing on Darwin's life and ways of working. It is a clarion call because of the editors' and authors' beliefs that there is still much to be done.

There are many reasons why Darwin is an invaluable resource for curriculum and pedagogy. For one thing, of course, he is the author of *On the origin of species*, one of the most important scientific books ever produced and perhaps the only one of such importance that can still profitably be read by non-experts and experts alike. But there is more to Darwin than the theory of evolution by natural selection. While the theory of evolution features in this book, many chapters make only limited reference to it. Instead they draw on other aspects of Darwin's life and work.

While Darwin's life – his academic shortcomings at school and university, the *Beagle* voyage, his views on religion and slavery, the wealth of information we have about his large family – mean that it is relatively easy to interest students in him, it is his ways of working, along with the theory of evolution by natural selection, that make him so suitable a resource for education, especially science education.

For a start there is the fact that *On the origin of species* is really one long argument – and the importance of argumentation is increasingly recognised in education (Erduran & Jiménez-Aleixandre, 2007; Walton, 2013). Related to this is the fact that evolution as an historical science, both biological and geological, provides a useful counterbalance to the paradigm of experimental physics. While Darwin was an outstanding experimentalist, he combined this with acute powers of observation and a tremendous ability to synthesise huge amounts of information, producing general laws as a consequence. In this he was aided by a veritable army, male and female, amateur and professional, of correspondents. In addition, Darwin was a genius at devising simple instruments from household materials and in the richness with which he reported his findings, especially his book *The expression of the emotions in man and animals* (Darwin, 1872), can be said to have anticipated aspects of multi-modality by over a century.

Of course, this book is not intended as hagiography and there is always the risk of simplification when historical figures are used in science education – few science teachers or educators are experts in the history of science. Nevertheless, editing this volume has confirmed in us the belief that, at the very least, Darwin's life and ways of working are a rich repository on which all those concerned to improve science education can draw.

The three of us have known each other for many years but the origins of this book are in the roles we have played in the Charles Darwin Trust. Carolyn Boulter and Dawn Sanders are two of the Trust's education consultants, having produced many curriculum resources and run countless workshops for the Trust. Michael Reiss is one of the Trust's trustees. The three of us were much heartened by the response we received when we approached potential contributors. Practically everyone enthusiastically agreed and produced their draft chapters in good time.

DARWIN'S HERITAGE

In Chapter 1, Randal Keynes, great-great-grandson of Charles Darwin and a trustee of the Charles Darwin Trust, provides a personal perspective on Darwin the scientist and his relevance for education. Darwin's life is traced from his time as a schoolboy through his university years, the *Beagle* voyage, his subsequent six years in London, his move with Emma to Down House, the decade spent on barnacles, his work on 'the species question' and his many years of experimentation. Keynes argues that Darwin's ways of working can be offered to students as an inspiration for an imaginative, creative and exciting approach to the life sciences in school classrooms and the world outside.

Dawn Sanders in Chapter 2 sees Down House and its surroundings as Darwin's living laboratory. Here, Darwin drew on every resource to hand – even the hair from Emma's head and whalebone (baleen) from one of her corsets. Furthermore, the outdoor, living laboratory of Downe connected Darwin not just to contemporaneous scientists but to gardeners, pigeon-fanciers and others in an extended social world. Despite his poor health, which meant that he rarely went further than he could walk in two to three hours, Sanders notes how the diversity offered by the local flora, fauna and habitats (both semi-natural and human-made) gave him opportunities to make the repeated experiments and observations needed for his work.

Cambridge University Library is home to the Darwin Correspondence Project, a unique undertaking to research and publish all of Darwin's 15,000 surviving letters. In Chapter 3, Sally Stafford describes how the project has worked in partnership with selected secondary schools to develop a series of online learning resources based on Darwin's correspondence. Through the letters we learn about Darwin as a person, his family life, his friends and peers, his ways of working, how he conducted his research and his scientific methods. As Stafford points out, the letters also show Darwin's almost child-like enthusiasm for every organism that he encountered and his enduring fascination with the natural world. Stafford provides three case studies, one in English, one in history and one in science, to show how secondary students can be both intrigued and inspired by his letters.

INTRODUCTION

DEVELOPING A SENSE OF PLACE

In Chapter 4, Paul Davies, Dawn Sanders and Ruth Amos highlight the role cultivated and other outdoor landscapes can play in developing children's understanding of the living world. They discuss how these can offer access to authentic environments for science and thus provide opportunities to see and actively participate in the discourses of 'real science' by using the tools and language of specific science disciplines. Furthermore, such environments can provide creative ways of learning and thinking together, which they illustrate by a case study of a residential biology field trip. Drawing on Hodgson Burnett's *The secret garden* (undercited in science education), Davies, Sanders and Amos also argue for more space for play – both in botanic gardens and school grounds.

Ola Magntorn argues in Chapter 5 that the notion of 'reading nature', i.e. the ability to recognise organisms and relate them to other organisms and to material cycling and energy flow in a specific habitat, is central to ecology. Reading nature is therefore an important component of ecological literacy. Magntorn goes on to argue that in many ways Darwin was the first person to read nature in this way and that students too can be taught to read nature. He illustrates this with a number of case histories including one where primary school students (aged 10 to 12 years) were helped to read a river ecosystem by focusing on a small freshwater shrimp *Gammarus pulex* and its ecology. This helped the students to understand the river ecosystem by starting with a single organism and gradually building up from it.

Travelling has long been seen as a great way of finding oneself. In Chapter 6, Sandra Selles explores the teaching and learning possibilities of two projects inspired by Darwin's manuscript records of his three-month visit to Rio de Janeiro in 1832. The more recent of these projects took place in 2008 and entailed a group of teachers, science educators, scientists, journalists and students following, over four days, a journey the 23 year-old Darwin took near Rio 176 years earlier. It is clear that not only did the project help many of the people on the route to learn about Darwin and his ideas about evolution and slavery, it also helped them to appreciate the importance of these places for his thinking.

Darwin had ten children and in Chapter 7 James Moore explores how their lives were affected by their father. The children of any age seem to have childhoods that are remarkable by our standards but Charles' and Emma's were especially distinctive. All of them grew up with their father working at home, many of them during his barnacle years. 'Then where does he do his barnacles?' one of them famously enquired on visiting a neighbour but seeing no dissecting table or microscope in his study. Once the barnacles were gone, their father settled some 90 fancy pigeons into two new garden lofts. At the same time Darwin began assembling a Noah's Ark of other exotic animal breeds, or their carcases, from all over the world. Poultry, puppies, rabbits and other creatures were used to build up an encyclopaedia of evidence for his 'big book' showing that domestic and farmyard species varied. Each differed slightly from individual to individual and the differences had been artificially selected by breeders to create new 'varieties' that if found in the wild would be classed as new species, thus mimicking natural selection. It is unsurprising that several of the boys achieved scientific distinction. The girls had the education considered appropriate at the time – very little – though Henrietta gradually became her father's in-house editor.

Darwin had a great belief in the power of observing things for oneself and in Chapter 8 Ruth Barlow demonstrates the value of this principle. While assisting in the delivery of courses with the Charles Darwin Trust, she found that students, no matter what their age, responded enthusiastically to contact with original artefacts from Darwin's life. Among the artefacts owned by the Charles Darwin Trust are many books by Darwin and his followers, scientific collections, such as Charles's own collection of beetles, and oddities like the slide that Charles had a local carpenter make to fit over the main staircase at Down House so that his children could play indoors on rainy days – which, as Barlow notes, is hardly the act of a typically stern Victorian father, which Charles certainly wasn't. Barlow goes on to show how a first edition of *On the origin of species*, whether viewed in the hand or online, can be used for teaching, as can Darwin's 'worm-stone micrometer' and his many specimens.

THE IMPORTANCE OF ACTIVE HANDS-ON ENQUIRY

In Chapter 9, Mike Corbishley reviews the ways in which evidence-based learning has developed since Darwin's time. In most schools in England at that time learning was by rote. The important subjects were the three Rs and scripture. Charles Darwin was not happy with the emphasis in the public schools (i.e. the famous fee-paying, independent schools) on classics and all but the eldest of his five sons were sent to Clapham Grammar School, which had been founded in 1834 because the headmaster was an enthusiastic supporter of the sciences. Darwin was a geologist before he was a biologist and he was well aware of developments in archaeological research, in particular the establishment of a chronology for prehistoric times based on scientific analysis and fieldwork. Corbishley goes on to show how archaeology teaching, whether in schools or outside of schools, can manifest a careful examination of evidence and respect for objects of which Darwin would have approved.

E. O. Wilson once memorably urged readers to explore the rich but often overlooked diversity of life found close at hand, as opposed to exotic locales, by taking their own 'Magellanic voyage of discovery' around the trunk of a single backyard tree. Taking a cue from Wilson, James Costa, in Chapter 10, encourages readers to emulate Darwin's voyage of discovery aboard his 'ship on the Downs' – Down House. Darwin's bustling home and its environs was his refuge and inspiration, its study, garden, meadows and woodlands the setting for an astonishing range of laboratory and field studies. As Costa says, Darwin's experiments and related observational investigations are so varied that they can be replicated, or adapted, for just about any age group and interest: behaviour, morphology, biogeography, plant growth, physiology and more.

INTRODUCTION

Charles Darwin was fascinated by child development and pioneered this field with scientific observations of his own children. In Chapter 11, Stephen Tomkins and Sue Dale Tunnicliffe trace how children recognise life and then name and categorise it. At six months of age babies are more startled by, and follow visually, an object that has independent movement unrelated to any other causality. This early knowledge of animacy develops so that by the time a child is six or seven years of age it begins to realise the irreversibility of being dead and inevitability of living things dying. Alongside such developing knowledge is a developing language in which to form and express such thoughts. Tomkins and Tunnicliffe conclude that Darwin's own childhood resonates with our present knowledge about the development of biological cognition.

Fossil hunting is a popular pastime. In Chapter 12, Shirley Simon describes her own experiences of such fossil hunting and relates this to scientific enquiry, both the kind in which Darwin engaged and the kind that science teachers try to foster in school. She notes that what was special about Darwin was what he chose to observe, how he asked questions about his observations and his ability to answer these questions. Simon argues that enquiry in school science essentially includes the intentional process of diagnosing problems, critiquing experiments, distinguishing alternatives, planning investigations, researching conjectures, searching for information, constructing models, debating with peers and forming coherent arguments. Each of these processes, she asserts, can be addressed through structured activities with students, but can present challenges for teachers who are more familiar with teaching about established scientific knowledge. Simon goes on to critique standard approaches to teaching about evolution, and suggests how science teaching can better develop enquiry and skills of argumentation.

In the final chapter in this section, Chapter 13, Peter Kennett and Chris King describe how the Earth Science Education Unit (ESEU) was formed in 1999 to provide a hands-on and interactive style of Continuing Professional Development for school science teachers and trainee (pre-service) teachers in the university sector. They go on to outline the content of a 1½ hour workshop on 'Charles Darwin, the Geologist', which they produced for the 2009 celebrations. The workshop begins with an 'icebreaker' activity that takes the form of a Darwin Quiz. Ten activities are then laid out on a 'circus' basis, where delegates are invited to carry out one or two activities only, to read the associated 'Darwin Connection' material and then to demonstrate their activity in the plenary session. A further eight activities are laid out for brief inspection and five more are described in an accompanying booklet but not displayed. The finale is a party popper 'volcanic eruption', which Kennett and King think Darwin would have loved, since he spent so much time in active seismic and volcanic regions and was well aware of their unpredictability.

CRITICAL THINKING ABOUT WHAT AND HOW WE KNOW

In Chapter 14, James Williams uses the examples from Darwin's theory of coral atoll formation (a triumph of his), his explanation of the then puzzling natural feature of 'parallel roads' in the highland valley of Glen Roy (a rare failure of his) and his painstaking collection of facts to support his theory of evolution alongside his later work on the movement of plants to show that science and 'the scientific method', far from being one approach can be conducted in different ways, from theory building to theory confirming. Williams goes on to show how the theory of evolution is predictive, thus fulfilling one of the central features of a scientific theory. He concludes that by examining how Darwin developed and worked as a scientist and looking in detail not just at his theory of evolution but also his other work as a geologist, we can discern various aspects of working scientifically that are helpful in explaining the nature of science to students.

The theory of evolution is often said to be 'controversial'. In Chapter 15, Ralph Levinson examines what precisely is required for something to be controversial. He points out that there are different types of controversy. These differences can be summarised as follows: differences where matters can be settled one way or the other when sufficient evidence can be available; differences of priority or significance; differences through meaning of a concept or term; differences of personal, communal or social interest; differences about a whole range of fundamental value positions. Levinson goes on to consider what science teachers might do when faced with students who refuse to countenance evolution as an explanation for the diversity of life. He notes that in his experience there are two main strategies often employed: the first is to avoid active teaching of the topic altogether and remind students of relevant parts of the textbooks to read; the second is to announce that this has to be learned for the examination and avoid any discussion. Levinson considers both to be understandable responses but unsatisfactory and likens the divide between science and creationism to a hazardous border that requires careful negotiation.

As Neil Ingram notes in Chapter 16, misconceptions in understanding evolution are common. Furthermore, there are evident political and religious implications for the evolution of life through a struggle for existence. In spite of the overwhelming evidence for evolution, it remains a controversial idea for many people. Ingram reviews common misconceptions about evolution and then examines how evolution and religion intersect. He concludes that the emphasis in science teaching should be on the evidence for the processes of evolution, and that discussion of ultimate causes should be discussed elsewhere (such as in religious studies lessons).

In Chapter 17, John Taylor outlines the 'Perspectives on Science' course, a course in the history and philosophy of science for 16-18 year-old students, and then describes how Darwin's life and work provide material for one of the major historical case studies in the course. The course was designed to promote discussion and debate of historical and philosophical questions associated with science and to make such debate a recognised part of the curriculum. It is now taught in schools and colleges as a designed programme for the 'Extended Project Qualification', which offers students the opportunity to engage in research and produce university-style dissertations. The emphasis throughout the course is on encouraging students to think for themselves. Students' attention is drawn to the community of scientists

INTRODUCTION

working at the same time as Darwin, such as Wallace, Cuvier, Lyell, Huxley, Hooker and Wilberforce, and to their interactions with Darwin himself. The idea of science as a social activity implies the possibility of conflict, or at least tension, and this is explored in the first activity of the evolution case study, entitled 'Darwin's dilemma'. This activity invites students to consider how they would advise Darwin to respond to the famous letter about natural selection that he received in 1858 from Alfred Russel Wallace.

Before Darwin, no botanist appreciated the significance of the insects often found on carnivorous plants. As Aaron Ellison relates in Chapter 18, it was Charles Darwin who used keen observations and literally hundreds of carefully designed experiments (Darwin, 1875) to demonstrate conclusively that these plants actively attract, trap, kill and digest insects and other small animals. Subsequent research has supported many of Darwin's conclusions about how carnivorous plants 'work' and shown how natural selection has led repeatedly to carnivory in a number of unrelated plant lineages. Ellison points out how good scientists are always trying to disprove their pet hypotheses. Scientific understanding advances most rapidly when existing explanations for observed phenomena are found wanting and new explanations are proposed and rigorously tested. The experiments described by Darwin in his work on carnivorous plants continue to provide an inspiring example of the inherent scepticism of science and of the power of such scepticism to lead to new knowledge, and a deeper understanding of the world around us.

In the summer of 1855 Charles Darwin surveyed the 13-acre hay meadow (Great Pucklands) near Down House with the help of Miss Thorley, his children's governess. As Karen James points out in Chapter 19, the survey was perhaps among the first intentional, comprehensive species counts in a geographically defined area. In an age when rare specimens were prized above all, Darwin's aim was radical: to identify all of the plant species growing on a small, unremarkable plot. During the summers of 2005, 2006 and 2007 a team from the Natural History Museum in London re-surveyed Great Pucklands meadow. The aims of the re-survey were to detect any changes in species number and diversity in the meadow since 1855, and to pilot and optimise procedures for high-throughput botany, pairing the collection and management of herbarium specimens with 'DNA barcoding', the creation of libraries of short, standardised, DNA sequences linked to representative specimens in established specimen repositories, for the eventual use in DNA-based identification of unknown samples. These aims were realised and the approach of DNA barcoding is being further developed by James and others for use with schoolchildren and other citizen scientists.

INTERDISCIPLINARY STUDIES

In the first chapter in this section, Chapter 20, Miranda Lowe and Carolyn Boulter look at Darwin's study of barnacles as an example of a Victorian scientist at work and show how students can follow in Darwin's footsteps and through that journey understand the importance of work by scientists today and see how scientific knowledge develops. Darwin began his barnacle work simply because he was tidying up the last of the specimens collected on his *Beagle* voyage. Using his dissecting microscope he was more than a little chuffed to discover that barnacles were crustaceans not, as Linnaeus and Cuvier had presumed, molluscs. The barnacle study grew and grew. His initial delight – 'After having been so many years employed in writing my old geological observations it is delightful to use one's eyes and fingers again' – palled somewhat: 'I hate the Barnacle as no man ever did before, not even a Sailor in a slow sailing ship'. Using the narrative of how Darwin worked with barnacles can provide deep insights for students into how scientists work and the processes of taxonomy, classification and phylogeny. Lowe and Boulter describe how they have developed for the Charles Darwin Trust a unit on barnacles which is called *Darwin's barnacles: evidence for evolutionary relationships*, which allows students to work with this process.

In Chapter 21, Martin Braund shows what the Arts, particularly drama, can offer science education. Braund argues that the learner of science benefits from engagement through performance, making abstract concepts understandable as they are connected to personal experiences of mime, dance and acted drama. Engagement through drama also contributes to learners' realisation of the nature of science and appreciation of viewpoints on scientific issues, thereby enhancing their scientific literacy. Darwin's work and life inspire many examples of this learning. Simulations of survival in nature, plays about Darwin's life and ideas and role-plays about modern applications of evolution and gene selection are examples included by Braund. These inspiring moments can bring school biology and science to life. However, the biology/science teacher often needs help to make the necessary 'border crossings', bridging the pedagogy of the drama teacher to that of the science teacher.

In Chapter 22, Tina Gianquitto discusses how Darwin's work helped writers and other contemporaries of his discover new ways about talking about old topics: love and marriage, moral sense and social instincts, even aesthetic sense and the perception of beauty. Interestingly, it was Darwin's botanical books that were especially significant in this regard. Darwin's plant studies were in part so popular because he employed basic observational and experimental methods using materials close at hand. Popular nature writers, such as Mary Treat – a correspondent of Darwin's and expert on carnivorous plants – made the connection between botanical study and moral and physical health explicit. Indeed, carnivorous plants aroused a host of contradictory feelings and views. Are they conscious, wilful organisms? Are they moral, immoral or amoral? Are they examples of exquisite evolutionary adaptation or are they degenerate, atavistic throwbacks, making their way by a sort of primitive violence? Are they flora or are they fauna? Darwin's re-mapping of the natural world placed many in the nineteenth century in a profoundly disturbing position, facing a paradigm shift that necessitated an entirely new way at looking at the world and its natural systems.

Margarita Hernández-Laille, in Chapter 23, analyses the inclusion of Darwin's theory of evolution in secondary school science books in England and Spain during the

INTRODUCTION

nineteenth century. In England, Darwin's ideas, even though they initially provoked controversy and criticism, were quickly introduced into school books. Indeed, the name Darwin and reference to his ideas entered English school classrooms even before the publication of *On the origin of species*, although it was not until after 1870 that the majority of school science books adopted a Darwinian approach. In Spain, the predominant position of the Catholic Church did not prevent the references to Darwinism which Spanish scientists introduced into their discourse shortly after the publication of *On the origin of species*. Nor did it take that long, albeit longer than in England, for Darwin's theory of evolution to enter the area of education in a society that was eager for modernisation. Although many teachers suffered considerable reprisals in the mid-1870s for defending science and introducing Darwinism into their classrooms, Spanish textbooks were nonetheless swift to incorporate Darwin's ideas.

DEVELOPING WORK WITH LEARNERS

In the first chapter in this section, Chapter 24, Vaughan Prain reviews Darwin's methods of enquiry and representing research, where he used writing and other forms of representation to raise and solve problems through extensive observation, written and visual records, reflection, claim-making, testing and re-representation. Prain then presents an overview of recent research on the role of writing, and more broadly representation, in learning in school science, and illustrates the implications of this research through reporting on classroom-based research on the topic of adaptation. In particular, Prain reports how his team worked with two years five and six teachers in a shared primary classroom to plan, implement and evaluate a unit on *Animals in the school environment* that included a rich range of teacher- and student-generated representational challenges, investigative activities, discussion and re-representation. Major concepts to be learnt included ecosystem, habitat, the diversity of animal populations, interactions between plants and animals in an ecosystem, animal structure and function and the adaptive purposes of behaviour. The types of drawing, the level of detail, the count of animals, the construction of a model centipede and the use of graphing all reveal how the students integrated meaning across modes, to reason about animal diversity. Teacher and peer verbal and other inputs were critical to this process.

In Chapter 25, Emma Newall explores how Darwin-inspired learning might help in the teaching of evolution by natural selection. She reports how the Charles Darwin Trust worked with a group of South London secondary schools in 2011 and 2012. A one-day workshop was developed to look at a range of Darwin-inspired topics including selective breeding, bee behaviour, climbing plants, Darwin's weed plot and intra-specific variation in plants. Some of these activities were undertaken in a classroom environment, but those involving plants were carried out in either the school grounds or a local park and the evaluations showed that being able to work outside was considered the best bit of the day by many students. More fundamentally, the activities enabled students to see the world in a new way.

The Charles Darwin Trust has developed a number of post-16 resources and in Chapter 26, Carolyn Boulter and Emma Newall explain the thinking behind these resources. An analysis of existing advanced level biology specifications (for 16-18 year-olds) showed that there were a number of topics that teachers often regarded as difficult to teach and students often considered dull that seemed likely candidates to benefit from a Darwin-inspired approach to learning. Three modules were therefore developed: one on Darwin's birds, one on Darwin's *Drosera* and one on Darwin's barnacles. Boulter and Newall argue that too much biology education concentrates on the molecular level at the expense of whole organisms. The next generation of biologists, both specialist and generalist, requires inspiration and a broader and more holistic biological education, which they hope the modules will help to provide.

In Chapter 27, Susan Johnson discusses how school grounds can be transformed for Darwin-inspired learning. All too often schools make little or no educational use of their grounds. One problem is that teachers often lack confidence in their knowledge and understanding of the outdoor environment and teaching in school grounds. Local concerns about health and safety when working out-of-doors, curriculum pressures and other considerations can also play a part. Johnson provides a rich assortment of activities that can take place in school grounds, many directly connecting with Darwin's own work.

In Chapter 28, Susan Johnson describes how a programme of Darwin-inspired learning can facilitate the transition as students move from their primary to their secondary schools. The intention of Darwin-inspired transition days is to make full use of the outdoor environment to explore the principles underpinning Darwin's work. Even seemingly unpromising school grounds or public parks have a small, grassed area, thickets of thorny plants, weeds, trees and climbing plants. In urban school playgrounds, tiny habitats for organisms are found between paving stones, on brick walls and the weedy edges of asphalt. Understanding plant life cycles, local habitats and the wildlife that may be attracted help to illustrate Darwin's big ideas and skills as a scientist

In the final chapter of this section, Chapter 29, Dawn Sanders proposes a biographical model for using the work of scientists in teaching science. She develops two biographical narrative-based approaches to Darwin-inspired learning: one that uses Boehm's statue of Darwin in the Natural History Museum, London; one that seeks to bring Darwin to life through his personal correspondence. Darwin's overcoat, as depicted in Boehm's statue, suggests a man for whom science was not practised solely indoors, a man whose garden was part of his life and science. Sanders suggests that the many pockets of possibilities in the waistcoat, jacket and overcoat of the statue allow students to imagine their contents, as Darwin worked in the grounds at Down House and beyond. Equally, Darwin's personal correspondence, as also noted in Chapter 3, provide a rich and increasingly accessible resource with

INTRODUCTION

which to appreciate Darwin's humanity, his powers of observation and the ways in which he both supports and confounds students' expectations of a great scientist.

EPILOGUE

Finally, in an epilogue the three of us summarise what is to us the essence of Darwin-inspired learning. We argue that an approach to learning inspired by Darwin can transform the ordinary, can help us to see with new eyes. Natural history is all around us but too often it is not noticed. Furthermore, a Darwinian approach to answering scientific questions shows how rich an authentic scientific approach to hypothesis formation and testing can be; too often, school learners are bored by an endless series of traditional hypothetico-deductive experimental narratives. There are common curiosities between the scientific and creative imagination. A Darwin-inspired approach to learning begins by paying attention, by close observation. Done well, school science can help develop 'everyday noticing' into 'scientific observation', the start of valid scientific investigation.

REFERENCES

Darwin, C. (1872). *The expression of the emotions in man and animals*. London: John Murray.
Darwin, C. (1875). *Insectivorous plants*. London: John Murray.
Erduran, S., & Jiménez-Aleixandre, M. P. (Eds.). (2007). *Argumentation in science education: Perspectives from classroom-based research*. Dordrecht: Springer.
Walton, D. (2013). *Methods of argumentation*. Cambridge: Cambridge University Press.

Michael J. Reiss
Institute of Education,
University of London,
UK

Carolyn J. Boulter
Charles Darwin Trust,
Institute of Education,
University of London,
UK

Dawn L. Sanders
Institute of Pedagogical, Curricular and Professional Studies,
Gothenburg University,
Sweden

DARWIN'S HERITAGE

RANDAL KEYNES

1. ENTERING DARWIN'S LIFE

INTRODUCTION

As a result of his fundamental contribution to human understanding, Charles Darwin touches all of our lives. I have a special connection with him as I am one of his great-great-grandchildren and a trustee of the Charles Darwin Trust, the organisation that uses the intellectual and cultural heritage of Darwin, through his approach to science and his work at Down House and in the immediate countryside, to inspire a deeper understanding of the natural world (Charles Darwin Trust, 2013).

In this chapter I begin by tracking some of Darwin's formative experiences and then connect these to what the Charles Darwin Trust understands by 'Darwin-inspired learning'.

SCHOOLBOY – EXPLORING AND EXPLOSIONS

Young Charles was 'back of the class' at school in Shrewsbury but from early childhood he loved exploring the countryside and examining plants and small creatures, collecting beetles and strange stones. His two grandfathers had both been closely involved in the wonderfully practical and adventurous experimental science of the Lunar Society in Birmingham, with Joseph Priestley a close colleague and friend. Charles's elder brother had a chemical laboratory in the tool-house and allowed Charles to assist him in making 'all the gases'. Charles helped eagerly and wrote in his autobiography that this was the best part of his education in his school years, 'for it showed me practically the meaning of experimental science' (Darwin, 1887).

In these two ways, with his exploring and collecting on his own in the countryside and then undertaking chemistry experiments with his brother in the tool-house, Charles grew into a young man 'of enlarged curiosity' as his uncle once perceptively remarked.

UNIVERSITY – FIELD TRIPS WITH EXPERTS

Finding little to interest him in his university studies, Darwin pursued his interests in natural history, studying birds and collecting beetles with student friends. Later, he criticised his earlier passion for beetle collecting, writing that he had been interested in little more about them than just 'getting them named', but he was fortunate also to find among his university lecturers and professors three outstanding naturalists who allowed him to accompany them on their field excursions, collect and study with them and develop his powers of observation and enquiry with their guidance. Each of them combined their expertise in field studies with bold interests in high science and global perspectives in the investigation of basic patterns of natural life. For Dr Robert Grant, the Lamarckian marine biologist in Edinburgh, it was links and distinctions between animals and plants that were of particular interest; for Professor John Henslow, the botanist in Cambridge, it was the global features of the plant kingdom; for Professor Adam Sedgwick, the geologist also in Cambridge, it was the deepest and broadest history of the earth's crust. Each of them in succession recognised the young man's absorption and fascination in what they were studying together and his potential as a scientist, and encouraged him in field-work and pursuing higher scientific enquiries.

THE *BEAGLE* VOYAGE

Henslow got Darwin onto the *Beagle* voyage as naturalist companion to the Captain. Darwin now had five years on his own as naturalist, five years of adventure exploring the world – sea and land, mountain and plain, continent and island. At that point in the history of natural science this provided an outstanding opportunity for an open-minded young investigator, and he used it well.

Darwin wrote vividly in his journal and letters home about his experiences on the voyage, especially those linked with some of the remarkable scientific insights he was developing. The importance of his observations on the Galapagos Islands is well known but he achieved much in addition. His geological and palaeontological studies changed how he saw the world. He came to see the surface of South America as pitching and heaving with geological changes – not least because of his first-hand experience of an earthquake in Chile – and he found patterns of succession between the extinct and living mammals of the Continent that Owen later made his 'law of succession', a key point for *On the origin of species*. His theory of the formation of coral reefs enabled him to trace global patterns of uplift and sinking, all hypothesised inductively and confirmed by careful observation as the *Beagle* sailed from archipelago to archipelago around the Pacific.

LONDON AND SPECIES THEORY

Back in London in 1836 Darwin lived and worked in the teeming, smoking city for six years. He delivered his many *Beagle* specimens to museum experts for identification and got their judgements on the Galapagos mockingbirds and finches he had collected. Gradually, he came to see the implications of his work for the 'species question' in taxonomy, a hot topic in natural science, and for what Sir John Herschel referred to in a letter to Charles Lyell as 'the mystery of mysteries, the replacement of extinct species by others'. Darwin started thinking hard about species and variation, the how and the why, and focused on possible processes for change.

As he read widely, Thomas Malthus' (1798) *An essay on the principle of population* alerted him to the importance of competition in nature. Eager to prove himself as a scientist, Darwin considered change with patterns in space (mockingbirds from Uruguay to Peru and then the Galapagos Islands), through time (fossil and living mammals in South America) and in taxonomy and embryology (comparative anatomy), and put together a first outline for a whole theory of natural life based on species change, his '1842 sketch'. He realised it would be rejected out of hand by almost all respectable scientists, and saw he would need to develop many parts of it in secret and test each rigorously against all the evidence he could find before he could offer it to the scientific community. Darwin's big ideas developed from his *Beagle* experiences and he drew on London's museums and libraries. Part of his genius was his ability to see the connections among a huge range of apparently disparate facts, enabling him to explain many things in widely different fields, each inexplicable in isolation but all making sense when seen together in his suggested framework. He saw at once in each topic many questions he'd like to put to many different people, and many experiments he'd like to try to see if they might provide any insights, but he couldn't do as much as he wanted while he was working and living in London, so he opened a book for all the points he wanted to pursue, scrawling simply on the cover, 'Questions and Experiments'.

Darwin's secret notebooks of 1836 to 1844, in which he noted his developing ideas in rapid, incisive comments, provide an outstandingly vivid display of one of the fastest and greatest achievements in scientific thinking. His historic jotting after first visiting Jenny, a young orangutan in the Zoological Gardens, to see how like or different from a human she might be, shows the breath-taking openness of his mind and boldness of his thinking: 'Man in his arrogance thinks himself a great work, worthy the interposition of a deity [i.e. specially created by God]. More humble and I believe true to consider him created from animals'.

DOWNE[1] – A PLACE TO WORK

When Darwin had written out the 1842 sketch, he could see that his idea might stand up and he decided to make it his life's work. To develop it he realised he'd need peace and quiet from social calls, and a garden and countryside to observe and experiment in, but he'd also have to be able to get to London easily to read books, examine museum specimens and consult experts. He decided with Emma, his wife, to move into the country. They found a small country house in a quiet part of Kent and moved there in September 1842 with their two young children. The couple were to live there, at Down House near Downe, for the rest of their lives, and Darwin made it his single workplace from then on. Darwin and Emma had looked at many properties in all directions out of London, and one important reason for their final choice of Downe was the variety of habitats he could find in that quiet neighbourhood, which he could explore, observe and collect in using the network of footpaths in every direction.

Once settled in Downe, Darwin created his 'thinking path' for daily walks in the grounds of his new home. He started botanical work with observations on a curious double flower he noticed in a neighbour's field, and embarked on a natural history of the neighbourhood modelled on *The natural history of Selborne* by Gilbert White (1789) whom he admired greatly as a naturalist who had made the natural life of his locality his special study.

Thinking all the time about his theory, Darwin produced a second fuller version, the two-hundred-page '1844 essay'. He was now ready to start field investigations around his home, but he then found another task he needed to concentrate on first, and spent most of the next eight years dissecting barnacles in his study.

BARNACLES

To command serious attention and carry weight when he eventually published his work on the origin of species through evolution, Darwin felt he needed first to gain experience in comparative anatomy and how it could be used in taxonomy, and then be able to show his expertise in the two subjects through a sound contribution to scientific understanding. Returning to his interest in marine biology on the *Beagle* voyage, he looked at the cirripedes, a group that included the barnacles and had remarkable varieties of form for living in different settings. He analysed the anatomical relations between the identified species and published a fresh taxonomy of them, for which in 1853, even before he had finished his work on them, he was awarded the Royal Society's Royal Medal, invaluable for him as a scientific recognition of his expertise.

EXPERIMENTS

As Darwin approached the end of his barnacle project in 1854 and planned to return to his species theory, he wrote to Hooker about his notes 'on the theory on which, as you know, I have been collecting facts for these dozen years. How awfully flat I shall feel if when I get my notes &c &c, the whole thing explodes like an empty puffball'[2]. Eventually on 9 September 1854 he finished the barnacle work, and then noted in his journal that on the day, 'Began sorting notes for Species Theory'.

A few weeks later, Darwin opened his book of 'Questions and Experiments' and set to work on investigations with living organisms. He did one on one of the ducks in the yard being fattened for Christmas, but then had to delay because of the cruel 'Crimean Winter' and only got going again as the snow melted away at last in March 1855. From that spring these experiments rapidly became a major part of his daily activity as a scientist. As he discovered what he could find out from them he began more and more, and soon had many in progress at any time. The whole body of investigative work that he carried out at Downe from this point until the end of his life stands after his 'species theory' as his second great achievement in science.

After 18 years working mostly indoors Darwin was now back working out of doors as he'd so enjoyed on the *Beagle* voyage. In his 27 years of investigating and experimenting at Downe he worked almost entirely within an area of a few square miles, but focusing on what he wanted, using what he could find there, and obtaining information and other resources from elsewhere, he had all he needed. Studying the natural life of the countryside around Down House as his primary resource for investigation, using his garden for botanical experiments and drawing on the London Zoological Gardens for other living animals, Kew Gardens for other living plants and the British Museum for preserved specimens and books, he made his surroundings, garden and home his open air laboratory and observatory for an ever-developing and extending programme of research on wild and domesticated animals and natural and cultivated plants.

With Darwin's investigations of living organisms we get to the heart of much of his best work and the value of Darwin-inspired learning.

DARWIN-INSPIRED LEARNING

Darwin-inspired learning is an approach to education about natural life, evolution and ways of investigating them, using Darwin's scientific work, the fierce debates at the time, and Darwin himself as a thinking, feeling person in his love for nature and his eagerness to help others find as much fascination and wonder in it as he did. Taking part in science education in Europe, Asia and the Americas, I've seen again and again how young people in Britain and around the world enjoy hearing about Darwin and using his experiences in their schoolwork about the natural world (Keynes, 2009).

If Darwin himself were to come into a science classroom today, he might be astonished to find what was being done there. He'd be eager to hear what natural life the class was studying, what they were asking about it and how they were looking for answers. He'd be amazed and delighted to hear what can now be explained to students about genetics as the mechanism for inheritance and evolutionary change. But in many schools he would be shocked to see the stress on textbooks and classroom instruction in order to reach school targets, and he'd be disappointed to find that students all too rarely ask their own questions about what they are observing and that there is all too often no opportunity in their lessons for them to work out themselves how to find out more.

The idea of Darwin coming into a science classroom isn't as fantastic as it might seem. In his letters to close friends we can sense his passion for hands-on engagement with the natural world and his eagerness to help his own children and other young people discover for themselves wonders like those he'd found.

Before the work of the Charles Darwin Trust, little use had been made of all we know about Darwin's scientific work for science education in schools. Many of the key points were scattered in separate places, or simply not thought through, and the links were difficult to find. In collaboration with other organisations including

English Heritage, the Natural History Museum and The Linnean Society, the Trust has worked to remedy this. What drove Darwin in all his work was the belief that natural life is immensely complex, but aspects of it can be understood if we can identify recurring features in the ceaseless evolutionary flux and work out its fundamental processes. Darwin's ways of working can be offered to students as an inspiration for an imaginative, creative and exciting approach to the life sciences in school classrooms and the world outside.

Noticing, Questioning and Testing

Throughout his life Darwin could find utter fascination in the endless wonders he found in the natural life around him. When one looks carefully, the utterly familiar can become deeply strange. Darwin found he needed then to search with an open mind for possible explanations, and in the search his fascination turned into science, quickly outreaching all other interests. Watching condors wheeling high above the Andes, Darwin wondered how they find their next meal, whether by scent or sight. Meeting some tethered condors later, he loosely wrapped a piece of carrion in paper and paraded it in front of them, with no response until the paper was opened, when they could see the meat and all tore at it together. Students can notice something distinctive in what a creature is doing, pose a question that intrigues, and then start thinking about ways to answer it.

Observing Closely

From his youth to old age, Darwin almost always had a hand lens on a ribbon round his neck and would put it to his eye at every opportunity to study some organism closely. He used it for observing moths and beetles, examining minute sea creatures on the *Beagle* voyage, peering intently into flowers, watching ants milk aphids and studying insect-eating plants engulf their prey. If students can pick up Darwin's habit and learn always to look closely, they will find so much that others miss.

Discerning Patterns and Exceptions

Each day that he was at Down House, Darwin walked on the Sandwalk, his thinking path, and was constantly alert both for the regular patterns that might have meanings and for exceptions that might point to another story. His children helped in his remarkable spotting and mapping of young male bumblebees' buzzing places in which he anticipated the eventual discovery of insects' chemical signalling systems, and he was first to identify seed dormancy as a factor in ecological succession by spotting one day some charlock seedlings emerging from the soil in a setting he'd never seen them growing in before.

Experimenting

One of Darwin's greatest contributions to the life sciences was to show again and again the value of moving on from careful observations of natural organisms to experiments with their living processes in order to detect and identify causative factors. For many laboratory chemists and physicists of the time, experimentation was a formal undertaking in a special place (a laboratory) with elaborate equipment. For his experiments with natural life, Darwin never had a laboratory of that kind but worked around his grounds and home with simple apparatus improvised from household odds and ends. He used kitchen jars and brushes, ribbon, pencils, clothes pegs, crockery, his wife's muslin and corset stays. This means that all his experiments, which revealed so much to the modern world about natural processes, can be repeated easily in a schoolroom or outdoor space, and prompt students to think of experiments of their own to try.

Measuring

Simple though Darwin's experiments were in the apparatus used, they show brilliant inventiveness in the many different ways they work to reveal what otherwise would have remained hidden. Many of his most productive investigations were rapid, tactical and exploratory, with careful thought given to how measurements could be made and used. Again, students can try out his methods and then vary them for different purposes of their own. They can do this with his wonderful sequence of discoveries in a few days tracing a wild cucumber's intertwining movements with a pencil in a flowerpot on his study desk. They can use his favourite broad bean, the still standard *Vicia faba,* with a clothes peg from a washing basket to translate the sideways strength of the growing bean root into a movement that can be measured and the measurement can then be translated again into a physical force. Each of the many other examples that can be used allow for variations in any other direction that students would like to work along.

'Fools' Experiments'

Emma Darwin often laughed with the family at her husband's experiments, and he was happy to laugh with them. He had a favourite kind he called 'fools' experiments', trials of wild possibilities that others wouldn't attempt but he enjoyed extremely. In one to find what attracts insects to plants, he took an artificial flower from Emma's bonnet, placed a drop of honey in the centre, dressed it with leaves and planted it in the flower bed. We know about this experiment because his two-year-old son spotted that the flower wasn't real from the other end of the garden and Darwin was surprised to see how soon in his development his son had learnt to distinguish between the natural and the artificial. He recorded the point in some notes he was making on his son's early development, and the paper he wrote from those notes is one of the founding texts of developmental psychology (Darwin, 1877; Keynes, 2005). Students can be inspired by Darwin's boldness and playfulness in trying out ideas that others might rule out as absurd. Asking his son to play his bassoon to some earthworms for a study of their capacity to hear is an example that springs to mind. Darwin's ability to switch his attention to a novel phenomenon was another of his special strengths. An experimenter with Darwin's alertness will always be watching for any points of possible interest in the entire field of view.

CONCLUSION

The Charles Darwin Trust was set up in 1999 with the aim of helping to advance scientific thought and education by using the life and work of Charles Darwin for inspiration. By 2005 the Trust was focusing on how the study of Darwin might contribute to enhancing science teaching and learning, and held a landmark seminar (Turney, 2005) to explore the possibilities of what we saw we could simply call *Darwin-inspired learning*. Throughout my writing of *Darwin, his daughter and human evolution* (Keynes, 2002) I had sought to give the reader an intimate view of how Darwin developed his ideas about human nature as he worked on his evolutionary theory while living closely with his wife and children in their country home. At the 2005 seminar I was particularly struck by the ways the educators suggested that the rich material about Darwin could be used for engaging education for the life sciences. It's wonderful that with all the information we have in his many writings, all his surviving correspondence and his personal papers, we can also visit so many of the places that were important for him in his work, find them just as they were in his time or only little altered, see the animals and plants he studied there, appreciate what he saw of their lives together and understand what he worked out about all the processes involved.

That said, for education, the students who can visit Down House and the surrounding countryside, or the Galapagos, are a lucky few. One great value of Darwin-inspired learning is that it can help students anywhere to find objects for study as Darwin did at Downe *but in their own surroundings* and investigate these in the simple ways he managed to, or in other ways his methods may suggest. Darwin's approach to the investigation and understanding of life has shown its ultimate value in all the insights that his work has led to. It has a high value also for science education as a vivid and engaging example for young enquirers to follow. With all Darwin tells us about his experiences and all he helps us to understand with his insights, he can truly inspire learning.

NOTES

[1] When Charles Darwin and his family moved to Down House, the spelling of the village was also Down, with no e. When the spelling of the villages name was changed to Downe some years later, Darwin decided not to change the spelling of his house, so it remained Down House.

[2] Charles Darwin to J. D. Hooker, 26 March, 1854. Darwin Correspondence Database, http://www.darwinproject.ac.uk/entry-1562. The Correspondence of Charles Darwin (1990). Frederick Burkhardt, Sydney Smith (Eds), Vol 5 1851-55 (pp. 186-187). Cambridge UK: Cambridge University Press. http://www.darwinproject.ac.uk/correspondence-volume-5.

REFERENCES

Charles Darwin Trust. (2013). *About us*. Retrieved December 28, 2013 from http://www.charlesdarwintrust.org/content/12/about-us

Darwin, C. (1877, July). A biographical sketch of an infant. *Mind, 2*, 285–294.

Darwin, C. (1887). *Autobiography*. Retrieved December 28, 2013 from http://www.victorianweb.org/science/darwin/darwin_autobiography.html

Keynes, R. (2002). *Darwin, his daughter and human evolution*. New York, NY: Riverhead Books.

Keynes, R. (2005). Darwin, William Erasmus (1839–1914). In *Oxford dictionary of national biography*. Oxford: Oxford University Press.

Keynes, R. (2009a). Darwin's ways of working: The opportunity for education. *Journal of Biological Education, 43*(3), 101–103.

Keynes, R (2009b) The Darwin Guide to recording Wildlife published online by the National Biodiversity Network http://www.nbn.org.uk/Tools-Resources/NBN-Publications/Darwin-Guide-to-Recording-Wildlife-pdf.aspx.

Malthus, T. R. (1798). *An essay on the principle of population*. London: J. Johnson.

Turney, J. (2005, March). *Darwin-Inspired learning. Report of a seminar organized by the Charles Darwin Trust, The Abbey, Sutton Courtney*. The Charles Darwin Trust.

White, G. (1789). *The natural history and antiquities of Selborne*. London: Benjamin White.

Randal Keynes
The Charles Darwin Trust,
UK

DAWN L. SANDERS

2. THE WORLD OF DOWNE

Charles Darwin's Living Laboratory

INTRODUCTION

Charles Darwin's achievements are all the more extraordinary when we reflect on the simple tools and domestic spaces in which he practised his post-*Beagle* enquiries. The relatively unchanged garden at Down House – with its glasshouse, kitchen-beds, lawn, hedgerows, adjacent woods and meadows – is a living monument to the observations, experiments, collections and continuous questioning clearly evidenced in his notes and letters. This chapter will examine Darwin's 'living laboratory' in the context of gardens as scientific spaces – from the experimental garden of Gregor Mendel to contemporary studies of ecological patterns and communities in a Leicestershire suburban garden. Drawing on Darwin's correspondence, notebooks and publications it will position Darwin within a social network of garden experimentation, and associated fieldwork, by both amateur and professional, male and female, correspondents. These historical explorations of Darwin's 'locale' (Kohler, 2011, p. 581) will set the scene for contemporary discussions of Darwin-inspired learning.

DARWIN AND DOWNE[1]

Many of the data for Darwin's post-*Beagle* works, and the reflective space for thinking and theorising about the origin of species, came from active experimentation with weeds, pigeons and various botanical experiments in his glasshouses or during perambulations in the Downe landscape. Indeed, in the conclusion to *On the origin of species*, Darwin refers to aspects of this locality in his 'entangled bank' metaphor: 'clothed with many plants of many kinds, with birds singing on the bushes, with various insects flitting about, and with worms crawling through the damp earth' (Darwin, 1859, p. 360). Jones (2009) has identified Downe as 'The Galapagos in the Garden of England' and highlights the rich range of experimentation and writing that emerged from Darwin's home in the Kent countryside.

WARDROBES AND CORSETS

Inside his house, Darwin was no stranger to the possibilities that his wife Emma's wardrobe, scullery and body offered his experiments: a whalebone from her corsets helped him to hypothesise the catapult-like pollinia mechanism on an orchid, clothes pegs assisted in his measurements of the forces involved in plant root movements, and one of Emma's hairs was placed on a *Drosera* leaf as part of his research into their sensitivity (Darwin, 1875). Human ephemera were a significant element in Darwin's experiments; tobacco smoke was blown on earthworms to gauge their response, ' a bit of old nail of my toe'[2] was positioned on the common sundew *Drosera rotundifolia*, and human urine added to the list of nitrogenous materials he placed on his 'beloved Drosera'[3]. In addition to his influential theory that 'life is a copiously branching bush, continually pruned by the grim reaper of extinction, not a ladder of perpetual progress' (Gould, 1989, p.35), Darwin's story has extensive cultural impacts; one being that no other individual has had so much influence on man's perception of nature (Worster, 1985). These cultural impacts also concern the practice of science itself, in particular 'indoor' and 'outdoor' science (Outram, 1996) and 'the lab-field border' (Kohler, 2002, p. 1).

PLACE: THE LAB-FIELD BORDER

A debate concerning the lab-field border emerged during the nineteenth century. It was preceded in the eighteenth century by discussions relating to 'indoor' and 'outdoor' science in which the French biologist, Georges Cuvier, was a principal protagonist (Outram, 1996). Within this spatial discourse, Darwin's work at Down House occupies a key juncture in scientific practice. Kohler (2002) describes the border between laboratory and field science as 'one of the most important in the cultural geography of modern science' (p.1). He also offers us a significant interpretative doorway into Darwin's outdoor scientific work, both in his garden and the local environs of Downe:

> Place must figure quite differently in lab and field practices. Laboratory workers eliminate the element of place from their experiments. Field biologists use places actively in their work as tools; they do not just work in a place, as lab biologists do, but on it. Places are as much the object of their work as the creatures in them. (Kohler, 2002, p. 6)

Darwin's correspondence gives us ample evidence for the importance of place, on both macro- and micro-scales, as the following extract from a letter to Hooker demonstrates:

> My observations, though on so infinitely a small-scale, on the struggle for existence, begin to make me a little clearer how the fight goes on: out of sixteen kinds of seed sown in my meadow, fifteen have germinated, but now they are perishing at such a rate that I doubt whether more than one will flower. Here

we have choking, which has taken place likewise on a great scale with plant not seedlings, in a bit of my lawn allowed to grow up ... What a wondrous problem it is – what a play of forces, determining the kinds and proportions of each plant in a square yard of turf! It is to my mind truly wonderful.[4]

Significantly, in relation to Darwin's correspondence networks, Kohler discusses the social identity of lab and field biologists and notes that: 'Labs are separate, a world apart from the world; nature connects field biologists to other social worlds' (Kohler, ibid, p. 7). This connection to 'other social worlds' is clearly exhibited by Darwin's interactions with his children, their governesses, women engaged in scientific practice, gardeners, pigeon-fanciers and the local chemist's son, as well as prominent scientists of the day, such as Gray, Hooker and Lyell – connections made through conversation, co-experimentation and correspondence.

DARWIN'S WAYS OF WORKING

Charles Darwin observed the living world through critical eyes. His extended observations and experiments, both on the voyage of the *Beagle* and at Downe, represented nature as multifarious strands of competitive interdependence. Although, as Beer points out, Darwin's 'descriptions of "the polity of nature"' give 'an impression of benign fullness' even as they draw attention to 'loss, failure and struggle' (Beer, 2009, p. 35). These dynamic relationships permeated the subsequent literature of the period; both poets and novelists drew on the rich imagery of his ideas and extended them to the realms of human interaction as demonstrated in the novels of George Eliot (Beer, 2009).

Darwin's carnivorous plant research exemplifies his critical observations in the field and experimental investigations in his greenhouse. The empirical studies conducted in both his house, and garden, were enriched by a network of global correspondents each exploring ideas related to carnivorous plant nutrition, form and function. His book *Insectivorous plants* (1875) continues to inspire the work of modern scientists (e.g. Chase et al., 2009). Charles Darwin first came across *Drosera rotundifolia* while walking in Sussex and was curious as to why there was such 'prodigious slaughter' of insects on its leaves (see Chapter 18). Darwin and his American correspondent Mary Treat (1830-1923) became fascinated by plant nutrition in relation to these carnivorous plants – both scientists researched a range of plants exhibiting different trapping mechanisms and corresponded in such matters over a period of five years (Sanders, 2009/10). Their studies were, in the main, conducted through observation in the field and experimentation in their homes and gardens.

Darwin was particularly interested in a plant exhibiting animal-like behaviours, as this extract from *Autobiographies* (Darwin, Neve & Messenger, 2002) affirms: 'The fact that a plant should secrete, when properly excited, a fluid containing an acid and ferment, closely analogous to the digestive fluid of an animal, was certainly a remarkable discovery' (p.81). At one point in his investigations he was said to exclaim, in a letter to Hooker: 'By Jove I sometimes think Drosera is a disguised animal'[5]. Mary Treat wrote detailed essays on carnivorous plants in popular magazines and in her book *Home studies in nature* (1885) (see Chapter 22). Like Darwin, she appears to cross the boundary between animal and plant with her description of bladderwort *Utricularia* 'digestion': 'These little bladders are in truth like so many stomachs, digesting and assimilating animal food'. (Treat, 1875 pp. 303–304)

OBSERVATION AND EXPERIMENT

Darwin's physical range was confined by his poor health – he rarely went further than the ground he could cover in a two- to three-hour walk. Despite these limitations, the diversity offered by the local flora, fauna and habitats (both semi-natural and human-made) gave him opportunities to make the repeated experiments and observations needed for his work. In addition, the local geological history and patterns of human settlement with their mixed methods of land management meant he could investigate natural communities in times of continuity and flux; for example, fields laid fallow, retained or changed levels of crop or animal production, land drainage methods and subsequent impacts on extant flora and/or moisture levels. Browne (2003) suggests 'the power of place' had a significant influence on his scientific interests; 'Living in the Kent countryside, with hop-fields all around, Darwin could not help but notice the twining tendrils that hitched the plants up their wires in the late-Spring sunshine' (Browne, 2003, p. 416). Furthermore, he was able to conduct and repeat investigations such as his weed plot experiment. Darwin wanted to know what life was like for a seedling plant. He carried out his weed-plot experiment at Down House from January to August 1857 (see Chapter 27) whilst investigating the struggle for existence articulated in his theory of evolution by natural selection, in *On the origin of species* (1859).

Figure 1. Weed-plot experiment. (© Susan Johnson)

Weeds are the plants, along with trees, with which children are often most familiar, even in urban environments – dandelion *Taraxacum officinale* seeds are blown away, cleavers *Galium aparine* stick to jackets and trousers. Darwin's weed-plot experiment brings alive the everyday dramas of our pavements, walls and back gardens. A patch of common plants becomes a miniature jungle where the struggle to survive is paramount, and competition rife. Darwin saw the struggle for existence as ruthless, universal and ceaselessly shifting, no less so with seed germination:

> With plants there is a vast destruction of seeds, but, from some observations which I have made, I believe that it is the seedlings which suffer most from germinating in ground already thickly stocked with other plants. Seedlings, also, are destroyed in vast numbers by various enemies. (Darwin, *On the origin of species*, 1859, p. 54)

Circa 15,000 letters survive from Darwin's time at Downe and represent a correspondence that extended across a global network. The study at Down House retains many of Darwin's original instruments and notebooks arranged as it would have been in the late 1850s while he was writing *On the origin of species*, reconstructed according to evidence provided by a photograph taken by his son, Leonard. Down House retains much original material and the immediate surrounds of Downe are relatively unchanged – in almost every case the setting is close to how it was in his time. His life at Downe was far from settled or 'humdrum', as Gillian Beer observes:

> He was still on his world journeys while he sat in his armchair, his mind packed with the materiality of the physical world and sharpened by exceptions noted. His greenhouse could harbour questions that unsettled the assumptions of the western world - and he determined to engage with those questions. (Beer, 2009, p. xvii)

Darwin's last book *The formation of vegetable mould through the action of worms* (1881) drew on his 'worm-stone' experiment – using a special mechanism designed by his engineer son Horace to investigate the displacement of soil by the action of earthworms. This was to be his final research project. English Heritage, an organisation which now manages Down House and its garden, reminds us 'by that time he was an internationally acclaimed figure in the scientific world and yet he was still doing simple experiments in his back garden'[6]. Of interest here is the significantly sceptical reception Darwin's research on earthworms received in the British horticultural press, more so than *On the origin of species* received in the same publications (Elliot, 2010), despite the book capturing the public imagination: 'a day or two after publication Murray exclaimed "3,500 Worms"' (Browne, 2003, p. 490).

One of Darwin's horticultural critics in the matter of earthworms was David Taylor Fish (1824-1901), head gardener at Hardwicke Hall, Suffolk. In 1881 Fish finally appears to have accepted Darwin's evidence of the contribution earthworm activity makes to the formation of soil, but his description of the earthworm as 'mean and despised' distracts the reader from its role as a 'wonderfully efficient drainer' (Fish in Elliot, 2010, p. 71). Prejudicial views of earthworms as pests persisted in horticultural circles long after Darwin's death (Satchell, 1983) and it was not until 1949 when Thomas Barrett's *Harnessing the earthworm* was published that 'concrete recommendations for encouraging earthworms and using them to make compost' (Elliot, 2010, p. 73) were offered to a gardening readership, which had been loathe to accept Darwin's evidence of their important role in the formation of vegetable mould and thus fertile soil.

Figure 2. Worm-stone. (© Susan Johnson)

SCIENCE IN THE GARDEN

Two of the greatest theories in biological science emerged from gardens in nineteenth century Europe. Mendel, 'the monk in the garden', working in a monastery in Brno, Moravia delivered his two-part lecture on Certain Laws of Inheritance in 1865 (Henig, 2000); Charles Darwin, in his garden in Downe, a small village in Kent, harnessed botany in his constant quest to acquire further evidence to support his theories in *On the origin of species* (Darwin, 1859). On the surface, Mendel's story could appear to be that 'of a gardener patiently tending his plants' (Henig 2000, p.4) but we know from authors such as Mawer (2006) that Mendel was both gardener and meticulous scientist. Mawer details Mendel's 'quantitative observation methods', using precise counting and defined characteristics and avoiding the imprecisely-defined terms 'size' and 'appearance' of his contemporary hybridists (Mawer, 2006, p.53). In addition, Mendel was careful to label and organise his experimental populations of the self-pollinating garden pea *Pisum sativum*. Indeed, his scientific use of the term 'control' in this experimental context was "almost certainly an all-time first" (Mawer, 2006, p. 55).

Darwin is very much the 'scientist in the garden', constructing his experiments with the assistance of various gardeners, some of whom were borrowed for their expertise on specific plants, such as tropical orchids (Elliot, 2010). Browne considers Darwin to be a man who 'loved to puzzle over the quietly complicated lives of plants' (Browne, 2003 p. 166). Despite the attention Darwin heaped on his 'twitchers, twiners, climbers and scramblers', his publication on climbing plants 'did not catch the public fancy any more than the digestive powers of *Drosera*' (Browne, 2003, p. 417). Both *Climbing plants* (1865) and *Insectivorous plants* (1875) were slow sellers amongst popular audiences. However, such publications aided the growth of his reputation amongst botanical scientists such as Gray at Harvard and Hooker in Kew.

The greatest contrast between Mendel and Darwin lies in the dissemination of their work among their scientific peers and the lack of an accepted language for the mechanisms of inheritance revealed by Mendel's experiments (Mawer, 2006). While Darwin was amassing publications and building powerful networks through which to develop his scientific discourse, Mendel was relatively isolated from the scientific community. It is this separation that distinguishes their scientific 'personas' (Daston & Sibum, 2003), not their investigative practice.

LONG-TERM MONITORING

Darwin's work in his garden, and close to home, follows in the tradition of the Selborne naturalist, Gilbert White, whose writing he admired (Browne, 2003). Both men were passionate observers of the natural world and made extensive notes of their observations, collected over many years. Contemporary Britain has Jennifer Owen's thirty-year study of her suburban garden in Leicester, the importance of which Ken Thompson notes, 'is the garden's ordinariness, coupled with the length of the project – three decades – that makes her results so valuable' (Thompson, 2010, p.754). Due partly to the Park Grass Experiment of Lawes and Gilbert, begun in 1856 at Rothampstead Research Station - the oldest agricultural research centre in the world - we know the principal drivers of vegetational change (Silvertown et al., 2006) and the importance of long-term ecological observations. But, as Silvertown et al. (2010) argue, 'Long-term experiments (LTEs) in particular can reveal the mechanisms that underlie change in communities and ecosystem functioning in a way that cannot be understood by long-term monitoring alone' (p.1). Darwin moved beyond close observation and monitoring and became experimenter, theoriser and critic in his own 'locale' (Kohler, 2012, p. 58). Kohler ascribes the term 'locale' to 'the connections between doing science and living lives' (2012, p. 581); Keynes makes such a connection explicit:

> Life and his science were all of a piece. Working at home on things he could study there, spending every day with his wife, children and servants, living at

a time when science meant knowledge and understanding in the broadest view, and dwelling on issues that bear directly on the deepest questions about what it is to be human, he could not keep his thinking on the natural world apart from feelings and ideas that were important to him in the rest of his life. (Keynes, 2002, p. 2)

The weed-plot experiment and his investigative work on plant movement, pollination, cross-fertilisation and insectivorous plant nutrition often required Darwin to be at his most 'patient and foot-slogging best' (Browne, 2003, p. 413). However, his Victorian readers were seemingly 'panting for gorillas and cave men' (Browne, 2003, p.194) and felt the author of 'the controversy (*On the origin of species*) had appeared to stroll into a greenhouse' (Browne, 2003 p. 194). Perhaps, the inability of humans to notice plants in their environment - a phenomenon described as 'plant blindness' (Wandersee & Schussler, 2001) - is not an issue solely confined to the modern era.

CONCLUSION

Darwin was as an eminent scientist who changed our views on the evolution of life with the publication of a book, not only read by scientists but also the wider populace. For some, his life is one of the greatest scientific lives ever lived. In this context, Downe and Down House, the place where Darwin spent the majority of his life, and from which he produced his major works, has emerged as a living laboratory. The practice of pilgrimage is not necessarily restricted to religious journeys and can equally apply to sites of scientific importance, as suggested by Sir Arthur Keith:

> To know Charles Darwin, we must first know Downe. Darwin, quite unwittingly, made these few acres of Kent upland an international possession. Down House, then, is a common heritage for truth-seekers of all countries and all centuries ... a permanent sanctuary for Darwinian pilgrims. In these gardens, orchards, meadows, and walks were slowly hammered, hot from fact, new doctrines, which, radiating out from here, permeated to the ends of the earth, giving humanity a new interpretation of living things and of its relationship to them. Human thought was forcibly and permanently thrust from its old time-honoured ruts. (Sir Arthur Keith speaking at the opening of the Darwin Museum, 1929)

In the modern world, Keith's term 'a common heritage for all truth-seekers' raises a powerful question for the site and its global relevance. Indeed, Down House and its environs could be seen to symbolise not only an important juncture for scientific praxis, but also the continuing discourse of science and faith, which has impacted on humanity since Copernicus (and possibly before). In this context, the house and its surroundings occupy a critical position in the history of human thought. But lying almost inaudibly below this grand narrative lies a more intimate story of Darwin as a man who had a 'most keen feeling' of the 'aliveness' of plants (Francis Darwin in Browne, 2003, p.417), whether they grew in a pot in his study, on benches in his greenhouse, in the garden beds of Down House or in the woods, fields and 'entangled' banks around Downe village. Their 'quietly complicated lives' (Browne, 2003, p.166) gave him much material with which to think and experiment (Kutschera and Briggs, 2009;Wycoff, 2009), so much so that he wrote:

> It has always pleased me to exalt plants in the scale of organised beings; and I therefore felt an especial pleasure in showing how many and what admirably well adapted movements the tip of a root possesses. (Darwin, Neve and Messenger, 2002, pp. 82–83)

At a time in human history when our burgeoning presence increasingly impacts on the tree of life, we would do well to reflect on Darwin's view that all organisms are inter-connected and 'the relation of organism to organism the most important of all relations' (Darwin, 1859, p.49). His house and garden, and the surrounding landscape, offered many opportunities to examine such relationships in depth and question how, and why, 'endless forms most beautiful and wonderful have been, and are being, evolved' (Darwin, 1859, p.360). Drawing inspiration from Darwin's life and science offers young people myriad possibilities to observe biological diversity closer to home, and experience at first hand, as Darwin did, the continuous struggle for life in the living world.

NOTES

[1] When Charles Darwin and his family moved to Down House, the spelling of the village was also Down, with no 'e'. When the spelling of the village's name was changed to Downe some years later, Darwin decided not to change the spelling of his house, so it remained Down House.
[2] (Cambridge University Library MS DAR 54:29).
[3] Charles Darwin to J.D. Hooker, 26 November, 1860. Darwin Correspondence Database, http://www.darwinproject.ac.uk/entry-2999 accessed on 28 November 2013.
[4] Charles Darwin to J.D. Hooker, 3 June, 1857. Darwin Correspondence Database, http://www.darwinproject.ac.uk/entry-2101 accessed on 25 November 2013.
[5] Charles Darwin to J.D. Hooker, 4 December, 1860. Darwin Correspondence Database, http://www.darwinproject.ac.uk/entry-3008 accessed on 28 November 2013.
[6] (http://www.english-heritage.org.uk/daysout/properties/home-of-charles-darwin-down-house/garden/open-air-laboratory/).

REFERENCES

Beer, G. (2009). *Darwin's plots: Evolutionary narrative in Darwin, George Eliot and nineteenth-century fiction* (3rd ed.). Cambridge: Cambridge University Press.
Browne, E. J. (1995). *Charles Darwin: Voyaging*. New York, NY: Alfred Knopf.
Browne, E. J. (2003). *Charles Darwin: The power of place*. London: Jonathan Cape.
Chase, M., Christenhuez, M., Sanders, D., & Fay, M. (2009). Murderous plants: Victorian gothic, Darwin and modern insights into vegetable carnivory. *Botanical Journal of The Linnean Society, 161*, 329–356.
Darwin, C. (1859/2008). *On the origin of species*. G. Beer (Ed.).Oxford: Oxford University Press.
Darwin, C. (1865). *Climbing plants*. London: John Murray.

Darwin, C. (1875). *Insectivorous plants*. London: John Murray.
Darwin, C. (1881). *The formation of vegetable mould through the action of worms*. London: John Murray.
Darwin, C. (2002). *Autobiographies*. M. Neve & S. Messenger (Eds). London: Penguin.
Daston, L., & Sibum, H. O. (2003). Introduction: Scientific personae and their histories. *Science in Context, 16*(1/2), 1–8.
Desmond, A. J., & Moore, J. (1991). *Darwin*. London: Michael Joseph.
Elliot, B. (2010). *Charles Darwin in the British horticultural press. Occasional papers from the RHS Lindley Library*. London: Lindley Library Royal Horticultural Society.
Henig, R. M. (2000). *The monk in the garden*. Boston, MA & New York, NY: Houghton Mifflin.
Jones, S. (2009). *Darwin's island: The Galapagos in the garden of England*. London: Little Brown.
Gould, S. J. (1989). *Wonderful life: The Burgess Shale and the nature of history*. London: Hutchinson.
Keynes, R. (2002). *Darwin, his daughter and human evolution*. New York, NY: Riverhead Books.
Kohler, R. (2012). Practice and place in twentieth-century field biology: A comment. *Journal of the History of Biology, 45*, 579–586.
Kohler, R. (2002). *Landscapes and labscapes: Exploring the lab-field border in biology*. Chicago, IL and London: The University of Chicago Press.
Kutschera, U., & Briggs, W. R. (2009). From Charles Darwin's botanical country-house studies to modern plant biology. *Plant Biology, 11*, 785–795.
Mawer, S. (2006). *Gregor Mendel: Planting the seeds of genetics*. New York, NY: Harry N. Abrams.
Outram, D. (1996). New spaces in natural history. In N. Jardine, A. Secord, & E. Spary (Eds), *cultures of natural history* (pp. 249–265). Cambridge: Cambridge University Press.
Sanders, D. (2009/2010). Behind the curtain: Treat and Austin's contributions to Darwin's work on insectivorous plants and subsequent botanical studies. *Jahrbuch für Europäische Wissenschaftskultur, 5*, 285–298.
Satchell, J. E. (1983). *Earthworm biology: From Darwin to vermiculture*. London: Chapman and Hall.
Silvertown, J., Tallowin, J., Stevens, C., Power, S., Morgan, V., Emmett, B., . . . Bardgett, R. (2010). Environmental myopia: A diagnosis and a remedy. *Trends in Ecology and Evolution, 25*(10), 556–561.
Silvertown, J., Poulton, P., Johnston, E., Edwards, G., Heard, M., & Biss, P. (2006). The park grass experiment 1856–2006: Its contribution to ecology. *Journal of Ecology, 94*(4), 801–814.
Thompson, K. (2010). Ecology begins at home. *The Garden, 135*, 754–755.
Treat, M. (1875). Plants that eat animals. *Gardeners' Chronicle*, 303–304.
Treat, M. (1885). *Home studies in nature*. New York, NY: American Book Company.
Wandersee, J. H., & Schussler, E. E. (2001). Toward a theory of plant blindness. *Plant Science Bulletin, 47*(1), 2–9.
Worster, D. (1985). *Nature's economy: A history of ecological ideas*. Cambridge: Cambridge University Press.
Wycoff, M. (2009). Scholar's Dilemma: 'Green Darwin' vs. 'Paper Darwin', An interview with David Kohn. *Evolution Education Outreach, 2*, 101–106.

Dawn L. Sanders
Institute of Pedagogical, Curricular and Professional Studies,
Gothenburg University,
Sweden

SALLY STAFFORD

3. 'PESTER THEM WITH LETTERS': USING DARWIN'S CORRESPONDENCE IN THE CLASSROOM

The Darwin Correspondence Project

Cambridge University Library has the largest single collection of Darwin's letters, notes and ephemera. It is home to the Darwin Correspondence Project, a unique undertaking to research and publish all of Darwin's 15,000 surviving letters, in print and online, reuniting those in the Library's collection with others from around the world. Funding from the Bonita Trust enabled the project to work in partnership with selected secondary schools to develop a series of online learning resources based on Darwin's correspondence. This chapter will examine how the letters fill in pieces of the Darwin jigsaw, offering fresh insight to his life and times. The three subsequent case studies demonstrate creative ideas for using the letters in the classroom. More importantly, perhaps, the emerging pupil comments reflect an increased understanding and a genuine enthusiasm and curiosity for learning about Darwin.

WHAT CAN THE LETTERS TEACH US ABOUT DARWIN?

The correspondence gives us a perspective on Darwin not found in his scientific work. Through the letters we learn about Darwin as a person, his family life, his friends and peers, his ways of working, how he conducted his research and his scientific methods. The letters also show his almost child-like enthusiasm for every organism that he encountered and his enduring fascination with the natural world.

After returning from the *Beagle* voyage, Darwin seldom left his home at Down House in Kent. As a result, science had to come to him. In a letter to the naturalist John Jenner Weir dated 6 March, 1868, Darwin wrote:

> If any man wants to gain a good opinion of his fellow man, he ought to do what I am doing – pester them with letters.[1]

Darwin wrote constantly to peers and colleagues seeking observations, findings and materials on all aspects of natural history. His connections in distant parts of the world (amounting to almost 2000 correspondents) enabled him to further his knowledge through making comparisons with what he was discovering on his own doorstep. As John Scott, a curator of the Royal Botanic Gardens of Calcutta wrote in response to Darwin's request:

> Worms are indeed abundant everywhere here: in the 'jungles' (dry and grass clad) lawns & rice fields.... As regards our lawns I indeed am mistaken if they are not even more troublesome than they are in Britain.[2]

Darwin sought evidence in the form of samples and specimens sent in the post and regularly received unsavoury parcels such as a diseased partridge foot, fish stomachs and 12 ounces of locust dung. In this way he amassed the raw material for examining and understanding the natural world and how it functioned. The letters reveal the breadth of his interests and the range of people that he 'pestered' with letters. His three young nieces did not escape his requests and were tasked with collecting flowers whilst on holiday in Wales. After writing to Darwin with the information that they had gathered 258 *Lythrum* specimens from a morning's walk, Darwin replied:

> My dear Angels!
> I can call you nothing else. I never dreamed of you taking so much trouble; your enumeration will be invaluable ... But I write now to ask will you be more angelic than angels & send me in tin, not tightly packed, with *little* damp (*not wet*) moss (perhaps tied around stems 2 or 3 flowers of *both* forms of Hottonia: I much wish to measure pollen and compare stigmas...[3]

The sheer volume of correspondence and the probing tone of Darwin's enquiries illustrate a life-long passion for scientific investigation. The letters also show how Darwin's curiosity was followed up by methodical recording and further testing. They convey the working processes of his scientific mind; they are works in progress, where ideas are teased out and tested, rather than polished, published works. The letters show that scientific discoveries are not instant, nor for Darwin at least, dependent on working in a 'state of the art' laboratory. They are often personal and sometimes funny or surprising. As such, they offer an introduction to Darwin, inspiring confidence to non-scientists to delve into his scientific writings or simply to find out more about him.

Beyond this, the letters offer an insight into the workings of mid-Victorian, middle-class Britain. The contradictory position of women, for example, in the newly emerging scientific world is revealed in a letter sent to Emma Darwin rather than to her husband, in which she is asked to awaken her 'feminine sympathies' to support Elizabeth Garrett Anderson in her application for a professorship at Bedford College for Girls. Edward Cresy wrote to Emma of the determined opposition that Anderson had already faced in seeking to qualify as a physician but that he knew her work to be 'of high order' and her 'industry and zeal' were 'beyond all praise'. Despite championing her work, Cresy simultaneously articulates the potential pitfalls facing intellectual women at the time:

> ... the very special career to which she has devoted herself has nothing impaired the charm of her manner or her social converse... she is neither masculine nor pedantic & except you knew her intimately you would only recognise a well bred English Lady.[4]

British politics and issues of the day are often discussed; Darwin was horrified at what he witnessed in the slave plantations in Brazil during his voyage around the world aboard HMS *Beagle*. In a letter to his friend John Herbert he reveals how pro-slavery propaganda permeated British culture at the time:

> It does ones heart good to hear how things are going on in England.— Hurrah for the honest Whigs.— I trust they will soon attack that monstrous stain on our boasted liberty, Colonial Slavery.— I have seen enough of Slavery & the dispositions of the negros, to be thoroughly disgusted with the lies & nonsense one hears on the subject in England.[5]

The correspondence provides a unique perspective on aspects of British history through a series of exchanges that happen over time. They enable the reader to witness events as they impact on Darwin's life, as well as the development of his own views and ideas. The letters can shed light on the causes of events and their impact and consequences. They provide a narrative that offers a distinct and personal angle on a key figure in and of his time.

LEARNING ABOUT DARWIN IN SCHOOLS

Charles Darwin features explicitly in the National Curriculum for England at both primary (elementary) and secondary (high school) levels. Darwin's theory of evolution through the mechanism of natural selection is addressed in the science curriculum and the impact of his ideas is explored in History and Religious Education. Yet in many classroom contexts pupil understanding of Darwin is limited to such key words as 'evolution' and 'Galapagos Islands'.

The correspondence is a useful vehicle for introducing Darwin's life and life's work, and for exploring some key issues and ideas from the period. His letters could form part of an investigation of nineteenth century language in english classes, accounts of his voyage around the world could be used in the geography classroom and his passionate views against slavery could feature in studies of black history. In short, learning about Darwin, his life, work and the impact of his ideas can occur across the schools' curricula. There is the potential for an entire school to devote a day to Darwin's letters as part of a curriculum enrichment or a day programme of deep learning. The case studies that follow took place with Key Stage 3 and 4 pupils (aged 11 to 15) at three schools in England. They reveal clear progression in learning about Darwin, his work and the times he lived in.

Case Study 1: English

A top set of Year 9 English pupils (ages 13 and 14) were tasked to compare Darwin's expectation of the *Beagle* voyage with the reality of his experience, as expressed over time in his letters home. Initially pupils were surprised to be studying Darwin in the context of an English lesson:

> I would imagine how you would study Darwin in science but like studying him in another subject you get to see a whole new side from the letters and things.

Part of the activity involved annotating passages from the letters to provide evidence for their argument. They also used direct quotation in their written responses:

> The journey turned out to be hard work but he found it 'most delightful and interesting'.

Pupils explored how the tone and language of the letter might change, depending on the recipient. They described how this worked:

> He seemed to be able to turn off work mode and be sociable; he wasn't serious when he was like, chit-chatting to his friends in his letters.

> There's the style when he knows the person he's writing to and the style when he doesn't, then there's the scientific style and then there's the personal style as well.

Pupils reflected on the different emotions expressed by Darwin at different times during the voyage:

> I think Darwin's voyage was not what Darwin expected. I think he missed the comfort and company of his friends back at home and everything was a little bit overwhelming at times.

The letters helped them to understand the importance of the offer to join the voyage and the scale of the potential dangers in going. Pupils read about Darwin's father's objections and debated whether they would have let their son go:

> I wouldn't have let him because in the 1800s people didn't tend to travel around as much, and he was like going all over the world and there was lots of dangers on board.

The question of actually going on the voyage proved fascinating for 13 year olds; they were interested in putting themselves in Darwin's shoes. There were strong expressions of opinion for and against leaving home, friends and family to join an expedition from which they might never return. It was hard for pupils to conceptualise surviving without the electronic resources that they now take for granted but some were entranced by the idea of discovering things that they had never encountered. They likened the journey to going to outer space.

> I would love to go, after years of him being brought up in England so far, it would be great to go out and explore and discover new things.

Although Darwin does not feature in the english curriculum, the letters were used successfully to examine social and historical variations in language and how language changes over time. As the teacher commented:

The pupils need to look at unfamiliar texts. In the exams, they won't be texts that they know.

The school is now expanding their study to explore what can be established about some of Darwin's correspondents by the tone and language of the letters and how the letters demonstrate the development of the relationship between correspondents. Outcomes of this investigation may take the form of creative writing assignments that culminate in a live performance.

The letters presented surprises to both pupils and teachers. They presented an opportunity to deepen an understanding of the breadth of Darwin's work and how he conducted his research. One pupil remarked:

I didn't think he'd done anything except for evolution.

Whilst a teacher commented:

I tended to think of Darwin as a one man band. Both the teachers and the students were surprised at the letters and especially the number from women.

Pupils were surprised to find out how he worked but clearly understood his practical and tactical method:

He used the correspondents to do some of the collecting for him; he used their results as well as his own.

I was surprised to find that he was so sociable, you always think of scientists and think of them as quite isolated people who just studied on their own, so I was quite surprised that he had so many contacts and the way he shared all his ideas.

The letters exude Darwin's exuberant personality; his excitement at the offer of the voyage, his desire to do as his father wished and his deeply felt homesickness when away. Through learning more about Darwin as a person, pupils were able to begin to negotiate an understanding of his scientific methods, expressed in sometimes complex nineteenth century language.

Case Study 2: History

Two Year 8 groups (ages 12 and 13) considered the question: 'How dangerous was Darwin?' during a one hour history class. The lessons focussed on the impact of the publication of *On the origin of species* in 1859 and *The descent of man* in 1871, as expressed via Darwin's correspondents, compared with responses that were aired in the popular press of the day. Difficulties in comprehension were assisted by access to dictionaries and teacher support; however pupils seemed to enjoy the challenge of translating the letter text, often prefacing their points with 'So basically, what he's saying is....'

Shortly after *On the origin of species* was published, Darwin received a letter from his Cambridge Professor of Geology, Adam Sedgwick, who confessed:

> I have read your book with more pain than pleasure. Parts of it I admired greatly; parts I laughed at till my sides were almost sore; other parts I read with absolute sorrow; because I think them utterly false & grievously mischievous.[6]

Sedgwick was afraid that Darwin had 'deserted' the 'true method of induction' and, as such, had started up 'a wild machinary'.

Pupils were surprised at the strength of feeling expressed by Sedgwick in opposition to the book and were engaged by the element of controversy:

> There's lots of offensive things, Darwin could be really upset about this letter, he probably was.

They repeatedly had to reflect on the context in which the book was written to understand its significance and the impact on its readers:

> They're dedicated to their religion. Now today we think, oh yeah, his theories are really well backed up with evidence and it seems to be the right thing to believe but back then they weren't so sure. They weren't open to ideas.

Pupils rationalised the negative responses:

> Perhaps people didn't want to believe it because it was so different from what they'd been brought up to believe.

> They sounded scared, because they'd believed in something for so long.

The letters were compared with images from the popular press including a French magazine, *La Petite Lune*, which depicted Darwin as an ape on its front cover (see Figure 1). Pupils were asked to analyse what they felt the image was trying to communicate:

> It's doubting his ideas, it's trying to prove that he's really false, saying, do you really think that we used to look like this?

> They think Darwin's ideas are unnatural, they mock him and his ideas.

The classes evaluated the value of the letters and press images as primary sources in terms of their reliability, bias and audience. Through studying the material they understood the reasons behind the potential controversy and the range of personal and public responses that Darwin's work had prompted. A pupil commented: 'He changed the world' but was corrected by another pupil: 'He changed the way the world understood the world'.

The letters enabled a shift in pupil understanding from considering Darwin as a traveller and explorer when questioned at the start of the class, to being able to describe his status as a contentious figure in Victorian society and as a real person, with whom they could empathise.

Figure 1. The cover of La Petite Lune, a Parisian satirical magazine showing Darwin as an ape, August 1878, by Andre Gill. (Classmark: DAR140.4:20 Reproduced by kind permission of the Syndics of Cambridge University Library)

Case Study 3: Science

Three Year 10 classes (ages 14 and 15) embarked on a lesson exploring what could be determined about Darwin's fascination with insectivorous plants through reading selected letters that he exchanged with American naturalist Mary Treat. Treat's work on butterflies was significant, leading Darwin to suggest that she might publish her work in a reputable scientific journal, as:

> Your observations and experiments on the sexes of butterflies are by far the best, as far as known to me, which have ever been made.[7]

Like Darwin, Treat worked at home where she created an observational enclosure that she referred to as her 'Insect Menagerie'. Emphasis was placed on the domestic contexts of both their work places; encouraging the notion that science can be carried out anywhere and that both Treat and Darwin were consummate observers and experimenters. This prompted the comment that:

> He was in his home so he couldn't use expensive equipment.

This comment was born out when pupils read about the types of materials that both scientists fed to insectivorous plants to assess the digestive mechanisms of different *Drosera* species (see Chapter 18). Although pupils didn't carry out the experiments themselves they understood the rationale for using nitrogen-rich substances that were commonly found at home such as roast beef and cheese. They were horrified to find that Darwin also tried feeding the plants urine and mucus:

> He put really disgusting stuff in the plants!

This led some pupils to think of Darwin as a 'mad scientist', but nevertheless one whose passion for science was clearly apparent.

The letters prompted useful discussions on the expectations for women's roles at the time and what barriers they might face in pursuing scientific work. Pupils argued that Treat was unusual because:

> ... women didn't have many rights back in Victorian times.

After learning about how much time Treat spent observing insect behaviour from her enclosure and the kinds of research that she and Darwin conducted separately, the pupils discussed their determination and dedication:

> I love science and everything but I wouldn't go that far!

> It depends how passionate you are about it; Darwin was obviously passionate about what he did, and that Mary woman, obviously she was too.

Based on their understanding of insectivorous plants from the information exchanged between Darwin and Treat, pupils were then asked to design their own carnivorous plant, ensuring that they explained how the plant could survive and reproduce (e.g. Figure 2). Responses to this task were creative and inventive but also rooted in a scientific understanding of how their plant might attract its prey, detain it and digest it:

> The brightly coloured leaves attract insects and the nectar entices them to stay long enough to be detected by the hairs.

> The plant releases enzymes to dissolve the insect.

Pupils agreed it was helpful to think about how Darwin developed as a scientist and that he wasn't always the man with the beard who knew about evolution. They started to think about how his career progressed:

> So I think that's why he started to collect loads of data, specimens and things, because he didn't know a lot about it.

His collaborative research method was discussed as something that was new and surprising to them:

> I thought he was a solitary person who just did science, it was nice to find out how much he worked with other people.

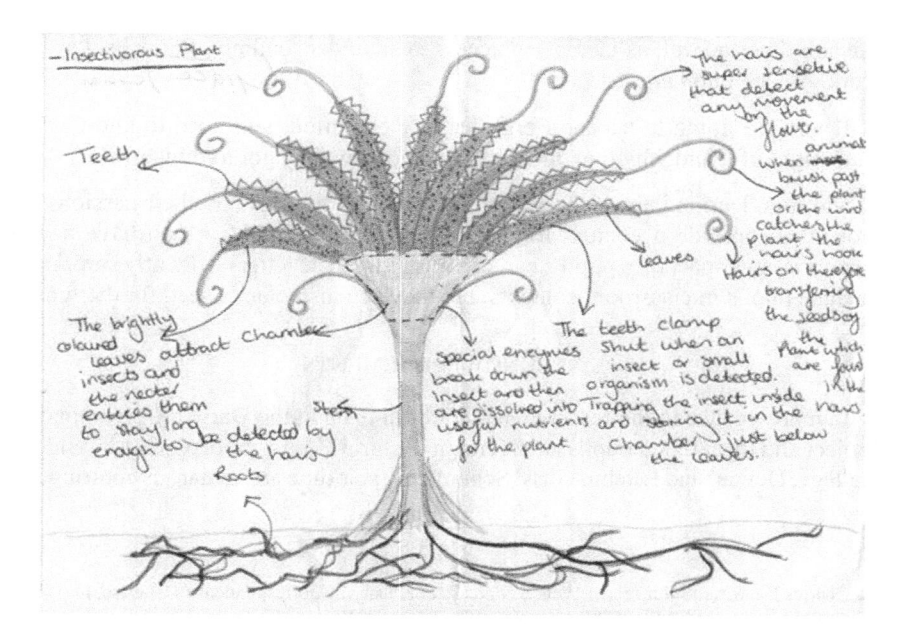

Figure 2. Pupil-designed insectivorous plant with its feeding and reproductive features labelled. (©Hitchin Girls' School)

He wasn't afraid to have a go – is this right? Do I do it this way?

The letters enabled the groups to understand more about Darwin's method, which helped to reinforce the idea that scientific discovery is underpinned by curiosity and the simple desire to find out more.

Their teacher concurred:

It's nice for them to see *real* science from someone they recognise.

She added:

It's been a massive help to my own Continuing Professional Development. There's lots of stuff that I didn't realise before.

CONCLUSION

Darwin remains embedded in British culture and will continue to feature directly and indirectly across many international schools curricula. If the starting point for pupils learning about Darwin is evolution, the letters add further pieces to the jigsaw of his life and times as well as increasing access to an understanding of how his key ideas work. As one pupil argued:

> If you are going to accept a big idea like evolution, you need to know who thought of it and why they thought of it and how they got to think of it.

In addition, learning about the personality of an individual and their passions does more than provide a context for specific curriculum study; it can have a wider inspirational impact on a pupil's career aspirations. The letters evidently surprise and intrigue pupils in classroom contexts, but they can also plant a seed for the future.

ACKNOWLEDGEMENTS

With many thanks to the research and editorial team at the Darwin Correspondence Project and to staff and pupils at Ulverston Victoria High School, Cumbria, Bideford College, Devon, and Hitchin Girls' School, for their time and generous contributions.

NOTES

[1] Charles Darwin to John Jenner Weir, 6 March, 1868. Darwin Correspondence Database, http://www.darwinproject.ac.uk/entry-5986 accessed on 29 August 2013.
[2] John Scott, Royal Botanic Gardens Calcutta, 22 March, 1872. Darwin Correspondence Database, http://www.darwinproject.ac.uk/entry-8249 accessed on 29 August 2013.
[3] Charles Darwin to Sophy, Margaret and Lucy Wedgwood, 4 August, 1862. Darwin Correspondence Database, http://www.darwinproject.ac.uk/entry-4373 accessed on 29 August 2013.
[4] Edward Cresy Junior to Emma Darwin, 20 November, 1865. Darwin Correspondence Database, http://www.darwinproject.ac.uk/entry-4940 accessed on 29August 2013.
[5] Charles Darwin to John Herbert, 2 June, 1833. Darwin Correspondence Database, http://www.darwinproject.ac.uk/entry-209 accessed on 29 August 2013.
[6] Adam Sedgwick to Charles Darwin, 24 November, 1859. Darwin Correspondence Database, http://www.darwinproject.ac.uk/entry-2548 accessed on 29 August 2013.
[7] Charles Darwin to Mary Treat, 5 January, 1872. Darwin Correspondence Database, http://www.darwinproject.ac.uk/entry-8146 accessed on 29August 2013.

Sally Stafford
Darwin Correspondence Project,
Cambridge University Library,
Cambridge,
UK

DEVELOPING A SENSE OF PLACE

PAUL DAVIES, DAWN L. SANDERS & RUTH AMOS

4. LEARNING IN CULTIVATED GARDENS AND OTHER OUTDOOR LANDSCAPES

INTRODUCTION

Much has been written on childhood experiences of gardens as places in which physical and imaginary experiences converge (e.g. Pollan, 1991). Similarly, recent research has examined the capacity of gardens and school grounds to provide artefacts and spaces for children to assimilate into imagined worlds (e.g. Malone & Tranter, 2003; Dowdell et al., 2011). In addition, a growing body of evidence affirms the rich educational opportunities provided by cultivated gardens and other outdoor landscapes (e.g. Rickinson et al., 2004; Malone, 2008).

The role that learning away from the traditional classroom plays in education has a long history; for example, Johann Comenius (1592-1670) argued that education should be a social process, much of which should occur outside of normal schooling (Braund & Reiss, 2004; Nundy, 2001). The educational theorists Pestalozzi (1746-1827), Froebal (1782-1852), Montessori (1870-1952) and Dewey (1859-1952) all highlight aspects of learning out-of-doors. In particular they see cultivated gardens as environments in which to engage in active learning. By the time of Darwin in the Victorian era, informal learning about science had become embedded in society, with the rapid advances in science and technology leading many people to visit science exhibitions and museums, as well as zoological and botanical collections; with these experiences being seen as important for 'lifelong learning' (Anderson, 1997; Braund & Reiss, 2004). In addition, creating personal collections of flowers and fossils and going on public excursions to observe and learn the names of plants and animals was part of the fabric of Victorian life, activities which extended across boundaries of class (Secord, 1994). Darwin himself was immersed in collecting beetles from an early age (see Chapter 7) and driven by a deep curiosity to explore the natural world (see Chapter 27).

Modern science lessons inhabit a range of environments beyond the classroom: science centres and museums, field visits, trips to universities and research institutions, botanic gardens and zoological collections (for example, Braund & Reiss, 2004; Sanders, 2007) along with the more local environments of parks, school gardens and adjacent streets (for example, Ross-Russell, 2001; Johnson, 2012). Darwin focused much of his science on learning out-of-doors and was interested in a broad range of both cultivated and other outdoor landscapes, whether it was the work he carried out on insectivorous plants in his glasshouses at Down House or his systematic surveys of the meadows surrounding his home (see Chapter 19). This chapter highlights the role cultivated and other outdoor landscapes can play in developing children's understanding of the living world.

LEARNING OUTSIDE THE CLASSROOM

Learning in outdoor environments can be highly organised, for example as part of developing an understanding of a specific part of the school curriculum, or more casual where parents encourage their children to look at living things in their local park. Whatever the setting, experiences of this type have been shown to have significant effects on children's cognitive and affective gains (Falk & Dierking, 2000; Nundy, 2001). However, focusing on one aspect of learning, for example the learner's understanding of specific scientific content somewhat misses the point of the richness that learning beyond the classroom has to offer (Braund & Reiss, 2004). Central to the significance that learning outside school plays in children's lives is that it affords them new and exciting opportunities to engage with science in diverse ways that encourage enquiry, curiosity and the establishment of positive relationships with the natural world (Orr, 1992).

Learning Science Outside the Classroom

Understanding how beyond-the-classroom experiences support learning is not straightforward. Falk and Dierking (2000) have devised a model that provides a useful framework to consider how these different environments might influence learning which focuses on the *personal, socio-cultural* and *physical contexts*. According to Falk and Dierking (2000), the personal context develops from a learner's emotional response to the learning setting and drives their interest, as well as motivation to know more. This might lead to both short-term and long-term changes in how a person thinks, behaves and, in the case of the natural world, interacts with and thinks about other living things (Orr, 1992). The physical context drives the personal response by engaging and intriguing the learner, often by challenging their beliefs about what it is they are learning about, as well as providing a stimulating environment which offers new and exciting opportunities. Often the learning setting allows access to what Braund and Reiss (2006) call 'rare materials' (p.1378), for example a botanical garden housing an unusual plant such as, the Titan Arum *Amorphophallus titanum* or the large Nepenthes *Nepenthes attenboroughii*, plants which are not commonly encountered in everyday life; such encounters can lead to powerful experiences, which Bebbington (2004) calls 'memorable moments' (p. 50).

The socio-cultural context of the Falk and Dierking model is a useful lens for examining what happens between learners in learning-beyond-classroom settings, and has important implications for Darwin-inspired learning. For learning to take place, it is mediated through interaction, most often through conversation with others (Wertsch, 1991); this can be face-to-face but can also occur through a host of communication devices. For Darwin, much of this occurred through letters and discussions with friends and colleagues, most notably Thomas Huxley the zoologist, the botanists Asa Gray and Joseph Hooker and the naturalist Alfred Russel Wallace, where ideas about their work were shared (Darwin Correspondence Project). For the modern learner, direct conversation still plays an important role in sharing, comparing and arguing about ideas, but this is now complemented by the affordances of digital technologies which can provide instant feedback (e.g. Berge & Muilenburg, 2013). Whatever its form, communication is set within cultural norms where our upbringing and the culture in which we are situated dictates much about how we feel we should act in a certain situation (Braund & Reiss, 2004). Learning outside of the classroom is very different to more formal schooling and brings with it different values and ideas which can be challenging to embrace (Nundy, 2001). Aikenhead (2006) and Braund and Reiss (2004) talk about the importance of understanding these different 'norms and values' in learning about science and remind us that they should be seen as opportunities. However, giving the learner freedom needs careful design and planning to support and guide the learning and, as Boyd (2013) has noted, requires teachers to become more confident in 'letting the children go' (Boyd, 2013, p.25).

Real Science Outside of the Classroom

Learning science within the classroom has often been criticised as not reflecting the way that 'real' science is carried out (Braund & Reiss, 2006; Hodson, 1998; Leach & Scott, 2002; Woolnough, 1998.). In contrast, learning-outside-the classroom experiences can offer access to authentic science environments and thus opportunities to see and actively participate in the discourses of 'real science' by using the tools and language of specific science disciplines. Taking a biology field visit as an example, at a beginning level, behaving like a real scientist would mean becoming familiar with the 'tools' of ecology, for example, using different sampling techniques. However, a more complete and meaningful understanding of the process of 'being a field ecologist' would mean knowing something of the approaches that ecologists take in collecting and analysing data, for example: using observations and readings to develop hypotheses, planning methodological approaches, which include using appropriate equipment to address the questions hypotheses raise, collecting the data, and modifying the collection method in light of the realities of working in the field, along with presenting and analysing the data and then drawing conclusions from the findings, as well as developing a sense of the significance of work of this type. This 'knowing something about ecology' thus encompasses an understanding of the nature of a specific habitat and the wider implications of understanding the complexities of relationships between living things. This linking together of ideas is challenging for many learners and is often described as occurring through a deep learning approach (Boyle et al.,

2007; Lublin, 2003), an approach in which settings beyond the classroom have been shown to play an important role (Drumer et al., 2008). In many ways Darwin helped define what we understand by 'doing science' and shaped the way we think about taking scientific approaches to solving problems and answering interesting questions; thus 'thinking like Darwin' (see Chapter 27) through school grounds investigations might provide such opportunities for 'authentic science' (see Chapters 27 & 28).

Creativity at the Centre of Learning Outside the Classroom

Despite outdoor learning experiences being shown to supporting learning, there is a body of literature highlighting a decline in their use in the UK (e.g. Fisher, 2001; Tilling, 2004; Lock, 2010), with pressures of the curriculum and lack of time often used to explain this reluctance to engage first-hand with the living world (Johnson, 2008). Settings outside the classroom allow students to learn in new ways, not always possible within the classroom context (see, for example, Blair, 2009; Boyd, 2013; Rickinson et al., 2004), and central to this is how a new, enriched environment can promote creative ways of thinking and learning together. Particularly in school science, the importance that social interaction plays in learning has become reduced to a narrow conceptualisation of Vygotsky's zone of proximal development (ZPD) (Vygotsky, 1978; for examples, see Holzman, 2010). Typical discussions of the role of Vygotsky's work in learning often ignore, or at best play down, the importance of collective social interaction *and* creativity in learning, instead focussing on the dyadic relationship and the 'more capable other' with its associated ideas of scaffolding proposed by Wood, Bruner and Ross (1976). A more comprehensive analysis of Vygotskian thinking has much to say about the nature of the learning environment and especially the role it has in development and thinking. According to Holzman (2010), the ZPD develops in a social setting that incorporates people doing things together. She argues that the ZPD is best understood in terms of a process rather than an entity, incorporating both the environment of learning and learning-leading-development, a notion she describes as the Vygotskian idea of the learner becoming 'a head taller' (Vygotsky, 1978, p.102). For Holzman, central to effective learning is playfulness, and she makes an interesting observation about the value placed on socially created learning in imaginative settings in schools, for example, a school play, as compared to the typical view of 'work' in schools where creativity and play are often rather limited, even discouraged or totally absent (Holzman, 2010). In thinking about learning in non-classroom settings, creativity and playfulness can be regarded as useful as they mediate between the learner and the social norms and values of the 'culture' they are becoming incorporated into. However, as Holzman (2010) points out, this does not mean that the learner is simply 'playing' at their role, for example being an ecologist, they are in fact taking on the role in a deep, internalised way.

LEARNING IN CULTIVATED GARDENS AND OTHER OUTDOOR LANDSCAPES

HIDDEN SPACES

There were other trees in the garden, and one of the things which made the place look strangest and loveliest was that climbing roses had run all over them and swung down long tendrils which made light swaying curtains, and here and there they had caught at each other or at a far-reaching branch and had crept from one tree to another and had made bridges of themselves. There were neither leaves nor roses on them now, and Mary did not know whether they were dead or alive, but their thin grey or brown branches and sprays looked like a sort of hazy mantle spread over everything, walls, and trees, and even brown grass, where they had fallen from their fastenings and run along the ground. It was this hazy tangle from tree to tree which made it look so mysterious. Mary had thought it must be different from other gardens which had not been left all by themselves so long; and, indeed, it was different from any other place she had ever seen in her life. (Hodgson Burnett, 1994 edition, pp.78–79)

This extract from the Victorian children's novel *The secret garden* represents the hidden 'other-worldness' that overgrown or dense vegetation can create for children's imaginations. The research examples of Åkerblom (2004), Blair (2009), Dowdell et al. (2011), Malone and Tranter (2003), and Sanders (2004) all give voice to the notion of cultivated gardens and school grounds as places where the 'unfettered play that children create in simple, hidden spaces' (Blair, 2009, p.35) can be fostered. Hart comments on the possible tensions that might arise if botanic gardens decide to develop 'a small corner of anarchy' where children under eight years of age can 'explore with many different kinds of materials that allow children to select, manipulate and construct things for themselves' (Hart, 2003, p.19). A challenge, highlighted by Hart, is how to provide space for imaginative 'play-based' learning activities in ways 'which do not threaten their larger goals as well as adults' sensibilities of what constitutes a "beautiful garden"' (Hart, 2003, p.16). Such discourses around garden aesthetics and functions do not begin and end with botanical gardens; schools also struggle with perceived tensions between 'unregulated exploration and play' and 'the formal educational curriculum' in their grounds (Malone & Tranter, 2003, p.289). These struggles have implications for the design of school grounds and children's interactions with them. In chapter 27 Johnson suggests that gatekeepers, in the form of policymakers, school leaders, curriculum frameworks and teachers, can facilitate or obstruct outdoor experiences in school grounds.

An Australian study by Malone and Tranter (2003) focused on the affordances of school grounds for 'cognitive play' and 'outdoor environmental learning'. 'Cognitive play' in their definition allows children to 'act on the environment and discover and understand relationships through their own behaviour'; such interactions are framed by the authors as 'unstructured informal learning'. Outdoor environmental learning, on the other hand manifests itself as 'the opportunities initiated by teachers or students to complement or supplement the formal curricula indoors' (Malone & Tranter, 2003, p.285). Their study draws on the earlier work of Titman (1994) which identifies four characteristics that children search for in school grounds:

- A place for doing
- A place for thinking
- A place for feeling
- A place for being (Titman, p.58).

Such preferences are not dissimilar to the range of indoor and outdoor places Darwin created in and around Down House, Kent (see Chapter 2).

The botanic garden can also provide opportunities for children to explore these ways of interacting with place (Sanders, 2004) but, as Malone and Tranter (2003, p. 299) comment, 'the philosophical value of the outdoor environment expressed by the school community is impacted by a number of variables'. Crucially, for botanic gardens, Malone and Tranter highlight one variable as being 'historical and policy orientated cultural norms'. 'Norms' are not only visible in school communities but are also embedded in the culture of many botanic gardens (Sanders, 2004). These past practices still resonate in some botanic garden attitudes to school visits, attitudes which focus on behaviour management and teacher-centred learning models. Giving children the space to 'discover for themselves the patterns and order that exist in the natural world', a space which, 'supports the link between experience and environmental cognition' (Malone & Tranter, 2003, p.300) may assist botanic garden educators to reflect on how learners perceive the nature and quality of their experience. In considering these relationships, botanic garden staff may also wish to review the balance between formal study and freer self-exploration, particularly if they hope to provide an environment for children that combines doing, thinking, feeling and being. As Titman observes:

> ...it is important to note that, in their terms, children operated on all these levels simultaneously. The environment was therefore required to offer the potential for children to 'do' and 'think' and 'feel' and 'be' all at the same time'. (Titman, 1994, p.58)

When asked about their favourite places in a UK botanic garden case study (Sanders, 2004, 2007) the children (aged 7-11) involved in the research focused on a wide range of spaces, but two key types of plant collections in the garden emerged:

- children enjoyed 'secret places', and 'the foresty bit';
- children highlighted the greenhouses, because they contained 'interesting' or 'exciting' plants. For some children, their favourite place was the greenhouse environment, because it made learning about plants 'easier to understand' and in their opinion made 'you learn more' (Sanders, 2004, p. 211).

This evidence suggests that children take a multi-faceted approach to the cultivated garden experience and respond to diverse aesthetics, in this case the contrast between the dense, freely-growing vegetation of 'the secret places' and 'foresty bits' against the 'exciting' and 'interesting' captive glasshouse collections. If botanic garden educators and horticultural staff took more opportunities to engage with learners' views of cultivated plant collections, then the resultant learning environments might provide further possibilities for each learner to become 'a theatre of perception' (Cobb, 1977, p. 29).

DARWIN-INSPIRED LEARNING THROUGH THE EXAMPLE OF A BIOLOGY FIELD VISIT

In contemporary Britain, the traditional biology field visit is often provided by specialist field centres and is tailored to the specific learning outcomes that meet the demands of awarding body specifications (Bebbington, 2004). While there is nothing wrong with this approach to using non-formal learning environments to develop an understanding of science, such tailoring can create a rather narrow and limited way of thinking about how and why students should engage with investigating the natural world at first hand. Darwin made extensive use of the gardens at Down House and the surrounding Kent countryside both in his studies and also in the way he introduced his children to the living world (see Chapter 7). He drew on different disciplines of science whilst investigating problems and a carefully designed field visit can support students both in learning about specific scientific content (Nundy, 2001) and also encouraging them to work as real scientists to develop an understanding of the relationship between humans and other living things (Orr, 1992).

As an example case study we show how a field visit to north Yorkshire, UK, supported students studying for a post-16 Advanced Level Biology qualification in what we describe as 'becoming a biologist'. The visit was conceptualised by the Head of Biology to mimic the approach taken on typical undergraduate biology field visits, where students work in a setting 'conducive to intellectual immersion' and without the 'distractions of the busy school day', and have the time and freedom to explore aspects of the natural world that interest them. Doing this involved the students following the Darwin-inspired meticulous methodical process (Johnson, 2004) of identifying a question of enquiry, developing an hypothesis that can be tested through an informed prediction, designing a methodology, gathering and analysing data and then interpreting findings by drawing considered conclusions.

The field visit involved the students working for five days in the three very different environments of the intertidal zone of a rocky shore, a freshwater stream and a managed heather moorland. Each day of the visit involved the students carrying out investigative work they had planned the previous evening on a variety of biological ideas, including factors affecting species distribution, human impact on the environment and relationships between different living things. Most of each day was spent in the field with students drawing on their own expertise and knowledge, working collaboratively, often with little support from teaching staff, to collect data to address their research questions. The approaches they took were often modified and adjusted in the light of challenges and difficulties they faced or in response to how their hypotheses developed throughout the day. The evenings were spent analysing and interpreting the data in a relaxed and informal environment, very different from the formal structures of school, with students working with, and identifying their peers and teachers as 'fellow biologists'.

As with a large number of other studies (e.g. Easton & Gilburn, 2012; Nundy, 2001; Rickinson et al., 2004), student development of conceptual knowledge and understanding of ecology concepts was an important and significant outcome of this field visit. Learning gain was observed for all students in terms of content and procedural knowledge and, importantly, through careful observation and analysis, students also developed a sophisticated understanding about the environments they were investigating as well as the methodological approaches that are taken in order to make sense of the complexities of the distribution of living things. In addition, they were able to make connections between what they were seeing; this kind of interplay between observables and theory is an example of the broader issue of the benefit that Abrahams and Millar (2008) identify as being afforded by practical work in school science. Significantly, many students developed a greater interest and appreciation of the natural world, and human interaction with the environment, when they talked about 'the stunning scenery' or the enjoyment of work in the beautiful surroundings of the heather moorland as well as the responsibilities for, and consequences of, maintaining this habitat. This raising of awareness was also apparent when the students made comparisons between their experiences of the natural world in their local environment and the excitement offered by exploring a new place.

The field visit provided an authentic experience that afforded the students unique learning opportunities. By working directly in the field, in diverse and novel environments (Cotton & Cotton, 2009), they were able to work as real ecologists. The students recognised that they were doing 'real science' (Braund & Reiss, 2006; Hodson, 1998; Lock, 1998, 2010) in a way that is quite different to the types of work they were familiar with in their typical school experience. Central to this happening was the careful design of the visit, both in terms of how it was conceptualised by the lead teacher and also the structural arrangements that were put in place. The visit provided opportunities for the students to use similar approaches to those taken by professional scientists and they appreciated the chance to explore different environments using the 'tools' of ecology and learning new skills, activities made much more meaningful because of the nature of the available space and, importantly, the context.

In school, there is often limited time to develop investigative work, with much work described as such, more often than not being only demonstrative (Abrahams & Millar, 2008). Through creative opportunities of the visit, the students independently took on the role of 'becoming biologists'; they developed new skills and knowledge but also began to experience the living world in new ways and 'see' nature as a biologist does, that is, develop the norms and values of 'biology culture' with the field visit mediating this change (Wertsch, 1994) in unique ways. The students were doing more than mimicking the role of an ecologist; they were starting to develop a mastery (Wertsch, 1992) of what it means to work as an ecologist and, occurring rapidly, over a matter of days, demonstrated the notion of 'becoming a head taller' (Holzman, 2010) as ecologists.

As ecologists, the students were able to be critical in their thinking, for example in their discussion of human interaction with the environment, to and draw upon, and relate to, a range of biological concepts in their explanations about what they were doing and finding out. The opportunity to work in three varied environments was important in providing 'creative encounters' (Holzman, 2010) for the students. These environments were new to many students, and far removed from their everyday urban living, and provided a setting to explore the natural world as well as to compare and contrast different environments using an ecological approach. The novelty appears to have been motivating for many, providing opportunities for the formation of significant memories (Bebbington, 2004; Nundy, 2001). Importantly, the establishment of these new experiences did not come about by chance but were methodically planned. This involved a range of important aspects of the visit: considering the types of habitats that would promote interest and provide contrasting learning experiences, giving students access to appropriate resources so that they could develop investigative approaches in ecology, and establishing a purposeful learning environment where students felt they had some autonomy over their learning. Consideration of these aspects by the Head of Biology sheds light on his perception of the purpose of field visits in relation to students becoming biologists and, in a wider sense, the purposes of a science curriculum. Aikenhead (2006) develops a useful 'categories of relevance' when considering this latter point, arguing that there are several positions that can be adopted when thinking about relevance of the curriculum, ranging from a fairly traditional teacher-centred approach of 'wish-they-knew' science to the much broader notion of 'science-as-culture'. For the Head of Biology, student-centred enquiry was a key feature of the design and success of the visit (the 'personal-curiosity' of Aikenhead, (2006) and something which was important to him as a biologist.

CONCLUSION

In many respects, cultivated gardens, and other landscapes, afford students access to special learning spaces and memorable opportunities. In the final page of *On the origin of species,* Darwin used a visual metaphor of an 'entangled bank' grounded in the close at hand – 'birds singing', 'worms crawling', 'insects flitting' (Darwin 1859, p.360) to provide a literary lens on his universal theory by allowing the reader to 'imagine hidden worlds' (Otis, 2002, p.xxxi.). We suggest that as students navigate through the outdoor classroom, they move between the imaginary and material world and, like Darwin, reconceptualise their understanding and thinking about science, and perhaps their place in nature too.

REFERENCES

Abrahams, I., & Millar, R. (2008). Does practical work really work? A study of the effectiveness of practical work as a teaching and learning method in school science. *International Journal of Science Education, 30*(14), 1945–1969.
Aikenhead, G. S. (2006). *Science education for everyday life: Evidence-based practice*. New York, NY: Teachers College Press.
Åkerblom, P. (2004). The impact and importance of school gardening in primary schools. In P. Wickenberg, H. Axelsson, L. Fritzén, G. Helldén, & J. Öhman (Eds.), *Learning to change our world? Swedish research on education and sustainable development* (pp. 75–88). Lund: Studentlitteratur.
Amos, R., & Reiss, M. (2012). The benefits of residential fieldwork for school science: Insights from a five-year initiative for inner-city students in the UK. *International Journal of Science Education, 34*(4), 485–511.
Anderson, D. (1997). *A common wealth: Museums and learning in the United Kingdom*. London: Department of National Heritage.
Bebbington, A. (2004). Learning at residential field centres. In M. Braund & M. Reiss, *Learning science outside the classroom* (pp. 55–74). London, UK: RoutledgeFalmer.
Berge, Z. L., & Muilenburg, L. (Eds.). (2013). *Handbook of mobile education*. London: Routledge.
Blair, D. (2009). The child in the garden: An evaluative review of the benefits of school gardening. *The Journal of Environmental Education, 40*(2), 15–38.
Boyle, A., Maguire S., Martin, A., Milsom, C., Nash, R., Rawlinson, S., Conchie, S. (2007). Fieldwork is good: The student perception and the affective domain. *Journal of Geography in Higher Education, 31*(2), 299–317.
Braund, M., & Reiss, M. (2004). *Learning science outside the classroom*. London, UK: RoutledgeFalmer.
Braund, M., & Reiss, M. (2006). Towards a more authentic science curriculum: the contribution of out-of-school learning. *International Journal of Science Education, 28*(12), 1373–1388.
Cobb, E. (1977). *The ecology of imagination in childhood*. Henley and London, UK: Routledge and Kegan Paul
Cotton, D. R. E., & Cotton, P. A. (2009). Field biology experiences of undergraduate students: The impact of novelty space. *Journal of Biological Education, 43*, 169–174.
Darwin, C. (1859). *On the origin of species*. G. Beer (Ed.) (Oxford Classics Edition). Oxford: Oxford University Press
Dowdell, K., Gray,T., & Malone, K. (2011). Nature and its influence on children's outdoor play. *Australian Journal of Outdoor Education, 15*(2), 24–35.
Dummer, T. J., Cook, I. G., Parker, S. L., Barrett, G. A., & Hull, A. P. (2008). Promoting and assessing 'deep learning' in geography fieldwork: An evaluation of reflective field diaries. *Journal of Geography in Higher Education, 32*(3), 459–479.
Easton, E., & Gilburn, A. (2012). The field course effect: Gains in cognitive learning in undergraduate biology students following a field course. *Journal of Biological Education, 46*(1), 29–35.
Falk, J. J. H., & Dierking, L. L. D. (2000). *Learning from museums: Visitor experiences and making of meaning*. New York, NY: AltaMira Press.
Fisher, J. (2001). The demise of fieldwork as an integral part of science education in United Kingdom schools: A victim of cultural change and political pressure? *Pedagogy, Culture and & Society, 9*(1), 75–96.
Hodgson-Burnett, F. (1994). *The Secret Garden*. London: Penguin.
Hodson, D. (1998). *Teaching and learning science: Towards a personalized approach*. Buckingham, UK: Open University Press.
Hart, R. (2003). Anarchy or order? Some dilemmas in designing landscapes for young children in botanical gardens. *Roots, 26*, 16–21.
Holzman, L. (2010). Without creating ZPDs there is no creativity. In M. C. Conner, V. P. John-Steiner, & A. Marjanovic-Shane (Eds.), *Vygotsky and creativity: A cultural-historical approach to play, meaning making and the arts* (pp. 27–40). New York, NY: Peter Lang.

Johnson, S. (2008). Teaching science out-of-doors. *School Science Review, 90*(331), 65–70.

Leach, J., & Scott, P. (2002). Designing and evaluating science teaching sequences: An approach drawing upon the concept of learning demand and a social constructivist perspective on learning. *Studies in Science Education, 38*(1), 115–142.

Lock, R. (1998). Fieldwork in the life sciences. *International Journal of Science Education, 20*(6), 633–642.

Lock, R. (2010). Biological fieldwork in schools and colleges in the UK: An analysis of empirical research from 1963 to 2009. *Journal of Biological Education, 44*(2), 58–64.

Lublin, J. (2003). *Deep, surface and strategic approaches to learning*. Belfield, Dublin: Centre for Teaching and Learning, UCD Dublin.

Malone, K., & Tranter, P. J. (2003). School grounds as sites for learning: Making the most of environmental opportunities. *Environmental Education Research, 9*(3), 283–303.

Malone, K. (2008). *Every experience matters: An evidence based research report on the role of learning outside the classroom for children's whole development from birth to eighteen years.* Report commissioned by Farming and Countryside Education for UK Department Children, School and Families. Wollongong, Australia.

Nundy, S. (2001). *Raising achievement through the environment: A case for fieldwork and field centres.* Peterborough, UK: National Association of Field Studies Officers.

Orr, D. W. (1992). *Ecological literacy: Education and the transition to a postmodern world.* New York, NY: State University of New York Press.

Otis, L. (2002). *Literature and science in the nineteenth century: An anthology.* Oxford: Oxford University Press

Pollan, M. (1991). *Second nature: A gardener's education.* New York, NY: Grove Press.

Rickinson, M., Dillion, J., Teamey, K., Morris, M., Choi, M. Y., Sanders, D., & Benefield, P. (2004). *A review of research on outdoor learning.* Shrewsbury, UK: Field Studies Council.

Ross-Russell, H. (2001). *Ten-minute field trips: A teacher's guide to using the school grounds for environmental studies.* Arlington, VA: National Science Teachers Association

Sanders, D. (2004). *Botanic gardens: Walled, stranded arks or environments for learning?* (Unpublished doctoral thesis). University of Sussex, UK.

Sanders, D. (2007). Making public the private life of plants: The contribution of informal learning Environments. *International Journal of Science Education, 29*(10), 1209–1228.

Secord, A. (1994). Corresponding interests: Artisans and gentlemen in nineteenth-century natural history. *The British Journal for the History of Science, 27,* 383–408.

Tilling, S. (2004). Fieldwork in UK secondary schools: Influences and provision. *Journal of Biological Education, 38*(2), 54–58.

Titman, W. (1994). *Special places, special people. The hidden curriculum of school grounds.* Godalming: World Wide Fund for Nature UK.

Vygotsky, L. (1978). *Mind in society.* Cambridge, MA: Harvard University Press.

Wertsch, J. V. (1991). *Voices of the mind: Sociocultural approach to mediated action.* Cambridge, MA: Harvard University Press.

Wertsch, J. V. (1994). The primacy of mediated action in sociocultural studies. *Mind, Culture, and Activity, 1*(4), 202–208.

Wood, D., Bruner, J. S., & Ross, G. (1976). The role of tutoring in problem solving. *Journal of Child Psychology and Psychiatry, 17*(2), 89–100.

Woolnough, B. 1998. Authentic science in schools, to develop personal knowledge. In J. Wellington (Ed.), *Practical work in school science. Which way now?* (pp.109–125). London: Routledge.

Paul Davies
Institute of Education,
University of London,
UK

Dawn L. Sanders
Department of Pedagogical, Curricular and Professional Studies,
Gothenburg University,
Sweden

Ruth Amos
Institute of Education,
University of London,
UK

OLA MAGNTORN

5. LEARNING TO READ NATURE TO UNDERSTAND THE NATURAL WORLD AND HOW IT WORKS

INTRODUCTION

The concept of *reading nature* is central to ecology. Its contributions to science education and its relation to Darwin and Darwinian learning are introduced, and discussed in this chapter. Reading nature is the ability to recognise organisms and relate them to other organisms and to material cycling, and energy flow in a specific habitat. It has to do with authenticity, where the natural world that we face outside is the book to be read and the tools we have to do so are our experiences from previous learning situations, both inside and out-of-doors. It is an aspect of ecology coined by Haeckel who referred to Darwin by writing 'in a word ecology is the study of all those complex interrelations referred to by Darwin as the conditions of the struggle for existence' (Stauffer, 1957, p. 141).

Darwin focused on species for developing his theories of evolution, and species are the point of departure for learning to read nature. The processes of developing the ability to read nature among students, ranging from primary school level all the way up to university students, has been my focus of interest for many years. The examples given here illustrate students' developing abilities to read nature in different habitats. In each habitat a key organism and its autecology is considered. Students' ideas of their own learning, as expressed in metacognitive interviews, are considered in relation to researchers' views of the key factors for learning to read nature. Another important aspect discussed in this chapter is the generalisability or transfer of students' abilities to read nature between different habitats.

Ecological Literacy

Ecological literacy primarily constitutes 'knowing, caring and practical competence' (Orr, 1992, p. 92). Ecological literacy also encompasses an understanding of 'how people and societies relate to each other and to natural systems, and how they might do so sustainably' (Orr, 1992, p. 92). In other words, ecological literacy entails knowing how the natural world works, the dynamics of our environment and how to preserve and maintain it. Ecological literacy is ideally about developing a rich knowledge base and multi-faceted beliefs and/or philosophies about the environment that lead to ecological sustainability. If we turn to the phrase 'reading nature', this ability is an important aspect of ecological literacy. This literacy has to do with an ability to recognise organisms outdoors and relate them to material cycling and energy flow. Reading in this context is strongly related to observation and interpretation of what you see.

LEARNING TO READ NATURE

Darwin's Ability to Read Nature

The knowledge of species and their ecology has a long history and it has certainly been a deep interest of the curious *Homo sapiens* to study and understand the surrounding natural world. Being able to distinguish between edible and poisonous plants or to be able to hunt suitable animals has been a matter of self-preservation. To observe and describe nature systematically in a scientific way is a much later phenomenon. The concept 'ecology' was not coined until 1866 when Ernst Haeckel defined ecology as the study of all of the complex inter-relations, referred to by Darwin as the 'conditions for the struggle for existence'. In a way, Darwin's account launched ecology as a discipline. His integration of the physical, geological and biological dimensions of places where the *Beagle* stopped, complemented by influential contemporary work by the English naturalist Alfred Russel Wallace, defined a new and synthetic way of looking at nature, or maybe the start of reading nature.

It is fascinating to read about Darwin's curiosity and passion for biodiversity expressed in the many letters to his friends. Randal Keynes, the great-great grandson of Darwin, writes:

> Darwin was an inspirational guide to his own children and many other young people who worked with him through his life. Not just as a teacher, more as a companion in an eager investigation, involving them in his special approach to observation and experiment, and then sharing the excitements, disappointments and triumphs with them. (Keynes, 2009, p.101)

A well-known example of Darwin's ability to read nature is his interest for earthworms and he writes to his niece:

> My dear Sophy,
>
> Will you be so kind in any of your walks as to observe whether there are any or many worm castings in the midst of Heath. It would be best to look where any grass-covered path crosses Heath, for if there are castings on the grass-covered paths or road & not amongst the Heath, it would show that heath is somehow unfavorable for worms. I ask because I find a memorandum in my notes, that 'there does not appear to be any worms amongst the Heath on Hayes common'.— If Lucy is with you, I know that she would readily look from her well-known affection for worms—I am also becoming deeply attached to worms.[1]

Another interesting example of Darwin's sharp eye and ability to read nature is an observation from his notes from Tahiti where he writes about the leaves of the banana plants adjacent to a waterfall: 'The leaves of the banana, damp with spray, possessed an unbroken edge, instead of being split, as generally is the case, into a thousand shards' (Darwin, 1871, p. 489) demonstrating that he had noted the changed leaf structure of the bananas living in this damper environment with mountainous 'lofty points' of 'the highest pinnacles' around them.

How Students Can Learn to Read Nature

I used the concept 'reading nature' when I started studying student-teachers' abilities to describe nature in an outdoor situation, for example in a beech forest, when they answered the questions 'what do you see here and why are these organisms living here?' This kind of literacy starts with an ability to discern and name the common plants and animals in an ecosystem. Species knowledge is of course only one aspect of this literacy. It is also about linking species to the environment, i.e. being able to explain why they live there and how they are related to the flow of energy and the cycling of matter. In my studies it soon turned out that the students were often frustrated at how difficult it was to answer such a deceptively simple question. It demanded their ability to connect the descriptive part of ecology, such as species identification and distribution of populations, with basic theories about the non-biological processes that occur in nature. They often expressed the view that this comprised much of what ecology is all about. "Of course one needs to be able to discuss ecology and take examples from nature" as many put it (Magntorn, 2007).

The Legacy of Linnaeus

Being a Swede I have to mention another person who lived 250 years ago who proved to have a lot in common with Darwin in his fascination for, and ability to read, nature – Carolus Linnaeus. Linnaeus received the royal assignment for describing nature and natural resources in the whole of Sweden. He was a superb observer who could relate details to the whole. His motto '*maxima in minimis*' (Linnaeus, 1737)[2] reflects his fascination for each insect or plant and how these relate to a holistic and larger picture of nature. Both Linnaeus and Darwin had a focus on organisms with questions considering taxonomy, adaptation or evolution, but they also showed a strong interest in the natural history of these organisms, in a time when the word ecology was yet to be coined. 'I have come to these conclusions by personally leading my pupils on wanderings through the tangled web of nature, in order to spur others to an examination and explanation of nature rather than the reiteration of perceived ideas!' Linnaeus quoted in Knapp (2002, p. 479). Both scientists had a great deal of Orr´s (1992) 'ecological literacy' and both were capable of reading nature using the scientific tools available to them at the time.

The Importance of Being Able to Read Nature for Teaching and Learning

How important is it then to have the bigger picture and to be able to discern and read nature? An overwhelming majority of the experienced teachers and student teachers I have met, and with whom I have discussed the ability to read nature, have said that it should be an important learning goal in biology teaching and part of the curriculum in school biology. It can also be regarded as an important aspect of education for sustainable development. Being able to recognise the natural world we have today is a pre-requisite for us to be aware of future changes in nature (Orr, 1992).

In the syllabuses for primary school biology all over the world, key ecological concepts and species identification, together with the ability to relate species to structures such as food chains and ecosystems, are central goals. The ecosystem concept is considered one of the most important, perhaps the most important in ecology. This can be illustrated by the response of members of the British Ecological Society who were asked to rank the most important ecological concept out of a list of the 50 most common (Cherett, 1989). A majority of respondents ranked 'the ecosystem' number one in importance. Most biology teachers would probably agree with this view of the ecosystem as a fundamental concept in biology, and in reading nature.

Important Features of Reading Nature from Research

In one of my studies, a teaching sequence was designed to help primary school students (10 to 12 years old) to read a river ecosystem, starting with the organisms with a special focus on a small freshwater shrimp *Gammarus pulex* and its ecology (Magntorn & Helldén, 2006). The ambition was to help the students to read the river ecosystem by starting with a single organism and gradually adding ecological and environmental aspects to its life and environment. This can be considered a bottom-up perspective and it proved a fruitful teaching design, helping the students to engage and learn more about an ecosystem and how it works, based on its biological and non-biological components. The teaching sequence was comprised of four steps starting with taxonomy (see Figure 1).

Knowledge of Species: What Is Its Name?

Taxonomy is the science of naming organisms and the idea is to describe nature by naming plants and animals with a specific system of two part names to enable shared understanding. Linnaeus expressed the importance of this taxonomic knowledge as *'Nomina nescis perit et cognita rerum'*, i.e. 'If we do not know the names the knowledge of things becomes meaningless' (Linnaeus, 1737, p. 11). This linguistic aspect of learning has been emphasised by, for example, Lemke (1990), who describes how science education often involves an ambition that students should acquire an unfamiliar scientific language that they can experience and compare

Phase 4: Systemic level
The relations between the shrimp and the living and the non living world. Cycling of matter and flow of energy

⇧

Phase 3: Synecology
The relations between the shrimp and other populations.

⇧

Phase 2: Taxonomy and autecology. Several organisms and their life cycles and adaptation the environment is studied

⇧

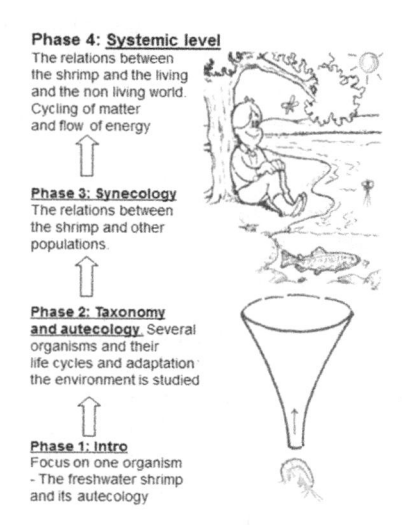

Phase 1: Intro
Focus on one organism - The freshwater shrimp and its autecology

Figure 1. A teaching approach beginning with an organism – a freshwater shrimp – a bottom-up perspective. (Peter Gehander. Smådjur i sötvatten, Kristianstad Naturskola, 1994)

to their everyday language. Knowledge about species names, for example, can be considered necessary in order to communicate about nature. Another aspect of this is that students often find it difficult to classify the animals and plants they see into a particular group, even if they sometimes have a correct name for them (Kattman, 2001). This knowledge about species has gradually declined in schools, making it even more difficult to describe an ecosystem in terms of its organisms (Magro, 2001; Bebbington, 2005).

Autecology: Why Does It Live Here?

The concept autecology represents ecological studies of each species and their habitat requirements, basically, to seek answers to the questions of why these organisms live here. This autecological aspect within the concept of reading nature is largely to do with how an organism is adapted to the environment it lives in, for example, what the differences are in the appearance and behaviour of an organism that lives in running streams compared to those in a lake, or how a ground beetle can be recognised as a predator on account of its rapid movement, its large eyes and powerful jaws, while a leisurely-moving caterpillar is a typical herbivore. This picture is a generalisation, which is frequently true, but, as is often the case in nature, there are exceptions. In education research, the importance of focusing on individual organisms is often emphasised and one example is provided by Tomkins and Tunnicliffe (2001) who describe primary pupils' fascination with the study of a crustacean, a brine shrimp of the genus *Artemia*. These aquatic animals were taken home as 'pets' and their development was described from day to day. Another example in line with this is Nyberg (2004, p. 326) who found strong support for the importance of the affective aspect when students were learning about life cycles, combining learning and caring for the organisms, an approach that both amazed students and stimulated their curiosity.

Systems Ecology: How Does It Relate to Everything Else?

If we shift the focus from individuals in an ecosystem and their autecology to the major processes in which all the organisms in an ecosystem take part, and where all the environmental factors that affect them are studied together as a unit, we get a different view. This view is all about models, focusing on the organisms' internal relations to one another in an ecosystem, such as food webs or food pyramids. In a broader context, it is the non-biological aspects of the organism related to the cycles of matter and flows of energy. To read nature is thus to be able to link together all these elements into a whole. And this is a tricky part of teaching ecology. Many teachers have found that students have difficulties with the abstract processes and 'invisible' elements of ecology that are central to reasoning about ecological processes (Helldén, 2004; Jordan et al., 2009).

An example of a central systems concept is photosynthesis, which is understood in many different ways by students. For instance, a common but alternative idea is that plants get their food entirely from the soil. Nutrient cycling has a historical foothold in the writings of Charles Darwin with his reference to the decompositional actions of earthworms. Darwin wrote about 'the continued movement of the particles of earth' (Darwin, 1881, p. 244). Even earlier, in 1749, Linnaeus wrote in his *Oeconomia Naturae:* 'We understand the all-wise disposition of the Creator in relation to natural things, by which they are fitted to produce general ends, and reciprocal uses' (Linnaeus, 1749, in Broberg, 1978, p. 123). In this book he captured the notion of ecological recycling: 'The "reciprocal uses" are the key to the whole idea, for the death, and destruction of one thing should always be subservient to the restitution of another; thus mould spurs the decay of dead plants to nourish the soil, and the earth then offers again to plants from its bosom, what it has received from them' (p. 127).

Ecological Puzzling

Alternative ideas about the recycling of matter are often seen in young students today (Wood-Robinson, 1991; Carlsson, 2002; Leach et al., 1996). Research demonstrates that bigger difficulties lie in the separation of energy and matter in an ecosystem. The idea that the consumption of energy is possible is a common notion when pupils deal with matter and transformation (Watson & Dillon, 1996; Hogan & Fisherkeller, 1996). Though ecological models, such as food webs, are presented to most students, research shows that when analysing this model, students often only focus on the effects on the next link of the model and seldom, or never is the so-called 'domino effect' noticed, that affects the whole chain, nor are any feedback mechanisms mentioned (Grotzer & Bell Basca, 2004).

When students reason about ecosystems they tend to see parts of the system as isolated from each other (Assaraf & Orion, 2005). One of the central points about the ability to read nature is that it is a combination of species knowledge and systems ecology structured in a meaningful way. Students who can read nature can use structure in the way that they observe nature. They are looking for functional groups, such as decomposers or predators, which they recognize and can link to the abstract processes, which they know take place in all ecosystems. Some of my students expressed it as, 'we know what happens in nature' (Magntorn & Helldén, 2005, p.1240), but they have to find out who performs it in that particular ecosystem. It makes sense and is a bit like puzzling with the living and non-living pieces where the student knows what the final puzzle will look like and reacts if any pieces are missing. This systems-ecological puzzle can be introduced early and my colleague Gustav Helldén (1992) has demonstrated, in longitudinal studies, how pupils' early experiences of basic processes and concepts can be very important in facilitating ecological learning later in life.

This brief summary gives an idea of the scope of ecology education research, conducted during the last two decades, in which students' difficulties in ecology have, amongst other things, been to understand the more abstract processes.

How Can We Know if the Students Can Read Nature?

As stated previously, one can see that an ecosystem is based on at least three levels: on the basis of the species, of populations and of the system as a whole. In my analysis, I include a method called 'structure-behaviour-function' analysis of complex systems (Hmelo-Silver & Pfeffer, 2004). 'Structure' refers to the parts of a system and the relationships between organisms, such as species in the ecosystem and their different autecologies. 'Function' refers to the various organisms' roles or functions in an ecosystem, such as decomposers that mineralise, release and circulate nutrients. 'Behaviour' refers to the dynamic mechanisms that influence ecosystems and lead to changes, such as how the ecosystem is changing due, for example, to eutrophication and how the food web will change and why. The ability to read nature is about being able to combine these levels for an ecosystem understanding and to reach this the student must be enabled to meet these levels in a structured way. Since they represent an increasing level of complexity the structural level is often the easiest to understand, and therefore an appropriate one with which to begin. It lays the foundation for further studies of ecosystem functioning and processes.

O. MAGNTORN

From Concrete to Abstract: Learning to Speak 'Ecologish'

I was initially interested in the student-teachers' ideas about the concept of reading nature and its relevance as a goal in ecology education. I was also very curious about how their ability to read nature would develop over a 10-week course in ecology and their own views on their learning in ecology during this course (Magntorn & Helldén, 2005). The students were in their seventh semester of the teacher education program with a focus on mathematics and science for grades 4-9 (10-15 year old pupils). During this course, they visited and studied seven different ecosystems. The interviews took place in a forest next to the university before the course began and again when the course had just been completed. The number of species that students could initially name was often counted on the fingers of one hand. The link between biological and non-biological factors was often difficult for them to describe. The majority of students, however, could explain photosynthesis and the cycling of water and carbon correctly in a general way. Another noticeable thing was the students' inability to link these abstract processes to what they actually saw in the ecosystem. They rattled the photosynthetic formula out without any reference to the actual trees and plants surrounding them. After the course, most students could recognise significantly more species in the ecosystem; another important change was that the students referred much more to the organisms they had around them in the forest. They knew where to find woodlice and lichens. They had insights about animal and plant autecology and could describe nature by using species knowledge and they referred to first-hand experiences in nature during the course. Human impact on nature, such as introduced species or maintenance of the vegetation and the natural succession of the ecosystem, were things many students still found difficult to describe.

The students' improved ability to read nature as a result of the course helped me to identify important aspects of student capability regarding their ecological literacy before and after instruction. The most interesting parts of the data were perhaps the metacognitive interviews after the course where they had to listen to their answers from the first and second field interviews and comment on their own knowledge and learning. Many students were totally amazed by how little they knew at the first interview and they felt that they saw nature with completely different eyes after the course. They commented on how their language had changed and the fact that they could now express themselves in a scientific way, which helped them to describe and explain nature. As one student expressed it 'I used to know something about nature in Swedish but now I know a lot more and I speak Ecologish, a better and more precise language' (Magntorn & Helldén, 2005).

Species knowledge and autecology, i.e. knowledge of an organism's requirements and adaptations to a habitat, was considered by most students to be very important. Excursions and field-work were considered the most valuable parts of the course in developing the ability to read nature. This is not surprising, but it was interesting that the students put forward various reasons for this statement. One student pointed to the occasions when they themselves were planning their environmental study;

another student appreciated when they were discussing with teachers in the field and when their teachers showed clearly what it was they were supposed to look at in the wild. The different approach to field studies was appreciated by many students, giving a clear indication of the need to vary the instruction to meet all students' demands. This aligns with a large study on quality in field studies (Rickinson et al., 2004): Field-work can have a positive impact on long-term memory, due to the memorable nature of the field-work setting and there can be re-inforcement between the affective and the cognitive, with each informing the other and providing a bridge to higher order learning (p. 24).

The results also convinced me that I should continue with my ambition to identify what knowledge students need in order to read nature and the importance of focusing on a limited number of organisms or aspects of an ecosystem. This is again supported by Darwin whose fascination for nature is quoted in the book *Darwin, his daughter and human evolution* (Keynes, 2002), when he describes his amusements for field work:

> Miss Thorley and I are doing a little botanical work for our amusement, and it does amuse me very much, making a collection of all the plants which grow in a field or wood … If ever you catch quite a beginner, and want to give him a taste for botany, tell him to make a perfect list of some little field or wood. Both Miss Thorley and I agree that it gives a really uncommon interest to the work, having a nice little definite world to work on, instead of the awful abyss and immensity of all British Plants. (p. 128)

From the Abstract to the Concrete System in a Forest Ecosystem

In the next study, we followed the students in a secondary class (Magntorn & Helldén, 2007). This time I started with the more abstract parts of reading nature. The teacher had three lessons of instruction on basic ecological concepts regarding the energy flow through an ecosystem and the cycles of carbon and water, before the students went out to study a nearby forest ecosystem. The non-biological aspects, such as light, moisture and soil conditions, were discussed and local plants and animals and their living conditions were studied. The students then built sealed ecosystems (microcosms) representing the forest, including relevant biotic and abiotic components and based on their own ideas. The given guideline was that the microcosms should stay sealed in the classroom for at least six months. Students also constructed food pyramids based on what they had found in the forest. The energy balance in the ecosystem was discussed. Students also made concept maps illustrating how their closed ecosystem worked. Finally, they had another excursion to the forest to summarise what they now knew about this ecosystem and to discuss succession and human impact on the forest.

Initially, students had difficulties relating the abstract processes to what they saw in the forest ecosystem. Studies of the decomposition process turned out to be important in helping the students get to grips with 'cycles thinking'. In the second interview students often indicated that they meant that something circulated in the soil as a result of the decomposition of the leaves. For some students, this 'something' was energy, and for others it was sugar or minerals. The food pyramid was used as a model to show the relationship between different groups of organisms in an ecosystem. This helped many students to understand the role of plants and animals as producers, consumers, predators or decomposers. It is interesting to compare students' superficial descriptions of trees and grass in the first interview with how elaborately in the second interview they discussed the processes and linked them to relevant organisms and ecosystem functioning.

Transferring Ecological Literacy to Another Ecosystem

We investigated students' abilities to transfer their 'ecological literacy' from one ecosystem, which they had studied to another, less known ecosystem. The students' first interviews took place in a forest where they had studied the ecology and the plant and animal life in order to learn how to 'read the forest'. Two months after their studies of the forest ecosystem they were taken to another, unfamiliar ecosystem – a pond. By the pond they were asked to answer the same type of ecological questions. This process of transferring the ability to read nature between ecosystems and being able to generalise the understanding of processes and functional groups existing in all common ecosystems, is important and valuable, since the students normally don't have the possibility to study more than a few ecosystems in their entire compulsory biology education. The first factor that influences successful transfer is the degree of mastery of the original ability. Without an adequate level of initial learning, transfer cannot be expected. It was therefore highly relevant to follow the students' learning and evaluate their ability to read nature after instruction. Research has indicated (Lobato, 2006) that transfer across contexts is especially difficult when a subject is taught only in a single context rather than in multiple contexts. When a subject is taught in multiple contexts, however, and includes examples that demonstrate wide applications of what is being taught, students are more likely to abstract the relevant features of concepts and to develop a flexible representation of knowledge (Bransford, Brown, & Cocking, 1999). The multiple contexts in this study are the forest and the pond ecosystem.

The class collected plants and animals from the pond and described their living conditions. They had to talk about the similarities and differences in comparison to the forest ecosystem. Later, the students built a mini-pond ecosystem under the same conditions as when they built their sealed forest ecosystem. The study was documented through numerous interviews and video recordings from both the forest and the aquatic ecosystem (Magntorn & Helldén, 2007a).

Although the students did not know the names of the species, they could use their knowledge of how certain organisms lived in a forest ecosystem, and they discussed the role of different organisms in the aquatic ecosystem. They asked themselves which organisms could be the producers and which animals would live on plants, and which are the predators or which contribute to the decomposition. They also discussed the distribution of organisms on the basis of the model of the food pyramid. This study shows that students did transfer their experience and knowledge gained from previous studies of an entirely different ecosystem (Magntorn & Helldén, 2007a).

The students concluded that the animals in the pond with rapid movements, large eyes and large mouth parts were probably predators even if they did not look exactly like the predators they found in the forest. This is in line with the ideas of Darwin, who saw the evolution and survival of the best-adapted organisms in the ecosystem and, for example, recognised that the features of a successful herbivorous lizard on Galapagos islands resembled the other herbivorous lizards, both on land and in the sea, whereas the predator lizards looked different (Darwin, 1995). The most difficult part for the students in my studies was to transfer and discuss spontaneously in a fruitful way the distinctions between energy and matter. The never-ending process of succession, slowly turning the pond into a willow thicket was rarely mentioned when they were asked about the long-term future of this pond. Here it is also interesting to relate to Darwin's clear ideas about succession in nature expressed when he writes:

> I will give only a single instance which, though a simple one, interested me. In Staffordshire, on the estate of a relation, where I had an ample means of investigation, there was a large and extremely barren heath, which had never been touched by the hand of man; but several hundred acres of exactly the same nature had been enclosed twenty-five years previously and planted with Scotch fir. The change in the native vegetation of the planted part of the heath was most remarkable, more than is generally seen in passing from one quite different soil to another: not only the proportional numbers of the heath-plants were wholly changed, but twelve species of plants (not counting grasses and carices) flourished in the plantations, which could not be found on the heath. Here we see how potent has been the effect of the introduction of a single tree, nothing whatever else. (Darwin, 1859, p. 71)

CONCLUSIONS

Implications for Teaching

By observing students on their journey towards a deeper understanding of ecology and by studying their ideas about nature, important insights have been gained. There is a hierarchy of subject content. It's about starting small. It's about developing a curiosity and an interest in the small. In my case this was the freshwater shrimp *Gammarus pulex,* but with reference to Darwin's fascination with earthworms, this land-based organism might be the central focus when studying a rich deciduous forest ecosystem. The concept of 'reading nature' is a dialectical relationship between natural history or experience-based knowledge on the one hand and the more abstract and non-visible aspects on the other. This means that these two worlds must meet in order to be able to read nature. If we start at the most basic level of reading nature, organisms should be introduced early. It is important that the teacher tries to help students to select appropriate organisms. The initial step when the key organism is chosen is to find out as much as possible about it. The freshwater shrimp, *Gammarus pulex,* was carefully chosen. It has an interesting biology and it is very common in the river. It's easy to find out some facts about it; at the same time it is not so well known. Studying biodiversity may be a goal in itself, but in my study it has been important to focus on a limited number of organisms and study them in more detail. Choosing a familiar organism can help prevent students losing interest (Magro et al., 2001). To provide practical, first-hand experiences and study, a small number of organisms which students themselves research and then use to build microcosms aroused great interest among the students. A year and a half after the teaching of the shrimp and the river, I asked the students what they remembered. They recalled many things including taxonomy and episodes from the instruction; one thing that all students remembered was the shrimp and the sealed ecosystems that they made (Magntorn, 2008). This proved to be an effective way of helping understand the abstract, invisible aspects of 'reading nature'.

NOTES

[1] Charles Darwin to K. Wedgwood, 8 October, 1880. Darwin Correspondence Database, http://www.darwinproject.ac.uk/entry-12745 accessed on 29 January 2014.
[2] http://www.linnaeus.uu.se/online/liv/9_4.html accessed on 29 January 2014.

REFERENCES

Assaraf, O. B., & Orion, N. (2005). Development of systems thinking skills in the context of earth systems education. *Journal of Research in Science Teaching, 42*(5), 518–560.
Bebbington, A. (2005). The ability of A-level students to name plants. *Journal of Biological Education, 39*(2), 63–67.
Bransford, J. D., Brown, A., & Cocking, R. R. (2000). *How people learn—brain, mind, experience and school.* Cambridge: Cambridge University School.
Carlsson, B. (2002). Ecological understanding 1: Ways of experiencing photosynthesis. *International Journal of Science Education, 24*(7), 681–699.
Cherrett, J. M. (1989). *Key concepts: The results of a survey of our members.* In J. M. Cherrett (Ed.), *Ecological concepts* (pp. 1–16). Oxford: Blackwell Scientific Publications.
Darwin, C. (1859). *On the origin of species.* London: John Murray.
Darwin, C. (1881). *The formation of vegetable mould, through the action of worms, with observations on their habits.* Fifth thousand (corrected), and with textual changes. London: John Murray.
Darwin, C. (2013). *The formation of vegetable mould through, the action of worms, with observations on their habits* (pp. 9–10). Hong Kong: Forgotten Books. (Original work published 1881).
Darwin, C. (1995). *The Galapagos Islands* (p. 20). London: Penguin Classics.
Dillon, J., Rickinson, M., Teamey, K., Morris, M., Choi, M.Y., Sanders, D., & Benefield, P. (2006). The value of outdoor learning: evidence from research in the UK and elsewhere. *School Science Review, 87*(320), 107–113.

Grotzer, T. A., & Bell-Basca, B. (2003). How does grasping the underlying causal structures of ecosystems impact students' understanding? *Journal of Biological Education, 38*(1), 16–29.

Helldén, G. F. (1992). Grundskoleelevers förståelse av ekologiska processer (Pupils' understanding of ecological processes.) (Doctoral Thesis). Stockholm: AWE International.

Helldén, G. F. (2004). A study of recurring core developmental features in students' conceptions of some key ecological processes. *Canadian Journal of Science, Mathematics and Technology Education, 4*(1), 59–76.

Hmelo-Silver, C. E., & Green Pfeffer, M. (2004). Comparing expert and novice understanding of a complex system from the perspective of structures, behaviours, and functions. *Cognitive Science, 28*, 127–138.

Hogan, K., & Fisherkeller, J. (1996). Representing students' thinking about nutrient cycling in ecosystems: Bi-dimensional coding of a complex topic. *Journal of Research in Science Teaching, 33*(9), 941–970.

Jordan, R., Gray, S., Demeter, M., Lui, L., & Hmelo Silver, C. (2009). An assessment of students' understanding of ecosystem concepts: Conflating ecological systems and cycles. *Applied Environmental Education & Communication, 8*(1), 40–48.

Kattman, U. (2001). Aquatics, flyers, creepers and terrestrials-students conceptions of animal classification. *Journal of Biological Education, 35*(3), 19–21.

Keynes, R. (2002). *Darwin, his daughter & human evolution.* New York, NY: Riverhead Books.

Keynes, R. (2009). Darwin's ways of working: The opportunity for education. *Journal of Biological Education, 43*(3), 101–103.

Knapp, S. (2002). Fact and fantasy. The zoology created by our imagination is far outstripped by that of reality. *Nature, 415*, 479.

Leach, J., Driver, R., Scott, P., & Wood-Robinson, C. (1996). Children's ideas about ecology 2: Ideas found in children aged 5–16 about the cycling of matter. *International Journal of Science Education, 18*(1), 19–34.

Lemke J. L. (1990). *Talking science: Language, learning and values.* Norwood, MA: Ablex Publishing Corporation.

Linnaeus, C. (1737). *Critica Botanica*, No 210. In A. Ellenius (1998). *Naturen som livsrum.* Stockholm: Natur & Kultur.

Linnaeus, C. (1749). *Oeconomia Naturae. In G. Broberg (1978). Om jämvikten i nature.* Stockholm: Natur & Kultur.

Linnaeus, C. (1758). *Systema naturae (10th ed.).* Stockholm: Laurentius Salvius.

Lobato, J. (2006). How design experiments can inform a rethinking of transfer and vice versa. *Educational Research, 32(1), 17–20.*

Magntorn, O., & Helldén, G. (2005). Student-teachers' ability to read nature: Reflections on their own learning in ecology. *International Journal of Science Education, 27*(10), 1229–1254.

Magntorn, O., & Helldén, G. (2006). Reading Nature: Experienced teachers' reflections on a teaching sequence in ecology: Implications for future teacher training. *NorDiNa- Nordic Studies in Science Education, 5*, 67–81.

Magntorn, O., & Helldén, G. (2007a). Reading new environments: Students' ability to generalise their understanding between different ecosystems. *International Journal of Science Education, 29*(1), 67–100.

Magntorn, O., & Helldén, G. (2007b). Reading nature from a 'bottom-up' perspective. *Journal of Biological Education, 41*(2), 68–75.

Magntorn, O. (2007). *Reading nature. Developing ecological understanding through teaching* (Doctoral thesis). Linköping University Department of Social and Welfare Studies, Linköping.

Magntorn, O. (2008). *The quality of memorable first-hand experiences in science education.* Paper presented at the 9th Nordic conference on science education, Reykjavik, Iceland.

Magro, A., Simmoneaux, L., Navarre, A., & Hemptinne, J. L. (2001, October). *The teaching of ecology in the agricultural secondary curricula in France: A new didactic approach. Proceedings of the III Conference of European Researchers in Didactics of Biology*, Santiago de Compostela, 197–205.

Novak, J. D. (1993). Human constructivism: A unification of psychological and epistemological phenomena in meaning making. *International Journal of Personal Construct Psychology, 6*, 167–193.

Novak, J. D., & Gowin, D. B. (1984). *Learning how to learn.* Cambridge: Cambridge University Press.

Nyberg, E. (2004). Life cycles – for caring and learning about organisms and their environment: A starting point towards an understanding of environmental issues.In I. P. Wickenberg, H. Axelsson, L. Fritzén, G. Helldén, & J. Öhman. *Learning to change our world* (pp.313–328). Lund: Studentlitteratur.

Orr, D. W. (1992). *Ecological literacy: Education and the transition to a postmodern world.* Albany: State University of New York Press.

Rickinson, M., Dillon, J., Teamey, K., Morris, K., Choi, M. Y., Sanders, D., & Benefield, P. (2004). *A review on outdoor learning.* Shrewsbury, UK: Field Studies Council, & National Foundation for Educational Research.

Shepardson, D. P. (2002). Bugs, butterflies and spiders: Children's understanding about insects. *International Journal of Science Education, 24*(6), 627–643.

Slingsby, D., & Barker, S. (2003). Making connections: biology, environmental education and education for sustainable development. *Journal of Biological Education, 38*(1), 4–6.

Stauffer, R. C. (1957). Haeckel, Darwin, and ecology. *Quarterly Review of Biology, 32*, 138–44.

Stauffer, R., & Haeckel, E. (1869). Darwin and ecology. Inaugural lecture, translation by W.C Allee. *Quarterly Review of Biology, 32*, 138–144.

Tomkins, S. P., & Tunnicliffe S. D. (2001). Looking for ideas: Observation, interpretation and hypothesis-making by 12 year-old pupils undertaking science investigations. *International Journal of Science Education, 23*(8), 791–813.

Uddenberg, N. (2003). Idéer om Livet. *En biologihistoria, Band 1*, 175–181.

Wood-Robinson, C. (1991). Young people's ideas about plants. *Studies in Science Education, 19*, 119–135.

Ola Magntorn
Department of Science & Mathematics Education,
Kristianstad University,
Sweden

SANDRA ESCOVEDO SELLES

6. WALKING WITH DARWIN IN RIO DE JANEIRO

Learning about Cultural and Historical Values

INTRODUCTION

Going on voyages into the unknown and visiting places which have never been visited before have fascinated many people throughout human history. In the last two or three centuries many Europeans have been challenged to leave their countries to explore other places in order to build up a body of knowledge of the world and to understand the place of humanity there. Many of them translated their experiences into information and understanding that they had to communicate to those they left behind. That is why they collected natural and cultural objects, wrote notes, journals and books, drew and painted, in order to build a solid record of what they had come across. Especially in the nineteenth century, people, mainly men, left Europe and went to Brazil to explore its different regions, concentrating their interest on the rain forest, its fauna, flora and geological resources, as well as on the lives of the indigenous people and slaves who lived there. There are many examples: Alexander von Humboldt (1769-1859); Auguste de Saint Hillaire (1779-1853); Carl von Martius (1794-1868); Johann von Spix (1781-1826); Prince Maximilian (1782-1867); Georg Langsdorff (1774-1852); Peter Lund (1801-1880) Alfred Russel Wallace (1823-1913), and, indeed, Charles Darwin (1809-1882) himself.

DARWIN'S TRAILS

Between the Past and the Present

Whereas the writings, discoveries and collections of all these have impacted on society and the culture of the time, Charles Darwin has given us an overwhelming contribution to scientific knowledge. Darwin's accounts, specimens, notes, diary, books and even his autobiography have been studied by many biologists, geologists and paleontologists, as well as sociologists, anthropologists and historians up to the present day. Charles Darwin's life and work have become a source of ceaseless interest amongst academics. That interest was also turned upside down when his ideas were seen during and after his lifetime as a threat to peace, morality and religious principles. It is over a hundred and fifty years since he published his book *On the origin of species by means of natural selection*. This and his other publications that followed in a sense all had their inspiration in his voyage around the world in HMS *Beagle*[1]. Looking back to those days, Darwin himself stated in his autobiography that 'The voyage of the Beagle has been by far the most important event in my life and has determined my whole career. ... I owe to the voyage the first real training of education of my mind' (Barlow, 1993).

Figuring out what made this experience of the voyage so unique may help us to understand why others in our time have reproduced in many ways Darwin's experience by producing Darwin trails of various kinds which follow the paths that he followed. Some are related to Darwin's voyage but others are more generally related to his life. In England, for instance, they either take into account Darwin's birthplace *The Darwin town trail*[2], or where he lived and worked *Darwin's landscape laboratory*[3]. The trails aim to get people to revisit these Darwin-related places and at the same time provide leisure, through hiking or other milder walks. In these examples, following the trails could mean an experience that combines leisure, physical activities, music, art and recreation underlined by a scientific and historical account and in close contact with the natural world. In a slightly different perspective, *The ancestor's trail*[4] is an annual event combining walking, science and art which retraces *Darwin's tree of life*, 'symbolically travelling back in time to our shared origins'. The experience gives the participants the opportunity to explore scientific aspects of evolution and biodiversity. In this case, there is a creative approach to education about evolution in the context of an outdoor trail. Participants are invited to perform the activities, bearing in mind the concepts of evolution that underlie them.

Exploring the Darwin Records

Despite the value of all of these trails, they rely on the historical presence of Darwin – the collections he made, the places where he was born and lived, the scientific evidence he was searching for or an experience that is symbolically related to evolutionary knowledge – rather than on other possible readings of the significance of his passage through these places. In other countries where Darwin stayed during his HMS *Beagle* trip the only accessible records to trace these places are Darwin's diary[5], field-work notebooks and letters written to his family and friends. Considering the lack of locally accurate maps at the time in Brazil and the changes in the environment since, it is understandable that it is not always easy to find these places today using his records.

That is why a number of questions arose in the year 2000, when reading Charles Darwin's *The voyage of the Beagle* (Darwin, 1909) about his stay in Rio de Janeiro, Brazil, in 1832. In particular, the passages which record his trip to an estate about 150 miles in the country after being invited by a British merchant who lived in the city. Which road had he followed? What had he described? What most attracted his attention? What were Darwin's social views of Brazil? How can we understand his views within the framework of the biological sciences and education today? From reading Darwin's diary and the reconstruction of his trip, I intended to answer some of those questions and to deepen the reflection on his writings which were at the very beginning of his thinking. Therefore, taking a perspective that explores Darwin's record during his *Beagle* expedition, I want to examine an authentic experience of following in his footsteps by paying attention to the flora and fauna, but also to the socio-cultural issues of his time.

Thus, in this chapter I explore the teaching and learning possibilities of two projects inspired by Darwin's manuscript records of Rio de Janeiro in 1832. The first small scale project was undertaken in 2000 and involved a group of biology school teachers and specialists from the city of Niterói, visiting the first stop of Darwin's trip in the country, the Itaocaia's village[6]. At this site, a workshop took place, exploring the ways in which it was possible to develop teaching strategies using Darwin's journey, his trail through the places he visited. Taking the environment as the central issue, this project explored the possibilities of an interdisciplinary approach to address environmental questions and to argue for the advantages of the use of a socio-historical strategy based on Darwin's accounts for enhancing biology teachers' and pupils' awareness. Later on, in 2008, as part of the beginning of the celebrations of Darwin's bicentenary and supported by federal government funds, it was possible to develop a second project involving science and biology school teachers on a four-day expedition to all the places visited by Darwin recorded in his diary.

As a result of both projects I argue that the work developed in situ using Darwin's records as a pedagogical source inspires a learning process with school communities that involves not only them but also the general public. Learning about Darwin and his evolutionary theory, and thinking about the controversies related to his ideas, producing curriculum material and cultural activities and, most of all, knowing that the young Darwin had walked in the same place significantly impacted on the teachers and also on people in the towns visited. As this chapter will document, both projects give an account of ways to motivate communities to search for their own stories, to deal with their memories, and to discover themselves as part of history and of other stories. This development of the *Darwin Trail* outside Rio with its focus on evidence from Darwin's papers and the importance of socio-cultural learning has inspired trails in other countries, such as Uruguay, Australia and Cabo Verde, for instance[7], even though not all have fully explored the educational potential.

DARWIN IN RIO DE JANEIRO, 1832

At the beginning of April 1832 Darwin arrived in Rio de Janeiro and spent approximately three months in the city while Captain FitzRoy went back to Bahia to check some cartographic measurements[8]. Darwin was continuously enchanted by it. Rio de Janeiro was, at the time, the capital of the Brazilian Empire. The opportunity to make an excursion to the Rio Macaé, 'some miles'[9] in the country of Rio, came soon after his arrival in the city. Darwin spent two more days making the arrangements to obtain passports for his 'riding excursion to Rio Macaé'. He showed his excitement about the trip in a letter to his sister Caroline: 'It is an uncommon and most excellent opportunity, and I shall thus see, what has been so long my ambition, virgin forest uncut by man and tenanted by wild beasts'. His reports of the trip take up nine pages of the entire chapter on Rio de Janeiro.

On 8 April of that year, leaving Rio de Janeiro, Darwin met a group of six people at Praia Grande, the name of the city of Niterói at that time, 'a village on the opposite side of the Bay'[10]. When 'crossing the hills behind Praia Grande', Darwin described the view as 'most sublime & picturesque. The colours were intense & the prevailing tint a dark blue; the sky & calm waters of the bay vied with each other in splendour'.

After passing through 'some cultivated country', Darwin saw a forest 'which in grandeur of all its parts' in his opinion 'could not be exceeded'. Following Darwin's description on a map of the region from the middle of the nineteen century, Serra da Tiririca[11] is the last major location. At noon they arrived at 'Ithacaia'[12], a 'small village' situated 'on a plain' where 'round the central houses'[13] were 'the huts of the negroes'. On the 1851 map, Itaocaia is marked as a hill with some plantations, most probably the village described by Darwin. Itaocaia's hill's special features were not ignored by him and he described it as 'one of the massive bare & steep hills of granite which are so common in this country'. Darwin's first view of the slaves in their huts impressed him deeply and reminded him of the Hottentots: 'the poor blacks thus perhaps try to persuade themselves that they are in the land of their Fathers'. He writes about Itaocaia's hill as a hiding place for runaway slaves who were all recaptured with the exception of an old woman who refusing to be taken 'dashed herself to pieces from the very summit'.

From Itaocaia, Darwin and his group went in the direction of the 'Lagoa Marica', an area marked by 'marshes and lagoons'. The road, according to Darwin, 'passed through a narrow sandy plain, lying between the sea & the interior salt lagoons'. After going through the region[14], Darwin had 'an excellent dinner' in one of the 'Vendas'[15] from where 'the distant wooded hills were seen over & reflected in the perfectly calm water of an extensive lagoon'[16]. Later, he 'continued to walk through an intricate wilderness of lakes' and entered the forest and after walking over '15 miles of heavy sand' stopped at São Pedro de Aldeia. After crossing the river São João, Darwin and his group went into the interior, following the River Macaé.

Darwin and his group finally arrived at the Fazenda Sossego, property of 'Manuel Figuireda', a relative of one of the members of the group. In this region, Darwin also visited another estate and his descriptions show that deforestation was already under way to cultivate coffee. His closer contact with slaves made him write that he was 'an eye-witness to one of those atrocious acts which can only take place in a slave country'. He stayed there for a few days. The group that returned to Rio de Janeiro was reduced to three people and they took another route: 'we then turned off, being determined to reach the city by the interior'. Back from the expedition, he organised his residence in a cottage in Botafogo on the bottom of the Corcovado Mountain and his reports focus on several excursions into the surrounding area. In his own words: 'I do not know what epithet such scenery deserves: beautiful is much too tame: every form, every colour is such a complete exaggeration of what one has ever beheld before'.

WALKING WITH DARWIN

In this section I use the accounts of two projects inspired by Charles Darwin's records reported previously. I want to explore, in a pedagogical perspective, the social, historical and cultural value of these projects not only for the teachers and students who took part in them, but also for the people of the localities visited that had been named by Darwin and identified by the project central team.

Revisiting Darwin's Walks on the Serra da Tiririca

In 2000 I was in charge of a project with a group of biology teachers, taking them to visit Itaocaia, the very first stop of Darwin's trip in the country in April, 1832. The village is located in Maricá, a city 25 miles from Rio de Janeiro. The farm visited by Darwin still stands, though with visible signs of changes. The project aimed to involve teachers in a reflection about possible ways to help students to understand environmental issues as part of a social, historical and cultural process. The choice of Darwin's writings was a way to provoke a discussion about the changes in the environment as it was recorded by him since his passage in Itaocaia. The development of the project, however, went beyond the first assumptions. It involved nine schools from Niteroi and Maricá, Rio de Janeiro in three stages: (1) a proposal for teachers to reflect on reading the extract from Darwin's *The Voyage of the Beagle*, complemented by a reading of other naturalists' accounts of the same region, and the use of maps[17]; (2) the actual walk to the farm in Itaocaia, Maricá, with the whole group of teachers followed by a workshop in the premises; (3) a follow up meeting with participating teachers two months later. In this meeting we gave as many opportunities as possible to the biology teachers to freely construct educational projects for their schools using the activity of re-visiting Darwin's walks as a starting point and forming multi-disciplinary teams. A full account of the project can be seen in Selles & Abreu (2002), Selles et al., (2001) and Cecchetti et al., (2001)[18] (see Figures 1 & 2).

Mapping Darwin's trail, reported in his diary, to Itaocaia required a search in libraries. The historical research, including the 1851 map, was conducted by historian Martha Abreu, who found it in the Brazilian National Library. This made it possible to reconstruct the route taken by Darwin. Through the use of maps and comparisons with Darwin's descriptions (reported earlier in this chapter), it was possible to identify places and changes that had occurred in both biological and social terms.

Figure 1. The road to Itaocaia Farmhouse. (© Sandra E Selles)

Figure 2. Itaocaia Farmhouse. (© Sandra E Selles)

The first thing that occurred to me while organizing this project was to reflect upon what Darwin saw in his passage and what can be seen today. Therefore, the starting point was to think about the contrasts between the environment visited by Darwin and the current Serra da Tririca which, despite signs of deforestation, flourishes. I argue for the contribution of history in this analysis through using an historical account for working with environmental questions with biology teachers. On the one hand, it widens the view of the environment itself, redefining it within human timescales, relocating limits, establishing boundaries and, at the same time, revealing a multiplicity of disciplinary approaches necessary for a more accurate analysis. On the other hand, a historical reading that helps us to see different meanings in Darwin's passage through the Serra da Tiririca is profoundly rich when analysed alongside his journal entries.

At several points in Darwin's journal we find descriptions of living things and minerals, and a great number of comparisons to the European species. Unlike naturalists who simply compiled collections of fauna and flora, the custom in Europe at the time, Darwin went further. He used the collections to address many questions about why things were the way they were.

Darwin also reported the (bad) habits of the *vendas'* owners and the manners of some people he encountered, specially the Brazilians. Lastly, he did not leave out comments about eating habits and food, regarding the latter as plentiful due to good crop yields – beans and rice –, the grassland for the cattle and the country's forests for hunting animals. However, among the several scenes that attracted the attention of Darwin, at least in this short period of time spent on the expedition to the Rio Macaé, the scenes of slavery fascinated him most.

From Darwin's first contact with the slaves in Itaocaia he continued to record his impressions throughout the trip to the Rio Macaé. In the last part of his report, 'the most interior piece of cleared ground', where Darwin was 'eye-witness' of 'a most violent and disagreeable quarrel' between the landowner and 'his agent'[19], in which the former made a threat about taking 'all the women & children [of the farm] from their husbands & selling them separately at the market at Rio ... I do not believe the inhumanity of separating thirty families ... even occurred to the owner'. If the threat had been carried out, Darwin lamented: 'can two more horrible & flagrant instances be imagined?' Recalling a fact that occurred later on involving his contact with a slave in a boat, he wrote in the diary his own feelings of 'surprise, disgust and shame' and he writes that this slave 'had been trained to a degradation lower than the slavery of the most helpless animal'.

I believe that contextualizing Darwin's account, particularly at the time of his trip through Rio de Janeiro, helps us to understand to what extent his reflections while in contact with the abundant Brazilian natural diversity – including the humans he encountered – occupied his mind later on when he elaborated his evolutionary theory. The richness of his views on this particular trip lies in the human issues, especially the impressions and reflections of slavery and the treatment given to the slaves by the Brazilians, rather than solely in the biological aspects of the environment. As Desmond & Moore (2009) remarkably document, both Darwin's grandfathers were deeply involved in the slavery abolition cause. This environment helped form the moral basis of Darwin's ideas and values concerning slavery. It is understandable that since his famous quarrel over slavery with FitzRoy early in the *Beagle* journey, the experiences with slavery affected him deeply and built up some reflections of the people he encountered, not only on this particular expedition but also throughout the entire voyage.

Darwin's Walk in Rio de Janeiro

Eight years after the first project, a group of teachers, science educators, scientists, journalists and students following Darwin's records fully retraced the 1832 expedition, now expanding it from Itaocaia's project aims. The work involved several schools in 12 municipalities of the state of Rio de Janeiro, launching the celebrations of the 2009 Darwin anniversary. This expedition would impress itself on the lives of the twelve towns and all of the people who took part in it. The leading group travelled by coach along the route the 23-year-old Darwin took 176 years ago, between 8 and 23 April 1832. Inspired by the 2000 curriculum development project, the ideas raised by Selles and Abreu (2002) helped students and teachers to reflect upon Darwin's contribution to modern thought and the role that Darwin's views on slavery played in the construction of his theory; it also helped local people to strengthen their feelings of belonging to the human and environmental histories of the place where they live.

The expedition organized by the project occurred between 26 and 29 November 2008, and it was supported by resources from the Brazilian Secretary of Science and Technology (MC&T), federal universities, Rio de Janeiro Department of Mineral Resources (DRM-RJ), British Council, local authorities and a number of other institutions. The Executive Coordination was the Casa da Ciência from the Federal University of Rio de Janeiro (UFRJ)[20]. I became part of the central team with Ildeu Moreira (MC&T), Fátima Brito (UFRJ), Kátia Mansur (DRM-RJ) and Jurema Holtz (hired producer). Among the team one of them played a remarkable role, not only due to his enthusiasm but also due to his kinship with Charles Darwin: Randal Keynes, his great-great grandson, came to Brazil for the first time to take part in the expedition.

As a matter of fact, the expedition was the climax of the project initiated months before November 2008. On the one hand some research was going on to get the most precise localisation possible of the places recorded by Darwin which were not completely identified as towns. On the other hand, educational and cultural plans were undertaken with each of the twelve municipalities to be visited by the expedition in order to invite school teachers to develop projects with the students – and even with the general public – taking into account Darwin's passage through the locality.

The project proposal included an unveiling of celebration plaques in twelve places (see Figure 3). Each of the plaques had information about the project and a quotation from Darwin's diary related to the place. Signs were also put along the roads to guide all travelers to know that Darwin once was there. The expedition left the Botanical Garden in Rio de Janeiro[21] and followed each of the places and towns in the order as they appear in the diary: Maricá, Saquarema, Araruama; São Pedro d'Aldeia, Cabo Frio, Barra de São João (Casimiro de Abreu); Macaé and Conceição de Macabu[22]. On the way back the expedition stopped in Rio Bonito, Itaboraí, and, finally, in Niterói. Not all of these localities can be precisely identified from Darwin's report, but the work of historical research allowed, to a great extent, accurate localisation. From the point of view of the integrity of the buildings, only the Fazenda[23] Itaocaia and Campos Novos preserve many traces of their original architecture.

Over four days the expedition followed Darwin's path, having a number of notable educational and cultural experiences (see Figures 4-7): children's performances about Darwin's decision to get married with Emma; a mock trial about the theory of evolution, recalling the 1860 public confrontation between Wilberforce, Hooker and Huxley; music and dance presentations; a referendum on evolution; a trip through the river São João (crossed by Darwin); a breakfast, including a menu Darwin ate, with amateur actors impersonating Darwin and his companions. A number of reviews were produced in the main Brazilian newspapers, international journalists were present, and other publications and documentaries that describe the four-day expedition have subsequently been produced (Moreira et al., 2009; Selles, 2009)[24].

Besides the unquestionable historical mark that the *Darwin's walk in Rio de Janeiro* left in each of the 12 towns, the pedagogical role played throughout the whole project needs to be highlighted. Taking into account that some of the towns are distant from the capital and have small populations, the enormous mobilisation of the schools, with their teachers working collaboratively in curriculum projects in advance of the expedition, was notable.

Figure 3. Randal Keynes unveiling of celebration plaques. (© Sandra E Selles)

Figure 4. Children's work related to the Beagle *voyage. (© Sandra E Selles)*

Figure 5. Randal Keynes and amateur actors impersonating Darwin and his companions at breakfast. (© Sandra E Selles)

Figure 6. Mock trial about the theory of evolution: 1860 public confrontation between Wilberforce, Hooker and Huxley. (© Sandra E Selles)

Figure 7. A trip through the river São João, crossed by Darwin. (© Sandra E Selles)

It is hard to describe all that I have experienced through the whole period of this project without valuing the efforts of the teachers and students of those remote towns. Learning about Darwin and about the evolutionary theory, learning about his views of slavery, thinking of the controversies related to it in order to make decisions, producing cultural and creative activities inspired by his accounts and, most of all, getting to know that he had stayed in their home towns, all of these have touched them. That is something that Darwin himself, at 23, could never have imagined. Led by curiosity and careful observation he was eager to understand what underlay what he saw. He was not only attracted by the geological formation, the beauty of the tropical forest and the fauna and flora, but also, the days of his trip to the Fazenda Sossego in the Rio Macaé were marked by his impressions of the way of life of the slaves and the injustice of slavery. However, the supposition that 176 years into the future, his records would form the basis of a pedagogical and cultural learning project would have been beyond any possible imagination.

What Darwin could never have imagined was that when the expedition revisited his journey, the project also challenged its inhabitants to search for their memories and find a place in history, rediscovering themselves as part of it. When he returned to his own country, Randal Keynes was probably carrying the legacy of his ancestor, added to by this unique experience. Perhaps he was sharing with us, from a different perspective, the re-union with the past, the reflections of what can be done in a pedagogical work that is based on historical readings of his great-great grandfather. Perhaps here it is not overdue to paraphrase the old Darwin saying that, from the cultural, historical and pedagogical viewpoint, the two projects were one of the most important events in my life.

HOW DARWIN INSPIRES LEARNING

Interchanges Between Biology, History and Education

In this chapter, I have argued how it is profitable to build bridges between history, biology, education and culture, inspired by Darwin's work and records[25]. Such liaisons expand school education by enhancing biology teachers' views about their school work as well as their worldviews. In other words, their knowledge of science acquired during their teacher-training education can be enriched by incorporating views from other disciplinary fields in order to better understand biology as a school subject. Serra da Tiririca as well as all the 12 places can be studied as a launch pad for the study of Darwin, and one which offers an opportunity to understand his thoughts from a wider perspective.

Above all, the opportunity provided by Darwin's passage through the places can be used to foster an understanding of this particular figure, central to biological thought and to many other areas of knowledge. As Mayr (1982, p. 875) points out: 'With the possible exception of Freud, there is no other scientist about whom so much has been written and continues to be written as about Darwin'. It is important to stress that history in a project of this type can be used in all sorts of models such as travelogues, oral history, use of memories and local history, since searching for famous personages cannot be the only criterion. Darwin's passage to Rio de Janeiro was a coincidental opportunity for enhanced reflections like the ones discussed here. Darwin's ideas travel through the frontiers of biology and need constantly to be re-addressed in relation to his biography and the intellectual milieu of his time, not to mention their impact in society and their appropriation.

The purpose is not only to invite teachers to revisit Darwin's walk, but to use the walk and journey to help them to understand Darwin in his own time, the influences that were upon him, and what he saw during his trip. An historical reading of Darwin fosters a deeper reflection in terms of the theoretical influences upon Darwinian thought. It especially helps to critically consider to what extent Darwin had these influences tacitly at work when encountering the Brazilian environment and how his theory was marked by them. In other words, this can help in understanding Darwin's contradictions and conflicts throughout his life (Desmond & Moore, 2009). Since initial biology teacher-training has not always had such concerns, the project inspired by Darwin's records is beneficial to biology teachers and to biology education.

What is most striking about Darwin's views on Brazil during his travels to the interior of the province of Rio de Janeiro is not Darwin the *sytematised naturalist,* or the *collector* eager to identify new species and to formulate theory. Darwin was an intellectual of his time, but he was not a scientist producing biological knowledge away from his social context. It is important for us to wonder (probably diverting from what is familiar to the biology teachers' scientific background) to what extent Darwin's ideas and doubts about the non-fixed origins of species were influenced by his direct experiences of the Brazilian fauna and flora and the diversity of Brazilians as well the rest of the people he encountered[26]. (A sound historical study about the impact of the view of slavery on Darwin's work can be seen in Desmond and Moore [2009]). Darwin was tormented by the idea of diversity and variation, and how to explain it in a robust theory was a goal he pursued through his life. This influenced him when he considered the different human beings that he encountered on his travels to the inland areas of Rio de Janeiro. In developing his evolutionary explanation, Darwin used his reflections on the exuberant diversity of life – for example, in the Serra da Tirirca – as much as his impressions about the racial differences and the different treatment given to slaves, and other people he encountered later on his trip[27]. Here, he was intrigued by the dilemmas of the equality as opposed to the diversity (a fuller discussion on this matter can be found in Selles and Abreu [2002]). These reflections used in biology and science education can expand practising and prospective biology teachers' horizons to include fruitful cross-curriculum discussions that can be integrated into their school work. Exploring an historical account such as Darwin's, inspired by his reflections, challenges us all to think about the possibilities for teaching biology beyond a factual history about his life and work on evolution.

NOTES

1. The HMS *Beagle* traveled throughout the world for five years, between 1831 and 1836. The British government wanted to identify strategic areas, mainly mines and navigation routes between the Atlantic and the Pacific, especially in South America, for investment and commercial control.
2. http://www.discoverdarwin.co.uk/darwin-town-trail/
3. http://www.darwinslandscape.co.uk/topic.asp?navid = 58&tid = 227
4. http://ancestorstrail.net/
5. 'Diary' and 'journal' are used throughout this chapter with the same meaning.
6. Brazilian people's and places' names, as Itaocaia, are written as they are correctly spelled in Portuguese, without commas. Commas are used as in Darwin's original writing.
7. Details of the projects in **Uruguay:** http://cienciaviva.fcien.edu.uy/docs/darwin/darwin1.php **Australia**: http://www.ccc.tas.gov.au/page.aspx?u=1198; http://www.wentworthfalls.org.au/bushwalks-around-wentworth-falls/charles-darwin-trail-/ **Cabo Verde**: http://raizafricana.wordpress.com/2010/01/07/cabo-verde-assinala-passagem-de-darwin/ accessed on 5 March 2014.
8. This section uses some parts written by Selles and Abreu (2002).
9. All the quotations used in this chapter are from: Darwin, C. (1952), and Darwin (1933). The former is known as 'Journal' and the latter as 'Diary' to distinguish them (cf. Lady Nora Barlow. Charles Darwin and the voyage of the Beagle. New York: The Philosophical Library, 1946).
10. Bay of Guanabara.
11. Serra da Tiririca is a State Reservation Park (Parque Estadual da Serra da Tiririca), a forest area on the top of hills located at the boundaries of the municipalities of Niteroi and Maricá in the State of Rio de Janeiro, Brazil. Darwin did not name Tiririca but it was already registered in the maps of the time of his trip.
12. Darwin misspelled Ithaocaia, but as can be seen on the 1851 map the place was written as Ithaocaia. The name no longer has an 'h'.
13. Currently, the farmhouse still exists.
14. The region – Lakes Region - is notable by a complex of lakes and lagoons.
15. In a facsimile of the 1839 first edition of Darwin's diary, 'venda' is translated as: 'The Portuguese name for an inn' (p. 22). Journal of Researches into the Geology and Natural History of the various countries visited by HMS Beagle, by Charles Darwin. New York London: Hafner Publishing Company, 1952.
16. The largest lagoon of the region is Lagoa de Araruama.
17. In the project, translations in Portuguese of the original publications were used.
18. http://www.canalciencia.ibict.br/pesquisa/0230-Darwin-ciencia-itinerante-e-interdisciplinar-Serra-Tiririca.html
19. Overseer.
20. www.casadaciencia.ufrj.br/caminhosdedarwin
21. Despite the fact that 1832 Darwin's trip did not leave from the RJ Botanic Garden, but from Niterói (Praia Grande), that place was visited many times by Darwin, from where he could make significant notes.
22. Not all towns are mentioned in Darwin's journal. Conceição de Macabu is closer to the most probable place where Fazenda Sossego was located. The state no longer exists.
23. Farm.
24. www.casadaciencia.ufrj.br/caminhosdedarwin
25. Some of the reflections of this section are driven from Selles and Abreu (2002).
26. In *The descent of man*, Darwin uses much of his travel observations and clearly reports them as example.
27. Reported in *The descent of man*, for instance.

REFERENCES

Barlow, N. (Ed.). (1993). *The autobiography of Charles Darwin 1809–1882* (p. 64). London: Norton & Company.

Moreira et al. Brasil, Ministério da Educação. (2009). *Salto para o Futuro*. Edição Especial. Caminhos de Darwin. Ano XIX boletim 16 - Novembro/2009.

Cecchetti, F., Araújo, A. F., Martins, L. D., & Carvalho, M. C. de A., (2001). Abordagem de conceitos darwinistas em jogo multidisciplinar. In *Anais do I EREBIO* (pp. 419–420). Niterói: SBEnBio.

Darwin, C. (1933). *Charles Darwin's diary of the voyage of the HMS Beagle diary*. Nora Barlow (Ed.) (1845 ed.). Cambridge: Cambridge University Press.

Darwin, C. (1952). *Journal of researches into the geology and natural history of the various countries visited by H.M.S. Beagle*. Facsimile reprint of the first 1839 edition. London: Hafner Publishing Company.

Darwin, C. (1909). *The voyage of the Beagle*. New York, NY: P. F. Collier & Son.

Desmond, A., & Moore, J. (1991). *Darwin. The life of a tormented evolutionist*. New York, NY: Warner Books.

Desmond, A., & Moore, J. (2009). *Darwin's sacred cause. Race, slavery and the quest for human origins*. London: Penguin Books.

Mayr, E. (1982). *The growth of biological thought*. Cambridge, MA: Harvard University Press.

Selles, S. E. (2009). A expedição Caminhos de Darwin: Memórias, histórias e reflexões sobre uma experiência pedagógica. *Revista da Sbenbio, 2*, 37–40.

Selles, S. E., & Abreu, M. (2002). Darwin na Serra da Tiririca: Caminhos entrecruzados entre biologia e a história. *Revista Brasileira de Educação, 20*, 5–20.

Selles, S. E., Pietszch, L. L., & Ferreira, M. J. M. (2001). Uso de registros históricos como tema gerador em projetos de educação ambiental. In *Anais do I EREBIO* (pp. 285–289). Niterói: SBEnBio.

Sandra Escovedo Selles
Faculdade de Educação,
Universidade Federal Fluminense,
Brazil

JAMES MOORE

7. GETTING THE KIDS INVOLVED – DARWIN'S PATERNAL EXAMPLE

Dropping in on the Darwins wasn't the done thing, not in the 1850s. Even the locals arranged their visits in advance, and the rest of the world had to plan ahead before travelling all the way to Down House, the 'ugly' flat-fronted pile just outside the Kentish village of Downe[1] where the family had lived since 1842. They liked it that way, especially Charles – no unexpected visitors, no unwanted guests. In an age of tumults, he and Emma had the security craved by rich *rentiers*, the 'fortifications for the self'[2] found on a country estate. Down House, an ex-parsonage, sat in 16 acres bordered by woodland and stony walls, the perfect sanctuary (or camouflage) for an ex-ordinand who harboured a heretical theory. It was a fulcrum 'at the extreme verge' of London from which he would move the world. A parson-naturalist's lifestyle went with the bucolic setting, and a large family was raised.[3] For the Darwin children as much as Charles himself, the secure environment fostered scientific learning, and they grew up not only familiar with the facts and methods behind Papa's strange obsession; they found out things for themselves.

Today we can drop in on the Darwins through historical sources. Family letters, recollections and other contemporary records give glimpses of what a casual caller at Down House – perhaps a science teacher – would have noticed in the 1850s when *On the origin of species* was being written. From these scenes we can trace how the lives of Darwin's novice naturalists were affected by their scientific home-schooling.

BOISTEROUS BOYS

As grown-ups, the children would remember leading a 'singularly quiet life', with practically no friends in the 'whole neighbourhood' and only brothers and sisters for companionship. But with so many of them at home, life in Down House was far from quiet. Emma had been averaging a baby every two years; now – in 1856 say – with Charles furiously gestating 'my big Book', the surviving sibs were 16, 13, 11, 9, 8, 6 and 5. The racket was ferocious, more than any schoolmaster would tolerate. Up and down the corridors, the patter of pint-sized feet was giving way to clodhoppers as raucous boys overran the retiring girls. 'Generally speaking, our manners were neglected', one of the five brothers confessed as a staid adult.

Typically, the younger set would make a bee-line for the drawing-room, 'jumping on everything & butting like young bulls at every chair and sofa'. Charles blamed the 'naughtinesses' on Emma's occasional absence and would mutter 'when the cat's away ...', but the canny kids thought Papa saw himself as one of the mice. There were rules and they were broken, yet no one could remember an 'angry word' from him. Once when he caught and admonished 5-year-old Leonard for prancing on the sofa, Lenny answered in a trice: 'Well then I *advise* you to go out of the room'. Charles didn't quite regard all his offspring with the 'perfect equality' remembered by one, but 'his respect for their liberty & ... personality' went so far that the tyke's insolence was treasured and jotted down. (Nor was Lenny past playing the grown-up when admonishing one of the staff, 'You ought to do what a child says to a maid'.)

Luncheons could be 'violent', auguring worse. After high tea in the schoolroom, the pack would thunder along a 'dark passage' in a 'sort of sham terror' and descend three flights with a 'rhythmic series of bangs' to find Mama and Papa trying to dine in peace. Indeed, with England at war in the Crimea from 1853, mock-violence stalked the estate. The boys took on ranks according to age, made wooden bayonets and marched off with knapsacks to pitch camp beside Papa's 'thinking path' the Sandwalk. Indoors there was 'much playing with tin soldiers' and 'hurling of darts'; a rope-trapeze suspended beside a stairwell topped off an assault course and led to more 'crashing and banging and shouting'. George, age 10, the self-made 'sergeant', would admit as a grown-up that 'the howls and screams must have been a great annoyance' but he still loved to think 'we were never stopped'. His young sisters took a less liberal view. 'I hate boys they are so plaguy tricky & bothersome', the elder Henrietta (Etty) scowled at age 7; to Elizabeth (Lizzy) when 6 they were just 'horrid' and 'beastly'. 'Georgy is such a soldiery boy', she pouted at the height of the Crimean conflict; 'he never speaks to a single girl'.

GOVERNESSES AND GIRLS

Gender divisions carried over into schooling. Emma seems to have engaged 'a series of very inefficient governesses ... rather from motives of pity than for their qualifications'. At any rate, Miss Pugh 'went mad', Mrs Grut 'left in high dudgeon', and though the 'competent' Miss Thorley stayed for eight years,[4] Miss Ludwig was sent packing after three when one of the boys developed an unhealthy attachment to her. Apparently the commitment to formal education in Down House was as easy-going as the discipline – for the girls. In Downe village, Charles had been involved in setting up a school for 'the poor' of both sexes, obviously not one for the Darwins. His boys went for private tutoring and then off to boarding schools; Etty and Lizzy stayed at home, learning what they could while surrounded by sad reminders of an elder sister.

Charles blamed Anne's lingering death in 1851 on some constitutional weakness inherited from himself. Not long after his voyage on HMS *Beagle*, he had fallen strangely ill, with kaleidoscopic symptoms. Twenty years later, he was still alarmingly unwell, despite the efforts of the medical specialists who failed to save his eldest daughter. After losing Anne at age 10, he watched the other children with mounting anxiety, fearing the hereditary flaw would kick in with deadly regularity as each reached the same age. Finally he decided that he was witnessing what he dreaded, and though there were no more fatalities (except a 19-month-old boy in 1858 who 'never learnt to walk or talk'), he settled into the belief, while writing his 'big Book', that most of his offspring were in some way physically or mentally defective. 'We are a wretched family & ought to be exterminated', he quipped to a friend.

Annie had shown talent; 'a second Mozart', Charles had called her, in fact 'more than a Mozart, considering her Darwin blood'. (This was to Emma, an able pianist, with a lesson or two from Chopin.) The child had even kept a 'little garden' with a flower patch, suggesting a botanical streak. But after the 'Darwin blood' felled her, Charles and Emma began to see her little sister's failing. Lizzy seemed slow for a five-year-old, talking with the 'oddest pronunciation' and 'peculiar phraseology'. She 'shivers' and makes 'extraordinary grimaces', Papa observed, and within a year she developed 'a great habit' of 'going by herself & talking to herself', Mama noted, while 'twiddling her fingers as Charles used to do'. And 'she does not like to be interrupted'. The 'poor little dear' required 'great effort' to do what others her age seemed to achieve with less. No one apparently questioned whether she or Etty was being held back by lack of stimulus.

At the age of 8, Etty had been marked for life after staying with Annie almost to the end. She would remember herself when 12 wandering 'about the lonely woods and lanes alone', heading for 'my breakdown'. Throughout her teens, into the 1860s, she suffered from a variety of real or imagined conditions, most of which her parents assumed were rooted in bad 'blood'. She became bedridden and was often wretched: sometimes her 'suffering was so pitiable' that Papa 'almost got to wish to see her die'. At 15 she tried a bit of botany and learnt to make out what was only too obvious to big brother William (Willy) 'that a Primrose had a central placenta & was one of the Primulaceae!' About this time she took a shine to Papa's pigeons and could distinguish some of the breeds. Nevertheless the girl nicknamed 'Body' grew into a professional invalid with a 'dangerous ... absorbing interest' in her own and everyone else's ailments. She preened herself as 'the older and cleverer sister', entitled to be 'impatient', while Lizzy played a submissive role, though she could be 'resentful and critical'. She even had the temerity to be 'sceptical about ... Etty's ill health'.

PROJECTS AND PRECEPTS

Pigeons were only the latest accession to the Down House menagerie. All creatures great and small found homes on the estate. Charles, listed as a 'Farmer'[5] in local directories, kept grazing cows, laying hens and a sprawling kitchen garden to feed the household; carriage and riding horses were stabled with the children's ponies, dogs and cats ran free. Pastured and wooded, the smallholding was a childhood paradise – an adventure playground, summer camp and petting farm all rolled into one. And that was before Papa's pet projects got underway.

In the 1850s he was just finishing the gargantuan self-imposed task of dissecting and describing all of the world's barnacle species, living and extinct. With time off for illness, the project dragged on for eight years. The kids had grown up with strange stalked and acorn-like crustaceans littering Papa's study, so that his habit of peering and picking at them 'seemed a commonplace human function, like eating or breathing'. On visiting a neighbour's study and 'seeing no dissecting table or microscope', one of the youngsters piped up 'with justifiable suspicion, "Then where does he do his barnacles?"' So far had Charles's research shaped his children's view of life.

With barnacles done, he settled some 90 fancy pigeons into two new garden lofts. At the same time he began assembling a Noah's Ark of other exotic animal breeds, or their carcases, from all over the world. Poultry, puppies, rabbits, livestock... all sorts of fascinating creatures were used to build up an encyclopaedia of evidence for his 'big Book' showing that domestic and farmyard species (like plants and indeed barnacles) were plastic. Each varied slightly from individual to individual and the differences had been *artificially* selected by breeders to create new 'varieties' that if found in the wild would be classed as new species, thus mimicking *natural* selection.

Most of the children probably understood what was at stake before reaching adolescence. At any rate, the youngest and sickliest boy learnt the lesson by age 11: after overhearing Papa talk about species, Horace came up to him, 'eyes open with astonishment', and demanded to know:

'Did people *formerly* really believe that animals & plants never changed?'

Papa: 'Oh yes'.
Horace: 'Well then what did they say about the kinds of cabbages & peas in the Garden?'
Papa: 'These were all due to man's agency'.
Horace: 'But do not wild plants vary?'
Papa: 'yes, within certain fixed but unknown limits'.

To this the boy 'shrugged his shoulders with pity for the poor people who *formerly* believed in such conclusions'!

'Whatever he said was absolute truth for us', Etty happily recalled. 'He always put his whole mind into answering any of our questions'. Not that other teachers weren't sometimes on hand. Charles's bosom friend, the Kew Gardens botanist Joseph Hooker, often visited Down House, but though he romped and picked gooseberries with the kids, the middle boy Francis (Franky) remembered him as a traditionalist, unlike Papa, favouring the classics and rote learning in schools. Thomas Huxley, a young medically trained zoologist, as sharp as a scalpel and mischievous, first stayed in 1856. Eventually he would shock the world as Charles's public arch-defender, which made the boys recall how privately he tried to shock *them* with 'anatomical stories'.

Oddly enough, it was an old-time parson-naturalist who shaped the children's learning more than any other, albeit indirectly. Revd John Stevens Henslow, Charles's botany professor and mentor at Cambridge University, was the pedagogical *éminence grise* in Down House, the role-model who shone through Papa's attentiveness to his own fledgling naturalists. Charles remembered Henslow as open, calm and generous; he treated everyone as equals, despite his own great knowledge, and made 'the young feel completely at ease with him'. He valued their 'most trifling observation' and dealt with their mistakes 'so clearly and kindly' that they 'only determined to be more accurate the next time'. On natural history rambles, he would pause to lecture spontaneously about some plant, bird or insect, and now as an improving Suffolk rector, Henslow gave similar talks to his 'poor parishioners' while teaching botany in their school.

So naturally Charles approached him to bring out 'some little Book to show how to teach Botany ... to children. How I wish you would: my children are always asking me, & I have no idea how to begin'. That may well be doubted, even if William, the eldest, was among the first to benefit from the 'lessons' that Henslow began to publish within weeks. Away for tutoring, Willy was 'making out all sorts ... of plants' new to his father. 'I suspect you require a dissecting microscope & some practice in dissection', Charles egged him on, recalling his own early lessons from Henslow; 'with patience you will surely get on. It is a pleasure just to know most of the British plants, as I find all agree'.

LEARNING AND LEISURE

By proposing him for the *Beagle* voyage, Henslow may have shaped his 'whole career more than any other', but Charles was still much more than Henslow's student. After all, how many fathers had lived to tell of a five-year circumnavigation aboard a ten-gun brig? Papa's vivid memories fired his children's imaginations. One sister was even emboldened to twit a big brother with the indubitable fact that although he might have ventured beyond the next village, he certainly had 'never been *quite* round the world'. Mementos from the *Beagle* became their playthings. Charles handed over his South American 'stirrups and spurs' for the nursery rocking-horse and a 'Patagonian bone spearhead to tie to sticks & throw about the garden'. The 'Gauchos bolas' got lost in the melée, as did the Australian 'throwingstick & spear', which however Papa taught the boys to replicate and toss impressively. Each souvenir had its back-story, each its lessons adapted for the Kentish countryside.

He could be generous with his presence if not unwell or preoccupied in the study. When he ventured outdoors, as Franky would recall, his 'companionship' gave a child a special feeling of 'honour & glory'. Summer games, autumn 'mushroom hunting' and 'winter sunrise' walks made delicious memories. Along the way Papa would point out 'all sorts of curious things' the kids hadn't noticed, showing them how to see, hear and even *feel* in a rural environment. Etty would remember the 'kind of sacred feeling' he had for orchids and the day when together they found his first bird's-nest orchid in a wood. 'I think he taught us all to have this peculiar feeling'. Others later summoned up the sounds heard with Papa that heralded the 'almost sacred ... changes of the seasons': 'the 'sharp cracking' of freshly frozen ice, the 'hooting of invisible owls', 'the querulous ... lambs' beside their mothers, 'the harsh warning of the jay'. Best of all, as adults they could still hear the sound of 'his heavy iron-shod walking-stick against the ground', the 'rhythmical click' that announced his presence, echoing down the years.

To walk, however, was to think. Charles carried his theory about on his shoulders, letting it drop only when distracted, though not always. Young Lenny once intercepted him in the garden and was astonished when, after 'a kindly word or two', Papa 'turned away as if quite incapable of carrying on any conversation'. This was so out of character that in a flash the 'strained and weary expression' on his face, the look of anguish, became a terrible revelation to Lenny, and it 'shot through my mind ... he wished he was no longer alive'. Life was precarious and short, Charles knew that better than anyone. He had a 'horror of losing time' and hated to waste a tick by doing anything more than once, unless it was an experiment. Back in the study, he would perch in front of a manuscript or his microscope working rapidly and obsessively right up to the limit of his endurance, which was often reached after just a few morning hours. The stints would go on for weeks or months until finally he broke down and had to leave home to recover.

His power of concentration was prodigious – it had to be. A tribe of marauders tested it daily. The kids viewed the study as 'a sort of sacred place not to be invaded in the morning without some really urgent cause', such as 'an absolute need of sticking plaister, string, pins, scissors, stamps, foot rule or hammer'. But these things were, of course, 'always to be found in the study' and nowhere else, so the temptation to transgress was often irresistible. After three or four intrusions in half an hour, Papa would turn to a child and say patiently, 'Don't you think you could not come in again. I have been interrupted very often'. The next one would be cautioned, 'You really mustn't come again', and so on. Lenny, irrepressible at 5 years old, came up with the perfect riposte. One morning 'when he knew there was very little chance of my coming out' – Charles, astonished, jotted this down – he barged into the study and announced, 'Well then, if you will come & stop with me on the lawn ... I will give you sixpence'. It was Emma's ploy for getting the children's co-operation: bribery.

BUTTERFLIES, BEETLES AND BEES

Papa's example was paramount and Papa had been a collector first of all. In this too he saw his 'Darwin blood' at work, the boys recapitulating not just his physical weakness, but also his youthful zeal for insects.

William, the eldest and healthiest (away at school when Annie died), was the first to show 'the hereditary principle, by a passion for collecting Lepidoptera'. Charles, delighted, nudged him: 'I am reading a Book on Chemistry, called "Familiar Letters on Chemistry", & this makes me often think of you in the evenings'. But at Rugby, Willy stuck with butterflies and moths, telling Papa his idea for 'breeding' them. 'I sh^d. like to hear what you do in Chemistry', his father wrote again, but by this time

'Gulielmus' was showing the 'contracting effects' of Rugby's classical curriculum on his former 'more extended interests' in 'the causes & reasons of things'. In summer 1857 he did take up photography and was seen 'rushing up & down the House' clutching glass plates in 'very dirty hands'. It was an expensive hobby, fit for a professional gent, and Charles began to think of 'making him a Barrister' ('though it is a bad trade'). Even so, William did some botanical work, and proved himself a keen observer when his father sought information on horse breeds for 'the Book', which, as he informed 'my dear old Gulielmus', now at Cambridge, 'will make a large-sized pamphlet'.

George, five years younger, followed Willy into 'ardent' lepidoptery. Charles wanted them to get beyond 'mere collecting' and identify their captures from descriptions in taxonomic manuals, like he did when afflicted with beetle-mania as an undergraduate. But the books had to be 'tolerably easy' and he found none suitable. All he could offer them was his old copy of Stephens' *Illustrations of British Entomology*, written in 'wretched latinised English', which obviously sent the wrong message. Too much Latin was dimming any hope that William would inspire Georgy to follow him beyond 'mere collecting'. And Georgy was showing scientific promise, with a 'strong mechanical turn'; soon he would get over his soldiery and, to Papa's relief, his other juvenile obsession, heraldry. Maybe he would become an 'engineer', provided he went to a 'less classical' school that taught 'general knowledge' and encouraged 'the observing or reasoning faculties'. In 1856 Papa settled on Clapham Grammar School in south London, a proprietary establishment kept by the astronomer Revd Charles Pritchard (later appointed Savilian Professor at Oxford).[6] The younger sons would follow Georgy, the first of them as a 'very unhappy "new boy"' sheltering under his wing.

This was Franky, the middle son, who stood slightly apart, a 'willing subordinate' to George and William but no less the head of a 'trio' with Leonard and Horace. All born within three years – Emma, turning 40, was at her most productive – the triumvirate stuck together when their big brothers went off to school. ('Lenny, Franky & Co^y. were rather awe-struck', Papa told Willy at Rugby, 'to hear that you had bought a cane to whip the Boys'.) By the time the youngest, Horace, was 5 years old, they all were netting moths and butterflies, which left their forlorn father wondering why 'all young & ardent lepidopterists despise from the bottom of their souls coleopterists' like himself.

Franky broke ranks first to pursue Papa's beloved beetles. At the age of 8 he had endeared himself to his father by suggesting a ghoulish experiment for 'the Book' – float a dead bird in water, then extract the seeds from its rotten crop and see if they sprout. Charles called this a 'profound' idea and wrote up the happy result in a section on the 'means of dispersal' of plants. As Franky went 'mad over beetles' in 1858, they grew closer. 'He froths at the mouth … in telling me his success', Papa whooped to Willy. The other day he caught 'Brachinus crepitans' of 'immo[r]tal … memory', and 'my blood boiled with old ardour' when he took 'a Licinus, – a prize unknown to me'. Franky would never forget 'the pleasure of turning out my bottle of dead beetles for my father to name, and the excitement, in which he fully shared, when any of them proved to be uncommon'.

Leonard, always the card, pursued his own choice of winged insects – 'Homoptera, Hemiptera & Orthoptera!', he loved using the 'big words' – before getting down to beetles with poor little Horace. The triumvirate even beat the *On the origin of species* into print. A few months before the manuscript went to press, the *Entomologist's weekly intelligencer* published a short notice, 'Coleoptera at Down', in which 'we three very young collectors ... Francis, Leonard & Horace Darwin', reported taking '*Licinus silphoides*, *Clytus mysticus*, and *Panagaeus 4-pustulatus*'. The author was, of course, a proud Papa. He hadn't seen any of his own captures in print until he was 20 years old.

Charles loved to watch the boys taking after him (except in illness), and he occasionally glimpsed a more endearing form of imitation. The children's impulse to add a mite to the balance of facts he was forever weighing could sometimes be as strong as their urge to invade the study.

Out of the mouths of babes came pedagogical home truths, most memorably from Lenny. In summer 1855 when Charles was trying to 'make out the names of all the common grasses', the boy handed him a new one, insisting in his downright way, 'I are an extraordinary grass-finder, & I must keep it particularly by my side all dinner-time'. Indoors and out, he saw Papa constantly tinkering with plants, so he came up to him one day bearing a flower and announced solemnly, 'I've a fact to do'. This was pure mimicry, there was no compulsion. George, with fresh memories in his twenties, praised his father's 'wisdom' for never trying 'to make us take an interest in science ... He thought that anything that a boy really takes to & sticks to of his own free will was good'. But when one of the kids – the boys at least – wished to learn something scientific, 'there was no amount of trouble which he would not take, & the result was of course far more powerful than if it had been at his urging'.

The children's greatest feat was another collective one: they contributed to a real scientific discovery. Charles got them all involved at one time or another, even Lizzy, in the summers of 1854 to 1861. Having taught them how to observe – never let 'what seem to be trifling facts pass' without suggesting an explanation – he now saw his lessons paying off.

Nine-year-old Georgy made the key initial observation in the Sandwalk. It was on a September day when, he remembered:

> as my father paced round ... I waited by the old ash tree at the end. On his coming round I told him that there was a humble bee's nest in the tree. This he declared to be impossible, but I stuck to it that there was, & that the bees were going & coming from it. Accordingly we walked there and presently a bee came & buzzed about & went away, and then another and another. That there was no nest was obvious but the fact excited his curiosity & he determined to investigate it ... [T]he bees were all males of Bombus Hortorum expelled from their nests & ... the ash-tree was a sort of house of call for them. They had a

high road along the hedge running to the kitchen garden with a number of similar houses of call. To discover this required many weeks as the bees flew too fast to follow. My father enlisted all of us children on the work....

Month by month, year after year, Charles's field-notes had the bees' flight-paths staying the same, their 'buzzing places ... fixed within an inch':

I was able to prove this by stationing five or six of my children each close to a buzzing place, and telling the one farthest away to shout out 'here is a bee' as soon as one was buzzing around. The others followed this up, so that the same cry of 'here is a bee' was passed on from child to child without interruption until the bees reached the buzzing place where I myself was standing.[7]

To help them track the bees, Papa made 'ingenious' use of a kitchen utensil, as George recalled:

[H]e tied a flour-dredger to the end of a stick & just as the bee was buzzing at the house of call he gave it a good dredging. We could see the bee much further when he was whitened all over ... We traced the bees over a line of 300 y[ar]ds or so, & then they disappeared like lightening [sic] over the corner of the kitchen garden wall.

They never figured out how the bees navigated – no one did until the twentieth century. But the observations made with Papa still added up to a minor breakthrough, one that George said 'we enjoyed immensely & so did he'. Lenny would remember it as both 'a game of play and ... a scientific inquiry', with his father joining in 'like a boy amongst other boys'.

ASSISTANTS AND APPRENTICES

The children learnt their science as Papa's assistants. One or two of the boys could even later be called his apprentices, but all of them followed in the footsteps of Charles's first apprentice, their neighbour John Lubbock.[8]

Five years older than William, he was himself an eldest child (of eleven) and namesake of the greatest parish landowner, a City banker who like Charles was a Fellow of the Royal Society. Socially the family connection might have stayed at this level. Young John had little in common with the isolated free-and-easy Darwin tribe. Unhampered by lingering illnesses like theirs, hardy and highly self-disciplined, he attended Church regularly, read incessantly, wrote poetry, joined the Kent militia, played cricket, hunted with dogs, went to parties and generally behaved himself like the old Etonian he was.[9] So too was his father, Sir John, 3rd Baronet, who in 1856 made him a partner in the family bank (later amalgamated with Coutts).

But one summer day when he was 14, John rode over to 'see Mr Darwin' and a beetle was caught.[10] Then another and another. Bitten by the bug, the boy had obvious talent. Charles obtained a microscope for Sir John to give to his son that Christmas and afterwards invited the boy over for 'half an hour's talk'. By 1850 John junior was lecturing to the Downe villagers on the larvae of the click beetle[11] (whose scarlet splendour Charles had prized at Cambridge); three years later, he published original descriptions of copepod crustaceans from the *Beagle* voyage, naming one *Labidocera darwinii*. Charles, then dissecting his own crustaceans (barnacles), crowed to America's leading authority in the field about this 'remarkably nice young man, only a little above 18 years old' but with 'great zeal', who 'may do good work in Natural History' if he can 'resist his future career of great wealth, business & rank'.

Eager to recruit and retain him, Charles quickly integrated John into his circle of close colleagues and secured his election to scientific societies. On the fateful weekend in April 1856 when Charles first tipped his hand on species to a select party staying at Down House (including Hooker and Huxley), John was the youngest naturalist present.[12] Charles saw him as a future ally and invested heavily with this particular banker.

By now John had unearthed part of a fossil skull of a species of musk ox previously unknown in England;[13] he was dissecting fly larvae and making, Charles reported, 'the most minute & beautiful drawings of their muscular system'; he had kept up his 'excellent work' on the crustacea and was preparing his first major scientific paper on one of the tiniest species, the water flea. Charles combed through the manuscript, jotting gentle criticisms and measured praise. 'I do most honestly admire your powers of observation & zeal; & you will do, much in Nat[ural]. History, notwithstanding your terrible case of "pursuit of knowledge under riches"' (which seemed 'as great a drawback as poverty'). But better to wait 'a little longer before publishing', he cautioned; 'you discuss ... such high points towards the close, that the premises ought to be extra certain'. For this reason he himself delayed publishing his theory of natural selection. John duly revised the manuscript for Charles to communicate to the Royal Society and within a year the paper was out in the *Philosophical transactions*, clinching John's election as a Fellow in 1858. He was 24 years old.

With a silver spoon in his mouth and Charles's microscope in hand, young John moved deftly up the greasy poles of science, politics and finance to become the most polymathic of public Darwinists (and eventually the first Lord Avebury). He got his social backbone by inheritance, but it was at Down House, while Charles was dissecting barnacles, that John himself first mastered lowly invertebrates – beetles, flies and fleas – winning his spurs in science and very soon, thanks to Charles, immortality in print.

In those years, the 'big Book' was no elephant in the study, far from it. If not privy to the theory, John was at least familiar with its vast empirical basis – so familiar in fact that out of the blue in 1857 he made a crucial correction to Charles's analysis in chapter four of the relative proportions of plant taxa around the globe.[14] 'He has pointed out to me the grossest blunder which I have made in principle ... I am the most miserable, bemuddled, stupid Dog in all England, & am ready to cry at vexation at my blindness & presumption'. So Charles moaned to Hooker. And to John his abject teacher confessed: 'You have done me the greatest possible service ... I am quite convinced yours is the right way ... I am quite shocked to find how easily I am muddled, for I had before ... concluded my way was fair. It is dreadfully erroneous. What a disgraceful blunder you have saved me from. I heartily thank you'. The thanking continued in the 1859 first edition of the *On the origin of species*, no less, where the 25-year-old 'Mr. Lubbock' is credited as a theory-minded 'philosophical naturalist' like Darwin himself and a keen observer of scale insects, worker ants and buff-tip moths. Further credits appeared in successive editions and many more in five other books published by Charles before his death.

They had been on familiar terms since John was in his teens, when Charles first began his letters with 'Dear Lubbock'. And they quickly got onto equal terms in science, always discussing subjects at the highest level of which John was capable. There was no 'talking down' to him. A stickler for accuracy, Charles came to trust John to notice the minutest detail, as if the observing eye were his own. In 1862, requesting advice on precisely where on clover blossoms visiting hive bees suck, Charles assured him, 'I cannot think of any other naturalist who w^d be careful' enough for the job.

That included his elder sons, William then 23, George 17 and Francis 14, who had continued to assist him over the years. Theirs was a different sort of apprenticeship. Richly privileged as they were, the Darwin boys felt themselves to be 'outside the pale of Eton-dom' and they were never part of the sporting set to which the eight great Lubbock brothers belonged. A cloud seems to have gathered about John, the future 4th Baronet, because when the Darwin boys were young he 'constantly rode over' to Down House and ensconced himself as 'a sort of pupil' in the sacred study. Perhaps they also begrudged Papa's being 'proud' to have 'discovered' their usurper and his boasting of John as an 'enthusiastic convert' who might even come to be seen as Papa's scientific heir. One thing certainly did rankle: after John married in 1856, his wife would refer to Charles casually as 'John's 2nd father', which demoted Papa rather. Crossly, the boys would 'parody this by calling ... John our second brother'.

DIVERGENT DESTINIES

William debuted in *On the origin of species* as 'my son' who had 'made a careful examination and sketch'[15] of a Belgian cart-horse. In later publications Charles credited him by name for observing insects, plants and worms. He was reliable, but his twig had been bent at school. After Cambridge, with his father's help he bought into a banking partnership and thereafter led a simple life, married but childless and devoted to 'all the classic works in all the languages he had ever known, or not quite forgotten'. Late for dinner, it was 'always because he was "just finishing a paragraph"'; and sometimes he could be 'caught hiding Homer under a pile of papers'. His lasting distinction was as the subject of Charles's early notes for a 'natural history of babies', published in 1877 as 'A biographical sketch of an infant'.

Henrietta, the second surviving child, never went on in education, though she possessed a lively mind beset by a morbid obsession. For all the 'cures' she endured in her teenage phase of dubious ailments, 'Body' might be seen as her father's main human experimental subject save that he experimented longer, more variously and more desperately on his own wretched corpus. Taking after Emma, who proofread the *On the origin of species*, Henrietta became the in-house editor of her father's *The descent of man*. Later she edited her mother's family letters for private circulation. In them Lizzy grows up to be 'Bessy' who plays a bit part in the family until the death of Emma, with whom she lived until the end, never quite able to manage on her own. In the published edition of the letters, Lizzy's birth is noted; Henrietta's other references to her are expunged.

George, boy soldier, bee hustler and leader at Clapham, was the first of the sons to achieve scientific distinction – Second Wrangler at Cambridge when 23, Fellow of the Royal Society (FRS) at 34 and Plumian Professor of Astronomy at Cambridge at 38. After the Wranglership, Charles began publicly crediting 'my son, Mr. George Darwin' for authoritative observations and calculations, even if his first response to the prize had been paradoxical. 'Only too much inclined to take a favourable view' of his sons' achievements, Frank would recall, he nevertheless doubted them for undertaking anything 'for which he did not feel sure ... they had knowledge enough'. Thus in 1868 he congratulated the new Second Wrangler 'with all my heart & soul', declaring, 'I always said from your early days that such energy, perseverance & talent as yours, would be sure to succeed'; then in the same breath he added, 'but I never expected such brilliant success'.

Dubious as pedagogy, but Charles's ambivalence spoke volumes. 'His doubts', Frank went on, 'were part of his humility concerning what was in any way connected with himself; his too favourable view of our work was due to his sympathetic nature, which made him lenient to every one'. Fathers don't always make ideal teachers.

Leonard and Horace, the youngest children, achieved less in science. They were sickly as adolescents, Horace the worse, and Charles put it all down to 'a curious form of inheritance'. Emma seems to have cured Horace by dispensing with the governess to whom he became attached, and though he started school late, found spelling hard and was known to the family as 'Skimp' ('to supply with meagrely'), he turned out to be brilliant with machines. At 23 he graduated from Cambridge with mathematical honours, at 27 he co-founded the Cambridge Scientific Instrument Company, becoming director at 40, and he was elected FRS at 52.[16] In his last book, published in 1881, Charles credited 'my son Horace'[17] for inventing a device to measure the subsidence resulting from earthworms burrowing beneath a stone. A 'worm-stone', and quite possibly the original one, still lies in the garden at Down House (see also Chapter 8 endnote 4).

Four of the brothers were Cambridge graduates, three were elected FRS and knighted, and the same three married with issue – the exception on each count was Leonard. Thinking himself 'the stupidest member of his family', he joined the Army at 18, entered the Royal Engineers at 21 and taught chemistry at staff schools before going into military intelligence at 35; he was elected a Liberal-Unionist MP at 42 and, defeated three years later, he wrote on economics until assuming the presidency of the Eugenics Education Society at age 61, the acme of his career.[18] Throughout his long life – he survived until 1943 – Leonard suffered from a severe case of his father's personal 'humility', now called low self-esteem. One who knew him for half a century remembered that an 'extremely disparaging attitude to himself was very characteristic of him at any age'.

Papa was partly responsible. In 1868 he could question the significance of Lenny's placing second in the Woolwich entrance exam (after George's triumphant '2nd' at Cambridge) – 'I shall be curious to hear how many tried' – because for a decade or more he had considered Lenny, if 'not stupid', at least 'slow & backward'. Tellingly, from his few distinct childhood memories Leonard jotted down this scene:

> I remember my father entering the drawing-room at Down ... when I, then a school-boy, was sitting on the sofa with *The Origin of Species* in my hands. He looked over my shoulder and said: 'I bet you half-a-crown that you do not get to the end of that book', and then left the room. If 'during the holidays' was an implied condition, I fear that he won his bet but never got his money.

Lenny at this time was at least 13 years old and primed to have a spontaneous interest encouraged. But Papa resorted to bribery, thinking cash might kick-start a sluggish learner. Evidently, a son whose insect 'collecting mania' had degenerated into 'the poor form of collecting Postage stamps' could not be expected to follow him in science, not for love rather than money. Lenny never forgot the lesson.

FRANCISCAN FACETS

Francis, beetle-buff and bird-floater, ears fine-tuned and eyes wide open to every facet of rural life, was the boy who followed most closely in Charles's footsteps. With a Cambridge MB at age 27, he moved from medicine (his father's first field) to botany, was elected an FRS at 34 and appointed reader in botany at Cambridge when 40. After losing his young wife in childbed, he lived at Downe with the baby and his parents, collaborating on plant experiments until his father's death six years later.[19]

Charles credited Frank in print more than any other son. Only Frank was named on a title-page, when in 1880 *The power of movement in plants* proclaimed 'assisted by Francis Darwin'. And Frank was the only field-naturalist. In adulthood, George and Horace would notice gross phenomena such as ripple-marks or pot-holes, William knew some geology; Leonard, the family philistine, could name 'the very commonest flowers and birds', and he 'never gardened'. Only Frank lived constantly in a world teeming with 'birds and beasts and flowers'. From an apprentice, he became the family aesthete, a musician, artist and popular writer; and it was he who edited the three-volume tribute to Papa, *The life and letters of Charles Darwin*, two further volumes of his letters and another transcribing early drafts of his theory.

Frank, the most reflective of the children, passed on to posterity more facets of Charles's pedagogy than the rest of the children together. *Respect* came first, respect for the children's freedom, individuality and ideas. Papa never demanded 'to know what we were doing or thinking unless we wished to tell'; and when they did, the kids felt themselves to be 'creatures whose opinions and thoughts were valuable'. *Praise* created this self-esteem; it was Papa's benediction. Francis never forgot his 'intense pleasure' as a small boy when his father showed delighted surprise at 'my knowledge of common trees and shrubs in a winter coppice'. It was a pleasure in short supply among Leonard's childhood memories. *Sympathy* lay at the root of Papa's encouragement. To him, it was the bedrock of 'the moral sense', what made each of them truly human. His 'constant sympathy in our pursuits', as Francis put it, runs through the children's recollections like a golden thread. It was his 'most loveable trait', William remembered, 'a sympathy that I *never* saw approached. So spontaneous and simple and delightful'.

Respect and praise for learners, rooted in paternal sympathy, radically distinguished the science-teaching ethos at Downe from the children's other schooling. *Practice* was the other indispensable facet, practice in observing, measuring, counting, recording and drawing. To Francis, the 'best teaching' he ever received was in 'how to play the flute, and how to use a microscope'. 'Both boys and girls', he believed, 'must be taught to use, not only their hands, but their eyes'; he had learnt both together seated at a microscope with Papa. Frank thought it 'piteous' that, when he was at school, no effort was made to 'keep alive the natural sharp-eyedness of children', as Papa had done. All was sacrificed to cramming and performance. 'The great Moloch of examination has constantly to be supplied with human children ... Some escape, but how many are reduced to ashes?' Charles would have agreed.

Nor was schooling the only problem. Cambridge left him wondering 'that fire did not descend from heaven and destroy a University which so sinned against the first elements of knowing, in neglecting the distinction between what we learn by our own personal experience and what we acquire from books'. Full of 'anger and contempt' at having to learn human anatomy by heart, he had retreated to his college rooms where, waiting for him one day, he found a dead porpoise sent by a 'thoughtful brother'. There and then, Frank proceeded to dissect the mammalian relative, to the horror of curious intruding staff.[20] In a study of his own.

NOTE ON SOURCES

This essay gives priority to the voices of Francis, George, Leonard, William and Henrietta as 'heard' in their primary sources listed in the bibliography. The recollections of George's grand daughters Margaret Keynes and Gwen Raverat are also heard and Charles himself speaks through the autobiography edited by Horace's daughter Nora Barlow and in the publications and correspondence volumes listed below, where Emma's voice is also present. George's great-grandson Randal Keynes has written frankly and memorably about his extended family and several of his works have been used. It would be tedious and confusing to give references to every phrase and word taken from these sources and would prevent easy reading. So while all sources are duly quoted, and can be traced by using the Darwin Correspondence

Project website (http://www.darwinproject.ac.uk/) and Darwin Online (http://darwin-online.org.uk/), references are kept to a minimum by citing only the other works in the bibliography, which lists every source used in the essay.

NOTES

[1] When Charles Darwin and his family moved to Down House, the spelling of the village was also Down, with no 'e'. When the spelling of the village's name was changed to Downe some years later, Darwin decided not to change the spelling of his house, so it remained Down House.
[2] Gay, Bourgeois experience, 403-60; Desmond and Moore, Darwin, ch. 20.
[3] Freeman, Darwin family.
[4] Healey, Emma Darwin, 198.
[5] Bagshaw, History, gazetteer and directory.
[6] Moore, 'On the education'.
[7] CD, Précis, in Freeman, Charles Darwin, p. 182.
[8] Patton, Science, politics and business.
[9] Grant Duff, Life-work, pp. 13-17.
[10] Diary of J. Lubbock, quoted in R. Keynes, "'I thought I'd try the telephone'", p. 80.
[11] Hutchinson, Life, 1:23.
[12] Desmond and Moore, Darwin, pp. 434-35.
[13] Hutchinson, Life, 1:37-39.
[14] Stauffer, Charles Darwin's 'Natural Selection', pp. 92-171; C. Darwin, On the origin, 53-58, 111-26.
[15] C. Darwin, On the origin, p. 164.
[16] Cattermole and Wolfe, Horace Darwin's shop.
[17] C. Darwin, Formation, p. 119.
[18] Edwards, Darwin, Leonard.
[19] Junker, Darwin, Sir Francis.
[20] F. Darwin, Rustic sounds, pp. 88-89.

REFERENCES

Bagshaw, S. (1847). *History, gazetteer and directory of the county of Kent* (2 volumes). Sheffield: Printed for the author by G. Ridge.

Barlow, N. (Ed.) (1958). *The autobiography of Charles Darwin, 1809-1882, with original omissions restored.* London: Collins.

Barrett, P. H. (1977). *The collected papers of Charles Darwin* (2 volumes). Chicago: University of Chicago Press.

Burkhardt, F., et al. (Eds.) (1985–2012). *The correspondence of Charles Darwin.* (19 volumes to date). Cambridge: Cambridge University Press.

Cattermole, M. J. G., & Wolfe, A. F. (1987). *Horace Darwin's shop: A history of The Cambridge Scientific Instrument Company, 1878 to 1968.* Bristol: Adam Hilger.

Darwin, C. (1859a). Coleoptera at Down. *Entomologist's weekly intelligencer, 6* (25 June), 99.

Darwin, C. (1859b). *On the origin of species by means of natural selection, or the preservation of favoured races in the struggle for life.* London, John Murray.

Darwin, C. (1881). *The formation of vegetable mould, through the action of worms, with observations on their habits.* London: John Murray.

Darwin, F. [Preliminary draft of] Reminiscences of my father's everyday life. CUL-DAR140.3, http://darwin-online.org.uk/.

Darwin, F. (1887). *The life and letters of Charles Darwin, including an autobiographical chapter* (3 volumes). London: John Murray.

Darwin, F. (1916). Memoir of Sir George Darwin. In G.H. Darwin *Scientific Papers* (5 volumes, 1907–1916). (vol. 5, pp. ix–xxxiii). Cambridge: Cambridge University Press.

Darwin, F. (1917). *Rustic sounds and other studies in literature and natural history*. London: John Murray. [reprints his RS memoir with corrections but abbreviated].

Darwin, F. (1920). *Springtime and other essays*. London: John Murray.

Darwin, G. H. [Recollections of Charles Darwin]. CUL-DAR112. Retrieved from http://darwin-online.org.uk/

Darwin, L. (1929). Memories of Down House. *Nineteenth Century, 106* (July), 118–123.

Darwin, W. E. (1883). [Recollections of Charles Darwin]. CUL-DAR112.B3b-B3f. Retrieved from http://darwin-online.org.uk/

Desmond, A., & Moore, J. (1991). *Darwin*. London: Michael Joseph.

Edwards, A. W. F. (2008). Darwin, Leonard (1850-1943). In *Oxford dictionary of national biography* (online ed.). Oxford: Oxford University Press.

Freeman, R. B. (1968). Charles Darwin on the routes of male humble bees. *Bulletin of the British Museum (Natural History), 3(6)*, 177–189.

Freeman, R. B. (1982). The Darwin family. In R. J. Berry (Ed.). *Charles Darwin: A commemoration 1882-1982: Happy is the man that findeth wisdom*. London: Academic Press.

Gay, P. (1984). *The bourgeois experience: Victoria to Freud* (Vol 1). *The education of the senses*. New York, NY: Oxford University Press.

Glazebrook, R. T. (2004). Darwin, Sir Horace (1851-1928). In *Oxford dictionary of national biography*. Oxford: Oxford University Press.

Grant Duff, U. (Ed.). (1924). *The life-work of Lord Avebury (Sir John Lubbock), 1834-1913*. London: Watts and Co.

Healey, E. (2001). *Emma Darwin: The inspirational wife of a genius*. London: Headline.

Hutchinson, H. G. (1914). *Life of Sir John Lubbock, Lord Avebury*. (2 volumes). London: Macmillan and Co.

Junker, T. (2004). Darwin, Sir Francis (1848-1925). In *Oxford dictionary of national biography*. Oxford: Oxford University Press.

Keynes, M. (1943). *Leonard Darwin, 1850-1943*. Cambridge: Cambridge University Press.

Keynes, R. (2001). *Annie's box: Charles Darwin, his daughter and human evolution*. London: Fourth Estate.

Keynes, R. (2005). Darwin, William Erasmus (1839-1914). In *Oxford dictionary of national biography* (online ed.). Oxford: Oxford University Press.

Keynes, R. (2008) 'I thought I'd try the telephone' – Darwin, his disciple, insects and earthworms. B. Gardiner, R. & M. Morris (ed). *The Linnean, Special Issue no. 9*, 79–96

Keynes, R. (2012). Darwin, Anne Elizabeth (1841–1851). In *Oxford dictionary of national biography* (online ed.). Oxford: Oxford University Press.

Kushner, D. (2013). Darwin, Sir George Howard (1842–1912). In *Oxford dictionary of national biography* (online ed.). Oxford: Oxford University Press.

Litchfield, H. E. (). Darwin Sketches for a biography. CUL-DAR 262.23.1. Retrieved from http://darwin-online.org.uk/

Litchfield, H. E. (1904). *Emma Darwin, wife of Charles Darwin: a century of family letters*. (2 volumes). Cambridge: privately printed at the University Press.

Litchfield, H. E. (1915). *Emma Darwin, a century of family letters, 1792-1896*. (2 volumes). London: John Murray.

Moore, J. (1977). On the education of Darwin's sons: The correspondence between Charles Darwin and the Reverend G. V. Reed, 1857-1864. *Notes and records of the Royal Society of London, 32*, 51–70.

Patton, M. (2007). *Science, politics and business in the work of Sir John Lubbock: A man of universal mind*. Aldershot: Ashgate.

Raverat, G. (1953). *Period Piece: A Cambridge childhood*. London: Faber & Faber.

James Moore
Open University,
UK

RUTH BARLOW

8. USING COLLECTIONS OF DARWINIANA IN DARWIN-INSPIRED LEARNING

As a research student, I sat in on an undergraduate lecture by my supervisor, stunned by how bored the students were. Admittedly, the eighteenth century isn't everyone's cup of tea, but these students had chosen to be there. So why were they bored? My supervisor had noticed it too. Was his lecturing so bad, he asked me. No, I replied, but the subject matter was not immediate enough for the level. What excited me was seeing him take an original manuscript, written three centuries previously, and show how he extracted philosophical, bibliographical, and aesthetic information from it. At the next lecture he did this, circulating a photocopy of the original manuscript of one of David Hume's most important works. The students were electrified to see, even in photocopy, Hume's own handwriting, his insertions and deletions, and his working practices. My professor showed them how seeing this and understanding it could shed light on the development of his philosophical thought. This was research and the students felt a privilege in having access to it and having that connection with Hume the philosopher, but also with Hume the man holding a quill, spilling ink, something few people in three hundred years had had.

While assisting in the delivery of courses with the Charles Darwin Trust, I have found that, no matter what the age of the students, they respond in a similar manner to contact with original artefacts from Darwin's life. Suddenly the gap in history contracts, and they can understand what Darwin did, how he did it, and why. It is exciting for both students and teachers. When we marry this historical approach to the techniques of Darwin-inspired learning, helping students to use research methods to discover facts for themselves, we have a very powerful tool in opening up Darwin's methods and conclusions to a wide range of students, and in a wider range of subjects than just biology. Among the artefacts owned by the Charles Darwin Trust are many books by Darwin and his followers, scientific collections, such as Charles's own collection of beetles, to oddities like the slide that Charles had a local carpenter make to fit over the main staircase at Down House so that his children could play indoors on rainy days – hardly the act of a typically stern Victorian father, which Charles certainly wasn't. Other collections at Down House, the Natural History Museum in London, the Cambridge University Library, the Museum of Natural History in New York, and many others, hold collections of specimens, notebooks, and artefacts that belonged to Charles, were used by him or those who worked with him.

In this chapter, I will consider three items of Darwiniana, all of them accessible to the public if you are within reach of the south of England, although reproduction images are easily and freely found on the web for teaching purposes for those living elsewhere. I will show how the principles of Darwin-inspired learning used to teach Darwin's theories within the historical context surrounding them can deepen the students' connection with, and understanding of, Darwin, his own research, and his time and place. Each will be laid out in the same format as lesson plans as published on the Charles Darwin Trust website (www.charlesdarwintrust. org) which they are intended to complement. The prompts are suggestions and as web resources improve and expand you will find it even easier to vary what follows to your needs.

A BOOK

Let us begin with perhaps the most iconic item of Darwiniana of all: a first edition of *On the origin of species*. Images from the first edition are widely available on the web[1] if your class is prevented from visiting a library, such as the Natural History Museum in London[2], which contains an original copy of the first edition on public view. It is an underwhelming book to look at: plain green covers and not very big. Why did this book revolutionise our understanding of all life on earth?

Even five years ago, what follows would not have been possible to implement except with a class of graduate-level bibliographers, but with web access and a growing body of resources available, this is now possible anywhere in the world.

Quotation

As many more individuals of each species are born than can possibly survive; and as, consequently, there is a frequently recurring struggle for existence, it follows that any being, if it vary however slightly in any manner profitable to itself, under the complex and sometimes varying conditions of life, will have a better chance of surviving, and thus be NATURALLY SELECTED. From the strong principle of inheritance, any selected variety will tend to propagate its new and modified form. (Darwin, 1859, p.5)

Lesson Outcomes

– Understand why *On the origin of species* caused such a revolution in scientific thinking.
– Use search engines and/or library catalogues and other bibliographic resources to discover what scientists thought about the natural world before Darwin.
– Examine how scientific ideas were communicated in the mid-nineteenth century.
– Describe the reactions to, and reception of, Darwin's ideas.

Suggested Activities for Students

- Encourage the class to discover what scientists thought about the evolution of animals and plants before Darwin published this book. Ask them to discuss what they find.
- Ask students to think about where the book was published. Why is that important?
- Can the students find out from secondary sources how long it took Darwin to write this work? What might be the reasons for that? Why did he finally buckle down to finishing the book and publishing it?
- Was the book successful? Did it sell well? What does that say about Darwin and his reputation in 1859? How did Darwin build that reputation?
- How did people receive the ideas contained in the book? Was it controversial? If so, what were the issues in question? How did this affect Darwin?
- Are any of these issues still being debated today? Why does the class think this is?
- Finally, if students have found contradictory evidence in written and electronic sources, (especially the well-known 'misquotations' – phrases many people attribute falsely to Darwin and to *On the origin of species*) how do they think they could discover the truth about what Darwin actually wrote?

Plenary Discussion

Lead the group through their findings. Do they make sense? Does what they have found surprise them? Do they think that there are any ways that the issues and controversies surrounding the book could be settled, either scientifically or theologically? Do they think deciding one way or another is necessary?

AN EXPERIMENT

Charles' youngest surviving son, Horace[3] was a successful civil engineer, interested in assisting and continuing his father's work. He founded the Cambridge Scientific Instrument Company which still exists as part of even bigger companies today.

In 1877 Horace designed and built a 'worm-stone micrometer' which enabled Charles to study the rate at which stones on the surface of the ground were buried by the action of worms beneath them. Charles and then Horace made measurements over a period of 19 years using this worm-stone at Down House, their home in Kent, where it (or one very like it[4]) can still be seen. Horace himself reported the final set of results in a paper to the Royal Society in 1901[5]. The data thus gained were the basis for Charles' book *The formation of vegetable mould, through the action of worms*[6] which was published in 1881 only six months before he died.

Quotation

Farmers in England are well aware that objects of all kinds, left on the surface of pasture-land, after a time disappear, or, as they say, work themselves downwards. How powdered lime, cinders, and heavy stones, can work down, and at the same rate, through the matted roots of a grass-covered surface, is a question which has probably never occurred to them:

> small objects left on the surface of the land where worms abound soon get buried, and that large stones sink slowly downwards through the same means. (Darwin, 1881, pp. 147, 156-7)

Lesson Outcomes

- Understand how an experiment such as this one was designed.
- Evaluate Darwin's evidence for his conclusions in *The formation of vegetable mould, through the action of worms*.
- Recognise that experiments sometimes take place over much longer periods of time than the students may be used to, in this case over decades.

Suggested Activities for Students

- Do the students think that they would go about finding evidence to support the theory in the same way today? If there are differences, what has changed between then and now to make that possible?
- Horace Darwin had to design the worm-stone so that the stone could move and yet the amount by which it had moved could be accurately measured. Ask the class to think about why this was innovatory in Victorian engineering.
- Ask the students to discuss the following: if Darwin had conducted measurements with the worm-stone for, say, 30 years and found no movement, should he have given up at that point? Or carried on? If so, for how long before he could conclude that the experiment was not going to produce any data which would prove that the soil moved?

Plenary Discussion

What have the students discovered about designing an experiment like this one? Do they understand why it took so long for Charles and then Horace to gather accurate data to support Charles' theory concerning earthworms? Why do your students think that Charles theorised that earthworms rather than any other organism were responsible for the formation of vegetable mould? Ask the class to discuss why Charles thought it so important to gather so much evidence in support of his theory before publishing.

A COLLECTION OF SPECIMENS

Charles Darwin amassed a large collection of specimens throughout a lifetime of studying nature, both wild and domesticated. At Down House he became fascinated by pigeon breeding, because it provided a microcosm of selection, as guided by the breeder, in other words artificial selection[7] which emphasises beauty or usefulness in human-bred organisms, as opposed to natural selection which emphasises only survival and reproduction. Darwin's work on pigeons helped to shape these theories. In 1867 he gave all his 120 pigeon specimens to the Natural History Museum in London, where they can still be seen today, most with Darwin's original labels which are now enabling researchers to cross-reference the specimens with Darwin's original research notes. This is providing new insights into Darwin's research methods[8].

Quotation

Although man does not cause variability and cannot even prevent it, he can select, preserve, and accumulate the variations given to him by the hand of nature in any way which he chooses; and thus he can certainly produce a great result. (Darwin, 1868, p. 3)

Lesson Outcomes

– Understand the distinction Darwin makes between natural and artificial selection.
– Recognise that human breeders knew that they could select traits in pigeons and other domesticated animals, even though they were unaware of Darwin's theories.
– Discover how studying the activities of pigeon breeders influenced Darwin's thinking on artificial selection.
– Consider the difference between breeding in Victorian England and that practised today, if any.

Suggested Activities for Students

– Look at the suggested websites and notice the differences between the breeds of pigeons[9].
– Notice that Darwin was both involved in pigeon breeding himself (though not for show!), and in communication with other pigeon breeders to discover more about how breeding changed the pigeons. Examine how Darwin's studies are much more in depth and detailed than those undertaken by hobby breeders – he kept the pigeons' skeletons after they died and maintained meticulous records of their traits and pedigrees.
– Examine Darwin's reasoning as he distinguished between natural and artificial selection through the breeding of fancy pigeons.

Plenary Discussion

- In Darwin's time, genes and DNA had not been discovered and scientists did not know how traits were inherited. If the students had lived in the mid-nineteenth century, how would they have explained this? Did Darwin explain this?[10]
- The traits that fancy pigeon breeders valued might actually have hindered the birds' survival in the wild. Ask the students to discuss the merits and demerits of different traits, whether they would help the pigeons win at shows or survive in the wild, and what is the difference in the selection process in each case.
- The Natural History Museum in London is trying to link Darwin's original labels (seen on display at the Museum and on their webpage – see note 7) attached to his pigeon specimens to his notes on each bird in order to discover more about his own research methods. What do the students think the Museum is looking for? What might be the significance of what the scientists find?

CONCLUSION

I've examined how close attention and observation of these three items of Darwiniana and placing them in their historical context can deepen understanding of Darwin's methods and interests. I hope I have inspired you to see that the same methods that make Darwin-inspired learning such a useful tool can be that much more powerful by adding a direct link to Darwin the man through such artefacts. I wish you joy on your historical journey to be, and to bring your students, closer to Darwin.

NOTES

[1] http://darwin-online.org.uk/EditorialIntroductions/Freeman_OntheOriginofSpecies.html
[2] http://www.nhm.ac.uk/nature-online/collections-at-the-museum/museum-treasures/darwin-origin-of-species-book/index.html
[3] http://darwin-online.org.uk/life25c.html.
[4] There is doubt over whether the worm-stone presently at Down House is the original one. Within the Darwin family, it is believed that the original stone was moved accidently in 1896 and then replaced in its present position, while scholars tend to think that it was lost but replaced by The Cambridge Scientific Instrument Company in 1929.
[5] See Horace Darwin's Shop by M. J. G. Cattermole and A. F. Wolfe (1987), p.7.
[6] http://darwin-online.org.uk/EditorialIntroductions/Freeman_VegetableMouldandWorms.html.
[7] The lesson plan for 'Artificial selection' is given at the Charles Darwin Trust website http://www.charlesdarwintrust.org/userfiles/uploaded/Files/Resources/KS3_M2_Artificial_Selection_Booklet_V5.pdf. See also the Charles Darwin Trust post-16 resource on Darwin's Birds: http://www.charlesdarwintrust.org/content/77/ both sites accessed on 10 February 2014.
[8] See http://www.nhm.ac.uk/nature-online/collections-at-the-museum/museum-treasures/charles-darwin-pigeons/ accessed on 11 February 2014.
[9] See http://darwinspigeons.com/, http://charlesdarwintrust.org/content/86/galleries_pigeons, http://www.youtube.com/watch?v = VFVueCs3gFI, http://vimeo.com/6786667 accessed on 12 February 2014.

[10] See On the origin of species, ch.1, Effects of habit and of the use or disuse of parts; correlated variation; inheritance, fifth paragraph beginning 'The laws governing inheritance are for the most part unknown'.

REFERENCES

Darwin, C. R. (1859). *On the origin of species by means of natural selection, or the preservation of favoured races in the struggle for life.* London: John Murray.

Darwin, C. R. (1868). *The variation of animals and plants under domestication.* London: John Murray.

Darwin, C. R. (1881). *The formation of vegetable mould, through the action of worms, with observations on their habits.* London: John Murray.

Ruth Barlow
The Charles Darwin Trust,
UK

THE IMPORTANCE OF ACTIVE
HANDS-ON ENQUIRY

MIKE CORBISHLEY

9. OBJECT LESSONS IN EVIDENCE-BASED LEARNING

Darwin's unique selling point and the reason why he was so successful in making the case for evolution was his absolute belief in evidence. (Owen, 2013, p. 138)

INTRODUCTION

One of Charles Darwin's sons, George, at the nearby house of another scientist, Sir John Lubbock (see below), asked 'Where does your father do his barnacles?' naturally supposing that all scientists carried out the same experiments (Keynes, 2001, p. 151). The public today, I believe, now understands that archaeologists are scientists, testing assumptions against carefully-collected evidence in the field. This chapter reviews the ways in which evidence-based learning has developed since Darwin's time and learning by rote has been largely displaced by enquiry in both formal and informal education in Britain.

BACKGROUND

The nineteenth century saw important changes and significant increases in the education of children in England. Well-off families educated their children at home in early childhood, then sending the boys away to boarding schools. While there were boarding schools for girls, parents generally preferred to continue to educate their daughters at home, as Gwen Raverat, Darwin's granddaughter explained in 1952 (1960, p. 61). Charles Darwin's wife Emma was educated at home. Charles Darwin was first educated at home and then sent as a boarder to Shrewsbury School at the age of eight. Long before his children had governesses, tutors and had attended school, Darwin took a keen interest in their development, both physical and mental and his observations were carefully set out in his notebooks.[1] Charles and Emma received an enlightened education where they were encouraged to ask questions. Both Charles and Emma were supporters of the methods recommended by the Swiss educationalist, Johann Heinrich Pestalozzi,[2] and 'wanted to encourage their children to think for themselves' (Keynes, 2001, pp. 122-3).

The Darwins supported the local school, set up and funded by Sir John Lubbock, by paying the fees of some children from poor families (Keynes, 2001, p. 143).

They employed tutors and governesses for their own children and had part of the first floor of Down House altered to accommodate a nursery and schoolroom. But of course Darwin himself was responsible for his children's interest in nature and the landscape, sometimes asking his children to help in experiments, for example, can earthworms hear music?[3], and they recollected particular walks with fondness (Keynes, 2001, p. 112). Raverat remembers that her father, George, on their frequent visits to Down House recreated some of those walks and that he 'adored a Roman road or prehistoric fort, and no one enjoyed a good dungeon, or a set of fine battlements, more than he did' (Raverat, 1960, p. 185).

In most schools in England at this time learning was by rote. The important subjects were the three Rs and scripture. Charles Darwin was not happy with the emphasis on classics in public schools, as he wrote to his second cousin, William Darwin Fox in 1852:

> No one can more truly despise the old stereotyped stupid classical education than I do, but yet I have not had courage to break through the trammels. After many doubts we have just sent our eldest Boy to Rugby. [4]

In another letter to Fox in 1853 Darwin wrote:

> Our second lad Georgie, has a strong mechanical turn: & we think of making him an engineer: I shall try & find out for him some less classical school,— perhaps Bruce Castle. I certainly shd like to see more diversity in Education, than there is any ordinary school: no exercise of the observing or reasoning faculties,—no general knowledge acquired.[5]

His younger four sons were sent to Clapham Grammar School which had been founded in 1834, because the headmaster was an enthusiastic supporter of the sciences. The nineteenth century also saw the beginnings of a formalised, not statutory, curriculum in schools. After a Royal Commission on education in 1858 recommendations were made for the government to issue instructions, in the form of codes, to improve and standardise teaching in schools. A revised code, The New Code, which was introduced in 1879, set out what each pupil should know in the compulsory subjects of Reading, Writing and Arithmetic from Standard I (6-year-olds) to Standard VI (11-year-olds). Later regulations allowed schools to teach other subjects, such as history, geography and science for specified hours each week.

DARWIN AND ARCHAEOLOGY

Darwin was well aware of the developments, in his own time, of archaeological research, in particular the establishment of a chronology for prehistoric times based on scientific analysis and fieldwork. Much of this was due to his close friendship with John Lubbock (later Sir John Lubbock) whose family moved into the property adjacent to Down House in the 1830s. In a recent biography of Lubbock, the author Janet Owen calls him 'Darwin's apprentice' (Owen, 2013,

p. 3). Darwin encouraged John Lubbock (25 years younger than himself) in his passionate enthusiasm for natural history. Lubbock published his own research as well as helping Darwin with his. For example, he worked on collections made during the voyage of HMS *Beagle*. Lubbock became a great collector, especially of prehistoric implements and ethnographic material and carried out research into the prehistory of the world. He had a particular enthusiasm for popularising the debate on human evolution and antiquity. He was part of a small but influential scientific community which made fundamental changes to the way science was conducted and published and helped spread Darwinist ideas (Owen, 2013, pp. 45-50 & 73). His book *Pre-historic times as illustrated by ancient remains and the manners and customs of modern savages*, first published in 1865, was particularly important in establishing the long antiquity of the world in the face of a chronology based on a calculation made from the *Book of Genesis* and first proposed in the seventeenth century. This calculation, for which there was no supporting scientific evidence, stated that the world was created in 4004 BC (Daniel, 1967, p. 110). As a key member of the scientific community Darwin was naturally interested in the evolution of races as well as plants, animals and geology. He was connected to archaeological discoveries through his own correspondence with other scientists and through frequent personal contact with John Lubbock who in 1884 married Alice the daughter of General Pitt-Rivers, the founder of modern scientific techniques in archaeological excavation and fieldwork.

TEACHING FROM TEXTBOOKS

In Britain, from the nineteenth century, prehistory was usually only defined in the context of the Roman invasion (Corbishley, 2011, pp. 128-129). The first textbooks, published in the nineteenth and early twentieth centuries were usually written by women for women (mothers, other female relations and governesses) who were educating children at home. Some of the most popular were *A History of England* by Mrs Markham (1819), *Little Arthur's History of England* by Lady Callcott (1834), *A First History of England* by Mrs Ransome (1903) and *Our Island Story* by Henrietta Elizabeth Marshall (1905). These books had a strong narrative structure and were meant to be read out by the teaching mother or governess to her children. Some books used other teaching devices. At the end of each chapter in Mrs Markham's history textbook there is a 'Conversation' where the children (named in her book as Richard, George and Mary) ask their mother questions to allow other information or statements to be made. These books were usually updated to include later periods not included in earlier editions. Mrs Markham's history, for example, was written originally in 1819 but was still being published by the end of the century. The books are written in a chatty style but usually without recourse to supporting evidence. This was particularly evident in sections, or in books, about prehistoric periods. Prehistoric peoples, for whom the authors had no evidence because they did not follow archaeological investigations or arguments, were portrayed as savages. An example of a typical description in an illustrated booklet for children of 1809 is that the Ancient Britons 'led a wild and simple life; their clothes were made from skins of animals. In warm weather they went almost naked' (Mills, 1809, p.1). Charles Dickens, in his *A Child's History of England*, calls them 'poor savages…no roads, no bridges, no streets. A town was nothing but a collection of straw-covered huts' (Dickens, 1898, pp. 9-10).

Although textbook authors generally did not understand or research evidence of the past, the evidence was there to be seen, for example on display in the British Museum and in other collections. A few textbook writers did present teachers and their pupils with supporting evidence. Outstanding amongst these were the authors Marjorie and C H B Quennell first published after World War I. Their two main series of books, *Everyday life in…* (for example *…prehistoric times*) and *A History of Everyday Things in England*, brought the past to life with lively text and illustrations (including their own artistic impressions) which they produced themselves from research into both archaeological and historic sources.

TEACHING FROM OBJECTS

A standard part of Victorian and Edwardian teaching was the use of both natural and manufactured objects, in particular but not exclusively, for teaching science. Teachers' manuals were keen to point out that children should experience real things and not just be told about them 'Gaining knowledge by full and careful examination of things and events in immediate experience is, then, the essential foundation of every real system of learning', (Welton, 1909, p. 78). For Welton, Professor of Education at the University of Leeds, this type of learning should include 'object lessons, nature study, out of doors study of geography, the first study of number, study of historical remains and of works of art' (1909, p. 78). He goes on to enlarge on the use of visiting ancient monuments:

> If pupils, then, are to be taken to see the remains of a castle or a monastery, they should be prepared to examine them intelligently, by means of a lesson in school which brings out the purpose such buildings served, and the kind of structure adapted to secure it. (Welton, 1909, p. 270)

Inside the classroom whole lessons were based on a single object, for example an apple which might be displayed as an object to draw in art or as part of natural history. May (1994, p. 21) shows two illustrations, one of a wooden cabinet called 'The Victoria' Cabinet of Objects for Object Lessons, sold by Cox & Company of London in 1902 (costing 40 shillings in Pitch Pine or 50 shillings in Hard Wood with Metal Fittings); the other illustration was of an adjustable wooden stand to display the object in front of the class and sold by the Educational Supply Association. But Welton also wrote that object lessons 'are often tedious, formal, and dull; interest is rarely aroused; and there is little or no call on the pupils' powers of observation and construction' (1909, p. 359). In 1910 HG Wells' Mr Polly certainly agreed. He was 'given object lessons upon sealing-wax and silk-worms; and potato bugs and ginger and iron and such-like things; taught various other subjects his mind refused to entertain' (Wells, 1953, p. 23).

EVIDENCE-BASED TEACHING AND LEARNING

Up to the second half of the twentieth century, history teaching in schools was dominated by learning by rote, the dates of kings, queens and wars and textbooks not written by historians or archaeologists. Until the creation of the National Curriculum in England and Wales, the history curriculum was *de facto* what teachers read about in textbooks. Sylvester (1994, p. 11), quotes the Board of Education report of 1923:

> 'I thought dates were quite out of date' is not an uncommon remark from a teacher of the recent generation. It is a reaction from the dry and excessive drill in dates and names...which distinguished the history methods of our grandparents.

Although some evidence-based resources for teachers and schools were available through the twentieth century, it was not until the 1970s that material was produced for history teachers which recognised the importance of archaeological as well as historical sources. The Schools History Project [6]:

> challenged the view of history as a 'received subject' which had dominated since 1900. Pupils were 'to do' history, not merely to receive it. They were to learn about the human past by looking in a chronological context at the sources, both primary and secondary, which historians use when they tell the story – the history – of the past. (Sylvester, 1994, p. 16)

The SHP produced pamphlets and packs of source material as well as textbooks for use in the classroom. These included several titles on archaeological themes, such as *What is history? Detective work: the mystery of the empty grave*. At about the same time the Council for British Archaeology published a series of *Bulletins* and books for teachers on using archaeological sites and materials as part of teaching history. In the 1980s the Education Department of English Heritage published a series of books, *Education on Site*, to encourage teachers to use archaeological excavations, ancient monuments and objects in their curriculum work.

A major spur to the use of primary source material in schools in England and Wales was the introduction of a statutory National Curriculum with the passing of the Education Reform Act 1988. The deeply controversial recommendations for the contents of each subject, especially history, delayed publication of the final report until 1999. But in the history curriculum were the seeds of universal change in 'doing' history in school (Corbishley, 2011, pp.119–123). Pupils, in primary and secondary schools, were required to be taught, through specific periods over time, to understand that the past has been, and is, interpreted; that they should use a range of sources to enquire about the past. These sources included visits to ancient sites and museums and studying objects. Helping teachers to develop their own enquiry skills, as well as those of their pupils and students, was clearly important – enquiry skills which scientists see as a normal part of their work. One writer, an experienced teacher trainer, explains the process of enquiry in history teaching as 'question – hypothesis – using the evidence to test the hypothesis – reformulation of hypothesis' (Dawson, 2009, p. 2).[7]

The Historical Association, which was founded in 1906, has worked hard since then to develop teachers' understanding of the subject and provide a range of research material and classroom guides.[8] The Office for Standards in Education (Ofsted) reported that schools were becoming familiar with what to many schools was a new area of teaching and an inspector noted of one teacher's lesson that:

> Not only was she teaching them to handle evidence, but she was also teaching them new words ... All pupils, including those with learning difficulties, learnt a lot in this lesson – speaking, listening, handling and interpreting evidence, developing vocabulary, drawing, writing and working together. (Ofsted, 2007, p. 15)

LEARNING FROM OBJECTS

Objects, unlike historical documents, are wordless. Archaeologists have to work hard to make them give up the information about themselves and the particular period of the past they are from. Close questioning puts the object at the centre of the investigation and the observers (children, students or adults) should be encouraged to ask questions – questions which they can be asked to devise themselves or may be presented to them (for example, Table 1). The question to start with should never be 'what is it?' or 'what is this object called?' This is the equivalent of a closed question in educational terms.

A learning activity, which is commonly used today in many museums and in schools, uses the examination of objects to study a particular period. For example, a school might visit a nearby museum which has a Roman collection to study the Romans as part of National Curriculum history. They may also use museum collections when they are studying the World War 11 but teachers will often source objects from this period from parents and grandparents or friends. These objects may often form the basis for a temporary school museum display and be supplemented with documents (such as ration cards and diaries) and by visiting adults with personal memories of living through the war. Museums will almost invariably put on object lessons for visiting schools and advertise activities for children and families at weekends and in the holidays. These may well be combined with activity sessions which look more generally at how archaeologists study the past (see Figure 1).

Still in use today is one of the first teachers' guides published by the then (1984) newly-formed Education Department in English Heritage called *Learning from*

Figure 1. A master class linked to the Living Collections exhibition in the Institute of Archaeology, UCL, created by postgraduate students as part of their coursework. This class for 12-year-olds was held in their school and bones were used as the main theme because it fitted in well with the Science curriculum. (© Mike Corbishley)

objects, written by three experienced museum education officers (Durbin et al., 1990, revised 1996). This book had an important impact on the way in which objects are used in museums, and in schools, to help pupils learn about specific periods of the past *and* about the ways in which archaeologists study objects and draw interpretations from them. Durbin et al. (1996, pp. 5-6) demonstrated that using objects can develop skills (such as in observing and examining), extend knowledge (such as the use of different materials) and develop concepts (such as design as a function of use). Their methods would have been understood by Charles and Emma Darwin and they would have seen historical object analysis as an obvious part of the educational ideas of Pestalozzi. Using the well-known educational technique of moving from the known to the unknown is a basic component of many of the exercises with objects described below.

Many museums and schools now use variations of an activity sheet (Durbin et al., 1996, p. 12) for pupils and students to use to analyse an object carefully. Table 1 provides a variation I use regularly with school groups, members of the Young Archaeologists Club (YAC) and masters' students at University College London.

This activity of close observation usually begins with modern objects and moves on to old or ancient objects. I always use 'mystery objects' in object-based educational exercises. The first point I make when holding up and passing around an object is that if anyone knows what the object is, they must not reveal it to the others. The objects need careful choosing and should fit the age and culture of the group doing the exercise (Corbishley, 2011, pp. 245-247) – for example, few students can ever work out what a clay pigeon is.

Table 1. Looking at an object activity sheet. (after Corbishley 1999, p. 17 adapted from Durbin et al., 1996, p. 12).

Think about...	...and ask about	What you have found out by looking	and then by researching
What does it look and feel like?	Colour? Smell? Sound? Made of? Natural or manufactured? Complete? Changed or mended? New or worn?		
How was it made?	By hand? By machine? Fixed together by what?		
What was it made for?	Used for what? Has its use changed?		
Is it well designed?	Does it do its job? Made of the best materials? Decorated? How decorated? Do you like the look of it? Do you think others would like its looks?		
What is it worth?	To those who made it? To those who used it? To you? To a museum?		

Children and adults who adopt this detective approach to studying objects are working in the same way that archaeologists work (and the same way as historians do with documentary material). The 'mystery' has been a favourite device to use in introducing archaeology to young people, for example matching the way that police detectives and archaeologists work, comparing a crime scene and its clues with an archaeological excavation and its material evidence (Corbishley, 2011, p. 208). Object games are now often used by schools (Corbishley, 1990, 2001, 2011, pp. 244-245) and museum educators and have been inventive in creating detective games. For example, Marion Green, the education officer at the Canterbury Archaeological Trust (CAT), suggests to teachers that they use the game 'A bagful of clues' to investigate objects from a handbag, a shopping bag or a briefcase to ask questions about the owners.[9] Recording the object can be in the form of drawing, photographs or making a video or audio recording. An excellent example of the last, and one that can be used with educational groups, is the book and radio series by Neil MacGregor *A History of the World in 100 Objects* (MacGregor, 2010).

CLASSIFICATION

One of the successful learning exercises with objects is to think about putting a range of objects into categories. One interesting teaching resource has been used by schools in Ireland where one of the activities in 'Archaeology in the classroom – it's about time!' involves categorising modern everyday objects into a series of topics familiar to children (Limerick, 2009).[10] Examples are Eating (fork, plate, cup, bowl), Recreation (chess pieces, cards, dancing shoes, football) and Education (chalk, projector, books, locker, blackboard, desk chairs, pens).

QUESTIONING THE LEARNER'S ASSUMPTIONS

Challenging the accepted view is a central part of a scientist's work, and no less for archaeologists. Forty (1986) gave several apt examples in his book, *Objects of desire*. He illustrated this point with nineteenth-century manufacturers' catalogues, for example, giving illustrations of men's watches which had Roman numerals while the watches for ladies all had Arabic numerals 'whose form – curvilinear rather than angular – may be judged more delicate' (Forty, 1986, p. 65). So today we might ask a class whether finding a comb in, say, an excavated ancient grave invariably means that this showed that it was the burial of a woman. This questioning can also cover the 'value' of an object. While some archaeological objects are given a monetary value (whether by treasure hunters and unscrupulous collectors or by the State for items under the legal provisions of Treasure Trove) archaeologists take a completely different view. The value of an object, for archaeologists, is what can be deduced from it to help us understand peoples and events in the past.

CARING FOR OBJECTS

Another educational activity which is sometimes carried out, especially in museums, is concerned with conservation and display. Even young children can be shown ways in which objects they use today will wear and deteriorate over time. Some museum conservators show how conservation techniques work and even set up simple conservation activities on material which the children can handle themselves. Other activities may include examining the ways in which a museum displays and interprets its collections, an activity which we have carried out in the YAC sessions in University College London.

MUSEUMS AND LEARNING FROM OBJECTS

While museums are now putting many of their collections online to be studied (and enjoyed) it is not as useful educationally as actually being able to handle the objects themselves. Some museums still maintain handling collections which can be used in schools. Newly-created museum displays try to help their visitors access, intellectually and physically, some objects themselves. The label 'Do touch!' is now becoming as usual as 'Do not touch'. Looking at objects as part of archaeological work is now normally used by a whole range of museums. For example, Bromley Museum is a local authority museum with part of the archaeology and ethnographic collections given by John Lubbock (above). Its museum education service provides school visits to the museum, with the opportunity for guided tours, object handling sessions, talks, archaeological 'excavation' and sorting of objects and visits to schools with loan boxes. Its events for children includes (in 2013) 'Hands on History' – 'handling real archaeology and making your own reconstructions' (Bromley Museum, 2013) [11]. The Museum of London (classified as a national museum) has, since its creation, regularly used objects for teaching sessions. It has self-directed and facilitated schools visits and a range of free leaflets and downloadable resources for teachers, including some for Special Educational Needs children and it regularly works with Special Schools and has a programme for hospital schools, using objects from its collections (Corbishley, 2011, pp. 191-199; Museum of London[12]). University College London has a number of museums open to the public as well as teaching and research collections. Its teaching and learning department regularly uses objects in its sessions for schools and has loan boxes with background information and activities based on a range of National Curriculum subjects (Corbishley, 2011, pp. 333-340; University College London[13]). Canterbury Archaeological Trust was set up in 1976 to provide an archaeological service in Canterbury and beyond. It has had an education officer since 1990 and provides a service similar to some museums with work in and for schools, providing access to and information about excavations, downloadable resources and activities for children, families and adult groups. It too now provides handling collections of archaeological objects to schools (Corbishley, 2011, pp. 91-92; Canterbury Archaeological Trust[14]).

Figure 2. The Big Dig at Whitefriars, Canterbury with a display of animal bone and activity sheets for children. Archaeological work began here in 2000 ahead of a new city-centre development, and over 55,000 people had visited the visitor centre with its displays, talks and activities by 2003. (© Canterbury Archaeological Trust)

CONCLUSIONS

In his own period Darwin was a particularly brilliant exponent and interpreter of a rising interest in and study of evidence, rejecting the concept of education as simply opinion and learning by rote. Activities based on real evidence and real objects collected by scientists, whether archaeologists or not, are now commonly to be found in informal learning activities for children and families, formal lessons in schools and project work with older students and adults. In formal education studying objects can help with the development of important skills, for example, close observation, critical thinking and questioning assumptions; it may also help to provide links with other subjects, such as science (see above Figure 1), geography, mathematics and language. Working with objects has even been shown to have therapeutic benefits for elderly people affected by the onset of dementia (Jacques, 2007, p. 160). Using objects in the classroom is an example of the major changes in the education of children in Britain since the 1970s, where the emphasis in teaching has changed from instructing children to encouraging children to learn.

NOTES

[1] Darwin Correspondence Project, (2013a). Darwin's observations of his children. Darwin Correspondence Database, http://www.darwinproject.ac.uk/observations-on-children accessed on 18 July 2013.
[2] Johann Heinrich Pestalozzi (1746-1827) was a social and educational reformer who had a profound influence on modern pedagogy. His school and his teaching methods were based on the principles that children should learn through their senses, going from the known (what they knew) to the unknown and using things and actions rather than simply being the recipients of a teacher's words and instructions. His ideas were spread by teachers and educationalists who visited his school and also by his published works, for example, *How Gertrude Teaches Her Children* published in 1801. A direct result of his educational ideas was the introduction and the popularity of the object lesson in schools in England.
[3] Darwin Correspondence Project. (2013b). Earthworms activity. Darwin Correspondence Database, http://www.darwinproject.ac.uk/earthworms-activity accessed on 18 July 2013.
[4] Darwin Correspondence Project (2013c). Charles Darwin to W. D. Fox, 7 March, 1852. Darwin Correspondence Database, http://www.darwinproject.ac.uk/entry-1476 accessed on 18 July 2013.
[5] Darwin Correspondence Project (2013d). Charles Darwin to W. D. Fox, 29 January, 1853. Darwin Correspondence Database, http://www.darwinproject.ac.uk/entry-1499 accessed on 18 July 2013.
[6] Schools History Project, (2013). About the SHP. http://www.schoolshistoryproject.org.uk/AboutSHP/index.htm accessed on 18 July 2013.
[7] Dawson, I. (2009). Developing Enquiry Skills. http://www.thinkinghistory.co.uk/EnquirySkill/downloads/DevelopEnquirySkills.pdf accessed on July 18 2013.
[8] Historical Association. (2013). About us http://www.history.org.uk/resources/about.html accessed July 18 2013.
[9] Canterbury Archaeological Trust. (2013). Archaeology in Education Service. http://www.canterburytrust.co.uk/learning/ accessed on 18 July 2013.
[10] Limerick Education Centre. (2005 & 2009). Archaeology in the Classroom It's About Time! http://www.itsabouttime.ie/ accessed on 18 July 2013.
[11] Bromley Museum. (2013). Museum Education Service. http://www.bromley.gov.uk/info/200070/museums_and_galleries/365/museum_education_service accessed on 18 July 2013.
[12] Museum of London. (2013). Homepage. http://www.museumoflondon.org.uk/london-wall/ accessed on 18 July 2013.
[13] University College London, (2013). Learning. http://www.ucl.ac.uk/museums/learning accessed on 18 July 2013.
[14] Canterbury Archaeological Trust. (2013). Archaeology in Education Service. http://www.canterburytrust.co.uk/learning/ accessed on 18 July 2013.

REFERENCES

Corbishley, M. (1990). *Archaeological detectives poster games*. London: English Heritage.
Corbishley, M. (Ed.). (1999). *Primary history: Using the evidence of the historic environment*. London: English Heritage.
Corbishley, M. (2001). *Time detectives: Poster games and teacher's notes*. London: English Heritage.
Corbishley, M. (2011). *Pinning down the past: Archaeology, heritage and education today*. Woodbridge: Boydell Press.
Daniel, G. (1967). *The Origins and Growth of Archaeology*. Harmondsworth: Penguin Books.
Dickens, C. (1898). *A Child's History of England*. London: Hazel, Watson & Viney.
Durbin, G., Morris, S., & Wilkinson, S. (1996). *Learning from objects* (2nd ed.). London: English Heritage.
Forty, A. (1986). *Objects of desire: Design and technology since 1750*. London: Thames & Hudson.

Jacques, C. (2007). Easing the transition: Using museum objects with elderly people. In E. Pye (Ed.), *The power of touch: Handling objects in museum and heritage contexts* (pp. 153–161). Walnut Creek, CA: Left Coast Press.
Keynes, R. (2001). *Creation: Darwin, his daughter & human evolution.* New York, NY: Riverhead Books.
MacGregor, N. (2010). *A History of the World in 100 Objects.* London: Allen Lane. Radio programmes. Retrieved July 18, 2013 from http://www.bbc.co.uk/ahistoryoftheworld/
May, T. (1994). *The Victorian classroom.* Princes Risborough: Shire Publications.
Mills, A. (1809). *Pictures of English history, in miniature.* London: Darton & Harvey.
Office for Standards in Education. (2007). *History in the balance: History in English schools, 2003–2007.* London: Office for Standards in Education.
Owen, J. (2013). *Darwin's apprentice: An archaeological biography of John Lubbock.* Barnsley: Pen & Sword Books.
Raverat, G. (1960). *Period piece: A Cambridge childhood.* London: Faber & Faber.
Sylvester, D. (1994). Change and continuity in history teaching 1900–1993. In H. Bourdillon (Ed.), *Teaching history* (pp. 9–23). London: Routledge.
Wells, H. G. (1953). *The History of Mr Polly.* London & Glasgow: Collins.
Welton, J. (1909). *Principles and methods of teaching* (2nd ed.). London: University Tutorial Press.

Mike Corbishley,
Institute of Archaelogy,
University College London,
UK

JAMES T. COSTA

10. SAILING THE BACKYARD *BEAGLE*

Darwin-Inspired Voyages of Discovery in Backyard and Schoolyard

INTRODUCTION

Charles Darwin returned home from his five-year voyage around the world aboard HMS *Beagle* in October 1836. As transformative as the experience was for him, the voyage he embarked upon in the coming months and years was even more so: by turns Darwin became convinced of species change, or transmutation, discovered its mechanism in the form of natural selection, became a respected member of several London scientific societies (and elected Secretary of one), published his first accounts of the *Beagle* voyage and a plethora of scientific papers, and became a devoted husband and father of two — all in the space of the five years following his return home. By the time Charles and his wife Emma were expecting their third child they decided to exchange bustling and sooty London for the quiet and healthful countryside. The family moved to Down House, just south of London in the small Kentish village of Downe[1], in September of 1842. Darwin undertook some travelling within the British Isles over the years, mostly on family holidays, but never left the country again: Down House became his anchor and base for the remaining 40 years of his life. The word 'anchor' is appropriate in this context. Darwin scholar Janet Browne saw Down House as Darwin's 'ship on the Downs', playing on the phrase 'The Downs' off the east Kent coast, a shallows or 'roadstead' where ships can lie safely at anchor outside of a harbour. She evocatively described the household as Darwin's 'self-contained, self-regulating scientific ship methodically ploughing onwards through the waves outside' (Browne, 1995, 530), made possible by his wife, children, servants, and a multitude of friends and acquaintances willing to lend a hand with specimens, information, or assistance with experiments. Pushing the simile a bit farther, to me the verdant and undulating 'downland' or Downs of southern England where the Darwins took up residence echoes the undulating sea, and Down House, like the trusty *Beagle*, was both domicile and laboratory amid a landscape that beckoned the explorer in Darwin.

Darwin's exploring did not, then, end with the conclusion of the *Beagle* voyage; it was just beginning. His home, garden, and surrounding woodlands and meadows became his centre of study as he pursued ever more lines of investigation in support of his evolutionary ideas. The diversity of evidentiary lines that he explored are reflected in the very structure of *On the origin of species*, with whole chapters devoted to domestication, variability, behaviour, hybridisation, fossils, geographical distribution, morphology, and more. Darwin showed how empirical observations in each area are consistent with his hypothesis of descent with modification by natural selection — the thread running through the book, collectively weaving 'one long argument' (1859, p. 459). In this respect Darwin's approach was inductive: he was being 'consilient' to use the term coined by the polymath Welshman William Whewell, the much admired philosopher and mathematician of Trinity College, Cambridge (see discussions of Darwin's method in Ruse, 1975; Hodge, 1991; Costa, 2009a,b). In the influential works *History of the inductive sciences* (1837) and *The philosophy of the inductive sciences, founded upon their history* (1840), Whewell treated the nature of scientific knowledge, and scientific method. In the latter he introduced his concept of the 'consilience of inductions' — the merging of independent inductive strands of evidence to form a stronger argument in favour of a hypothesis. In Whewell's words:

> the Consilience of Inductions takes place when an Induction, obtained from one class of facts, coincides with an Induction, obtained from another different class. This Consilience is a test of the truth of the Theory in which it occurs. (1840, 1, p. xxxix)

The greater the number of such inductive strands pointing to a common explanation, the greater the confidence that the explanation is correct. Whewell argued that this is a powerful means of gaining scientific insight:

> ... the cases in which inductions from classes of facts altogether different have thus jumped together, belong only to the best established theories which the history of science contains... I will take the liberty of describing it by a particular phrase; and will term it the Consilience of Inductions.... (1840, 2, p. 230)

Yet Darwin's approach was not purely inductive (Szathmáry, 2006; Costa, 2009a). He had a framework of evolutionary ideas, from the concept of species change giving rise to a branching genealogical pattern over time to a specific mechanism for this process (natural selection), and these guided the sorts of questions he asked and the various lines and leads that he pursued. In this respect Darwin's method was thus also deductive, looking for evidence in the places that his theory predicted he ought to find some. Depending on the subject and question his approach was sometimes observational, sometimes experimental. Often, in private letters and open ones published in such venues as the *Gardeners' Chronicle*, he asked others to duplicate his studies and share the results.

Darwin's new understanding of species naturally led to a new way to look at the natural world. In the 1923 work *La prisonnière* [The Captive], volume 5 of the series *In search of lost time*, French novelist and philosopher Marcel Proust commented that real voyages of discovery consist 'not in seeking new landscapes but in having new eyes.' Darwin's actual voyage of discovery ultimately gave him 'new eyes', and through them even the long-familiar pastoral landscape of England was transformed. The most mundane or seemingly trivial details of the structure, behaviour, distribution, or relationship of species were now seen in a new, evolutionary light, pregnant with meaning. Often the most basic questions about these things had not only been unanswered, but the right questions had not even been asked. With his new eyes, Darwin embarked upon what was to become a life-long passion: 'experimentising', dreaming up 'fool's experiments' to test his ideas. But his new and unconventional way of looking at the natural world required unconventional approaches to understand it.

'EXPERIMENTISER'

The mid- to late nineteenth century was a period of transition in the practice of western science, with the rise of norms for experimental approaches and data analysis, and, just as importantly, the rise of the institutional laboratory as the proper site for the conduct of scientific research. This shift reflected the tension between what historians have termed country-house versus laboratory science, the former associated with the pursuit of science by the privileged wealthy or aristocratic, a tradition that was steadily giving way to a scientific enterprise based on meritocracy and government sponsorship in this period (Schaffer, 1998; Opitz, 2006; Livingstone, 2003; Lightman, 2011). The very term 'scientist' had only arisen in the 1830s, one of many terms coined by Whewell:

> As we cannot use physician for a cultivator of physics, I have called him a physicist. We need very much a name to describe a cultivator of science in general. I should incline to call him a Scientist. Thus we might say, that as an Artist is a Musician, Painter, or Poet, a Scientist is a Mathematician, Physicist, or Naturalist. (Whewell, 1840, 1, p. cxiii)

Darwin might be considered the last of the great Victorian 'country house' scientists, but far from representing an old and outdated mode of scientific enquiry, Darwin's research program in many respects blazed new paths in anticipating the rise of experimental approaches in organismic and field biology. As 'the field was colonized by the laboratory approach', as Secord (1996, p. 449) put it, Down House, with its experimental garden plots, adjacent greenhouse and workroom, and study which functioned as a laboratory offering more controlled conditions for closer observation, can be seen as a forerunner of the kind of early twentieth century research station described by Opitz (2011, p. 73) as a 'marriage of field and laboratory'.

The range of Darwin's 'experimentising', including his observational studies, is remarkable. Over nearly five decades they broadly encompassed myriad enquiries into plant and animal structure, physiology, and inter-specific interactions, as exemplified by this list of selected topics he pursued:

- seed transport and longevity, from flotation and viability in salt water to animal carriage;
- insect behaviour: ants and aphids, pollination, slave-making ants, and the construction of bees' cells;
- competition and diversity: seedling plots, meadow plant censuses;
- pollination mechanisms and the effects of cross-fertilisation;
- carnivorous plants: modes of insect capture and digestive physiology;
- earthworms, from action in altering the landscape to sense perception;
- movement in plants: tendril circumnutation, circadian movement of leaves, and phototropism in shoots, tendrils, and root radicles;
- flower structure in relation to pollination, including trigger-action stamens, different forms of flowers on the same individual plants, and the phenomenon of di- and tristyly.

Some were short-lived, one-off experiments (including the occasional dead end), while others were ongoing investigations that he kept up for years. Many, especially the later botanical experiments, were reported in detail in his six botanical books published between 1862 and 1880. Darwin's 'fool's experiments', as he self-deprecatingly called them, were not quaint diversions: the data and other information they yielded were often communicated as scientific papers (see collections in Barrett et al., 1977; van Wyhe, 2009), and made their way into his many books as empirical evidence backing up arguments. Therein lie lessons for us today. Darwin's approach is scientific enquiry at its most elemental: real insight into the natural world can be gained through a straightforward process of questioning and creative approaches to trying to answer those questions. His approach epitomised the experimental philosophy, in which reason, observation, and experiment represent the 'holy trinity' of scientific investigation.

Philosopher John Dewey (1925, 2), in his essay 'Experience and Nature', pointed out that in the natural sciences there is a 'union of experience and nature', whereby 'the investigator assumes as a matter of course that experience, controlled in specifiable ways, is the avenue that leads directly to the facts and laws of nature.' This is the empirical tradition that began to take its modern form through the experimentalism of the seventeenth and eighteenth centuries. More importantly in Dewey's essay, however, is his point that experience of the natural world — including, I suggest, the kind of basic hands-on experimentation Darwin did so well — is not restricted to scientists: the experiences of nature '...is the same for the scientific man and the man in the street. The latter cannot follow the intervening reasoning without special preparation. But stars, rocks, trees, and creeping things are the same material of experience for both' — as are, say, floating seeds. Dewey emphasized that 'these commonplaces take on significance when the relation of experience to the formation of a philosophic theory of nature is in question'. In other words, the experiences or observations of mundane phenomena — Dewey's 'commonplaces' — take on greater significance when we realize that in them we gain insight into the very workings of nature. Darwin's experiments focused precisely on such mundane phenomena: he experimented on the local and extrapolated to the global, even universal. Some areas of enquiry are, of course, only probed with sophisticated technology and analytical approaches, but Darwin's example reveals others accessible with nothing more than everyday items (flowerpots and string, rulers and glue, hand lenses and a timer...) creatively put to good use. Those many areas of enquiry accessible to probing at an elemental level have great instructive potential for students today. Darwin's 'ship on the Downs' is also ours for the sailing: many of the experiments and observational investigations that Darwin undertook at his home can just as easily be undertaken elsewhere — any home or garden, classroom or schoolyard.

GERMINATING IDEAS

Consider Darwin's investigations into seed transport and longevity pursued in the 1850s: these not only provide an outstanding example of Darwin's working method, but also exemplify the kinds of experiments readily accessible today. His transport studies began with the flotation of seeds in salt-water, and the related questions of viability and germination success following salt water exposure. He eventually undertook related side projects along these lines, for example the germination success of seeds eaten by fish in turn eaten by predacious birds — imagining that this mimicked a natural process of dispersal if the bird disgorged or defaecated the seeds with the remains of its meal after flying to distant shores (the seeds would be naturally fertilised too). The related seed longevity studies stemmed from his curiosity over long-buried seeds: just how extensive is the seed bank, and how long can seeds lie dormant in soil or pond mud? A well-stocked seed bank meant that seeds must occasionally get transported when bits of soil or mud they are embedded in adhere to the feet of, for example, water birds. To put these investigations into perspective, they relate to Darwin's overarching interests in geographical distribution of species.

Understanding the determinants of geographical distribution was of the highest importance for Darwin's theory: why are species distributed as we see them? Given that distribution is not random, what principles govern the differences, from a global scale (between and within continents, and between continents and islands) to the local (valleys separated by lofty mountain ranges, for example, or vegetation zonation from low to high elevation along a single mountain)? Two phenomena were especially puzzling. One was species disjunctions, where the same species exists as two or more widely separated populations. Another was endemic species of isolated islands, species that are unique, yet tend to show the closest taxonomic affinity to species of the nearest mainland. Explaining disjunctions in particular was at the heart of the debate over single- vs. multiple centres of creation: was each species created at one point on the globe and subsequently spread according to the vagaries of geological and climatic changes, or could a given species have been created simultaneously at two or more different points? Most naturalists preferred the single-origin view, perhaps not least because it was closer to theological orthodoxy (multiple centres of creation meant that species could not have been created in the biblically proscribed pairs, since each disjunct population required its own pair of progenitors). Accordingly, they considered physical mechanisms to explain disjunctions. Some cases could be explained by species' powers of migration, but believing this to be limited, land bridges, continental extensions of past geological ages, were advanced as the preferred explanation (see Browne, 1983, pp. 111–114). These vast continental bridges are not to be confused with the land bridges of continental shelves, which are exposed when sea level drops low enough, linking any islands on the shelf with the continental mainland (e.g. Tasmania, Sri Lanka, Long Island). Rather, this school of thought posited bridges that extended out into or completely across oceanic basins, physically linking the remotest islands to continents, and in some cases continent to continent. A century before continental drift and plate tectonics was confirmed, at a time when it was believed that continents may experience uplift and subsidence but never lateral movement, and wed to the idea of single centres of origin for species, continental extensions were considered the most plausible explanation for odd species disjunctions: the species of Atlantic islands like the Azores that were identical with those of Europe, or the commonalities of species found on the scattered sub-Antarctic islands.

Darwin puzzled over every aspect of species distribution, remarking in a letter to his botanical correspondent Sir Charles Bunbury that it was a 'grand game of chess, with the world for a board'[2]. He also believed that species originated at single centres, but through descent with modification rather than special creation, but he was highly critical of the continental extension idea, maintaining that there was no geological evidence for bridge-like land extensions in the abyssal sea. To explain disjunctions and island endemism he felt that the capacity of species to disperse great distances, and even survive chance transoceanic journeys to land at the remotest oceanic islands, was severely underestimated. He believed that island endemics are the descendants of ancestral colonists, and disjunctions are essentially historical artifacts: indicators of past changes in the landscape and climate that opened and closed migration corridors over time. In his view dispersal over land and sea is facilitated by shifting landscape and climate over geological time. He subscribed to Lyell's vision of earth history where corridors of movement open and close repeatedly: volcanic islands create stepping-stones in the seas and eventually erode away, slowly uplifted mountain chains bar the movement of some species while creating routes of migration for others, other land areas subside and are flooded by the sea, climate alternates between glacial and warm periods, and so on (Rudwick, 1998; Wilkinson, 2002). He even explored the possible role of icebergs in transporting organisms, as they were known to transport boulders great distances (e.g. Darwin, 1839).

In Darwin's day pure dispersal was understandably difficult to accept as a general explanation for patterns of disjunction and island-continent relationships, but he steadfastly maintained that dispersal was key. However, in the ensuring discussions and arguments with fellow naturalists, it soon became evident that data were lacking on the most basic relevant questions. In regard to his belief that plant species have naturally colonised even the remotest islands, this begs the practical question: can seeds survive exposure to sea water? Vegetation bearing seeds or fruits may get swept out to sea regularly, but if they soon sink or the seeds perish in salt water the question of chance colonisation of islands is moot. The need for such basic information set the stage for Darwin's experiments with seed flotation and viability, and related studies of seed longevity, bird transport, and more.

He first undertook seed-soaking experiments in his cellar, setting up many different kinds of seeds in jars, floating them in artificial sea water made with a recipe developed for salt-water aquariums. In April 1855 he published a short query in the *Gardeners' Chronicle and Agricultural Gazette*, which opened:

> I have begun making some few experiments on the effects of immersion in sea-water on the germinating powers of seeds, in the hope of being able to throw a very little light on the distribution of plants, more especially in regard to the same species being found in many cases in far outlying islands and on the mainland. (Figure 1; see also van Wyhe, 2009, p. 246)

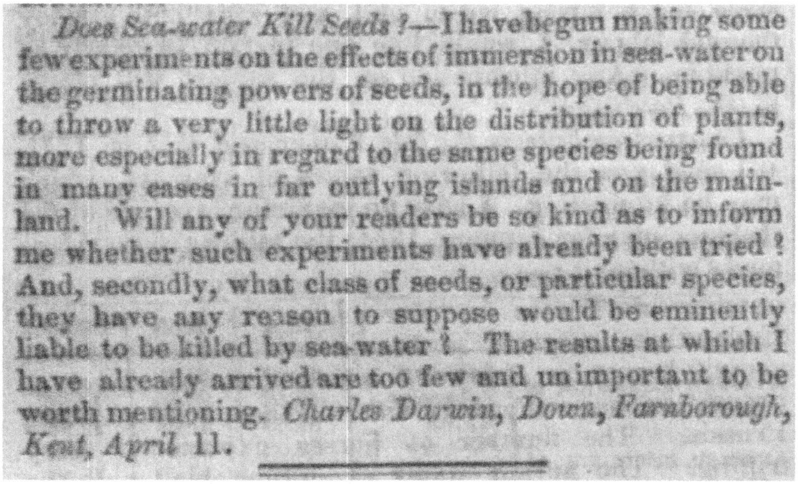

Does Sea-water Kill Seeds ?—I have begun making some few experiments on the effects of immersion in sea-water on the germinating powers of seeds, in the hope of being able to throw a very little light on the distribution of plants, more especially in regard to the same species being found in many cases in far outlying islands and on the mainland. Will any of your readers be so kind as to inform me whether such experiments have already been tried ? And, secondly, what class of seeds, or particular species, they have any reason to suppose would be eminently liable to be killed by sea-water ? The results at which I have already arrived are too few and unimportant to be worth mentioning. *Charles Darwin, Down, Farnborough, Kent, April* 11.

Figure 1. Darwin's query to readers of the Gardeners' Chronicle and Agricultural Gazette (no. 15, 14 April 1855, p. 242) concerning the vitality of seeds exposed to salt water. (courtesy of the Biodiversity Heritage Library [www.biodiversitylibrary.org] and the Missouri Botanical Garden).

The next month he followed up with a longer paper reporting on his own efforts:

> As you have done me the honour to notice favourably my wish to ascertain experimentally the power of resistance in seeds to the injurious action of seawater, you may perhaps like to have a report....

But more than this, Darwin first set out the reasons to conduct such experiments:

> As such experiments might naturally appear childish to many, I may be permitted to premise that they have a direct bearing on a very interesting problem...namely, whether the same organic being has been created at one point or on several on the face of our globe.

Darwin then described then-current proposals for continental extensions, citing the claim of geologist Edward Forbes that a once-vast extension of the European continent into the Atlantic explained the distribution of species found in Ireland, northern Spain, and the Azores (Forbes, 1846) critically maintaining that:

> To imagine such enormous geological changes within the period of the existence of now living beings, on no other ground but to account for their distribution, seems to me, in our present state of ignorance on the means of transportal, an almost retrograde step in science..... (van Wyhe, 2009, pp. 247–249)

The alternative hypothesis, in other words, had not been tested: perhaps odd distributions can be explained simply by powers of dispersal. In the paragraph that follows Darwin gave his methods:

– Artificial salt-water was made using the recipe of 'Mr Bolton, 146, Holborn Bars', noting that it had been tested 'by better chemists than men, namely by numerous sea animals and algae having lived in it for more than a year.'
– Experimental design: two approaches were taken, one in which 'the seeds were placed in separate bottles, holding from 2 to 4 oz. each, out of doors in the shade' (reporting the average temperature to be 44° F), and the other in which he placed the seeds 'in a quart bottle in a tank filled with snow and water.' Samples of the seeds were planted daily under controlled conditions ('in glasses on my chimneypiece'), along with seeds that were not exposed to salt water, and the germination success or failure recorded.
– Seeds of 23 species were used, including a host of garden vegetables (onion, carrot, beet, celery, lettuce, beans, peas, cabbage, cress, radishes, and others), in addition to other agricultural plants such as flax, oats, and barley. Darwin does not say how many seeds of each were placed in salt water initially.

Darwin next reported his results: 18 of the 23 species germinated after exposure to salt water, some surviving only a few days but others germinating well even after 42 days' exposure. Much detail was given here, including the comparative germination success in the ice-cold water treatment vs. ambient treatment. Darwin concluded by noting, first, that based on an average ocean current speed of 33 nautical miles per day, which he gleaned from a popular physical atlas, his seeds surviving 42 days' exposure could theoretically be carried as far as 1400 miles. Next, however, he noted that most of his seeds sank in the salt water. That would seem to render meaningless all the previous results, but, undaunted, Darwin pointed out that naked seeds are less likely to find their way to sea than seeds in fruits or on whole plants or parts of plants, and that these would float more readily. This proved not to be the case: the following November Darwin published a progress report in the *Gardeners' Chronicle,* reporting a great many instances of seed germination after as much as 137 days of salt-water immersion, but also acknowledging that sinkage was a problem:

> I always meant to try [floating vegetation bearing seeds], and I have now done so with sorrowful result; for having put in salt-water between 30 and 40 herbaceous plants and branches with ripe seed of various orders, I have found that all (with the exception of the fruit of evergreens) sink within a month, and most of them within 14 days. (van Wyhe, 2009, p. 253)

He dejectedly concluded that 'as far as I can see, my experiments are of little or no use...in regard to the distribution of plants by the drifting of their seeds across the sea', except as negative evidence.

A year later Darwin read a final, longer, paper on the subject at the Linnean Society, reporting his results together with those of the Rev. M. J. Berkeley, who was inspired by Darwin's query to try the experiment. Berkeley tested the seeds of 53 species, and separately had published his results in the *Gardeners' Chronicle* in 1855. Darwin had meantime tested a host of other species, in particular several that were reported to have been deposited on the coast of Norway by the Gulf Stream. The total number of species tested between the two of them totaled 87, and the paper included a lengthy tabulation of the germination success rates by plant family. Darwin again acknowledged the problem of sinkage, but here he chose to view the glass as half-full: a great many seeds tested floated for 10 days or so before sinking, and very few were killed by 10 days' exposure. Thus, given an average ocean current speed of 33 miles per day, he concluded that 'some plants might under favourable conditions be transported over arms of the sea 300 or even more miles in breadth, and if cast on the shore of an island not well stocked with species, might become naturalised' (van Wyhe, 2009, p. 261).

Darwin's results may have been 'sorrowful', but did not take the wind out of his sails altogether. Even while conducting these immersion experiments he attempted a number of spin-off versions: if seeds have a hard time dispersing simply by floating, maybe they get farther with a little help from animals — specifically, fish and birds, in some cases the two together. He tried feeding seeds to fish at the Zoological Gardens with the idea that birds like herons might eat fish stuffed with seeds, and then transport them great distances. In another variant his 8-year-old son Francis suggested that seed-eating birds with full crops might somehow end up dead in the water and float the seeds to distant shores. In a letter to Hooker sent in December 1856, Darwin wrote:

> I must tell you another of my *profound* experiments! Franky [Francis] said to me, 'why sh[d] not a bird be killed (by hawk, lightning, apoplexy, hail &c) with seeds in crop, & it would swim.' No sooner said, than done: a pigeon has floated for 30 days in salt water with seeds in crop & they have grown splendidly & to my great surprise even tares (Leguminosae, so generally killed by sea-water) which the Bird had naturally eaten have grown *well.*[3]

These experiments did not always go well; the fish at the Zoological Garden more often than not spit his seeds out, dimming the prospects that herons carrying seed-stuffed fish serve as good dispersal agents. He wrote a dejected letter about it to his cousin William Darwin Fox:

> I am rather low today about all my experiments ... the fish at the Zoological Gardens after eating seeds would spit them all out again ... all nature is perverse & will not do as I wish it...[4]

However, other studies showed that birds were good dispersal agents: he collected and germinated seeds from bird droppings, as well as from clumps of earth adhering to their feet. Turning his attention to the related problem of how aquatic organisms colonize lakes and ponds, which can be thought of as 'islands' on the land, he successfully experimented with duck's feet suspended in aquaria full of snails, positing that snails can be carried by migrating waterfowl once unsuspectingly climbing 'aboard' their feet when the birds sleep.

In the ups and downs of these various experiments, perhaps the first important lesson they offer for any student, or budding scientist, is perseverance.

SINK OR SWIM: A DARWIN-INSPIRED EXPERIMENT IN DISPERSAL

Darwin's experiments ultimately bolstered his arguments for the possibility of natural colonisation of even the most remote of oceanic islands. The results, along with those of other experiments (including the floating bird experiment suggested by young Francis) were duly reported in *On the origin of species* under 'means of dispersal' (Darwin, 1859, pp. 358–362). What lessons do Darwin's dispersal experiments hold for students today? I suggest that, like many of his experiments, they epitomise the process of scientific enquiry insofar as they entail (1) posing a testable question, or hypothesis; (2) devising a means of answering that question though experimental design (thinking through materials needed, set-up, execution, standardisation or control of variables, replication); and (3) making sense of the results, whether or not they support the initial hypothesis (and why). The scientific pursuit is often an iterative process, and the results of experiments like these may in turn inspire a next round of questions, spin-offs like Darwin's myriad parallel experiments on dispersal. Let's next consider how Darwin's seeds in salt-water experiment can be replicated today in the classroom as a case study in Darwin-inspired learning.

Darwin's 'seeds in salt-water' experiments were aimed at determining, first, how long seeds might retain their vitality after exposure to salt water, and second, how long they float vs. sink in salt water. He performed several versions of this experiment using many species, from garden vegetables to common weeds to seeds of various tropical plants procured from his friend Joseph Hooker at Kew Gardens. We can follow Darwin's lead and use readily-available vegetable or garden flower seeds.

A. Salt-water

Begin with artificial salt-water, as Darwin did using a commercially available salt and mineral preparation. This can be purchased from online aquarium supply retailers (Instant Ocean® and Natural Sea Aquarium Salt Mix from Oceanic Systems, Inc. are inexpensive brands), or from a local pet shop or aquarium supply store. (Real sea water is teeming with microorganisms, which will die and foul the water in short order, so artificial salt-water is preferable.) Home-made 'sea water' is an alternative; there are many recipes, but for the purposes of this experiment the following one is simple. For each litre of water dissolve:

– 27 g pure (not iodized) table salt
– 4 g magnesium chloride
– 2.6 g magnesium sulphate (Epsom salts)
– 1.3 g plaster of Paris

B. Materials

The following materials are needed:

– seeds of at least six species (e.g., assorted vegetable and wildflower seed packets are readily available from garden centres),
– 100-500 ml beakers or flasks (or even plain jam jars), one for each plant species; The bottom of a 2-litre plastic beverage bottle will work too.
– pipette or turkey baster,
– forceps,
– plastic wrap (cling film),
– labeling tape and marker,
– for seed planting: petri dishes or similar transparent chambers *or* one or more germination flat (ideally, partitioned into individual planting units) or paper cups, with potting soil.

C. Procedure

1. Prepare the salt-water in an aquarium tank, carboy, or large flask, depending on volume, and keep at room temperature. Measure 300 ml salt water for each

beaker or flask. (If the vessel does not have a 300 ml measurement mark, make one with a marker or tape as a reference for maintaining the water level.) Place the beakers or flasks in a location, out of direct sunlight, where the experiment will be run, to avoid agitating the water surface and disturbing the seeds after they are placed in the water. Once positioned, using fingers or forceps carefully place (not drop)10 seeds of a single species onto the water surface in each vessel, labeling the vessel with the date, time, and plant species. Repeat for each of the remaining seed species, one species per beaker or flask. Loosely cover the mouth of each vessel with plastic wrap; some water will evaporate, and a pipette or baster can be used to replenish evaporated water. To do this, carefully dispense water along the inner wall of the vessel so as to minimise agitating the water surface. (An optional variant for larger classes is to set up replicates. For example, a class of 24 students could set up four replicates of each of six plant species.)
2. Record the status of the seeds daily, recording for each vessel/species the number still floating and the number that may have sunk. This can be continued indefinitely, as Darwin did by removing seeds at intervals to see how long they would remain viable after prolonged exposure to salt-water, but it will be more practical for most people to run the experiment for a set period of time — one, two, three weeks, or whatever pre-determined length. Larger groups with replicates of each seed species might harvest one replicate per species after, say, one week of exposure, a second replicate after two weeks, etc. Alternatively, all replicates can be floated for the same period of time in order to obtain descriptive statistics on seed performance among replicates.
3. At the conclusion of the time-span determined for the experiment, record the number of floating vs. sunken seeds for each species. First retrieve the floating seeds from each vessel using the slotted spoon, taking care not to sink any seeds. Then retrieve the sunken seeds. Keep each species and/or replicate separate. It is also desirable to keep still-floating vs. sunken seeds of each species separate. Rinse seeds in fresh water and plant the seeds using one of the two following methods:
   – *Paper toweling method.* Use separate dishes for floaters and sinkers of each species and replicate. Place one piece of saturated paper toweling on the bottom of the dish, saturate with water, and place seeds. Saturate the second piece of paper toweling and place over the bottom piece, covering the seeds. Place the lid on the dish to seal moisture. Ensure that all dishes are labeled (species, floater vs. sinker, date).
   – *Soil method.* Carefully plant each set in adjacent units of the germination flat. (If the flat does not have individual planting units, use string to grid off the flat.) If paper cups are used, plant floating and sunken seeds in separate cups. Repeat for each replicate as necessary, water, and cover the flats or cups with plastic wrap.

When all seeds are planted, expose dishes, germination flats, or cups to indirect sunlight (not direct sunlight) or a growth lamp. Monitor daily and record numbers of seeds of each category (species, floating vs. sunken, etc.) observed to germinate.

At the conclusion of the experiment the data can be tabulated noting number and percentage of seeds sinking and remaining afloat for the experimental period, and the number and percent germinating for each category. The results can then be related back to Darwin's original puzzle: is it possible that some species can colonise remote islands simply by floating there as seeds? I tried a version of this experiment with an intrepid group of educators in a field course taught at Highlands Biological Station (Highlands, North Carolina, USA) in the summer of 2011. Garden vegetable seeds were used: lettuce, onion, radish, carrot, and squash. The results, presented in Table 1, were informative albeit expected in some respects and unexpected in others. Flotation vs. sinkage varied considerably, and while overall germination was higher with floating seeds, in some cases sinking seeds had a higher germination rate. While this experiment was run for a small fraction of the length of Darwin's version, it is instructive to consider that even a version of this brief duration can yield results worth discussing.

The conditions under which the experiment was run hardly mimicked the conditions of the open sea, but nonetheless the results serve to underscore Darwin's findings: the seeds of some species do remain afloat, at least for the duration of the experiment. This in turn raises the question of how far they might be carried in that time. Darwin pointed out in a letter to Hooker that 'many sea-current go a mile an

Table 1. Results of a short trial of Darwin's salt-water seeds experiment, conducted by educators in the Evolution in the Blue Ridge field course held at Highlands Biological Station, Highlands, North Carolina, summer 2011. The experiment was run from 20 – 27 June 2011, and germination rates recorded after two weeks (11 July 2011).

Experimentiser	Species	Seeds (N)	Floaters Total No.	No. Germ.	%	Sinkers Total No.	No. Germ.	%
Alyssa	Lettuce	40	7	5	71.4	33	28	84.8
Susan	Onion	10	4	4	100	6	5	83.3
Gloria	Radish	9	8	7	87.5	1	1	100
Paula	Carrot	50	50	14	28	0	n/a	n/a
Hannah	Carrot	50	50	24	48	0	n/a	n/a
Tom	Radish	10	8	0	0	2	1	50
Megan	Onion	10	10	3	30	0	n/a	n/a
Leslie	Onion	10	10	4	40	0	n/a	n/a
Mark/Jena	Squash	20	2	2	100	18	18	100
Randi	Lettuce	60	45	27	60	15	0	0

hour: even in a week they might be transported 168 miles: the Gulf-stream is said to go 50 & 60 miles a day', based on data from a contemporary physical atlas.[5] Indeed, this is likely to be an underestimate for some currents: with a maximum estimated surface velocity of 5.6 mph, the Gulf Stream could carry floating seeds over 130 miles per day. This is a simple analysis that students can perform based on their own results. The sunken seeds, too, are informative — Darwin's spirits may have initially sunk when he saw how many of his seeds did, but he realised that among other insights sinkers still shed light on the extent to which seeds might remain viable after salt-water exposure. In my students' experiment, most sinkers germinated despite their week-long immersion, just as Darwin found.

CONCLUSION

Darwin's seed dispersal experiments in all of their at-times-quirky permutations are emblematic of a fundamental and effective mode of scientific enquiry, one that, owing to the absence of specialised or sophisticated scientific equipment, is also fundamentally *accessible* to modern audiences. I have long argued that we can profitably draw on Darwin's own writings in teaching today's generation about Darwinian ideas, arguments, and modes of enquiry (e.g. Costa, 2003), but I believe that drawing on Darwin's deeds as well as his words has even greater potential to instruct. Darwin's experiments and related observational investigations are so varied that they can be replicated, or adapted, for just about any age group and interest: behaviour, morphology, biogeography, plant growth and physiology, and more. This is 'MacGyver science,' to invoke the 1980s American adventure television series starring Richard Dean Anderson, in which random odds and ends (rubber bands, paper clips, pencils, string, ruler, etc.) were creatively assembled into problem-solving tools. It's all in seeing the creative potential of objects at hand, and in learning how to think in terms of asking basic questions that can be tested.

Darwin's voyage on his 'ship on the Downs' provides us with exciting navigational tools, charting our own course of experiments, demonstrations, and observations of natural phenomena all to a purpose — with the potential to steer today's students toward a deeper understanding of the natural world and the essence of scientific inquiry, as well as of Darwin as a scientist and a person. The eminent naturalist E. O. Wilson had microbial diversity in mind when he commented that 'a lifetime can be spent in a Magellanic voyage around the trunk of a single tree' (Wilson, 1994, p. 364). For me this evokes the diversity of Darwin's experiments in home, garden, and meadow: questions remain to be asked about the natural world even close at hand, under our noses. What's more profound may be the light bulb that lights up, the sudden realisation that through such mundane experiments on humble earthworms, flowers, or seeds, insight might be gained into the most profound ecological and evolutionary phenomena shaping life on earth. In other words, local backyards and school yards, bedroom labs and classrooms everywhere have the potential to be a Down House; we can all sail a backyard *Beagle* there in the pursuit of Darwin-inspired projects, and insights.

ACKNOWLEDGEMENTS

I thank editors Carolyn Boulter, Michael Reiss, and Dawn Sanders for the invitation to contribute to this volume, and for their helpful comments and criticisms on an earlier draft of the chapter. I am grateful to Randal Keynes for many stimulating discussions of Darwin's experimental work, and to the participants in the 2011 *Evolution in the Blue Ridge* field course at Highlands Biological Station for their enthusiasm for 'teaching Darwin with Darwin' and replicating Darwin's experiments.

NOTES

[1] When Charles Darwin and his family moved to Down House, the spelling of the village was also Down, with no 'e'. When the spelling of the village's name was changed to Downe some years later, Darwin decided not to change the spelling of his house, so it remained Down House.
[2] Charles Darwin to Sir Charles Bunbury, 21 April, 1856. Darwin Correspondence Database, http://www.darwinproject.ac.uk/entry-1856 accessed on 15 December 2013.
[3] Charles Darwin to J. D. Hooker, 10 December, 1856. Darwin Correspondence Database, http://www.darwinproject.ac.uk/entry-2018 accessed on 18 December 2013.
[4] Charles Darwin to William Darwin Fox, 7 May 1855, Darwin Correspondence Database, http://www.darwinproject.ac.uk/entry-1678 accessed on 18 December 2013.
[5] Charles Darwin to J. D. Hooker, 13 April 1855. Darwin Correspondence Database, http://www.darwinproject.ac.uk/entry-1667 accessed on 18 December 2013.

REFERENCES

Barrett, P. H. (Ed.). (1977). *The collected papers of Charles Darwin* (vol. 1). Chicago, IL: University of Chicago Press.
Browne, J. (1983). *The secular ark: Studies in the history of biogeography*. New Haven, CT: Yale University Press.
Browne, E. J. (1995). *Charles Darwin: Voyaging*. New York: Alfred Knopf.
Costa, J. T. (2003). Teaching Darwin with Darwin. *BioScience, 53*, 1030–1031.
Costa, J. T. (2009a). Darwinian revelation: Tracing the origin and evolution of an idea. *BioScience, 59*, 886–894.
Costa, J. T. (2009b). *The annotated origin: A facsimile of the first edition of On the origin of species*. Cambridge, MA: Harvard University Press.
Darwin, C. R. (1839). Note on a rock seen on an iceberg in 61° south latitude. *Journal of the Royal Geographical Society of London, 9*, 528–529.
Darwin, C. R. (1859). *On the origin of species by means of natural selection, or the preservation of races in the struggle for life*. London: John Murray.
Darwin Correspondence Project Database. Retrieved from www.darwinproject.ac.uk/
Dewey, J. (1925). *Experience and nature*. Chicago and La Salle, IL: Open Court.
Forbes, E. (1846). On the connexion between the distribution of the existing fauna and flora of the British Isles, and the geological changes which have affected their area, especially during the epoch of the Northern Drift. *Memoirs of the Geological Survey of Great Britain, and of the Museum of Economic Geology in London, 1*, 336–432.

Hodge, M. J. S. (1991). Discussion note: Darwin, Whewell, and natural selection. *Biology and Philosophy, 6*, 457–460.

Lightman, B. (Ed.). (1997). *Victorian science in context*. Chicago, IL: University of Chicago Press.

Livingstone, D. (2003). *Putting science in its place: Geographies of scientific knowledge*. Chicago and London: University of Chicago Press.

Opitz, D. L. (2006). 'This house is a temple of research': Country-House centres for late Victorian science. In D. Clifford, E. Wadge, A. Warwick, & M. Willis (Eds.), *Repositioning Victorian sciences: Shifting centres in nineteenth-century scientific thinking* (pp. 235–259). London: Anthem Press.

Opitz, D. L. (2011). Cultivating genetics in the country: Whittingehame Lodge, Cambridge. In D. N. Livingstone & W. J. Withers (Eds.), *Geographies of nineteenth-century science* (pp. 73–98). Chicago, IL: University of Chicago Press.

Rudwick, M. J. S. (1998). Lyell and the principles of geology. In D. J. Blundell & A. C. Scott (Eds.) *Lyell: The past is the key to the present* (Vol. 143, pp. 3–15). London: Geological Society, Special Publications.

Ruse, M. (1975). Darwin's debt to philosophy: An examination of the influence of the philosophical ideas of John F. W. Herschel and William Whewell on the development of Charles Darwin's theory of evolution. *Studies in the History and Philosophy of Science, 6*, 159–181.

Ruse, M. (1979). *The Darwinian revolution*. Chicago, IL: University of Chicago Press.

Secord, J. A. (1996). The crisis of nature. In N. Jardine, J. A. Secord, & E. C. Spary (Eds.), Cultures of natural history (pp. 447–459). Cambridge: Cambridge University Press.

Schaffer, S. (1998). Physics laboratories and the Victorian country house. In C. Smith & J. Agar (Eds.), *Making space for science: Territorial themes in the shaping of knowledge* (pp. 149–180). Basingstoke: Macmillan.

Szathmáry, E. (2006). Darwin for all seasons. *Science, 313*, 306–307.

Van Wyhe, J. (Ed.). (2009). *Charles Darwin's shorter publications 1823–1883*. Cambridge: Cambridge University Press.

Whewell, W. (1840). *The philosophy of the inductive sciences, founded upon their history*. 2 volumes. London: John W. Parker.

Wilkinson, D. M. (2002). Ecology before ecology: Biogeography and ecology in Lyell's 'Principles'. *Journal of Biogeography, 29*, 1109–1115.

Wilson, E. O. (1994). *Naturalist*. Washington, DC: Island Press.

James T. Costa
Highlands Biological Station & Department of Biology,
Western Carolina University,
USA

STEPHEN P. TOMKINS & SUE DALE TUNNICLIFFE

11. NAMING THE LIVING WORLD

From the Infant's Perception of Animacy to a Child's Species Concept

INTRODUCTION

Children have an astonishing ability to relate to, talk about, identify and then name organisms in a mental framework shared with their peers; some even become naturalists and bioscientists as well. In this chapter we outline some of the ideas, supported by research evidence, which contribute to this ontogeny of just one aspect of science capability. At its pre-linguistic start it is a matter of an infant's perception of an object being alive rather than unresponsively inanimate. At pre-school, huge strides are then made in first naming, essentialising the identity, and then talking about organisms, and their ordinate grouping. At primary school, children's capability and confidence in identifying, categorising and classifying organisms grows apace. At its most developed this skill-set leads to an adult's understanding of biodiversity in its systematic and evolutionary framework. We will not concern ourselves with the latter, for it is the initial confidence in relating to and recognising the natural world, and talking about it with others, that opens the larger box in which natural science later operates. This initial confidence is nurtured through every child's physical, natural and social environment. Alongside any child are his or her peers, parents and teachers, all of them being key players. Charles Darwin himself was no stranger to such ideas about child development; indeed, he pioneered this field with scientific observations of his own children. He was also fully aware, and most acknowledging of, his own ontogenetic development in natural science and he wrote feelingly of it in his autobiography. The component parts of this *one aspect* of scientific thinking and competency are reflected in Darwin's own record of his early life. Darwin is in no way peculiar or singular in this respect, but his own developed nature in this one area is a delightfully illustrative example of the pathway from childhood observing and naming, through social discourse and reasoning to a fully-fledged hypothetico-deductive science.

ANIMACY AND FIRST TALK

Animacy

Very young children, under the age of one year, readily recognise objects that manifest a state of being alive or being seemingly animate. It should not surprise us that infants are innately able to detect an object's motion or sounds (Gelman & Spelke, 1981). Thus at six months they are more startled by, and follow visually, an object that has independent movement unrelated to any other causality (Leslie, 1979) – so the passing cat may be more interesting to a baby than its dangling toy. This hard-wiring, to be aware of other organisms, has obvious adaptive value for the infant human. However, what starts in a child's mind with a mere response to perceptual processing of motion, rapidly develops further to a fuller concept of the animacy of that object. This is not a biological concept of a living object versus a dead one, but a matter of degree of significant liveliness. Classically, Piaget (1929) saw this as a situation in which the child imputes human character to the autonomously moving object. This has been criticised since as being simplistic. Confusion is found in very young children as to whether animatronic toys are 'alive' or not – e.g. in comparing a real mouse to a clock-work one. In this respect Carey (1985) maintained that very young children early on start to use many more different cues to make a conceptual judgement about animacy. These would include the animate object's responsiveness and its interactive behaviour. Thus, the pre-school child will be both attracted to and well engaged with quite diverse concepts that surround the animate nature of those things that they encounter. They will be learning extensively long before any very formal teaching begins. The unresponsiveness of many biological living things makes them different and therefore seemingly inanimate. So much so that to say to a young child of four that 'plants are alive' is a fairly meaningless suggestion. Significantly, Jakkola (1997) found that it is only children between the ages of between four and six who begin for the first time to use the concept of 'life' and being 'alive' to predict and explain biological phenomena. This is the age at which a biological construction of their knowledge about life begins. Interestingly in this context, Spreece and Brent (1985) assert that the irreversibility of being dead and inevitability of living things dying does not embed itself conceptually until children are at least six or seven years old. In summary, animacy provides the first interest in objects for infants, but much else, like language, is also dawning in their lives at the same time.

Language

There is comparatively little research into pre-school children's development of language in biological naming (Tunnicliffe & Ueckert, 2011). The research emphasis is very much on older pupils and on their later skills and concept development. Great strides in learning, however, begin with a child's first talking. This is a vital stage:

> Children, we now know, need to talk, and to experience a rich diet of spoken language in order to think and learn. Reading, writing and number may be acknowledged as curriculum 'basics' but talk is the true foundation for teaching. (R. Alexander, 2008)

At the foundations of learning biology we therefore need to be encouraging observation and the narratives about the living world that children encounter and in our planning of experiences for young children. It is perhaps surprising that theories of learning have not been derived from making a better biological study of young children's language development. Human language is a biological adaptation that has evolved to make 'meaning' more clear to others of our species. We therefore learn a language *from* our parents but we also learn *through* that language.

NAMING AND THE CONCEPT OF IDENTITY

Once perception of objects develops (whether by sight, sound, smell, feel or taste) children rapidly start to construct a concept of identity for an object. This is of course now assisted hugely by language. The 'dogginess' of a dog is clear to the mind of a two year old. Susan Gelman (2005) describes this as 'essentialism'. She emphasises that, very largely, children's concepts are formed by the language which they hear being used by others, in association with that child's own early observations. Thus, naming reinforces learning through discussion and talk and so becomes embedded in mental constructs.

How did the simplest naming originate? Many simple object name-makings may well have originated from an onomatopoeic start (e.g. with the bird names - cuckoo, peewit, hoopoe), some namings are highly conserved but undoubtedly evolve (e.g. mama, mam, mamai, mummy, mum). Others change over time so much as to retain no obvious sound connection with their original form (e.g. cat, dog, rabbit). This naming is an inherent human need (Bruner, Goodnow & Austin, 1956). Namings are rapidly picked up by infants. A two-year-old boy had five words for animals and five words for plants in his first 104 words (Tunnicliffe, 2013). New names are constructed by those who learn. Such names may then persist into a language and culture (e.g. creepy-crawlies). New names are often figurative. The San Bushmen of the Kalahari until recently had no language name, of their own, for a helicopter. Today their San language has a vivid compound word-descriptor that translates literally as 'dragonfly-motorbike' (*pers. comm.* J. L. Tomkins). As children acquire their early language, they begin to label more phenomena and then gradually, with increasing linguistic facility, narrative begins. Narratives are important in learning science. Ogborn et al. (1996) argue that science knowledge can be reworked into story-like forms, not merely to add to its 'liveliness' or 'interest', and not merely to show it 'applied' to some real context, but more fundamentally to act as an involving, memorable and efficient knowledge carrier. Stories are knowledge in a reworked form.

Very young speaking children (of, say, 2-4 years old) quickly, if not entirely clearly, communicate their knowledge of living things as their own concepts form. Carey (1985), writing of conceptual change in childhood, argues that between the ages of four and ten all children undergo a period of conceptual re-organisation of their understanding of animals and other living things. Once that restructuring has taken place, an 'intuitive biology' emerges from this basic start. We would not argue with this idea, for it is only through the process of putting living things into categorical compartments that one can arrive at a systematic understanding of other living things. How does this categorisation begin?

CATEGORISATION

The Fundamentals of Categories

Bruner, Goodnow and Austin (1956) pointed out that we would all be overwhelmed with information if we were denied the ability to categorise those things which we meet in life that we need to get to know. This next anecdote serves well. A four year-old boy, out with his parents, was observed collecting so many pine cones that he could not carry them all in his hands. He had to make a decision: which to retain and which to discard? He considered his dilemma. His solution was to identify some distinguishing attributes. These he decided on were size, texture, and a certain shape. He eliminated cones which did not match his criteria (quoted *verbatim* from Tunniclffe & Ueckert, 2011). Once we have defined a category it extends beyond its group members and defines for us, and itself, a notional frame that is just waiting for other missing pieces to fall into that group with it. Children know that tables, stools, chairs, armchairs and sofas are all 'furniture' but that super-ordinate group is not initially as easy a concept to think of as each constituent member on its own. The logic or rationale of groupings is not easy either. Strawberries, pillar-boxes and fire-engines certainly do not group naturally together despite having one blazing colour in common.

The theory of categorisation is a vastly complex scene involving not only philosophy and psychology but also considerable applications in science and control technologies. Most simply, a category is defined entirely by those members in it having certain shared attributes. Every attribute has to be there in any member. Thus if a member has all those attributes they have to be in that category. The boundaries of the category are discrete: there are no fuzzy edges. By making a mental picture of the categorical attributes, one is able to test whether a new candidate is in that category or not. As was most ably pointed out by Ellen Markman (1989) categories (such as species) are themselves divided into sub-ordinate groups (such as taxonomic races or sub-species) as well as being nested into the super-ordinate groups (like taxonomic genera and classes). Children do not arrive at these ideas easily nor perhaps did we historically.

The Human-Centredness of Category

How should children set about grouping living things? Yorek and Narli (2009) found that children construct their own ideas of living things very much around themselves. They called this 'an animistic anthropocentric conceptual model'. They also noted that when Aristotle (350 BCE) initially developed his own biological classification,

Scala naturae, he saw it as a chain of beings from the simplest life up to humans. Yorek, Sahin and Aydin (2009) conducted an interesting investigation into the criteria for grouping organisms, expressed by middle secondary pupils, and found that when removed from the constraints of taught systematic biology students developed their own empirical classes for animals e.g. swimmers in water, flyers in the air and walkers on land. This simple thinking has deep roots and is again not dissimilar from ideas that were ventured by Aristotle, who no doubt built on his own native culture in ancient Greece. Interestingly Linnaeus, who knew Aristotle's teaching, also reflected on our human need to group things. Sometime after first publishing his own *Systema naturae* (1735), Linnaeus wrote (1751) of an intuitive system of ordering which he felt all people might possess. He described 'a natural instinct [that] teaches us to know first those objects closest to us, and [then] more distantly [from us] the smallest ones: for example, Man, Quadrupeds, Birds, Fish, Insects, Mites, or first the large Plants [and] last the small Mosses'. He too perceived our natural anthropocentricity. The genius in his *Systema naturae* was to free classification from anthropocentrism, at least somewhat, by a mental leap to a 'natural classification' of mutual hierarchical affinity based on the kinship of *each* and *every* species to the rest of nature and not just in affinity to ourselves. This requires a tree construction, as Darwin re-discovered, where each extant species is a leaf at the end of a branch. We accept this, now, as our target concept for teaching systematics, but it is certainly not entirely intuitive. Today, humans might be freed even further from anthropocentrism if we no longer needed to be the top leaf on the tree.

Categorisation as a Universal

Darwin (1859) built on those Linnaean ideas for he clearly had a feeling for grouping being a reality that was just waiting to be made clear:

> ... from the most remote period in the history of the world organic beings have been found to resemble each other in descending degrees, so that they can be classed into groups under groups. This classification is not arbitrary like the grouping of stars in constellations. (Darwin, C., 1859, p.431)

Was Darwin right to state that this ordering is universally plain? Today, Atran and Medin (2008) have made a most thorough folk-biology study of categorisation and its character, specifically addressing the ways different peoples organise naming and how and whether this relates to scientific systematics. They studied Amerindians in Guatemala, such as the Itzá-Mayan, in contrast with several urban and rural cultures in North America. First, they concluded that all cultures certainly have a classification into 'species-like groups' (e.g. robins, blackbirds, thrushes). Secondly, they found that for all cultures all such generic types (not of necessity true species) are recognised as having an 'essence' that defined their nature: niche, ecology, behaviour, character etc. Thus, for the British, robins are small red-breasted birds, commonly found in woods and gardens, which sing sweetly, eat insects and seeds and which people often find quite tame. This 'essentialism' accords with Gelman's view and although something of a metaphysical construct, for those in science education, it is well regarded as a valuable construct in psychology. Thirdly, Atran and Medin also found that *all* folk biology cultures have super-ordinate and sub-ordinate categories for expressing the affinity of these generic species – so Charles Darwin was right. Many such groupings are naturalistic or utilitarian, but do often accord well to biological systematics. Although in many cultures cockroaches, snakes and lizards might all be super-ordinately grouped as 'creeping things', these peoples might also acknowledge that each of these animals have sub-ordinate category differences.

Children Learning to Categorise

Early years primary school children encounter very many organisms or representations of organisms in their daily lives. Animals feature much more than plants. For example, domestic, farm and exotic animals are well known through books and field trips, visits to museums, zoos, farms and nature centres (Tunnicliffe, 1995). We know that recognising animals (knowing their essence) is a complex procedure but young children use the appearance of an animal to group it and readily use exemplars. Thus, to talk about 'pet animals', 'farm animals', or 'zoo animals', immediately introduces a familiar but categoric super-ordinate framework. This level of categorisation, into a defined perimeter collection, is an example of the simplest and most important start that a teacher can make (Tunnicliffe & Ueckert, 2011). Young children display a gradually increasing competence in their use of the *appearance* of an animal or plant to classify it further and use exemplars, matching what they see with what they have experienced previously. They come to realise that what they are observing represents a natural kind and thus the object has certain shared characteristics with other members of the same group and, therefore, shared membership.

Such early cognitive development, in understanding living things, is very informal, with children learning gradually from the world around them and often not from formal teaching. This may create some conceptual problems for later *biological* understanding as the systematic concepts are not always intuitive. Older children frequently use exemplars, matching what they see to what they have as a mental model and can also use both unique features and commonplace ones in identifying a species. Thus 'an African lion' can be both 'a member of the cat family', generically, and also a 'carnivore', ecologically. Only later do the sub-ordinate groupings gather easily into the super-ordinate groupings, for this is much harder. The systematic mental model evolves and develops. Thus, that 'cat' will also be a 'mammal' and the mammal belongs to the category 'vertebrate'. That group, in turn, is a 'chordate' as well as an 'animal', and so, the cat is finally one of many 'living things'. All this takes some long time to understand and only comes with conceptual change over years. That one's domestic cat has the identifying features for being in each of the nested categories to which it belongs from its pet name of 'pussy' to its membership of the animal kingdom is not easy to follow. True hierarchical classification skills require the classifier to use abstract thought and this certainly involves much embedded knowledge.

THE EXTINCTION OF EXPERIENCE

Categorising may be difficult to learn but it ought to be well motivated by interest. E. O. Wilson (1984) hypothesised that all humans have an innate desire to be with, to understand and so order their knowledge and interest in other living things. He called this *biophilia*. However, of the deepest concern to those teaching life science in all schools today is the haemorrhage of first-hand knowledge about the natural world that has occurred in developed societies with adults and children of all ages. Initially, Nabhan and St Antoine (1993) referred to this as the 'extinction of experience' of nature. Louv (2005), later described it as a 'nature deficit disorder'. Atran & Medin (2008) noted the loss of knowledge about living forms in white urban North America. The situation in many urbanised cultures appears to be dire. It seems that with greater formal education and removal from the environment in which humans originally sought their food comes an increasing loss of knowledge of nature amongst both children and adults alike. This is borne out for children by some of the research we describe below. Addressing it is of both cultural and human survival importance. This is certainly not for want of classification ability in children, as was shown by Balmford et al. (2002) who noted that between the ages of four and eight years old, children's identification of common species of British wildlife improved from 32% to 53% whilst their knowledge of the names of Pokémon characters improved from 7% to 78%. Many English children knew the identity of more than 100 synthetic species from this one Japanese game set.

CHILDREN'S NAMING OF PLANTS AND ANIMALS

In the course of researching children's interest in plants and animals (Tunnicliffe, 2001; Tomkins & Tunnicliffe, 2007), children's observations of brine shrimps (Tomkins & Tunnicliffe, 2001), children's conversations in zoos (Patrick & Tunnicliffe, 2013), at museum-based natural history dioramas (Tunicliffe, in press) and in early primary education (Patrick & Tunnicliffe, 2011) we have reported on just some issues raised by children's observing, naming and classifying both animals and plants. The children who were listened to or interviewed displayed a remarkable consistency in the comments generated in such situations, but there were many differences also. Young children at the Piagetian concrete stage of learning need many visual clues and are unlikely to be able to use a true taxonomic hierarchy. Even though young children are able to divide objects hierarchically, they do not understand a true hierarchical taxonomy and teaching this should not be attempted with them. This does not mean that they are without the earliest formulations of a 'species concept': there are clearly different 'kinds' of plants and animals. Although this need not be a genetic conception Springer (1999) looking for the roots of biological conceptual thinking found that four to five year olds mostly have already acquired a 'theory of kinship' about the relationship between a mother and her child: cats produce only kittens and dogs only puppies. In the naming of the kinds of plants and animals, the inability of very young children to articulate their own ideas can be frustrating to a teacher or parent. But as the definition of their own ideas improve, and as vocabulary develops, young children's progression in the use of anecdote and simile is also often an impressive reflection of their early learning

The Naming of Animals

With respect to animals, 'interest' is always high. The child psychologists Schiefele (1991) and Krapp (1999) drew attention to this power of 'interest' in motivation and learning. Earlier, Markman (1989) emphasised the importance of naming itself as the first step in providing a handle for a concept. But she also emphasised that names are fluid adjuncts to a developing concept and are not immutable categories for the child, i.e. names will be expected to alter in their meaning.

Right from the start, pre-school vocabulary builds fast. We have found that a sample of 92 primary age pupils used 11 different names just to describe the mealworms which they observed. Older 11 and 12 year-old pupils, observing brine shrimps without formal instruction, developed their own vocabulary very rapidly in order to describe their observations of a novel animal (Tomkins & Tunnicliffe, 2001). Employing systemic network analysis in many of these papers Tunnicliffe (1995 and 1998) established some consistent gender differences in naming animals; girl-only groups refer to names less than do boy-only groups but the former describe more affective relations and inferred animal activities. Girl-only groups generated significantly more emotive attitudes – expressing their 'likes and dislikes'. In zoos, 75% of children's conversations relate to animal namings; however, zoological labels, which give systematic naming information, are very rarely read. Even though the younger secondary children, who might read such information, are able to divide objects hierarchically, Tunnicliffe has found that younger children do not understand the hierarchical taxonomy, such as the labels, used in traditional animal collections. Whilst children notice prominent features of any object, Tversky (1989) noted that they do not readily notice the criterial attributes of animals that zoologists use unless the features, and the rationale for their use, are specifically pointed out. Pupils viewing dioramas in museums relate these static exhibits very well to the required curricular objectives in classification and ecology (Tunnicliffe, 2013). Such displays, which call for name learning, may lead to highly generative discussion.

In a study reporting the dialogue of a family making zoo visits, the majority of categorisation of animals, 39 out of the 60 names given to animals, were expressed in everyday language at the genus/order level, 11 were at the species level, e.g. red-crowned crane and 10 were at a super-ordinate class level, e.g. bird, fish, etc. (Patrick & Tunnicliffe, 2012). Children certainly readily elaborate from all namings in story telling and in the synthesis of their own ideas. There are other confounding complexities in naming because animals do not always have the same form during their life cycles, e.g., egg → tadpole → frog, &/or egg → larva → pupa → imago (adult butterfly). The 'extinction of experience' (see above), which afflicts contemporary children, was expressed well by a UK study in which a museum taxidermy specimen of a common starling *Sturnus vulgaris*, realistically mounted on a stick, was presented to four groups of nine children who were asked to say what it was. Without exception all the children recognised it as a bird, some even justifying their classification quite ably. However for this ubiquitous British bird species, only a small minority recognised it as a 'starling', most children making a species identity attempt which included such bird species as parrot, woodpecker, thrush, blackbird, crow, pigeon and blue tit (Patrick & Tunnicliffe, 2013).

The Naming of Plants

The naming of plants starts with more difficulty. Carey (1985) established that children aged four to seven years have a clear animal concept, but that they have no meaningful concept of 'living things', which would include plants, as being distinct from inanimate objects. Plants and animals are therefore not naturally grouped together by children at age six. However, children by age nine have a developing concept of plants, and plants are now mentally-mapped as being 'alive'. This initial conceptual difficulty lies at the root of what Wandersee and Schussler (2001) saw as a tendency to 'plant blindness' in both children and adults. Even the word 'plant' has its conceptual problems at the outset. In a small study in an English primary school, children aged five were asked what the word 'plant' meant to them (Tunnicliffe & Uekert, 2011). The children did not know what 'plant' meant other than as a verb, to put seeds in the ground, or in other words 'to plant'. Patrick and Tunnicliffe (2011) have also written extensively on children's conceptions of plants. Certainly children use their own strategies to identify plants (Uno, 2009), so it is essential that children have a more direct interaction with plants to make a significant difference to their knowledge (Askham, 1976). We would add to Askham's observation that it should be a better and earlier experience as well.

Tunnicliffe's work in Kew Gardens (2001) reinforces this view. In this admittedly 'exotic' plant situation, children focused on particular parts of the plants such as their leaf shapes and sizes, prickly stem, colourful flower or an obvious fruit or pattern in the leaf of the veins. They did not use these observations to justify the name of the plant, but interest was there. In over half of the analysed conversations, interest in anatomical features predominated and this was the largest category. But not knowing the names of plants seems to be the biggest problem for children who are thereby less able to discuss them. Lack of an appropriate vocabulary, because their adult mentors (in or out of school) do not refer to plant phenomena, is a stumbling block in learning.

In a study of 104 pre-school and primary-age children from UK (England) and the United States (Texas), Patrick and Tunnicliffe (2011) found a steady increase in competence in naming with a child's age (see Figure 1). UK children named domesticated, farmed and wild plants with roughly equal frequency. In the USA farmed plants but not wild ones were better known. The exotic plants in both samples were least named (there was therefore no correlation with the well-known exotic-animal equivalents which are so popular with children). All the age groups identified home/garden/yard as the location where they saw plants most often (England 53%, USA 56%). Alarmingly, schools, as places where plants were to be seen, scored below 'the shops', 'wild natural areas' and 'outside' (England 7%, USA 3.5%)!

A further problem with naming plants is that a plant may not be seen as one organism. While 'Z' is for zebra, 'A' is for more than apple: an apple tree has leaves, blossoms, pollinators and fruits (apples), with flesh, pips and apple juice; it has roots, a trunk and branches, that you can climb and swing from. It is something multifarious. Thus, visiting plants in botanic gardens and formal gardens, on farms, in meadows and in woods for the purposes of learning is all the more needed. In this, as in gardening and growing one's own food, there is a great nature deficit to be addressed, not least by schools.

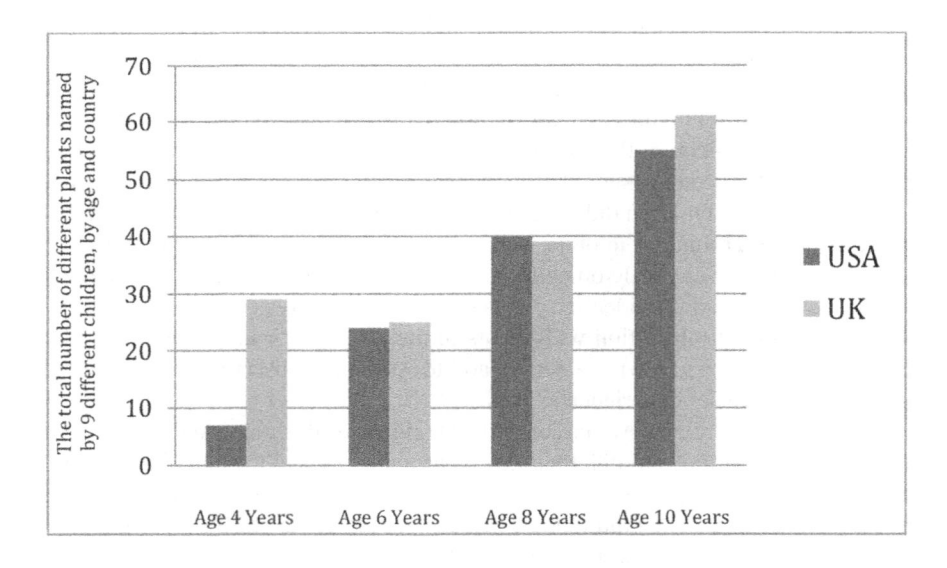

Figure 1. The increasing competence displayed by children of primary age in naming those plants with which they were familiar. (Patrick & Tunnicliffe, 2011)

ON CONVERSATIONS AND COLLECTING THINGS

Talking

A focus of much research described above has been on the conversations that children have with their teachers and peers. The merits of discourse in the development of scientific thinking is well established; we know that a strong social *milieu* is conducive to children clarifying their own understanding, expanding their vocabulary and expression, and sharing their knowledge with others (Driver, Newton & Osborne, 2000; Alexander, 2008). Talking is also supportive of the skills of observation. Children need training in looking with accuracy, testing pre-formed ideas and so questioning meaning as expressed by others.

Collecting Things

Many children are avid collectors on their walks. It is almost tempting to assume that this behaviour is a hard-wired human adaptation for survival.

Significantly, it was the originator of Pokémon, Tajiri Satoshi, who from a childhood of collecting and observing insects then recognised the loss of wildlife in his urbanised home area and so then designed Pokémon characters to create a more 'biodiverse' environment for children (Sanders, 2010). The attribute of collecting persists in many children beyond childhood and we feel that it is probably both under-researched and under-used by teachers. Employing children's interests in what they notice is obviously a way into children's minds and through that to their learning about what they encounter. What children collect will have some intrinsic interest for them and the objects may well fit into some narrative of theirs, imagined or real. Beyond that, any collection (whether it is dolls, Pokémon characters, pebbles, tree leaves or sea shells) will be the vehicle that leads to better thinking and so the furthering of a child's cognitive skills (Durbin et al., 1990).

DARWIN'S OWN CHILDHOOD IN SCIENCE

Finally, we pose two questions:

- Did Darwin's own childhood resonate with our present knowledge about the development of biological cognition?
- Did his own behaviour as a pupil, parent and teacher reflect his own upbringing and pedagogic experience?

In response to both these questions an affirmative, 'Yes indeed', might be facile or trivial but there are many events and traits in his life that do need to be remarked upon for their resonance with this topic.

Pre-schooling

Darwin was a much-loved child in a wealthy and enlightened household (see Figure 2), (Barlow, 1958; Browne, 1995). His large 'sisterhood', three elder sisters and one younger and his hugely admired elder brother, Erasmus, were his peers and indeed his resident pre-school teachers until he was over eight years old. He undoubtedly had a caring and rich early-learning environment with his siblings. He wrote in his autobiography (Darwin, in Barlow, 1958) 'I can say in my own favour that I was as a boy humane, but I owed this entirely to the instruction and example of my sisters'.

Figure 2. Charles Robert Darwin, aged six. (Darwin Heirlooms Trust)

Collecting in His Early School Years

It was not until Darwin's mother's tragic death, when he was only eight, that he went to a local school. The trauma of her death almost ablated his subsequent memory of her and might possibly have made him seek more solace in his own natural history pursuits out-of-doors. He wrote of this important period of his childhood:

> By the time I went to this day-school my taste for natural history, and more especially for collecting, was well developed. I tried to make out the names of plants, and collected all sorts of things, shells, seals, franks, coins, and minerals. The passion for collecting, which leads a man to be a systematic naturalist, a virtuoso or a miser, was very strong in me, and was clearly innate, as none of my sisters or brothers ever had this taste. (Darwin, *Autobiography*, 1873: in Barlow, 1958.)

He was, by this admission, compulsive in his systematic acquisition of 'specimens' and later in his serious beetle-collecting days, as an undergraduate, quite competitively so as well (van Wyhe, 2009). There was a breadth to his collecting. He was familiar with garden plants and growing them from an early age. He was familiar with wild flowers. Rocks in all their diversity, butterfly and beetle hunting, fishing and later shooting were enduring and compulsive pursuits. The biodiverse Shropshire countryside of his childhood and teenage was central. His developing intellect and wonder were also clear to his family though he was seemingly a bit dreamy and neither a keen or very successful learner in school. He wrote 'I have heard my father and elder sister say that I had, as a very young boy, a strong taste for long solitary walks; but what I thought about I know not' (Darwin, 1873 in Barlow, 1958). From an early age he certainly read avidly in natural history and he doubtless lived in a world of his own creative imaginings as pre-school children often do. He evidently hated school, but loved his escape from it into his reading, collecting and countryside activities. His initial discovery of his own sociality was revealing. He wrote of his early childhood discovery of 'telling lies' to surprise people, and then of his discovery that he was not, subsequently, necessarily believed. He was certainly acquisitive of new ideas as well as of his own personal observations. His home experiments in Chemistry with Erasmus were also fun and most formative of his subsequent experimental approach. Unquestionably, though, it was his early collecting that schooled him to look for difference, whether it was in the angles of crystals or in the variety of beetles. He wrote careful labels for the specimens in his home museum 'cabinet'.

Darwin's Mentors

To be schooled strictly, as he was at Shrewsbury (from aged 9-16 years) under Dr Butler, in both writing and narrative expression certainly taught Darwin to marshal his ideas. He was later aware of, and must indeed have puzzled over, his own grandfather's rather obviously un-evidenced writing about evolution, and in his late teens learned to his surprise, through Robert Grant at Edinburgh, of Lamarck's work. At Cambridge he discussed with John Stevens Henslow, his most significant mentor, the latter's puzzlement over the exact nature of 'species'. So whether it was walking and talking with Grant or Henslow or tussling to systematise his natural history observations, his early entertainment of conflicting views must have been intrinsically valuable to his own subsequent hypothesis-making and experiment. To be nicknamed by Cambridge academics as 'the man who walks with Henslow' tells us that he had already developed his appetite for ideas and new observations. John Medows Rodwell, one of Darwin's more scholarly Cambridge peers, later wrote of Henslow's chance remark to him: 'What a fellow that Darwin is for asking questions!' (van Wyhe, 2009).

Although the young Darwin often worked in the field with assistance, as was expected then of a gentleman-naturalist, he learned from his mentors many vital practical skills in collecting, dissection, taxidermy and plant pressing. Indeed, his anxiety about the quality of his practical skill was evident in his correspondence with Henslow on *Beagle* specimens. His keenness to acquire naturalist's skills is exemplified at Edinburgh, in his late teens, by his learning to stuff birds. His teacher was John Edmonstone, a former black slave from Guyana. Darwin was hugely privileged in the opportunities that he had for collecting and sharing discoveries in the countryside not only with his own family, and especially the Wedgwoods, but also with another significant mentor when he was at Cambridge. This was Leonard Jenyns the country-parson naturalist whom Darwin perhaps most sought to emulate. He was an influential friend and, like Darwin, entranced by entomological collecting. Jenyns was nine years older than Darwin and five years younger than Henslow. His sister Harriet was married to Henslow, and so he was uncle to Henslow's children. Jenyns also imparted important natural history disciplines. As a schoolboy, Jenyns had admitted, 'a fondness for order, method and precision'. Like Darwin, he was also partial to solitary walks 'wrapped up in observing, admiring and reflecting'. These were significant influences in the making of Darwin as a naturalist.

Mentor-models and Parents

Lastly, we need to consider Darwin's own understanding of teaching others. We see much evidence of his own social gentleness and humanity. He described his own father (Robert Darwin) as:

> ... the wisest man I ever knew.. . His chief mental characteristics were his powers of observation and his sympathy, neither of which have I ever seen exceeded or even equalled. (Darwin, 1873; in Barlow, 1958)

The youthful Charles Darwin would have observed much of Henslow's treatment of his own family and students. He wrote later in testimony to the life of Henslow:

Nothing could be more simple cordial and unpretending than the encouragement that he afforded to all young naturalists ... he had the remarkable power of making the young feel completely at ease with him ... He would receive with interest the most trifling of observation in any branch of natural history; and however absurd a blunder one might make, he pointed it out so clearly and kindly that one left in no way disheartened, but only determined to be more accurate the next time. (van Wyhe, 2009)

One important story of Darwin's time at Cambridge, which might have occasioned this tribute, was of the young Darwin's discovery, through his own observation, of the germination of pollen grains and pollen-tube growth. He excitedly wrote a paper for Henslow under the full misapprehension that his observation was a novel discovery. Henslow went to some lengths to commend him, first, on his microscopy technique and very careful observation and accurate recording before, finally but gently, letting Darwin know how well published the phenomenon was but in so doing emphasising how good it was that his findings were consonant with the findings of others. This was quality teaching. Thus when Charles and Emma Darwin began their own large family at Downe they would have had ample role-model experience of teaching children natural history (see Chapters 1,2 & 7). This pedagogy would undoubtedly have included training in observation, in collecting skills, in encouraging curiosity and in asking those all-important questions.

CONCLUSION

This chapter has aimed to trace a conceptual ontogeny in children's minds from animacy to a species concept. At some way along their journey school children arrive at a categoric way of thinking about the different kinds of plants and animals and their kinship as species. In this they recapitulate humanity's ideas of categories and their utilitarian or naturalistic groupings. Learning science at school provides the strong frame. We recognise that the idea of species as evolutionary groups is at a high conceptual level. Indeed, biologists themselves cannot even agree on the concept entirely, and some venture that 'the species concept' is more of a human need than a biological reality (Hey, 2001). What we are sure of is that unless children have exposure to biodiversity ('hands-on' and 'minds-on'), observing living things in nature, in collections and exhibitions, they will neither understand biology discourse nor experience Darwin-inspired learning.

REFERENCES

Alexander, R. (2008). *Towards dialogic teaching: Rethinking classroom talk.* Cambridge, MA: Dialogos.
Askham, L. A. (1976). The effects of plants on classification behavior in an outdoor environment. *Journal of Research in Science Teaching, 13*(1), 49–54.
Atran, S., & Medin, D. (2008). *The native mind and the cultural construction of nature.* London: MIT Press.

Balmford, A., Clegg, L., Coulson, T., & Taylor, J. (2002). Why conservationists should heed Pokémon. *Science, 297*(5564), 2367b.
Barlow, N. (Ed.). (1958). *The autobiography of Charles Darwin 1809–1882*. With the original omissions restored. London: Collins.
Browne, J. (1995). *Charles Darwin: Voyaging*. New York, NY: Knopf.
Bruner, J. S., Goodnow, J. J., &. Austin, G. A. (1956). *A study of thinking*. New York, NY: John Wiley.
Carey, S. (1985). *Conceptual change in childhood*. Cambridge, MA: MIT Press.
Darwin, C. (1859). *On the origin of species by means of natural selection*. London: John Murray.
Darwin, C. (1873). *The autobiography of Charles Darwin 1809-1882*. London: Collins.
Durbin, G., Morris, S., Wilkinson, S., & Corbishley, M. (1990). *A teacher's guide to learning from objects*. London: English Heritage.
Driver, R., Newton, P., & Osborne, J. (2000). Establishing the norms of scientific argumentation in classrooms. *Science Education, 84*(3), 287–312.
Gelman, R., & Spelke, E. (1981). The development of thoughts about animate and inanimate objects: Implications for research on social cognition. In J. H. Flavell & L. Ross (Ed.), *Social cognitive development* (pp. 43–66). Cambridge, MA: Cambridge University Press.
Gelman, S. (2005). *The essential child: Origins of essentialism in everyday thought*. Oxford: Oxford University Press.
Hey, J. (2001). The mind of the species problem. *Trends in Ecology and Evolution, 16*(7), 326–329.
Jakkola, R. (1997). The development of scientific understanding: children's construction of their first biological theory. (Unpublished PhD thesis, MIT). Quoted in Slaughter, Jakkola & Carey in M. Siegal & C. Peterson. (1999). Children's understanding of biology and health. Cambridge: Cambridge University Press.
Krapp, A. (1999). Interest, motivation and learning: an educational-psychological perspective. *European Journal of Psychology of Education, 14*(1), 23–40.
Leslie, A. M. (1979). *The representation of perceived causal connection* (PhD thesis). Oxford.
Linnaeus, C. (1735, et sequ to 1758). *Systema naturae*. English edition (1964). Nieuwkoop: B. De Graaf,
Linnaeus, C. (1751). *Philosophia botanica*. Stockholm: G Kiesewetter.
Louv, R. (2005). *Last child in the woods: Saving our children from nature-deficit disorder*. Chapel Hill, NC: Algonquin Books.
Markman, E. M. (1989). *Categorization and naming in children: Problems of induction*. Cambridge, MA: MIT Press.
Nabhan, G. P., & St Antoine, S. (1995). The loss of floral and faunal story: The extinction of experience. In S. R. Kellert & E. O. Wilson (Ed.), The biophilia hypothesis (pp. 229–250). Washington, DC: Island Press.
Narli, S., Yorek, N., Sahin, M., & Usak, M. (2010). Can we make definite categorization of student attitudes? *Journal of Science and Technology Education, 19*, 456–469.
Ogborn, J., Kress, G., Martins, I., & McGillicuddy. K. (1996). *Explaining science in the classroom*. Buckingham, UK: Open University Press.
Patrick, P. G., & Tunnicliffe, S. D. (2011). What plants and animals do early childhood and primary students name? Where do they see them? *Journal of Science Education Technology, 20*(5), 630–642.
Patrick, P. G., & Tunnicliffe, S. D. (2013). *Zoo talk*. Dordrecht: Springer.
Piaget, J. (1929). *The child's conception of the world*. London: Routledge and Kegan.
Sanders, D. (2010). All netted together: Is there a need for a cultural consilience in the face of extinction? *Kew Bulletin, 65*(4), 677–680.
Spreece, M., & Brent, S. (1985). Children's understanding of death: A review of three components of a death concept. Child development, 55(1), 671–686.
Schiefele, U. (1991). Interest, learning and motivation. *Educational Psychologist, 26*, 299–323.
Springer, K. (1999). How a naive theory of biology is acquired. In M. Siegal & C. Peterson (Eds), *Children's understanding of biology and health*. Cambridge: Cambridge University Press.
Tomkins, S. P., & Tunnicliffe, S. D. (2001). Looking for ideas: observation, interpretation and hypothesis making by 12 year old pupils undertaking science investigations. *International Journal of Science Education, 23*(8), 791–813.

Tomkins, S. P., & Tunnicliffe, S. D. (2007). Nature tables: Stimulating children's interest in natural objects. *Journal of Biological Education, 41*(4), 150–155.
Tunnicliffe, S. D. (1995). *Talking about animals: Studies of young children visiting zoos, a museum and a farm.* (Unpublished PhD thesis). King's College, London.
Tunnicliffe, S. D. (1998). Boy talk: Girl talk. Is it the same at animal exhibits? *International Journal of Science Education, 20*(7), 795–811.
Tunnicliffe, S. D. (2001). Talking about plants: Comments of primary school groups looking at plants as exhibits in a botanical garden. *Journal of Biological Education, 36,* 27–34.
Tunnicliffe, S. D., & Reiss M. J. (1999). Building a model of the environment: How do children see animals? *Journal of Biological Education, 33*(4), 142–148.
Tunnicliffe, S. D., & Ueckert, C. (2011). Early biology: The critical years for learning. *Journal of Biological Education, 45*(4), 173–175.
Tunnicliffe, S. D. (2013). *Talking and doing science in the early years.* London: David Fulton.
Tunnicliffe, S. D. (in press) Naming and narratives at natural history dioramas. In S. D. Tunncliffe & A. Scheresoi (Eds.), *Natural history dioramas: History, construction and educational role.* Dordrecht: Springer.
Tversky, B. (1989). Parts, partonomies and taxonomies. *Developmental Psychology, 25,* 983–995.
Uno, G. (2009). Botanical literacy: What and how should students learn about plants? *American Journal of Biology, 96,* 1753–1759.
Wandersee, J. H., & Schussler, E. E. (2001). Toward a theory of plant blindness. *Plant Science Bulletin, 47,* 2–9.
Wilson. E. O. (1984). *Biophilia.* Cambridge, MA: Harvard University Press.
van Wyhe, J. (2009). *Darwin in Cambridge.* Cambridge: Christ's College.
Yorek, N., & Narli, S. (2009). Modeling of cognitive structure of uncertain scientific concepts using fuzzy-rough set and intuitionistic fuzzy sets: Example of the life concept. *International Journal of Uncertainty, Fuzziness and Knowledge- Based Systems, 17*(5), 371–380.
Yorek, N., Sahin, M., & Aydin, H. (2009). Are animals 'more alive' than plants? Animistic-anthropocentic construction of life concept. *Eurasia Journal of Mathematics, Science & Technology Education, 5*(4), 369–378.

Stephen P. Tomkins
Homerton College,
University of Cambridge,
UK

Sue Dale Tunnicliffe
Institute of Education,
University of London,
UK

SHIRLEY SIMON

12. SCIENTIFIC ENQUIRY

Searching for and Interpreting Evidence to Construct Arguments

Pitch up in a car park in southern England on a sunny afternoon in August when the tide is going out and you might see a group of families with their buckets and nets amassing for an expedition. At first glance they appear to be on their way to search for the usual crabs in rock pools; however, these families are suspending this popular seaside hunting activity for an hour or so to focus their attention on something else: the search for evidence. They are hunting for dinosaurs, at least the footprints left many millions of years ago by dinosaurs. But dinosaur footprints are not obvious (see Figures 1a and 1b), and most of us need support and guidance on what to see – how to interpret the evidence. Hence the group have a guide who leads a procession across the sandstones at low tide to find the exact spot where footprints were left by a wandering dinosaur and can tell them about the evidence – how long ago, which kind of dinosaur. On this particular site off the south coast of England several different sets of prints can be seen, in different layers of sediment, travelling in different directions and being laid down thousands of years apart.

The ravages of wind and tide continue to expose new sets of prints in different layers, adding further evidence of these family favourites. What questions arise

Figure 1a. Dinosaur footprint. (© Shirley Simon)

Figure 1b. Three dinosaur footprints. (© Shirley Simon)

once you have seen the footprints? Why are they here? How were they preserved? How many different kinds are there? Can we tell something about their lives? To search for some answers one might go to a nearby town where there is a dinosaur museum designed for families and school visits. The guides come from here and the expeditions are organised through the museum. But does the visit sustain that stimulating experience of the sunny summer afternoon at the edge of the sea? I shall return to this question ...

IDEAS AND EVIDENCE IN SCIENCE

The experience and subsequent questions outlined above can be seen as a stimulus to the process of scientific enquiry, not unlike the kind of enquiry Darwin engaged in as he looked at nature and asked questions that he set about solving. What was special about Darwin was what he chose to observe, how he asked questions about his observations, and his ability to answer these questions. It would be very easy to miss the dinosaur footprints whilst 'crabbing' in the rock pools in this special location; it takes a keen eye to spot them. Darwin trained himself to observe and find this kind of phenomenon; school students can learn something of these observational skills and how to think in a Darwinian way.

Enquiry is an important feature of education and is often known as 'enquiry-based learning' (Edelson, Gordon & Pea, 1999). Enquiry in school science can be defined in different ways but essentially includes the intentional process of diagnosing problems, critiquing experiments, and distinguishing alternatives, planning investigations, researching conjectures, searching for information, constructing models, debating with peers, and forming coherent arguments (Linn, Davis & Bell,

2004). Each of these processes can be addressed through structured activities with students, but can present challenges for teachers who are more familiar with teaching about established scientific knowledge. Research focusing on the construction of arguments using argumentation activities has shown this aspect of enquiry to be particularly challenging, as many teachers are unfamiliar with strategies involving a more open classroom dialogue (Simon, Erduran & Osborne, 2006). Teaching enquiry requires a mind-set change on the part of the teacher, away from an approach where the teacher often presents the concepts and information, including results of experiments even before the student carries them out, to an approach where the teacher creates the atmosphere to allow for student observation, experimentation, planning, and, through teacher guidance, students can construct their knowledge. Asking students to question the evidence for that knowledge or question why one theory is more acceptable than an alternative theory can be problematic for some teachers. Much research has been conducted on the ways in which the process of enquiry can be taught, and how argumentation in science teaching can be established through certain teaching strategies (Osborne, Erduran & Simon, 2004a), and how developing the skills of argument (Kuhn, 1991) can enhance students' learning through weighing up evidence, distinguishing alternatives and strengthening arguments in the light of opposition. Through working with teachers I have come to value the importance of the design of the activity itself (Simon & Richardson, 2009); teachers' own beliefs, values and experience of a range of teaching strategies determines their own development, but having good ideas for classroom activities that stimulate interest to carry out an enquiry or construct arguments is essential.

Most teachers are not in a position to take their students to coastal environments, yet a visit to see something that fascinates and raises questions like the visit to the seaside described in my opening passage could lead to an enquiry. Seeing the different sets of dinosaur footprints inspired me to ask about the existence of animals and plants in different locations and habitats in different time periods. Central to this enquiry would be weighing up evidence to find the best explanation for events occurring over long periods of time and constructing arguments using that evidence. Darwin's life is inspirational for appreciating the value of such a scientific enquiry, as he and others of his time were focused on using evidence to explain changes in events over time. As a young man and budding naturalist, Darwin's voyage on the *Beagle* made him an eager observer and collector. When the *Beagle* reached land Darwin made long excursions and collected many specimens, made notes and sketches, and kept a journal of what he saw. Influenced by Lyell's *Principles of Geology*, Darwin's observations and collections led him to explore the contents of rocks, through which he found the bones of extinct species such as the giant ground sloth *Megatherium*. The journey provided the stimulus for Darwin to proceed with a lifetime of enquiry. Fortunate to be born into privilege, and having made a name for himself through the voyage on the *Beagle*, Darwin was able to spend all his time reflecting on the significance of his findings and setting up experiments to test out his ideas. One outcome of Darwin's work, published at a time when others, notably Wallace, were coming to similar conclusions about evolution, was his book *On the origin of species* (Darwin, 1859). In my reading of Darwin's work, and about the times and influences on his thinking (Eiseley, 1961), I have come to realise the importance of Darwin's use of argument as the culmination of his process of enquiry. Darwin observed, discovered, collected, experimented, weighed up evidence, made inferences, but critically, in *On the origin of species*, presented his argument. Moreover, Darwin communicated his ideas with others whilst constructing his argument; he corresponded with many eminent scientists of the time, including Joseph Hooker, Thomas Huxley and Richard Owen. Weighing up evidence and arguments with others is an important argumentation process in establishing scientific knowledge and understanding.

Darwin makes reference to the process of argument many times throughout *On the origin of species*, and here I make reference to the sixth edition (Darwin, 1872). Early in the book he talks about 'balancing the facts and arguments on both sides of each question' (p. 2); arguments being of 'great weight' (p. 18); of 'several interesting lines of argument, from geographical distribution, analogical variation ...' (p. 39). As the book unfolds his own argument, Darwin draws on a range of others' arguments, critiquing these and weighing them up against the evidence of his own theory: 'we must not, however, push the foregoing argument too far' (p. 113); 'it may be urged as a most forcible argument' (p. 255); 'most of the arguments which have convinced me that all the existing species of the same group have descended from one progenitor, apply with nearly equal force' (p. 286).

Darwin was thus concerned in expressing argument in terms of the nature of evidence, his own or presented by others, the strength of evidence and the validity of application. In conclusion, Darwin writes of this book, 'As this whole volume is one long argument, it may be convenient to the reader to have the leading facts and inferences briefly recapitulated' (p. 404). He follows this by looking at 'the other side of the argument' (p. 410), and finally claims that those arguments that have the 'greatest weight extend very far' (p. 424). Key to the power of Darwin's theory is the construction of the argument, drawing on different sources of evidence and evaluating these. As Faller-Fritsch (2008) notes in his case for teaching evolution, *On the origin of species* shows 'how creative thought provides evidence from several independent sources, and ways of evaluating the strength of this evidence' (p. 40).

TEACHING IDEAS AND EVIDENCE: PEDAGOGIC CHALLENGES AND ACTIVITY DESIGN

I have referred above to the pedagogical challenges that teaching enquiry and argumentation present, and in particular to the design of good activities. That the teaching of evolution might involve activities where students weigh up evidence in the tradition of Darwinian thinking led me to explore how teachers might approach the topic. In a conversation with a teacher recently I asked how the idea of natural selection was approached in his lessons. The reply I got was 'well I am not a biologist but in year 7 (11-12 year olds) we give out worksheets about a load of finches which they fill in. I don't do discussion or debate very often'. There is nothing unusual about this comment, so in searching for the finches task from an existing curriculum (Nuffield, 2008) the following activity was found and described as a discussion activity, though for much older students (16-17 years). The activity is introduced with reference to Darwin's voyage in the *Beagle* and his visit to the Galapagos Islands. Students are asked to read a story about how Darwin's observations of the distribution of finches could be explained by natural selection. Teachers are advised that this could be a good pair or small group activity. The story and questions are as follows:

A long time ago, a small flock of sparrow-like birds called finches were blown out to sea by a fierce storm. They lost their bearings but flew on in search of the mainland, going further and further out to sea. At the point of exhaustion, 600 miles from home, they spotted a speck of land - an island in the middle of the sea. They were saved and could rest, drink and feed before returning home. But this island was perfect: it had abundant seeds and other food, plenty of shelter, nesting sites and (amazingly) no predators or other birds to compete with. Life was much harder on the mainland. There was no need for the birds to move on. Their numbers grew – until they became just a bit too numerous for the little island. Some found it hard to find enough food for themselves or their offspring, and young birds were driven away from areas where food was available. Some birds were forced to fly across the sea to nearby islands. There, they found new territories, also with no predators or other birds to compete with. As the plants and their seeds were just a little different on each island, some birds were better than others at finding and eating the new food sources. Birds which could break open fruits and eat the seeds survived well enough to produce lots of babies. Eventually, after a very long time, all the islands became occupied by these birds but the finches on each island were slightly different.

Scientists believe that this story is just the sort of scenario that happens when new, volcanic islands like the Galapagos are colonised by animals (and plants). It shows how a theory has to include a plausible mechanism to explain events. The questions in this activity are similar to those which a scientist like Darwin would have to deal with when presenting his theory to other (sceptical) scientists. Answer the following questions about the story using Darwin's theory and discuss your answers with a partner or in a small group:

1. Explain why it is unlikely that more than one flock of birds would find the islands in this way at the same time.
2. Suggest two possible reasons why there were no predators on the island.
3. Why were there no other birds to compete with? (see Q1.).
4. Why might some finches survive better than others on the same food sources?
5. Why were the finches slightly different on each island?

The teacher's guide to this activity provides some possible answers that focus on the distance of the islands from the mainland, their volcanic nature and relative 'newness'. It is pointed out that other animals could not get to the islands so easily as birds, and that the size and shape of the finches' beaks indicate that they had evolved to feed on seeds and other food that was different on each island.

I have included this activity as it is presented as a discussion activity and focuses on some of Darwin's key evidence from his voyage, but it is not very inspiring as an argumentation activity. The guide to teachers focuses on question and answer rather than discussion of interesting evidence for and against different arguments. No wonder our teachers reduce such ideas to 'worksheet' activities. How does the teacher plan the groups? Where is the stimulating issue and evidence for discussion? Teachers trying to excite students into scientific enquiry and argumentation need better activities than this for discussion and argument.

A much more stimulating example that requires reasoning and argument from evidence can be found in the Royal Society of Chemistry (RSC) collection called *Tricky tracks* (RSC downloaded 2013). In this activity students are presented with three diagrams showing animal tracks and are asked the following questions:

Carefully study Tricky tracks 1 and write a short account of what you think has happened.

1. Now collect *Tricky tracks 2* from your teacher.
2. What do you **observe** in *Tricky tracks 2*?
3. Why are the two animals heading towards the same point?
4. Now collect *Tricky tracks 3* from your teacher.
5. What do you **observe** in *Tricky tracks 3*?
6. What do you **observe** in *Tricky tracks 1*?
7. Based on what you have found out so far, do you **think** we can ever know what has really happened?
8. What could you do to find out more about the situation?

The difference (and problem) here is that the activity is not presented as a discussion activity, though it does lend itself to being so. Students could discuss in pairs or small groups their ideas to explain the tracks, and what evidence they draw on to argue for what they think has happened. The possible answers here can be more extended than those of the finches activity, suggesting the much richer possibilities this activity presents for questioning evidence. The teacher is advised to accept all possible accounts for question 1, for questions 2, 4 and 5 they should encourage observation, whereas for questions 6 and 7 it is pointed out that we can never know what has really happened, we can only imagine what has happened, thus all theories put forward are valid. The tracks could be identified using a key and hence more could be found out about the behaviour of the animals which would support some theories and not others.

So, though the activity using the finches is more closely related to the substance of Darwin's work and the evidence he used for his theory of evolution, it can so easily be reduced to a worksheet activity that does not necessarily develop enquiry or skills of argumentation. The second activity provides more focus on the nature of evidence in supporting an argument, but has less focus on scientific content. However, we could go back to our dinosaur footprints, and draw on that more stimulating topic to follow up our *Tricky tracks* activity. This would probably require looking at the changing environment over time, and thinking about the variation occurring between dinosaurs and how certain dinosaurs would be adapted to these environmental changes. The task is to construct good discussion/debating activities that would interest students.

On visiting Down House I engaged in an interactive activity which showed an evolutionary chart of big cats, some of which were extinct, some not. The pictures of the cats were placed on tiles, half of which were in fixed positions, the other half were moveable. The task was to look at evidence in the tails, body shape and teeth to decide where each cat should be placed on the chart. If a moveable tile was placed correctly, a light would show 'yes'. The activity was challenging and took much trial and error as well as judgement based on evidence. It showed how difficult it can be assimilating evidence to chart changes. A school argumentation activity that can help students to understand and appreciate arguments for classification was developed in argumentation curriculum activities (Osborne, Erduran & Simon, 2004b). This activity uses cards with statements about the features of creatures that can be used as evidence to classify them in a certain way. The first activity to be developed using this design was called *Euglena*, where characteristics of *Euglena* were presented on cards and the task was to use the cards as evidence for classifying it as plant or animal. The real solution was neither, which did not detract from the value of the activity in stimulating discussion, argument and decision-making based on evidence, but did leave the students feeling a little short changed! A further version of this design was developed using the axolotl (Davies, Simon & Trevethan, 2013), again with statement cards that could be used to classify it as fish, reptile or amphibian. In this case one of the options is correct (amphibian), though initially students do not know which one, so arguments can be presented by different students and shared and their evidence base weighed up to see how valid they might be. Teaching this activity still requires careful consideration of how to handle different outcomes of argumentation. Most students convince themselves (and others) that axolotl is a fish; it requires a good class discussion of the weight of evidence to help students determine the most compelling argument. These activities demonstrate how science is a human activity; we impose order on the differences between organisms because of the relationships between them of the kind Darwin observed. Debates about classification are on-going, based on evidence, and the most significant evidence presented for the axolotl being an amphibian is that it does not have scales, even though it has lots of fish features.

THE DINOSAUR MUSEUM

After finding the dinosaur footprints and seeing how interested large groups of families were in finding these, I wanted to answer some questions – the dinosaur museum had little to offer in direct answer to the question of how the footprints came to be there.

However, we know that for dinosaur footprints to survive, the impression has to be made in soft clay, then baked dry by the sun and then covered in sediment. In this way the footprints can persist in spite of being buried under layers of sediment. That we could see different prints exposed in different layers of rock makes more sense when we understand this. In the museum I looked for activities that would help students look for evidence to support arguments about dinosaurs. The worksheets for children were useful aids for busy parents, with 'fill the gaps' and spaces for drawings, but they did not really focus on evidence. What I did find took me back to Darwin, and gave me an idea for the kind of argumentation activity that has proved very popular – that of role play and debate. On a series of posters, summarised in Hutt (2012), I found a story that begins with Richard Owen, the founder of the Natural History Museum and one of Darwin's greatest critics. Writing of a discovery made near my dinosaur footprints in the year 1854, the poster display of Owen's account reads:

> Part of the skeleton of a young *Iguanodon*, the entire body of which was probably under two yards in length, was discovered in the year 1849. The mass of stone in which this skeleton was imbedded was broken into two parts in its extraction. The workman disposed of one part to one collector, and of the other to another. One collector therefore had that portion which contained the most important part of the skeleton, consisting of seventeen vertebrae, the pelvis, the right hand foot, portions of ribs, part of the left femur, right tibia and fibula. The other portion of the block includes eleven caudal vertebrae, the right femur and (portions) of the tibiae.

Unfortunately the skull was missing from this small dinosaur (about one metre long when entire). At this time, when dinosaurs were new to science, the importance of assembling evidence to try to assimilate the dinosaur was not appreciated, so 'mistakes' were made. When Owen saw the fossil he decided it was a young *Iguanodon*, a plant-eating dinosaur, the bones of which had already been discovered in sites across southern England. Owen's decision that the fossil was a young *Iguanodon* seemed to satisfy everyone until 20 years later, when William Fox, a local curate, found bits of another skeleton and this one had a skull. Fox, like Darwin, had time on his hands to indulge his hobby and was the kind of amateur Darwin liked to work with. Thomas Huxley, a prominent scientist, saw this fossil and decided that it was the same species as the one found earlier, but that they were neither of them *Iguanodon*. His evidence, presented on the poster, was:

> The teeth of this reptile leave no doubt as to its distinctness from *Iguanodon*; and, as I shall immediately bring forward evidence to prove, that difference is generic. I propose, therefore, to name it *Hypsilophodon foxii*.

Thus, Huxley claimed to have recognised a new dinosaur, named for the high ridges on the teeth, and after the man who found it. Fox, being anxious to have corroboration of the evidence regarding his fossil, decided to share the find with Owen, who chose to disagree with Huxley:

The conclusion of the author as to the generic relationship of the species to which this unique fossil skull belonged, were not, however, satisfactory to its discoverer, and he, consequently, placed the specimen in my hands.

Thus began an argument between these two palaeontologists, Owen and Huxley, as Owen claimed that the two fossils were a new species of *Iguanodon*, and he invented a new name *Iguanodon foxii* (Fox's Iguana tooth). This disagreement fuelled the existing feud between Owen and Huxley, already at loggerheads over Darwin's ideas about natural selection. So, who was correct? Was this a new species of *Iguanodon*, or a new genus *Hypsilophodon*? Well Huxley was correct, as many similar finds have proved since 1869. So what makes Owen disagree? One can speculate the following:

– Owen was misled by the similarity of the bones of the two dinosaurs (*Hypsi* and *Iggy*) and needed to see the complete skeletons. He only had bits of limbs, backbones and an incomplete jaw.
– Owen was a famous palaeontologist and did not want to admit his mistake.
– Owen did not want to accept that his protagonist Huxley was correct and he was wrong.
– Should Owen have examined the evidence more closely and admitted his earlier mistake?

One can also speculate as to what Fox would have made of this disagreement between the scientists. Such debates can provide the substance of role play to enhance the ideas and evidence of the times and the influence of the people – they are scientists but they have emotions and personality conflicts. Students can think about how they would portray Fox, Owen and Huxley, what their debate helped us to understand about evidence and the discoveries of the time, set in the context in which Darwin lived and wrote. Interestingly, Darwin himself rarely engaged in public debates; he left that to Huxley.

INSPIRED – BY DARWIN, THE VICTORIANS AND MY LOCAL ENVIRONMENT

Writing this chapter has prompted me to look around and see what might inspire students of today in exploring evidence from the past; to think about fossils, evolutionary theory and to see Darwin's life and work in the context of his time and peers, and also in the light of recent pedagogical ideas of teaching science. In doing so I have used my knowledge and experience of teaching argumentation to think about how evidence we can see today provides us with insights to the past, and how we can inspire students to explore that evidence and construct arguments about it. Such work needs a guide, a teacher or parent to know what to use and how to look for evidence. It remains to say that all the families I watched on the beach that day walked past several dinosaur casts (see Figure 2) without a second glance, though they were clearly situated along the base of the cliff for all to see. You need Darwin's eyes to see what is worth noticing.

Figure 2. Dinosaur cast. (© Shirley Simon)

REFERENCES

Darwin, C. (1859). *On the origin of species by means of natural selection, or the preservation of favoured races in the struggle for life*. London: John Murray.
Darwin, C. (1872). *The origin of species by means of natural selection, or the preservation of favoured races in the struggle for life* (6th ed.). London: John Murray.
Davies, P., Simon, S., & Trevethan, J. (2013). Retrieved from http://www.pstt.org.uk/ext/cpd/argumentation/
Edelson, D. C., Gordin, D. N., & Pea, R. D. (1999). Addressing the challenges of inquiry-based learning through technology and curriculum design. *The Journal of the Learning Sciences, 8*(3, 4), 391–450.
Eiseley, L. (1961). *Darwin's century: Evolution and the men who discovered it*. New York, NY: Anchor Books
Faller-Fritsch, B. (2008). Teaching evolution: A case of better late than never. *School Science Review, 90*(331), 37–42.
Hutt, S. (2012). *Where dinosaurs roamed*. London: West Wight Landscape Partnership.
Kuhn, D. (1991). *The skills of argument*. Cambridge, UK: Cambridge University Press.
Linn, M. C., Davis, E. A., & Bell, P. (2004). *Internet environments for science education*. Mahwah, NJ: Lawrence Erlbaum Associates.
Nuffield. (2008). Retrieved from http://www.nuffieldfoundation.org/science-society/activities-evolution
Osborne, J., Erduran, S., & Simon, S. (2004a). Enhancing the quality of argument in school science. *Journal of Research in Science Teaching, 41*(10), 994–1020.
Osborne, J., Erduran, S., & Simon, S. (2004b). *Ideas, evidence and argument in science. In-service training pack, resource pack and video*. London: Nuffield Foundation. Retrieved from http://www.nationalstemcentre.org.uk/elibrary/resource/6906/ideas-resources; http://www.nationalstemcentre.org.uk/elibrary/collection/1470/ideas-evidence-and-argument-in-science-ideas-pack
RSC. (downloaded 2013). Royal Society of Chemistry. Retrieved from http://media.rsc.org/Nature%20of%20science/NSci-Bbox1.pdf
Simon, S., Erduran, S., & Osborne, J. (2006). Learning to teach argumentation: research and development in the science classroom. *International Journal of Science Education, 28*(2–3), 235–260.
Simon, S., & Richardson, K. (2009). Argumentation in school science: Breaking the tradition of authoritative exposition through a pedagogy that promotes discussion and reasoning. *Argumentation, 23*, 469–493.

Shirley Simon
Institute of Education,
University of London,
UK

PETER KENNETT & CHRIS KING

13. USING DARWIN TO TEACH EARTH SCIENCE

The Development of the Darwin Workshop Methodology

All too many teachers in the UK have suffered 'whole school' Continuing Professional Development (CPD) days, where a highly paid consultant is brought in to cover the latest fad in 'target setting' or 'Health and Safety regulations', and the costs are justified by insisting that all members of staff must attend. More often than not, the only expectation is that they should listen, and try to refrain from nodding off in front of an interminable presentation on the data projector! What would the science staff rather be doing? Usually it would be planning future lessons, and sharing expertise on a departmental basis, possibly carrying out practical work to develop confidence and to find out any possible problems.

Even when CPD is delivered in a more focussed, subject-orientated way, it is all too common for the presenter to speak from the front, and maybe to demonstrate a few practical activities, but seldom to provide an opportunity for delegates to carry out any investigations on their own. Still less is there any incentive to report back on the outcome. Sadly, research has shown that such methods are largely ineffective, as summarised by Adey:

> There is universal condemnation in the research literature on professional development for the one-shot 'INSET day' as a method of bringing about any real change in teaching practice. (2004, p.161)

With this in mind, the Earth Science Education Unit (ESEU) (ESEU website) was formed in 1999, with funding from Oil and Gas UK (then known as UKOOA), to deliver a more hands-on and interactive style of CPD to practising science teachers in schools and trainee (pre-service) teachers in the university sector. On the spot evaluations have shown that the method is valued by participants. The effectiveness of the workshops was substantiated by research carried out on all schools visited by ESEU in 2003/4 (Lydon & King, 2009) and in 2007/8 (King & Thomas, 2011). Most schools which responded (33% response rate in 2003/4; 31% response rate in 2007/8) had modified their schemes of work, with levels of change that ranged from 'significant' (all new ESEU activities incorporated), to 'modest' (some activities included). The 2009 Lydon and King paper noted the addendum of Adey (2004):

> Perhaps the only exception to this rule is the introduction of a very specific technical skill, such as the use of [a] new piece of software. (Adey, 2004, p.161)

It went on to comment:

> The evidence ... indicates that this exception should be extended to include the transmission of practical science teaching ideas (and fostering of skills and confidence in using them, with the associated building of knowledge and understanding), where training is delivered by a well-trained provider, within a well-structured workshop which provides opportunities for exploration, practice, and peer feedback. (Lydon & King, 2009, p. 81)

As the research evidence has indicated, a crucial factor in such workshops has been the involvement of the delegates. During the course of a typical 1½ hour ESEU session, an 'icebreaker activity' is followed by a 'circus' of about eight related activities. Participants are usually only allowed time to carry out one of these, but at least a third of the session is reserved for them to take turns to report on their findings and to demonstrate the activity. For example, one sub-group may have been asked to build up layers of sand and flour in an empty plastic box and then to deform the layers by pushing with a board, resulting in a series of folds and faults in the layers. In the discussion they are prompted to consider what patterns they discerned; whether there were any conflicts of expectation; whether they could apply any of the principles of physics to the outcome, and to consider how realistically they thought the activity represented the 'real world'.

Figure 1. Folding and faulting in an empty chocolate box. (© Peter Kennett)

Once all the sub-groups have reported to the whole group, the session closes with a plenary Earth science activity, usually something spectacular, such as a simulation of volcanic eruptions using exploding party poppers.

In order to develop such workshops, the ESEU adopted the principle of the 'writing weekend', which had already been found effective by the voluntary Earth Science Teachers' Association. A group of ESEU facilitators, all of whom had a background in the Earth sciences at various levels, were incarcerated in a laboratory for two days, with a technician on hand to supply requests for equipment. After an initial gathering where the aims and objectives of the project were outlined, members were allocated part of an overall 1½ hour workshop and then dispersed into small groups to 'brainstorm' with each other, and to develop and test practical ideas in the laboratory. Demonstrations of their work were given to the whole group and the method refined. Nobody was allowed to go home without handing in their notes. Of course, the rigour of such gatherings was mitigated by being well-fed, watered and housed.

Having thus established the method of working, it was subsequently used repeatedly, for example: to develop the Joint Earth Science Education Initiative (JESEI) (see JESEI website); to devise workshops for the upper primary curriculum in Scotland; to develop materials for the teaching of biology, chemistry and physics through an Earth context for the Wellcome Trust Creative Science initiative and to develop ESEU's 'Earth physics' workshops. In all such cases, the ESEU's own team was enhanced by the addition of specialists in their own field, whether primary teachers in Scotland, biologists, chemists and physicists for JESEI or for Creative Science, or representatives from the Institute of Physics for the 'Earth physics' workshops.

During the Association for Science Education Conference in January 2009, the authors were approached by the National Science Learning Centre in York, pointing out that 2009 was the bicentenary of the birth of Charles Darwin. Darwin made significant geological observations, even though these are frequently eclipsed in the popular mind by his biological work. Could the authors develop a 1½ hour workshop on 'Charles Darwin, the Geologist', for presentation at York, please? 'Oh, by the way, the workshop is in March!'

Clearly, there was no time to summon a team for the traditional writing weekend, so the authors worked on their own to devise the workshop, relying where possible on existing practical activities to exemplify Darwin's geological work. The 1989 Penguin abridged edition of *Voyage of the Beagle* provided the main source of information about Darwin's travels, enhanced by quotations from his journals, with further comment on Darwin himself from *Charles Darwin* by C. Aydon (2002).

WORKSHOP – CHARLES DARWIN, THE GEOLOGIST

Introduction

How does one bring Darwin's geological work to life for twenty-first-century students? How accessible are quotations from his notebooks of the 1830s? Was he ahead of his time, or was he 'wrong', judged by our current understanding of the Earth? Is there scope for teaching 'How science works'? Can we find practical and investigative activities which will model some of Darwin's experiences?

With these challenges in mind, the 'Darwin the Geologist' workshop was developed, using the tried and tested ESEU format. The workshop was published in the Darwin bi-centenary year (2009) as an internal ESEU document (Kennett & King, 2009) and much of the information below is taken directly from the booklet that accompanies the workshop.

The 'icebreaker' activity takes the form of a Darwin quiz (in the writing of which we found a few surprises ourselves). Ten activities are laid out on a 'circus' basis, where delegates are invited to carry out one or two activities only, to read the associated 'Darwin connection' material and then to demonstrate their activity in the plenary session, see p. 182. A further eight activities are laid out for brief inspection and five more are described in the accompanying booklet but not displayed. The finale is the party popper 'volcanic eruption', which we think Darwin would have loved, since he spent so much time in active seismic and volcanic regions and was well aware of their unpredictability. The workshop is summarised in Table 1.

Answers to the Darwin Quiz Sheet (see p. 182)

1. a) About 18 months. He got off whenever he could and travelled in the hinterland
2. d) 75%
3. c) Yes – before and during the voyage of the *Beagle*
4. c) Finding fossil shells
5. b) Falkland Islands
6. d) Numbers
7. c) Building a wormery
8. d) Geological Society
9. c) Herbert Spencer
10. c) Agnostic. Darwin wrote towards the end of his life:

> It seems to me absurd to doubt that a man may be an ardent theist and evolutionist. I have never been an atheist in the sense of denying the existence of God. I think that generally, an agnostic would be the most correct description of my state of mind. (Darwin to J. Fordyce, 1879)

11. d) In Westminster Abbey (at Huxley's instigation, not Darwin's wish nor that of his family).
12. c) Drilling for basalt. In 1947 Darwin's theory was tested by drilling on the Bikini and Enewetak atolls of the Marshall Islands in the Pacific Ocean.

Table 1. Activities exemplifying some of Darwin's geological insights C = Circus during workshop: L = Activities for brief inspection: X = Activities not displayed, but with Darwin connections: *Earthlearningidea activity

Activity	Darwin connection
Icebreaker – Darwin Quiz	Darwin in general
Circus of activities during workshop	
C1. Dig up the dinosaur*	*Megatherium* fossils near Bahia Blanca
C2a. Quake shake* C2b. Earthquake prediction*	Earthquake at Valdivia and Callao
C3. Tsunami*	Tsunami damage at Talcuhano
C4a. A valley in 30 seconds* C4b. The Himalayas in 30 seconds*	Concepcion and Peuquenes: origin of marine fossils high up in the Andes
C5a. Crystallisation* C5b. Erosion and transport*	Bahia, Brazil. Speculating about the origin of granite and its subsequent exposure by erosion
C6. Wax volcano*	Witnessing a distant volcanic eruption from Chiloe
C7. Crystal settling	James Island lavas, Galapagos Islands
Finale – Party poppers*	Volcanoes and earthquakes in general
Activities for brief inspection	
L1. What is a fossil?*	*Toxodon* fossil near Montevideo
L2. Surviving an earthquake*	Earthquake at Concepcion: Pile of books
L3a. Geobattleships* L3b. Earthquake distribution on world map	Earthquake at Concepcion cf. England: Speculating about 'subterranean forces'
L4. Grinding & gouging*	Erosion by floating ice? – or grounded ice?
L5. Stone rivers (reading sheet)	Falkland Islands - Darwin stumped!
L6. Darwin's 'big coral atoll idea'*	Darwin's cross sections, vindicated today
L7. Darwin's 'big soil idea'*	Repeating Darwin's wormery observations
Activities not displayed	
X1. Evolution of the horse	Fossil horse tooth at Santa Fe
X2. Extinction of the dinosaurs	Fossil mammals at Bahia Blanca
X3. Student molecules – modelling seismic waves*	Valdivia and Concepcion
X4. Gold panning	Central Chile
X5. Radioactive countdown	Darwin and the age of the Weald, Kent, UK

Table 2. The 'Icebreaker' activity – Darwin quiz sheet

1. How long did Darwin spend at sea actually living on the *Beagle*?
   a) about 18 months
   b) just over 3 years
   c) 4 years
   d) almost 5 years
2. What percentage of the scientific notes that Darwin made on the voyage of the *Beagle* were geological ones?
   a) 0%
   b) 25%
   c) 50%
   d) 75%
3. Did Darwin believe in the immutability of species (that species are fixed)?
   a) No – never
   b) Yes – but only before the voyage
   c) Yes – before and during the voyage
   d) Yes – always
4. What was Darwin's remedy for mountain sickness?
   a) a good walk before bed
   b) drinking tea
   c) finding fossil shells
   d) spending as much time as possible in lowland areas
5. In which group of islands did Darwin spend the most time during the voyage of the *Beagle*?
   a) Cape Verde Islands
   b) Falkland Islands
   c) Galapagos Islands
   d) Mauritius Islands
6. Darwin was not good at:
   a) drawing
   b) writing
   c) remembering
   d) numbers
7. Darwin 'discovered' how soil formed by:
   a) digging pits
   b) mapping areas of different soils
   c) building a wormery
   d) making experimental soils
8. Of which learned society was Darwin made the Secretary in 1838?
   a) Royal Geographical Society
   b) Royal Society
   c) Institute of Biology
   d) Geological Society
9. Who coined the term 'survival of the fittest'?
   a) Thomas Huxley
   b) Charles Darwin
   c) Herbert Spencer
   d) Joseph Hooker
10. Darwin was a/an:
    a) creationist
    b) theist
    c) agnostic
    d) atheist
11. Where is Darwin buried?
    a) in Shrewsbury Cathedral
    b) with the Wedgwood family at St Peter's Church in Maer, Shropshire
    c) beside his wife at St Mary's Church, Downe, Kent
    d) in Westminster Abbey
12. Darwin's theory of atoll formation was later tested by:
    a) mapping atoll shapes
    b) observing coral growth
    c) drilling for basalt
    d) mapping atoll distribution

CIRCUS OF ACTIVITIES DURING THE WORKSHOP

C1. Dig up the dinosaur[1]

Darwin was either incredibly lucky in stumbling upon fossil remains or else was guided by local people. His finds even included a Mylodon bone (extinct giant ground sloth) that still had skin attached to it, displayed on TV by Sir David Attenborough in 2009. Near Bahia Blanca, Darwin wrote:

> We may feel certain that the bones have not been washed out of an older formation, and embedded in a more recent one, because the remains of one of the Edentata were lying in their proper relative position (and partly so in a second case); which could not have happened, without the carcass had been washed to the spot where the skeleton is now entombed *(Voyage of the Beagle,* 1989, p. 97*).* [Edentata include sloths, armadillos and anteaters *ed.*]

The 'Dig up the dinosaur' activity consists of burying a dismembered wooden model dinosaur skeleton in a sand tray, which has a grid marked out on it by elastic bands. Participants are invited to 'dig for the bones' using spoons and paint brushes, and to mark round the outline of each piece on an accompanying sheet of A3 paper, with the grid drawn to the same scale. This ensures that they can then 'think like Darwin' and decide whether the animal became buried where it died, or if it had been washed down in a river and the bones disarticulated and even mixed up with others. The skeleton may then be reconstructed, once all the bits have been recovered from the sand (plywood dinosaur skeleton 'jig-saws' can be purchased for around £2 each from UK toyshops).

Figure 2. Dig up the dinosaur (carefully) (© Peter Kennett)

C2. Earthquakes – Introduction

Darwin experienced at least one earthquake, at Valdivia, in Chile in February 1835. He wrote:

> The day has been memorable in the annals of Valdivia, for the most severe earthquake experienced by the oldest inhabitant. I happened to be on shore,

and was lying down in the wood to rest myself. It came on suddenly, and lasted two minutes; but the time appeared much longer. The rocking of the ground was most sensible. (*Voyage of the Beagle*, 1989, p. 228)

He later visited areas which had been devastated by earthquakes, including Callao in Peru, where in 1746 liquefaction of unconsolidated ground had destroyed buildings:

It has been stated that the land subsided during this memorable shock: I could not discover any proof of this; yet it seems far from improbable, for the form of the coast must certainly have undergone some change since the foundation of the old town; as no people in their senses would willingly have chosen for their building place the narrow spit of shingle on which the ruins now stand. (*Voyage of the Beagle*, 1989, p. 265)

C2a. Quake Shake[2]

The liquefaction of unconsolidated ground and subsidence that can result can be simulated by taking a tray of very wet sand and placing on the surface two heavy masses (e.g. large steel nuts, or sections of lead pipe). If the tray is shaken steadily from side to side, the water wells up and increases the pore water pressure. This reduces the bearing strength of the sand. One mass topples over and begins to sink in; the other does not. Why? Children wrestle with this conundrum and the last thing they think of is that their teacher has 'cheated' by placing a small platform of wood or metal below the sand on one side of the tray! Primary teachers usually seize on this illustration and relate it across the curriculum to 'the house on the rock and the house on sand', but it does show what Darwin had probably understood about the ruination of Callao.

C2b. Earthquake Prediction – When Will the Earthquake Strike?[3]

Darwin's experience of the earthquake at Valdivia shows that earthquakes may occur without apparent warning, but students need to appreciate that the stresses which lead up to rock failure are often built up gradually. This can be modelled using a few house bricks and an elastic rope (bungee). The bungee is attached to the middle brick in a pile of three or four and pulled steadily. Tension is built up in the bungee and also in the onlookers until friction between the bricks is overcome and they suddenly begin to slide over one another. The vibration may be felt through the bench, and can sometimes be demonstrated by watching for ripples in a dish of water placed alongside. So, '... was most sensible' in 1835 means '... was easily felt' today (see Darwin quote p.228). The ripples may also be used to help understand the passage of seismic waves. Although not known as such in Darwin's time, he and his companion tried to estimate the direction from which the vibrations had come (and found it very difficult).

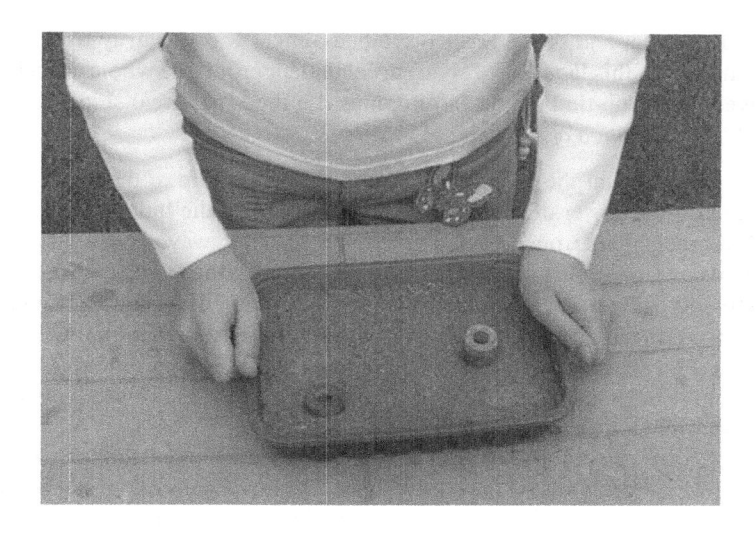

Figure 3. Liquefaction in a sand tray. (© Peter Kennett)

Figure 4. Building up the tension for a brick earthquake. (© Peter Kennett)

C3. Tsunami: What Controls the Speed of a Tsunami Wave?[4]

The mayor-domo of the estate quickly rode down to tell us the terrible news of the great earthquake of the 20th (February 1835); 'that not a house in Concepcion, or Talcuhano, (the port) was standing; that seventy villages were destroyed; and that a great wave had almost washed away the ruins of Talcuhano.' Of this latter fact I soon saw abundant proof; the whole coast being strewed over with timber and furniture, as if a thousand great ships had been wrecked.. .. (*Voyage of the Beagle*, 1989, p. 229)

It is only recently that the general public has become aware of the name 'tsunami' and of the terrible power of such waves. Initial reports of the Indonesian earthquake of 26 December 2004 erroneously referred to the resultant wave as a 'tidal wave', but within two days the geologist's term was being quoted in the media and has remained in use, notably with the catastrophic tsunami in Japan in 2011. Indeed, 'tsunami' is a Japanese word meaning 'harbour wave'. We have also become familiar with tsunami warning systems based on buoys carrying sensors. What controls the speed at which a tsunami may be transmitted across an ocean? Why does the destructive power of a tsunami vary with the coastal profile?

A simple investigation may be carried out using a clear-sided tank, ideally a long wave tank, but a fish tank will do. Add about 10 mm of coloured water to the tank and raise one end of it a few centimetres. Then let it drop from this height onto the bench and time the passage of the surface wave along the length of the tank (or five reflections of the wave, in the case of a fish tank). Will the wave travel more quickly or more slowly if the depth of water is doubled? Try it. The participants are usually divided in their predictions, which engenders a good discussion (the activity clearly shows the deeper the water, the faster the wave).

To model the way in which a tsunami can cause more destruction when it hits a sloping beach, rather than a cliff, a beach may be constructed in modelling clay and tested in the tank.

Figure 5. Timing a 'tsunami' in a wave tank. (© Peter Kennett)

C4. Folding and Faulting – Introduction

The origin of mountain ranges has fascinated scientists for generations, and many of Darwin's days ashore involved trips up into the Andes. Like many before him Charles was aware of the occurrence of marine fossils at considerable altitudes, as shown by this extract:

> Even at the very crest of the Peuquenes, at the height of 13,210 feet, and above it, the black clay-slate contained numerous marine remains, amongst which a gryphaea is the most abundant, likewise shells, resembling turritellae, terebratulae, and an ammonite. It is an old story, but not the less wonderful, to hear of shells, which formerly were crawling about at the bottom of the sea, being now elevated nearly 14,000 feet above its level. The formation probably is of the age of the central parts of the secondary series of Europe [i.e. Mesozoic]. (*Voyage of the Beagle*, 1989, p. 239)

But how did the fossils get there? Until as late as the 1950s, most geologists tended to think of uplift as being caused by movements acting in a vertical sense, although the explanations left much to be desired. It took the plate tectonic revolution of the late 1960s to show that lateral forces were far more commonly the cause. Small wonder then, that Darwin did not apply 'lateral thinking' and tried to explain his observations by vertical movements of the Earth. He did, however, suspect a link between seismic and volcanic activity, which is now an important feature of plate tectonics:

> The elevation of the land to the amount of some feet during these earthquakes appears to be a paroxysmal movement, in a series of lesser and even insensible steps, by which the whole west coast of South America has been raised above the level of the sea. In the same manner, the most violent explosion from any volcano is merely one in a series of lesser eruptions: and we have seen that both these phenomena, which are in so many ways related, are parts of one common action, only modified by local circumstances. (*Voyage of the Beagle*, 1989, p. 239)

C4a. A Valley in 30 Seconds[5]

To encourage students to appreciate the vertical movement of blocks of land, albeit sinking rather than being forced upwards, layers of sand and flour are built up in one half of a plastic box, constrained against a vertical board. When the board is gently moved away, keeping it upright, a normal fault develops in the layers. The fault is steep, i.e. at a high angle to the horizontal, and is typical of rocks which have been under tension. They are commonly seen in rock exposures such as in quarries and coal mines.

Figure 6. A normal fault in a chocolate box. (© Peter Kennett)

C4b. The Himalayas in 30 Seconds[6]

The effects of lateral forces causing compression may be investigated by building up the sand and flour layers across the base of the whole box and then pushing the board from one end. At first, the layers become folded, but before long, low angle thrust faults develop as one layer is forced over another. The whole mass rises above its original elevation, simulating the rise of a mountain chain at a destructive plate margin (where two plates collide). It has taken modern geologists to appreciate the existence of plates and to realise that their boundaries do not necessarily coincide with the coastlines. In the case of the Andes, the East Pacific plate is descending beneath the South American plate and the intervening sediments, fossils and all, are being lifted up to form the mountains. We can forgive Darwin for not reaching this conclusion 130 years sooner (see Figure 1.)

C5. How Did Granite Form?

In the generation before Charles Darwin, there had been a furious dispute between the 'plutonists', who believed that crystalline igneous rocks such as granite formed from molten material, and the 'neptunists', who averred that it formed by crystallisation from aqueous solution. Darwin was strongly influenced by Charles Lyell, who had adopted Hutton's 'plutonist' reasoning. Furthermore, Lyell argued against the current 'catastrophist' view that geological processes happened on a short time scale, and promoted 'uniformitarianism', loosely summarised as, 'the present is the key to the past'. The influence of all these threads can be discerned in Darwin's notebooks and clearly led him to ponder many geological problems. An example is his thinking about how granite formed and how it came to be exposed at the Earth's surface:

> Throughout the coast of Brazil, and certainly for a considerable space inland, from the Rio Plata to Cape St Roque, lat. 5° S, a distance of more than 2,000 geographical miles, wherever solid rock occurs, it belongs to a granitic

formation. The circumstance of this enormous area being thus constituted of materials, which almost every geologist believes to have been crystallized by the action of heat under pressure, gives rise to many curious reflections. Was this effect produced beneath the depths of a profound ocean? or did a covering of strata formerly extend over it, which has since been removed? Can we believe that any power, acting for a time short of infinity, could have denuded [eroded] the granite over so many thousand square leagues [a vast area]? (*Voyage of the Beagle*, 1989, pp. 50-51)

The two activities below bring together the topic of crystallisation and the rate of erosion, which could then reveal a buried granite.

C5a. Crystallisation[7]

If granite had crystallised beneath 'the depths of a profound ocean', then as the liquid rock (magma) emerged it would have crystallised very quickly and would have produced very small crystals. If, however, the magma had been intruded into 'a covering of strata...', then the insulating effect of the overlying rock would have ensured that it crystallised very slowly, producing large crystals. We can test the relationship between cooling rate and crystal size by the use of a relatively 'safe' chemical, 'Salol' (Phenyl salicylate or Phenyl 2-hydroxybenzoate), which melts at 42°C. The Salol is melted carefully, to little more than its melting point, and a drop or two added to three pairs of glass slides, the second slide being used in place of a cover slip. One pair of slides is at room temperature: another pair has been heated and the third pair is taken from a freezer. The crystals on the cold slide usually set almost instantly and are very small: the warm slides produce large crystals, very slowly, whilst the results on the room temperature slides are intermediate. Granite has large crystals, so it can be inferred that it is more likely to have been intruded below a cover of other rocks than to have erupted onto an ocean floor.

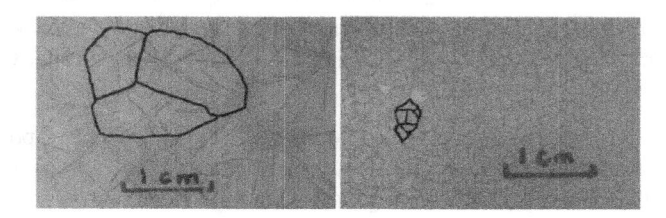

Figure 7. Salol crystals cooled on (a) a pair of slides at room temperature (medium) and (b) a pair of slides from the freezer (fine). (© Peter Kennett)

C5b. Erosion and Transport [8]

So, how can we demonstrate what sort of 'power, acting for a time short of infinity, could have denuded the granite...'? Today, we refer to this process as erosion, and students enjoy a very noisy way of investigating the susceptibility to erosion of a range of rock types. Taking due precautions for asthmatics, fragments of several different rock types are shaken in a plastic bottle for 15 seconds or so, and the effects noted, before the 'shake' is repeated. Most rocks will soon show rounding of their edges and corners, and if they are weighed before and after each phase of shaking, the loss of mass may be measured and plotted.

Figure 8. School pupils enjoying a destructive activity. (© Peter Kennett)

C6. Wax Volcano[9]

Darwin clearly anticipated a link between earthquakes and volcanoes, and probably suspected that the formation of granite from once-liquid magma was linked to the eruption of lavas. The following quotation is typical, written after watching an eruption from Chiloe in January and seeing earthquake devastation at Concepcion in February 1835:

> With respect to the cause of the paroxysmal convulsion in particular portions of the great area which is simultaneously affected, it can be shown to be extremely probable, that it is owing to the giving way of the superincumbent strata, (and this giving way probably is a consequence of the tension from the general elevation) and their interjection by fluid rock – one step in the formation of a mountain chain. On this view we are led to conclude, that the unstratified mass forming the axis of any mountain, has been pumped in when in a fluid state, by as many separate strokes as there were earthquakes. (*Voyage of the Beagle*, 1989, p. 239)

USING DARWIN TO TEACH EARTH SCIENCE

Students can usually understand the surface effects of a volcanic eruption, since they have seen so many superb images on television, but trying to visualise what happens below ground is more challenging. The 'wax volcano' helps to overcome this difficulty, although it pays not to give it the title first.

Melt about 1 cm of coloured candle wax into the bottom of a 500 ml glass beaker. Let it set and then add about 1 cm of clean washed sand and top up with cold water, preferably iced. Ensure the safety of the group and then start heating the base of the beaker with a Bunsen burner, or a Gaz burner, whilst asking the students what they expect to happen. They will usually use their hands to explain as much as their voices, and inevitably, there will be a wide range of views. The presenter cannot be too sure either, which makes it all the more exciting. Suddenly, a plume of molten wax will rise to the surface and spread out to form a 'lava lake' – that's the easy bit. If the water has remained cold, some of the wax will usually rise so far into the sand and water, then stop and set. This replicates the intrusion of magma below a 'covering of strata'. It will only be revealed when the 'surface rocks' have been 'eroded away', which can be simulated by pouring off some of the water, once everything has solidified.

Participants can be asked to discuss in what respects the model gives the opposite result to what they have already learned (the surface 'lava' sets more slowly than the intrusion, since the air temperature is warmer than that of the cold water).

Figure 9. The 'wax volcano' after an eruption of wax onto the surface and the intrusion of wax into the cold water. (© Peter Kennett)

191

C7. Crystal Settling

During the course of a five-week stay in the Galapagos Islands, Darwin studied more than just tortoises and finches. By following a giant tortoise trail up into the hills on James Island, he found a lava (a trachyte) which was paler in colour and of lower density than the more common basalt. He inferred that fractional crystallisation had occurred in an underlying magma chamber – a conclusion which was way ahead of its time. His evidence was only corroborated in 2007/8, when geologists also followed a giant tortoise trail to locate the trachyte (one wonders if it was the same tortoise, given their longevity!). Darwin wrote:

> Lavas are chiefly composed of three varieties of feldspar, varying in specific gravity [relative density] from 2.4 to 2.74; of hornblende and augite, varying from 3.0 to 3.4; or olivine, varying from 3.3 to 3.4; and lastly, of oxides of iron, with specific gravities from 4.8 to 5.2. Hence crystals of feldspar, enveloped in a mass of liquefied, but not highly vesicular lava, would tend to rise to the upper parts; and crystals or granules of the other minerals, thus enveloped, would tend to sink. (Quoted by Gibson, 2009)

The principle may be demonstrated in the lab, although it is not strictly analogous to molten rocks, by half-filling a boiling tube with sodium ethanoate and heating it gently over a Bunsen flame until it dissolves in its own water of crystallisation. Two spatulas of copper sulphate crystals are stirred in and the mixture is allowed to cool. After half an hour or so, two distinct layers of crystals are usually observed, with the white sodium ethanoate lying above the blue copper sulphate.

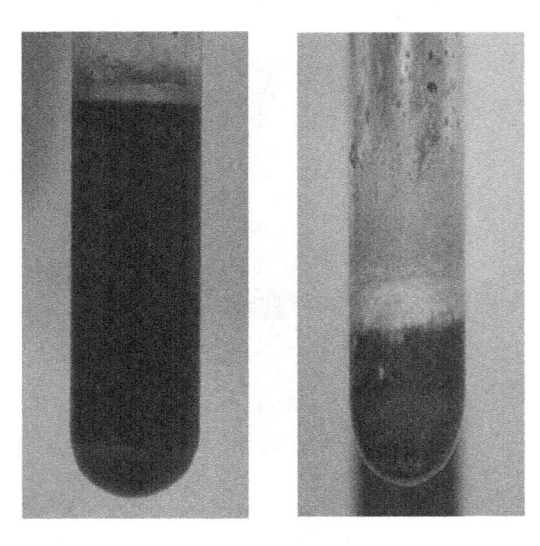

Figure 10. Two stages in crystal settling a) the hot solution of sodium ethanoate and copper sulphate, b) the cold tube showing two distinct layers. (© Peter Kennett)

Feedback

After all activities C1 to C7 have been completed, each sub-group demonstrates its activity to the whole group, teasing the science and the practical applications out of each one.

Finale[10]

Once all the activities have been demonstrated, the participants are invited to consider how predictable a 'volcanic eruption' might be. Several party poppers are set up in clamp stands, with each pull cord tied into a loop. Each popper represents a volcano. How many 100 g masses will it take to set them off? Will they all be the same? Predictions should be discussed before the activity starts and then volunteers are asked to add the masses to a mass hanger on their popper carefully, one by one. The disparity is amazing – so far the total mass needed to set off a party popper has varied from 300 g to 3600 g. The Earthlearningidea (ELI) website contains a set of cards giving real observations which accompany volcanic activity, which can be used to make the activity even more realistic.

Figure 11. Party poppers in action – one went off much sooner than expected. (© Peter Kennett)

OTHER ACTIVITIES

Space does not permit details of the other activities given in Table 1 to be elaborated, but descriptions of many of them may be found on the Earthlearningidea website, as indicated in the table, although mostly without their Darwin links. The Earthlearningidea (ELI) website also contains more than 190 other activities for teaching Earth science (King et al, 2013). Suffice it to note that:

- Activity L4 – 'Grinding and gouging' shows Darwin's ability to change his mind when presented with sufficient evidence. At first he followed Lyell's view that floating ice alone was responsible for transporting erratic blocks, but later revisited Cwm Idwal in Snowdonia in North Wales and realised that ice could also be a powerful erosive agent as it scoured the land surface, which we model in the lab with gritty ice cubes dragged over hardboard.
- Activity L5 – 'Stone rivers' provides a comprehension exercise based on the Falkland Islands section of Darwin's journals, where he was puzzled by these unique features. They are now regarded as being of periglacial origin.
- Activity L6 – Darwin's 'big coral atoll idea'. He was intrigued by the origin of coral atolls (island rings) in tropical seas and proposed that they were formed by corals growing upwards at the same rate as a hidden roughly circular volcanic structure sank beneath them. His hypothesis was tested more than a century later when the Bikini and Eniwetak Atolls were drilled and revealed exactly the sequence of coral and lava which he had predicted. Activity L6 asks participants to model this idea by folding paper sheets, and also gives the method for a demonstration in a fish tank.
- Activity L7 – Darwin's 'big soil idea'. After his return from the *Beagle* expedition, Darwin became engrossed in the origin of soils and experimented with wormeries to demonstrate the vital work of these lowly creatures. The activity shows how to build and run a simple wormery, linked to Darwin's notes.

CONCLUSION

The preparation of the 'Darwin the Geologist' workshop highlighted the impact that geology had on Darwin and Darwin's impact on geological thinking. It showed that there are many opportunities for practical and interactive activities to be presented in the classroom, based on Darwin's research and experiences.

Presentation of the workshop has shown that ESEU's strategy of presenting practical hand-on activities in short interactive workshops continues to be successful, with strong post-course evaluation and the research-based probability of making real impact in classrooms. Most ESEU secondary workshops are available free of charge to schools and teacher-training institutions in the UK (apart from the travelling expenses of a nearby facilitator). The 'Darwin the Geologist' workshop is not free of charge, but a fee can be negotiated for presenting it and the workshop materials can also be made available for a small fee. Please contact the ESEU at the address below for details.

Darwin made a major contribution to geological thinking and his work provides the opportunity for bringing some of this thinking into today's classrooms in novel ways that encourage the development of the critical thinking skills and investigational skills of the pupils of today, helping them to 'think like Darwin thought'.

ACKNOWLEDGEMENTS

We are most grateful to the members of the ESEU Central Team at Keele for their work in making the 'Darwin the Geologist' workshop materials suitable for presentation and internal publication. The ESEU is funded by 'Oil and Gas UK' to disseminate Earth science-based teaching materials, with no editorial requirements relating to oil and gas. ESEU is most grateful for this continued funding.

REFERENCES

Adey, P. (2004). *The professional development of teachers: Practice and theory.* Boston: Kluwer Academic Publishers.
Aydon, C. (2002). *Charles Darwin.* London: Constable.
Darwin, C. (1989). *The Voyage of the Beagle: Charles Darwin's Journal of Researches* (J. Browne & M. Neve, eds.) London: Penguin Classics
Earthlearningidea (ELI). Retrieved May, 2013 from http://www.earthlearningidea.com/ with individual activities shown by suffices:
  1 Dig up the dinosaur – become a fossil hunter and dig up a dinosaur
  2 Quake shake – will my home collapse?
  3 Earthquake predication – when will the earthquake strike?
  4 Tsunami – what controls the speed of a tsunami wave?
  5 A valley in 30 seconds – pulling rocks apart
  6 The Himalayas in 30 seconds! Making a miniature mountain range in an empty box
  7 Why do igneous rocks have different crystal sizes?
  8 Rock, rattle and roll – investigating the resistance of rocks to erosion...
  9 Volcano in the lab – modelling igneous processes in wax and sand
  10 Take a 'Chance' on the volcano erupting – how hazardous is the volcano?
Earth Science Education Unit. (ESEU). Retrieved May, 2013 from http://www.earthscienceeducation.com/
Gibson, S. (2009). Early settler: Darwin the geologist in the Galapagos. *Geoscientist, 19*(2), 19. Retrieved May, 2013 from http://www.geolsoc.org.uk/Geoscientist/Archive/February-2009/Early-settler-Darwin-the-geologist- in-the-Galapagos
Kennett, P., & King, C. (2009). *Darwin the geologist.* Staffordshire: Earth Science Education Unit internal publication: ESEU, Keele University, ST5 5BG.
King, C., & Kennett, P. (2010). Darwin Geólogo: Una selcción de actividades de earthlearnigideas y Earth Science Education Unit. *Enseñanza de las Ciencias de la Tierra, 18*(2), 182–193.
King, C., & Thomas, A. (2011). Earth Science Education Unit: Report on the two year pilot and ten year national rollout (p. 27). Staffordshire: The Earth Science Education Unit internal report, Keele University.
King, C., Kennett, P., & Devon, E. (2013). Earthlearningidea: A worldwide web-based resource of simple but effective teaching activities. *Journal of Geoscience Education, 61,* 37–52.

Joint Earth Science Education Initiative (JESEI). (). Retrieved May, 2013 from http://www.esta-uk.net/jesei/index.htm

Lydon, S., & King, C. (2009). Can a single, short CPD workshop cause change in the classroom? *Professional Development in Education*, 35(1), 63–82.

Peter Kennett & Chris King
Earth Science Education Unit,
Keele University,
UK

CRITICAL THINKING ABOUT WHAT AND HOW WE KNOW

JAMES D. WILLIAMS

14. DARWIN THE SCIENTIST

Working Scientifically

INTRODUCTION

When Charles Darwin was moved to describe himself as a scientist in one of his notebooks, he wrote 'I, a geologist' (Darwin, 1838, p.40). For the majority of people, Darwin is cited most often as a great biologist whose theory of evolution is central to the science of biology, a theory so central that Theodosius Dobzhansky (1900–1975) wrote his now famous essay, *Nothing in biology makes sense except in the light of evolution* (Dobzhansky, 1973).

Darwin as a man was complex. Many have speculated on the illnesses that plagued his later life, the speculations range from Chagas and Ménière's disease to hypochondria. Others have given reasons as to why he delayed publication of his theory, from not wishing to upset his devoutly religious wife to wanting to be sure – by gathering enough scientific evidence – that his 'theory' was indeed correct.

We know much about the circumstances surrounding Darwin's work and how he came up with his theory. The tensions and angst that the letter from Alfred Russel Wallace (1823–1913), that arrived on 18 June 1858, describing 'Darwin's theory' almost exactly, is also well documented[1].

Much less is written about Darwin the scientist and how he conducted his scientific work. Questions that centre on Darwin, his geological, botanical and evolutionary ideas and how he came to his conclusions about natural selection and evolution are useful discussion points on the nature of science and working scientifically in the secondary science classroom. What sort of a scientist was Darwin? Did he employ a particular 'scientific method' in his work and, as he worked across various disciplines (from geology to biology), how did this affect his approach to science?

After establishing the origins of the terms 'scientist' and 'biologist', Darwin's early life will be examined briefly to establish how he acquired his interests and skills in science. Darwin's time on the *Beagle*, mostly charting the geology of the countries visited, developed his early skills as an observational field scientist, but it is when he returns to England that he begins to theorise and more fully develop the scientific methodologies that underpinned his future scientific work.

Using the examples from Darwin's theory of coral atoll formation, his explanation of the then puzzling natural feature of 'parallel roads' in the highland valley of Glen Roy and his painstaking collection of facts to support his theory of evolution alongside his later work on the movement of plants, this chapter will set out to show that science and 'the scientific method', far from being one approach can be conducted in different ways, from theory building to theory confirming. Where science is conducted can also vary from the laboratory to the field, to experiments in home settings.

THE ORIGINS OF THE TERM 'SCIENTIST'

Describing those who work in the various scientific disciplines as 'scientists' is relatively recent with respect to the history of scientific discovery; less than 200 years old. The term, originally coined by William Whewell (1794–1866) in 1834, was intended to replace 'natural philosopher'. Prior to the nineteenth century, 'the sciences' were specialized branches of philosophy that included grammar, logic, rhetoric, arithmetic, music, geometry and astronomy. Science, or the study of science, was synonymous with philosophy and many of the methods employed were philosophical. As the sciences grew in number, attempts to redefine the branches of philosophy resulted in a demarcation between moral philosophy, natural philosophy and metaphysics (Ross, 1962). The term science in its strictest sense simply means 'knowing' or 'knowledge', it was also the name given to a skill acquired through practice.

From the late seventeenth century through the eighteenth and nineteenth centuries, the terms 'science' and 'scientific' became more associated with knowledge acquired through experiment or observation. During this time 'experimental science' and 'experimental philosophy' were being used interchangeably. Natural philosophy was being divided into two distinct branches – speculative and experimental:

> Experimental philosophy was originally a method for acquiring knowledge of nature. On the positive side it emphasised observation and experiment and negatively it decried hypotheses and speculation. Experimental philosophers believed that only when a sufficient number of observations and experiments had been performed was the natural philosopher in a position to theorise. Experimental philosophers' opposition to hypotheses and speculation was based, in part, on the danger of pre-possession, that is, allowing speculative hypotheses to predetermine the way observation was interpreted. Experimental philosophers also criticised the speculative philosophers' lack of recourse to observation, their premature theorising on the basis of speculative hypotheses and especially the way they constructed systems of natural philosophy. (Anstey & Vanzo, 2012, p. 500)

BIOLOGY – THE EMERGING 'NEW' SCIENCE

The word biology, with its meaning of 'knowledge of life' or the 'science of life', can be traced back to 1766, in the title of a book by the German meteorologist Michael Christoph Hanow (1695–1773). The use of the word to describe the discipline that we would now recognize as biology really took hold in the late eighteenth and early nineteenth centuries. It was independently coined by four naturalists: Thomas Beddoes (1799); Karl Friedrich Burdach (1800); Gottfried Reinhold Treviranus (1802); and Jean-Baptiste Lamarck (1802) (Coleman, 1978).

During the eighteenth and nineteenth centuries biology, with its sub disciplines of zoology and botany, developed as a professional scientific subject. From applying experimental techniques, derived from chemistry and physics, to the study of living things and investigating how living organisms interact with their surrounding environment, the work of explorers such as Alexander von Humboldt (1769–1859) – an inspiration to Darwin – laid a foundation for biology as well as the development of related disciplines such as biogeography, whose champion was Darwin's co-discoverer, Alfred Russel Wallace.

During this period scientists began to question 'accepted' knowledge, such as the idea that plants and animals do not change over time (immutability). Cell theory was developed and revolutionise the basis on which we understand how living things are constructed. How life began was also being questioned and the theory of spontaneous generation was rejected by the end of the nineteenth century.

The scene was being set for the development of a revolutionary theory to explain the observations being made about how living things grow and develop and how the ever-growing diversity of flora and fauna could be explained as explorers visited new countries and new environments were discovered. These ideas were synthesised in Darwin and Wallace's theory of evolution by natural selection.

DARWIN – THE MAKING OF A SCIENTIST

School was not, for the young Darwin, a positive and developmental experience. 'Nothing could have been worse for the development of my mind... the school as a means of education to me was simply a blank' (Darwin, 1958, p.9). By his own account, Darwin felt that he was below the common standard in intellect.

As a child Darwin was a passionate collector, minerals being one of his enduring loves. From the age of 10, after a visit to Wales, he started collecting insects. One of Darwin's brothers, Erasmus (named after his grandfather), was interested in chemistry and built a chemical laboratory in an outhouse of the family home. The young Darwin became interested and worked with his brother. This, he believed was the best part of his 'education' as it showed him 'the meaning of experimental science' (Darwin, 1958, p.11). His love of chemistry earned him the nickname 'Gas' at school.

As he failed to excel in school, the young Darwin was sent to Edinburgh University at the age of 16 to follow the family tradition and train as a physician. His training was never completed as he found anatomy and dissection 'disgusting'. At Edinburgh he also studied geology, but that was also for him 'dull'.

Having failed to qualify in medicine, Darwin was moved to Cambridge to become a clergyman – a respectable career for the son of a gentleman and physician. It was here he developed a passion for collecting beetles and his love of geology was ignited by the clergyman, botanist and geologist John Stevens Henslow (1796–1861). Accompanying the geologist Adam Sedgwick (1785– 1873) on a field trip to North Wales, Darwin began to learn the skills of a field geologist, skills that would be invaluable on his *Beagle* voyage.

Throughout his childhood and during his university education Darwin was gaining various skills and experiences that would equip him as a naturalist and explorer. Through collecting minerals, insects and beetles he developed keen observational skills and grasped classification. Working with his brother taught him experimental skills. Looking at the geological features of North Wales showed Darwin how to interpret natural structures.

Having completed his theology degree, Darwin's next adventure was to travel with Captain Robert FitzRoy as companion and geologist on board the Royal Navy ship HMS *Beagle*.

SCIENCE ON THE *BEAGLE*

Darwin's initial role on board the *Beagle* was to act as a companion for the Captain and to study the geology of the countries visited. The post of naturalist on board Royal Navy ships was traditionally given to the ship's surgeon. On board ship, Robert McCormick had this role as well as looking after the health of the captain and crew, but McCormick requested leave from the *Beagle* as he felt his role as naturalist was being undermined by the Captain's companion, Charles Darwin. Dubbed 'Philos'[2] by the captain, Darwin used his previously gained skills to understand the natural history of the various countries visited:

> On first examining a new district nothing can appear more hopeless than the chaos of rocks; but by recording the stratification and nature of the rocks and fossils at many points, always reasoning and predicting what will be found elsewhere, light soon begins to dawn on the district, and the structure of the whole becomes more or less intelligible. (Darwin, 1958, pp. 28-29)

Here Darwin is clearly using a hypothetico-deductive approach. He begins with general observations then develops an initial explanation (hypothesis) which allows him to predict (and deduce) what will be found elsewhere and he then tests those predictions through further field observations.

Although famous for his work as a 'naturalist' on the *Beagle*, a common misconception is that Darwin spent most of his time collecting plants and animals and that it was this which inspired and led directly to his formulation of a theory of evolution. In fact during the whole of his voyage, his pages of notes on geology vastly outnumbered those on animals: 1,383 pages to 368 (Herbert, 1991, p.163).

Even when he did collect animal specimens, e.g. the finches of the Galapagos, he was not the most meticulous recorder of locations. The various finches that he gathered were sometimes misidentified and he failed to note the various islands from where the specimens were collected. In this respect Darwin had failings as a field scientist, but it is worth remembering that he was still only 26 years of age and spent only five weeks on the islands. Evidence from his correspondence shows that he was more interested in the geology of the area than the exotic flora and fauna:

> In a few days' time the Beagle will sail for the Galapagos Islands. I look forward with joy and interest to this, both as being somewhat nearer to England and for the sake of having a good look at an active volcano. (F. Darwin & Seward, 1903, p. 26)

The significance of the finches was only realized after Darwin's return and after extensive examination by the ornithologist John Gould (1804–1881). The name 'Darwin's finches' was only given to the collection in 1936 in his honour.

Darwin's skill in dissection, something he hated as a medical student, was developed as he dissected barnacles collected during the voyage and observed their structure through a dissecting microscope. This marked the start of his long work on barnacles, resulting in a monograph that is still used today as a defining work on the various species and varieties of barnacles.

The voyage of the *Beagle*, while undoubtedly providing Darwin with a mass of observations and a thorough grounding across the sciences, was not in itself sufficient to arrive by induction at a theory of evolution. The process of induction, or inductive thinking, begins not with any hypothesis, but with the data itself. From looking at the data or examining the observations, general conclusions are drawn up. On his return to England, Darwin started to theorise, initially not in biology, but in geology.

INDUCTION, DEDUCTION AND HYPOTHETICO-DEDUCTIVE REASONING

Put simply, we can think of induction and deduction as either theory building or theory testing. Inductive reasoning in science takes general observations and facts and builds an explanation for those facts – theory building. True inductive reasoning does not start with a theory; any hypothesis also would come not before the collection of any observations or data, but from an initial examination of any observations/data.

In strict deductive thinking you start with premises that you accept to be 'true' and from the available data or observations, make a deduction, for example:

- Insects have three body segments and six legs
- A spider has two body segments and eight legs
- Therefore a spider is not an insect

The first two statements (premises) are true leading to a true conclusion.

Hypothetico-deductive reasoning is theory testing. It is the process of testing explanatory ideas, hypotheses or theories. Strictly speaking, deductive reasoning is 'truth preserving'; if the initial premise (s) is/are true then the conclusion must also be true. Put another way, if the theory is true, then any prediction from such a theory is also true. Karl Popper, however, showed that it is not possible to prove any scientific theory is true; you can only show that a theory is false. The test of any theory then is whether or not the predictions that the theory generates can be shown to be correct (in which case the theory is supported) or false, in which case the theory cannot be 'true'. No matter how much support a theory may gain from confirmed predictions, just one failed test means that the theory must be rejected or modified to take account of the new evidence.

DARWIN'S FIRST THEORIES

Darwin's first theories resulted in both success and abject failure. On the one hand he devised a theory to account for the formation of island coral atolls; this was, much later, proven to be correct and a stunning intellectual achievement. He also proposed a theory to account for the 'parallel roads' – a natural phenomenon – found in Glen Roy, Scotland, which proved completely incorrect.

Using his knowledge of raised beaches observed in Chile, Darwin proposed that similar features at Glen Roy were created in the same way. He theorized that the whole region had gradually risen out of the sea and the ledges that formed the 'roads' on the sides of the valley were fossilized raised beaches. Unlike the beaches in Chile, Darwin found no fossils to support his theory. Undaunted he presented his theory to the Geological Society of London in 1839. Soon after, his ideas were dismantled by the Swiss geologist Louis Agassiz who correctly proposed that the roads were the result of an ancient glaciation.

This event may well have been a factor in Darwin's delay in publishing his theory of evolution. Many years later, in 1863 he wrote to a young scientist, John Scott, offering advice on publishing:

> I would suggest to you the advantage at present of being very sparing in introducing theory in your papers (I formerly erred much in geology in that way) let theory guide your observations, but till your reputation is well established be sparing in publishing theory. It makes persons doubt your observations. (Darwin, 1863)

Clearly the incorrect conclusion of his Glen Roy theory had a lasting effect on Darwin. Yet this did not deter him from publishing another geological theory on the formation of coral reefs in 1842. This theory was much better received and confirmed as correct 100 years later when the United States Atomic Energy Commission carried out test drillings at the Pacific Enewetak Atoll in 1952.

DARWIN'S METHODOLOGY

In his autobiography Darwin was clear about the methodology he used to arrive at his theory of evolution. He claimed to use 'true Baconian principles and without any theory collected facts on a wholesale scale' (Darwin, 1958, p.42). This has been disputed by Ayala (2009) who sees a contradiction between what Darwin wrote in his autobiography and what he actually did in the course of developing his theory of evolution. From the evidence of Darwin's own notebooks and accounts of his time after returning from his *Beagle* voyage, including his failed Glen Roy roads theory, it seems that he did indeed have ideas/hypotheses to explain how evolution works and he subsequently took a long time to try and gather evidence to support and test his ideas. In this sense, Darwin was not working on strict Baconian principles. He was not proceeding by accumulating experimental facts and moving towards a general theory to explain them – this being the inductive principle that underpins the Baconian method.

Years later Darwin admits as much in a letter to Asa Gray: 'my work will be grievously hypothetical & large parts by no means worthy of being called inductive; my commonest error being probably induction from too few facts' (Darwin, 1857). Yet at this point he had spent nearly 20 years gathering evidence to support his theory and within a year would be pushed to publish with the arrival of Wallace's letter.

The notion of conducting an experiment in evolution is, in itself, problematic. We know that evolution takes place in populations and involves large timescales. Where speciation has been observed in nature, e.g. in *Drosophila*, cichlid fish and even morphological speciation in mice, the resultant species is still very closely related and morphologically similar to its predecessor. This has led to such instances being called microevolution and, as such, distinct from macroevolution, e.g. the evolution of birds from dinosaurs or whales from land mammals.

Much of modern biology is conducted experimentally, yet the theory of evolution by means of natural selection is often not at the core of this experimental work (Skell, 2005). That said evolution is used often in explanations and generalisations from experimental work.

Darwin had developed theories which, at the time, were accepted as inductive in nature, e.g. his theory of coral island atoll formation. In the case of the coral atolls, the prevailing idea was that they formed by growing on the submerged remains of volcanoes, specifically around the rim of the craters. For Darwin, however, this did not ring true. Having studied marine life in Edinburgh, during his failed attempt at medicine, he knew that the creatures that made up the coral atolls could not survive in deep water. Even before he left on his voyage on board the *Beagle* Darwin had formulated an idea as to how such atolls could form. Instead of the reef building on the rim of a submerged volcano the reef would build up on the slopes of a volcano protruding from the sea. As the ocean floor subsided and the peak of the volcano disappeared, the reef would remain. So Darwin developed a hypothesis and, on his voyage on the *Beagle*, that hypothesis was tested and at that time was the best explanation. To be truly 'inductive' in nature Darwin would have to have made many observations and only then generated his theory from the observed facts.

How Darwin worked was not simply to observe, collect facts and then generate a 'theory', but to start with a hypothesis, collect data to support or refute the hypothesis and in so doing arrive at a general theory. This way of working shows Darwin to be much more of a hypothetico-deductive scientist than an inductive scientist. By his own admission, Darwin had conceived of his idea of natural selection as early as

1838. The following 20 years were spent gathering evidence to support (or refute) this idea. The idea of natural selection we may indeed call a hypothesis at this stage. It is a speculative explanation that needs to be tested. How Darwin tested his hypothesis is evident in his work on barnacles, orchid fertilisation, climbing plants etc. All these were tests in some way or other of his earlier 'hypothesis' of natural selection. So why did Darwin say that his method of scientific working was 'Baconian' when clearly it was not?

Ayala (2009) surmises that there were two possible reasons. The term hypothesis was, unlike its use in modern science, mostly applied to metaphysics, a branch of philosophy concerned with the nature of 'being'. As such it would not have been used in the newer experimental philosophies which were more concerned with explanations of natural phenomenon than understanding the nature of 'being'. While Darwin did undoubtedly develop hypotheses in the modern sense of the word he is unlikely to have admitted this in any description of how he worked fearing that he would be seen to be working on metaphysics rather than investigating natural phenomena and deriving explanations for those natural events. Darwin did not wish for his ideas to be classed as metaphysics and so he avoided using the term.

THE POWER OF PREDICTION

One of the most powerful aspects of any scientific theory is the ability to make predictions on the basis of that theory. Can the theory of evolution be predictive? One simple illustration of the predictive power of evolution comes from a later work by Darwin, *The descent of man*:

> In each great region of the world the living mammals are closely related to the extinct species of the same region. It is therefore probable that Africa was formerly inhabited by extinct apes closely allied to the gorilla and chimpanzee; and as these two species are now man's nearest allies, it is somewhat more probable that our early progenitors lived on the African continent than elsewhere. (Darwin, 1901, p. 240)

At the time little was known about human evolution. Although fossilized remains of Neanderthals had been discovered in 1829, the discovery was made in Belgium, not Africa. *Dryopithecus*, also mentioned by Darwin, had been found in France, but the idea of a migration out of Africa seemed the correct inference to Darwin as a result of looking not just at the relationship between modern humans and our ancestors, but also at their probable diet and characteristics.

OBJECTIONS TO DARWIN'S THEORY

When *On the origin of species* was published in 1859 its reception has often been stated as a huge success – a sell-out. However, its reception in scientific circles generated a range of views from immediate acceptance to complete rejection. In pre-Darwinian Victorian Britain many naturalists, including, initially, Darwin himself, did not question theistic interpretations of the natural world. The idea of the creation of separate 'types' of plants and animals was not questioned; many scientific texts of the day were testaments to God's creative works. The very popular *Natural Theology* by William Paley, published in 1802 – famous for his watchmaker analogy and more recently used in a modified form by Intelligent Design creationists – was an influential book. Another publication, the very ambitious Bridgewater Treatise series of books published in the 1830s and 1840s, was written by the most eminent natural philosophers of the day.

Even after Darwin and Wallace's theory was announced and the publication of *On the origin of species,* texts linking science to the Bible were still very popular, such as *Moses and geology or the harmony of the bible with science* (Kinns, 1882), a book endorsed by Queen Victoria with a long list of subscribers from clergymen to scientists and members of the aristocracy.

The objections to Darwin's ideas came principally in two forms: firstly, an objection on the grounds that it was a wholly naturalistic explanation for the development and diversity of life and, as such, challenged the prevailing accepted metaphysical explanations which naturalists had been trying to reconcile with the science of the day; and secondly, that Darwin's methodology was not rigorous and so threw into doubt the validity of his conclusions (Rudolph & Stewart, 1998).

DARWIN THE EXPERIMENTAL SCIENTIST

Darwin's first experience of true experimental science was, as described earlier, undertaken in the homebuilt chemistry lab constructed by his brother Erasmus. This was not his only brush with experimental science. Working with his son Francis, he published *The power of movement in plants* (Darwin, 1880). Darwin's work on plants is less well known that his other work, but he dedicated over twenty years to their study. Unlike his English contemporaries who, rather than experiment on plants, simply classified them, Darwin investigated their physiology. One of his most important discoveries in botany is an explanation of the movement of plants, particularly in response to gravity. He determined that the response was most sensitive in the tip of growing roots and that if the tip was removed, the plant root did not grow downwards if laid horizontally, but continued growing horizontally until a new tip grew. Only then would the root return to growing downwards. These findings contradicted the explanations of root growth in response to gravity by a German botanist, Julius Sachs (1832–1897) who did not agree that the tips of the roots were the site of sensitivity and control.

Sachs attacked Darwin's ideas not with counter evidence, but by criticizing his experimental skills and the fact he was conducting such experiments at his home, whereas Sachs had a scientific laboratory and instruments at his disposal:

> In such experiments with roots not only is the greatest precaution necessary, but also the experience of years and extensive knowledge of vegetable physiology,

to avoid falling into errors, as did Charles Darwin and his son Francis, who on the basis of experiments which were unskillfully made and improperly explained, came to the conclusion, as wonderful as it was sensational, that the growing point of the root, like the brain of an animal, dominates the various movements in the root. (Quoted in Chadarevian, 1996, pp. 17-18)

Such a criticism, either on experimental design, precision and rigour, or on the expertise of the scientist, is not uncommon in science today. A key aspect of scientists' current work is ensuring that the experimental design, procedures and the actual data collected are available for both scrutiny and replication. Replicating experiments is one way of verifying and testing the validity of any new science being presented. A failure to replicate experiments can mean that the new science is rejected, e.g. cold fusion science.

DARWIN'S THEORIES AS ILLUSTRATIONS OF 'WORKING SCIENTIFICALLY'

Darwin and his scientific work is helpful in showing that when scientists work, they do not follow one single method and that science can be conducted in a range of ways, from field science to laboratory-based experimental science. Darwin also shows us that thinking skills, logic etc. are vital components in the work of the professional scientist. Examining his successful and unsuccessful theories we can also see where he went wrong and how, in the case of his Glen Roy theory, he was less than rigorous in his scientific working.

Darwin's theories, geological and biological, illustrate his use of inference. They serve in more than one way as illustrations of aspects of 'working scientifically' in the classroom.

While Darwin claimed in his autobiography to use inductive reasoning, it is clear that this is not the whole story. He used, mostly, hypothetico-deductive reasoning, where he started with ideas or hypotheses he thought were correct and sought evidence to support them.

CONCLUSION

Examining how Darwin developed and worked as a scientist and looking in more detail, not just at his theory of evolution but also his other work as a geologist, we can see various aspects of working scientifically that are helpful in explaining the nature of science to children. Seeing how Darwin used evidence to support his theories is a good illustration of hypothetico-deductive working. It also illustrates how, in ignoring a lack of evidence in one instance, it meant that he invoked a completely incorrect, though plausible, theory which in the light of new and better evidence was overturned and shown to be wrong.

Darwin's run-in with Sachs illustrates how scientists can sometimes defend their ideas badly, by attacking the scientist rather than their evidence or conclusions. Amateurs accounted for the majority of Victorian scientists. Today science is mostly a professional pursuit and making new discoveries may require very expensive equipment and laboratory facilities. Certain fields, such as astronomy, are still areas where the informed amateur can make scientifically worthwhile discoveries. Home-based science is still possible and new discoveries are still made. The case of the BBC radio experiment on the homing instincts of snails, devised by a non-scientist and conducted in conjunction with a practising scientist, shows that even simple questions, if investigated correctly, can yield interesting results to the body of scientific knowledge (Brooks, 2010).

Investigations of Darwin and Wallace's ideas over the past 160 years shows that far from being a speculative hypothesis, the theory of evolution by means of natural selection has stood the test of time. This does not mean that modifications have not been made or that the theory is no longer being tested. One of the strengths of science that needs to be conveyed is that, rather than seeking to be a static and permanent body of knowledge and a description of natural phenomena, it seeks to find explanations (theories) which, in the light of new evidence, can and will be modified or rejected.

NOTES

[1] Many biographies of Darwin and Wallace describe the events surrounding the arrival of Wallace's letter. e.g. Browne, J. (2002) *Charles Darwin: the power of place*, London: Jonathan Cape; Fichman, M. (2004) *An elusive Victorian: the evolution of Alfred Russel Wallace*, Chicago: University of Chicago Press.

[2] Darwin's nickname came from the Captain's view of him more as the ship's philosopher than naturalist. Over his lifetime Darwin had a range of nicknames including 'the Sage of Down' with T. H. Huxley's calling him 'the Czar of Down' or 'the Pope of Science'.

REFERENCES

Anstey, P., & Vanzo, A. (2012). The origins of early modern experimental philosophy. *Intellectual History Review*, 22(4), 499–518.

Ayala, F. J. (2009). Darwin and the scientific method. *Proceedings of the National Academy of Sciences*, 106(Supplement 1), 10033–10039.

Brooks, R. (2010). BBC - Radio 4 - So you want to be a scientist? - The Experiments - homing snails experiment. Retrieved August 15, 2013 from http://www.bbc.co.uk/radio4/features/so-you-want-to-be-a-scientist/experiments/homing-snails/results/

Chadarevian, S. D. (1996). Laboratory science versus country-house experiments. The controversy between Julius Sachs and Charles Darwin. *The British Journal for the History of Science*, 29(1), 17–41.

Coleman, W. (1978). *Biology in the nineteenth century: problems of form, function and transformation* (Cambridge Studies in the History of Science). Cambridge: Cambridge University Press.

Darwin, C. (1857). *Charles Darwin to Asa Gray, 29 November, 1857*. Retrieved August 31, 2013 from Darwin Correspondence Database website: http://www.darwinproject.ac.uk/letter/entry-2176

Darwin, C. (1863). *Charles Darwin to John Scott, 6 June, 1863*. Retieved August 15, 2013 from Darwin Correspondence Database website: http://www.darwinproject.ac.uk/letter/entry-4206

Darwin, C. (1880). *The power of movement in plants*. London: John Murray.

Darwin, C. (1901). *The descent of man and selection in relation to sex*. London: John Murray.

Darwin, C. (1958). *Autobiography and selected letters*. London: Dover Publications.

Darwin, C. (1838). Notebook M: Metaphysics on morals and speculations on expression. Retrieved August 15, 2013 from Darwin online website: http://darwin-online.org.uk/

Darwin, F., & Seward, A. C. (Eds.). (1903). *More letters of Charles Darwin. A record of his work in a series of hitherto unpublished letters* (Vol. 1). London: John Murray.

Dobzhansky, T. (1973). Nothing in biology makes sense except in the light of evolution. *The American Biology Teacher, 35*(3), 125–129.

Herbert, S. (1991). Charles Darwin as a prospective geological author. *The British Journal for the History of Science, 24*(2), 159–192. doi: 10.1017/S0007087400027060

Kinns, S. (1882). *Moses and geology*. London: Cassell.

Ross, S. (1962). Scientist: The story of a word. *Annals of Science, 18*(2), 65–85.

Rudolph, J. L., & Stewart, J. (1998). Evolution and the nature of science: on the historical discord and its implications for education. *Journal of Research in Science Teaching, 35*(10), 1069–1089.

Skell, P. (2005). Why do we invoke Darwin? *The Scientist, 19*(16), 10.

James D. Williams
School of Education and Social Work,
University of Sussex,
UK

RALPH LEVINSON

15. TEACHING EVOLUTION IN SCHOOLS

A Matter of Controversy?

INTRODUCTION

In a clip from YouTube Richard Dawkins says 'Who cares about creationists? They don't know anything'.[1] Like Dawkins, I agree that creationism has nothing to offer as an explanation for the origins and diversity of life on this planet. Although I am not a professional biologist everything I have read and heard, including Darwin's *On the origin of species*, has so far convinced me that evolution is a fact, and that while there are different explanations to account for evolution none have to date undermined it. But I wonder whether the more one rails against creationism and creationists the more likely that the latter will feel impelled to push their case. Ruse (2007) suggests that comments such as Dawkins' tend to alienate young people coming from a creationist background grappling with the complexity and enormity of the change of worldview that the fact of evolution offers. If those to whom you are closest, who you love and who have sustained you are called 'ignorant' and worse, it is hardly likely to endear to you those who see you as ignorant as you try and 'cross the border' (Aikenhead, 1996) into a different way of thinking about nature.

This chapter focuses on the nature of controversy in teaching evolution. In so doing my sights are set on young people at school whose beliefs are challenged, rather than those creationists fighting a cynical battle to make their views heard (Pennock, 2007). To take another quote from Dawkins in the same YouTube clip about Darwinism. 'It's not a controversial issue. It's absolutely certain. It's about as certain as the fact that the Earth and other planets orbit the Sun'. From one perspective, that of the scientific community, Dawkins is right. But from an everyday perspective it seems odd that people like Dawkins spend much of their working lives writing books, appearing on the media, dedicating websites to a matter which is uncontroversial. To understand whether teaching evolution in schools and dealing with creationist viewpoints is controversial or not I want to explore what is meant by controversy to shed light on this dispute. This has, I will argue, pedagogic implications.

THE NATURE OF CONTROVERSY

Controversy presupposes different points of view or perspectives on a matter under consideration. At a basic level almost all conversations are controversial; it would hardly be worth talking to each other at any length if we agreed on everything; such interchanges would be tiresome. Most conversations do not necessarily reveal deep differences because people tend to keep company with those whose views they are sympathetic to. But it is often when people are most perturbed by something someone says that they start to examine more closely their own viewpoints. For example I listen occasionally to a programme on BBC Radio 4 called *The moral maze* where contemporary issues are discussed by a panel whose members have different perspectives. I like this programme partly because one of the panellists expounds views (including, incidentally, those in defence of creationist teaching) which are almost always completely antithetical to mine and which I often find repellent. Occasionally she says something which challenges an unexamined belief which forces me to reconsider or more thoroughly justify that belief. Part of that process involves an inner conversation which goes something like this:

Inner voice 1: What X has said is ridiculous.
Inner voice 2: Perhaps. But why did you say that it's ridiculous?
Inner voice 1: Because for all right-thinking people such and such is the case and X says that it's not true.
Inner voice 2: So why do you think it's true?

And so on. In other words, conversations which involve differences can be inner dialogues often prompted by what others have said.

Such a provocation is therefore educational, although uncomfortable. Hand and Levinson (2012) have argued that participants taking extreme positions in a controversial issue help others to think carefully about where their views might appear on the spectrum. From another research perspective, studies in cognitive psychology demonstrate that when individuals disagree about solutions to a problem and both get it wrong they make greater cognitive gains than those who agree about the solution to the problem whether wrong or right (Schwarz et al., 2000).

Most definitions of controversy take a normative view. For example, take the following depiction: controversial issues are those '.. . about which there is no one fixed or universally held point of view. Such issues are those which commonly divide society and for which significant groups offer conflicting explanations and solutions' (Crick, 1998, p.56). Hess (2009) teases out her definition of controversy in the context of controversial political issues (i.e. those predominantly in the public domain and of public importance). She identifies some key pre-requisites of controversial issues: that they are open questions with answers that are both strikingly different and legitimate. There are problems, however, with these descriptions of controversy. They assume that what is at question is commonly and publicly known. But that is not always the case even in broadly open and democratic societies. There may be marginalised groups who are unwilling to make their views public. Consider the case of a young person brought up in a fundamentalist religious community (plenty of these exist, of course, in the midst of highly secular societies) who, having been able to listen to views outside their own community, doubts the existence of God or indeed that all life was created in a week about 6000 years ago. It would require enormous courage, and possibly recklessness, to put forward such ideas to their own community for deliberation. The same could be said about someone with decidedly creationist views sitting in a meeting of a humanist association although one might speculate why they were there in the first place. In other words, it is not enough to say that controversy is where we see or hear it (witness also my point above about *inner* dialogue), there need to be certain conditions present such as tolerance, respect, openness and honesty for such views to be aired and to be made public, what have been referred to as appropriate dispositions (Bridges, 1979) or communicative virtues (Burbules & Rice, 1991). Conditions like these do not always arise naturally; frequently, they have to be taught and nourished.

But these accounts of controversy lack an epistemic dimension. To say that a view is legitimate is to allow that the view is acceptable not just because lots of people believe in it but because there are good reasons for it. This is the view of controversy as expounded by Dearden (1981): 'a matter is controversial if contrary views can be held on it without these views being contrary to reason' (Dearden 1981, p.38). 'What is controversial', argues Dearden, is 'precisely the truth, correctness or rightness of view, which presupposes that at least it makes sense to search for these things even if we do not attain them' (Dearden 1981, p. 40). What follows from Dearden's view is that an exchange is controversial, or has the potential to be controversial, if reasons are given (i.e. evidence drawn from attested theoretical foundations which are consistent with a given point of view). Controversial issues can be taught – students can learn how reasoning supports a particular perspective, something which can be drawn from pedagogies associated with critical thinking (Bailin & Siegel, 2003). For a controversy to take place there needs to be sound and different reasons proposed, as well as an appropriately receptive but critical social atmosphere.

DIFFERENT LEVELS OF CONTROVERSY

These, then, are the basic conditions that operationalise controversy. In Levinson (2006) I pointed out that there are different types of controversy. Briefly these differences can be summarised as follows:

1. Differences where matters can be settled one way or the other when sufficient evidence can be available. Sometimes this evidence might be uncertain and difficult to interpret.
2. Differences of priority or significance.
3. Differences through meaning of a concept or term.
4. Differences of personal, communal or social interest.
5. Differences about a whole range of fundamental value positions.

What comes to mind in the last case is Thomas Kuhn's (1962) theory of scientific revolutions. Kuhn argues that a shift occurs in theory about such matters as an Earth-centred/Sun-centred universe, Divine creation/evolution, oxygen/phlogiston. These shifts are so fundamental in explaining the world that thinkers of the old schools and new schools use ideas and language which are incommensurate and incompatible, the new concepts simply do not fit into the conceptual frameworks and language of the old-school thinkers. These different ways of thinking are called paradigms. Language, concepts and evidence are interlinked within each paradigm but cannot be used in the paradigms that have come to replace them. Explanations of species diversity from a literal biblical creationist point of view are simply incompatible with those of an evolutionist. You cannot be an evolutionist and a literal creationist. However, differences of view can lie within paradigms, for example, different explanations for mechanisms of natural selection.

A prominent example of a recent controversy within the natural selection paradigm is the explanation for the formation of new species. Darwin maintained that evolutionary change takes place gradually (a phenomenon known as phyletic gradualism) over time but more recently this has been challenged. Palaeontological evidence shows that trilobites barely changed morphologically over tens of millions of years much less than might be expected through a gradual change. Eldredge and Gould (Gould, 1982) claimed that speciation occurs only in rapid bursts in terms of geological time, followed by long periods of morphological stoicism, or *stasis*. They termed this profile of speciation 'punctuated equilibrium', which was consistent with Mayr's theory of allopatric speciation. If the mutation rate had been steady during this period then one might have expected to have seen this exhibited in gradual phenotypic variation, punctuated equilibrium therefore managed to account for the relative lack of change. However, Eldredge and Gould's thesis has been radically rebutted by Dawkins and Dennett (1995).

Another example is the 'selfish gene' theory (Dawkins, 1986) or gene-centred theory in which evolutionary survival is driven by the success of genes to replicate themselves through phenotypic carriers, i.e. organisms. The evolutionary role of the organism, therefore, is to ensure the success of competing genes through reproduction. Opposition to this theory has come from biologists who conceive of it as far too reductionist, with evidence and arguments to show that selection acts at various levels of complexity, not just at the level of the genotype (Rose, 1997). Much of the controversy surrounding these differences revolves around the interpretation of evidence and the meaning of concepts, for example, Daniel Dennett, has written expansively defending and qualifying reductionism.

CREATIONISM/EVOLUTION DIFFERENCES

The examples I briefly described above are controversies between protagonists in explaining mechanisms of evolution and natural selection which relate to explanations about natural selection but do not call evolution into question. These controversies are based upon agreed scientific criteria; to put it colloquially, the protagonists agree on what they disagree about, hence there are mutually agreed starting points, language and concepts in which to frame disagreements. The problem when science teachers are faced with students who subscribe to creationist perspectives is very different. In this case there is 'no agreement about whole frameworks of understanding relevant for judgment' (Levinson, 2006, p. 1212).

In my experience there are two main strategies often employed by science teachers when confronted with a refusal by students to countenance evolution as an explanation for the diversity of life. The first is to avoid active teaching of the topic altogether and remind students of relevant parts of the textbooks to read. The second is to announce that this has to be learned for the examination and avoid any discussion. Both are understandable responses but unsatisfactory.

Some years ago I attended a meeting at a school for about a hundred young people aged between 14 and 16 years where a debate was presented between two creationists and two scientists on evolution. Almost all the young people ended up supporting the creationist position which highlighted closeness to God and the uniqueness of the human condition, and was framed in rousing language. The scientists presented good compelling scientific arguments which largely fell on deaf ears; the choice was one between a warm inspiring glow and a self-conscious, challenging and stark landscape. The challenge faced when teaching evolution in many cases is not only a scientific one but a metaphysical one. To focus on the scientific argument may well only result in a short-term gain with sullen acquiescence of the student.

The above episode illustrates the problem for science teachers when introducing evolution in schools. But an episode from my experience as a teacher educator has taught me that the dividing line between creationist perspectives and evolution is not always clear; it can be complex and diffuse (Alexakos & Pierwola, 2013). In a session I was running for student teachers on teaching evolution a young woman, Orla (not her real name), who had demonstrated a profound and convincing understanding of Darwinian evolution approached me after the session. Her problem, she said, was that at one level natural selection made sense to her but despite reading everything she could on evolution (far more widely and deeply than I had read, and I suspect more than the other student teachers in the group) she had doubts, she could not quite convince herself that it was a plausible explanation. She had no religious belief she could claim, and she was sceptical about non-materialist explanations of the origin and diversity of life. But she had existential doubts which she found difficult to articulate precisely. Addressing creationist positions she felt put her in a pedagogic dilemma because she empathised with some of the pupils' doubts.

There are two points to make here: first, there are a wide variety of creationist (or rather, non-Darwinian) positions ranging from literal and rigid readings of the bible to views that are a reflection of uneasiness at Darwinian theory; secondly, that to have an understanding of evolution is not to dismiss creationist positions and to have creationist sympathies is not to disparage evolution. There is, if you like, a fuzzy border between the paradigms in which people can live with incompatible concepts and meanings simultaneously, a pre-requisite for passing from one conceptual framework to another.

How then to support young people in coming to an understanding of evolution in the face of a creationist background? As evidenced by Orla, understanding evolution does not necessarily pre-suppose wholehearted acceptance. Aikenhead and Jegede (1999) have likened challenges of cultural and religious backgrounds to learning accepted science as crossing borders. They identify four types of crossings: smooth, managed, hazardous and impossible. The first two occur when there are minimal differences between microcultures (that of the cultural background of the student and the culture of science) so that crossing the border is barely noticeable or can be managed with a little adaptation. It is the latter two that often face science teachers from creationist students. Some of the conditions for being able to cross borders that are deemed hazardous or impossible are flexibility, playfulness and ease, i.e. that we can be comfortable adopting different roles in different cultures. This can be achieved through collateral learning (Aikenhead & Jegede, 1999). Collateral learning involves students holding on to discrepant explanations about a particular concept. There are a number of different ways in which this can take place. Students may retain different explanations side by side without any overlap or conflict (parallel collateral learning). Such learning may occur when students who have creationist beliefs are able to learn about evolution so the two explanations are compartmentalised without any overlap. On the other hand, students may hold contrasting and conflicting ideas about evolution but one of the ideas influences the other so that a shift in conceptions begins to take place (dependent collateral learning). How this shift is handled by the teacher is crucial and relies on the teacher being able to envisage and empathise with the student in terms of the shift in conceptions that is taking place. In some cases it is perfectly possible, and even desirable, to compartmentalise different ways of thinking, so that we can get on with life. Most people use language which is contextually sensitive. For example, almost everyone knows what is meant when someone says: 'Shut the door to keep out the cold. It's freezing in here'. It is unscientific language since 'cold' is not a physical entity and it's very unlikely that the conditions are freezing. But such a plea is likely to bring about the required action of closing the door. Scientifically you would have to say 'Shut the door because there is a large temperature gradient between the internal environment within the walls of the house and everything outside it'. Anyone who used the latter form of language would be scientifically correct but most reasonable people would avoid such a pedant like the plague. Understanding evolution, however, is quite different because what is at stake is not just normal everyday communication but fundamental ideas about who we are, i.e. worldviews. At some point it is unavoidable that there will be a conflict of ideas.

That is where the fuzzy border between the two worldviews of science and creationism comes into play. It is an area where collateral learning can take place for hazardous and impossible border crossing. But it can only be achieved by negotiation and dialogue so that those struggling to cross the border can feel at ease; it means communicating using language and concepts which are meaningful to different parties. Listening is therefore an important aspect of supporting this border crossing.

The purpose of listening is both to understand what the other is saying and to grasp the motive for saying it so that concepts are constructed which make communication possible. For John Dewey (Waks, 2011), listening enhances mutual co-operation where all voices are heard so that the act of learning can be carried out. Both parties, teachers and students, need to make every effort to grasp what the other is saying. There is a special onus on the teacher because s/he can best draw on experiences of the student to identify the most appropriate way of doing this. Hence Dawkins' dismissal of creationism would be unconducive to border crossing.

One strategy for enhancing listening and hence dialogue in a group is to give time to parties to explain what their view is of, for example, human origins. This might be with a class of 14 year-olds where there is an atmosphere of mutual respect between teacher and students and between students. The teacher might ascertain that there are diverse views in the classroom. This could be done, for example, by getting students to write down on a card how far they felt that the human species was created in one act by a divine being and asking them to arrange the cards along a line from those close to Darwinian perspectives to those with literalist creationist perspectives. Students could be grouped in pairs where they have similar views and then grouped with a pair of students with very different views. Call the first pair (1) and the second pair (2). Pair (1) has then to explain their ideas to pair (2) in a certain amount of time, say, three minutes. Pair (2) has then to respond to pair (1), not with a rebuttal, but to try and amplify and explain pair (1)'s position even better than pair (1) has done. The purpose of this exercise is to make sure that pair (2) understands what pair (1) is trying to say in terms which both parties understand. Then the exercise is now reversed with pair (2) explaining their position to pair (1). Only when both pairs have clarified each others' position can they begin to critically analyse each others' ideas in a respectful way. It is important to recognise that students may be going through an inner struggle and to reach a position where students can identify this struggle in a conducive and respectful atmosphere is an important step forward.

How the class moves on lies in the skill of the teacher and his/her knowledge of the class. But when faced with students with ardent creationist beliefs it may be better to discuss the origins of variation within non-human species and leave the origin of human species for the time being, although there is no reason why human variation and its underlying biology cannot be discussed. It may need to take time for ideas to come together but if concepts such as variation, gene selection and speciation are commonly recognised and understood, the conditions for controversy and consideration of evidence and theories come into play.

SOME PRACTICALITIES

Enhancing listening and dialogue in the context of teaching evolution comes with certain qualifiers. The idea of crossing borders is to recognise that borders can be crossed in both directions. The DCSF guidance to teachers:

> …there is a real difference between teaching 'x' and teaching about 'x'. Any questions about creationism and intelligent design which arise in science lessons, for example as a result of media coverage, could provide the opportunity to

explain or explore why they are not considered to be scientific theories and, in the right context, why evolution is considered to be a scientific theory.[2]

This seems to me to expect a lot of science teachers, particularly in a world where performance targets and examination results are prioritised. Given the particular realities and constraints in schools and the importance of supporting the teaching of controversies within science, it may well be better to create a space for discussion of creationist-evolution worldviews beyond science lessons at first. While doubt and uncertainty have to be embraced in understanding science, such doubts should not lead to undermining validated scientific explanations at school, whether wholly materialist or not.

Consider the dilemma. Suppose that facilitating a discussion about creationism-evolution led to some very persuasive literalist creationist students beginning to convince others of the creationist position. Despite the teacher clearly explaining the difference between evidence and belief such a movement began to take place. One option is to accept that this is the risk of opening up any discussion; another is that it would be wrong to suppress such views but that explanations drawing on evidence and theory have validity within science lessons.

Nor need this space be religious education lessons; historical aspects of evolution, or lessons based on philosophy (Worley, 2012) could provide a grounding before starting a course in science lessons on evolution. There is an important distinction, in terms of their status as controversies, between alternative theoretical explanations of natural selection that come within the accepted Darwinian framework and creationism-evolution. The former rely on critical and agreed modes of supplying evidence and examining arguments as controversies, the latter is a very different type of disagreement; it is not a scientific controversy, but it is a difference that has to be taken seriously pedagogically. And if pupils do have doubts that Darwinian biology lacks the dimension of wonder and speculation, reading the last few pages of *On the origin of species* should at least remediate that misapprehension.

NOTES

[1] http://www.youtube.com/watch?v = R9uhE4CT2xM.
[2] (http://humanism.org.uk/wp-content/uploads/1sja-creationism-guidance-180907-final.pdf)

REFERENCES

Aikenhead, G. S. (1996). Science education: Border crossing into the subculture of science. *Studies in Science Education, 27*, 1–52.
Aikenhead, G. S., & Jegede, O. J. (1999). Cross-cultural science education: A cognitive explanation of a cultural phenomenon. *Journal of Research in Science Teaching, 36*(3), 269–287.
Alexakos, K., & Pierwola, A. (2013). Learning at the 'boundaries': Radical listening, creationism, and learning from the 'other'. *Cultural Studies of Science Education, 8*, 39–49.
Bailin, S., & Siegel, H. (2003). Critical thinking. In N. Blake, P. Smeyers, R. Smith, & P. Standish (Eds), *The Blackwell guide to the philosophy of education* (pp. 181–193). Oxford: Blackwell Publishing.

Bridges, D. (1979). *Education, democracy and discussion.* Slough: NFER Publishing Company.
Burbules, N., & Rice, S. (1991). Dialogue across differences: Continuing the conversation. *Harvard Educational Review, 61*(4), 393–416.
Crick, B. (1998). *Education for citizenship and the teaching of democracy in schools.* London: Qualifications and Curriculum Authority.
Dawkins, R. (1986). *The blind watchmaker.* London: Penguin.
Dearden, R. F. (1981). Controversial issues in the curriculum. *Journal of Curriculum Studies, 13*(1), 37–44.
Dennett, D. (1995). *Darwin's dangerous idea: Evolution and the meanings of life.* London: Penguin.
Gould, S. J. (1982). Punctuated equilibrium: A different way of seeing. *New Scientist, 94*(1301), 137–148.
Hand, M., & Levinson, R. (2012). Discussing controversial issues in the classroom: Some helps and hindrances. *Educational Philosophy and Theory, 44*(6), 615–629.
Hess, D. (2009). *Controversy in the classroom.* New York, NY: Routledge.
Kuhn, T. (1962). *The structure of scientific revolutions.* Chicago, IL: University of Chicago Press.
Levinson, R. (2006). Towards a theoretical framework for teaching controversial socio-scientific issues. *International Journal of Science Education, 28*(10), 1201–1224.
Pennock, R. T. (2007). How not to teach the controversy about creationism. In L. S. Jones & M. J. Reiss (Eds.), *Teaching about scientific origins.* New York, NY: Peter Lang.
Rose, S. (1997). *Lifelines.* London: Viking/Allen Lane.
Ruse, M. (2007). The warfare between Darwinism and Christianity: Who is the attacker and what implications does this have for education? In L. S. Jones & M. J. Reiss (Eds), *Teaching about scientific origins.* New York, NY: Peter Lang.
Schwarz, B. B., Neuman, Y., & Biezuner, S. (2000). Two wrongs may make a right ... if they argue together! *Cognition and Instruction, 18*(4), 461–494.
Waks, L. J. (2011). John Dewey on listening and friendship in school and society. *Educational Theory, 61*(2), 191–205.
Worley, P. (2012). *The philosophy shop.* Carmarthen: Crown House Publishing.

Ralph Levinson
Institute of Education,
University of London,
UK

NEIL INGRAM

16. THE 'ATTENTIVE AND REFLECTIVE OBSERVER'

Darwin-Inspired Learning and the Teaching of Evolution

INTRODUCTION

Evolution has grown into a *big* idea, which continually bursts out of whatever container it is put in. Dobzhansky's maxim that 'Nothing in biology makes sense except in the light of evolution' is as imperative now as it ever was, because of the significant new impetus generated by contemporary observation and research (Dobzhansky, 1973). This is a new generation of Darwin-inspired learning.

The beating heart of evolution is the 'origin of species by means of natural selection' and the 'preservation of favoured races in the struggle for life', just as it was in 1859 for Charles Darwin.

Radical and unexpected new observations are continually being made and the theory of evolution adapts to accommodate each of them. For example, the universality of the genetic code across all organisms and all times is a remarkable phenomenon. Yet surely, given the right circumstances, might we not occasionally expect new variants to arise, taking their place to be tested by natural selection?

Their absence can be explained by the premise that once a stable functioning genetic code evolved, almost all further changes act to stabilise the genetic code. The universality of the code suggests that this was a major prerequisite for the evolution of cellular life.

Exciting new observations (Rinke et al., 2013) of variants in *Gracilibacteria* that have 're-coded' the opal stop codon (UGA) to make the amino acid glycine show that variations to the code may occasionally arise that are not deleterious, even if they are rare and restricted to a limited number of genera of bacteria.

Such observations strengthen and reinforce the basic tenets of Darwin's theory, rather than undermine it. Their significance can be debated and interpreted, but the presence of rare variants strengthens the argument that the genetic code is developing by natural selection, rather than by a preformed plan.

The Evolution of Evolution

Over time, the theory of evolution has evolved, embracing Mendelian genetics, pedigree analysis, chromosome and mutation theory and ecology. Fisher's *The genetical theory of natural selection* (Fisher, 1930) was written to show that natural selection was a force powerful enough to build complex organisms. It led to an emphasis on studying the process of evolution, rather than its end products. In doing so, evolution became more reductionist and less inductive.

Most recently, the genetic code, genomics, proteomics, epigenetics and horizontal gene transfer are new currents that are continuing to shape the form of the theory. Genomic analyses are helping to construct evolutionary pathways, by allowing us to read genomes like maps across time.

The extraordinary achievement of Charles Darwin is that the framework for interpreting the story of life remains much as he developed it. The framework is flexible and very forward thinking. The remarkable uniformity of the genetic code implies that there was a single (universal) common ancestor from which all organisms that have ever existed or ever will exist are descended. Darwin foresaw this in *On the origin of species*:

> Therefore I should infer from analogy that probably all the organic beings which have ever lived on this earth have descended from some one primordial form, into which life was first breathed by the Creator. (Darwin, 1859, p. 484)

Confirming that there was a single Universal Common Ancestor 3.5 billion years ago is difficult, and it was only recently that Theobald (2010) produced statistical evidence that confirms Darwin's foresight.

Thomas Henry Huxley's reaction to reading *On the origin of species* is said to have been: 'How extremely stupid not to have thought of that!' (Darwin, F., 1887, p. 198). The simplicity is such that it can be encapsulated as three observations and four deductions.

– Observation 1: All species have a great potential to increase in number.
– Observation 2: The numbers of most species remain approximately constant.
– *Deduction 1: There is a struggle between individuals for existence. Many individuals die before they can reproduce.*
– Observation 3: Much variation within populations is inherited. Organisms have inherited characteristics.
– *Deduction 2: Some inherited characteristics adapt organisms to survive in their environments.*
– *Deduction 3: Natural selection will favour those individuals that have the most effective inherited characteristics.*
– *Deduction 4: Over the generations natural selection will gradually change the inherited characteristics in a population, and may lead to the production of new species. This is evolution by natural selection.*

(after Berry, 1977; Mayr, 1982)

Older children at school can appreciate the elegant simplicity of this argument. Yet the biological and philosophical implications of this theory are so immense that it takes time and considerable practice for students to grasp its subtlety. Because of this, misconceptions in understanding evolution are common, and often actively promoted. There are evident political and religious implications for the evolution of life through a struggle for existence. Teachers of evolution at all levels of education wrestle with the paradox that one of the easiest ideas to teach is one of the hardest for students to learn.

In spite of the overwhelming evidence for evolution, it remains a controversial idea for many people. Teaching evolution in schools is still controversial for many students and their parents, and many people of widely differing religious perspectives would concur with Bishop Wilberforce, in his review of *On the origin of species:*

> With Mr Darwin's 'argument' we may say in the outset that we shall have much and grave fault to find. But this does not make us the less disposed to admire the singular excellences of his work. (Wilberforce, 1860, p. 227)

Powerful voices on the extreme sides of the debate are strident: moderate views occupying the centre ground tend to be drowned out. In the field of Darwin versus religion, there seems to be 'no neutral ground'[1].

Darwin is one of the few scientists whose biography forms part of the narrative of teaching. The *mythos* of Charles Darwin has almost the same stature as the *logos* of his ideas. Given the almost universal fascination with the back-story, are we presenting the most contemporarily relevant 'Darwin' to the world?

Misconceptions, controversy and mythology, then, will therefore form the substance of the remainder of this chapter.

MISUNDERSTANDING EVOLUTION

The deductions outlined in the previous section have been applied piecemeal to many different species in the story of life. As we shall see, a convincing narrative has been constructed.

Even so, arguments that question this claim still persist. This section will consider a few of these misconceptions. As with any other aspect of teaching, misconceptions are best dealt with by encouraging students to reflect critically on the significance of evidence. I will take an evidence-based approach here, emphasising where possible, contemporary thinking. I will consider both limitations of evidence and philosophical considerations.

The Limitations of Evidence

Darwin's theory argues that, as a result of natural selection, a new species evolves from an existing species. In time, the new species may replace the earlier one. If this is so, then intermediate forms might be expected to be found in the fossil record:

Intermediate varieties, from existing in lesser numbers than the forms which they connect, will generally be beaten out and exterminated during the course of further modification and improvement. (Darwin, 1859, p. 287)

Darwin recognised that one weakness of his theory was the absence of fossils of transitional species. Darwin proposed that the 'extreme imperfection of the geological record' was caused partly by the conditions under which fossils form. It is a matter of chance whether transitional species were preserved as fossils.

Of course, some intermediate fossils are now recognised. *Archaeopteryx*, a transitional form between dinosaurs and birds, was discovered as early as 1861, and provided independent verification of Darwin's thinking (see Ostrom, 1976, for a review).

Recent discoveries of coloured bristles on the theropod dinosaur *Sinosauropteryx* (Zhang et al., 2010) are also examples of transitional fossils. The bristles are precursors of feathers and appear as orange and white rings down its tail. The discovery raises the possibility that the bristles acted as warning and communication signals. This is because the bristles were only present as a crest down the midline of the back and round the tail and so would have had only a limited function in thermoregulation.

Feathers evolved from these prototype bristles and their genes were available for natural selection to use when building structures that eventually became wings.

Developmental genetics has revealed that most of an organism's genes are shared by other species throughout the living world. The diversity we see within, for example, the animal kingdom seems principally to rely on the use of similar combinations of genes, used and re-used in different ways. Genes can be duplicated and then modified for different functions.

Jacob (1977) proposed the metaphor of 'bricolage', to explain the action of natural selection as a 'tinkerer' using genes and structures that are to hand to achieve its effects, rather than by creating a clearly formulated 'plan', characteristic of a human engineer. Wilkins (2007, p. 8591) suggests that the evolution of certain reptilian jaw joint bones into two of the middle ear bones of the mammalian ear is a 'classic example of such evolutionary tinkering'.

Some transitional human fossils are recognised and accepted, suggesting that humans are not exempt from evolution. The hominid *Australopithecus afarensis*, (Aahton et al., 1981) is thought to be a transitional form between bipedal modern humans and their ape-like ancestors that were quadrupeds. The pelvis is far more human than ape-like, with short, wide iliac blades and a wide sacrum, positioned directly behind the hip joint.

A revolution is occurring as it is increasingly accepted that genomes are a repository of evolutionary information that can be read and compared to pathways constructed from fossil and comparative anatomy. This allows new ways of thinking about evolution to arise. For humans, recent techniques that allow genomes to be sequenced from fossils are showing that human evolution is indeed a bricolage, with a complex mosaic pattern.

The traditional view is that Neanderthal humans were a separate species to modern (Cro-Magnon) humans. The Neanderthals, regarded as brutish and incapable of sophisticated communication and abstract (symbolic) thought, became extinct in Europe about 28,000 years ago, after the arrival of modern humans to Europe from Africa (Stringer, 2012).

This view has been challenged by the occurrence of other anatomically distinct types of human (such as the Denisovans and Flores) and also by some evidence for admixture of their archaic DNA into the modern human genome. Between 1% and 4% of Neanderthal DNA is found in Eurasians, who are all descended from a small group of modern humans who left Africa about 60,000 years ago (Green et al., 2010).

The possibility of further interbreeding between Asian Denisovans and modern humans is suggested because between 4% and 6% of the genome of Melanesians (such as from Papua New Guinea) is an admixture from a Denisovan population (Reich et al., 2011), suggesting that recent human evolution is a mosaic of small groups of humans encountering each other and interbreeding. The classical picture of isolated morphological and biologically distinct 'species' is being reconsidered.

That species formation is labile is supported by other studies of species formation, such as the adaptive radiation of cichlid fish in East African lakes (Kocher, 2004) where over 2000 new species have formed in the last two million years. The species show clear morphological and behavioural differences, and gene flow is restricted largely by strong visual cues when selecting mates (Figure 1). Post-mating isolating mechanisms have yet to evolve.

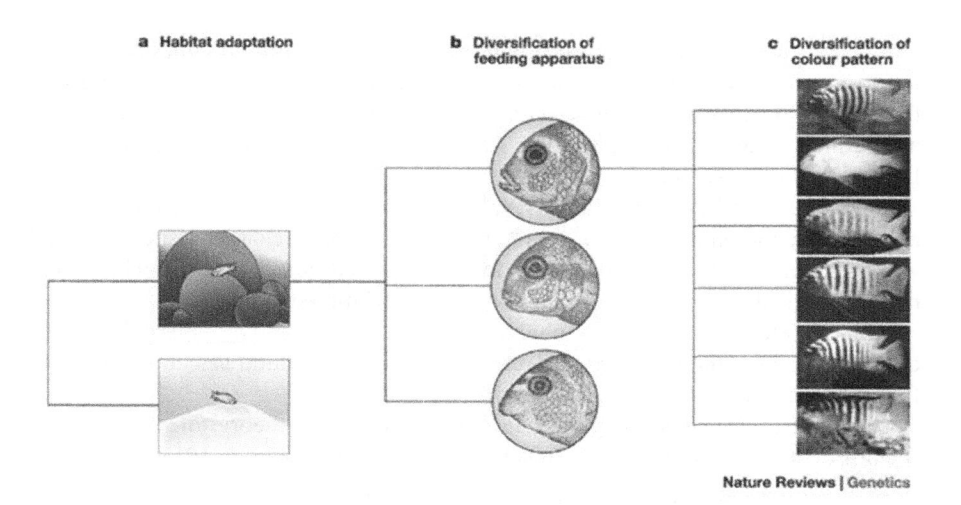

Figure 1. Speciation in Cichlid fish in East Africa. (©Thomas D. Kocher, Nature Reviews Genetics, 5, 288-298, April 2004)

A number of rare cichlid species in the lakes are currently endangered by human activity and this illustrates the fragility of newly formed species. About 200 endemic species in Lake Victoria are endangered, due to the introduction of a predatory Nile perch to boost fishing. This represents 70% of the total number of species of cichlids currently in the lake (Witte et al., 1992).

Philosophical Considerations

Charles Darwin collected observations of many organisms from different environments and read and consulted widely with the scientific community. Gradually, over nearly 30 years, he allowed his theory to coalesce around the empirical evidence. It is the epitome of the approach to science called inductivism. Darwin made generalisations about the evolution of all organisms in the past and the present, using particular examples of organisms as empirical evidence.

One criticism of inductivism, suggested by Popper, is that the generalisations can be challenged by a single example that does not fit the pattern (Popper, 1994). The generalisation that 'all swans are white' can be disproved by the occurrence of a single black swan. So, why has this not happened for evolution?

Every species that has ever existed has its own unique evolutionary biography, and the theory of evolution is inclusive enough to account for each of these stories. Each biography is like a strand in a coiled rope. The strength of the rope is distributed across the many fibres that compose it. There are so many independent pieces of evidence supporting the theory that no serious evidence-based objection to the theory has been proposed.

Natural selection selects those organisms with the maximum fitness. This has led to claims that evolution is tautological. Put at its simplest, critics claim that through the process of natural selection, the 'fittest' survive. However, the 'fittest' are defined as the ones who survive. A tautological theory is not testable and of limited predictive value.

In practice, whilst differential survival and reproductive success are the levers of natural selection on populations, there are always adaptive characteristics involved within organisms that can be independently measured and monitored. This is the methodological basis of studying microevolution within populations.

Natural selection acts on the phenotype of an organism. The inheritable bases of the phenotype (the genes) are selected indirectly, and natural selection alters the frequency of alleles in the population.

Creationist groups sometimes question whether the theory of evolution is scientific, often citing statements by philosopher Popper (1976, p. 195):

> Darwinism is not a testable scientific theory, but a metaphysical research program – a possible framework for testable scientific theories.

Popper recognised the power of trying to falsify hypotheses using repeatable experimental conditions (Popper, 1934, p. 23). Darwin's inductive observations, which were largely a reading of the fossil record and comparative anatomy on extant forms, did not lend itself to Popper's methodology.

Later, Popper (1977) retreated from this extreme position, stating that the neo-Darwinian formulation of Darwin's own theory of natural selection supported by the Mendelian theory of heredity, by the theory of the mutation and recombination of genes in a gene pool, and by extension, the decoded genetic code is:

> ... an immensely impressive and powerful theory ... The Mendelian underpinning of modern Darwinism has been well tested, and so has the theory of evolution which says that all terrestrial life has evolved from a few primitive unicellular organisms, possibly even from one single organism.

The Origins of Life

The development of organic macromolecules from inorganic precursors and the emergence of life from biochemical systems do not form part of the theory of evolution. Natural selection accounts for the development of life on Earth, not its formation.

Charles Darwin speculated in a letter (Darwin, 1887, p. 19):

> It is often said that all the conditions for the first production of a living organism are now present, which could ever have been present. But if (and oh! what a big if!) we could conceive in some warm little pond, with all sorts of ammonia and phosphoric salts, light, heat, electricity, &c., present, that a protein compound was chemically formed ready to undergo still more complex changes, at the present day such matter would be instantly devoured or absorbed, which would not have been the case before living creatures were formed.

The formation of life remains problematic, speculative and uncertain. There are many alternative theories, involving a 'primordial soup' in an atmosphere of reducing gases, with life forming on clays containing iron, sulphur and zinc molecules, under the influence of UV radiation forming self-replicating and catalytic RNA molecules.

Sharov and Gordon (2013) apply statistical modelling to the rate of nucleotide evolution, and estimated an origin of the first nucleotide base pair of at least 9.7 ± 2.5 billion years. The Earth itself is estimated at only 4.54 billion years in age, suggesting that bacterial spores on Earth might have been seeded by panspermia from outer space. Panspermia is an ancient theory, recently pioneered by Hoyle and Wickramasinghe (1981, pp. 35-49).

RELIGION AND EVOLUTION

The review of the *On the origin of species* by Bishop Wilberforce in *The Quarterly Review* makes it very clear that it was not appropriate for Charles Darwin to:

... apply his scheme of the action of the principle of natural selection to MAN himself, as well as to the animals around him. (Wilberforce, 1860, p. 258)

The uniqueness of Man at the heart of God's Creation was, and is, sacred to many who hold the Abrahamic faiths. Similar arguments are sometimes made in classrooms around the world today. The tension between religious belief and evolution is not a historical artefact, and this section explores the tensions from a variety of different viewpoints.

Watchmakers and Ultimate Causes

Evidence for the evolution of life is essentially value-free, although it is often misappropriated when discussing final causes, such as the purpose or goal of life. A consideration of final causes is traditionally regarded as being beyond the limits of science, and scientific evidence used in this way is relocated from science into metaphysics. The language that science teachers use needs to be carefully chosen so as to avoid stepping over the boundary.

Paley (1809) uses a watchmaker analogy in his book, *Natural theology*. He says that on finding a watch on the ground:

There must have existed, at some time, and at some place or other, an artificer or artificers, who formed [the watch] for the purpose which we find it actually to answer; who comprehended its construction, and designed its use. (Paley, 1809, p. 385)

This argument suggests that just as the complexity of the watch implies a designer, so the complexity of the natural world implies a Creator God.

Richard Dawkins' famous rebuttal to Paley (Dawkins, 1986) is that that natural selection is the 'blind watchmaker' that can produce the complexity of living organisms without a pre-determined plan. He goes on to argue that there is no need to use the complexity of living organisms as evidence of the existence of God as a divine Creator.

By arguing in this way, both Paley and Dawkins are moving science into metaphysics. Both arguments are teleological because they are suggesting that (different) final causes exist in nature, which can be inferred from scientific evidence.

Teleology and the Language of Teaching Evolution

Humans find teleology innately appealing: we like to think about final causes. Kelemen (2004, p. 295) has described children as 'intuitive theists' because her experiments suggest that young children around the age of five have a 'broad tendency to reason about natural phenomena in terms of purpose and an orientation toward intention-based accounts of the origins of natural entities'. In other words, they believe that the natural world has been designed for a purpose.

Childhood intuitive theism appears to be consistent with how very young children learn about cause and effect. They live in a world of designed objects, where everything has a purpose (a cup is *for* drinking and *not for* wearing as a hat). Since all effects have causes, children are trained to look for and expect causes. If there are causes, then why not ultimate causes? Everything seems to require a purpose, to be *for* something. There may be evidence that this tendency is 'hard-wired into the brain' (Abrahams & Reiss, 2012, p. 413).

Kelemen's research is important, because she suggests this is a natural stage of children's cognitive development, which weakens at about 10 years of age. The dictum 'give me a child until he is seven and I will give you the man' (attributed to the religious order of the Society of Jesus) illustrates how critical these years are for the formation of values and worldviews, including religious and secular perspectives.

There are implications here for science teaching and for any idea of teaching of evolution in primary education. Kelemen comments:

> The implication is that children's science failures may, in part, result from inherent conflicts between intuitive ideas and the basic tenets of contemporary scientific thought. (Kelemen, 2004, p. 299)

Similarly, the impact of the teaching of evolution on the development of children's worldviews should also be considered.

Teleological language is commonly used in school biology education. Children might be told that 'lions' teeth are shaped to kill and eat zebra', which is only a small semantic step away from the childhood teleological notion that 'the purpose of lions' teeth is to kill zebra' or that 'lions' teeth are designed to kills zebra'. This may explain some of the difficulty adults have untangling observations about evolution from reflections on intention and final causes.

Chance and Necessity

The role that chance plays in macroevolution is also controversial. Gould (1989, p. 14), reflecting on the explosion of Cambrian fossils found in the Burgess Shale, wrote: 'Wind back the tape of life to the early days of the Burgess Shale; let it play again from an identical starting point, and the chance becomes vanishingly small that anything like human intelligence would grace the replay'.

Conway-Morris, who worked on the Burgess Shale fossils, disagrees and claims that Gould's famous statement arose from his 'personal credo about the nature of the evolutionary process':

> [Such a view, with its] emphasis on chance and accident, obscures the reality of evolutionary convergence. Given certain environmental forces, life will shape itself to adapt. History is constrained, and not all things are possible. (Conway-Morris, 1998, p. 50)

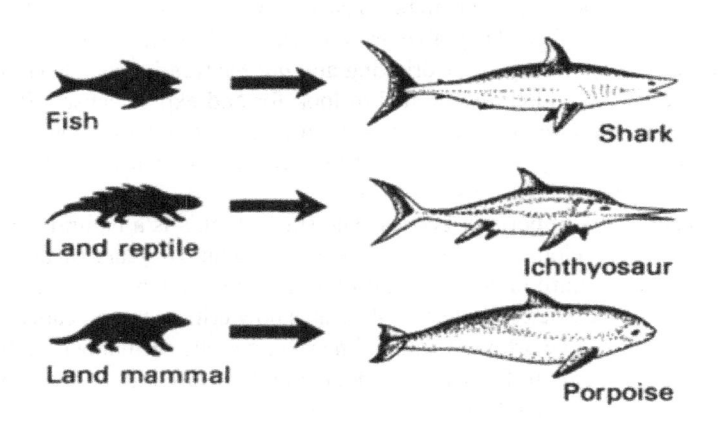

Figure 2. Examples of convergent evolution. (From http://rpdp.net/sciencetips_v2/ images/L12D3_5.gif)

Conway-Morris believes that if the tape of life were re-wound and played again, a creature with human-like intelligence and self-awareness would surely have evolved:

> ... although perhaps not from a tailless, upright ape. Almost any planet with life, in my view, will produce living creatures we would recognize as parallel in form and function to our own biota.

There is a widespread presumption that all evolutionary scientists must, *de facto*, be humanists or atheists, and this appears not to be true. The quotation from Dobzhansky that is included in this chapter's title is part of a paper for American teachers that espoused theistic evolution. Ayala, Berry, Collins, Conway-Morris, Fisher, Peacocke and Wright have all written extensively about evolution, whilst having a Christian faith.

Medewar, not a believer, advocated that there were 'limits to science' (1984), with ideas of beauty, values, origins and the existence of God being unknowable. Gould (1999) extends this idea by proposing that science and religion each have 'a legitimate magisterium, or domain of teaching authority', and these two domains do not overlap. This is his idea of NOMA, non-overlapping magisteria.

Although initially attractive, this idea is difficult to use in practice, because the magisteria inevitably overlap. The effects of faith, meditation and prayer on a believer, for example, can be observed in a brain scanner.

Polanyi, a chemist and a philosopher of science, argued that it is the reductionist philosophy that underpins scientific investigations that leads to the conclusion that God is unnecessary in the world. There is little doubt that science reduces the complexity of the world to generalisations. For example, early in his career, Dawkins reduced human life and culture to the activity of selfish genes and self-replicating memes. For Polanyi:

> Darwinism has diverted attention for a century from the descent of man by investigating the conditions of evolution and overlooking its action. Evolution can be understood only as a feat of emergence. (Polanyi, 1958, p. 390)

Polanyi regards evolution as consisting of a number of significant steps of emergence, such as the development of the genetic code, the appearance of eukaryotic cells, multi-cellularity and the like. These steps culminate in the emergence of human knowledge and conscious self-awareness. (Teilhard de Chardin calls this final step the 'noosphere'.) Each stage of emergence acts as an 'ordering principle' for future evolution.

> And evolution, like life itself, will then be said to have been originated by the action of the ordering principle, an action released by random fluctuations and sustained by fortunate environmental conditions. (Polanyi, 1958, p. 390)

This model, which is closer to Conway-Morris than Gould, implies that the natural selection watchmaker might not be as 'blind' as Dawkins believes. Teilhard de Chardin, a palaeontologist and radical Catholic Priest, described an end to evolution, a maximum level of complexity and consciousness towards which he believed the universe was evolving. He called this the Omega Point (Teilhard de Chardin, 1961, p. 257).

Is the Teaching Evolution a Controversial Issue?

The metaphysical speculations of the previous section arise as reflections on the empirical data, a process that would have been familiar to Charles Darwin.

'Biblical creationism' and her hand-maiden, 'Intelligent design', are of a different kind. Here, the evidence of the Bible is held to be unquestioningly true and scientific evidence that disagrees with the narrative has to be discredited. There are varieties of belief within creationism, but the general tenets are of a young Earth, creation within seven 'days', a global flood, and limited evolution from the basic 'kinds' that were saved by Noah in the Ark.

Intelligent design, as proposed by Behe, argues that some biological systems are too complex to have evolved from simpler, or 'less complete' predecessors, through natural selection. He returns to the 'argument from design', originally proposed by Paley. Behe proposed that the cornerstone of intelligent design was that of 'irreducible complexity', which was defined as any system that is:

> composed of several well-matched, interacting parts that contribute to the basic function, wherein the removal of any one of the parts causes the system to effectively cease functioning. (Behe, 1996, p. 39)

The evolution of the flagella of bacteria is regarded as an example of irreducible complexity because it consists of a molecular motor requiring the interaction of about 40 different protein parts. Behe argues that the absence of any one of these proteins causes the flagella to fail to function.

It appears that the flagella have been modified from existing protein transport systems in bacteria (Wong et al., 2007). The genes controlling the process seem to have been cloned and modified by natural selection, rather than being newly developed. The example is now regarded more as 'bricolage' than intelligent design.

Biblical creationism is often allied with right-wing politics and has powerful influence in different parts of the United States and Europe. There is concern, too, amongst some Muslim communities that human evolution is contradictory to the teaching of the Qur'an. The recent evidence of human evolution presented earlier can be seen to further dislocate Man from its place at the top of the created order.

The teaching of evolution may be becoming increasingly controversial and seeking regional or national guidance on what is permissible may be needed. Reiss (2011) has proposed that we consider students' personal beliefs on the origins of life as part of their 'worldviews'. Worldviews are coherent collections of concepts and theorems that we use to construct a 'global image of the world, and in this way to understand as many elements of our experience as possible'. Although worldviews may be complex, possibly containing mutually incompatible ideas, they need to be treated sensitively and with respect.

My personal view is that the emphasis of our teaching should be on the evidence for the processes of evolution, and that discussion of ultimate causes (be they emergent, intelligent designs, NOMA or noospheres) should be discussed elsewhere (such as in religious studies lessons). That said, I believe that science teachers should answer any questions that the children ask, especially if they are helping students to understand the evidence for the processes of evolution.

THE 'ATTENTIVE AND REFLECTIVE OBSERVER': PRESENTING DARWIN TO THE MODERN WORLD

Darwin's story forms an integral part of the teaching of evolution and, in conclusion, it is worth re-assessing its relevance to contemporary society.

Darwin, for example, is often presented as disproving Lamarck (1809), who proposed that characteristics acquired during an organism's life are passed onto future generations. Darwin did not know how variation arose, but did not support the idea that it could originate through parental experiences.

Recent scientific evidence for epigenetics suggests that the environment can affect the expression of genes, and that some of these changes can be passed onto future generations. This blurs the distinction between Lamarck and Darwin, although we are not sure whether these changes can persist long enough for natural selection to act on them. Even so, there is a danger that we might be introducing potential misconceptions in our teaching by over-emphasising the fallacy of Lamarckism early in our teaching.

Huxley's British Association debate with Bishop Wilberforce is sometimes taught in science lessons (Lucas, 1979) to show that Darwin's ideas caused immediate controversy with the established Christian church. Given the tensions between science and religion outlined in the previous section, I wonder if a discussion of this aspect is a distraction from a careful consideration of the evidence for the processes of evolution? Might this kind of discussion be more profitably discussed in history or a joint science/religious studies lesson?

The Charles Darwin story is multi-faceted, and there are other aspects of his life that could be emphasised, especially in primary education.

Darwin was an attentive and reflective observer, who recorded his observations with meticulous accuracy. Darwin's writing is full of such examples, such as his descriptions of earthworms producing vegetable mould or the various finches on the Galapagos Islands. All of Darwin's work is freely available on line, and we can celebrate his talent as an observer and an author.

Darwin was also an extraordinarily prolific letter writer and the records of his correspondence allow the richness of his intellectual life to be exposed and recognised. The theory of evolution, although formulated in a country house in England, was a collaborative effort from so many people across the world, that through his writings we can be inspired to see how science progresses through observation, reflection and conversation.

Darwin was a brave man: he took risks as an explorer and as a map-maker. This was literally true of his voyage on the Beagle, and his journal stands the test of time as a model of how to write a travel book. It is also metaphorically true of his journey towards understanding the origin of species over the next 30 years of his life.

Darwin's scientific work is worthy of celebration. He chose his thoughts and words carefully. He chose to emphasise the evidence rather than speculation on ultimate causes. We all aspire to be attentive and reflective observers, and, above all, the teaching of evolution in schools should inspire wonder and respect for the natural world.

NOTE

[1] From 'Precious Angel' by Bob Dylan (1979): 'Ya either got faith or ya got unbelief and there ain't no neutral ground'.

REFERENCES

Aahton, E. H., Flinn, R. M., Moore, W. J., Oxnard, C. E., & Spence, T. F. (1981). Further quantitative studies of form and function in the primate pelvis with special reference to Australopithecus. *Transactions of the Zoological Society of London, 36*, 1–98.

Abrahams, I., & Reiss, M. (2012). Evolution. In P. Jarvis & M. Watts (Eds), *The Routledge international handbook of learning* (pp. 411–418). Abingdon: Routledge.

Behe, M. J. (1996). *Darwin's black box: The biochemical challenge to evolution.* New York, NY: Simon and Schuster.

Berry, R. J. (1977). *Inheritance and natural history.* London: Bloomsbury.

Conway-Morris, S. (1998). Showdown on the Burgess Shale. *Natural History, 107*(10), 48–55. Retrieved August 23, 2013 from http://www.stephenjaygould.org/library/naturalhistory_cambrian.html

Dawkins, C. R. (1986). *The blind watchmaker.* New York, NY: W.W. Norton.

Darwin, C. (1859). *On the origin of species by means of natural selection, or the preservation of favoured races in the struggle for life.* London: John Murray.

Darwin, F. (Ed.). (1887). *The life and letters of Charles Darwin, including an autobiographical chapter* (Vol. 2, p. 198). London: John Murray.

Dobzhansky, T. (1973). Nothing in biology makes sense except in the light of evolution. *American Biology Teacher, 35,* 125–129.

Fisher, R. A. (1930). *The genetical theory of natural selection.* Charleston, SC: Nabu Press.

Gould, S. J. (1989). *Wonderful life: The Burgess shale and the nature of history.* New York, NY: W. W. Norton.

Gould, S. J. (1999). *Rocks of ages: Science and religion in the fullness of life.* New York, NY: Ballantine Books.

Green, R. E., Krause, J., & Briggs, A. W. (2010). A draft sequence of the Neanderthal genome. *Science, 328*(5979), 710–722.

Hoyle, F., & Wickramasinghe, N. C. (1981). *Evolution from space.* London: J.M. Dent and Son.

Jacob, F. (1977). Evolution and tinkering. *Science, 196*(4295), 1161–1166.

Kellemen, D. (2004). Are children 'intuitive theists?' *American Psychological Society, 15*(5), 295–301.

Kocher, T. D. (2004). Adaptive evolution and explosive speciation: The cichlid fish model. *Nature Reviews Genetics, 5,* 288–298.

Lamarck, J. B. (1809). *Philosophie Zoologique.* Oxford: Oxford University Press.

Lucas, J. R. (1979). Wilberforce and Huxley: A legendary encounter. *The Historical Journal, 22*(2), 313–330.

Mayr, E. (1982). *The growth of biological thought.* Cambridge, MA: Belknap Press of Harvard University Press.

Medewar, P. B. (1984). *The limits of science.* London: HarperCollins.

Ostrom, J. H. (1976). *Archaeopteryx* and the origin of birds. *Biological Journal of the Linnean Society, 8,* 91–182.

Paley, W. (1809). *Paley's natural theology: With illustrative notes* (Vol. 2). London: Charles Knight.

Polanyi, M. (1958). *Personal knowledge: Towards a post-critical philosophy.* Chicago, IL: University of Chicago Press.

Popper, K. R. (1934). *The logic of scientific discovery.* London: Routledge.

Popper, K. R. (1976). *Unended quest: An intellectual autobiography.* Glasgow: Fontana/Collins.

Popper, K. R. (1977). *Natural selection and the emergence of mind.* A talk delivered to Darwin College, Cambridge, November 8, 1977. Retrieved August 1, 2013 from http://www.informationphilosopher.com/solutions/philosophers/popper/natural_selection_and_the_emergence_of_mind.html

Popper, K. R. (1994). Zwei Bedeutungen von Falsifizierbarkeit [Two meanings of falsifiability]. In H. Seiffert & G. Radnitzky (Eds), *Handlexikon der Wissenschaftstheorie* (pp. 82–85). München: Deutscher Taschenbuch Verlag.

Reich, D., Patterson, N., Kircher, M., Delfin, F., Nandineni, M. R., Pugach, I., . . . Stoneking, M. (2011). Denisova admixture and the first modern human dispersals into Southeast Asia and Oceania, *The American Journal of Human Genetics, 89*(4), 516–528.

Reiss, M. J. (2009). Imagining the world: The significance of religious worldviews for science education. *Science & Education, 18,* 783–796.

Rinke, C., Schwientek, P., & Sczyrba A. (2013). Insights into the phylogeny and coding potential of microbial dark matter: Nature. Retrieved August 1, 2013 from http://www.nature.com/nature/journal/vaop/ncurrent/full/nature12352.html?utm_content=buffer175a7&utm_source=buffer&utm_medium=twitter&utm_campaign=Buffer

Sharov, A. A., & Gordon, R. (2013). Life before earth. Retrieved August 1, 2013 from http://arxiv.org/pdf/1304.3381v1.pdf

Stringer, C. (2012). *The origin of our species.* London: Penguin.

Teilhard de Chardin, P. (1961). *The Phenomenon of man.* London: Harper Torchbook.

Theobald, D. L. (2010). A formal test of the theory of universal common ancestry. *Nature, 465*, 219–222.

Wilberforce, S. (1860). [Review of] On the origin of species, by means of natural selection; or the preservation of favoured races in the struggle for life. By Charles Darwin, M. A., F.R.S. London, 1860. *Quarterly Review, 108*, 225–264. Retrieved August 1, 2013 from http://darwin-online.org.uk/content/frameset?pageseq=1&itemID=A19&viewtype=text

Wilkins, A. S. (2009). Between 'design' and 'bricolage': Genetic networks, levels of selection, and adaptive evolution. *Proceedings of the National Academy of Sciences, 104* (Supplement 1), 8590–8596.

Witte, F., Goldschmidt, T., Wanink, J., van Oijen, M., Goudswaard, K., Witte-Maas, E., & Bouton, N. (1992). The destruction of an endemic species flock: Quantitative data on the decline of the haplochromine cichlids of Lake Victoria. *Environmental Biology of Fishes, 34*(1), 1–28.

Wong, T., Amidi, A., Dodds, A., Siddiqi, S., Wang, J., Yep, T., . . . Saier, M. H. (2007). Evolution of the bacterial flagellum: Cumulative evidence indicates that flagella developed as modular systems, with many components deriving from other systems. *Microbe, 2*(7), 335–340.

Zhang, F., Kearns, S. L., Orr, P. J., & Benton, M. J. (2010). Fossilized melanosomes and the colour of Cretaceous dinosaurs and birds. *Nature, 463*, 1075–1078.

Neil Ingram
Graduate School of Education,
University of Bristol,
UK

JOHN L. TAYLOR

17. DARWINIAN CASE STUDIES WITHIN A POST-16 PROGRAMME FOR THE HISTORY AND PHILOSOPHY OF SCIENCE

The Perspectives on Science Course

The Perspectives on Science (PoS) programme is a course in the history and philosophy of science for 16-18 year-old students. PoS was designed to promote discussion and debate of historical and philosophical questions associated with science and to make such debate a recognised part of the curriculum. The course ran in the UK as a pilot AS level qualification between 2004 and 2008, making it equivalent to half an A level, the main academic qualification taken by 16–18 year-olds. Since then it has been taught in schools and colleges as a designed programme for the 'Extended Project Qualification', which offers sixth-form students the opportunity to engage in research and produce university-style dissertations.[1]

A feature of the PoS course is the use of a taught course as a basis for the development of the skills and conceptual frameworks which students then utilise in their project work. The taught course contains a series of case studies, designed to stimulate discussion and debate in the classroom, to highlight significant points about the nature of science and to facilitate the development of skills in research and argument.

Darwin's life and work provide material for one of the major historical case studies in the PoS course. The course also contains materials designed to encourage exploration of the philosophical implications of Darwinism, specifically its implications for the philosophy of mind and the philosophy of religion. The emphasis throughout the course is on encouraging students to think for themselves. At no point are students told 'what to think' about controversial matters of history, philosophy or theology.

Development of the capacity for independent learning has been identified as one element in Darwin-inspired learning. In the PoS course, this is seen to happen through open discussion and debate during the taught-course phase and in subsequent research-project work. In what follows, I will use examples from course materials to illustrate aspects of the history and philosophy of science in which Darwin-inspired learning takes place, and recount a number of episodes in which students can be said to have found such inspiration in their project work.

C.J. Boulter et al. (Eds.), *Darwin-Inspired Learning*, 237–242.
© 2015 Sense Publishers. All rights reserved.

J. L. TAYLOR

LEARNING FROM DARWIN ABOUT THE HISTORY OF SCIENCE

In the introduction to his seminal work *Structure of scientific revolutions*, Thomas Kuhn remarked that 'History, if viewed as a repository for more than anecdote or chronology, could produce a decisive transformation in the image of science by which we are now possessed' (Kuhn, 1962, p.1). Kuhn's work was, of course, influential in precipitating just such a transformation, the result of which was to bring to the fore the social – and at times political – nature of science. We may not wish to go as far as Kuhn did in some of the more rhetorically forceful passages of SSR in viewing paradigm shifts as irrational episodes, driven by factors extrinsic to science itself. But the existence of episodes of deep-seated, revolutionary change within science, and the recognition that the path along which such change unfolds cannot be understood without an appreciation of the surrounding social context, now constitute received wisdom concerning the nature of science.

Whilst the PoS course does not contain explicit instruction about the 'nature of science' (since the emphasis is on equipping students to develop their own philosophical ideas), nonetheless, the choice of case study materials and questions is designed to encourage students to appreciate certain aspects of science. In particular, the case study of Darwinian evolution aims to illuminate the nature of science by showing some of the ways in which scientific knowledge emerges within a particular social context, and how, in turn, science raises questions for society. In place of science as an activity of accumulation of fixed, uncontentious facts, a picture emerges of science as a human activity, shaped by the social context within which it takes place, and in turn exerting significant social and cultural pressure.

So, for example, students' attention is drawn to the community of scientists working at the same time as Darwin, such as Wallace, Cuvier, Lyell, Huxley, Hooker and Wilberforce, and to their interesting and significant interactions with Darwin himself. The idea of science as a social activity implies the possibility of conflict, or at least tension, and this is explored in the first activity of the evolution case study, entitled 'Darwin's dilemma'[2]. This activity invites students to consider how they would advise Darwin to respond to the receipt of a letter from Alfred Russel Wallace, in which Wallace explains his own theory of evolution by natural selection, an idea which Darwin himself had been developing for the previous 20 years.

Darwin's Dilemma

> For any scientists who value their work, priority is vital. The first person to announce a discovery or propose a theory draws the fame associated with it. Darwin held in his hand the paper that could take away his priority of development of the theory of natural selection, his life's work. He thought of three options:
>
> 1. He could destroy the letter, ignore it completely, and announce the theory himself. If Wallace ever enquired about it he could say that he had never received the letter.

2. He could put the letter to one side while he announced his theory. In a few months' time he could reveal the letter as if it had just arrived,
3. He could do as Wallace requested and forward the letter for publication and thereby lose priority.

What should Darwin do?

- Justify each course of action and comment on the outcome.
- Bear in mind that the postal service from the jungles of south-east Asia was slow and unreliable.

A second aspect of the social nature of science comes into focus when students are invited to reflect upon the cultural impact of Darwinism. The implications of evolution, in a range of spheres of human life, remain the focus of controversy, and this provides an excellent context within which students can carry out research as a preparation for involving themselves in the debate.

Darwinism Today

Hold a debate on one or more of the following propositions. Prepare for the debate by setting out arguments and evidence for and against the propositions:

- Evolutionary theory has contributed to racial hatred in the world today.
- The human race has ceased to evolve.
- Darwin's theory of evolution by natural selection is as good a theory as Newton's Law of Gravitation.

Activities such as the 'Darwinism today' debate enable active learning of aspects of the history of science whilst also helping facilitate the development of the skills required for the writing of successful Extended Project dissertations. Students who find such debates particularly engaging occasionally choose to make this the starting point for their full extended project. One PoS student, who planned to go to university to read history, was intrigued to discover that Darwinian evolution figured in propaganda for the Nazi eugenics programme carried out during World War 2. He decided to carry out an investigation of the history of purported associations between evolution and the eugenics movement.

DARWIN AND THE PHILOSOPHY OF SCIENCE

In a research study of the PoS course, it was found that some of the best classroom discussions happened in the context of the exploration of controversial issues (Levinson, Hand & Amos, 2012). One significant aspect of the inspiration which Darwin provides for PoS students is that the significant, deep-seated and persistent philosophical controversy which his work has provoked provides an excellent starting point for classroom discussion and debate.

How should such sensitive and potentially inflammatory matters be handled? The model used to approach such teaching in the PoS course is based on frameworks: the broad intellectual outlooks which structure debate about controversial questions. So, for example, in exploring philosophical issues related to the question of whether there is evidence of design in the universe, students are introduced to the perspectives of naturalism, intelligent design, theistic evolution and relativism (a term used to denote SJ Gould's NOMA approach)[3]. In the 'Discussing design' activity, they are invited to reflect on the strengths of the arguments for and against these philosophical positions and to present their own point of view in discussion. They are also asked to evaluate whether any of the four frameworks can be considered 'scientific' and to relate this question to what they have learned from discussion of the nature of science. The question of whether Popperian falsification provides a criterion for demarcating science from pseudo-science or non-science is raised[4]. The frameworks approach is also used in exploring whether Darwinism favours materialism over mind (or soul) body dualism.

Discussing Design

Make a survey of a range of different viewpoints on the question of intelligent design, then define your own viewpoint in relation to these, giving reasons for the choice you have made and considering objections to it. Be prepared to make a brief oral presentation of your argument to the rest of your class. To help with your presentation, make notes summarising your point of view and the arguments you call upon to support it. Try to lay out your argument (s) in the form of premises followed by the conclusion.

Though situated mid-way through the philosophy of science section, discussion of creation and evolution can be one of the most fruitful starting points for engaging students' interest in matters philosophical. Since students often have some familiarity with these matters, perhaps through discussions in religious studies classes, they are better able to begin discussing questions about, say, the design argument, than more abstract questions about the epistemology or metaphysics of science. Moreover, within most groups there will be students who hold the strongly divergent views which can so helpfully catalyse the process of argumentative enquiry.

As well as stimulating debate, and thus encouraging students to reflect on their own beliefs in relation to those of others, the exploration of philosophical frameworks for relating creation and evolution opens up scope for focused exploration of the nature of science. Valuable philosophical analysis often proceeds contrastively, and putting scientific and religious ideas side-by-side can enable a fruitful juxtaposition of contrasting ways of thinking. If, for example, it is felt, with Popper and others in the empiricist tradition, that there is a criterion of demarcation between science and non-science, then this will plausibly involve reference to the generation of falsifiable predictions; and if the intent of the theorising of the devotees of creationism is to sustain specific doctrines about such matters as the age of the Earth, in the light of strongly falsifying evidence, then there are indeed grounds for locating creationism, not within the domain of science, but within a sphere of metaphysical belief.

Within the conceptual space of discussion of matters of science and religion, Darwin inspires learning, since he inspires controversy, and controversy acts as a catalyst of the process of formation of intellectual independence. When faced with divergent views, each of which can apparently be given argumentative support, the question as to where the truth lies becomes pressing. Controversy is the grit in the oyster, around which the pearl of independent thought may coalesce.

There is value in handling such sensitive matters within the context of the study of the history and philosophy of science – away from the media spotlight which invariably accompanies mention of the 'teaching' of intelligent design within science lessons. The value of a philosophical approach to this contentious issue, and the 'measured, intelligent way' that the question of the science/religion relationship is handled in programmes such as Perspectives on Science has been noted (Baggini, 2009).

The emphasis in the PoS course is on the value of discussion as a starting point for critical, reflective enquiry into the open questions of philosophy. It should be emphasised, however, that this pedagogical approach does not imply commitment to epistemic relativism, according to which any viewpoint is considered equally valid. On the contrary, the approach embodies belief in the importance of critical examination of the logic of arguments and the coherence of concepts as essential parts of the process of the pursuit of truth. Of central importance is the understanding that philosophical and ethical questions are essentially contestable and that developing as an intellectually self-sufficient individual involves learning to identify and respond to counter-arguments to one's beliefs[5]. Such an approach is highly congruent with Darwin's own intellectual approach, which drew heavily on his own commitment to honest yet critical enquiry. It is this approach which the PoS course encourages students to take, as these three concluding brief examples of Darwin-inspired learning illustrate:

- In a PoS seminar discussion on the question of design, the facilitator asks the group, from a sixth-form science college, whether they all believe in evolution. Two students say that they do not. They explain their reasons, based on their religious beliefs. The facilitator asks them why they think that so many scientists do accept evolution. 'That's a good question,' one of the students responds.
- A student with an interest in the relationship of science and religion decides to use his Extended Project to explore the extent to which Darwinism has contributed to the decline in religious belief. He begins with a literature review in which he explores the historical development of Darwinian evolution before going on to look at theories about secularisation.
- A visiting lecturer, speaking about science and religion, asks a group of students whether any of them are creationists. One girl – a Muslim – puts her hand up. During a subsequent PoS seminar, the teacher asks her to present her views to the

rest of the class. She agrees. Following her presentation, the students in the group respond with polite though probing questioning.

Each of these examples represents a step on a journey of philosophical enquiry. And this, perhaps not coincidentally, at another level, mirrors Darwin's own journey with respect to matters philosophical and scientific, a journey along a thinking path.

NOTES

[1] The 'Extended Project Qualification' was launched in the UK in 2008. It offers 16 – 18 year-old students the opportunity to carry out an independent research project on a topic of their own choice. The majority of projects take the form of written dissertations, although scientific investigations, performances and artefacts are possible outcomes.
[2] The Darwin case study materials were written by Peter Ellis. The extracts here all come from Swinbank and Taylor (2007).
[3] Stephen Jay Gould's NOMA approach articulates the idea that science and religion represent 'non-overlapping magisteria'; that is to say, statements made in either domain neither conflict with nor agree with those of the other. See Gould (1999).
[4] Without foreclosing philosophical discussion of possible alternatives, it is suggested in the PoS guidance to teachers that ID is treated as a philosophical framework, not a scientific one. At no point in the course is it suggested that there is serious controversy, within the scientific community, about the scientific credentials of Darwinian evolution.
[5] For further discussion of the philosophical pedagogy embodied within the PoS course and other, cognate approaches to the Extended Project Qualification, see Taylor (2012).

REFERENCES

Baggini, J. (2009, February 10). Science and religion don't have to be enemies. *Herald Scotland*. Retrieved September 5, 2013 from http://www.heraldscotland.com/science-and-religion-don-t-have-to-be-enemies-1.839271
Gould, S. J. (1999). *Rocks of ages: Science and religion in the fullness of life*. New York, NY: Ballantine Books.
Kuhn, T. (1962). *Structure of scientific revolutions*. Chicago and London: University of Chicago Press.
Levinson, R., Hand, M., & Amos, R. (2012). What constitutes high quality discussion in science? Research from the Perspectives on Science course. *School Science Review, 93*(344), 114–120.
Swinbank, E., & Taylor, J. (Eds). (2007). *Perspectives on science: Student book*. Oxford: Heinemann.
Taylor, J. (2012). *Think again: A philosophical approach to teaching*. London and New York: Continuum.

John Taylor
Rugby School,
UK

AARON M. ELLISON

18. THEY REALLY DO EAT INSECTS

Learning from Charles Darwin's Experiments with Carnivorous Plants

INTRODUCTION

Carnivorous plants. The idea of plants eating animals conjures up visions of giant Venus's flytraps making meals of humans in a Little Shop of Horrors or Triffids marauding across the English countryside. And indeed, these strange plants have inspired countless children's books and science-fiction movies. But carnivorous plants have their serious side as well, and botanists, zoologists, and ecologists have been studying them for nearly 500 years (Figure 1).

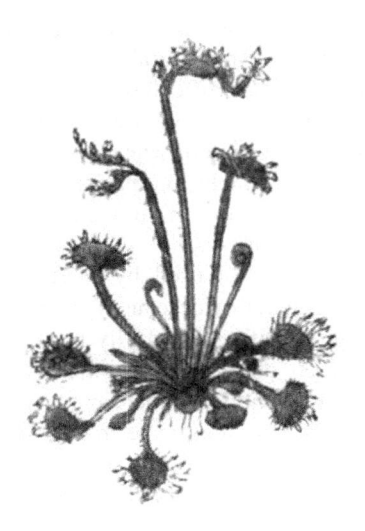

Figure 1. The first carnivorous plant to be illustrated in any flora was a sundew, Drosera cf. rotundifolia *(from Dodoens, 1554). We now know this to be a carnivorous plant, but there is no evidence that Dodoens thought it was carnivorous. Rather, he thought it was a type of moss and he called it a 'Ros solis' (Lat: dew of the sun)*

Linneaus (1753) named the majority of carnivorous plant genera, but neither he, nor other botanists of the 1500s, 1600s and early 1700s, seriously considered that the insects found associated with these plants were anything but nuisances to be avoided (Juniper, Robins & Joel, 1989). It was Charles Darwin, who in the mid-1800s used a series of keen observations and carefully designed experiments (Darwin, 1875), to demonstrate conclusively to his colleagues that these plants actively attract, trap, kill and digest insects and other small animals. Subsequent research has supported many of Darwin's conclusions about how carnivorous plants 'work' and shown how natural selection has led repeatedly to carnivory in a number of unrelated plant lineages.

THE IMPORTANCE OF EXPERIMENTS

Many other chapters in this book have emphasized the importance of observations: getting to know the world and the organisms around us. Darwin himself was a masterful observer. His observations of geological phenomena (see Chapter 13) and geographic variation among species led him inexorably through a series of deductions to the startling conclusions elaborated in *On the origin of species* (1859). Although Darwin himself did not do any conclusive experiments to support his hypothesis that evolution proceeded by natural selection, he pointed in *On the origin of species* to a type of experiment—artificial selection for plant and animal traits—practised routinely by farmers. But genetics was still far in the future, and farmers breeding new varieties of cattle, swine or wheat knew only that selective breeding worked, not how it worked. The conclusion that improved breeds could arise from artificial selection could be ascribed to a multitude of causes, ranging from particles of inheritance to divine intervention.

Experiments are the central tool used by scientists to identify cause-and-effect relationships and to separate true causes from false ones. In most cases, scientists first state a range of different, ideally mutually exclusive, *hypotheses*: proposed explanations for an observed phenomenon based on first principles (e.g. mathematical or physical axioms or theories) or other available information derived from observations or previous experiments (Chamberlain, 1890; Platt, 1964; Taper & Lele, 2004). The essential objective of any scientific experiment is to falsify (*not prove!*) one or more of these hypotheses. After several rounds of this process of observation → hypothesis generation → experimentation → hypothesis rejection, only one hypothesis should remain standing. Superficially, this process resembles the deductive method (and maxim) of Arthur Conan Doyle's famous detective, Sherlock Holmes: 'when you have eliminated the impossible, whatever remains, however improbable, must be the truth' (Conan Doyle, 1890 p. 111). But unlike detectives and courts of law, for whom or which 'beyond reasonable doubt' is sufficient to convict, scientists are ever-skeptical of the 'truth' and persist in trying to falsify even their seemingly most bullet-proof hypotheses (Popper, 1959). In other words, good scientists are always trying to *disprove* their pet hypotheses.

Scientific understanding advances most rapidly when existing explanations for observed phenomena are found wanting and new explanations are proposed and rigorously tested. The experiments described by Darwin in *Insectivorous plants* continue to provide an inspiring example of the inherent skepticism of science and of the power of such skepticism to lead to new knowledge and a deeper understanding of the world around us.[1]

CAN PLANTS REALLY BE CARNIVOROUS?

The Pre-Darwinian View

In the years before Darwin began studying carnivorous plants, botanists had routinely ignored or elided their observations that dead insects were found stuck to or inside the leaves of what we now know as carnivorous plants (Gerard, 1633, is a notable early exception to this otherwise general rule). On the other hand, they routinely put forth a wide range of reasons to explain why plants such as sundews *Drosera*, butterworts *Pinguicula*, bladderworts *Utricularia* and pitcher plants *Sarracenia* (in the Americas), *Nepenthes* (in Southeast Asia), and *Cephalotus* (in Australia) all had strange sticky glands, elaborately shaped leaves or other mysterious structures (summarised in Juniper, Robins & Joel, 1989). For example, some had suggested that the gooey surfaces of butterwort leaves prevented insects that were too small to be effective pollinators from reaching the flower. It was also asserted that the water-filled pitchers of *Sarracenia* provided refuges for insects fleeing predation by frogs, and that flies would be released by the Venus's flytrap *Dionaea muscipula* after they ceased struggling.

Only the Australian pitcher plant *Cephalotus follicularis* was suspected of actually using insects for food. In December 1800, Robert Brown, a naturalist traveling with Matthew Flinders' expedition around Australia, observed and collected *Cephalotus* in south-west Australia. Brown observed that dead ants filled the plant's water-filled pitchers and Flinders wrote:

> Amongst the plants collected by Mr. Brown and his associates, was a small one of a novel kind, which we commonly call the pitcher plant. Around the root leaves are several little vases lined with spiny hairs, and these were generally found to contain a sweetish water, and also a number of dead ants. It cannot be asserted that the ants were attracted by the water, and prevented by the spiny hairs from making their escape; but it seemed not improbably, that this was a contrivance to obtain the means necessary either to the nourishment or preservation of the plant (Flinders, 1814, p. 64).

By the late 1700s and early 1800s, increasing evidence from careful observations of living specimens, such as those described above by Brown and Flinders in Australia, was leading to new thinking about many of these plants. For example, John Ellis, in his description of the Venus's flytrap wrote:

> Each leaf is a miniature figure of a Rat trap with teeth: closing on every fly or other insect that creeps between its lobes, and squeezing it to Death. (Ellis, 1770, caption Plate 1)

In the full description of *Dionaea*, Ellis further adds (italics in the original):

> ... that nature may have some view towards its *nourishment*, in forming the upper joint of its leaf like a *machine* to catch food. (Ellis, 1770, p. 37)

But Ellis also asserted (1770, p. 37) that *Dionaea* could not distinguish between live insects (prey) and 'a vegetable or mineral substance'. A century later, Darwin would use experiments to show otherwise.

In the intervening decades, the leaves and stalked glands ('tentacles') of sundews were clearly seen to move and 'imprison' insects (Sowerby, 1790, p. 867). Macbride (1818, p. 52) observed that flies walking unsteadily on the rim of the tube-shaped leaf of the yellow pitcher plant *Sarracenia flava* would lose their footing as an 'impalpable or loose powder' on the rim suddenly gave way, leaving only a surface of 'perfect smoothness' off which the fly slipped and fell into the pitcher.[2] Hooker (1858, p. 5080) noted that the pitcher of *Nepenthes villosa* is 'a great provision of nature for decoying and for the destruction of insects'. The observational stage was now set for Darwin's experiments.

DARWIN'S EXPERIMENTS WITH CARNIVOROUS PLANTS

Darwin's central achievement, described in *Insectivorous plants* (Darwin, 1875), was to use controlled, manipulative experiments to distinguish fiction from fact. The facts accumulated by Darwin's experiments with carnivorous plants eventually led to the development of new and testable theories of the evolutionary origin of carnivorous plants and how natural selection allows them to persist among their non-carnivorous relatives.[3]

Darwin's Experiments with Sundews

More than two-thirds of Insectivorous plants recounts Darwin's experiments with the round-leaf sundew *Drosera rotundifolia* (see Figure 2). This small plant, with leaves barely two centimetres across, grows throughout the northern hemisphere in bogs and fens. It can be nestled in and among Sphagnum mosses, its sticky, glistening leaves barely visible in the relatively giant forest of moss, or it can form dense, very visible aggregations on open mudflats.

Darwin opens *Insectivorous plants* with a short paragraph that is remarkable for its clarity, concision, and richness of data and hypotheses:

> During the summer of 1860, I was surprised by finding how large a number of insects were caught on the leaves of the common sun-dew (*Drosera rotundifolia*) on a heath in Sussex. I had heard that insects were thus caught, but knew nothing further on the subject. I gathered by chance a dozen plants,

bearing fifty-six fully expanded leaves, and on thirty-one of these dead insects or remnants of them adhered; and, no doubt, many more would have been caught afterwards by these same leaves, and still more by those as yet not expanded. On one plant all six leaves had caught their prey; and on several plants very many leaves had caught more than a single insect. On one large leaf I found the remains of thirteen distinct insects. Flies (Diptera) are captured much oftener than other insects.... . As this plant is extremely common in some districts, the number of insects thus annually slaughtered must be prodigious. Many plants cause the death of insects, for instance the sticky buds of the horse-chestnut (*Aesculus hippocastanum*), without thereby receiving, as far as we can perceive, any advantage; but it was soon evident that *Drosera* was excellently adapted for the special purpose of catching insects, so that the subject seemed well worthy of investigation. (Darwin, 1875, pp. 1-2)

The 'surprise' in the opening sentence points out how few reliable facts were known about sundews in spite of its widespread distribution and abundance.[4] From the description, the reader can derive an estimate of the probability of insect capture by leaves (31/56 = 0.55; cf. Dixon, Ellison & Gotelli, 2005; Ellison & Gotelli, 2009), an estimate of the upper bound of the maximum number of insects caught per leaf (13), and an hypothesis that flies are the most frequently captured insect. Finally, Darwin compares sundews to horse-chestnuts. The latter, like many other plants armoured with spines, bristles or sticky hairs, kills insects but do not derive benefits from them. In contrast, he hypothesises that sundews appear to be 'excellently adapted' to capture insects, and presumably derive some benefit from doing so.[5]

Darwin then proceeds to describe in detail the range of experiments he used to determine: whether *Drosera* is responsive to different kinds of stimuli; if the

Figure 2. The round-leaf sundew Drosera rotundifolia *with an entrapped ant. (© Aaron M. Ellison)*

response is sensitive to temperature, the kind of substance stuck to the leaf or various poisons; and whether and how it digests and absorbs nutrients from material stuck to the leaves. Throughout, Darwin works with a variety of artificial prey—bits of meat and other animal parts, liquids (including human urine) and salts containing nitrogen (ammonia), phosphorus from chemical salts or infused from leaves, as well as glass, cinders, his wife's hair, chalk—caused to land on and stimulate the sundew's sticky leaf pad once or repetitively. Unlike with real insect prey, Darwin was able to control carefully the precise chemical composition and exact amounts of each of these substances—in one case as little as one twenty-millionth of a grain (3.3 nanograms) of ammonium phosphate [$(NH_4)_3PO_4$]—and their precise placement on the leaf. Such precision and control is now seen as the *sine qua non* of a scientific experiment, and permits rigorous testing and evaluation of scientific hypotheses.

At the same time, it is important that the artificial conditions of the garden or a laboratory experiment are relevant to the messier conditions of the 'real world' (for further discussion, see Chapter 2). Darwin was certainly aware of this need. For example, when reporting his results of how 'motor impulses' appeared to be transmitted from one part of the leaf to another, he wrote:

> I will give here a case not included in the above thirty-five experiments [on transmission of motor impulses]. A small fly was found adhering by its feet to the left side of the [leaf] disc. The tentacles on this side soon closed in and killed the fly; and owing probably to its struggle whilst alive, the leaf was so much excited that in about 24 hrs. all the tentacles on the opposite side became inflected; but as they found no prey, for their glands did not reach the fly, they re-expanded in the course of 15 hrs.; the tentacles on the left side remaining clasped for several days. (Darwin, 1875, p. 237)

But after this (and several other specific and unique examples), Darwin returns to the 'general results' from the controlled experiments.

After conducting literally hundreds of experiments on *Drosera rotundifolia*, and observing half a dozen other species of sundews he had growing in his greenhouse, Darwin was able to draw a number of key conclusions. The leaves capture insects using a sticky fluid poised at the ends of the tentacles densely arrayed on each leaf's surface. These tentacles move inward and envelop the prey. Movement is stimulated more by animal substances than by inert ones, and only when the glands are touched more than twice. Thus, a raindrop or a passing breeze does not trigger the prey-capture response. The sensitive parts of the leaves are the glands, tentacles and cells immediately beneath them. The movement of tentacles spreads across the leaf surface in a manner similar to a reflex or a motor impulse seen in animal neurons. Finally, the leaves truly dissolve insect prey and the glands absorb the digested nutrients. Meat is more readily digested and absorbed than cartilage, and the plants are especially sensitive to direct additions of nitrogen and phosphorus.

Darwin's experiments did not provide direct proof that sundews grew better when fed additional prey (see also Note 6). He had done an experiment in which

200 sundews were transplanted from the field into small dishes. All of the plants were covered with gauze so that insects could not be captured by any of the plants. Then, half of the plants were fed additional roast meat, and half were left unfed ('starved'). All of the plants died, however; Darwin's son Francis wrote that 'the experiments intended to decide the question [i.e. provide direct proof that sundews or other carnivorous plants get a substantial benefit from capturing, digesting, and absorbing prey] only failed through an accident' (F. Darwin, 1878a, pp. 222-223). Francis Darwin repeated the experiment in 1877, with better success (F. Darwin, 1878a, 1878b). In the season in which they were fed, the fed plants grew somewhat better—exclusive of flowers, fruits, and seeds they were just over 20% heavier than the starved plants—but more dramatically, the fed plants produced more than twice as many seeds as the starved plants, and the seeds of the fed plants weighed nearly twice as much as the seeds of the starved plants (F. Darwin, 1878a). Francis only harvested half of the plants, however; the remainder were left to overwinter (as dormant winter buds, or hibernacula). When they re-sprouted in the spring, they were not fed at all, but they continued to grow, using nutrients stored in the hibernacula. After about 10 weeks (from mid-January to 3 April 1878), the plants were harvested, dried, and weighed. The plants that had been fed the previous season were just over twice as heavy as the plants that had been starved the previous season.[6] Unknown to Francis Darwin at the time he did his experiment, Kellermann & von Raumer had done a similar experiment with *Drosera rotundifolia* fed aphids (Kellermann & von Raumer, 1878); the results, compared explicitly in F. Darwin (1878b) were qualitatively identical.

Despite the revolutionary nature of his findings—the experiments described in *Insectivorous plants* overturned nearly a century of botanical dogma[7]—Darwin is characteristically modest at the close of his general summary:

> I have now given a brief recapitulation of the chief points observed by me, with respect to the structure, movements, constitution, and habits of *Drosera rotundifolia* [ed]; and *we see how little has been made out in comparison with what remains unexplained and unknown* [ed]. (Darwin, 1875, p. 277)

In fact, our scientific understanding of the mechanisms by which sundews attract, capture, kill and digest prey has changed little since 1875. On the other hand, we now know much more about how carnivorous plants evolved and how the nutrients from the prey are partitioned among growth, respiration and reproduction.

Darwin's Experiments with Other Carnivorous Plants

Darwin repeated on a range of other carnivorous plants many of the experiments that he had conducted on *Drosera rotundifolia*. For example, he showed that only repeated stimulation in short succession of the trigger hairs of the Venus's flytrap would cause the leaves to close over their prey. As rain did not stimulate the inflection of the sundew's tentacles, the flytrap was similarly 'indifferent to the heaviest shower of rain' (Darwin, 1875, p. 291). Darwin explored digestion and absorption of a wide range of nutrients and other chemicals not only in *Dionaea* but also in the waterwheel plant *Aldrovanda vesiculosa*, the dewy-pine *Drosophyllum lusitanicum*, the rainbow plant *Byblis gigantea*, the flycatcher bush or vlieëbos *Roridula dentata* and many species of butterworts *Pinguicula*, bladderworts *Utricularia* and lobster-pot plants *Genlisea*.[8] As importantly, returning to his hypothesis about the difference between carnivorous plants and other plants with sticky leaves or buds, Darwin explored the ability of other plants to digest and absorb nutrients. In two saxifrages *Saxifraga umbrosa* and *S.* cf. *rotundifolia*, a white-edged cultivar of the Chinese primrose *Primula sinensis*, a pink *Pelargonium zonale,* the cross-leaved heath *Erica tetralix,* sweet four o'clock *Mirabilis longiflora* and cultivated tobacco *Nicotiana tabacum*, Darwin found repeatedly that their glandular hairs or other structures were immobile and unable to absorb nutrients.

WHERE DARWIN WENT WRONG: THE EVOLUTION OF CARNIVOROUS PLANTS

Although *Insectivorous plants* was published sixteen years after *On the origin of species*, Darwin does not dwell extensively on how carnivorous plants might have evolved. He does refer, albeit obliquely, to relationships among carnivorous plants and suggests homologies among their key structures.[9] These references suggest that he was at least developing a theory as to their evolutionary origin. Several lines of evidence pertain.

First, Darwin considered the sticky glands of all the Droseraceae (*Drosera, Dionaea, Aldrovanda, Drosophyllum, Roridula, Byblis*; but see Note 9) to have the homologous trait of being able to absorb nutrients:

> These octofid [eight-part] projections [on the leaves of *Dionaea*] are no doubt homologous with the papillae on the leaves of *Drosera rotundifolia.* (Darwin, 1875, p. 288)

> By comparing the structure of the leaves, their degree of complication, and their rudimentary parts in the six genera, we are led to infer that their common parent form partook of the characters of *Drosophyllum, Roridula*, and *Byblis*. The leaves of this ancient form were almost certainly linear, perhaps divided, and bore on their upper and lower surfaces glands which had the power of secreting and absorbing. (Darwin, 1875, p. 358)

> The above-named three genera, namely *Drosophyllum, Roridula*, and *Byblis*, which appear to have retained a primordial condition, still bear glandular hairs on both surfaces of their leaves; but those on the lower surface have since disappeared in the more highly developed genera, with the partial exception of one species, *Drosera binata*. The small sessile glands have also disappeared in some of the genera, being replaced in *Roridula* by hairs, and in most species of *Drosera* by absorbent papillae. *Drosera binata*, with its linear and bifurcating leaves, is in an intermediate condition... . A further slight change would

convert the linear leaves of this latter species into the oblong leaves of *Drosera anglica*, and these might easily pass into orbicular ones with footstalks like those of *Drosera rotundifolia*. (Darwin, 1875, p. 360)

The parent form of *Dionaea* and *Aldrovanda* seems to have been closely allied to *Drosera*.. ... (Darwin, 1875, p. 360)

Darwin similarly considered the production of digestive enzymes by these six genera of the Droseraceae to be homologous, although evidence for digestion by the unrelated (but see Note 9) *Pinguicula* and *Nepenthes* presented a 'remarkable problem' (Darwin, 1875, p. 361). Conversely, the third characteristic of the Droseraceae—the ability of leaves, hairs, and glands to move when stimulated[10]— was not seen as a homologous trait:

It should, however, be borne in mind that leaves and their homologues... have gained this power [of movement when stimulated], in innumerable instances, independently of inheritance from any common parent form... . We may therefore infer that the power of movement can be by some means readily acquired. (Darwin, 1875, pp. 363-364)

Darwin's hypotheses regarding homologies and the evolution of carnivorous plants have been supported only partially by subsequent data (reviewed by Ellison & Gotelli, 2009; see also Note 9). In part, this reflects the fact that strong selection in nutrient-poor environments has led repeatedly to the evolution of carnivory in a wide range of plant lineages (Albert, Williams & Chase, 1992; Adamec, 1997). That there are only a few ways that plants have evolved carnivory—sticky traps, pitfall traps, bladders and lobster-pots—led Darwin erroneously to identify homologies in homoplasies (similar traits arising in unrelated species as a result of similar selective pressures). But perhaps more importantly (in the context of this chapter), it was impossible for Darwin in the nineteenth century, just as it is for us today, to use controlled experiments to distinguish among hypotheses for the origin of different species, genera and higher taxa.

CARNIVOROUS PLANTS SINCE DARWIN AND THE CONTINUING IMPORTANCE OF EXPERIMENTS

Changes in our understanding of how carnivorous plants 'work' have proceeded in fits and starts. Darwin's work, summarized in *Insectivorous plants*, overturned several centuries of botanical 'truths' about carnivorous plants. His detailed descriptions of how carnivorous plants capture and digest insects and other small invertebrates, as well as how they absorb nutrients, but not carbon, from their prey have, by and large, stood the test of time.[11] Darwin's emphasis on experimental demonstration of the ability of truly carnivorous plants to actively capture, entrap, kill and digest prey, and then to absorb the nutrients of the digested prey (characteristics which, along with a mechanism for prey attraction, constitute the 'carnivorous syndrome' [Juniper, Robins

& Joel, 1989, p. 3]) has consigned many other suggested 'carnivorous' plants to the dustbin of hopeful fantasies. Although we now recognise many more carnivorous plant species, only two (or perhaps three) truly carnivorous plant genera have been discovered since *Insectivorous plants* was published: the carnivorous bromeliad *Brocchinia* (and possibly *Catopsis*; Frank & O'Meara, 1984; Givnish et al., 1984) and the liana *Triphyophyllum peltatum* (Green, Green & Heslop-Harrison, 1979).

Intensive experimental research on carnivorous plants re-emerged in the 1940s and again in the 1980s, supporting some of Darwin's hypotheses and overturning others. The new sets of hypotheses and theories developed in the 1980s (Givnish et al., 1984) have been re-examined critically in the last 15-20 years, and again some of the hypotheses have been supported but others have not (e.g. Ellison & Farnsworth, 2005; Ellison & Gotelli, 2009; Ellison & Adamec, 2011). At each of these times, and in all of these cases, experiments have been the critical tool used to advance scientific understanding.

Carnivorous Plants as Educational Tools

The fascination that carnivorous plants hold for children of all ages, the general ready availability of these plants from commercial growers and biological supply companies and the ease with which they can be grown both in glasshouses and in classroom terraria[12] create opportunities for a wide range of enquiry-based projects (see also discussions in Chapters 10, 13 & 27). The questions that Darwin asked about carnivorous plants, and the hypotheses that he tested, continue to be relevant to ecologists and evolutionary biologists today. For example, what is the range of adaptations shown by plants and animals? How do plants obtain nutrients when they are otherwise scarce? How does competition for these scarce nutrients lead to natural selection, new adaptations and evolutionary change? How do particular species fit into broader assemblages, food webs and ecosystems? What can we do to conserve these botanical curiosities as more and more land is used extensively and intensively for a growing human population, and the climate continues to change?

Darwin's observations and experiments themselves—enumerating and quantifying the types of insects captured and consumed by carnivorous plants, determining what nutrients are absorbed by individual leaves and what environmental stimuli cause the plant to move and capture its prey—can be encouraged and repeated using simple tools. Technology unavailable to Darwin, but now seen increasingly in secondary schools, such as high-speed web-cams, isotope mass spectrometers and DNA sequencers, can yield new insights into the physiological ecology and evolution of carnivorous plants (e.g. Forterre et al., 2005; Butler & Ellison, 2007; Butler, Gotelli & Ellison, 2008; Ellison et al., 2012). Carnivorous plants are also being used to address questions such as how to identify and forecast tipping points in ecological systems (Sirota et al., 2013). Such experiments require only some pitcher plants, a ready supply of prey (e.g. ground-up ants or wasps) and a probe for measuring dissolved oxygen; these experiments are already being adapted for classroom use.[13] The information garnered from these experiments is likely to be useful in determining how to prevent catastrophic 'regime shifts' in ecosystems.

CONCLUSION

The key feature of any well-designed experiment is to identify a small number of hypothesised critical processes which, when carefully examined, allow the testing and (potential) falsification of one or more plausible hypotheses. All well-designed experiments have 'treatments', in which the process of interest is excluded or manipulated, and 'controls', in which the same process is unmodified. Of course, there is some variability in each individual replicate to which a treatment is applied or a control is assigned (and so all good experiments have replicates in all treatment and control groups). In botanical experiments, such variability may be caused by genetic differences among individuals; unappreciated environmental variation within a controlled environment chamber or greenhouse, such as light quantity or temperature in the centre of a bench or at its edge; or uncontrollable processes in the field. Nonetheless, the hallmark of a successful experiment is that the 'signal' (the effects of the experimental manipulation) adequately exceeds the 'noise' caused by small-scale differences in genotype, growth chambers, greenhouses or site characteristics in the field. Experiments also provide a degree of control over when, where and how a biological process is activated or manipulated, and they enable repeatability in both time and space that can never be achieved with observational studies. As a consequence of all of these attributes, from long before Darwin's time until today, experimental results provide the 'gold standard' of scientific evidence.

There are mechanical 'rules' for good experimental design: the most important is adequate numbers of independent replicates of both treatment and control individuals. But effective application of the scientific method—repeated hypothesis development, testing and rejection—still requires a lot of creativity and new thinking. Darwin's research with carnivorous plants remains an inspiring example of how to test hypotheses effectively and skeptically and generate new theories of how the world works.

NOTES

[1] The scientific method of falsification and the inherent skepticism of scientists is the fundamental point of contrast between science and religion; unlike science, religion requires faith and a suspension of disbelief.

[2] A similar phenomenon, termed 'aquaplaning' (Bohn & Federle, 2004, p. 14138) was experimentally demonstrated for the unrelated Asian pitcher plant *Nepenthes rafflesiana* by Bauer, Bohn and Federle (2008), but Macbride's observations have not yet been tested experimentally for any species of *Sarracenia*.

[3] Within a year of the publication of *On the origin of species*, Darwin had already moved on to the problem of the evolution of carnivory in plants. As he wrote to Charles Lyell in 1860 (F. Darwin 1911, p. 492):

… at the present moment, I care more about *Drosera* than the origin of all the species in the world.

A. M. ELLISON

4   Darwin references an 1860 bibliography on prior works on *Drosera*, but notes (*Insectivorous plants*, p. 1) that '[m]ost of the notices published before 1860 are brief and unimportant'.
5   In the second edition of *Insectivorous plants* (1893), Darwin adds a section on pp. 15-16 describing subsequent experiments of the benefits, in terms of growth and especially reproduction that *Drosera* obtains from additional prey. These latter experiments were actually done by Charles Darwin's son Francis (F. Darwin, 1878a, 1878b), who, unlike his father, was able to successfully demonstrate experimentally that *Drosera rotundifolia* plants 'profit by their carnivorous habitats' (F. Darwin 1878a, p. 222). The lack of attribution of these experiments to Francis Darwin apparently resulted from a proof-reading error (Randal Keynes, personal communication, 13 November 2013).
6   Francis Darwin's experiment (F. Darwin, 1878a, 1878b) is an example of what we now call a 'Before-After-Control-Impact' (or BACI) experiment. The plants themselves were first collected in the field, and then divided into two groups. Half were starved (the 'control') and half were fed (the 'impact'). The measure of effect is the change from the initial to the final state (hence 'before' versus 'after'). The same 'before' versus 'after' effects were tested on the plants that were allowed to overwinter (F. Darwin, 1878b). For additional details on BACI designs, see Gotelli & Ellison (2012).
7   Mainstream botanists from the 1700s on had followed Linnaeus's lead in denying that plants could either deliberately entrap insects or use the nutrients obtained from captured prey. In the second (revised) edition of *Insectivorous plants* (1893), Francis Darwin wrote (p. 243):

Linnaeus was unable to believe that the plant could profit by the captured insects. .. he consequently regarded the capture of the disturbing insect as something merely accidental and of no importance to the plant. Linnaeus' authority overbore criticism if any was offered; his statement about the behaviour of the leaves [in this case, of the Fly-trap] was copied from book to book.

8   Darwin, like other botanists of the time, considered these plants to be members of the sundew family (Droseraceae), in which were placed all of the sticky-trapping carnivorous plants. Analyses done in the last 20 years have shown not only that most of these non-carnivorous plants are unrelated to the Droseraceae, but also that *Byblis* and *Roridula* are neither related to the Droseraceae nor to each other. Furthermore, Darwin, in discussing Hooker's observations on digestion of insects by the Asian pitcher plants (*Nepenthes*), wrote (pp. 361-362):

The six genera of the Droseraceae have probably inherited this power [of digestion] from a common progenitor, but this cannot apply to *Pinguicula* or *Nepenthes*, for these plants are not at all closely related to the Droseraceae.

In fact, there is now strong support for asserting that the Droseraceae (which includes only *Drosera, Dionaea, and Aldrovanda*) is ancestral to, and the sister family of, the clade that includes *Nepenthes* (Nepenthaceae) and *Drosophyllum* (Drosophyllaceae). See Ellison & Gotelli (2009) for a detailed discussion of convergent evolution among, and current hypotheses for, phylogenetic positions of carnivorous plants

9   The concept of homology, or the correspondence of (morphological) traits of different organisms resulting from common evolutionary history, is another of Darwin's fundamental contributions to evolutionary biology (Ghiselin, 2005).
10 Five years later, Darwin published an entire book on movement in plants (Darwin, 1880).
11 Darwin's understanding of the mechanism by which *Utricularia* bladders trap their prey is a notable exception. Darwin thought that small aquatic crustaceans pushed their way into the bladder, but this turns out not to be even close to an accurate description of the actual mechanism, in which Treat observed the role of 'trigger hairs' (Treat, 1875-see Chapter 2) and which Lloyd (1942) described as a nearly ideal mousetrap. The bladderwort's trap is a purely mechanical, vacuum trap. Tripping the 'trigger hairs' opens the vacuum seal, and the animal that hit them is sucked into the bladder, which rapidly (within 10 milliseconds) reseals and resets Lloyd's (1942, pp. 266-267) 'better mousetrap'.
12 It is important to note, however, that carnivorous plants such as *Drosera rotundifolia* and other sundews, *Sarracenia* species, and many bladderworts *Utricularia* and butterworts *Pinguicula* native to temperate climatic zones go dormant for at least six weeks, and often as much as four-six months,

in the winter. Careful planning of classroom experiments is required to ensure that experiments are conducted when the plant is actively growing. D'Amato (2013) provides detailed guidelines on carnivorous plant cultivation.

[13] See the London-based INQUIRE project. See http://www.inquirebotany.org/en/discussions/pitcher-plants-as-ecosystems-ibse-626.html.

REFERENCES

Adamec, L. (1997). Mineral nutrition of carnivorous plants: A review. *Botanical Review, 63*(3), 273–299.

Albert, V. A., Williams, S. E., & Chase, M. W. (1992). Carnivorous plants: Phylogeny and structural evolution. *Science, 257*(5076), 1491–1495.

Bauer, U., Bohn, H. F., & Federle, W. (2008). Harmless nectar source or deadly trap: *Nepenthes* pitchers are activated by rain, condensation and nectar. *Proceedings of the Royal Society B: Biological Sciences, 275*(1632), 259–265.

Bohn, H. F., & Federle, W. (2004). Insect aquaplaning: *Nepenthes* pitcher plants capture prey with the peristome, a fully wettable water-lubricated anisotropic surface. *Proceedings of the National Academy of Sciences, USA, 101*(39), 14138–14143.

Butler, J. L., & Ellison, A. M. (2007). Nitrogen cycling dynamics in the carnivorous northern pitcher plant. *Sarracenia purpurea. Functional Ecology, 21*(5), 835–843.

Butler, J. L., Gotelli, N. J., & Ellison, A. M. (2008). Linking the brown and green: Nutrient transformation and fate in the *Sarracenia* microecosystem. *Ecology, 89*(4), 898–904.

Chamberlin, T. C. (1890). The method of multiple working hypotheses. *Science* (Old Series), *15*(366), 92–96.

Conan Doyle, A. (1890). *The sign of four*. London: Spencer Blackett.

D'Amato, P. (2013). *The savage garden, revised: Cultivating carnivorous plants*. Berkeley, CA: Ten Speed Press.

Darwin, C. (1859). *On the origin of species by means of natural selection, or the preservation of favoured races in the struggle for life*. London: John Murray.

Darwin, C. (1875). *Insectivorous plants*. London: John Murray.

Darwin, C. (1880). *The power of movement in plants*. London: John Murray.

Darwin, F. (1878a). Insectivorous plants. *Nature, 17*(429), 222–223.

Darwin, F. (1878b). The nutrition of *Drosera rotundifolia. Nature, 18*(449), 153–154.

Darwin, F. (1911). *The life and letters of Charles Darwin, including an autobiographical chapter*. New York, NY: D. Appleton & Co.

Dixon, P. M., Ellison, A. M., & Gotelli, N. J. (2005). Improving the precision of estimates of the frequency of rare events. *Ecology, 86*(5), 1114–1123.

Dodoens, R. (1554). *Cruijdeboeck*. Leyden, The Netherlands.

Ellis, J. (1770). *Directions for bringing over seeds and plants from the East Indies, and other distant countries in a state of vegetation. To which is added, the figure and botanical description of a new plant, Dionaea muscipula or Venus's Flytrap*. London: L. Davis.

Ellison, A. M., & Adamec, L. (2011). Ecophysiological traits of terrestrial and aquatic carnivorous plants: Are the costs and benefits the same? *Oikos, 120*(11), 1721–1731.

Ellison, A. M., & Farnsworth, E. J. (2005). The cost of carnivory for *Darlingtonia Californica* (Sarraceniaceae): Evidence from relationships among leaf traits. *American Journal of Botany, 92*(7), 1085–1093.

Ellison, A. M., & Gotelli, N. J. (2009). Energetics and the evolution of carnivorous plants: Darwin's 'most wonderful plants in the world'. *Journal of Experimental Botany, 60*(1), 19–42.

Ellison, A. M., Butler, E. D., Hicks, E. J., Naczi, R. F. C., Calie, P. J., Bell, C. D., & Davis, C. C. (2012). Phylogeny and biogeography of the carnivorous plant family Sarraceniaceae. *PLoS ONE, 7*(6), e39291.

Flinders, M. (1814). *A voyage to Terra Australis; undertaken for the purpose of completing the discovery of that vast country* (Vol 1). London, UK: W. Bulmer & Co.

Forterre, Y., Skotheim, J. M., Dumais, J., & Mahadevan, L. (2005). How the Venus flytrap snaps. *Nature, 433*(7204), 421–425.

Frank, J. H., & O'Meara, G. F. (1984). The bromeliad *catopsis berteroniana* traps terrestrial arthropods but harbors *Wyeomyia* larvae (Diptera: Culicidae). *Florida Entomologist, 67*(3), 418–424.

Gerard, J. (1633). *The herbal or general history of plants, revised and enlarged by Thomas Johnson.* London: Norton & Whittakers.

Ghiselin, M. T. (2005). Homology as a relation of correspondence between parts of individuals. *Theory in Biosciences, 124*(2), 91–103.

Givnish, T. J., Burkhardt, E. L., Happel, R. E., & Weintraub, J. D. (1984). Carnivory in the bromeliad *Brocchinia reducta*, with a cost/benefit model for the general restriction of carnivorous plants to sunny, moist, nutrient-poor habitats. *American Naturalist, 124*(4), 479–497.

Gotelli, N. J., & Ellison, A. M. (2012). *A primer of ecological statistics* (2nd ed.). Sunderland, MA: Sinauer Associates.

Green, S., Green, T. L., & Heslop-Harrison, Y. (1979). Seasonal heterophylly and leaf gland features in *Triphyophyllum* (Dioncophyllaceae), a new carnivorous plant genus. *Botanical Journal of the Linnean Society, 78*(2), 99–116.

Hooker, W. J. (1858). *Nepenthes villosa* from Kina-Baloo, Borneo. *Curtis's Botanica Magazine, 14*(3rd series), 5080.

Juniper, B. E., Robins, R. J., & Joel, D. M. (1989). *The carnivorous plants.* London: Academic Press.

Kellermann, C., & von Raumer, E. (1878). Vegetationsversuche an *Drosera rotundifolia*, mit und ohne Fleischfutterung. *Botanische Zeitung, 36*(14), 209–218, 225–229.

Linnaeus, C. (1753). *Species plantarum, exhibentes plantas rite cognitas, ad genera relatas.* Stockholm, Sweden: Laurentius Salvius.

Lloyd, F. E. (1942). *The carnivorous plants.* New York, NY: Ronald Press.

Macbride, J. (1818). On the power of *Sarracenia adunca* to entrap insects. *Transactions of the Linnean Society of London, 12*, 48–52.

Platt, J. R. (1964). Strong inference. *Science, 146*(3642), 347–353.

Popper, K. (1959). *The logic of scientific discovery.* London: Routledge.

Sirota, J., Baiser, B., Gotelli, N. J., & Ellison, A. M. (2013). Organic-matter loading determines regime shifts and alternative states in an aquatic ecosystem. *Proceedings of the National Academy of Sciences, USA, 110*(19), 7742–7747.

Sowerby, J. (1790). *English botany.* London: R. Hardwicke.

Taper, M. L., & Lele, S. R. (Eds). (2004). *The nature of scientific evidence.* Chicago, IL: University of Chicago.

Aaron M. Ellison
Harvard Forest,
Harvard University,
USA

KAREN E. JAMES

19. DNA BARCODING DARWIN'S MEADOW

A Twenty-first-century Botanical Inventory at Historic Down House

CHARLES DARWIN'S 1855 SURVEY OF A MEADOW NEAR DOWN HOUSE

If ever you catch quite a beginner, and want to give him a taste for Botany, tell him to make a perfect list of some little field or wood... it gives a really uncommon interest to the work, having a nice little definite world to work on, instead of the awful abyss and immensity of all British Plants.[1]

In June 1855 Charles Darwin wrote to Joseph Hooker that he intended to survey the 13-acre hay meadow (Great Pucklands) near Down House, and reported with delight – 'Hurrah! Hurrah!' – that he had identified his first grass.[2] He and Miss Thorley, his children's governess, began the survey that month[3] and by the end of that month had identified 28 species of grass[4]; by July, they were up to 35 species[5]. They were still conducting the survey in August when he wrote to John Henslow that he was puzzled by an umbellifer.[6]

Darwin's objectives in doing the survey were his and Thorley's 'amusement' (Darwin to Hooker, 5 June 1855) and 'to show the degree of diversity in our British plants on a small plot' (Darwin, 1857, p. 230); the survey was, perhaps, among the first intentional, comprehensive species counts in a geographically defined area in history. In an age when rare specimens were prized above all, their aim was radical: to identify all of the plant species growing on a small, unremarkable plot. He described the field and the result of the survey as follows:

I selected a field, in Kent, of 13 acres, which had been thrown out of cultivation for 15 years, & had been thinly planted with small trees most of which had failed: the field all consisted of heavy very bad clay, but one side sloped & was drier: there was no water or marsh: 142 phanerogamic plants were here collected by a friend during the course of a year; these belonged to 108 genera, & to 32 orders out of the 86 orders into which the plants of Britain have been classed.

This narrative appeared in the second part of his original 'big species book' written from 1856 to 1858 (Darwin, 1857, p. 230), but about half-way through writing the book, on June 18, 1858 Darwin received the now famous letter from Alfred Russel Wallace which enclosed his February 1858 manuscript 'On the tendency of varieties to depart indefinitely from the original type [7], which spurred him to write what he called 'an abstract' of the book: *On the origin of species*. In Chapter IV of that work, Darwin substituted his later count on a 3-foot by 4-foot patch of his lawn for the original Great Pucklands meadow survey (Darwin, 1859, p. 114; Randal Keynes, pers. comm.).

THE NATURAL HISTORY MUSEUM'S 2005-2007 RE-SURVEY OF THE MEADOW

The field that Darwin and Thorley surveyed, Great Pucklands meadow, is part of a larger area including Down House and the surrounding countryside (see Figure 1) that is the subject of a World Heritage Site bid '*Darwin's Landscape Laboratory*'.[8] During the summers of 2005, 2006 and 2007 a team from the Natural History Museum in London (NHM) re-surveyed Great Pucklands meadow (see Figure 2). As Darwin used Great Pucklands meadow in 1855 to develop his botanical identification skills – to get 'a taste for botany'[9] – so the team used the meadow to further develop procedures for plant identification 150 years later.

The aims of the re-survey were to (1) detect change (if any) in species number and diversity in the meadow since 1855, and (2) pilot and optimise procedures for high-throughput botany, pairing the collection and management of herbarium specimens together with 'DNA barcoding', the creation of libraries of short, standardized, DNA sequences linked to representative specimens in established specimen repositories, for the eventual use in DNA-based identification of unknown samples. Specifically,

Figure 1. Satellite image[10] (left) indicating the relative locations of Down House (top right) and Great Pucklands meadow (bottom right) on the south-west corner of Downe village in Kent. (Top right, bottom right © Karen James)

Figure 2. The NHM re-survey in 2007 of Great Pucklands meadow (top left) involved plant identification (top right), specimen collection (bottom left) and sampling for DNA barcoding (bottom right). (Top right, bottom left © Karen James; top left, bottom right: screen capture from the 2009 BBC programme, Jimmy Doherty in Darwin's Garden)

the NHM team aimed to evaluate a selection of short regions of DNA that had been identified as potential candidates for DNA barcoding (Chase et al., 2007; Kress & Erickson, 2007).

Though the DNA barcoding data from these specimens have been reported and analysed as part of a peer-reviewed, consortium-authored paper that recommended a 'DNA barcode for land plants' (CBOL Plant Working Group, 2009), that paper did not allow space to report or discuss the results of the re-survey, nor the DNA barcoding results in isolation from the larger consortium data set. This chapter provides an opportunity to discuss the importance of Charles Darwin's original survey of Great Pucklands meadow with the children's governess, Miss Thorley in relation to a twenty-first-century re-survey and the use of DNA barcoding in the context of a potential science learning environment.

The NHM team carried out preliminary surveys in 2005 and 2006, recording, but not collecting, 161 vascular plant species. In 2007 single specimens from 141 species – 138 flowering plants, two conifers and one fern (see Table 1) – were collected, along with digital photographs and Ordinance Survey National Grid references (not shown).

Table 1. List of seed plant species collected by the NHM team (2007) as per Stace (1997).

Order	Family	Taxon
Alismatales	Araceae	*Arum maculatum*
Alismatales	Araceae	*Lemna minor*
Apiales	Apiaceae	*Anthriscus sylvestris*
Apiales	Apiaceae	*Chaerophyllum temulum*
Apiales	Apiaceae	*Daucus carota*
Apiales	Apiaceae	*Heracleum sphondylium*
Apiales	Apiaceae	*Pimpinella saxifraga*
Apiales	Apiaceae	*Sanicula europea*
Apiales	Apiaceae	*Torilis japonica*
Apiales	Araliaceae	*Hedera helix*
Aquifoliales	Aquifoliaceae	*Ilex aquifolium*
Asparagales	Hyacinthaceae	*Hyacinthoides non-scripta*
Asterales	Asteraceae	*Achillea millefolium*
Asterales	Asteraceae	*Arctium minus*
Asterales	Asteraceae	*Centaurea nigra*
Asterales	Asteraceae	*Cirsium arvense*
Asterales	Asteraceae	*Hypochaeris radicata*
Asterales	Asteraceae	*Lapsana communis*
Asterales	Asteraceae	*Leucanthemum vulgare*
Asterales	Asteraceae	*Senecio erucifolius*
Asterales	Asteraceae	*Senecio jacobaea*
Asterales	Asteraceae	*Senecio vulgaris*
Asterales	Asteraceae	*Sonchus asper*
Asterales	Asteraceae	*Taraxacum officinale* agg
Asterales	Asteraceae	*Tragopogon pratensis*
Asterales	Asteraceae	*Crepis capillaris*
Asterales	Asteraceae	*Crepis vesicaria*
Brassicales	Brassicaceae	*Alliaria petiolata*
Brassicales	Brassicaceae	*Sisymbrium officinale*
Caryophyllales	Amaranthaceae	*Atriplex patula*
Caryophyllales	Caryophyllaceae	*Cerastium fontanum*
Caryophyllales	Caryophyllaceae	*Stellaria graminea*

(*Continued*)

Table 1. (Continued)

Order	Family	Taxon
Caryophyllales	Caryophyllaceae	*Stellaria holostea*
Caryophyllales	Polygonaceae	*Polygonum aviculare*
Caryophyllales	Polygonaceae	*Rumex acetosa*
Caryophyllales	Polygonaceae	*Rumex crispus*
Caryophyllales	Polygonaceae	*Rumex obtusifolius (x pratensis)*
Caryophyllales	Polygonaceae	*Rumex sanguineus*
Caryophyllales	Polygonaceae	*Rumex x pratensis*
Cornales	Cornaceae	*Cornus sanguinea*
Dioscoreales	Dioscoreaceae	*Tamus communis*
Dipsacales	Adoxaceae	*Adoxa moschatellina*
Dipsacales	Adoxaceae	*Sambucus nigra*
Ericales	Primulaceae	*Primula vulgaris*
Fabales	Fabaceae	*Lathyrus pratensis*
Fabales	Fabaceae	*Lotus corniculatus*
Fabales	Fabaceae	*Trifolium dubium*
Fabales	Fabaceae	*Trifolium pratense*
Fabales	Fabaceae	*Trifolium repens*
Fabales	Fabaceae	*Vicia sepium*
Fabales	Fabaceae	*Vicia tetrasperma*
Fagales	Betulaceae	*Carpinus betulus*
Fagales	Betulaceae	*Corylus avellana*
Fagales	Fagaceae	*Castanea sativa*
Fagales	Fagaceae	*Fagus sylvatica*
Fagales	Fagaceae	*Quercus ilex*
Fagales	Fagaceae	*Quercus robur*
Gentianales	Gentianaceae	*Centaurium erythraea*
Gentianales	Rubiaceae	*Galium mollugo*
Geraniales	Geraniaceae	*Geranium dissectum*
Geraniales	Geraniaceae	*Geranium molle*
Geraniales	Geraniaceae	*Geranium robertianum*
Lamiales	Lamiaceae	*Glechoma hederacea*

(*Continued*)

Table 1. (Continued)

Order	Family	Taxon
Lamiales	Lamiaceae	*Lamium album*
Lamiales	Lamiaceae	*Origanum vulgare*
Lamiales	Lamiaceae	*Prunella vulgaris*
Lamiales	Lamiaceae	*Stachys sylvatica*
Lamiales	Oleaceae	*Fraxinus excelsior*
Lamiales	Oleaceae	*Ligustrum vulgare*
Lamiales	Orobanchaceae	*Odontites vernus ssp. serotinus*
Lamiales	Plantaginaceae	*Plantago lanceolata*
Lamiales	Plantaginaceae	*Veronica chamaedrys*
Lamiales	Plantaginaceae	*Veronica chamaedrys*
Malpighiales	Euphorbiaceae	*Mercurialis perennis*
Malpighiales	Hypericaceae	*Hypericum perforatum*
Malpighiales	Violaceae	*Viola reichenbachiana*
Malvales	Malvaceae	*Tilia x europea*
Myrtales	Onagraceae	*Epilobium hirsutum*
Myrtales	Onagraceae	*Epilobium montanum*
Myrtales	Onagraceae	*Epilobium parviflorum*
Myrtales	Onagraceae	*Epilobium tetragonum*
Poales	Brassicaceae	*Capsella bursa-pastoris*
Poales	Cyperaceae	*Carex sylvatica*
Poales	Juncaceae	*Luzula campestris*
Poales	Poaceae	*Agrostis capillaris*
Poales	Poaceae	*Agrostis vinealis*
Poales	Poaceae	*Alopecurus pratensis*
Poales	Poaceae	*Anisantha sterilis*
Poales	Poaceae	*Anthoxanthum odoratum*
Poales	Poaceae	*Arrhenatherum elatius*
Poales	Poaceae	*Bromopsis ramosus*
Poales	Poaceae	*Bromus commutatus*
Poales	Poaceae	*Bromus hordeaceus*
Poales	Poaceae	*Dactylis glomerata*

(Continued)

Table 1. (Continued)

Order	Family	Taxon
Poales	Poaceae	*Deschampsia cespitosa*
Poales	Poaceae	*Elymus repens*
Poales	Poaceae	*Festuca ovina*
Poales	Poaceae	*Festuca rubra*
Poales	Poaceae	*Holcus lanatus*
Poales	Poaceae	*Lolium perenne*
Poales	Poaceae	*Melica uniflora*
Poales	Poaceae	*Phleum bertolonii*
Poales	Poaceae	*Phleum pratense*
Poales	Poaceae	*Poa annua*
Poales	Poaceae	*Poa pratensis*
Poales	Poaceae	*Poa trivialis*
Poales	Poaceae	*Vulpia bromoides*
Ranunculales	Ranunculaceae	*Clematis vitalba*
Ranunculales	Ranunculaceae	*Ranunculus acris*
Ranunculales	Ranunculaceae	*Ranunculus auricomus*
Ranunculales	Ranunculaceae	*Ranunculus bulbosus*
Ranunculales	Ranunculaceae	*Ranunculus repens*
Rosales	Rosaceae	*Agrimonia eupatoria*
Rosales	Rosaceae	*Crataegus laevigata*
Rosales	Rosaceae	*Crataegus monogyna*
Rosales	Rosaceae	*Fragaria vesca*
Rosales	Rosaceae	*Geum urbanum*
Rosales	Rosaceae	*Malus domestica*
Rosales	Rosaceae	*Potentilla reptans*
Rosales	Rosaceae	*Potentilla sterilis*
Rosales	Rosaceae	*Prunus avium*
Rosales	Rosaceae	*Prunus spinosa*
Rosales	Rosaceae	*Rosa arvensis*
Rosales	Rosaceae	*Rosa canina* agg.
Rosales	Rosaceae	*Rubus fruticosus* agg

(*Continued*)

Table 1. (Continued)

Order	Family	Taxon
Rosales	Rosaceae	*Sorbus aria*
Rosales	Ulmaceae	*Ulmus glabra*
Rosales	Ulmaceae	*Ulmus procera*
Rosales	Urticaceae	*Urtica dioica*
Sapindales	Sapindaceae	*Acer campestre*
Sapindales	Sapindaceae	*Acer pseudoplatanus*
Saxifragales	Grossulariaceae	*Ribes rubrum*
Solanales	Convolvulaceae	*Calystegia sepium*
Solanales	Convolvulaceae	*Convolvulus arvensis*
Solanales	Solanaceae	*Solanum dulcamara*
-	Boraginaceae	*Myosotis sylvatica*
Pinales	Pinaceae	*Picea abies*
Pinales	Taxaceae	*Taxus baccata*

Leaf samples from each specimen were taken for DNA extraction. High-throughput laboratory methods for 'sequencing', that is, reading, the chosen DNA barcode region from animal tissue samples (Hajibabaei et al., 2005) were adapted for plant material. Six plant DNA barcoding candidate loci – *rpoC, rpoB, rbcL, matK, trnH-psbA* and *atpF-atpH* (Chase et al., 2007; Kress & Erickson, 2007) – were isolated and amplified via PCR[11], then sequenced and deposited in GenBank (CBOL Plant Working Group, 2009).

GREAT PUCKLANDS MEADOW: 150 YEARS ON

Whether, and how, the flora of Great Pucklands meadow has changed in the 150 years since Darwin and Thorley did their survey is naturally of great interest. Have environmental changes, such as land-use change or climate change, affected a change in plant communities or phenology, that is, the timing of biological events such as flowering? Repeat surveys can reveal the biotic response to landscape and environmental change (Walther et al., 2002), and citizen scientists - young and old - may be involved in these studies; thus, a demonstration that Great Pucklands meadow has remained largely unchanged since Darwin's time would add to the justification for including not just Down House but the grounds around it in a proposed World Heritage Site.

Darwin must have made a list of the species he recorded in the meadow, for he wrote of comparing the flora of Great Pucklands with that of Ashdown Common in

Table 2. Number of seed plant species, genera, families, and orders recovered by Darwin and Thorley (1855) and the NHM team (2005-2007).

	Species	Genera	Families	Orders
Darwin and Thorley, 1855	142	108	-	32
NHM, 2005-2006	160	112	44	27
NHM, 2007	140	106	44	27

Sussex, noting that 'the vegetation was ... considerably different in other respects, no less than nine of the 34 orders, not being found on [Great Pucklands].' (Darwin, 1857, p. 230). Alas, Darwin's species list is yet to be discovered (Randal Keynes, pers. comm.). Therefore it is only possible to compare the *number* of species, genera and orders recorded by Darwin with the number recorded during the repeat survey.

In 1855, Darwin and Thorley collected 142 seed plants belonging to 108 genera and 32 orders (Darwin, 1857, p. 230). In 2005 and 2006 the NHM team recorded 160 seed plants and one fern, the seed plants belonging to 112 genera, 44 families and 27 orders; in 2007 the NHM team re-found and collected 140 of the seed plants and the fern, the seed plants belonging to 106 genera, 44 families and 27 orders (Table 2).

Of the 160 seed plant species recorded in 2005 or 2006, 20 were not re-found (and therefore not collected) in 2007. This discrepancy may be the result of annual fluctuations in (1) the composition of the flora, (2) environmental factors that affect the timing of flowering and thus conspicuousness of some species, or (3) the identity, number of, total time spent by, and attentiveness of team members.

The number of seed plant species and genera collected by the NHM team in 2007 (140 and 106, respectively) is similar to the number Darwin reported finding in 1855 (142 and 108, respectively). At the level of order, however, the numbers diverge; the NHM team's collection spanned 27 orders while Darwin's survey spanned 32 orders. On first consideration, this might seem to suggest that the similarity between the numbers of species and genera is coincidence, and that the flora of Great Pucklands meadow changed significantly between 1855 and 2007. However, there is another potential explanation: the flora has remained relatively constant, and the NHM team and Darwin found largely the same species, but British plant taxonomy has changed in the interim, such that the orders to which those species are assigned have changed or been combined and/or renamed.

The NHM team used the second edition of Clive Stace's *New flora of the British Isles* as the primary reference for the resurvey (1997). This flora classifies British seed plants into 62 orders, while Darwin wrote that he was using a classification system with 86 orders (Darwin, 1857, p. 230). Floras he may have used as his reference include John Lindley's *Synopsis of the British flora* (1829) (Sandra Knapp, pers. comm.), one of two editions of John Stephens Henslow's *A catalogue of British plants* (1829, 1830) (Mark Spencer, pers. comm.), and the fourth or seventh edition of William Hooker's *British flora* (1838 and 1855, respectively) (David Kohn, pers. comm.). Disappointingly, a cursory count of the orders listed in these floras fails to identify one with exactly 86; Lindley (1829) lists 103 flowering plant orders, Henslow (2nd edition, 1830) lists 98 plant orders, 91 of those being seed plant orders, Hooker (4th edition, 1838) lists 106 plant orders, 99 of those being seed plant orders, and Hooker (7th edition, 1855) lists 113 plant orders, 107 of those being seed plant orders. Thus the identity of the flora Darwin used as a reference for his survey remains elusive. Nevertheless, Stace (1997) classifies British seed plants into 24 fewer orders than the reference Darwin used, consistent with the hypothesis that changes in British plant taxonomy – rather than dramatic changes to the species assemblage of Great Pucklands meadow – underlie the difference in number of orders identified in 1855 and 2007.

Darwin went on to compare the species composition of Great Pucklands with that of 40 acres of uncultivated ground at Ashdown Common in Sussex, which was surveyed for him by 'another friend' (Darwin, 1857, p. 230). There, 106 species belonging to 82 genera and 34 orders were recorded. Darwin notes that the greater number of orders in this meadow over Great Pucklands was a result of the presence of water and marsh plants on the former. Even so, he notes 'the vegetation was … considerably different in other respects, no less than nine of the 34 orders, not being found on [Great Pucklands]' (Darwin, 1857, p. 230). A repeat of Darwin's Ashdown Common survey might add depth, breadth, and significance to the Great Pucklands re-survey.

DNA BARCODING

For DNA barcoding to be used successfully in research and its applications, two conditions must be met: the DNA barcoding region or regions must be universal, that is, present and amplifiable by PCR from the biological samples to be studied, and the DNA sequences of that region or those regions must be usable for discriminating species. Floristic and faunistic studies, that is, studies that explore the diversity of species in a geographically defined area, provide an ideal context for evaluating the universality of DNA barcoding regions because they tend to include a taxonomically broad range of species.

As a floristic study, then, the Great Pucklands meadow re-survey presented an opportunity to test the universality of a selection of candidate regions that had been proposed for use in plant DNA barcoding: *rpoC*, *rpoB*, *rbcL*, *matK*, *trnH-psbA* and *atpF-atpH* (Chase et al., 2007; Kress & Erickson, 2007). As noted earlier in this chapter, PCR amplification success rates from the Great Pucklands meadow specimens collected in 2007 have already been reported and analysed as part of a consortium-authored paper (CBOL Plant Working Group, 2009), but that paper did not allow space to report or discuss the DNA barcoding results in isolation from the larger consortium data set. Figure 3 provides an overview of PCR amplification

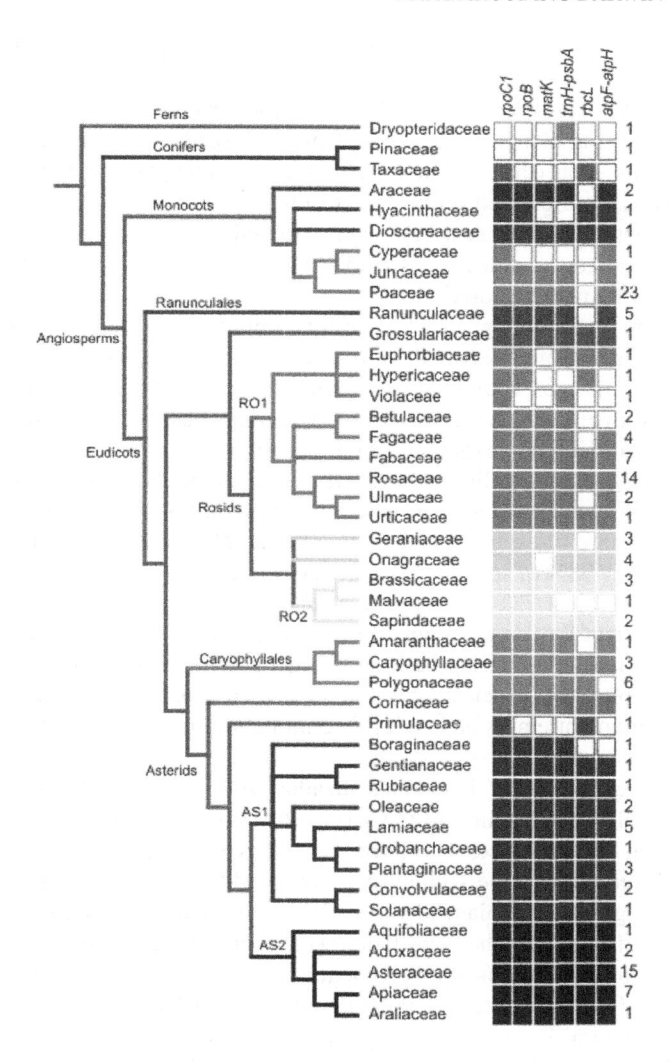

Figure 3. Phylogenetic context of included taxa and sequencing success of tested loci. The cladogram depicts the major land plant lineages (Angiosperm Phylogeny Group, 2003; Moore et al., 2007; Smith et al., 2006) modified to include only the families from which taxa were sampled for this study. The PCR amplification success of each locus is indicated, and the number of taxa sampled (n) from each family; shaded boxes indicate success in at least one taxon tested and white boxes indicate failure in all taxa tested.

success rates from the Great Pucklands meadow specimens in a phylogenetic context.

Higher PCR success rates were achieved among eudicots (one of the two major groups of flowering plants, comprising plants with seeds that bear two cotyledons) than among monocots (the other major group, comprising plants with seeds that bear one cotyledon), conifers and ferns. This result is unsurprising considering that the PCR conditions that were used had been designed for eudicots; thus, universality is highest in eudicots and decreases with phylogenetic distance. Beyond this trend, there are no other notable correlations.

In addition to providing an ideal testing opportunity for the universality of DNA barcoding regions, geographically-defined floras are also well-suited to the application of DNA barcoding for its intended purpose, that is, the identification of specimens to the species level. DNA barcoding has been shown to be more successful in floristic contexts than in the context of monographic studies, that is, studies with a geographically unrestricted but taxonomically narrow focus (Kress et al., 2009). When applied to 296 species of woody trees, shrubs, and palms found within a 50-hectare forest plot in Panama, for example, DNA barcoding was able to correctly identify 98% of specimens to the species level (Kress et. al, 2009), whereas on a global scale, just 72% of specimens can be correctly identified to the species level (CBOL Plant Working Group, 2009). The reason for this useful discrepancy is that there is often little overlap between the geographical ranges of closely related species pairs, or 'sister species', and it is the presence of sister species that is most likely to confound attempts at species discrimination through DNA barcoding in a given research context.

Thus the flora of Great Pucklands meadow holds promise for the successful application of DNA barcoding in the service of future research and/or educational endeavours at Down House. The library of DNA barcoding reference sequences generated through this project might be used in addition to or in conjunction with other technology-enabled plant identification tools such as Columbia University's prototype 'Leafsnap'[12] for the identification of plant specimens, or for the validation of identifications by 'plant-blind' students and citizen scientists (Wandersee & Schussler, 2001). This concept is being piloted as part of Tree School, a collaboration between the Natural History Museum, London, and the Cothill Educational Trust, engaging 10-15-year-old schoolchildren in building DNA barcode libraries during immersive, 5-day programmes (Hopkins & James, 2010) and BioTrails, a new collaboration of the Mount Desert Island Biological Laboratory, Acadia National Park, and the Schoodic Institute supported by an award from the National Science Foundation[13]. If implemented at Down House, such a technology-assisted citizen-science project might complement existing and proposed methods for teaching plant identification and stimulating interest and awareness (Stagg & Donkin, 2013). Findings from, and procedures developed through, such activities could in turn be applied to a wider suite of case studies addressing what Darwin called 'the awful abyss and immensity of all British Plants'.[14]

ACKNOWLEDGEMENTS

The author thanks Down House and its staff for access to Great Pucklands meadow in 2005, 2006 and 2007, and other members of the team from the Natural History Museum in London who helped design and carry out the repeat survey, sample collection and processing, DNA barcoding, and analysis, including Frederick Rumsey, Mark Spencer, Mark Carine, Anna Dennis, Christopher Davis, Steve Russell, Michael Grundmann, Julia Llewellyn-Hughes, Johannes Vogel, and Harald Schneider. Randal Keynes and David Kohn kindly provided expert assistance with locating and interpreting historical information. Sandra Knapp provided counts of families and orders from Stace (1997). Funding for the project was provided by the Natural History Museum and Whatman International, Ltd.

NOTES

[1] Charles Darwin to J. D. Hooker, 15 June, 1855. Darwin Correspondence Database, http://www.darwinproject.ac.uk/entry-1700 accessed on 21 February 2010.
[2] Charles Darwin to J. D. Hooker, 5 June, 1855. Darwin Correspondence Database, http://www.darwinproject.ac.uk/entry-1693 accessed on 21 February 2010.
[3] Charles Darwin to J. D. Hooker, 15 June, 1855. Darwin Correspondence Database, http://www.darwinproject.ac.uk/entry-1700 accessed on 21 February 2010.
[4] Charles Darwin to J. S. Henslow, 27 June, 1855. Darwin Correspondence Database, http://www.darwinproject.ac.uk/entry-1705/ accessed on 21 February 2010.
[5] Charles Darwin to J. D. Hooker, 5 July, 1855. Darwin Correspondence Database, http://www.darwinproject.ac.uk/entry-1711/ accessed on 21 February 2010.
[6] Charles Darwin to J. S. Henslow, 23 (Aug–Sept, 1855?). Darwin Correspondence Database, http://www.darwinproject.ac.uk/entry-1748/ accessed on 21 February 2010.
[7] The manuscript was later presented together with extracts from Darwin's own writings on the subject of natural selection at the Linnean Society on 1 July, 1858 (Darwin and Wallace, 1858).
[8] http://www.darwinslandscape.co.uk/).
[9] Charles Darwin to J. D. Hooker, 15 June, 1855. Darwin Correspondence Database, http://www.darwinproject.ac.uk/entry-1700 accessed on 21 February 2010.
[10] Imagery © 2013 Bluesky, DigitalGlobe, Getmapping plc, Infoterra Ltd & Bluesky, Landsat, The GeoInformation Group.
[11] Polymerase Chain Reaction (PCR) is a standard molecular biology method that isolates and amplifies a region of interest for further investigation, which may include the determination of the DNA sequence of that region.
[12] (http:leafsnap.com/).
[13] Grant No. DRL-1223210.
[14] Charles Darwin to J. D. Hooker, 15 June, 1855. Darwin Correspondence Database, http://www.darwinproject.ac.uk/entry-1700 accessed on 21 February 2010.

REFERENCES

The Angiosperm Phylogeny Group. (2003). An update of the Angiosperm Phylogeny Group classification for the orders and families of flowering plants: APG II. *Botanical Journal of the Linnean Society, 141*, 399–436.

CBOL Plant Working Group. (2009). A DNA barcode for land plants. *Proceedings of the National Academy of Sciences, USA, 106*(31), 12794–12797.

Chase, M. W., Cowan, R. S., Hollingsworth, P. M., van den Berg, M., Mandrinan, S., Petersen, G., . . . Carine, M. (2007). A proposal for a standardised protocol to barcode all land plants. *Taxon, 56*(2), 295.

Darwin, C. R. (1857). On natural selection. In R. C. Stauffer (Ed.), *Charles Darwin's natural selection: Being the second part of his big species book written from 1856 to 1858*. Cambridge, UK: Press Syndicate of the University of Cambridge.

Darwin, C. R. (1859). *On the origin of species by means of natural selection, or the preservation of favoured races in the struggle for life* (1st ed.). London: John Murray.

Darwin, C. R., & Wallace, A. R. (1858, August). On the tendency of species to form varieties; and on the perpetuation of varieties and species by natural means of selection. *Journal of the Proceedings of the Linnean Society of London, Zoology, 3*, 46–50.

Hajibabaei, M., DeWaard, J. R., Ivanova, N. V., Ratnasingham, S., Dooh, R. T., Kirk, S. L., . . . Hebert, P. D. N. (2005). Critical factors for assembling a high volume of DNA barcodes. *Philosophical Transactions of the Royal Society B: Biological Sciences, 360*(1462), 1959–1967.

Henslow, J. S. (1829, 1835). *A catalogue of British plants, arranged according to the natural system, with the synonyms of De Candolle, Smith, Lindley, and Hooker*. Cambridge: Deighton & Stevenson.

Hooker, W. J. (1838). *The British flora: Comprising the phaenogamous, or flowering plants, and the ferns* (4th ed.). London: Longman, Rees, Orme, Brown & Green.

Hooker, W. J., & Arnott, G. A. W. (1855). *The British flora: Comprising the phaenogamous, or flowering plants, and the ferns* (7th ed.). London: Longman, Brown, Green, & Longmans.

Hollingsworth, M., Clark, A. A., Forrest, L. L., Richardson, J., Pennington, R. T., Long, D. G., . . . & Hollingsworth, P. M. (2009). Selecting barcoding loci for plants: Evaluation of seven candidate loci with species-level sampling in three divergent groups of land plants. *Molecular Ecology Resources, 9*, 439–457.

Hopkins, D., & James, K. E. (2010). Tree school: A new innovation for science and education. In P. L. Nimis & R. Vignes Lebbe (Eds.). *Tools for identifying biodiversity: Progress and problems* (pp. 395–400).

Kress, W. J., & Erickson, D. L. (2007). A two-locus global DNA barcode for land plants: the coding rbcL gene complements the non-coding trnH-psbA spacer region. *PLoS ONE, 2*(6), e508.

Kress, W. J., Erickson, D. L., Jones, F. A., Swenson, N. G., Perez, R., Sanjur, O., & Bermingham, E., (2009). Plant DNA barcodes and a community phylogeny of a tropical forest dynamics plot in Panama. *Proceedings of the National Academy of Sciences, USA, 106*(44), 18621–18626.

Moore M. J., Bell C. D., Soltis P. S., & Soltis D. E. (2007). Using plastid genome-scale data to resolve enigmatic relationships among basal angiosperms. *Proceedings of the National Academy of Sciences, USA, 104*, 19363–19368.

Smith, A. R., Pryer, K. M., Schuettpelz, E., Korall, P. Schneider, H., & Wolf, P. G. (2006). A classification for extant ferns. *Taxon, 55*, 705–731.

Stagg, B. C., & Donkin, M. (2013). Teaching botanical identification to adults: experiences of the UK participatory science project 'Open Air Laboratories'. *Journal of Biological Education, 47*(2), 104–110.

Stace, C. A. (1997). *New flora of the British Isles* (2nd ed.). Cambridge: Cambridge University Press.

Walther, G. R. (2002). Ecological responses to recent climate change. *Nature, 416*, 389–395.

Wandersee, J. H., & Schussler, E. E. (2001). Towards a theory of plant blindness. *Plant Science Bulletin, 47*, 2–9.

Karen E. James
Mount Desert Island Biological Laboratory,
USA

INTERDISCIPLINARY STUDIES

MIRANDA LOWE & CAROLYN J. BOULTER

20. DARWIN'S BARNACLES

Learning from Collections

INTRODUCTION

The collection of both recent and fossilised barnacles that are amongst those that Darwin studied, are now stored within the Natural History Museum (NHM) in London. Occasionally parts of this collection of over 180 fossil and 1,500 extant barnacle specimens are put on public view as part of special exhibitions. Barnacles are marine invertebrates belonging to the group known as Cirripedes (Latin meaning 'curl-footed' referring to the feeding limbs which filter food from the water, see Figure 1). This is a diverse group and contains the sessile acorn barnacles that encrust the rocks of all shorelines and the hulls of boats, stalked or goose-necked barnacles fixed to piers and floating material, and parasitic barnacles living on or within other animals.

Many specimens in the Natural History Museum collection are dried material, cemented to trays, others are preserved in alcohol; in addition, there are some barnacles and parts of specimens stored as microscope slides. The collection contains numerous specimens still used for the identification of species and accessed by scientists from across the world.

Figure 1. Barnacles Semibalanus balanoides *feeding. (Kim Hansen, Wikipedia)*

Figure 2. A type specimen of Litoscalpellum giganteum *in front of the illustrations by G. B. Sowerby. (© Carolyn J. Boulter)*

WHY DID DARWIN STUDY BARNACLES?

Darwin had been interested in invertebrates since his years as a student in Edinburgh when Robert Edmond Grant[1] involved him in collecting from the seashore. But Darwin's inspiration for the study of all the known barnacles began when he found 'Mr Arthrobalanus' (later named *Cryptophialus minutus*) during his expedition on the *Beagle* (Newman, 1993). This was a shell-boring barnacle that he had found on the Chilean shore. Like many others it was stored in alcohol, for the journey back with him to England. It had no shell and was parasitic and he labelled it as belonging to the sessile acorn barnacles. But its differences troubled him. Nearly 10 years after its discovery, when he had been working on the publication of his experiences of the *Beagle* voyage, all that remained to be described were the marine invertebrates. In 1846 Darwin decided to spend a short time studying these organisms before working full time on his species theory. After describing the flatworms and then the arrow worms he had collected off the coast of South America he turned to barnacles (cirripedes). He recalled the strange tiny parasitic barnacle from South America and wondered again how it would fit into the classification of cirripedes in general. Using his dissecting microscope he discovered developing eggs at the base of the specimen and saw different larval stages. This suggested to him that barnacles were indeed crustaceans, not molluscs as Linnaeus and Cuvier had classified them because of their outer shell and inner cavity. Darwin became totally engrossed in the study of barnacles. Encouraged by his friend Joseph Hooker, with whom he exchanged 1,400 letters during his lifetime[2], he decided it might take a couple of years to describe all the species and work out a classification that might provide evidence of the process of speciation and an example of how this group had evolved, and of a common ancestor, for his book *On the origin of species*.

Darwin's scientific laboratory[3] was set up in his home at Down House and he really enjoyed the work; writing to Hooker in November 1846:

> As you say there is an extraordinary pleasure in pure observation; not but what I suspect the pleasure in this case is derived from comparisons forming in one's mind with allied structures. After having been so many years employed in writing my old geological observations it is delightful to use one's eyes and fingers again.[4]

He began to write to his contacts across the world for specimens and the barnacles started arriving by post to Down House.

Fourteen months after Darwin started his barnacle studies, late in 1847, John Edward Gray, keeper of the zoological collections at the British Museum and himself a barnacle expert, suggested that he prepare a monograph of the entire sub-class, as the entire classification of barnacles was regarded as being in disarray and there was no definitive work on them. Darwin asked for permission to borrow barnacles in batches from the museum collection:

> I am well aware that my request is an unusual one; but I would most respectfully beg to call the attention of the Trustees to the fact that specimens are sent out mounted, & that one specimen of every species of Cirripede must be disarticulated for the characters to be ascertained, & the parts of the mouth dissected.[5]

Unusually, his request was granted. He studied 153 extant species in total (Castilla, 2009) and the work stretched out from the two years he had envisaged into eight. By October 1852 he wrote, 'I hate the Barnacle as no man ever did before, not even a Sailor in a slow sailing ship'.[6] But was driven on by a desire to complete the classification work and publish all his findings. Darwin had possessed a passion for collecting from his school days which he later saw as the basis for his development into a systematic naturalist (Darwin, 1887). In the nineteenth century collecting was a significant pastime in Britain for many members of the public as well as specialists, and for those collectors able to travel across the empire writing travel narratives and assembling collections back home, was a way to make an authoritative name scientifically and socially (Hancock, 2007).

HOW DARWIN WORKED WITH THE BARNACLE COLLECTION

Darwin's scientific method was to look at the external plates of the barnacles, if they were present, then dissect the internal organs and finally to examine the larval stages. The work involved close observation of each species, dissection and description:

> I find by experience that each species takes me between 2 & 3 days, & each new genus, as many weeks. Every portion requires examination under the microscope & and all the minute organs under a high Compound power.[7]

Darwin bought the best dissecting microscope (see Figure 3) designed in Paris and made in London to obtain the highest resolution possible at that time. This enabled him to identify organs such as cement glands and sex organs and to compare similar structures across species.

Under the influence of the new guidelines for taxonomy that Owen[8] was formulating he took on the concept of homologies (structures that had arisen from the same embryological segments of the body). 'For Darwin homology revealed phylogenetic relationship rather than just similarity in the basic plan of organisation' (Richmond,

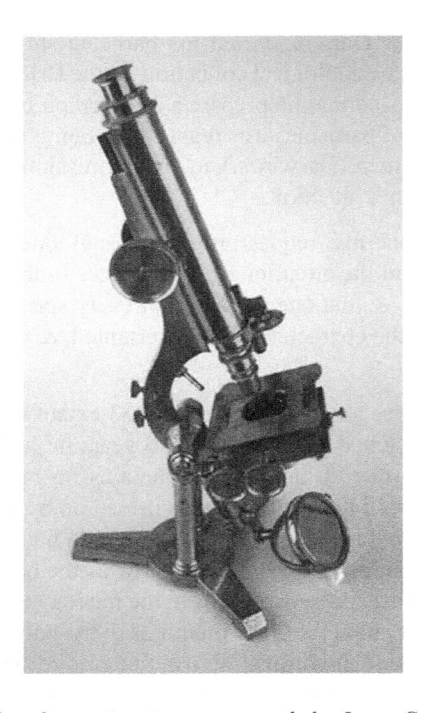

Figure 3. Darwin's achromatic microscope, made by James Smith in 1846. (By kind permission of the Whipple Museum, Cambridge.)

2007 online). These homologies could be established through embryology. For instance, he observed how the free-swimming cyprid larva[9] stuck itself onto the rock as it metamorphosed into the sedentary barnacle using cement glands which, at the time he believed to be the transformed ovaria. By his own admission in his autobiography he had 'blundered dreadfully' (Darwin 1887, p. 79) as this was later shown to be inaccurate. Despite such a set back to his theory, homological similarities suggested evolutionary relationships between the species and provided an idea of how the barnacles had evolved from a common ancestral crustacean.

Darwin's comparisons led to the identification of new genera and species and the establishment of a system of classification, which is the basis of current-day barnacle classification. He not only used similarities shown by homologies in his decisions about species but also the loss of useless organs (such as the last abdominal segments and abdominal swimmerettes of the ancestral crustacean). In addition, he saw that homologous organs were sometimes transformed, such as the original thoracic limbs for walking and swimming into cirri for feeding (see Figure 4).

It was the barnacle *Cryptophialus minutus* that initially caught his attention and led him into his study, but it was the genus *Ibla* that later held his attention. *Ibla* had small rudimentary males parasitic on the female and he then discovered some species of *Ibla* and *Scapellum* with minute males attached to a hermaphrodite body. This prompted him to write to Hooker in 1848 suggesting the evolution of sexuality through hermaphrodite into bisexuality. He claimed his species theory had convinced him this must be so.

As he worked through the barnacle species, Darwin was constantly thinking about his theories of species change and how the barnacle groups were related and might appear in a phylogenetic tree which showed their evolutionary relationships. The issue of the immense variation of barnacles was both a joy, (as it was evidence

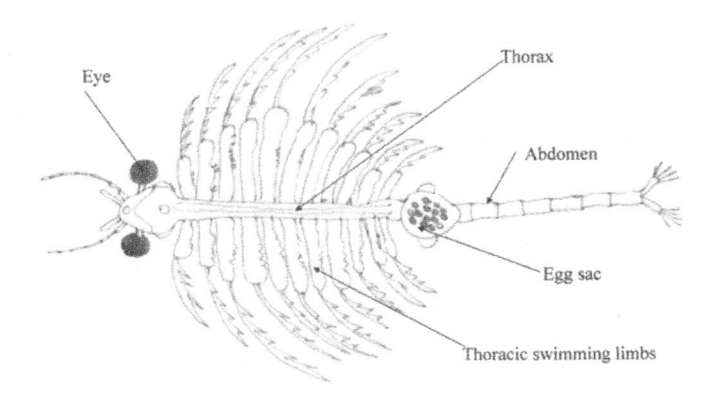

Figure 4. Sketch of an adult female brine shrimp Artemia *to show crustacean morphology. (© Carolyn J Boulter)*

of the raw material for selection), and a difficulty in defining where intra-specific variation stopped and species began. As Darwin reflected to Hooker in June 1850:

> At last I am going to press with a small, poor first fruit of my confounded cirripedia,viz.the fossil pedunculated cirripedia. You ask what effect studying species has had on my variation theories; I do not think much; I have felt some difficulties more; on the other hand I have been struck (& probably unfairly from the class) with the variability of every part in some slight degree of every species; When some organ is *rigorously* compared in many individuals I always find some slight variability, & consequently that the diagnosis of species from minute differences is always dangerous. I had thought the same parts of the same species more resembled than they do anywhere in Cirripedia objects cast in the same mould. Systematic work w^d be easy were it not for this confounded variation, which, however, is pleasant to me as a specularist though odious to me as a systematist.[10]

Today we recognise as separate species some of those Darwin grouped together as showing variation. His theory of gradual species change led him to be cautious.

In all this labour Darwin had the support of many naturalists, such as Hugh Cuming, a shell collector who made his own barnacle collection available, scientists, such as John Gray, and collectors from across the world. He lists those who helped him in the acknowledgements to his cirripede volumes and includes Mr Samuel Stutchbury from Bristol who supplied fresh specimens, William Thompson from Ireland who sent, 'the finest collection of British species and their varieties' and Revd Richard Thomas Lowe for his collection from Madeira (Darwin, 1854, p. vii). He was often in correspondence with Joseph Hooker about the finer points of the morphology and Hooker helped with the dissection and drawings.Darwin's children took their father's barnacle work as entirely natural and assumed all fathers had a room in which to study their barnacles. His work bore fruit in the volumes on the extant and fossil cirripedes published in 1851, 1852, 1854 and 1855, and illustrated by the Sowerby family.[11]

Darwin's methodology is discussed in other chapters (4, 10 & 18) of this volume. His work on barnacles shows his inductive drive to examine every known barnacle and to deduce their classification and their evolutionary connections from morphology and life histories. But his work also demonstrates the strong hold that his theory of natural selection and the mutability of species held on his barnacle years. He knew he needed to justify what he wanted to say in his major work about evolutionary trees, variation and natural selection and so he persisted in the work. The barnacle work is referred to at several points in *On the origin of species*[12] to justify claims for the species theory. In particular, he writes that: 'larvae can show the common affinity of disparate adult forms (the law of embryonic resemblance); that ancient forms resemble the embryo; that the barnacles emerged in the Mesozoic era, that very diverse forms of males and females are included in the same species; that the loss of organs from larva to adult is a response to selection pressure in a settled existence; that homologous organs are adapted for other uses; and that useless organs are lost to save energy'. The reasons for Darwin's long obsession with the barnacles has often been said to have been driven by his desire and need for status as a scientist. However some disagree and the issue has been discussed extensively (Scott, 2003). The drive, however motivated, required him to study every known barnacle and led to collections being gathered in institutions such as the Natural History Museum after his work was over.

THE USE OF COLLECTIONS TODAY

Many natural science collections today provide a vital resource for researchers, biological recorders, environmental consultants, science educators and the wider public. Darwin described 53 new species of extant barnacles. The specimens of these new species are commonly known as 'types' in the scientific community and form the original basis for a species description and are still used for comparison or further identification of new species. They are an irreplaceable resource for taxonomic and biodiversity research (Cordoro, 2009).

Collections in museums, like the barnacle collection in the NHM, are repositories of extensive information of changes through time and can be used to inform decisions about sustainability, so that regeneration and improvement of habitats can take proper account of the natural world.

They can be used as a means for understanding issues, and many scientific studies are proof of this. Certain aspects of deep-sea barnacles of the central Pacific are poorly studied and the recent scientific work of Poltarukha & Mel'nik (2012) has tried to resolve this. Most publications are devoted to the barnacles of underwater mountains, e.g. Mid-Pacific Mountains (Rao & Newman, 1972). Data on the barnacles of deep-sea ferromanganese nodule field areas are fragmentary but important for nature conservation, and more research would ensure that reliable data provide a sound basis to policy and action in environmental management worldwide and for UK Biodiversity Action Plans.

Specimens from the past are also valuable as a means of understanding the diversity and evolution of a group like the barnacles, as it exists today. In a similar way the effects of climate change can be monitored using named, dated and located specimens. James Carlton (2011) traces the effect of climate change on the barnacles of the East Coast of the USA. The spread of invasive species by commercial shipping can also be traced using collections.

COLLECTIONS FOR TEACHING AND LEARNING

The Crisis in Taxonomy and Systematics

The 2008 *House of Lords Science and Technology Report* [13] highlighted the crisis in the fields of taxonomy and systematics. The subsequent NERC report[14] focused on the special nature of collections and the need to maintain over 500 biological and geological collections in the UK, as well as enhancing the training of taxonomists for recruitment in industry and conservation. The NERC report called for a national strategy for taxonomy and systematics and pointed out the special nature of collections compared to the infrastructure of other scientific disciplines. Collections remain valuable as sources for research data for taxonomy indefinitely; the UK has a very large number due to its colonial past; many volunteer scientists are involved in high quality unpaid scientific work; the research field is expanding fast with new techniques from molecular biology and web-based communication. The results of taxonomic investigations have wide-ranging destinations from environmental science to the oil industry. There is therefore now a widely recognised need, not only for more stable funding for maintaining and making collections available, but also for a clear pathway through education from school, though undergraduate to postgraduate training in taxonomy and systematics.

The new molecular techniques require very small samples for the production of data which is stored and manipulated electronically. This has led to a questioning of the need for collections with all the problems of maintenance and storage space. Cordero (2009) considers that:

> The preservation of biodiversity requires an appreciation of traditional approaches in biological research in conjunction with modern ones. Therefore efforts must be made to train 21st century students in museum based research. (p. 60)

Raising the Awareness of Collections for Learning

Collecting specimens was the foundation of Darwin's work; it was the major task he set out with on his *Beagle* voyage and it was that search and the collections themselves that prompted his reflections on the origin of species for which he has became so famous. On the bicentenary of his birth in 2009 and during the *Darwin 200* celebrations, many of these collections went on show in museums and allowed the public to become aware of and to learn about the significance of these and other collections. The awareness of the significance of collections for learning led in 2012 to the first international congress for Teaching Innovation in Natural History, focusing on scientific collections. Another example is The Real World Science Project[15], a collaboration of nine museums with natural history collections across the UK that aims to enrich and enhance science teaching and learning at upper primary and secondary levels in school. The learning activities which use each museum's collections, aim to engage and inspire secondary school students to study science further, to pursue a science-related career or gain confidence as a scientifically literate individual who feels more prepared to discuss scientific issues.

Darwin-Inspired Learning: A Unit on Evidence for Evolutionary Relationships

Using the narrative of how Darwin worked with collections can provide deep insights for older students into how scientists work and the processes of taxonomy, classification and phylogeny. The Charles Darwin Trust has developed a unit around barnacles for 16 to 18 year olds which allows students to work with this process (see Chapter 26). The unit is called *Brilliant barnacles: evidence for evolutionary relationships* and is divided into three sections, each of which deals with the evidence for evolution in this group. The first section is about the evidence Darwin himself used from the morphology and life histories of barnacles. It encourages students to use the light microscope to examine crustacean structure in another crustacean, the brine shrimp, and compare its nauplius larva with representations of barnacle nauplii to look for similarities of form and function (homologies). The second section is about how Darwin built the tree of life[16] using his morphological studies of the barnacle collection. Students use data cards of a selection of the barnacles Darwin studied to build their own tree of life and then examine how scientists today have modified the tree through evidence from molecular studies (a maximum likelihood consensus tree). In the third section, students work with data from a paper by Benny Chan (2008), examining the feeding setae of three barnacle species (ones which Darwin also studied) using scanning electron microscopy (see Figure 5). This provides evidence for relationships using new SEM technology to extend vision.

Figure 5. Students examine evidence from scanning electron micrographs. (© Carolyn J. Boulter)

Figure 6. Miranda Lowe with Pollicipes elegans, *a stalked barnacle.*
(© Carolyn J. Boulter)

In order to engage students in the work of a scientist working with collections today, videoed interviews with Miranda Lowe (Figure 6) are available on the importance of the barnacle collections at the NHM and elsewhere, as well as a practice exam question on classification and taxonomy together with analyses of syllabuses and extension activities.

From such study, students can get an understanding of Darwin's big ideas and some of the questions that guided his work which link closely to their biology courses. Darwin's ways of working give insights into how scientists work, especially when allied to present day scientists' descriptions of their work with barnacles.

The collection of barnacles at the Natural History Museum prompted the development of the post-16 unit described here on classification and phylogeny. Our journey through the barnacle years alongside Darwin has been fascinating. The hope is that students will also be inspired by Darwin's life and his methods, along with those of today's scientists, and may come to understand the importance of systematics and taxonomy and the role of collections.

NOTES

[1] Autobiography, pp. 49-50 Darwin online
[2] Darwin Hooker letters Darwin Correspondence Project
[3] Darwin's study laboratory was in his house at Downe and has been reconstructed and is under the care of English Heritage. His garden greenhouses and the land round Downe was his 'outdoor laboratory'.

[4] Charles Darwin to Joseph Hooker, 6 November, 1846. Darwin Correspondence Database, http://www.darwinproject.ac.uk/entry-1018 accessed on 10 February 2014.
[5] Charles Darwin to J. E. Gray, 18 December, 1847. Darwin Correspondence Database, http://www.darwinproject.ac.uk/entry-1139 accessed on 10 February 2014.
[6] Charles Darwin to W. D. Fox, 24 October, 1852. Darwin Correspondence Database, http://www.darwinproject.ac.uk/entry-1489 accessed on 10 February 2014.
[7] Charles Darwin to J. E. Gray, 18 December, 1847. Darwin Correspondence Database, http://www.darwinproject.ac.uk/entry-1139 accessed on 10 February 2014.
[8] Richard Owen was Professor of Comparative Anatomy and classified the mammals from the Beagle. He set up the Natural History Museum in 1881. Owen introduced the term homology with the aim of describing common design among organisms.
[9] The barnacles go through two larval stages, a free swimming nauplius with many limbs which metamorphoses into a cyprid which is shelled and able to move freely, find a suitable rock and cement to it prior to metamorphosing in the sedentary adult form.
[10] Charles Darwin to Joseph Hooker, 13 June, 1850. Darwin Correspondence Database, http://www.darwinproject.ac.uk/entry-1339 accessed on 10 February 2014.
[11] Joseph Sowerby illustrated the first two volumes and George Bettingham Sowerby Jr illustrated the barnacles in the third volume.
[12] From the first edition (1859), p.148, p.151, p.191, p.304, p.424, p.440, p.441, p.448
[13] http://www.publications.parliament.uk/pa/ld200708/ldselect/ldsctech/162/16202.htm.
[14] http://www.nerc.ac.uk/research/programmes/taxonomy/documents/national-strategy.pdf.
[15] http://www.nhm.ac.uk/education/real-world-science/index.html
[16] The tree of life is the only illustration in *On the origin of species* and students examine this in this unit.

REFERENCES

Carlton, J. T., Newman, W. A., & Pitombo, F. B. (2011). Barnacle invasions: Introduced, cryptogenic, and range expanding cirripedia of North and South America. In J. T. Carlton, W. A. Newman, & F. B. Pitombo (Eds), *Invading nature: Springer series in invasion Ecology, 6*(3), 159–213.
Castilla, J. C. (2009). Darwin taxonomist: Barnacles and shell burrowing barnacles *Revista Chilena Historia Natural, 82*,477–483.
Chan, B. K. K., Garm, A., & Høeg, J. G. (2008). Setal morphology and cirral setation of thoracican barnacle cirri: Adaptations and implications for thoracican evolution. *Journal of Zoology, 275*, 94–306.
Cordero, G. A. (2009). Encouraging students to utilize museum resources in ecology, evolutionary and conservation biology. *Bulletin of the British Ecological Society, 40*(4), 59–60.
Darwin, C. R. (1852). *A monograph on the sub-class Cirripedia, with figures of all species. The Lepadidae or pendunculated cirripedes*. London: Ray Society.
Darwin, C. R. (1854). *A monograph on the sub-class Cirripedia, with figures of all species. The Balanidae*. London: Ray Society.
Darwin, C. R. (1859). *On the origin of species by means of natural selection, or the preservation of favoured races in the struggle for life*. London: John Murray.
Darwin, C. R. (1887). Autobiography. In F. Darwin (Ed.), *The life and letters of Charles Darwin*. London: John Murray.
Hancock, M. W. (2007). Boffins books and Darwins finches: Victorian cultures of collecting (Dissertation). Kansas State University, KS.
Newman, W. A. (1993). Darwin and cirripedology. In Truesdale, F. (Ed.), *History of Carcinology (Crustacean Issues 8)*, 349–434. Rotterdam: Balkema.
Rao, M. V. L., & Newman, W. A.(1972).Thoracic cirripedia from the guyots of the mid Pacific Mountains. *Transactions of the San Diego Society of Natural History, 17*, 69–94.
Richmond, M. (2007). *Darwin's study of the cirripedia*. Darwin online.
Scott, R. (2003). *Darwin and the barnacle*. London: Faber & Faber.
Polarukha, O. P. & Mel'nik, V. F. (2012). New records of deep-sea barnacles (Cirripedia: Thoracica: Scalpelliformes) from the Clarion-Clipperton region, Pacific Ocean. *Zootaxa, 3297*, 34–40.

M. LOWE & C. J. BOULTER

Miranda Lowe
Natural History Museum,
London,
UK

Carolyn J. Boulter
Charles Darwin Trust,
Institute of Education,
London,
UK

MARTIN BRAUND

21. DARWIN-INSPIRED DRAMA

Towards One Culture in Teaching and Learning Science

Both the known and the unknown, the two worlds of our ancestors, nourish the human spirit. Their muses, science and the arts, whisper: Follow us, explore, find out. (Wilson, 1998, p. 233)

The relationship between 'the Arts' and 'the Sciences' has both fascinated and troubled educationists. Darwin's connection with the arts changed radically over his lifetime. In his early years he embraced cultural activities loved by so many early Victorians. But later, as his science advanced, he became increasingly estranged from poetry, literature and theatre. Darwin's changing and ambivalent relationship with the arts reminds us of what C. P. Snow called the 'two cultures' and the inherent dangers that perceiving this division and continuing it holds for education. In this chapter I show what the arts, particularly drama, can offer science education. The learner of science benefits from engagement through performance, making abstract concepts understandable as they are connected to personal experiences of mime, dance and acted drama. Engagement through drama also contributes to learners' realisation of the nature of science and appreciation of viewpoints on scientific issues, thereby enhancing their literacy of science. Darwin's work and life inspire many examples of this learning. Simulations of survival in nature, plays about Darwin's life and ideas and role plays about modern applications of evolution and gene selection are examples included in this chapter. These inspiring moments can bring school biology and science to life. However, the biology/science teacher often needs help to make the necessary 'border crossings', bridging the pedagogy of the drama teacher to that of the science teacher.

DARWIN AND THE 'TWO CULTURES'

As a young man struggling to make sense of what others thought should be his professional destiny, first in medicine and later theology, Darwin wholeheartedly embraced the arts as did many in fashionable society of the early nineteenth century. At this stage of life there were no conflicts between his growing interests in science and nature and cultural connections to poetry, opera, ballet, fine arts and theatre. Even when at school in Shrewsbury, the adolescent Darwin turned to the plays of Shakespeare and the poetry of Byron to relieve the tedium of rote learning from the classics and other school subjects, which he found so abjectly boring (Desmond & Moore, 1992, p. 16). Edinburgh's Theatre Royal provided welcome relief from the horrors of medical dissections by way of ballet or other 'terpsichorean delights' (Desmond & Moore, 1992, p. 23).

As his interests turned towards science, especially avid collecting and fascination with South American landscapes, plants, animals and fossils on the voyage of the *Beagle*, Darwin turned to Rossini's operas to relieve the tedium of scientific 'downtime' in Montevideo. In the busy days collecting on the voyage, Darwin expressed his experiences (for example, of summiting the Andes and of collecting in the dense rainforests of Brazil) in terms of the imagery of Tennyson, the landscapes of artist Claude Lorrain and choruses of Handel's *Messiah*. Darwin often used the term 'sublime' as if to recognise that the beauty of what he saw was beyond mere rationalisation and theory.

Yet, after the *Beagle's* voyage, as he became progressively more engrossed with validating evidence and constructing theory, Darwin became noticeably estranged from the arts. For example in a letter to Joseph Hooker in 1868 he wrote:

> I have tried lately to read Shakespeare, and found it so intolerably dull that it nauseated me. I have also almost lost my taste for pictures and music. I am glad you were at the 'Messiah', but I dare say I should find my soul too dried up to appreciate it; and then I should feel very flat, for it is a horrid bore to feel as I constantly do, that I am a withered leaf for every subject except Science. The loss of these tastes is a loss of happiness. My mind seems to have become a kind of machine for grinding out general laws out of large collections of facts. It sometimes makes me hate Science. (Darwin, cited by Fleming, 1961, p. 219)

It seems that as his science progressed Darwin increasingly set the atomising nature of his science above the integrating vision provided by the arts. Fleming likens Darwin's atrophy for aesthetics and estrangement from the arts as transformation from an aesthete and broader intellectual, able to draw equally on science and the arts, to an 'analytical man' concerned only with scientific facts and theories. Hence, the title of Fleming's paper, 'Charles Darwin, The Anaesthetic Man' (1961). It seems that later, in his increasingly scientific life, Darwin could not find the emotional space or mental capacity to integrate the arts, yet this was the very aspect of intellectual life that might have made him more emotionally complete and at peace with himself at a time of increasing self-doubt. Towards the end of his life his regret for not having embraced the arts is plain to see. In his autobiography, published after his death, he wrote:

> ... if I had to live my life again, I would have made a rule to read some poetry and listen to some music at least once every week; for perhaps the parts of my brain now atrophied would thus have been kept active through use. The loss of these tastes is a loss of happiness, and may possibly be injurious to the intellect, and more probably to the moral character, by enfeebling the emotional part of our nature. (Darwin, 2005, p. 115)

The 'Two Cultures'

In many ways, Darwin's changing relationship with the arts is a fascinating example in a debate that has continued to affect educational thinking for some time. The schism in western intellectual thought, seen as a cultural divide between the arts and sciences, found its most famous expression when physicist and novelist C. P. Snow delivered his landmark Rede lecture on *Two cultures and the scientific revolution* at the Senate House, Cambridge in May 1959. For Snow it was mainly the ignorance and lack of education in the sciences, particularly for the 'governing classes', that was his chief concern. While being well versed in the classics and the arts were seen as essential attributes for those who wanted to get on in society, ignorance of science and the fundamental principles on which the world works were seen as conferring no real disadvantage.

The perception that studying the arts is intrinsically and intellectually different to studying sciences stems from a worldview in which thought is divided into two separate realms. As Morris puts it, the first (the science one) is 'tangible, measureable and real and the other (the arts one) is immaterial, intangible, unquantifiable and imaginary' (Morris, 2006, p. 152). In this way science is seen as a reductionist enterprise reducing the world, as Darwin started to do, to its most simple and understandable parts. But, as Darwin soon realised, grand ideas such as his require much synthesis and integration of parts to create a whole. Science is then a more creative enterprise, yet few science teachers in schools or their pupils seem to recognise the creativity of science. It is no wonder that poorer attitudes of pupils to science are the result, particularly when studying science gets harder and seemingly more remote from the real world it is supposed to explain.

A more enlightened view of science ought to take in how it has changed in the history of human thought. Czech scientist and poet, Miroslav Holub, sees science as best understood in terms of a slow transition involving three paradigms (Holub, 1993). The first scientific paradigm was essentially that of the Greeks, that today would be regarded as more philosophical than scientific, being based more on axioms from which theorems could be deduced by the application of logic than on empiricism. Holub sees this first science being gradually replaced by the science of the Renaissance, relying more on measurement, observation and the empirical testing of competing hypotheses. This second scientific paradigm is still dominant and characterises much of present-day school science and, I would argue, is partly responsible for its sterility in the eyes of many pupils. Holub's third science includes post-classical physics in which unpredictability and more open-mindedness abound. Here there are critical roles for imagination, metaphor and analogy. Words don't and cannot now mean all they normally stand for and the steadfast language of the second science, including the conventions of, for example, equations and chemical formulae, are not enough. The language of science and its capacity to explain through traditional methods is under stress. It is here at this level that the arts, especially drama, have potential for learning science.

WHAT DRAMA CAN OFFER LEARNING IN SCIENCE

A Model for Drama and Learning Science

Learning science can be seen as rationalising between two worlds of knowing: the learner's world and the scientist's. The learner's world draws on everyday experience, commonly used terms and language and what has been gleaned from science as presented knowledge from media and from family, friends and school. The scientist's world of knowing, which is the eventual target for learning change, has specific rational explanations for the world based on applications of concepts and theories mediated through empiricism. A model to represent this view of learning science is shown as Figure 1.

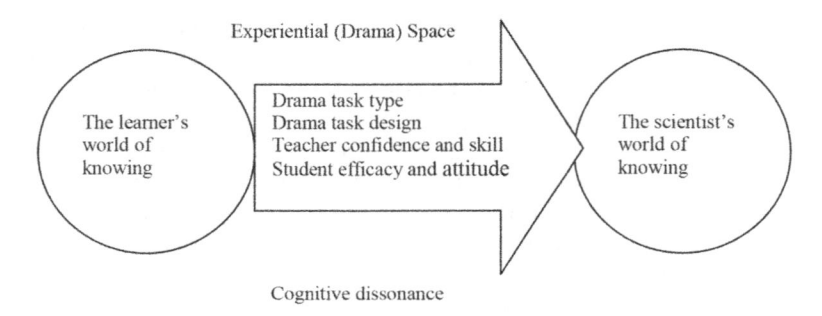

Figure 1. A model for drama as a way of learning science. (© Abrahams & Braund)

In this model, 'cognitive dissonance' is the 'distance' between the two worlds of knowing and the 'experiential space' is the nature of activity and effort, used by the teacher, to reduce the amount of cognitive dissonance and so close the gap between the two worlds. Of course the experiential space could be occupied by any one of a number of teaching methods: group discussion, practical work, watching video, computer work, board work and so on, but in this case it is drama that is the chosen method.

The central arrow of the model in Figure 1 represents aspects of drama as a pedagogical tool most likely to affect learning. Many science teachers are nervous of using drama methods to teach science either because they believe the class will descend into chaos or, at a deeper level, they may believe that they lack the pedagogical skills and training of the drama teacher that can make these methods work. As suggested by Figure 1, understanding the nature of the type of drama to be used (scripted plays, scripted role plays, improvised role plays, physical simulations, mime and dance), how the task is planned and designed and the teacher's confidence and skill at organising, deploying and debriefing activities are all important. Pupils' efficacies and attitudes to the task, in this case drama, always affect outcomes, but there is a feeling of many who have used these techniques that this is not so much of a problem. So far, drawing on this model, there has been hardly any research into how drama might work best in science classrooms, though some recent work by the author and colleagues is available to suggest how teachers can make the most of the Darwin-related activities discussed later (Abrahams & Braund, 2012, pp. 46-49).

How Drama Helps Science Learning

Reviewing literature on drama in science, Marianne Ødegaard sees drama contributing to three areas of learning: about *concepts,* about the *nature of science* and about *science's interactions with society* (Ødegaard, 2003). There is some evidence that Ødegaard's first justification for science drama, *conceptual understanding,* is advanced through use of drama. For example, simulations to understand circuit electricity have been used with students training to become teachers and pupils in primary schools and improved understanding of current, voltage and resistance has been found (Braund, 1999). In biology, concepts in photosynthesis and about cell division (Ødegaard, 2001) have been advanced using drama activities. Improvement of learners' understandings of ecological concepts, such as feeding inter-relationships, has been noted from using role plays where learners act out the components and inter-relationships of food chains and webs (Bailey, 1994).

As far as educating about the *nature of science* is concerned, Ødegaard claims that 'stories of science' offer learners new insights into the reality of the processes of scientific practice (Ødegaard, 2003, p. 85). Solomon, Duveen, Scott and McCarthy (1992) see activities, such as plays about the history of science, challenging positivistic-empiricist views as they show how science theories have been developed and are open to challenge and re-construction.

The use of drama to teach about *science's interactions with society*, Ødegaard's third justification, has been said to improve pupils' empathy and identification with socio-political situations of science and even to have the capacity to challenge or change learners' worldviews (Aikenhead, 1996). In South Africa lessons have been observed where role-plays helped raise the content and level of argumentation about the ethics of trade in organs for xenotransplantation (Braund et al., 2007). In a similar vein, analysis of students' discourse following short role-plays on who should have rights of access to genetic information have been seen to help in development of group argumentation skills (Dawson, Hill, Barlow & Weitkamp, 2009). Thus, drama can help in the deployment and development of argumentation in science by anchoring scientific debate and ideas in pupils' real worlds (Duschl & Osborne, 2002).

TEACHING DARWIN-RELATED SCIENCE USING DRAMA

In this section I provide examples of drama activities to teach about Darwin, his life and ideas and to address controversies in modern science related to evolution and genetics. Activities link with Ødegaard's three purposes for science drama described above using types of drama commonly seen in school science: scripted drama, defined role play discussions and simulated role play/games. Each of the activities is discussed in relation to some of the literature suggesting effective ways to use drama and emerging research.

Teaching Concepts: Using Simulation Role-Play/Games

The idea of using simulations, that are effectively types of games, is that they provide analogues for the concepts to be learned (Braund, in press). In the first example, of 'Reed Warblers and Cuckoos', the concept is colour variation conferring different survival rates of prey (caterpillars) so that individuals with better survival chances are more likely to breed. In the second example, 'The Blackbird Game', the concept concerns survival behaviour of birds that again confers differential survival and better breeding chances. In both cases pupils' roles are to 'play' organisms involved in prey selection. Science teachers have often used analogy or metaphor in their teaching to try to connect pupils with, sometimes abstract, ideas. The value of drama is that these methods provide memorable, enjoyable and highly active examples where pupils are part of the process the teacher wants to explain.

Teachers often like to use warm-up activities to get pupils tuned into these teaching methods. This can involve practising a pre-version of the game or a slightly different activity, for example such as 'Fruit Salad', where each pupil sitting in a circle of the class is given the name of a fruit and at the call of that fruit's name must go to the centre of the circle (Abrahams and Braund, 2012).[1]

Reed Warblers and Cuckoos

This game-simulation can be played outside or in a classroom or school hall and is suitable for pupils in the age range 11-16 years, depending on the level of the concepts developed. The idea is that a pupil or the teacher plays 'the cuckoo' who wears a 'tongue' made from card carrying *velcro* strips to which the caterpillars collected as prey by the other pupils playing 'reed warblers' are attached. A teacher acting as the cuckoo is shown as Figure 2.

The game starts when the cuckoo calls 'feed me'. The 'reed warblers' search for and capture caterpillars, represented by different coloured wool strands (about 15 in each of 12 different colours should do), some brightly coloured which stand out against various backgrounds, others having more camouflaged colours. The rule that reed warblers can only retrieve one caterpillar at a time to return to the cuckoo's tongue helps prevent over-zealous collection of bunches of caterpillars. The wool 'caterpillars' can be stuck onto the cuckoo's tongue from top to bottom in order of retrieval, providing a record of colours of prey selected as predation continues. The patterns can be discussed in terms of changes in relative selection pressure as more

Figure 2. The 'cuckoo' showing the card 'tongue' with captured wool 'caterpillars' attached. (© Abrahams & Braund)

brightly coloured and obvious individuals are selected out. If the game is played in the school grounds, then a distinct area can be pegged out that includes grass, bushes and trees, and any remaining caterpillars on each background can be counted when the game has terminated. I have seen the game played in a classroom where camouflaged military netting was suspended above pupils' heads with the wool 'caterpillars' laid just inside the netting.

A feature of drama, like some other interactive learning activities, is that it has potential to generate additional misconceptions through comparison with reality. In this case it is necessary for pupils to appreciate that cuckoos are not normally fed by more than one pair of reed warblers. How good the drama is as an analogue for nature can be part of discussion that follows the drama-game. In some of my observations of drama used in science classrooms I have noticed that teachers do not spend enough time debriefing or discussing the drama. This was particularly noticeable for student teachers who were drama specialists. They seemed to assume that the potential of the drama to establish learning was so powerful that nothing else was needed to embed concepts or address shortcomings of simulations (see Braund et al., 2013). As with most learning events, consolidation by the teacher and reflection by learners makes fuller impact of the activity more likely.

The Blackbird Game

As with the previous drama this simulation-game deals with survival chances of prey animals. In this case predation is related to evolved and inherited behaviour: blackbird flight patterns in woodland. The game can be played by any number, but if the class is large you can use two or more groups. The concepts can be extended for more able and older students and the basic game is suitable for pupils aged from 9-14 years.

Ten to fifteen pupils are arranged in a large circle. These pupils represent trees in a wood or forest. The space inside the wood is a clearing. Blackbirds are fist-sized, 'scrunched-up' balls of black paper or bean bags given to about half of the pupils acting as trees. A warm-up activity might be to practise throwing and catching the 'birds' around and across the circle. A pupil is asked to enter the centre of the circle to play the predator, a 'sparrowhawk'. The game starts as one 'blackbird' is thrown around the circle from one pupil acting as 'a tree' to another who must catch it. The aim is for the 'sparrowhawk' to catch the 'blackbird' before it reaches the safety of another 'tree'. Once a blackbird is caught it is removed from the game. The teacher can establish rules to prevent the sparrowhawk from grabbing blackbirds when not in flight or to deal with sparrowhawks who are too good at catching the prey by telling them they can only catch with one hand.

I like to play the game several times without much direction to see if the 'trees/blackbirds' can learn that, if they throw short distances around the circle, rather than throwing across the open circle, the prey has more chance to survive. If this doesn't happen naturally, I 'direct' a few 'trees' to start doing this. Later in the game I progressively ask more than one tree to throw blackbirds ending up with all of the blackbirds simultaneously 'flying' around and across the circle. This is great fun and good for pupil concentration and catching skills. The selection-survival point here is that flocking behaviours have evolved to make it difficult for predators to seize a bird from a host of fast moving individuals. This stage of the game is shown in Figure 3.

As an extension or for differentiation, a white ball of paper, representing an albino-mutant blackbird can be introduced to the game. You should find that the white mutant, even in flocking behaviour, is selected/predated more than each black one. The discussion following the game can include questions on why mutant blackbirds are so rare in the population (because so few of them survive to breed and pass on their genes and so are selected out).

Figure 3. Pupils playing the 'blackbird game'. At this point the 'sparrowhawk' in the centre of the circle is trying to catch one of the several 'blackbirds' thrown by 'trees'.
(© Abrahams & Braund)

Teaching About Darwin's Ideas and the Nature of Science: Using Scripted Plays

Fels and Meyer's prediction that many science teachers find it hard to adopt and use a pedagogy of drama for science lessons (Fels & Meyer, 1997) might mean that science teachers are more nervous of types of drama with high rates of pupil autonomy and interaction, such as in the games described above. Perhaps the 'safest' form of drama to start using, for more reticent or less practised teachers, is the 'scripted play'. This is where I started my personal journey in using drama to teach science. From this there is a progression, as experience and confidence grows, to using role-plays where the roles and ideas are suggested (see later) to freely improvised drama simulations where the scenario, phenomenon, event or process is provided but pupils make up their own ways of showing these (Abrahams and Braund, 2012, pp. 1-5).

For some time, teaching about the ideas of science and how they came about has been seen as an important component of learning science. This found its most obvious expression in the national curriculum of England when a section called 'How Science Works' was introduced in 2000. Behind teaching about the ideas of science is the contention that a science education that does not recognise the intellectual efforts made by scientists, both in the present and in the past, to contribute to knowledge and provide explanations for scientific phenomena is, at best, only partially valid and, at worst, intellectually bereft. In the words of Osborne, Erduran and Simon, who produced a teaching pack developing this style of teaching:

> To ask school students to accept and memorise what the science teacher says without any concern for the justification of those beliefs is poor currency. Poor currency because it leaves them unable to explain those beliefs to anybody else but, more importantly, poor currency because it fails to lay bare the enormous intellectual achievement of those who first realised the scientific explanation and the struggle they had in winning the hearts and minds of a sceptical public (Osborne et al., 2004, p. iii)

So it is important for pupils to see that the ideas of Darwin did not exist, frozen in time, in a historical vacuum. Darwin pondered the ideas of Lamarck to see how his ideas challenged these. His ideas in turn challenged Christian fundamentalist orthodoxy of the late nineteenth century, and still do. Today, there is more evidence of evolution, and modern genetics provides explanations for variation and selection, though Darwin's essential notion of speciation through natural selection remains one of the most robust theories of science.

To teach about Darwin's ideas and to show how these ideas developed and are seen by some as controversial, I wrote four short plays, orginally intended for the Salters Science teaching scheme on Evolution for pupils aged 14-16 years. The plays and the accompanying teachers' guide and pupils' questions are available on the website for *Performing science* (Abrahams & Braund, 2012[2]). In the first play, 'The giraffe's long neck', players discuss how ontological reasoning, that organisms evolved features to fit changes in the environment, might explain how different extant and extinct organisms came about and how these ideas were regarded as heretical at the time. The second play, 'The voyage of the *Beagle*', deals with the relationship between Darwin and his father, who was originally opposed to the trip, and Fitzroy, the *Beagle's* captain. 'The great debate', the third play, deals with Darwin's reluctance to publish his great idea and how his friends encouraged him, focusing finally on the defence of *On the origin of species* by Huxley in the well-known debate with Bishop Wilberforce at the Oxford Union. The final play, 'Whatever happened to Genesis?', shows that Darwin's ideas continued to be and still are challenged by creationists. The example in the play is the trial of Tennessee biology teacher John Scopes who was brought to trail in the 1920s for attempting to teach evolution according to Darwin.

The idea is that these plays are used to stimulate discussion, rather than as polished dramatic performances. Drama through plays has most power in science teaching when pupils are actively involved to construct 'holistic empathy'; in other words, they may have empathy with the characters they play, but they also construct an understanding of the story as a whole and its true meaning from the entire narrative. I have found it best to allocate each play (which has between 6 and 8 parts) to a different group of pupils and then to get each group to read, prepare and rehearse, if they want, and finally to perform to the rest of the class who can ask questions about the play and the ideas and controversies represented.

Teaching about Darwin as Part of Science's Interactions with Society

One of the justifications for a science education for all is based on a broader rationale than just to educate an elite set of pupils from which to recruit future generations of scientists and technologists. In this broad rationale the public understanding of science is seen as important to equip school leavers with the ability to engage in debates and take decisions based on science that are most likely to impact their lives. An example of this 'life knowledge' is about genetic selection, one of the twenty-first century's most important post-Darwinian legacies.

The Y Touring Company funded principally by the Wellcome Trust has been active in facilitating uses of drama in the public understanding of science. For example, they have been leaders in using short plays, digitised as films, to focus debate for learners about uses of bio-technology and thinking on bio-ethics. Evaluation shows there have been specific and marked shifts in learners' attitudes to science as a result of pupils' engagement in these activities (Reiss, 2010). One of their earliest plays, *The gift*, tells the story of three generations of the Kaye family affected by a genetically inherited disease called Friedreich's ataxia[3]. One child of the Kaye family, Annie, inherits the double recessive form of a gene causing the ataxia from her parents who are both heterozygote carriers. The lack of a dominant gene in Annie means the defect is fully expressed and the condition affects her cerebellum, causing loss of balance and muscular coordination. This is devastating news for her and her family, in part because Annie is a very talented sportswoman destined for future honours. Annie's brother Ryan, who is not affected by the condition but carries the recessive gene, is devastated by news of Annie's inheritance and later in life becomes a geneticist dedicated to treating and eradicating genetic diseases. When he marries he is shocked to find that his wife also carries the recessive gene for Friedreich's ataxia. Using his knowledge and position as a geneticist he puts his wife in for treatment for superovulation, whereby she produces several ova one of which he selects for fertilisation as having the dominant (good) gene for the condition. This is legal but he goes further in selecting one of the fertilised embryos for gender and for genetic traits conferring extreme athleticism. Thus Ryan is charged with going beyond the geneticist's code of conduct by operating 'genetic selection' for what he sees as additional benefits for his family. Much later, the son Mark, the result of this 'selection', finds out about his father's actions and is upset, regarding himself as some sort of 'freak of science'.

There are a number of ways of using materials associated with *The gift* to teach about genetics and bio-ethics. The genetics futures website provides a full script of the play, a digitised downloadable film, newspaper articles telling various aspects of the story as it unfolds in time, a synopsis and role cards for each member of the Kaye family. I think one of the best ways to use the materials is to provide a synopsis of the story and go over it with the class and provide some of the news articles for them to read – this could be done as pre-lesson homework. In class, groups could role-play members of the Kaye family as they meet to consider Mark's situation and his feelings about being a 'genetic freak'. Some license might be needed here as some family members, particularly Annie, would probably not be alive in Mark's time!

As noted for the Darwin plays discussed in the last section, it is important for each role-player to establish holistic empathy through the whole storyline rather than only having empathy or antipathy with their own roles. Whole class discussion of the ethical issues that emerge from the outcomes of discussions and opinions expressed from each group should be principal outcomes, rather than arriving at a right or wrong resolution to whatever question the teacher poses.

ONE CULTURE FOR LEARNING SCIENCE

Even after explaining the virtues and advantages of using drama to teach science, including extensive drama workshops, I still find a persistent 'two cultures' rhetoric. One of our student teachers in South Africa said this:

> I don't really see where the link is with drama. I spoke to my husband about it and he's an engineer ... so he just loves the science and maths and everything and he says he also can't make the link because to him science is content and I do think it's like that ... it's like science is a serious subject and drama is just for having fun.

I am not saying this opinion is typical, but it does seem that for some teachers drama goes beyond what they are prepared to do to teach science. It could be that the student teacher quoted above just has a view of science that precludes any kind of interactive teaching that is pupil-centred. She may also assume the didactic transmissive methods that led to her own success at school are appropriate to use with her pupils. I have found this 'teach as I was taught' view to be quite a common feature among trainee teachers.

However, there are some rays of hope for the future of science teaching. The two cultures view is beginning to break down. For example, Nobel astrophysicist George Smoot sees the two cultures idea as outmoded, irrelevant in the modern world. Smoot claims we are entering a 'third culture' more heavily dominated by science and technology:

> Basically, in terms of whatever war [between the two cultures] has been going on, I think it is has finished. I don't characterise it by saying we [the scientists] have won. I think everybody has won. We are living in a profound science culture and the big events that are affecting people's lives are scientific ones (Adams, 2007[4]).

For Smoot's view on science to result in a more modern science education, teaching will needs to move to one culture for learning, one which truly embraces the advances in our understanding of the psychology of learning. In an article with Michael Reiss (Braund & Reiss, 2006) we argued that, while our understanding of the ways in which pupils learn science advanced in the second half of the twentieth century, the paradigm for teaching science in schools remains stuck with a late nineteenth-century view of science, seen mainly as laboratory-based activity and reductionist principles. In contrast, science today is multi-disciplinary and located in a number of situations that include field work, computers, discussion and thought experiments as well as lab work. Unfortunately for pupils in many schools Darwin, if he were alive today, would recognise and feel quite comfortable with much of what goes on in the name of school science.

It is widely recognised that the arts, including drama, play a significant part in developing overall intellectual capacity. The contribution of drama to creative and critical thinking, including advancing skills in scientific argumentation, is of particular importance (Duschl & Osborne, 2002). In South Korea there is a government initiative aimed at fostering students' creativity through the inclusion of arts subjects in a STEM-focused curriculum. The idea is to broaden the curriculum from 'STEM' to 'STEAM': science, technology, engineering, the arts and mathematics.

Darwin's work, his life and his ideas lend themselves to learning activities that involve learners in highly interactive methods. Drama activities are memorable not only because they can be highly enjoyable but because they help establish meaningful and long-lasting links between the science and the dramatic events. As a pupil having just completed a drama in science lesson put it:

> I liked doing the drama because you can learn and you can do it yourself. It's a quicker way of learning than from books and stuff even from video ... You will know what it would feel like and that kind of thing, like maybe we could remember about how we moved and how we acted in the grade exams.

Perhaps dramatic Darwin activities might even improve pupils' performances on examination questions about selection and evolution. But I hope that examination success is not the only justification for a more holistic science education that embraces and uses the arts.

NOTES

[1] For descriptions of these 'warm-ups' see Index 1 of *Performing Science*, Abrahams and Braund, 2012, pp. 125-131.
[2] Abrahams & Braund, 2012, pp. 28-29 or e.mail martin.braund@york.ac.uk.
[3] www.geneticfutures.com/thegift.
[4] http://www.theguardian.com/science/2007/jul/01/art.

REFERENCES

Abrahams, I. & Braund, M. (2012). *Performing science: teaching physics chemistry and biology through drama*. London: Continuum.

Adams, T. (2007). The new age of ignorance. *The Observer*, 1 July 2007.
Aikenhead, G. (1996). Border crossings into the subculture of science. *Studies in Science Education*, 27, 1-52.
Bailey, S. (1994). *The Ecogame*. Risley, Warrington, Cheshire: BNFL Education Unit.
Braund, M. (in press). Drama and learning science: an empty space, *British Educational Research Journal*.
Braund, M. (1999). Electric drama to improve understanding in science, *School Science Review*, 81(294), 35-42.
Braund, M. & Reiss, M. (2006). Towards a more authentic science curriculum: the contribution of out-of-school learning, *International Journal of Science Education*, 28(12), 1373–1388.
Braund, M., Lubben, F., Scholtz, Z., Sadeck, M. & Hodges, M. (2007). Comparing the effect of scientific and socio-scientific argumentation tasks: lessons from South Africa. *School Science Review*, 88(324), 67-76.
Braund, M., Ekron, C., & Moodley, T. (2013). Critical episodes in student teachers' science lessons using drama in grades 6 and 7, *African Journal of Research in Mathematics, Science and Technology Education*, 17(1-2), 4-13.
Darwin, C. (2005). *The Autobiography of Charles Darwin*. New York: Barnes and Noble Publishing.
Dawson, E., Hill, A., Barlow, J., & Weitkamp, E. (2009). Genetic testing in a drama and discussion workshop: exploring knowledge construction. *Research in Drama Education*, 14(3), 361-390.
Desmond, D. & Moore, J. (1992). *Darwin*. London: Penguin Books
Duschl, R. & Osborne, J. (2002). Supporting and promoting argumentation discourse, *Studies in Science Education*, 38, 39-72.
Fels, L. & Meyer, K. (1997). On the edge of chaos: co-evolving world(s) of drama and science, *Teaching Education*, 9(1), 75-81
Fleming, D. (1961). Charles Darwin, the anaesthetic man. *Victorian Studies*, 4(3), 219-236.
Holub, M. (2001). Poetry and science: the science of poetry/the poetry of science. In K. Brown (Ed.), *The measured world: on poetry and science*, (447-68). Athens, Georgia: University of Georgia Press.
Morris, A. (2006). The act of the mind: thought experiments in the poetry of Jorie Graham and Leslie Scalapino. In R. Crawford (Ed.), *Contemporary poetry and contemporary science*, (146-166). Oxford: Oxford University Press.
Ødegaard, M. (2001). The drama of science education. How public understanding of biotechnology and drama as a learning activity may enhance a critical and inclusive science education. Unpublished Dr.scient. Dissertation. Norway: University of Oslo.
Ødegaard, M. (2003). Dramatic science. A critical review of drama in science education. *Studies in Science Education*, 39, 75-101.
Osborne, J., Erduran, S. & Simon, S. (2004). *Ideas, evidence and argument in science (IDEAS PROJECT)*. London: Kings College, University of London
Reiss, M. (2010). Science education, theatre and 'Y Touring'. Available online at: www.theatreofdebate.com/ytouring21/Blog accessed 10 February 2012.
Solomon, J., Duveen, J., Scott, L., & McCarthy, S. (1992). Teaching about the nature of science through history: Action research in the classroom. *Journal of Research in Science Teaching*, 29, 409-421.
Wilson, E.O. (1998). *Consilience: the unity of knowledge*. New York: Alfred K. Knopf.

Martin Braund
Cape Peninsula University of Technology,
Cape Town,
South Africa

TINA GIANQUITTO

22. EVOLUTIONARY NARRATIVES

Darwin's Botany and US Periodical Literature

Darwinian language and theories made multiple inroads to US literary and cultural texts in the late nineteenth and early twentieth centuries. As the human place in nature fundamentally shifted from one at the top to one among many, evolutionary theory provided writers with a new vocabulary to describe human affairs and interactions with other living organisms. However, what is often lost in a *general* understanding of the impact of evolutionary theory on US literature are the *specifics* of Darwinian theory. Critics (Jones & Sharp, 2010; Gianquitto & Fisher, 2014) have recently begun to create a more nuanced understanding of the conceptual impact of Darwinian evolution on American literature (see for instance, *Darwin in Atlantic Cultures* and *America's Darwin*), displacing the idea that US writers, if they concerned themselves with evolution at all, relied almost solely on themes common to Spencerian social Darwinism (the 'struggle for existence' and 'survival of the fittest') to represent the particular qualities of American social, economic and industrial society toward the close of the nineteenth century.

Scholars of American literature are increasingly looking beyond *On the origin of species* and examining Darwin's later works, especially *The descent of man and selection in relation to sex* (1871) and *The expression of the emotions in man and animals* (1872), which, as Bert Bender (1996, p. 7) argues, had 'far greater impact ... for writers and other students of human nature' in the late nineteenth and early twentieth century. These key documents of Darwinian theory helped writers and others discover new ways about talking about old topics: love and marriage, moral sense and social instincts, even aesthetic sense and the perception of beauty. Darwin's portrayal of the lives of both human and non-human organisms and especially the seeming fascination with '*obscene* processes', as John Ruskin put it (as cited in Smith 2006, p. 167), that marked Darwin's later works – a fascination with plant digestion, as in the case of carnivorous plants, or with morphological changes developed in the context of sexual desire, or with physiological expressions of emotions that link humans to non-human kin – add both unmistakable texture to Darwin's arguments for evolutionary progress *and* put even more distance between the human and the divine.

If we turn directly to Darwin's writings as primary source materials, we are able to track more accurately the deployment of evolutionary ideas in the US scene. This reliance on primary sources – *On the origin of species*, *The descent of man*, and

The expression of the emotions, the plant studies, etc. – encourages more careful consideration of the multiple interpretations of 'evolutionary theory' at work in US literary culture. Darwin's study *Insectivorous plants* (1875) – and the surprising impact that text had on American literary culture – can offer a rich and, perhaps for students, unexpected avenue for discussing the wide-ranging effects Darwin's books had on a culture both fascinated and repulsed by evolutionary theory. Indeed, the explosion of interest in insectivorous plants after the publication of Darwin's book, which can be seen in the number of articles on them in popular magazines of the time, functions as a useful – and unusual – starting point for a classroom discussion of what, exactly, is at stake in evolutionary theory in the American scene.

Other chapters in this book deal with Darwin's experimental plant research (see for instance Keynes, Sanders and Ellison); this chapter will consider ways to discuss in the classroom the literary and cultural dimensions of Darwin's plant studies. Carnivorous plants can be effectively deployed to highlight those elements of evolutionary theory that were especially problematic for American audiences, namely, the displacement of a divine force animating the natural world, the profound element of chance and contingency that marked life according to the evolutionary scheme, and, finally, fears of both common descent and of degeneration or atavism, that arose in a culture fraught by racial and ethnic divides.

As noted, many scholars and others look to the furore over *On the origin of species* and *The descent of man* to gauge American responses to evolutionary theory. Of course, Darwin's depiction of both the 'struggle for existence' and the lines of common descent linking all organic beings (including, significantly for post-Civil War America, whites and non-whites) rattled an American public riven by war and the legacy of slavery, as well as by a swelling immigrant population. And yet, perhaps surprisingly, Darwin's botanical works, which form the majority of his published texts after the publication of *On the origin of species* in 1859, found great purchase in the US, where school children of all ages took botany lessons and leisure-time botanists are said to have numbered in the tens of thousands. To help students grasp the ways in which Darwin's studies were popularised, it is important to stress the immense popularity of botanical study throughout the century (Elizabeth Keeney [1992] offers the best overview of the topic.) Articles in the popular periodical press (newspapers and magazines) encouraged this leisure pursuit, and as Sally Shuttleworth and Geoffrey Cantor (2004, p. 7) note, periodical editors introduced readers to scientific ideas and helped influence their opinions in scientific controversies. Periodicals were essential to the dissemination of evolutionary ideas as well as to the cultural conversation about evolution generally in the US in the nineteenth century, and periodicals, especially those geared to a general audience, 'established both the platforms and the necessary conditions' for debating such controversial topics as evolution (Shuttleworth, et al., p. 8). For instance, the *Atlantic Monthly*, one of the most influential magazines of the era, 'carried the first major American exposition and defense of Darwin' written by Darwin's earliest and most vocal American supporter, the Harvard botanist Asa Gray. By the time *The descent of man* was published in 1872, 'the essential tenets of Darwinism were well entrenched in the magazine' (Sedgwick, 1994, p. 10). The periodical press likewise introduced American audiences to evolutionary plant studies – Darwin's 'unanswerable arguments in favour' of evolutionary theory – and offered Darwin's revolutionary views on flowers such as orchids, primulas, climbing plants and insectivorous plants as regular fare for readers (Gibson, 1881, p. 82).

Magazine articles not only presented Darwin's findings, however; writers, 'following Mr. Darwin', described the methods they used to perform their *own* research into floral mechanisms and encouraged readers to do the same (Herrick, 1885, p. 235). As Robin Schultze (2013, p. 42) argues, such a programme of direct engagement with the natural world resonated in an era when educators increasingly turned to nature study as a means to promote mental and physical fitness (with its evolutionary and eugenic overtones) and to protect against the threat of 'mass racial decay' posed by 'swelling ranks of immigrant children', the 'prolific spawn of supposedly degenerate racial stocks'. As Schultze (2013, pp. 43-44) observes, the 'typical American classroom' encouraged 'imitation' and rote learning; in failing to challenge students' minds, such educational practice threatened to 'drag the nation back down the phyletic ladder'. Nature study, on the other hand, provoked the imagination and encouraged progressive mental activity, not regressive lassitude. 'Investigate everything', botanical textbook writer George G. Groff (1889, p. 5) encouraged pupils. 'Take nothing for granted.' Evolutionary-minded readers were familiar with the tenets of natural theology that had guided their study of the natural world earlier in the century—nature was the divine will manifest on earth and to study nature was to connect the human with the divine. Darwinism may have displaced the notion of nature as the expression of the divine mind, but for proponents of nature study, the natural world nevertheless remained 'inherently moral ... because of its relation to fundamental material truths' (Schultze, 2013, p. 44). These truths were observable to anyone who looked outside.

Darwin's plant studies were no doubt so popular because he employed basic observational and experimental methods using materials close at hand. For instance, in his investigation of *Drosera*, Darwin (1875a, p. 92) describes the various digestible substances he fed to the plant, including hard-boiled egg, roasted meat, muscle tissue, cartilage, bone, enamel, and milk – all of which were notably 'acted on by the gastric juice of the higher animals in the same manner' (see Chapter 18). It is easy to imagine the home-bound scientist reaching for anything at hand in the other, non-digestible materials that were also tried – 'particles of glass, coal-cinder ... stone, gold-leaf, dried grass, cork, blotting-paper, cotton-wood, and hair rolled up into little balls' (Darwin, 1875a, p. 22). As is well known, Darwin's reliance on home-based study was no doubt influenced by his poor health. As he describes in his 1865 essay on 'Climbing plants', observations on the precise movements of twining tendrils were made 'in a well-warmed room to which [he] was confined during the night and day' (Darwin, 1865, p. 2). When he published a more complete account of the movements of climbing and twining plants, Darwin clarified that he had been confined to the room 'by illness' (Darwin, 1875b, p. 3). Illness also notably characterised his work with insectivorous plants. As Janet Browne (2002, p. 147) points out, Darwin turned to the study of vegetable stomachs as a way to help him navigate both his own and his daughter Henrietta's persistent sicknesses. Browne writes: 'The question of stomachs persistently seeped into his thoughts – Henrietta's stomach, his own stomach, leaves as stomachs ... To investigate his leaves was to search for the essence of the Darwin family weakness, the bane of his life'.

Popular nature writers, such as Mary Treat – a correspondent of Darwin's and expert on carnivorous plants – made the connection between botanical study and moral and physical health explicit. Treat (1866, p. 39) opens her 1866 essay 'Botany for invalids' with the following recommendation: 'If weak, nervous, dyspeptic individuals knew how much they might be benefited by the study of Botany, that it is almost a panacea for many of their diseases, would it not be more generally prosecuted?' Although Treat had not yet been introduced to Darwin, she might have been gratified to learn that the great naturalist himself followed this course of treatment. This domestic touch was undoubtedly part of the naturalist's appeal with the general public, even as Darwin's 'country-house styles of investigation' was coming under increasing criticism by proponents of laboratory- based botanical research (Browne, 2002, p. 477).[1]

Despite the seemingly violent nature of insectivorous plants, they were not left out of the nature study picture. Readers of the *American Educational Monthly*, for instance, were encouraged to model Darwin and procure sundews in order to 'test the process of devouring' for themselves (Carnivorous Flowers, 1875). Specimens could be purchased through seed catalogues or, with approximately 45 species native to locales across the country, could be found during almost any walk to a local bog. For such active observers, these plants could tell quite a bit about the human relationship to non-human kin. For Italian criminal anthropologist Cesare Lombroso (2006, [1884], pp. 167–8), for instance, 'zoology' formed the basis of his study into innate criminal behaviour (the 'born' criminal), and, in the third edition of his influential text *Criminal man*, he turned to Darwin's studies of insectivorous plants to understand the 'dawn of criminality'. From these studies Lombroso concludes that 'premeditation, ambush, killing for greed...are derived completely from histology or the microstructure of organic tissue—and not from an alleged will'. Others, again, such as Mary Treat, imagined insectivorous plants not as criminals and murders, but rather as 'avengers of their kingdom', waging a just battle for their survival (Treat, 1885, p.139). These kinds of conflicting presentations of insectivorous plants in the American literary imagination demonstrates, as I have argued elsewhere (Gianquitto, 2014), that these plants embodied the multiple and often contradictory response to the evolutionary narrative in the American scene[2]. The possibility that plants could act violently and with 'premeditation', as Lombroso argues, prompted some profound questions: Are insectivorous plants conscious, wilful organisms? Are they moral, immoral or amoral? Are they examples of exquisite evolutionary adaptation or are they degenerate, atavistic throwbacks, making their way by a sort of primitive violence? Are they flora? Or are they fauna?

'WICKED DEAR LITTLE PLANTS': CARNIVOROUS PLANTS IN US PERIODICAL LITERATURE

The explosion of interest in insectivorous plants after the publication of Darwin's book in 1875 functions as a useful – and unusual – starting point for a classroom discussion of what, exactly, is at stake in the discussion of evolutionary theory. Classroom exercises that focus on the astonishing variety of 'literary' carnivorous plants – plants that appear in the hundreds if not thousands in language of flower books, poems, novels, periodical essays and short stories – from pre-1875 and post-1875 sources can help unpack for students the profound conceptual impact of even seemingly obscure texts, such as *Insectivorous plants*, on the American imagination. Plants like the sundew and the pitcher plant were transformed virtually over night, from bejeweled exemplars of moral behaviours (Dall, 1860) to murderous wretches, as readers absorbed the consequences of Darwin's account of 'wicked dear little' plants (Darwin)[3], who survive by the 'premeditated slaughter' of unsuspecting insects (Carnivorous Flowers, 1875)[4]. While some (Hunt, 1882) bemoaned the 'vegetable wickedness' arising in a natural world bereft of a benevolent god, others meditated on the elements of chance and contingency – perfectly demonstrated by the fly on the cusp of a *Sarracenia*'s pitcher – that seemed to characterise life in late-nineteenth-century America, where chance – as opposed to divine grace – *seemed* as likely as anything to determine who would gain economic and social advantage in a rapidly transforming landscape.

Carnivorous plants especially displayed a fundamentally disturbing truth about the natural world: fixed borders – between individuals, between races, between species, between flora and fauna – blurred under the evolutionary lens. The boundary-blurring nature of insectivorous plants illustrated what T. H. Huxley (1876) called 'the border territory between the animal and vegetable kingdoms'[5]. Or, as writer Robert Arnold (1881) put it in his essay 'Vegetable animals':

> Most persons are in the habit of thinking them [animals and vegetables] entirely different, but who can draw the line of distinction between them? ... There are animals that have not muscles, or nerves, or mouths, or stomachs; yet they move, they eat and they digest ... Animals feel. So do plants; and it may be that their sensibility is owing to their having a nervous system ... Animals sleep. So do plants ... Animals eat and drink. Plants eat and drink, too, and some are exceedingly fond of animal food ... It is said that animals have instinct, at least, if not reason, and that vegetables have not. Do not be too sure of that. Mr Darwin saw the tendril of a climbing plant voluntarily withdraw from a hole in the wall after it had chosen it and remained fixed in it for thirty-six hours; and it is a fact that the tentacles and leaf of the sundew will move a little

distance upwards after a fly – and catch him, too! ... Professor Huxley says: 'The difference between an animal and a plant is one of degree rather than of kind, and the problem of whether, in a given case, an organism is an animal or a plant may be essentially insoluble. So, to be on the safe side, I shall call such things as the sundew, Venus's flytrap, and so forth, vegetable animals'.

When Darwin looked at nature, he did not see fixed forms and easily comprehensible functions. Instead, he saw a world where form was mutable, continually responding to the changes in the environment. In the case of carnivorous plants, Darwin demonstrated that plant carnivory 'evolved independently' in several different subclasses of plant, a 'habit', as Peter Ayers (2008) explains, that 'was an adaptation to nutrient-poor habitats'. Darwin (1875a, p. 363) calmly explains, perhaps to the alarm of his readers, that such a habit is not necessarily unusual, as natural selection predicts that:

> ... *any* ordinary plant having viscid glands, which occasionally caught insects, might thus be converted under favourable circumstances into a species capable of true digestion. It ceases, therefore, to be any great mystery how several genera of plants, in no way closely related together, have independently acquired this same power.

Darwin's observation is remarkably double-edged, representing on one hand 'exquisite' adaptation to significant environmental challenges (Darwin, 1860, p. 60), while on the other degeneration or the 'morbid derivation from an original type' (Chamberlain, 1985, p. 265). The reaction is best seen in Mable Mapes Dodge's (1904) poem *Carnivorous plants*:

What's this I hear,
My Molly dear,
About the new carnivora?
Can little plants
Eat bugs and ants,
And gnats and flies?
Why, – bless my eyes!
Who is the great diskiverer?

Not Darwin, love,
For that would prove
A sort of retrograding;
Surely the fair
Of flowers is air,
Or sunshine sweet.
They shouldn't eat
Or do aught so degrading!

These issues of adaptation (progress) and degeneration ('retrograding'), as well as other evolutionary connundra, are nicely presented in another poem of the era, Edith Thomas's (1891) *The sundew speaks*, from the *Atlantic Monthly*. The poem offers a good starting point for classroom discussions of 'literary' carnivorous plants, as it outlines some of the central concerns raised by Darwin's evolutionary theory generally and by his work on insectivorous plants in particular. Thomas opens the poetic section of her piece 'Notes from the Wild Garden' with a warning:

> If, in this gathering, a certain grotesquery in flowers, rather than their loveliness, seems to be given emphasis, I can only say that, beside those flowers first notable for their beauty, there are others more conspicuously suggesting pathos … flippancy of character … audacity, hauteur … and vain-glory.

Much like Darwin, Thomas seeks out the 'aliveness' of the flowers she encounters in the wild, seeking common ground and even, for imaginative purposes, a common language. However, her conversation with the 'truculent' and combative sundew highlights not just the familiar but also the uncanny (Thomas, 1891, p. 177); she captures the uneasy feeling that, disgusted as we may be by the 'abnormal', 'unnatural' and 'monstrous' diet of the sundew, its actions belie a common, if distant, past (Carnivorous flowers, 1875):

> A prying creature bore me from my place,
> Me much admired, but started back apace
> When one who trimmed a *hortus siccus* said,
> 'Observe how this same tender plant is fed.'
>
> For when some few trapped midges were espied,
> Straightway my ruddy filaments were dyed
> As rank on rank of sanguinary spears, --
> Hypocrisy lurked in my jeweled tears!
>
> And why, forsooth, my table do you chide?
> No vegetarian you, flesh food denied,
> Who now call down with lead the wingèd kind,
> Now bid the field, the stream, your diet find!
>
> Moreover (still the Sundew urged the case),
> It were but fair the chased at length gave chase,
> And, since so long my compeers have fed flesh,
> Some plant should tangle *yours* in cunning mesh!

At the most obvious level, Thomas's humorous poem takes aim at the hyperbole often found in some rather hysterical pronouncements on the carnivorous habits of these plants, and the adjectives deployed to describe carnivorous plants signal a reversal in perception post-1875. Where once 'Sarracenia / Waves over her cups banners of purple, and / Sundew, at her feet, glitters with diamonds' (H. T.,

1871), phrases such as 'murderous', 'wicked', 'evil', 'treacherous', 'predatory', 'bloodthirsty', 'repulsive' and 'degraded' were common descriptors post-1875[6]. It is worth noting that the US in the late-nineteenth century was a place where tremendous changes were being wrought by, among other things, industrialisation, urbanisation and especially the influx of 'new' immigrants, primarily from southern and eastern Europe. It is worth pointing out the suggestive connections between the fierce and fearful nativist (eugenic) reaction to this degenerate 'immigrant tide' and the language of degeneration that characterised discussions of plants at the same historical moment. Students might be encouraged to search for articles on carnivorous plants in online databases such as either of the 'Making of America' websites to locate other examples for discussion.[7] In the closing stanza of *The sundew speaks*, Thomas both gestures toward other popular manifestations of literary killer plants (especially the giant 'man-eaters' common to South American adventure/ travel stories) and playfully considers a possible future where roles will be reversed and the hunted will become the hunter.[8]

The playfulness of Thomas's poem underlies its more serious considerations. Among the chief topics raised by the poem is the obvious one of teleology; the self-conscious sundew, with its rational challenge to the ostensibly rational botanist, calls into question a teleological conception of the natural world that places humans firmly at the apex of both consciousness and creation. Along the way, the sundew also challenges the supposed moral authority that follows upon that position at the head of creation, asking, 'And why, forsooth, my table do you chide?' The sundew reminds the poet that *all* organisms must struggle to survive. Or, as a writer for *The New York Tribune* put it:

> If someone were to tell you that an animal ate a plant you would think nothing of it, for it is the natural order of life that the higher forms of life should make use of the lower ones to help them exist, as do we humans who feed upon animals. But if someone were to tell you that a plant eats the animal you would probably say: 'Pooh I don't believe it!'. ('A plant that had indigestion', 1902)

As Thomas considers the potential role of reason, consciousness or directed action in plant life (again, as the sundew 'urged the case'), she takes her cue from Darwin, who described the sundew as a 'wonderful plant, or rather a most sagacious animal'[9]. One of the revolutionary aspects of Darwin's work on carnivorous plants was his assessment that the plants digest animal food by deploying an enzyme analogous to pepsin. But the analogies between flora and fauna did not stop there. In discussing the plant with Joseph Hooker, Darwin postulated that the plant 'possesses matter at least in some degree analogous in constitution & function to nervous matter'[10]. Darwin did not go *quite* so far in his published observations of the plant, insisting, instead, that while plants did not possess anything akin to a brain or 'a central organ, able to receive impressions from all points, to transmit their effects in any definite direction, to store them up and reproduce them', the leaves of the *Drosera* are nevertheless able 'to transmit a motor impulse to a distant point, inducing movement'. He explains:

With Drosera the really marvellous fact is, that a plant without any specialised nervous system should be affected by such minute particles; but we have no grounds for assuming that other tissues could not be rendered as exquisitely susceptible to impressions from without if this were beneficial to the organism, as is the nervous system of the higher animals. (Darwin 1875a, pp. 26, 128, 273)

Darwin's audience, no doubt troubled by these speculations, was led to its own series of questions about sensory perception and consciousness. It would be worth exploring with students the profound implications of Darwin's conclusions about movement, digestion, and volition in plants. Such a stance led many to question the supposed and supposedly well-established distinction between flora and fauna, and perhaps hinted at deeper obligations that might exist not only between peoples, but also between human and non-human beings. As an one commentator in an article published in the *New York Times* in 1894 ('Do certain plants think') was led to ask:

... are those plants that are endowed with the power of motion as a result of sensation capable of connecting the sensation of touch with their movements by any process of thought? What is thought? ... Is there any connection between these similar actions of these plants and animals, and if so, are they not due to the same cause?[11]

As this kind of speculation demonstrates, Darwin's re-mapping of the natural world placed many in the nineteenth century in a profoundly disturbing position, facing a paradigm shift that necessitated an entirely new way at looking at the world and its natural systems. Darwin's plant studies opened up a whole new world to a public already jarred by natural and sexual selection. Some accepted with ease the news that plants ate animals; others, it appears, needed convincing. Why? What should it matter if plants ingest animals? Students should be encouraged to consider that Darwinian generalisations startled a fascinated public into recognising that the terms of evolution levelled the playing field and placed humans and non-humans on equal footing in the mechanisms of nature. It matters, because if one accepts the explicit argument that plants display even the most rudimentarily analogous systems (nervous, digestive) and, further, share lines of descent with humans, it necessarily placed an increased emphasis on humans and non-humans as parts of and participants in distinct yet interrelated communities. Evolutionary theory prompted writers and others to ponder the kinds of connections that existed between humans and the lowly plant (Can plants think? What is thought?). In doing so, they may have made tentative steps towards considering other kinds of connections that might exist between individuals. In an era rife with struggles over the rights of many – Native Americans, African Americans, immigrants, labourers, children, women, as well as non-human animals – such language would have profound and potentially disruptive echoes.

NOTES

[1] See also Ayers (2008, p. 97–114).
[2] For a more comprehensive discussion of the topic of the reception and impact of carnivorous plants in the American scene, see Gianquitto, T. (2014, pp. 235–262).
[3] Darwin used this phrase to describe the *Drosera* in a letter to Charles Lyell in 1860. Charles Darwin to Charles Lyell, 24 Nov, 1860. Darwin Correspondence Database, http://www.darwinproject.ac.uk/entry-2996 accessed on 28 July 2013.
[4] Transcendentalist and reformer Caroline Helaey Dall associated the *Drosera* with 'opportunity for devotion'.
[5] Huxley likened 'those acts of contraction following upon stimuli,' such as the closing of the lobes of the *Dionaea* in response to a slight touch, to animal 'reflex.'
[6] (1908). Beware, oh, ye vegetable eaters, (1908); The New York Tribune (1886); Thomas, E. M. (1886); 'Predatory plants', (1883); 'A plant that had indigestion', (1902); Pyne, E. (1891). Pyne was a British author whose essay was reprinted for American audiences.
[7] See 'Making of America' (University of Michigan site): http://quod.lib.umich.edu/m/moagrp/ and 'Making of America' (Cornell University): http://moa.library.cornell.edu. Both of these sites are open access.
[8] Two recent anthologies provide a great overview of the many kinds of carnivorous plant fiction popular in the late nineteenth, early twentieth centuries: Arment, C. (Ed.). (2008); and Arment, C. (Ed.). (2010).
[9] Charles Darwin to Asa Gray, 4 August, 1863. Darwin Correspondence Database, http://www.darwinproject.ac.uk/entry-4262 accessed on 29 July 2013.
[10] Charles Darwin to Joseph D. Hooker, 26 September, 1862. Darwin Correspondence Database, http://www.darwinproject.ac.uk/entry-3738 accessed on 29 July 2013.
[11] Do certain plants think. (1894). *New York Times*. This essay was widely republished. At the turn of the century, The New York Tribune, playfully recalling the upheaval of *Insectivorous plants*, published an article reviving the discussion of plant consciousness: 'Beware oh, ye vegetable eaters! Lowly onion may be a sentient creature. Scientists of repute now tell us plants have memory, feelings, sight and hearing.'

REFERENCES

A plant that had indigestion. (1902). *The New York Tribune*, October 26, B14.
Are plants able to think? (1900). *Current Literature*, 29(3) (September), 338.
Arment, C. (Ed.). (2008). *Flora curiosa: cryptobotany, mysterious fungi, sentient trees, and deadly plants in classic science fiction and fantasy*. Landisville, PA: Coachwhip Publications.
Arment, C. (Ed.). (2010). *Botanica delira: more stories of strange, undiscovered, and murderous vegetation*. Landisville, PA: Coachwhip Publications.
Arnold, R. (1881). Vegetable animals. *Christian Union*, (July 27), 24, 4; American Periodicals p. 78.
Ayers, P. (2008). *The aliveness of plants: the Darwins at the dawn of plant science*. London: Pickering & Chatto.
Bender, B. (1996). *The descent of love: Darwin and the theory of sexual selection in American fiction, 1871-1926*. Philadelphia: University of Pennsylvania Press.
Beware, oh, ye vegetable eaters. (1908). *The New York Tribune*, October 25, B7.
Browne, J. (2002). *Charles Darwin: the power of place*. Princeton: Princeton University Press.
Carnivorous Flowers. (1875). *The American Educational Monthly*, July, 313.
Chamberlain, J. E. (1985). Images of degeneration: turnings and transformations. In *Degeneration: the dark side of progress*. Chamberlain, J. E. & Gilman, S. L. (Eds). New York: Columbia University Press, pp. 263-289.
Dall, C. H. (1860). *Women's right to labor; or, low wages and hard work in three lectures. Delivered in Boston, November 1859*. Boston: Walker, Wise.

Darwin, C. R. (1860). *On the origin of species.* 2nd edition. London: Murray.
Darwin, C. R. (1865). On the movement and habits of climbing plants. *Journal of the Linnean Society (Botany),* 9, 1– 18.
Darwin, C. R. (1875a). *Insectivorous plants.* London: John Murray.
Darwin, C. R. (1875b). *The movement and habits of climbing plants.* London: John Murray.
Do certain plants think. (1893). *New York Times,* June 25.
Dodge, M. M. (1904). Carnivorous plants. In *Poems and verses,* p. 134. New York: Century.
Jones, J. E., & Sharp, P. B. (Eds.). (2010). *Darwin in atlantic cultures: evolutionary visions of race, gender, and sexuality.* New York: Routledge.
Gianquitto, T. (2014). Criminal botany: progress, degeneration, and Darwin's insectivorous plants. In *America's Darwin: Darwinian evolution and U.S. culture.* Gianquitto, T. & Fisher, Lydia (Eds.). Athens, GA: University of Georgia Press.
Gianquitto, T. & Fisher, Lydia (Eds.) (2014). *America's Darwin: Darwinian evolution and U.S. culture.* Athens, GA: University of Georgia Press.
Gibson, W. H. (1881). Among our footprints. *Harper's New Monthly Magazine,* 64(379) (December), 65-82.
Groff, G. G. (1889). *The book of plant descriptions, or record of plant analyses.* Lewisburgh, PA: Geo. G. Groff.
Herrick, S. B. (1885). Orchids. *The Century,* 30(2) (June), 230-240.
H. T. (1871). The Marsh. *The Religious Magazine and Monthly Review,* 46(1) (July), 19.
Hunt, J. G. (1882). Natural history studies. *Friends' Intelligencer,* 39(1) (18 February), 10.
Huxley, T. H. (1876). On the border territory between the animal and vegetable kingdom. *Macmillan's Magazine: The Popular Science Monthly,* 8(8) (1 April), 641.
Keeney, E. (1992). *The botanizers: amateur scientists in nineteenth-century America.* Chapel Hill: University of North Carolina Press.
Lombroso, C. (2006). *Criminal man.* trans. Gibson, M. & Rafter, N. H. Durham, NC: Duke University Press.
Predatory Plants. (1883). *The Advance,* 18 (Sep 27), 648.
Pyne, E. (1891). Garden of Death. *Eclectic Magazine of Foreign Literature, Science, and Art,* 53(116) (June), 778-780.
Ruskin, J. quoted in Smith, J. (2006). *Charles Darwin and Victorian visual culture.* New York: Cambridge.
Schultze, R. (2013). *The degenerate muse: American nature, modernist poetry, and the problem of cultural hygiene.* New York: Oxford.
Sedgwick, E. (1994). *The Atlantic Monthly 1857-1909: Yankee humanism at high tide and ebb.* Amherst, MA: University of Massachusetts Press.
Shuttleworth, S. & Cantor, G. (2004). Introduction. In *Science serialized: representations of the sciences in nineteenth-century periodicals.* Cantor, G. & Shuttleworth, S. (Eds.). Cambridge: MIT Press.
Thomas, E. M. (1886). Through magic windows. *The Book Buyer,* 3(2) (December 1), 432.
Thomas, E. M. (1891). Notes from the wild garden. *Atlantic Monthly,* 68(406) (August), 172-178.
Travers, H. (1912). Are plants conscious? *The Theosophical Path,* 2(3) (Mar 1), 162.
Treat, M. (1866). Botany for invalids. *Herald of Health,* 8, 39-40.
Treat, M. (1885). 'Utricularia clandestina', *Home studies in nature.* New York: American Book Company.

Tina Gianquitto
Division of Liberal Arts and International Studies,
Colorado School of Mines,
USA

MARGARITA HERNÁNDEZ-LAILLE

23. DARWIN IN NATURAL SCIENCE SCHOOL TEXTBOOKS IN THE NINETEENTH CENTURY IN ENGLAND AND SPAIN

INTRODUCTION

This chapter analyses the inclusion of Darwin's theory of evolution in secondary-school natural science manuals during the nineteenth century. These manuals are considered, not only as a source of curricular information and knowledge for discipline development, but also as an object of research and an ideological transmitter of individual moments in history.

The teaching of natural sciences during the nineteenth century in England and Spain included drawing, dissections, field trips, museum visits, creating school gardens, etc., depending on the kind of school. Schools even had natural history museums, some of which are in existence, as is the case of Eton College. Moreover, each school could have its own specific pedagogical approaches to the natural sciences, dependent on the school's culture. In Spain, for example, there were many differences between the teaching of natural sciences in most schools and in the Institución Libre de Enseñanza (ILE), where textbooks were not much used in classrooms and students learned natural theories by observation through field trips and through experimentation in the school laboratories. It is difficult to know which pedagogical approaches were used in classrooms in different historical periods. However, textbooks are a useful instrument in the field of historical research in education.

This research on the teaching of Darwinism through school manuals stems from a desire to reveal the inter-relationship between natural sciences and education, and focusses on England and Spain, with a view to comparing how teaching took place and evolved in these two countries, each with a different political and social context, and dissimilar attitudes to science and religion.

Victorian England played an important role in scientific development, largely as a result of the influence of the French and Industrial Revolutions, but the introduction of science teaching came up against severe difficulties. The conservativism of the English aristocracy and bourgeoisie was significantly reflected in the gap between most areas of science and technology when compared with other states in Northern Europe. Whereas on the continent, state participation in education speeded up the development of science teaching, in England, the blocking of state investment in this area led to the creation of a voluntary school system, based on personal initiative and supported by private funding. A great many efforts were made to change this education system, and 1860 marked the start of a decisive transition period which culminated in 1870 with Forster's Education Act. This Act established a universal system of elementary schools that were required to abide by the Cowper-Temple Clause, which stated that no catechism or religious formulary of any particular tendency could be taught in schools with municipal funding. Between 1872 and 1875, the Devonshire Royal Commission published eight reports on scientific instruction and the progress of science, with a view to improving the situation. In 1895, the Liberal Bryce Commission was called upon to draw up a report on developing the organisation of a national secondary education system and from 1899 onwards, grants for the teaching of science and technology proliferated. In 1902, the Balfour Education Act defended secular education, and secondary education was introduced on a widespread basis.

In Spain, the introduction and dissemination of Darwinism followed a different path from the one taken in England, and the controversies that arose were very different in their intensity and duration, particularly with regard to the attitude of the Church which, in Spain, was implacable, and loyally supported by the most staunchly conservative groups. In reality, Darwinism destroyed the Aristotelian scholastic theory which defended species fixism and an absence of evolutionary past; this Darwinian notion was intolerable in these social strata. However, the restoration of the monarchy in 1875 gave a major boost to scientific culture and the natural sciences, even though, in the field of education, the Orovio's Royal Decree ordered that teachers had to submit to choosing their school manuals from a list of authorised textbooks, and comply with the law ordering that students be taught according to Catholic dogma, which remained in force until 1923. This was the educational context in which Charles Darwin revealed to the world his theory of evolution by natural selection, the teaching of which was fundamental for its understanding and dissemination.

The analysis of natural science school manuals used in English and Spanish classrooms in the nineteenth century, included in this chapter, reveals when, how and with what values Darwinism was introduced into schools in both countries, who their authors were, which publishers issued them and what resistance they found along the way.

DARWIN IN NATURAL SCIENCE SCHOOL MANUALS IN ENGLAND IN THE SECOND HALF OF THE NINETEENTH CENTURY

Charles Darwin's ideas were quickly introduced into English school manuals in the second half of the nineteenth century. Some teachers and scientists explicitly referred to Darwin in them, whilst others did not name him.

There were also anti-Darwinist British authors, like John Hutton Balfour, whose *Class book of botany being an introduction to the study of the vegetable* k*ingdom*, published in 1852 for the first time, refuted Darwin, stating that 'the doctrine of transmutation of species is disproved by the best physiological reasoning, and its application to geological phenomena is altogether gratuitous and futile'[1]. He also claimed that the theory of evolution was a speculative doctrine with dangerous tendencies and in 1875 said that:

> We cannot but honour the man [Darwin], who, by his genius and talent, has been enabled to develop one of the great laws of nature [...]; but we have no sympathy with that discoverer [Darwin] in science, who, puffed up with intellectual superiority, puts the laws which he has elucidated in the place of the Creator, whose personality and ever-working omnipresence he ignores'[2].

At the same time, some of the natural science school manuals published sought to align religion with science, such as *Introductory text-book of geology* by David Page, which, between 1857 and 1867, accepted the transformation of our planet whilst reconciling it with the action of a Supreme Being[3].

English Darwinian School Manuals Which Did Not Quote Darwin

One of the first authors to teach Darwin's ideas in English schools was Thomas Henry Huxley. Many of his lessons, essays and sermons – which informed about the most recent evolutionary discoveries – were published and used as school books. In 1854, he published 'On the educational value of the natural history sciences', a lesson imparted at St Martin's Hall, the contents of which were totally evolutionist. In other lessons published, Huxley spoke of Darwin, praising his work or showing teachers how to communicate science to their pupils.

In 1866, Huxley published *Lessons in elementary physiology*, in which he included the most advanced knowledge about this science and its teaching. This book was then reprinted for the following twenty years[4]. In the same year, Daniel Oliver published *Lessons in elementary botany*. In 1871, Henry Alleyne Nicholson published *An introductory text-book of zoology for the use of junior classes* and Huxley published *A manual of the anatomy of vertebrated animals* to inform comparative anatomy students of the relationship between the anatomical structure of the orang-utan, the gorilla and the chimpanzee and that of man, and the classification and organisation of mammals. In 1874, M. Foster published *Physiology* and two years later, assisted by J. N. Langle, *A course of elementary practical physiology*. Alleyne Nicholson also omitted Darwin in 1879 in his Darwinian *A manual of palaeontology*.

The early 1880s saw the publication of *An elementary text-book of botany* by K. Prantl and S. H. Vines, which introduced the transformation process of the plant structures resulting from continuous cell modification. At the same time, *Botany for children: an illustrated elementary text-book for junior classes and young children* by Revd George Henslow appeared. In 1882, Henry Edmons published *Elementary botany. Theoretical and practical*. Four years later, Archibald Geikie issued *Class-book of geology*, which, though it did not quote Darwin, developed the theory of evolution perfectly, tracing the species back to a common ancestor. By the end of the decade, *Animal biology. An elementary textbook* by Conwy Lloyd Morgan had also been published.

In 1891, Edith Aitken published *Elementary textbook of botany* for the use of schools and in 1893, Herbert George Wells provided reasoned arguments for descent from a common ancestor in the second part of his *Textbook of biology. Invertebrates and plants*. By the end of the century, Francis Darwin referred to the struggle for existence and natural selection in *The elements of botany*, though without mentioning his father, Charles.

English Darwinian School Manuals Quoting Darwin

One of the school manuals that did include Darwin's ideas before the publication of *On the origin of species* was *Advanced text-book of geology, descriptive and industrial* by David Page, who, in 1856, already considered Darwin an authority on the study of South American coral reefs. In the second edition of 1859, Page explicitly declared himself a Darwinist and even cited Darwin on more occasions than in the first. From that moment until 1876, David Page alternated textbooks where he defended evolution as compatible with God Creation with others in which he declared himself a staunch advocate of Darwinism[5].

Another author of Darwinian English natural science books was the geologist Joseph Beete Jukes, who, in 1862 published *The student's manual of geology*, citing Darwin on many pages and offering a detailed analysis of his theory. In 1863, Charles Lyell accepted Darwin's theory of natural selection for the first time in *Geological evidences of the antiquity of man: with remarks on theories of the origin of species by variation*. Between 1864 and 1867, in *The principles of biology*, Herbert Spencer commented that:

> Mr Darwin has shown in many cases that the forms and positions of the essential organs of fructification are such as to facilitate the actions of insects in transferring pollen from the anthers of one flower to the pistil of another – an arrangement produced by natural selection.[6]

A manual of zoology by Henry Alleyne Nicholson was published in 1870, and explained the proposals of 'the doctrine of the development of species by variation and natural selection – propounded by Darwin – and commonly known as Darwinian theory'.[7] In 1871, Lyell published the first edition of his Darwinian *The student's elements of geology*. In 1873, Beete Jukes again named Darwin, as he had in 1862, to defend his theory of gradualism in *The school manual of geology*. In 1876, James Geikie published *Geology*, J. D. Hooker *Botany* and Alexander Macalister defended the theory of natural selection in *An introduction to animal morphology and systematic zoology*. In 1877, Nicholson issued a school manual on the history of the earth in which he asserted that:

> Palaeontology is in favour of the view that the succession of life-forms upon the globe has been to a large extent regulated by some orderly and constantly-acting law of modification and evolution […].[8]

The same year saw the publication in England of *Text-book of structural and physiological botany* by Otto Wilhelm Thomë and Alfred William Bennett, which had first been published in Germany in 1869 as a textbook for German technical schools. Its contents defended evolutionist ideas, insisting that Darwin had shed considerable light on carnivorous plants and their habits. In 1877, Huxley's *A manual of the anatomy of invertebrated animals* explained the general principles of biology and expounded his arguments on the initial causes of the phenomenon of life and the environment's tendency towards variation, with the struggle for existence resulting in a gradual evolution of simpler animals and plants into more complex ones, transmitted through inheritance as Darwin had shown. The first edition of his essay *Physiography: an introduction to the study of nature* also appeared in 1877.

In 1882, Sir Archibald Geikie cited Darwin in his *Text-book of geology*. The same year saw the publication of *The frog: an introduction to anatomy and histology* by Milnes Marshall, and *Synopsis of the classification of the animal kingdom* by Alleyne Nicholson. A year later, Robert Bentley issued a guide on the study of the structure and physiology of plants. In 1887, Milnes Marshall and Herbert Hurst wrote *A junior course of practical zoology* and Nicholson, in his seventh edition of *Manual of zoology for the use of students* claimed that virtually all scholars were in agreement that species had originated through a process of evolution and development, although not all coincided on the manner in which this evolution had taken place.

In 1888, Arabella Burton Buckley published the fourth edition of a school manual in which she said that 'The theory of natural selection, or the Darwinian theory as it is often called, was chiefly worked out by the great naturalist Charles Darwin'[9]. A year later, Robert J. Harvey Gibson published *A textbook of elementary biology*, which referred to the 'evolution school, led by Darwin and Wallace'.

In the final decade of the nineteenth century, Darwinian textbooks were published one after another with ever greater frequency. In 1891, in *The making of flowers*, Henslow[10] explained the importance of the adaptation of insects in plant fertilisation including many references to the observations and works of Darwin. In 1895, in *A text-book of zoogeography*, Frank Evers Beddard asserted that:

> it is not necessary now to argue against the doctrine of special creation; evolution in some form or other is almost universally accepted; and the facts of distribution, as Darwin himself showed in great detail, are among the most convincing proofs of the untenability of any such belief as special creation.[11]

In the same year, in *An introduction to the study of zoology*, B. Lindsay acknowledged the importance of the contribution made by Darwin and his theory, claiming that 'closely associated with the spread of "Darwinian theories" came the recognition of the fundamental unity of animal and vegetable life'[12]. In 1897, Thomas Jeffery Parker and William Aitchenson Haswell, zoologists and biology teachers in New Zealand and Sydney, published *A text-book of zoology*, both volumes of which cited Darwin and his *On the origin of species* in their respective introductions. The second volume also included an exhaustive explanation of the theory of evolution by natural selection. Also in 1897, in *A text-book of geology*, William Jerome Harrison the Elder stated that 'the generally accepted theory of the formation of coral islands is that [which] was first advanced about 1845 by Charles Darwin'[13]. In 1899, a posthumous textbook by Thomas Jeffery Parker was published, which maintained that 'the point of view [about the God's Creation] underwent a complete change when, after the publication of Darwin's Origin of Species in 1859, the Doctrine of Descent or of Organic Evolution came to be generally accepted by biologists'[14].

DARWINISM IN NATURAL SCIENCE SECONDARY SCHOOL MANUALS IN SPAIN IN THE LAST THIRD OF THE NINETEENTH CENTURY

Most natural science school manuals published in nineteenth-century Spain defended the theory of the divine creation of the Earth and the beings that lived on it.

However, numerous authors sought to bring religious beliefs into line with scientific truths, among them Manuel María José de Galdo, who from 1848 onwards, asserted in eight of the ten editions of his *Manual de historia natural* that 'far from being hostile to religion, the culture of the sciences is its most steady and solid support'[15]. In a new edition of this book, published in 1894, Galdo stopped seeking to reconcile religion with science. Other reconciliatory school manuals included *Curso de nociones de historia natural* (1860) by Serafín Casas Abad; *Compendio de historia natural* (1874) by José Monlau; *Programa de historia natural* (1877) and *Elementos de historia natural* (1880) by Emilio Ribera Gómez; *Nociones de historia natural* (1879) by Manuel Díaz de Arcaya; *Curso de historia natural, fisiología e higiene según los principios de Santo Tomás de Aquino* (1883) by Rev. Martínez-Vigil and *Elementos de historia natural y fisiología e higiene* (1883) by José Albiñana.

Other natural science textbook authors declared themselves anti-Darwinist. In 1861, Laureano Pérez Arcas published *Elementos de zoología*, stating, 'Indeed, in his theory, Darwin confuses variability, which is transitory, with mutability [...]. Even in fossils the numerous intermediate forms that would be necessary to prove that certain species give rise to others have not been found [...]'[16]. In 1889, Felipe Picatoste was still asserting that 'science has been unable to explain either the principle or the succession of organic species, however many hypotheses may have been put forward'[17], and he considered that the transformation of species could be cited as one of the many 'scientific eccentricities' that had sought to explain the generation of species. By the start of the last decade of the nineteenth century, the ultramontane Ortí y Lara had brought out the second volume of *Curso abreviado de filosofía natural*, where he asserted one of the reasons proving the falsity of the doctrine of evolution to be 'that living creatures of superior degree had not descended from those of inferior degree', and claimed, as proof of this assertion, that 'the transformation of an inferior degree of life in another essentially superior one, would mean the destruction of the specific being of the respective living creature'[18].

There were even authors whose textbooks denied the scientific validity of geology and geogeny[19], as reflected by the words of Luis Pérez Mínguez in the 1893 edition of *Nociones de historia natural e ideas generales de geología*, which stated that these two sciences were the ones that 'had supplied most arms to those who have been looking for weapons to aim at our Religion', and that 'even today, both Geology and Geogeny are a long way from being true sciences', adding that 'the fundamentals of Geology are a long way from being absolute and incontrovertible truths, and they can therefore neither serve as support for, nor destroy, an institution whose fundamentals are in the heavens'[20]. In 1897, in his *Elementos de historia natural*, Demetrio Fidel Rubio y Alberto described Darwin's theory on the origin of species as a 'theory as seductive as it is untrue, supported by hypotheses that are all but gratuitous, without having been able to cite a single fact from observation or experience which confirms it'[21]. A year later, in his *Historia natural*, Fidel Faulín Ugarte expressed the view that 'no species, however much variety or changes it presents, had transformed into a new type, either by gradual variation or by abrupt change' and that 'as things stand today, transformism (and even more so Darwinism), lacks the evidence to demonstrate the evolution of all beings'[22]. In 1899, Manuel Mir y Navarro criticised advocates of Darwinism in his *Programa-sumario de elementos de historia natural: con principios de fisiología e higiene*.

However, despite the power of the Catholic Church and the restrictive legislation of nineteenth-century conservative governments, Spain had no shortage of natural science textbooks of a Darwinian nature, some of whose authors cited Darwin and others who chose not to do so.

Spanish Darwinian Natural Science Manuals that Did Not Explicitly Cite Darwin

The first Spanish author to introduce Darwinian concepts into a natural science textbook was Rafael García Álvarez, secondary school teacher at the Instituto de Granada. In the second edition of his *Nociones de historia natural*, published in 1867, he asserted that:

> the theory of analogies and homologies has also given rise to the unity of composition, not just of different animals, but also of the different organs of each of them, leading some naturalists to the theory of the transformation and variability of species, an effect of the changes that have occurred in organisation as a result of the prolonged action of the influences to which they were subjected.[23]

He goes on to say that:

> ... the animal kingdom taken as a whole represents a plan of gradation, in which animality rises from a minimum in which it borders on vegetability and reaches a maximum of development crowned by humanity, whose synthesis and ascendant series has been given the name animal series or scale.[24]

In 1874, Rafael García Álvarez openly declared himself Darwinian in his *Tratado elemental de fisiología general y humana*, although he did not cite Darwin. This manual for young people studying at secondary level made reference to certain authors who considered that:

> the whole immense variety of complex organisms which have been occurring over the series of ages up to the present era, are the effect of slow metamorphoses that have taken place gradually over time. This theory, supported by the philosophers of antiquity and modern naturalists, is known by the name of the theory of transformism or genealogic descent, and is currently the subject of many studies and enlightened discussions in the field of science.[25]

In 1874, in *La evolución en la naturaleza*, Enrique Serrano Fatigati also praised Haeckel's research on the variability of form, adopting the view that these constituted 'a monument of glory for humanity'.

In 1888, Odón de Buen y del Cos published *Cartilla de historia natural*, written to 'infiltrate in childhood the healthy principles on which the study of nature is founded today, and to develop a spirit of observation, without prejudice and without fundamental errors'. This booklet was written in the style known as *lecciones de cosas*, in which a teacher leads his pupils to the observation that 'everything in nature works, everything is transformed', stating that 'creatures which associate are the strongest', and advising them to live in harmony with their fellow beings in order to endure 'the struggle for life'[26]. In 1891, Odón de Buen published *Diccionario de historia natural* on nature teaching, accompanied by wonderful colour illustrations. In the same year, Rafael García Álvarez introduced his Darwinian ideas explicitly in his textbook *Elementos de historia natural*, asserting, though without citing Darwin, that evolution:

> ... is the law or principle by virtue of which everything in Nature tends to pass from the undefined to the defined, from the simple to the compound, from the homogeneous to the heterogeneous and from the uncomplex to the complex [...], everything appears to obey this law, which applied in our globe reveals to us the numerous transformations [...] and very varied forms in which life has manifested itself since the incalculable age of its appearance until the present moment, which is known by the name of the theory of evolution. [...]. Life is not subject to, nor is it the effect of, any agent or vital principle as was thought before.[27]

In 1894, José de Galdo published *Taxonomía y cuadros sinópticos de historia natural*, where he claimed it to be 'natural that life should have started from sarcodic and cellular forms; that after the protozoa came the mesozoa, and that, finally, the metazoa should gain further ground and development, with their supreme organisation emerging sanctioned in man'[28]. Likewise, in 1894, Félix Gila y Fidalgo published *Tratado de historia natural* defending Darwinian ideas, though without citing Darwin, and in 1897, the Darwinian Manuel Cazurro Ruiz issued *Programa de un curso elemental de historia natural con nociones de fisiología e higiene*. At the end of the century, Salvador Calderón Arana published the first edition of his *Nociones de historia natural*, where he explained the significance of fossils and the similarity between the human genus and other animals.

Spanish Darwinian Natural Science School Manuals Which Explicitly Cited Darwin

From the 1870s onwards, natural science manuals were also published in Spain in which the authors named Darwin explicitly. In 1873, Augusto González Linares quoted Darwin in his *Ensayo de una introducción al estudio de la historia natural*.

In 1877, Peregrín Casanova Ciurana published *Estudios biológicos*, considered the first Spanish biology book with openly Darwinian contents. Its first volume, on *General biology*, cited Darwin on numerous occasions. It reads as follows:

> The evolutionary doctrine is contrary to the doctrine of fixism; it is the theory of change and transformation [...]. It contains a complete philosophy of the whole Universe [...]. It does not bring any supernatural agent into its explanation of all the events, because this would be to depart from the limits of Science [...][29].

He adds that:

> ... many know Darwin by name, though very few know about his ideas, much less understand them, and yet [...] he has warranted the hatred of uncultured people for whom the name of Darwin is synonymous with the devil[30].

Rafael García Álvarez also defended Darwinism in 1883, citing Darwin in his *Estudio sobre el transformismo*.

In 1890, Ignacio Bolívar Urrutia, Salvador Calderón y Arana and Francisco Quiroga Rodríguez published *Elementos de historia natural*. The book was thoroughly Darwinian and contained clear explanations about natural selection, the struggle for existence and all the other concepts advocated by Darwin in his theory, such as variability and inheritance. The three authors explicitly cited the English scientist, asserting that he was responsible for the huge impetus that had been injected into the biological sciences of the day.

In 1894, in the first part of the aforementioned *Elementos de historia natural*, Jose de Galdo for the first time cited 'Carlos Roberto Darwin', considering him 'one of the world's most noteworthy figures'. In 1895, the second part of this book appeared, which not only explicitly cited Darwin but filled its pages with his doctrine. Galdo made it clear in his book that there were few differences between the brains of the higher anthropoidea and primitive man, a circumstance that could be demonstrated were it not for the disappearance of certain types of humans with very deficient brain development or if certain anthropoid forms that were 'perhaps victims of the struggle of culture against savagery' had been conserved. The year 1895 also saw the publication of second editions of *Elementos de historia natural* by Bolivar, Calderón and Quiroga, and *Tratado elemental de zoología* by Odón de Buen, which maintained that:

> ... the modern age begins in 1859, when Charles Darwin published his memorable book entitled *On the origin of species*, which produced a profound revolution in Biology ...

and that:

> the predominance of the evolutionary transformist school, which prescribes the accidentality of organic forms and their slow modification by adaptation to the environment and natural selection, which merges in the unity of the biological plan, is the most salient feature of contemporary zoology.

In his *Historia natural*, Odón de Buen insisted, in 1896, on the notability of Darwin and his theory, asserting that 'the concept we must form of life is an *evolututionary concept*'. Another of Odón de Buen's works was *Tratado de elementos de botánica* which was published in 1897, where he quoted Darwin's exact words on plant circumnutation movements. Also in 1897, José Gogorza y González included manifestly Darwinian declarations in his school manual *Elementos de historia natural*, asserting that *On the origin of species* 'had given a satisfactory explanation to a portion of events that had previously not had one [...] and is today accepted by most scholars'. In 1899, Odón de Buen published the eighth edition of *Programa de un curso de zoología*, into which he introduced the Darwinian line.

CONCLUSIONS

The above analysis would suggest that different policies in education, in general, and educational legislation on textbooks, in particular, exerted considerable influence on the transmission of new knowledge about evolution through its teaching in nineteenth-century England and Spain.

In England, Darwin was considered a revolutionary of science and his works were recognised and respected in every scientific area, even though they initially provoked controversy and criticism. The name Darwin and reference to his ideas entered English school classrooms even before the publication of *On the origin of species*, although it was not until after 1870 that the majority of school science manuals adopted a Darwinian approach.

In Spain, Darwin was also adopted very early on in certain naturalist circles. The predominant position of the Catholic Church did not prevent the references to Darwinism which Spanish scientists introduced into their discourse shortly after the publication of *On the origin of species*. Nor did it take long for Darwin's theory of evolution to enter the area of education in a society that was eager for modernisation. Although many teachers suffered considerable reprisals in the mid-1870s for defending science and introducing Darwinism into their classrooms[31], Spanish textbooks were nonetheless swift to incorporate Darwin's ideas.

In conclusion, it becomes clear that, despite the differences between the political and social situation in Spain and England at that time, Darwinism was introduced into natural science school manuals in both countries, although in Spain they were published at a later date than in England.

NOTES

[1] Balfour, J. H. (1852). *A class book of botany being an introduction to the study of the vegetable kingdom.* 2 vol. Edinburgh: Adam and Charles Black, p. 8.

[2] Balfour, J. H. (1875). *A manual of botany being an introduction to the study of the structure, physiology, and classification of plants.* Edinburgh: Adam and Charles Black, pp. xii–xiii.

[3] Page, D. (1857). *Introductory text-book of geology.* Edinburgh and London: William Blackwood (3rd edn). (4th edn in 1860; 6th edn in 1864; 7th edn in 1867.)

[4] T. H. Huxley's *Lessons in elementary physiology editions*: 1st edn 1866; new edition 1868; reprinted 1869, 1870, 1871 and March and May 1872; new edition October 1872; reprinted 1873, 1874, 1875, 1876, 1878, 1879 (from 6th edn), 1881, 1883, and January, February, May, September, November 1884; new edition 1885; reprinted 1886, 1888.

[5] Page, D. (1861). *Advanced text-book of geology, descriptive and industrial.* Edinburgh and London: William Blackwood and Sons (3rd edn). (4th edn 1867; 6th edn 1876.)

[6] Spencer, H. (1864). *The principles of biology.* Vol. I. London & Edinburgh: Williams and Norgate. p. 153.

[7] Nicholson, H. (1870). *A manual of zoology.* 2 vol. Edinburgh: [s. n.], pp. 35–36.

[8] Nicholson, H. (1877). *The ancient life-history of the earth. A comprehensive outline of the principles and leading facts of palaeontological science.* London & Edinburgh: William Blackwood and Sons, pp. 372–374.

[9] Buckley, A. (1888). *A short history of natural science for the use of schools and young persons.* London: Edward Stanford. (4th edn), p. 463.

[10] The clergyman, teacher and botanist George Henslow was the younger son of John Stevens Henslow, Darwin's professor of botany during his time at Christ's College, in Cambridge, who was perhaps the most influential person in Darwin's development towards his theory of evolution. J. S. Henslow was very interested in variation between members of the same species and Darwin learnt much from him on that topic. They became great friends and because they took walks together, Darwin was known as 'the man who walks with Henslow'. It was also J. S. Henslow who suggested to Captain FitzRoy that Darwin should be taken on the voyage of the Beagle, and who received and looked after the specimens sent by Darwin to him from the different parts of the world.

[11] Beddard, F. E. (1895). *A text-book of zoogeography.* Cambridge: University Press, p. 131.

[12] Lindsay, B. (1895). *An introduction to the study of zoology.* London: Swan Sonnenschein & Co., p. 59.

[13] Harrison, W. J. (1897). *A text-book of geology.* London: Blackie & Son Ltd, p. 152.

[14] Parker, T. J. (1899). *A manual of zoology.* London: Macmillan, p. 9

[15] Galdo, M. M. J. (1848). *Manual de historia natural.* Madrid: Imprenta de Higinio Reneses, p. 183.

[16] Pérez Arcas, L. (1863). *Elementos de zoología.* Pinto: Imprenta de Gabriel Alambra (2nd edn). p. 141. (1st edn 1861).

[17] Picatoste Rodríguez, F. (1889). *Elementos de historia natural.* Madrid: Librería de la Viuda de Hernando y Cª, p. 198.

[18] Ortí y Lara, J. M. (1892). *Curso abreviado de filosofía natural.* V. II. Madrid: Sociedad editorial de San Francisco de Sales, pp. 92–94.

[19] Geogenia is the branch of geology that studies the origin and transformation of Earth.

[20] Pérez Mínguez, L. (1893). *Nociones de historia natural e ideas generales de geología.* Valladolid: Imp. Y Librería Nacional y Estrangera [sic] de los Hijos de Rodríguez, Libreros de la Universidad y del Instituto (9th edn), p. 265.

[21] Rubio y Alberto, D. F. (1897). *Elementos de historia natural con principios de fisiología e higiene.* Madrid: Librería de Hernando y Cia. (2nd edn), p. 107.

[22] Faulín Ugarte, F. (1898). *Historia Natural (elementos) con nociones de anatomía y fisiología humanas*. Madrid: Establecimiento tipográfico 'Sucesores de Rivadeneyra', p. 411.
[23] García Álvarez, R. (1867). *Nociones de historia natural*. Granada: Imprenta de D. Francisco Ventura y Sabatel, impresor de SS. MM (new edition), p. 208.
[24] Ibidem, p. 209.
[25] García Álvarez R. (1874). *Tratado elemental de fisiología general y humana*. Granada: Imprenta de Indalecio Ventura, p. 48.
[26] Buén y del Cos, O. (1888). *Cartilla de historia natural*. Madrid: José Matarredona, pp. v, 31, 74.
[27] García Álvarez, R. (1891). *Elementos de historia natural*. Granada: Indalecio Ventura, p. 228.
[28] Galdo, M. M. J. (1894). *Taxonomía y cuadros sinópticos de historia natural*. Madrid: Viuda de Hernando y Cª., p. 144.
[29] Casanova Cuirana, P. (1877). *Estudios biológicos. I. La biología general*. Valencia: Ferrer de Orga, pp. 403–404.
[30] Ibidem, p. 405.
[31] After the Orovio's Royal Decree of February 26th of 1875, ordering that students be taught according to Catholic dogma and that teachers had to submit to choosing their school manuals from a list of authorised textbooks, many teachers, defenders of freedom of science and freedom of teaching, refused to comply with this law. The professors Francisco Giner de los Ríos, Laureano Calderón y Arana, Augusto González Linares, Nicolas Salmerón y Gumersindo de Azcárate, among others, were removed from their teaching positions and some of them were even confined. Because of that, university's reaction began and protests, writings and resignations of professors took place continuously. These serious political and social events related to the Spanish educational system are known as the 'second university question'. One year later, in 1876, some of the ceased teachers founded the Institución Libre de Enseñanza, which was always devoted to the cultivation and propagation of science, and Darwin was appointed honorary member.

REFERENCES

Choppin, A. (2000). Los manuales escolares de ayer a hoy: El ejemplo de Francia. *Revista Historia de la Educación*, 19.
Choppin, A. (1992). The Emmanuelle textbook project. *Journal of Curriculum Studies*, 4.
Delgado, B. (1983). Los libros de texto como fuente para la historia de la educación. *Revista Historia de la Educación*, 2.
Herlihy, J. G. (1992). *The textbook controversy: issues, aspects and perspectives*. Norwood (USA) : Ablex.
Gomez Rodriguez de Castro, F. (1998). Le programme Manes: Les manuels scolaires dans l'Espagne contemporaine (1808-1990). *Histoire de l'education*, 78.
Göran, A. (1972). *Historia en las escuelas de secundaria superior. Enseñanza y libros de texto (1820-1965)*. Uppsala: [s. n.].
Hernández-Laille, M. (2010). *Darwinismo y manuales escolares en España e Inglaterra en el siglo XIX (1870-1902)*. Madrid: UNED.
Johnsen, E. B. (1996). *Libros de texto en el calidoscopio*. Barcelona: Ediciones Pomares-Corredor, S.A.
Pingel, F. (1999). *Unesco Guidebook on textbook research and textbook revision*. Hannover: Unesco, with the support of the Georg Eckert Institute for International Textbook Research.
Selander, S. (1990). Análisis de textos pedagógicos. Hacia un nuevo enfoque de la investigación educativa. *Revista de Educación*, 295.
Tiana Ferrer, A. (2000). *El libro escolar, reflejo de intenciones políticas e influencias pedagógicas*. Madrid: UNED.

Darwinian natural science school textbooks used in England since the publication of On the origin of species.

Aitken, E. (1891). *Elementary textbook of biology*. London: Longmans, Green & Co.

Beddard, F. E. (1895). *A text-book of zoogeography.* Cambridge: University Press.
Bentley, R. (1883). *Students guide to structural and physiological botany.* London: J. & A. Churchill.
Darwin, F. (1899). *The elements of botany.* Cambridge: University Press.
Edmons, H. (1882). *Elementary botany. Theoretical and practical.* London: Longmans, Green & Co.
Foster, M. (1874). *Physiology.* London: Macmillan and Co.
Foster, M., & Langley, J. N. (1876). *A course of elementary practical physiology.* London: Macmillan & Co.
Geikie, A. (1882). *Text-book of geology,* London: Macmillan & Co.
Geikie, A. (1885). *Text-book of geology.* London: Macmillan & Co.
Geikie, A. (1886). *Class-book of geology.* London: Macmillan & Co.
Geikie, J. (1876). *Geology.* London & Edinburgh: W. & R. Chambers.
Gipson, R. J. H. (1889). *A textbook of elementary biology.* London: Longmans, Green & Co.
Harrison, W. J, the elder (1897). *A text-book of geology.* London: Blackie & Son Ltd.
Henslow, G. (1880). *Botany for children: An illustrated elementary text-book for junior classes and young children.* London: Stanford.
Henslow, G. (1891). *The making of flowers.* London: Society for Promoting Christian Knowledge.
Hooker, J. D. (1876). *Botany. Science primers.* Professors Huxley, Roscoe & Balfour Stewart (Eds.). London: Macmillan & Co.
Huxley, T. H. (1866). *Lessons in elementary physiology.* London: Macmillan & Co.
Huxley, T. H. (1877). *A course of elementary instruction in practical biology.* (3rd edn). London: Macmillan & Co.
Huxley, T. H. (1871). *A manual of the anatomy of vertebrated animal.* London: J. & A. Churchill.
Jukes, J. B. (1862). *The student's manual of geology.* Edinburgh: Adam & Charles Black.
Jukes, J. B. (1873). *The schools manual of geology.* (2nd edn). Edinburgh: Adam & Charles Black.
Lindsay, B. (1895). *An introduction to the study of zoology.* London: Swan Sonnenschein & Co.
Lyell, Ch. (1878). *The student's elements of geology.* (3rd edn). London: John Murray.
Macalister, A. (1876). *An introduction to animal morphology and systematic zoology. Part I. Invertebrate.* London: Longmans, Green & Co.
Marshall M., & Hurst H. (1887). *A junior course of practical zoology.* London: Smith, Elder & Co.
Marshall, M. (1882). *The frog, an introduction to anatomy and histology.* Manchester: J. E. Cornish.
Morgan, C. L. (1889). *Animal biology. An elementary textbook.* (2nd edn). London: Rivingtons.
Nicholson, H. A. (1870). *A manual of zoology.* 2 vol. Edinburgh: [s. n.].
Nicholson, H. A. (1871). *An introductory text-book of zoology for the use of junior classes.* Edinburgh & London: [s. n.].
Nicholson, H. A. (1877). *The ancient life-history of the earth. A comprehensive outline of the principles and leading facts of palaeontological science.* Edinburgh & London: William Blackwood & Sons.
Nicholson, H. A. (1879). *A manual of palaeontology for the use of students with a general introduction on the principles of Palaeontology.* 2 vol. (2nd edn). Edinburgh & London: William Blackwood & Sons.
Nicholson, H. A. (1882). *Synopsis of the classification of the animal kingdom.* Edinburgh & London: William Blackwood & Sons.
Page, D. (1859). *Advanced text-book of geology descriptive and industrial.* (2nd edn). Edinburgh & London: William Blackwood and Sons.
Parker, T. J. (1899). *A manual of zoology.* London: Macmillan.
Parker, T. J., & Haswell, W. A. (1897). *A text-book of zoology.* 2 vol. London: Macmillan.
Prantl, K., & Vines, S. H. (1880). *An elementary text-book of botany.* London: W. Swan Sonnenschein & Allen.
Spencer, H. (1864-1867). *The principles of biology.* 2 vol. London & Edinburgh: Williams & Norgate.
Thomë, O. W., & Bennett, A. W. (1877). *Text-book of structural and physiological botany.* Translation and English edition of the 4th German edition, recommended by Revd Alexander Irvin, of Wellington College. London: Longmans, Green & Co.
Wells, H. G. (1893). *Textbook of biology. Part 2, Invertebrates and plants.* London: W. B. Clive.

Darwinian natural science school textbooks published in Spain since the last third of the nineteenth century.

Bolivar Urrutia, I., Calderon y Arana, S., y Quiroga y Rodriguez, F. (1890). *Elementos de historia natural.* Madrid: Establecimiento Tipográfico de Fortanet.
Buen y del Cos, O. (1888). *Cartilla de historia natural.* Madrid: José Matarredona.
Buen y del Cos, O. (1891). *Diccionario de historia natural.* Barcelona: Imprenta de Salvador Manero Bayarri.
Buen y del Cos, O. (1895). *Tratado elemental de Zoología.* (2nd edn). Barcelona: Imprenta Gutenberg).
Buen y del Cos, O. (1897). *Tratado de elementos de botánica.* Barcelona: Manuel Soler.
Buen y del Cos, O. [1896]. *Historia natural.* 2 vol. Barcelona: Manuel de Soler.
Calderon Arana, S. (1899). *Nociones de historia natural.* Madrid: Establecimiento Lipotipográfico de J. Palacios.
Casanova Cuirana, P. (1877). *Estudios biológicos. I. La Biología General.* Valencia: Ferrer de Orga.
Cazurro Ruiz, M. (1897). *Programa de un curso elemental de historia natural con nociones de fisiología e higiene.* Gerona: Imprenta Paciano Torres.
Galdo, M. M. J. (1894–1895). *Elementos de historia natural.* 2 vol. Madrid: Librería de la Viuda de Hernando y Compañía (Novísima ed.).
García Álvarez, R. (1867). *Nociones de historia natural.* Granada: Imprenta de D. Francisco Ventura y Sabatel, impresor de SS. MM.
García Álvarez, R. (1874). *Tratado elemental de fisiología general y humana.* Granada: Imprenta de Indalecio Ventura.
García Álvarez, R. (1883). *Estudio sobre el transformismo.* Granada: Ventura Sabatel.
García Álvarez, R. (1891). *Elementos de historia natural.* Granada: Indalecio Ventura.
Gila y Fidalgo, F. (1894). *Tratado de historia natural.* Tomo II. Santiago: Tip. de José Mª Paredes.
Gogorza y González, J. (1897). *Elementos de historia natural.* Salamanca: Estereotipia Tipología de Francisco Núñez Izquierdo.
González de Linares, A. (1873). *Ensayo de una introducción al estudio de la historia natural.* Madrid: Imprenta y Estereotípia de M. Rivadeneyra.
Serrano Fatigati, E. (1874). *La evolución en la naturaleza.* Madrid: Imprenta, Estereotipia y Galvanoplastia de Aribau y Cª.

Margarita Hernández-Laille
MANES (UNED),
Madrid,
Spain

DEVELOPING WORK WITH LEARNERS

VAUGHAN PRAIN

24. WRITING AND REPRESENTING TO LEARN IN SCIENCE

INTRODUCTION

The material and symbolic tools for undertaking and representing science activity have changed so much since Darwin's time. From medical science researchers using synchrotron microscopy at a spatial resolution of 3 to 5 microns to analyse artificially-coloured chemical maps of the effects of different drugs on cells, to astronomers generating and analysing digital imagery of distant galaxies, scientists now use a vast array of verbal, visual and mathematical resources to make discoveries and excite public interest in their work. Despite this huge increase in technological resources and expertise, Darwin's methods still inspire learning and breakthroughs across many settings.

RESEARCHING AND REPRESENTING IN SCIENCE

In this chapter I briefly review Darwin's methods of enquiry and representing research, where he used writing and other forms of representation to raise and solve problems through extensive observation, written and visual records, reflection, claim-making, testing, and re-representation. I then present an overview of recent research on the role of writing, and more broadly representation, in learning in school science, and illustrate the implications of this research through reporting on classroom-based research on the topic of adaptation, and some current options for bioscience study by senior secondary biology students. As recognised in Darwin's work, scientific explanations rely on modal interdependence, where visual, linguistic and mathematical modes are integrated to make evidence-based claims about phenomena first for the self, and then for wider professional and public readerships.

DARWIN'S REPRESENTATIONS OF RESEARCH

For Darwin, writing functioned as a major reasoning tool with which to imagine, speculate, clarify and justify explanations, propose causes, annotate models and solve problems. Famously he speculated on his voyage on the *Beagle* that if the birds on the Galapagos were 'only varieties', and 'if there is the slightest foundation for these remarks the zoology of archipelagos will be well worth examining: for such facts undermine the stability of species' (Barlow, 1963, p.262). In expressing tentatively the possibility of evolution, this brief note instantiates Darwin's characteristic openness to inferences from facts, his rigorous doubt, and his reasoning acuity. As claimed by Kohn, Murrell, Parker and Whitehorn (2005), his voyage journals record his painstaking struggle not only to draw on but also to question the teaching and representations of his mentor, Henslow, on how species originate. Annotations, diagrams and notebooks were key tools in an exacting logical process where he made precise observations, framed questions and uncertainties, carried out investigative experimentation, generated and tested theories, and re-represented his claims for different readerships.

He also recognised that writing, as one explanatory mode and tool, had to be integrated with other modes to build persuasive causal accounts of phenomena. To this end he used others' illustrations as data from which to build evidence-based accounts for such topics as climbing plants (Darwin online, 2013a) and insectivorous plants (Darwin online, 2013b). His *On the origin of species* has only one illustration, but it is iconic, and a considerable amount of mathematical data is also integrated into this text. In reasoning that the construction of hexagonal cells by honeybees was due to instinct, Darwin used geometric drawing and raft building of bubbles and fossil objects to develop a multi-modal case for this claim (Darwin Project, 2013). He also appreciated that to excite broader public interest in his work he had to vary his writing style from technical to more popular. His celebrated metaphor of 'an entangled bank' (Darwin online, 2013c, p.490) at the end of *On the origin of species* poetically captures his profound sense of the wonder and mystery of the interconnectedness of macro and micro worlds and of the intricate laws governing these worlds. While Darwin left no records of his reflections on the value or effectiveness of writing as an enquiry resource in general, or its usefulness in his own case, his practices over his career confirm its key role in his personal meaning-making, reasoning processes, and extended attempts to persuade others of his claims.

RESEARCH ON LEARNING THROUGH WRITING IN SCIENCE

Writing as a crucial mode for learning in science has been researched extensively over the last 20 years, with researchers aiming to (1) identify what is or might be known and learnt by the writing process, and (2) explain how, and under what conditions, writing promotes learning. Two dominant accounts of how writing serves learning have guided classroom research. The genrist approach (see Halliday & Martin, 1993; Veel, 1997), drawing on cognitive processing theory (Johnson-Laird, 1983) assumes that scientific language organises and represents scientific thought, and that students need to be inducted into the particular purpose-built language practices of this subject. From this perspective, knowing and reasoning in science depends on students' acquisition of subject-specific writing skills, evident in the writing practices of scientists (Halliday & Martin. 1993). By contrast, advocates of a 'learning through writing' approach (Sutton, 1992; Hand, 2007; Rowell, 1997), drawing predominantly on claims about effective conditions for learning, assert that to acquire the new literacies of science, students needed to write in diverse ways for different readerships to clarify understandings for themselves and others.

Both perspectives assume that writing operates as a symbolic tool for abstracting and knowing in this subject, where drafting and revising strategies enable students to build and review links between classroom activities, conceptual understandings, and their expression. Both perspectives agree that writing functions as an epistemological tool to organise understanding for the self and others. Both also assume that this capacity for the linear organisation of thought makes writing well-suited to specifying evidence-based claims about natural phenomena, and is therefore a fundamental resource for disciplinary reasoning, as exemplified in Darwin's writing. The genrist approach emphasises the necessity of fidelity to disciplinary norms of expression and discourse structure, whereas the writing-to-learn approach stresses personal meaning-making through links to natural language and everyday communicative contexts. The genrist viewpoint assumes that the languages of science add up to a broadly stable, denotative, representational system that must be learnt in order for students to demonstrate science literacy. According to Martin (2000), Veel (1997), and others, students will learn effectively the rules and meanings of the particular language practices of science through the following teaching strategies: detailed analysis of linguistic features of textual examples; joint construction of genres with their teacher; and through an explicit extensive teacher focus on key textual function/form relationships and their rationale. Classroom research based on this perspective has largely taken the form of case studies of reputed exemplary implementation (Martin, 2000; Scheppegrell, 1998; Unsworth, 2001).

'Learning through writing' researchers, such as Keys, Hand, Prain and Collins (1999), Rivard and Straw (2000), Rowell (1997), and others, assert that students should be encouraged to write in diverse forms, for different purposes, and for varied readerships. Descriptive studies of diversified science-writing tasks were reported to have positive effects on students' attitudes towards, and engagement with, the subject (Prain & Hand, 1996). Comparative studies of contrasting treatments conducted by Hand and his colleagues (Hand 2007; Hand, Gunel & Ulu, 2008) indicated strong learning gains when students made and justified claims, gathered and represented evidence, and reflected on the progression of their ideas. These researchers claim that writing serves learning when (1) writing tasks are designed to require students to elaborate and justify claims about a topic, (2) the target readership is meaningful for the students, (3) students are provided with sufficient planning support, and (4) students engage in purposeful backward and forward search of the fit between their intentions and achieved meaning as they draft their texts.

These two perspectives provide crucial insights into (1) the complexity of the demands of writing tasks in science, and (2) likely conditions to promote learning through writing. While student induction into scientific representational norms is clearly necessary to develop student competence in this subject, making this induction engaging and meaningful requires a rich range of learning opportunities of the kind the writing-to-learn research sought to identify. Darwin's writing is an exemplary enactment of this dual process in his own learning.

WRITING WITHIN MULTIPLE MODES OF REPRESENTATION IN SCIENCE

Both agendas assumed that writing was the dominant learning mode, whereas recent research has also focused increasingly on modal interdependence in interpreting and constructing science texts, and the importance of visual representations (Ainsworth, 2008; Ainsworth, Prain & Tytler, 2011; di Sessa, 2004; Gilbert, 2005; Lemke, 2004). These researchers place more emphasis on the critical role of 'meta-representational competence' (diSessa, 2004, p. 293), or a knowledge of when, why and how to integrate different representational modes to undertake science enquiry and make evidence-based claims. This multi-modal focus also implies skill in 'visualisation' (Gilbert, 2005, p. 9), or visual/spatial reasoning (Ainsworth, Prain & Tytler, 2011), the capacity to construct appropriate meanings from and across multiple visual and other science representations at micro, meso and macro levels of processes and models. Lemke (2004, p. 41) noted that students needed to 'integrate multiple media simultaneously to re-interpret and re-contextualise information in one channel in relation to that in the other channels', with students having to translate, integrate and re-interpret meanings across verbal, visual and mathematical expressions, as well as connect these modes to earlier experiences of science activity. This is evident when students interpret the individual and relational meanings between a diagram, an accompanying text, and its referents in the world. Equally, students participate in similar processes when they construct their own text to clarify or elaborate on the meaning of an accompanying graph, photograph or diagram. For Lemke (2008, p. 2), writing's forte is its capacity to enable 'reasoning about relations among categories' because it operates primarily by categorical contrasts and exclusions around classification of entities, and relations between subjects and objects. Quantitative meanings such as rates and angles of change, and alterations to shape and motion are more suited to visual and mathematical representation. In this way, Lemke argued that science is necessarily about reasoning across interdependent modes of measurement and explanation. He further argued that the use of natural language, and by implication writing, enables links to be made between qualitative observation and linguistic reasoning about verbal categories, concepts, and their justification. Darwin clearly enacts this process regularly in his writing, such as in the weed experiment in *On the origin of species*.

In researching strategies and practices that enable learning, cognitive scientists now claim that learners employ a very rich range of both formal and informal interpretive meaning-making strategies (Abrahamson, 2009; Klein, 2008; Lemke, 2008; Lehrer & Schauble, 2013). In summarising this diverse literature, Klein (2006) argues that this research increasingly focuses on the role of student perception, motor actions, feelings, embodiment and pattern identification and completion, as significant strategies students use to learn. For Lemke (2008), positive student feelings are crucial to student identity work and identification with science learning, while research on visualisation has repositioned visual-spatial reasoning and representation work as critical to learning science concepts and their application in different contexts (Lehrer & Schauble, 2013). For Abrahamson (2009), even when students are interacting with computer-based programs, they are reasoning through dynamic interplay with the artefacts, perceptual stimuli, intuitive pattern-spotting, use of personally expressive resources, mental simulations, and embodied guesses. In these interactions they draw on the affordances of both their bodies as biomechanical systems and the properties of available material and symbol resources of the classroom, including peers and teachers, to learn.

All these insights into what enables or constrains student learning generally, and in science in particular, point to crucial conditions for achieving quality learning in this subject. They suggest the need for students to experience challenging, pleasurable, diverse tasks that enable creative mastery in this subject through an appealing variety and meaningful sequence of practices. At the same time, students need to be inducted meaningfully into the reasoning processes and representational norms of this subject, including scientific writing. In the next section, I report on a classroom-based research program that aimed to achieve these outcomes (see Tytler, Prain, Hubber & Waldrip, 2013), as well as current computer-based bioscience programs for senior secondary biology students (Gene Technology Access Centre, 2013).

LEARNING ABOUT ANIMAL DIVERSITY

In this example, we worked with two year-5/6 teachers in a shared primary classroom to plan, implement, and evaluate a unit on *Animals in the School Environment* that included a rich range of teacher and student-generated representational challenges, investigative activities, discussion, and re-representation. Major concepts to be learnt included: ecosystem, habitat, the diversity of animal populations, interactions between plants and animals in an ecosystem, animal structure and function, and the adaptive purposes of behaviour. Students were expected to learn about methods for studying animals, and generate their own representations to explore ideas and develop understanding of target concepts.

The students were taught how to sample and draw representations using tables, graphs, diagrams and cross sections in relation to animal diversity and animal classification, which they then applied to studying mealworms. Students collected data on animals and plants in the school-ground habitat, and then gathered animals for small-group study. They were required to describe the diversity of these animals in their logbooks, characterise their structure and behaviours, and explain how these were adaptive to their habitat (see Figures 1 and 2 for examples).

The specificity of detail in these logbooks points not only to the students' high levels of engagement, but also to the ways in which writing and other modes are necessarily interdependent in meaning-making as the students integrate visual, verbal

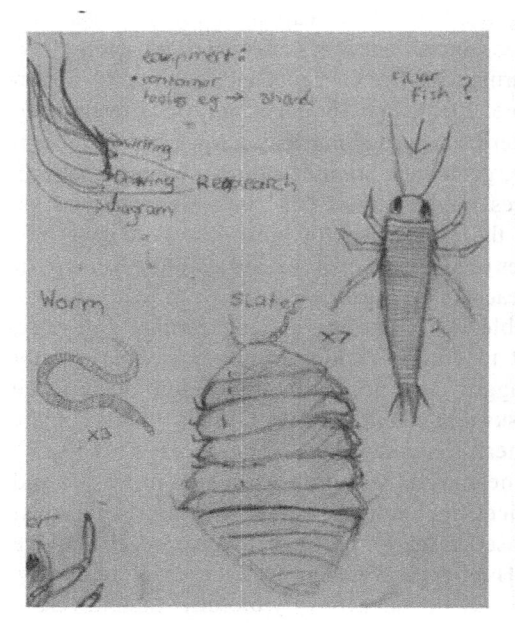

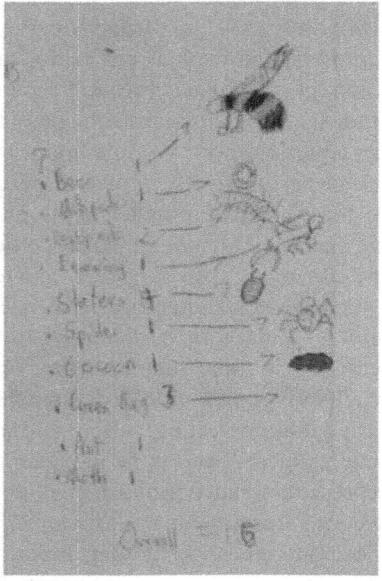

Figure 1. Student notebook sketches. (© Sense)

and mathematical modes to clarify and communicate emerging understandings. The types of drawing, the level of detail, the count of animals, and the use of a graph to characterise the population, all reveal how the students integrate meaning across modes, to reason about animal diversity. Teacher and peer verbal and other inputs are also clearly critical to this process. Learning the languages and reasoning moves of science is embedded meaningfully in an enquiry where students are addressing the challenge of how to represent adequately their understanding of this diversity. The changing annotations flag how the students used the graphs to guide both data collection and to prompt new reasoning processes and conclusions. Writing here is clearly a necessary component in these processes but not sufficient to enable or characterise all the students' meaning-making or learning outcomes.

Two boys in this class observed centipede behaviour closely and then constructed a jointed model with elastic connections to attempt to capture the animal's undulant movement. As with all the representational challenges in this class, the students were expected to draw on and extend their current representational resources to address this problem. The 3D model that they produced (see Figure 4) indicates a strong understanding of the nature of the jointed body and the sequence of leg movement. The two boys made preliminary drawings of the arrangement of the centipede's legs, as well as a close-up of the animal cleaning its antenna (Figure 3), and these

WRITING AND REPRESENTING TO LEARN IN SCIENCE

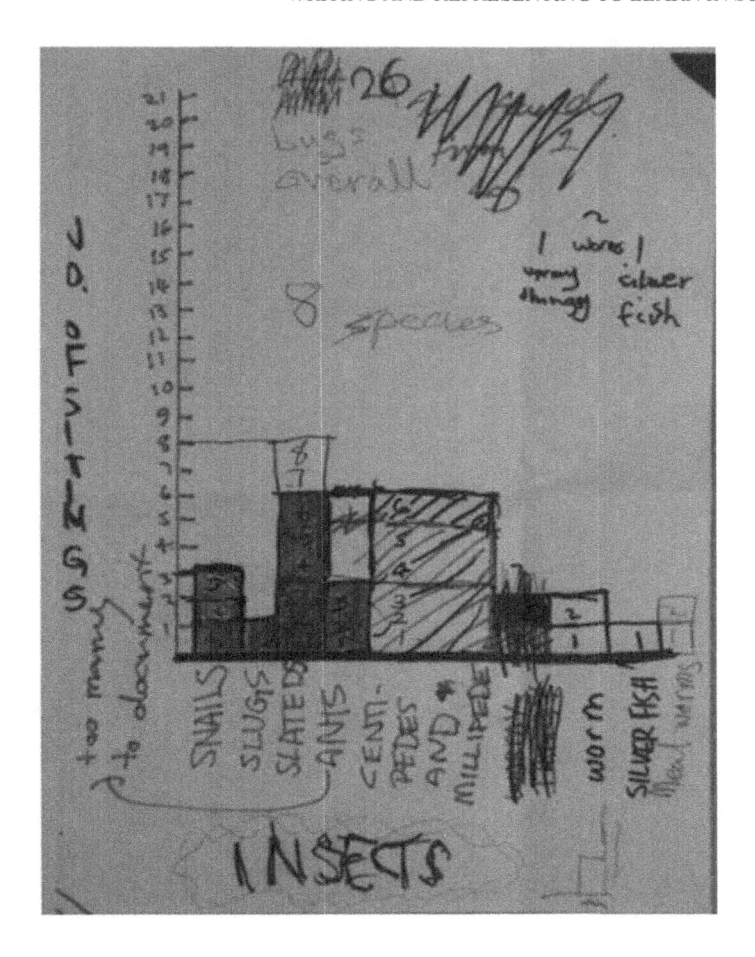

Figure 2. Student graphical representation of animal population. (© Sense)

observations were subsequently reflected in the constructed model, and in the verbal descriptions made by the boys to the class in explaining this model.

The two boys drew on many resources, including writing, to reason about how centipedes move, and how to design a model that explains this movement. They used past knowledge and experience in constructing objects, their understanding and experience of their own bodily movement and the movement of other animals, as well as symbolic resources such as learnt verbal, visual and mathematical representations of past science lessons. They also drew imaginatively on perceived qualities in their raw materials and their capacity to visualise a product or a possible outcome as they tackled this non-routine task. Their reasoning processes varied across different stages of the process. Initially their talk, sketches, and decisions

333

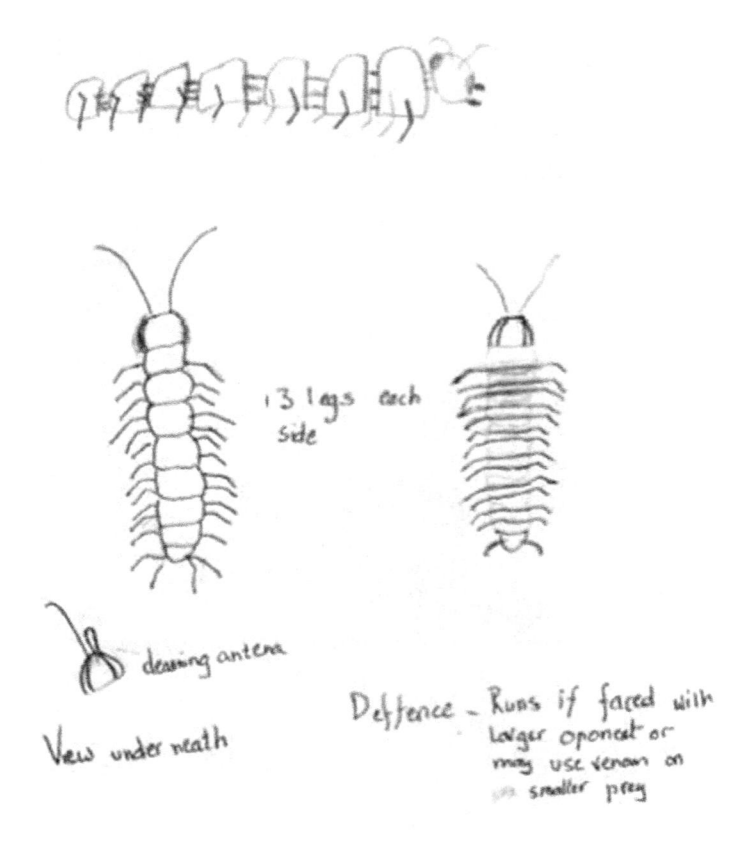

Figure 3. Centipede notebook entry. (© Sense)

on model design enabled them to organise perceptions of the precise nature of how the legs and body moved. Constructing drawings involved identifying key centipede parts important to movement, and abstracting these elements in a creative visual reasoning process. This then led to successive transformations across multiple representations, from labelled drawing, ongoing talk, a design drawing focusing on joints, model construction, and then embodied characterisation in a spontaneous role-play of the centipede's movement when they later demonstrated their understanding to the class.

Different representational tasks within this process provide different affordances that constrain and productively focus the students' attention. Drawing enables the relation between segments and leg attachments to be specified, with the design drawing requiring an account of the characteristics of the joints. Annotated writing enables them to categorise parts and specify the exact nature of their claim about

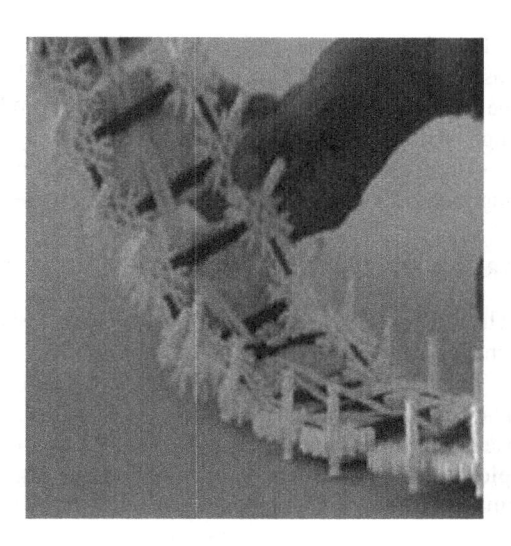

Figure 4. Centipede model showing elastic attachment of segments. (© Sense)

the movement. Creating a 3D model forces consideration of the material properties that would allow appropriate movement, such as the choice of elastic over hard sections.

The 3D model shows the boys' close awareness of the nature of the jointed body and the leg movement sequence. In presenting the model to the rest of the class, one boy moved the model so that individual sections undulated. He gestured, moved the model, and commented that 'instead of moving in straight lines it moves like a snake'. The other boy gestured to signify the undulation, and added, 'so we used elastic so it could move properly'. Their 3D representation combined with their verbal accounts functioned as reasoning tools. As one boy said:

> How we found out, how it moves is (moves the model) it went like (uses right hand to simulate the undulating movement). I also think it did this (moves hands) one set of legs forward and the other (raises both hands and moves them in a left – right, left – right motion).

At this point he moved very close to and just behind the other boy in order to represent the next consecutive segment. Both students then used their hands and their entire body, gesturing and moving in complete synchronicity as an embodied account of their understanding.

This example of primary students addressing a representational challenge highlights the complexity of factors and strategies that contribute to quality learning in primary school science, where writing is one of many resources that contribute to the processes and products of learning. The students, as in all science learning, have to make durable links between past knowledge, new experiences, manipulation of objects and other enquiry processes, as they invest all their available representational resources, including writing, into personal meaning-making about the target concepts. What the students can know or learn through writing in this topic depends on their ability (and motivation) to make strong links across all these elements. Whether student writing can serve informal and formal reasoning processes in this context also depends on these linkages.

LEARNING BIOSCIENCE BEYOND PRIMARY SCHOOL

Beyond primary school, there are now many net- and computer-based programs and resources for students to use to learn about the extensive evidence for evolution. For example, the Gene Technology Access Centre (GTAC, 2013) based in Melbourne, Australia, offers teachers and secondary students diverse opportunities to practise contemporary bioscience applications such as basic DNA manipulation techniques in relation to topics such as cell and protein structure, algal bloom, forensic investigation, immune response, and digestion and bacterial transformation. Students can participate in field experiences, and interact with material models, animations, simulations, and with peers and teachers to learn advanced concepts as they undertake bio-informatics tasks drawing on global databases in real time.

In one program, year 12 biology students can explore evolutionary relationships between five tiger subspecies through learning about their distribution and morphological characteristics. In this program students spend half a day at Melbourne Zoo investigating pelts, real tigers, and breeding books to determine the officially recognised number of tiger subspecies in the world. They then return to the Centre to perform DNA sequencing to look at molecular evidence using *Biology workbench* (SDSC, 2013), a web-based tool that enables access to many popular protein and nucleic acid sequence databases. Students can explore molecular homology as a way to define evolutionary relationships, using wet lab tasks and bio-informatics tools to distinguish between patterns in DNA sequences in the tiger subspecies. This program enables students to run gene sequence alignments of the tiger populations, using similarities and variation between sequences to construct a phylogenetic tree they can then analyse to identify an additional tiger subspecies.

In another program, 'From hominoids to hominims', students undertake a simulated palaeontological study to explore the characteristics of half-scale model skulls of four extinct hominins, and the modern human, chimpanzee, and gorilla. From these resources they can draw inferences about trends in the evolution of morphology, locomotion, diet, and hominins' cognitive capacity by examining and comparing anatomical and dental structures, such as cranial volume and jaw shape evolution. In a follow-up computer-based enquiry, they can use molecular homology to identify phylogenetic relationships, constructing phylogenetic trees based on mitochondrial DNA sequences to investigate evolutionary relationships between modern humans and other hominoids. Similarly, the Charles Darwin Trust has also developed Year 12 (post 16) modules on phylogeny and classification of barnacles moving from morphological evidence to DNA sequences and scanning electronic microscopy (see Chapters 20 & 26).

In developing representational and meta-representational competence in relation to understanding and applying concepts in these subjects, these students are concurrently (1) expanding their understanding of topic-specific technical terms and procedures, (2) making meaningful links between macro and micro features/models in these topics, (3) building their understanding of generic requirement in science discourse on this topic, and (4) deepening their understanding of the bases for evidence-based claims about evolution. Writing is clearly a crucial epistemological resource in this learning. Through this tool students can explore, reason, speculate about, revise, refine, organise, explain and apply their understandings of topics to new contexts, making permanent records of their claims, findings and conceptual understanding. However, as these accounts of science learning in practice make clear, this tool needs to be used in tandem with all the other available embodied, verbal, visual and mathematical resources for student meaning-making.

CONCLUDING REMARKS

We now know so much more about the comprehensive evidence for evolution and the complex factors that contribute to effective student learning about this topic, including the key role of writing. While terminology, genres, and the means for studying and communicating this knowledge continue to change, the necessity for teachers to engage students' feelings and imagination in undertaking science enquiry in this field remains. In this regard, Darwin's research methods and writing continue to offer exemplary leads on how to achieve this goal.

REFERENCES

Abrahamson, D. (2009). Embodied design: Constructing means for constructing meaning. *Educational Studies in Mathematics, 70*, 27–47.
Ainsworth, S. (2008). The educational value of multiple representations when learning complex scientific concepts. In J. Gilbert, M. Reiner, & M. Nakhlel (Eds.), *Visualization: Theory and practice in science education* (pp. 191–208). New York, NY: Springer.
Ainsworth, S., Prain, V., & Tytler, R. (2011). Drawing to learn in science. *Science, 333*, 1096–1097.
Barlow, N. (Ed.). (1963). Darwin's ornithological notes. *Bulletin of the British Museum (Natural History) Historical Series, 2*(7), 201–278.
Darwin online. (2013a). Climbing plants illustrations. Retrieved October 7, 2013 from http://darwin-online.org.uk/graphics/Climbing_plants_illustrations.html
Darwin online. (2013b). Insectivorous illustrations. Retrieved October 7, 2013 from http://darwin-online.org.uk/graphics/Insectivorous_Illustrations.html.
Darwin online. (2013c). *On the origin of species*. Retrieved October 7, 2013 from http://darwin online.org.uk/content/frameset?pageseq=1&itemID=F376&viewtype=text
Darwin Project. (2013). The evolution of honey comb. Darwin correspondence database. Retrieved from http://www.darwinproject.ac.uk/the-evolution-of-honey-comb
diSessa, A. (2004). Metarepresentation: Native competence and targets for instruction. *Cognition and Instruction, 22*(3), 293–331.

Gene Technology Access Centre (GTAC). (2013). Retrieved August 3, 2013 from http://www.gtac.edu.au

Gilbert, J. (2005). Visualisation: A metacogntive skill in science and science education. In J. Gilbert (Ed.), *Visualisation in science education* (pp. 9–28). Netherlands: Springer.

Halliday, M., & Martin, J. (1993). *Writing science: Literacy and discursive power*. London: Falmer Press.

Hand, B. (Ed.). (2007). *Science inquiry, argument and language: A case for the science writing heuristic*. Rotterdam: Sense Publishers.

Hand, B., Gunel, M., & Ulu, C. (2008). Sequencing embedded multimodal representations in a writing to learn approach to the teaching of electricity. *Journal of Research in Science Teaching, 46*(3), 225–247.

Johnson-Laird, P. (1983). *Mental models: Towards a cognitive science of language, inference and consciousness*. Cambridge, MA: Harvard University Press.

Keys, C., Hand, B., Prain, V., & Collins, S. (1999). Using the science writing heuristic as a tool for learning from laboratory investigations in secondary science. *Journal of Research in Science Teaching, 36*(10), 1065–1084.

Klein, P. (2006). The challenges of scientific literacy: From the viewpoint of second-generation cognitive science. *International Journal of Science Education, 28*, 143–178.

Kohn, D., Murrell, G., Parker, J., & Whitehorn, M. (2005, August 4). What Henslow taught Darwin. *Nature, 436*, 643–645.

Lehrer, S., & Schauble, L. (2013). Representational re-description as a catalyst for conceptual change. In B. Brizuela & B. Gravel (Eds.), *Show me what you know: Exploring student representations across STEM disciplines* (pp. 244–250). New York, NY: Teacher College Press.

Lemke, J. (2008). Identity, develoment and desire. Critical questions. In C. Caldas-Coultard & R. Iedema (Eds.), *Identity trouble: Critical discourse and contestations of identification* (pp. 17–42). London: Macmillan Palgrave.

Martin, J. (2000). Design and practice: Enacting functional linguistics. *Annual Review of Applied Linguistics, 20*, 116–126.

Prain, V., & Hand, B. (1996). Writing and learning in secondary science: Rethinking practices. *Teaching and Teacher Education, 12*, 609–626.

Rivard, L., & Straw, S. (2000). The effect of talk and writing on learning science. *Science Education, 84*, 566–593.

Rowell, P. A. (1997). Learning in school science: The promises and practices of writing. *Studies in Science Education, 30*, 19–56.

Scheppegrell, M. (1998). Grammar as resource: Writing a description. *Research in the Research in the Teaching of English, 25*, 67–96.

SDSC (2013). Biology Workbench. Retrieved August 3, 2013 from http://workbench.sdsc.edu

Sutton, C. (1992). *Words, science and learning*. Buckingham, UK: Open University Press.

Tytler, R., Prain, V., Hubber, P., & Waldrip, B. (2013). *Constructing representations to learn in science*. Rotterdam, The Netherlands: Sense Publishers.

Unsworth, L. (2006). Towards a metalanguage for multiliteracies education: Describing the meaning-making resources of language-image interaction. *English Teaching: Practice and Critique, 5*(1), 55–76.

Veel, R. (1997). Learning how to mean: Scientifically speaking. In F. Christie (Ed.), *Genre and institutions: The language of work and schooling* (pp. 161–195). London: Cassell Academic.

Vaughan Prain
Faculty of Education,
La Trobe University,
Melbourne,
Australia

EMMA NEWALL

25. ROUTES TO CONCEPTUAL CHANGE IN TEACHING AND LEARNING ABOUT EVOLUTION

Experiences with Students Aged between 11 and 16 Years

INTRODUCTION

I regard my own experience of Darwin-inspired learning as the continuation of a highly personal journey. My academic and professional life is rooted in the laboratory, but since joining the Charles Darwin Trust as an educator in 2008, I have become aware that I am still on this childhood journey of discovery.

I grew up in a small fishing town and spent much of my time exploring the local coastline. This was simply play, something that all children do. I had normal curiosity and imagination, and particular things would interest me, small things that I remember to this day. Until recently, this experience had receded from my memory somewhat. As I grew up and pursued my interest in science, I was studying biology at the abstract, molecular level. Working with the Charles Darwin Trust and developing my own conception of Darwin-inspired learning has led me to think again about these early experiences. I am an experimental biologist, but I am also a biologist in the fundamental sense of the word. I want to understand the living world and that desire for understanding began in childhood, but the significance of this did not become apparent to me until much later. Working with secondary school students from young 11 year-olds to those at 16, approaching adulthood, has given me the opportunity to observe children's experiences of biological science both formally and informally. Practising Darwin-inspired learning has revealed a number of insights into how children learn and how young scientists can be developed and go on to follow their own journeys of discovery.

PEDAGOGICAL ORIGINS: DARWIN-INSPIRED LEARNING

Darwin-inspired learning is an idea that developed through the work of the Charles Darwin Trust, both by wide consultation and through the experience in teaching and learning of the educators involved. Darwin's own life and the way he worked were the inspiration. It developed out of the idea that his approach to understanding the natural phenomena he observed could be adopted by people of all ages. He learnt directly from nature, through observation, and questioning, using this to develop ideas and explanations (Ayala, 2009). This is a highly democratic approach; it requires no specialist equipment or training, just curiosity and the opportunity to make observations and ask questions.

Darwin-inspired learning is explored throughout this volume, but in brief it:

– encourages a sense of place and direct engagement with the natural world using environments local to students, and those of Downe and other places Darwin worked.
– has a pedagogy of enquiry which places importance on active learning through seeking out experiences and questions, solving problems, and dialogue between teachers and pupils, and between learners;
  – teaching that facilitates imagination and thoughtful hands-on enquiry as well as the delivery of high-quality, engaging content
  – teaching that engages critical, creative thinking about how we know and how scientists work.
  – encouraging inter-disciplinary studies, with Darwin as the context, between science and literature, writing and expression, history, religious studies, geography, horticulture, dance and drama, design and technology, numeracy, music and art (Charles Darwin Trust, 2012).

This pedagogical approach is constructivist in essence, being based on the idea that children build on their own experiences and ideas in any learning situation (Piaget, 1950). Rosalind Driver in the 1970s and '80s carried out a number of studies into how children learn in school science lessons and developed the concept of 'alternative frameworks' (Driver, 1978). Her conclusions were based on the suggestion that learning is personal. To any new learning situation we bring our own experiences, pre-conceived ideas and expectations. We experience learning through these filters or lenses, and these profoundly affect how we assimilate new knowledge and understand concepts. These highly personal interpretations that we all develop are also resistant to change, and new information alone does not necessarily dislodge erroneous conceptions (Driver, 1985). Posner (1982) discusses 'accommodation'. This is not just the re-interpretation of ideas; accommodation requires a student to make a conceptual change which needs both dissatisfaction with existing conceptions and a plausible alternative which opens up potential new areas of enquiry. These are demanding requirements which need a teacher to have a detailed understanding of the science they are teaching and a full understanding of students' misconceptions. I would argue that nowhere in the curriculum is this more relevant than in the teaching of evolution by natural selection.

MISCONCEPTIONS: LANGUAGE, INTUITION AND EXPERIENCE

Darwin's theory of evolution is a fundamental concept in science and within the academic world of biological scientists is not under dispute. It is an excellent example of evidence-based science. Darwin himself provided a huge body of evidence for his ideas, which have subsequently been built on by the work of many, many scientists.

Although his theory has been refined over the last 150 years, Darwin's basic idea still stands. Despite this, it is associated with controversy and public resistance, and misconceptions of the science abound (Cleaves & Toplis, 2007). Teachers in the UK report challenges to their teaching of evolutionary biology by students (Cleaves & Toplis, 2007) and a BBC (2006) Gallup poll of 200 adults revealed that 39% believed that either creationist principles or Intelligent Design can explain the origins and variety of life on Earth. This is a challenge for educators, particularly as worldviews play such a large part in resistance and misconceptions, but rejecting a student's religious perspectives is not likely to be a successful teaching strategy (Reiss, 2008).

Misconceptions of both Darwinian science and Darwin himself are common in the school and the general population. A significant body of research exists into the nature of these misconceptions and a number of common themes emerge (Borun, 1993; Evans, 2006; Helm & Novak, 1983; Williams, 2009). These misconceptions are held not just by school-age students, but also university science graduates and, perhaps most worryingly, some science teachers (Cleaves & Toplis, 2007; Williams, 2009).

The reported misconceptions fall into the following broad categories:

– Views about the status of humans: these are based on ideas that we are not part of the animal kingdom, that we hold some special status in nature. Also, that if we have evolved, that we are the ultimate end product of a linear process from simple to complex forms.
– Teleological views encompassing belief in an active, directional process with a goal; for instance, that natural selection provides for an organism's needs.
– Lamarckian ideas; for instance, the belief that individual organisms actively adapt to their environment over time and pass on an adaptation to their offspring. This contrasts with the process Darwin proposed which is based on random variation in a population. This variation generates a range of characteristics within the population. If a characteristic is favourable it may become more common in the population, leading to species change.
– Misunderstanding of scientific terminology, such as the word 'theory'. Many people have a lay understanding that is synonymous with terms such as 'hunch' or 'best guess'. This fosters the idea that the theory of evolution is controversial and not fully accepted (Borun, 1993; Williams, 2009).

Language itself is also part of the problem and it plays a crucial role in teaching science. Teachers need to decode the technical language of science, allowing students to access scientific ideas. However, language is subtle and small differences in interpretation can lead to student misunderstandings. For instance, teachers may refer to a 'belief' in evolution as a short-hand means of describing an acceptance of ideas based on evidence, or 'design' as an explanation for adaptation. Also, the everyday understanding of words such as 'theory' and 'hypothesis' lead to descriptions of evolution as 'not a fact, only a theory', without an understanding of the scientific status of the concept (Williams, 2009).

The concepts that underpin evolution by natural selection are, on the surface, fairly simple. The existence of variation, inheritance, adaptation, competition and predation in the natural world outside our window may in some ways seem obvious. However, in teaching I have observed that they are highly susceptible to personal interpretation, or are taken for granted with no appreciation of their significance. Students may develop an intuitive understanding of the natural world based on stories they heard or read as children, family beliefs and lay talk in their own social circle and in the media. Such intuitive interpretations can produce barriers to learning alternative views (Brunby, 1984). For instance, a fundamental concept in evolutionary biology is the idea of species change, but this fact may be far from apparent to a child who wakes up every morning to a world where species are seemingly unchanged from the day before.

The fact that biological concepts are inter-related rather than discrete ideas may also contribute to students' difficulties in understanding, and can render them problematic to investigate. Biological adaptation is an example of a concept with which students often struggle, but is crucial to understanding selection and is linked to variation (Clough & Wood-Robinson, 1985). All these concepts need to be understood, but also the connection between them appreciated for the theory of evolution to be grasped. The nature of language again may serve to confuse, as a 'folk' or non-scientific understanding of the word 'adaptation' can mean 'a change in response to a stimulus'. From this we can explain how students may view the process as a conscious change made by an individual and confuse acquired and inherited characteristics (Clough & Wood-Robinson, 1985).

Chi (1998) puts forward the view that misconceptions about the mechanism underlying species change cannot be resolved merely by teaching Darwinian principles. Rather, it is necessary for students to understand that evolution is a process, like diffusion or conduction. It is not a discrete event. This requires an understanding of biology at the level of the population as well as the individual, and of time on a geological scale. Students need to have an appreciation of the micro and macro worlds and how they are linked. These are big ideas which are difficult for many students to grasp, requiring a high degree of abstract thinking.

Children's ideas begin forming at an early age and there is evidence that children start to develop their own beliefs about how species have arisen before they even start school (Samarapungavan, 2011). Samarapungavan argues that empirical evidence suggests that although religious beliefs do affect understanding of speciation, for instance, they alone are not the only barrier to such understanding. Ontological essentialism also plays a part, this being the Aristotelian idea that species exist unchanged over time, that their identity is fixed as a set of 'essential' characteristics. Many students, although they may accept natural selection as a mechanism to explain small changes in a species, do not make the connection with speciation on a macro scale (Samarapungavan, 2011). She suggests that students often maintain differing explanations of natural phenomena, such as inheritance in co-existence, as Darwin himself did in his writings, but that it is possible for these 'alternate conceptions' to be a starting point for discussion and argumentation. Evolution is at present taught in a piecemeal manner whilst biology, as a science in practice, is increasingly moving towards a systems approach (Ideker, 2001). This can explain in part why students do not appreciate the extent and the inter-relatedness of evidence to support evolution by natural selection. Secondary school teaching and learning does not always reflect how biology works.

PARALLELS AND LESSONS LEARNT FROM GENETICS EDUCATION

Working as I have within the realm of medical research and clinical genetics, I have had the opportunity to observe and reflect on the parallels between genetics and evolution in terms of teaching and learning. They overlap in regard to the science. Many of the concepts are linked, and understanding of both is necessary to understand the theory of evolution by natural selection. However, genetics, like evolution, is also susceptible to common misconceptions which are influenced by people's personal beliefs and experiences. Many people's ideas of heredity, how traits are transmitted form parent to child, do not fully reflect the reality, which is more subtle and complex (Venville, 2004). Like evolution, genetics is an area of biology that often appears in the general media and is associated with a degree of controversy. This everyday exposure can result in the public perception that we all generally know a certain amount about the science. Such seeming familiarity can generate a partial and skewed understanding. For instance, terms such as DNA, gene and chromosome are often used inaccurately and interchangeably by the media and in everyday conversation (Lewis & Kattman, 2004). Again, as with evolution, genetics tends to be taught in a piecemeal way, looking at either the macro or the micro level, resulting in a lack of holistic understanding (Lewis & Kattman, 2004; Castro, 2006). Teachers are also susceptible to misconceptions and may compound students' erroneous ideas by the use of ambiguous language (Lewis & Kattman, 2004; Castro, 2006). The basic concepts of genetics are often misunderstood by students; they are familiar with key terms but not with their full meaning, and do not have a good understanding as to how concepts are connected (Lewis, 2000). Lewis et al. (2000), carrying out research with a cohort of mixed ability state school students, reported a lack of understanding of the basics within this group, which resulted in an inability to grasp more complex topics. The evidence suggests that students need to understand the basic concepts and to build up an idea of how they are connected before they can understand overarching ideas or their application. This is also crucial in evolution, which requires an understanding of the mechanisms behind selection which are fundamentally connected to theories of inheritance and the role of genes.

Interestingly, Lewis (2000) also reported that the use of metaphors and analogies, a common approach to explaining complex topics, can encourage misconceptions. For instance, the barcode and blueprint metaphors do not allow for a full explanation of the fact that gene sequences are used to create proteins and can in turn foster overly deterministic ideas about the role of genes.

A study into the application of genetic knowledge by students between the ages of 11 and 16 years through an essay competition in the United States, revealed a significant degree of variability in students' knowledge and understanding, and some common misconceptions. These misconceptions, like those affecting understanding of evolutionary principles, were found to be shaped by personal experiences and are difficult to modify (Mills Shaw et al, 2008). To add further weight to the argument, a review of high school students by the National Assessment of Education Progress (NAEP) in the United States in 2000 revealed a multiplicity of deficits in student understanding, including in the topics of evolution, classification, mutation and inheritance (see Table 1). All of these concepts are inter-connected and are fundamental ideas in biological science.

Table 1. *NAEP test results for student understanding of core genetics concepts, grades 8 and 12 (in 2000). (Adapted from Mills Shaw et al., 2008)*

Theme	Students with unsatisfactory answers (%)
Classification	58
Theory of evolution	45
Reproduction	39
Evolutionary relationships	70
Darwin's theory of evolution	47
Genes	30
Mutation	58
Interpreting genetic material	83
Genetic DNA	56
Recombinant DNA usage	58

The backdrop to this problem of knowledge and understanding is one of rapid progress in the scientific world. New evidence to support evolutionary theory from genetic and genomic research is mounting, but are students equipped to understand it, given these findings? The work of Mills Shaw (2008) suggests the greatest areas of misunderstanding are in the application of genetic principles because of lack of appreciation of the complexity involved.

Students make broad leaps without demonstrating an understanding for the multiple factors that play a role (Mills Shaw, 2008, p. 1164). They often demonstrate a lack of understanding of the connection between an organism's characteristics and the role of genes in determining its anatomy and physiology. An observation backed up by other studies is the perception of genetic determinism or, again, in parallel with evolution, genetic essentialism (Condit, 1999); the idea prevailing that there is one gene for one trait and that complex aspects of behaviour and disease are attributed to genes. This perception is reflected in the media with stories of discoveries of 'the gene for X', whether this is sexuality, criminal behaviour, intelligence or cancer (Mills Shaw et al., 2008; Dougherty, 2009). The reality is that multiple genes, producing multiple protein products, act in combination with other DNA sequences, gene products and environmental factors to produce the vast majority of traits. Once again, student appreciation of the complexity is lost because of the loss of connection between ideas and because of their lack of understanding of the basics. Thinking in this way is challenging for young people emerging as scientists. It requires the ability to synthesise ideas and critically evaluate evidence. Mills Shaw (2008) suggests that students need to have support to develop their critical thinking skills if they are to apply knowledge. How able are all students to achieve these higher order skills? Is this something schools need to look at for all, or are they thinking principally about the next generation of biological scientists? Will one approach fit all, or do we need to diversify in terms of teaching and learning strategies?

Clinical genetics has allowed an insight into the impact of cultural, including religious, beliefs on notions of inheritance and disease, through research examining the ideas and opinions of patients visiting genetics clinics. Shaw and Hunt (2008), in a study of British Pakistani families visiting UK genetics clinics, found a variety of alternative explanations for the cause of genetic disease. Many reflected misconceptions held by the general UK population, but some were culturally and ethnically specific, which raises questions for teachers working in ethnically diverse schools and re-inforces the premise that teachers need to have a thorough understanding of the source and nature of misconceptions. As with the general population, this group of patients incorporated the medical genetic information they received into their prior understanding of illness, leading to a hybrid understanding which can be both helpful and obstructive to understanding (Shaw & Hunt, 2008). The picture is complex indeed and presents a significant challenge to hard-pressed teachers.

DARWIN'S WAYS OF WORKING: OBSERVATION, QUESTION, NARRATIVE

Given the complexity of competing worldviews and alternate conceptions, what can Darwin's ways of working contribute to teaching and learning? Darwin did not work in a formal laboratory setting. Although he used scientific equipment for investigations and scientific writings as references in his study at Down House, he also took his work out into the world. This was most obviously demonstrated on his journey across the globe on the *Beagle*, but also on expeditions closer to home. In addition, he engaged in innumerable conversations and correspondence with animal breeders, farmers, market gardeners and amateur naturalists nationally and internationally but, perhaps most crucially of all, in his local environment, his garden and the countryside that surrounded his home in rural Kent (Desmond & Moore, 1991; Keynes, 2001; Jones, 2008).

Darwin spent 40 years working from his own home and using his garden and local environment as his laboratory (see chapters 1 and 2). His approach began with observation. He had a huge curiosity and a desire to understand (Desmond & Moore, 1991), a characteristic apparent in most young children. However, his curiosity persisted and Darwin-inspired learning, using his methods as inspiration, aims to foster and maintain this curiosity as the starting point to generating questions and developing explanations. This is the objective, but what have we as educators for the Charles Darwin Trust achieved? Does Darwin-inspired learning promote understanding of the concepts underpinning more complex biology? Does it foster understanding of complexity and allow students to appreciate the inter-connectedness of both natural life and ideas? It would not be realistic, given the short interventions with 11– 16-year-old students that the Trust has been able to provide, for us to claim a high degree of impact; and in the absence of in-depth evaluation we cannot say for certain what effect these interventions have had on students and teachers. However, we do have our own reflections and observations to begin exploring impact, and the words of the children and staff involved, via their formal feedback directly after the sessions.

The Trust worked with a group of South London high schools in 2011 and 2012. The schools were academies and their intake was mixed ability, but with a significant number of economically disadvantaged students. We developed a one-day workshop for a group of year 7 students (11–12 year olds), focusing not just on science but also on design and technology and mathematics. This workshop was held a number of times with different groups of students over this period. Groups of between 15 and 20 students took part in several short sessions looking at a range of Darwin-inspired topics. These were:

– Selective breeding
– Bee behaviour and honeycomb formation
– Climbing plants: adaptation
– Darwin's weed plot: competition
– Intra-specific variation in plants
– Darwin's Facebook: communication and collaboration

Each was designed to address basic concepts and, in combination, to encourage students to begin to make connections between both observations and ideas. Some of these workshops occurred in a classroom environment, but those involving plants were carried out either in the school grounds or in a local park.

The student feedback was enlightening. Students were asked what the best bit of the day was, which revealed a variety of answers but certain themes predominated. A significant proportion of students replied that being able to work outside was the best bit of the day. This came up again and again in student responses (Charles Darwin Trust, unpublished data):

> Going to the park because we investigated freely and we learned all about different plants.

> The wildlife workshop. I liked exploring while learning massively about nature.

There is a significant body of evidence to support the positive impact of learning outside the classroom (Eyre & Marjoram, 1990; Nundy, 2001; Cerini et al., 2003;

Braund & Reiss, 2006). My observations as a Trust educator would certainly bear this out. The children appreciated the freedom to explore and indulge their curiosity about nature. There was an element of play in their behaviour. They used their imagination, they worked together. Put simply, they behaved like children. There was also evidence of learning in their comments. Studies into the development of children's skills in science support the role of play. One study indicated that even very young children are able to understand that investigation requires something that can be found out and a means of doing so. Their play incorporates these ideas through exploration and experimentation (Cook, 2011).

One workshop focused on intra-specific variation. Students logged leaf size in different plants in the same species. On being introduced to the task some remarked that they are 'just' plants and they are all the same. Variation is essential for selection to occur. Uniformity would not allow selective advantage, but students tended at first not to notice this variation and if they did they did not appreciate its potential significance. Students have difficulty making the connection between variation, selection and the cumulative effects on the traits of a species (Clough, 1985). I am not able to claim from these interventions that students had a full appreciation of the concept of variation and selection, but their initial perceptions were challenged and they had a positive experience that allowed them to consider Darwin's ideas and think critically about their own assumptions. These included challenging their habitual negative image of botanical science, as the following 'best bits' responses indicate:

> When I was in the first workshop about variation. It was quite fun and I found out some new and interesting plants.

> Looking at leaves

A telling comment from one student hinted at the fact that students are not getting the opportunity to work outside, even if a school possesses a dedicated wildlife area:

> When I was in the part of the school that I had never known about which was a nature area. I enjoyed plotting down onto my chart and looking at plants.

Another theme students particularly mentioned in their feedback was Darwin's Facebook session, where they explored how Darwin collaborated in his work. They were introduced to the great array of people from different walks of life that Darwin consulted across the world. Students were surprised that he corresponded with non-scientists a great deal and that he valued the knowledge and experience of a great number of diverse people:

> Darwin's Facebook as that's when I learnt the most about Darwin and his friends.

> It was interesting to know other people thought like him.

Other 'best bits' were more general in nature:

Learning about Darwin

Exploring, finding out new things and experimenting with new things.

Learning many new and interesting things about the things that surround us.

Darwin-inspired learning allows students to investigate in an open-ended manner. And they are encouraged to ask questions. The answer is not necessarily important, but the act of noticing is key. As Keynes (2009) describes in his article on Darwin's ways of working and their potential for education:

> Pupils can notice something remarkable in what a creature is doing, spot an intriguing question and start thinking about ways to answer it. (Keynes, 2009, p. 102)

Questions were a cornerstone of Darwin's work and his inspiration is used to stimulate the curiosity of students. Research begins with questions, and answers cannot be reached without them:

> A sarcastic soul once observed that the primary function of our schools is to impart sufficient facts to make children stop asking questions. Those with whom the schools did not succeed become scientists. I never made good grades in school, at times I nearly failed, and I never stopped asking questions. (Schmidt-Nielsen, 1994, p. 1)

This quotation from an eminent physiologist alludes to an idea that I have been thinking about ever since I began reflecting on Darwin-inspired learning and my experiences as an educator. That is that we have two tasks; we want all children to engage with the natural world and their own environment, to notice and ask questions, but we also want to develop young scientists, new Darwins possibly? A Darwin-inspired approach can, I believe, serve both functions. Whilst working with young people I have seen students' excitement at having the opportunity to explore and investigate in a humble green space in their own school. I have seen their curiosity emerge, their enjoyment of collecting and observing grow. Some, I believe, have had an enjoyable experience and engaged with some new ideas, others wanted to see as Darwin and develop their own questions and ideas. Will they become the biologists of the future? Obviously I cannot say, but I believe Darwin-inspired learning does have the potential to be transformative.

Helping students to understand Darwin's theory and the concepts that underpin it is not just about informing them of the principles; it can require them to see the world in a new and different way (Sinatra, 2008). This is conceptual change, which is a difficult thing to achieve and presents a challenge to educators. Educators are faced with the fact that students' prior experiences, ways of understanding and deeply held beliefs may conflict with the knowledge they are presented with at school. Sinatra et al. (2008) present a thoroughly researched set of principles for teaching evolution and avoiding misconceptions. They suggest that teachers begin by first understanding their students' pre-conceived ideas, and provide the opportunity for them to critically consider and reflect on alternative ideas. Teachers also need to consider the language they use and avoid anthropomorphic or intentional language in explanations. Finally, the use of familiar and relevant contexts to teach the evolutionary concepts and direct engagement with nature are, they claim, more likely to support conceptual change. Darwin-inspired learning, as it has been developed and practised by the Charles Darwin Trust, uses a very similar approach, placing a great emphasis on the direct investigation of the central concepts but in places such as school grounds and local green spaces:

> Conceptual change research suggests that the degree of engagement, that is, how deeply students become involved in the content through discussion, debate, dialog, and/or experimentation, relates to the likelihood of change. (Sinatra, 2008, p.194)

Why is observation so crucial? Randal Keynes writing about Darwin's ways of working encapsulates the idea: 'When you look carefully, the utterly familiar can become deeply strange.' (Keynes, 2009, p. 103).

This new way of seeing can begin that process of conceptual change and may be an experience a student will never forget. Darwin-inspired learning to me embodies three central ways of knowing: questions, observations and narrative. These allow us to see and appreciate the world in a new and different way. They are part of the journey I am still on.

REFERENCES

Ayala, F, J. (2009). Darwin and the scientific method. *Proceedings of the National Academy of Sciences, 106*(suppl.), 10033–10039.
BBC. (2006). Britons unconvinced on evolution. Retrieved from http://news.bbc.co.uk/1/hi/sci/tech/4648598.stm
Borun, M, Massey, C., & Lutter, T. (1993). Naïve knowledge and the design of Science Museum exhibits, *Curator, 36*(3), 201–219.
Braund, M., & Reiss, M. J. (2006). Towards a more authentic science curriculum: the contribution of out-of-school learning. International Journal of Science Education, 28, 1373–1388.
Brunby, M. (1984). Misconceptions about the concept of natural selection by medical biology students. *Science Education, 68*(4), 493–503.
Castro, J. Retrieved from http://www.csun.edu/~jcc62330/coursework/690/Assignments/castro_misconception.pdf
Cerini, B., Murray, I., & Reiss M. J. (2003). *Student review of the science curriculum: Major findings.* London: Planet Science.
Charles Darwin Trust . (2012). Retrieved from http://charlesdarwintrust.org/content/19/darwin-inspired-learning
Cleaves, A., & Toplis, R. (2007). In the shadow of intelligent design: The teaching of evolution. *Journal of Biological Education, 42*(1), 30–35.
Clough, E., & Wood-Robinson, C. (1985). How secondary students interpret instances of biological adaptation. *Journal of Biological Education, 19*(2), 125–130.
Cook, C., Goodman, N. D., & Sculz, L. E. (2011). Where science starts: Spontaneous experiments in preschoolers' exploratory play. *Cognition, 120*, 341–349.

Desmond, A., & Moore, J. (1991). *Darwin*. London: Penguin Books.
Dougherty, M. J. (2009). Closing the gap: Inverting the genetics curriculum to ensure an informed public. *American Journal of Human Genetics, 85*, 6–12.
Driver, R., & Easley, J. (1978). Pupils and paradigms: A review of literature related to concept development in adolescent science students. *Studies in Science Education, 5*, 61–84.
Driver, R., Guesne, E., & Tiberghein, A. (1985). *Children's ideas in science*. Milton Keynes: Open University Press
Evans, M. E. (2006). Teaching and learning about evolution. In M. E. Evans & J. Diamond (Ed.). *Virus and the whale: Exploring evolution in creatures small and large*. Arlington, VA: NSTA Press.
Eyre, D., & Marjoram, T. (1990). *Enriching and extending the national curriculum*. London: Kogan Page.
Ferrari, M., & Chi, M. T. H. (1998). The nature of naive explanations of natural selection. *International Journal of Science Education, 20*(10), 1231–1256.
Helm, H., & Novak, J. D. (1983). Misconceptions in science and mathematics. *Proceedings of the First International Seminar on Misconceptions in Science and Mathematics*. Ithaca, NY: Cornell University Press.
Ideker, T., Galitski, T. & Hood, L. (2001). A new approach to decoding life: Systems biology. *Annual Review of Genomics: Human Genetics, 2*, 343–372.
Jones, S. (2008). *Darwin's Island: The Galapagos in the garden of England*. London: Hachette Digital.
Keynes, R. (2001). *Darwin, his daughter and human evolution*. New York, NY: The Berkley Publishing Group.
Keynes, R. (2009). Darwin's ways of working: The opportunity for education. *Journal of Biological Education, 43*(3), 101–103.
Lewis, J., Leach, J., & Wood-Robinson, C. (2000). All in the genes? Young people's understanding of the nature of genes. *Journal of Biological Education, 34*(2), 74–79.
Lewis J., & Kattman, U. (2004). Traits, genes, particles and information: re-visiting students' understanding of genetics. *International Journal of Science Education, 26*, 195–206.
Mills Shaw, K. R., Van Horne, K., Zhuang, H., & Broughman, J. (2008). Essay contest reveals misconceptions of high school students in genetics content. *Genetics, 178*(3), 1157–1168.
Nundy, S. (2001). Raising achievement through the environment: A case for fieldwork and field centres. Peterborough, UK: National Association of Field Studies Officers.
Piaget, J. (1950). *The psychology of intelligence*. London: Routledge and Kegan Paul.
Posner, G. J., Strike, K. A., Hewson, P. W., & Gertzog, W. A. (1982). Accommodation of a scientific conception: Toward a theory of conceptual change. *Science Education, 66*(2), 211–227.
Rees, P. A. (2007). The evolution of textbook misconceptions about Darwin. *Journal of Biological Education, 41*(2), 53–55.
Reiss, M. J. (2008). Teaching evolution in a creationist environment: an approach based on worldviews not misconceptions. *School Science Review, 90*(331), 49–56.
Samarapungavan, A. (2011). Ontological assumptions about species and their influence on students' understanding of evolutionary biology. In R.S. Taylor & M. Ferrari (Eds.), *Epistemology and science education: Understanding the evolution vs. intelligent design controversy*. London: Taylor & Francis.
Schmidt-Nielsen, K. (1994). About curiosity and being inquisitive. *Annual Review of Physiology, 56*, 1–12.
Shaw, A., & Hurst, J. A. (2008). What is this Genetics, Anyway? Understandings of genetics, illness causality and inheritance among British Pakistani users of genetic services. *Journal of Genetic Counselling, 17*, 373–383.
Sinatra, G. M., Brem, S. K., & Evans, M. (2008). Changing Minds? Implications of conceptual change for teaching and learning about biological evolution. *Evolution Education Outreach, 1*, 189–195.
Venville, G., Gribble, S. J., & Donovan, J. (2004). An exploration of young children's understandings of genetics concepts from Ontological and Epistemological perspectives. *Science Education, 89*(4), 614–633.
Williams, J. D. (2009). Belief versus acceptance: Why do people not believe in evolution? *Bioessays, 31*(11), 1255–1262.

CONCEPTUAL CHANGE IN TEACHING AND LEARNING ABOUT EVOLUTION

Emma Newall
Charles Darwin Trust,
UK

CAROLYN J. BOULTER & EMMA NEWALL

26. DEVELOPING A MODEL FOR POST-16 TEACHING AND LEARNING

INTRODUCTION

- What can a nineteenth-century gentleman scientist have to contribute to contemporary science education post-16?
- What place can Darwin-inspired learning have in training future scientists, when the biology research world appears to be dominated by the micro-level and technologically-driven science of genomics[1]?

As educators for the Charles Darwin Trust, we are sometimes asked these questions. In order to explore them we started our work with an examination of the curriculum specifications and the textbooks for the post-16 stage in England.

Towards the end of his life Darwin himself reflected back on his qualities as scientific naturalist:

> Looking back as well as I can at my character during my school life, the only qualities which at this period promised well for the future, were, that I had strong and diversified tastes, much zeal for whatever interested me, and a keen pleasure in understanding any complex subject or thing (Barlow, 1958, p. 27).

From the school texts and curricula we studied, students could learn little about Darwin's passion for understanding complex subjects and the large diversity of organisms that he researched, nor about the manner in which he pursued his scientific questions. When he does feature in textbooks the content focuses on his Galapagos observations and the famous finches. In fact, these feature only briefly in his writings, and much of his theoretical and investigative science was carried out in his home at Downe and in the Kent countryside (see Chapter 2). So, the significance of his contribution to our perception and understanding of biology as a *way of knowing* is seldom described at all. To understand whether this matters for today's students we went on to examine some aspects of the development of science and education, especially in biology, since Darwin took his daily walks round the Sandwalk at Down House (see Chapter 7), returned to his greenhouse to set up experiments on climbing plants or boiled down pigeon carcasses to look for variation.

THE TWO CULTURES AND THE SCIENTIFIC REVOLUTION

The education for young gentlemen of Darwin's generation in England was dominated by the classics[2] as he recalled in his autobiography:

> Nothing could have been worse for the development of my mind than Dr. Butler's school, as it was strictly classical, nothing else being taught except a little ancient geography and history. The school as a means of education to me was simply a blank. During my whole life I have been singularly incapable of mastering any language. Especial attention was paid to verse-making, and this I could never do well. (Barlow, 1958 p.27)

Perhaps against his better judgement in the light of his own experience, Darwin sent his oldest son to Rugby and his fears were realised about the restrictions of a classical education[3] (Desmond & Moore, 1991, p. 400). The next sons had a more liberal schooling at Clapham School and the daughters were educated at home (see Chapter 7). Even if Darwin's early formal education had been unmemorable, he later added experience of medicine at Edinburgh University and training for the Anglican ministry at Cambridge, disappointing his father by finding neither attractive. For as long as he could remember Darwin had collected beetles and as a young man spent long hours in the countryside shooting and skinning game. These, and the other experiences and skills gained on the *Beagle* voyage, fed into his life's work as a scientific naturalist, explaining the natural world and its organisms, and the processes of the world, both living and geological. He was also deeply engaged in literature and his reading of novels was extensive, as his library shows (Rutherford, 1908).

During the years of the expansion of science in the early twentieth century, the classics continued to be seen as an essential background for a cultured person and science as unnecessary. The tension erupted in 1959 when the scientist and novelist, C. P. Snow, delivered the Rede lecture in Cambridge with the title 'The two cultures and the scientific revolution'[4]. Snow's address was cutting, when he spoke of scientists who had given up on reading Dickens, and humanities professors who were ignorant and derisory about the Second Law of Thermodynamics. He criticised an education system that forced children to specialise too early and the snobbery that guided them towards the classical and traditional professions and away from science and industry. The effect of the lecture was widespread and the reaction vitriolic especially in 1962 from F. R. Leavis (republished 2013). Fifty years after this lecture, on the 150th anniversary of the publication of *On the origin of species* in 2009, there was still extensive comment on the issues that Snow had raised so many years earlier[5].

The Context of Science Education Today

C. P. Snow suggested that 'the way out of all this ... is of course by rethinking our education' (Snow, 1959). The education system in England had been thoroughly reformed in 1944 under a coalition wartime government and its free and universal provision implemented by the Labour government after the Second World War. The 1960s saw the effects of an education for all being worked out with ideas such as 'the rise of the meritocracy' (Young, 1961), visions of a liberal, classless society, and attempts to make the curriculum appropriate for the full range of abilities. The backlash (Cox & Boyson, 1977) demanded a return to a traditional curriculum and criticised the popularist curriculum designed for the less academic starting with pupils' interests and the exploration of themes. This is the context of science education today, a constant tussle between the needs of what Fensham (1985) called 'elitist' science and 'popularist' science education. Various reforms of the whole school curriculum, notably the Education Reform Act of 1988, brought in tight definitions of the curriculum in science and rigorous progammes of testing and comparison intended to raise standards. The dilemma of how to provide for the complete range of abilities and needs in science education has not been solved and remains an important factor affecting student choices to study science later in school post-16. A report into secondary school student views in 2005 concluded:

> Contemporary science lessons demonstrate many similarities with the ways secondary science was taught a century or more ago. These students are demanding a twenty-first century identity for science. (Bevin, Brodie & Brodie, 2005, p. 18)

During a period from the 1990s, a marked downturn in UK students studying science post-16 occurred (Roberts, 2002). This was most acute in the physical sciences. Uptake in science courses post-16 and at university has since improved and the biological sciences are a particularly popular choice. Degrees falling under the category of the biological sciences were the most popular science degree choice in UK university applications in 2013 (UCAS, 2013). Although a greater investigation of student choices is required, there is an apparent rise in the popularity of the biomedical and sports science degrees and a downturn in more classical biology subjects, particularly botany (Drea, 2011). Unlike in Darwin's day, there is now a vast range of university courses available to aspiring biologists apart from the classical ones of zoology and botany, medicine and pharmacy. The scientific developments of the last century within the topics of environment, microbiology, human and evolutionary biology have given rise to many. Within evolutionary biology alone there are courses covering: systematics, palaeontology, evolutionary ecology, evolutionary behaviour, evolutionary morphology and physiology, molecular evolution and evolutionary developmental biology. In addition, the rise of genetics and genomics and the increasing use of mathematical or computational biology provides a bewildering choice for school leavers.

However, the point at which students today specialise at age 16 years is a crucial turning point. For many students it is still the moment when they have to decide between advanced studies in sciences or in the arts. Since the debate articulated by C. P. Snow, educational researchers have been tracking student choices and trying to work out what factors influence their choice for or against science. Research investigating student attitudes revealed a general mismatch between the reality of science and its practitioners and student perceptions of it (Hill & Wheeler, 1991, Osborne et al., 2003). Research questioning students' attitudes demonstrated that they wanted a curriculum that allowed greater autonomy, that they felt was more relevant and contemporary in content and that allowed them to exercise their creativity (Osborne et al., 2003). The debate continues and the age of 16 years remains a filter which narrows down the number of candidates able to make a positive choice two or three years later to go to study science at university.

If at the stage of university entrance students turn away from science in greater numbers this leads to severe shortages of scientifically trained graduates. In some biological areas such as systematics (see Chapter 20), botany and field-based research, the crisis is severe at a time when the skills of identification and analysis of the biosphere are vital[6]. In economies dependent on science, technology, engineering and mathematics (STEM) skills, the lack generally in the workplace causes grave concern[7]. But alongside is another concern, that of the seemingly limited public understanding of science and, as in the case of the British government, the lack of ministers with anything but basic scientific training. This is equally important to having sufficient career scientists in a world where awareness of science, especially of biology and how it is carried out, is needed to make informed decisions about wellbeing, both of humans and the wider environment.

WHAT CAN DARWIN-INSPIRED LEARNING OFFER?

Much of biology today is based on the ideas that Darwin developed in the nineteenth century, but how easy is it to link Darwin and his approach to the biology that students need to know now? In developing our materials we took topics directly from the Advanced Level specifications of English awarding bodies for biology (2012) which broadly cover the same content as one another. Although we could probably have found some linkage with most topics, we knew from experience as teachers and from in-service courses we were running, that some topics proved difficult to teach and were regarded as rather dull. These were also topics with close links to Darwin's work – phylogeny and classification, genetics and adaptation, especially in plants. So we hoped that we could provide some inspiration in these areas for budding specialists and generalists alike. As mentioned earlier, students want science to be relevant and contemporary as well as giving them autonomy. So the first task was to draw up the introductory part of our model which links the topics to the contexts in biology both for Darwin and for the present day. There are so many contextual areas within which new scientific understanding arises and is used: technological, social, economic, religious, political, gender, medical, communications and transport.

The Context of Darwin's Work

Darwin was working within the Victorian period (1837-1901), moving to Downe in 1842. It was a time of political stability in England and a time of belief and hope in the advancement of science and engineering engendered by the Great Exhibition in 1851 which Darwin did visit though initially somewhat reluctantly (Desmond & Moore, 1991, pp. 391-395). It was an age of social reform and the Darwin family was closely involved in the anti-slavery movement directly supported by their relations, the Wedgwoods. Darwin was not unaffected by the voices for the emancipation of women and worked with many women in areas such as the study of digestion in carnivorous plants (see Chapter 18). Not only were new areas of study in biology emerging, to join the traditional ones of botany and zoology, but also new technologies were developing including flash photography, the culture of micro-organisms and the development of achromatic microscope lenses (see Chapter 20). The public services expanded under the optimism and wealth generated by industry. Transport, sewage and water systems were being installed across the land. Darwin's own father had invested in the development of the roads and canals which created some of the wealth that Darwin himself was able to rely upon for his gentleman's existence in the depths of the Kent countryside. The postal service developed and could be relied upon several times a day if necessary and was used by Darwin to communicate with collectors and colleagues at home and across the world.

The Context of the Present Day

In many ways Darwin's ways of working were very different from those of contemporary researchers in evolutionary biology. We wanted our modules to encourage students to make connections between Darwin's work and that of current scientists, and to expand their understanding of how science and scientists worked in the nineteenth century and work today.

After Darwin, with the professionalisation of science, the gentleman (or lady) naturalist took a back seat and the pursuit of science became an economic necessity in developed countries. Science became largely associated with work carried out in separate laboratories with expensive technical equipment and scientists dedicated to following the line of research associated with and funded for that laboratory. Much of the data from today's scientific enterprises, especially in the realm of genomics, is entirely numerical, and mathematical modelling is increasingly used to represent and explain evolutionary and other theories. The academic discipline of evolutionary biology came into existence with the neo-Darwinian evolutionary synthesis in the 1930s and 1940s, integrating the discoveries of genetics (started by Mendel's experiments in the 1860s) both at the cellular and population levels to explain how evolution proceeds. In 1953 Watson and Crick's discovery of the structure of the genetic code of DNA set in motion the development of theory and technology in the fields of genetics and developmental biology.

The human genome mapping project and the genomic studies of the natural world that have followed have generated a mind-blowing amount of data, too large for us to analyse and understand without the aid of information technology. At first sight, Victorian science and natural history have little to offer such an exponential explosion of data. Up to the dawn of genomic technology, molecular biology, the principal research discipline that led to this revolution, often used an approach whereby the system was reduced to its basic components, with individual investigators focusing on small parts of complex molecular systems. This is necessary to unpick what is happening at a molecular level. However, the enormous amounts of data produced by whole genome sequencing mean that this approach alone will not serve to help us understand the whole picture. For instance, the new science of metagenomics, which has only been possible as a result of advances in high-throughput DNA sequencing, has taken our understanding of microbiology to another level. The study of microbiology blossomed in the nineteenth century with the development of more powerful microscopes and lab cultivation methods that allowed scientists to isolate and study single micro-organism species. This understanding, although very important, was artificial and did not allow any understanding of how micro-organisms behave in the real world on an ecological level. Without this understanding our ability to combat infectious disease is limited. Metagenomics allows mixed microbiological samples to be taken and analysed direct from the environment. The entire genetic code of many organisms can be analysed at the same time, allowing the identification of previously unknown micro-organisms. This is because many micro-organisms cannot be cultured in a lab environment and without this technology it is hard to understand how they will behave in a community. This re-introduces the levels of the organism and the ecosystem, a far more Darwinian way of working. It allows us to develop an understanding of the complex interactions at work in the natural world by looking at the genes of an entire community.

Darwin researched a wide range of interests in collaboration with a few friends; today, scientists focus on much narrower ranges of interest and have more prior knowledge to build upon. The result has been increased specialisation and the likelihood that most scientists will be working in teams. Darwin's communication was facilitated by the postal service; today electronic communications provide the medium for collaboration and the review of findings[8].

Darwin, the Father of Biology?

A major reason for placing Darwin at the centre of our modules for biology education is the notion, commonly held by many contemporary biologists, of Darwin as the original biologist; if you like, a common ancestor of biologists. Prior to Darwin, biology was a fragmented discipline, but his theory of evolution by natural selection unified biology as a science (Mayr, 2004). We begin from the standpoint that Darwin *is* the father of biology and an examination of the current curriculum confirmed that his ideas have relevance to almost everything students are taught. As the title of Dobzhansky's famous essay exemplifies:

> Nothing in biology makes sense except in the light of evolution. (Dobhzansky, 1973).

As we have demonstrated, science is a process that exists in a historical context. New ideas relate to prior knowledge. Nowhere is this more apparent than in the development of evolutionary biology (Stott, 2012). Darwin's theory is a fundamental, and still unifying, concept. His work remains highly relevant and is the cornerstone of biology today, effectively influencing every intellectual discipline within biology. However, it is not a static idea; scientists over the last 150 years have modified and re-interpreted his ideas in the light of new technologies and advances in knowledge. His work, and that of the scientists following in his footsteps, offers extensive opportunities to explore how science works and examine biology as a *way of knowing*.

Having explored some of the general contexts that could inform our thinking about the situation of Darwin's time, and our own, we turned to finding the specific ways of approaching the topics in biology for our modules. Many of Darwin's published works were concerned with organisms, e.g. worms, orchids, barnacles and climbing plants, and so we took organisms as our primary focus.

The Place of the Organism: Levels of Complexity

This chapter started with a question about the place of Darwin-inspired learning when biology research is increasingly focused on the micro level of genomic investigations. From our reading of Darwin's work we realised that the organism is at the centre of all his investigations and theories. Greene (2005) gives a spirited rationale for placing organisms as a central focus in biology (see also Chapter 5). He suggests: that as organisms lie at the central point of the hierarchy of biological complexity they are essential for understanding the lower molecular and the higher population and ecosystem levels; that the study of new organisms often sets off new research; that data about organisms underlie conservation; and that in themselves organisms promote human curiosity and are a major reason why many students become biologists. Bartholomew (1986) discusses these biological 'levels of integration' or levels of complexity, from the micro to macro, from the molecular to the ecosystem level, and he argues that:

> The most satisfactory understanding of a given biological phenomenon or event incorporates many levels of integration, ideally from the molecular to the ecological (Bartholomew, 1986, p. 326).

Thus the three modules each take a group of organisms with which Darwin worked as the focus. The current post-16 modules[9] are:

1. *Funky pigeons* (Darwin's birds: Revealing the biology of inheritance and selection).
2. *Brilliant barnacles* (Darwin's barnacles: Evidence for evolutionary relationships).
3. *Murderous plants* (Darwin's *Drosera*: Investigating adaptation and competition in carnivorous plants).

Big Ideas and Questions

Given these foci, we looked for Darwin's questions, prompted by these organisms and his 'big ideas' and the theories he was developing in species change, nutrition in plants, trees of life, common ancestry and natural selection. Each module links both Darwin's questions and those of present-day scientists. Part of the reason for engagement with present-day science was to find contemporary scientists using these organisms to explore similar topics. This was fascinating and enabled the research of practising scientists to be integrated into the course work. For example, we included recent data from papers on barnacle classification using scanning electron microscopy and genomic data, on carnivory in plants (Ellison & Gotelli, 2009) (see Chapter 18), and on barnacle taxonomy (Pérez-Losada & Candell, 2003) and recent studies (Grant & Grant, 2009) on evolution in Galapagos finches. A result was the production of video interviews with scientists explaining their current work on pigeon variation, barnacle classification and conservation of *Drosera* and how such work had been influenced by Darwin.

We have shown that in order to understand evolutionary processes you need to be able to switch between levels of complexity and integrate these understandings and have a holistic and dynamic view, a perspective which Darwin took and which is now receiving more emphasis in post-genomic biology (Richardson, 2010). We suggest Darwin's ways of working allow such an understanding to develop for specialist and generalist alike. For Darwin there was no single route to understanding and this is also the case with students. We do know that working out-of-doors in the natural world enhances this thinking (see Chapter 5) and that paying attention to the organism is the starting point (see Chapter 11), and that collecting and classifying have an important place.

Ways of Working

So, the final feature of the model concerns ways of working and relates directly to the way teachers structure learning for their students. Darwin himself encouraged active learning in his own children through questioning, problem solving, investigating and dialogue (Keynes, 2001) (see Chapters 7 and 27). Randal Keynes in Chapter 1 has described the inspiration of Darwin for learners following in his experimental footsteps. In our modules students are encouraged in the same way to engage with Darwin's ways of working – collecting information in notebooks, using everyday materials for investigation, questioning and theory building. Critical thinking is also supported and links to ways of working – how do we assess the credibility of evidence? How do we resolve scientific dilemmas?

The materials stress how Darwin observed and experimented using the living laboratory of his home and garden (Chapter 2), how he questioned and investigated, and how he engaged in critical thinking, and with the natural world. They are designed to encourage teachers to support students in gaining the hands-on experience of 'being a scientist' and working like Darwin. In taking students back into Darwin's life and science the modules also encourage students to reflect on contemporary scientific practice and see how science develops through theoretical, technical and cultural change (see Figure 2).

Figure 1. Post-16 students investigate Drosera *in Darwin's greenhouse at Down House (© Charles Darwin Trust).*

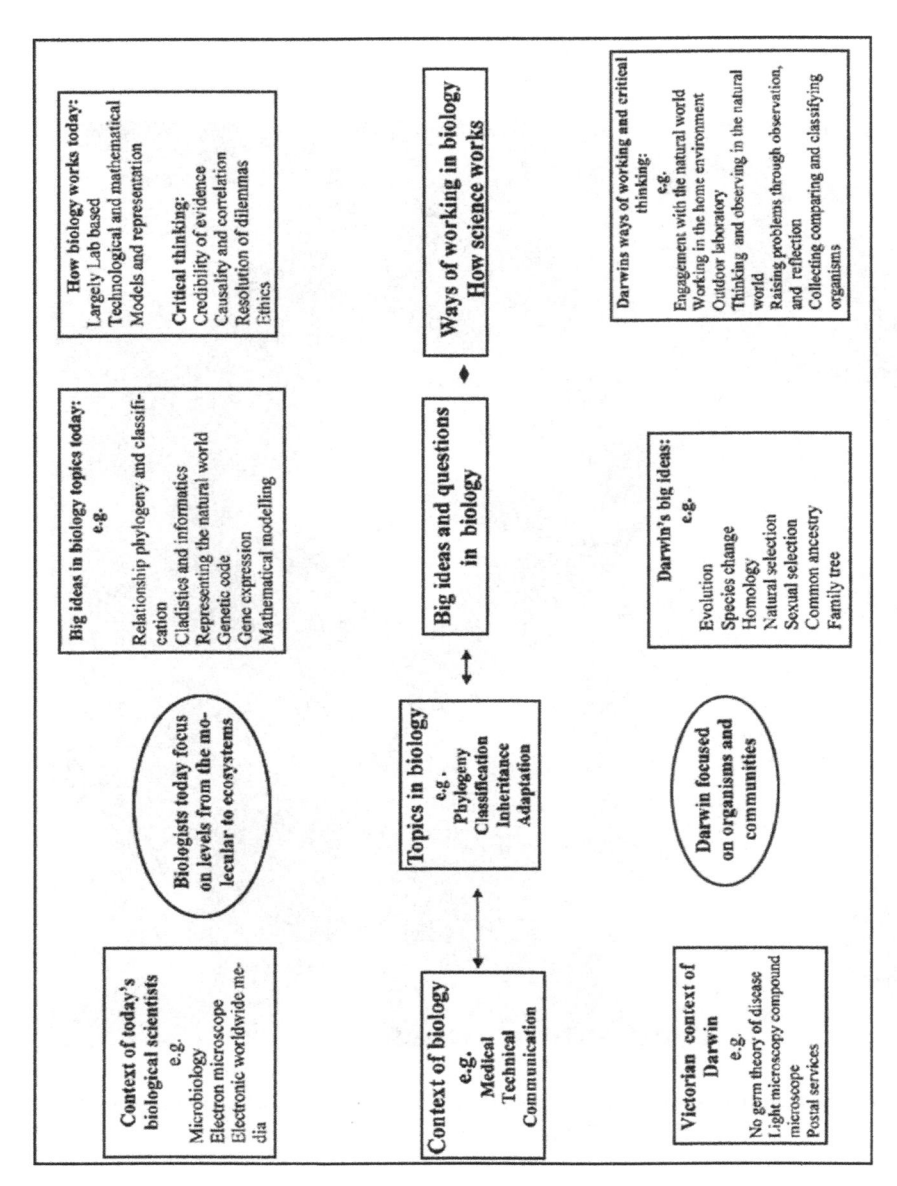

Figure 2. A model for designing a post-16 unit (Boulter, Newall & Sanders for Charles Darwin Trust)

CONCLUSION

The questions with which this chapter began have prompted the educators at the Charles Darwin Trust to develop the model, to write the modules and to consider the reasons why Darwin should be included as a starting point for enrichment modules in the post-16 biology curriculum. Although Darwin did not understand the molecular mechanism of biological inheritance himself, his legacy is apparent in the work of the scientists that came after him. Our new understanding of the molecular world is being used alongside Darwin's ideas to increase our understanding of evolution, speciation and phylogeny. Nowhere is Darwin's legacy more keenly felt than in these fundamental areas of biology today (Edwards & Moles, 2009; Micheneau et al., 2009; Weller, 2009). It could be argued that evolution is more important to biological research than it has ever been and that by integrating biology at the macro and micro levels we may yield a much greater knowledge. However, for this to happen, the next generation of biologists, both specialist and generalist, require inspiration and a broader, and more holistic biological education, which we hope our modules will help to provide. Darwin himself was passionately interested in the natural world at all levels and would, we are sure, be fascinated and delighted to see where his work has led. He has a great contribution to make to school science to enhance our understanding of *how science works* and *biology as a way of knowing*.

NOTES

[1] Genomics is a discipline in genetics that applies recombinant DNA, DNA sequencing methods, and bio-informatics to sequence, assemble, and analyse the function and structure of genomes (the complete set of DNA within a single cell of an organism).
[2] The classics entail the study of Latin and Greek literature and languages but can include the study of the culture of the Ancient Mediterranean world or is used in a general sense to mean traditional.
[3] Charles Darwin to W. D. Fox, 7 March, 1852. Darwin Correspondence Database, http://www.darwinproject.ac.uk/entry-1476 accessed on 18 December 2013.
[4] C. P. Snow (1959). The Rede Lecture, 1959. Cambridge University Press. http://s-f-walker.org.uk/pubsebooks/2cultures/Rede-lecture-2-cultures.pdf accessed on 18 Dec 2013.
[5] http://www.nytimes.com/2009/03/22/books/review/Dizikes-t.html?pagewanted = all&_r = 0.
[6] Especially see Tim Radford http://www.theguardian.com/science/2004/mar/19/taxonomy.science accessed on 18 December 2013.
[7] In Australia: http://education.qld.gov.au/projects/stemplan/docs/stem-discussion-paper.pdf In USA: http://nms.org/Education/TheSTEMCrisis.aspx accessed on 18 December 2013.
[8] http://undsci.berkeley.edu/article/modern_science Modern science what is changing? accessed on 18 December 2013.
[9] http://www.linnean.org/Education+Resources/Secondary_Resources/darwin_inspired_learning.

REFERENCES

Barlow, N. (Ed.). (1958). *The autobiography of Charles Darwin*. London: Collins.
Bartholomew, G. (1986). The role of natural history in contemporary biology. *BioScience, 36*(5), 324–329.
Bevins, S., Brodie, M., & Brodie, E. (2005). A study of UK secondary school students' perceptions of science and engineering. In *European Educational Research Association Annual Conference*, Dublin, 7-10 September 2005.

Chan, B., Garm, A., & Høeg, J. (2008). Setal morphology and cirral setation of thoracican barnacle cirri: adaptations and implications for thoracican evolution. *Journal of Zoology*, 275, 294–306

Charlesworth, B. & Charlesworth, D. (2009). Anecdotal, historical and critical commentaries on genetics: Darwin and Genetics. *Genetics*, 183, 757-766.

Committee on Metagenomics: Challenges and functional applications, National Research Council, (2007). The New Science of Metagenomics: revealing the secrets of our microbial planet. The National Academies Press.

Cox, C. & Boyson, R. (1977). *Black papers*. London: Temple Smith.

Desmond, A., & Moore, J. (1991). *Darwin*. London: Penguin.

Dobhzansky, T. (1973). Nothing in biology makes sense except in the light of evolution. *American Biology Teacher*, 35, 125-129.

Drea, S. (2011). The end of the botany degree in the UK. *Bioscience Education*, Vol. 17-2.

Edwards, W. & Moles, A.(2009). Re-contemplate an entangled bank: t*he power of movement in plants* revisited. *Botanical Journal of the Linnean Society*,160(2), 111–118.

Ellison, A. & Gotelli, N. (2009). Energetics and the evolution of carnivorous plants—Darwin's 'most wonderful plants in the world'. *Journal of Experimental Botany*, 60(1), 19–42.

Fensham, P. (1985). Science for all: a reflective essay. *Journal of Curriculum Studies*, 17(4), 415-435.

Grant, P. & Grant, R. (2009). The secondary contact phase of allopatric speciation in Darwin's finches. *Proceedings of the National Academy of Science*, 10, 1073.

Green, H. (2005). Organisms in nature as a central focus for biology. *TRENDS in Ecology and Evolution*, 20(1), 23 -27.

Hill, D. & Wheeler, A. (1991). Towards a clearer understanding of students' ideas about science and technology: an exploratory study. *Research in Science and Technological Education*, 9, 125–136.

Kelly, G. J., Carlsen, W. S. & Cunningham, C. M. (1992). Science education in sociocultural context: perspectives from the sociology of science. *Science Education*, 7(2), 207-220.

Keynes, R. (2001). *Darwin, his daughter and human evolution*. New York: The Berkley Publishing Group.

Leavis, F.R. (re-published 2013). *Two cultures?* The significance of C. P. Snow. Cambridge, UK: Cambridge University Press.

Mayr, E. (2004). *What makes biology unique?* Cambridge, UK: Cambridge University Press.

Micheneau, C., Johnson, S. & Fay, M. (2009). Orchid pollination: from Darwin to the present day. *Botanical Journal of the Linnean Society*, 161(1), 1–19.

Oxford Cambridge and RSA Examinations (OCR). (2008). AS Biology student book. Edinburgh: Heinneman.

Osborne, J., Simon, S. & Collins, S. (2003). Attitudes towards science: a review of the literature and its implications. *International Journal of Science Education*, 25 (9), 1049-1079.

Pérez-Losada, M., Høeg, J. & Candell, K. (2003). Unraveling the evolutionary radiation of the thoracican barnacles using molecular and morphological evidence: a comparison of several divergence time estimation approaches. *Systematic Biology*, 53(2) 244-264.

Richardson, A. (2010). Darwin and reductionisms: Victorian, neo-Darwinian and postgenomic biologies. *Interdiscipimary Studies in the Long Nineteenth Century*, 11. www.19.bbk.ac.uk accessed on 10 December 2013.

Roberts, G. (2002). Set for success: the supply of people with science, technology, engineering and mathematics skills, review. London: Department for Education and Science.

Rutherford, H.W. (Ed.). (1908). Catalogue of the library of Charles Darwin now in the botany school, Cambridge. Cambridge, UK: Cambridge University Press.

Stott, R. (2012). *Darwin's Ghosts: the first evolutionists*. London: Bloomsbury.

Universities and Colleges Admissions Service (UCAS) (2013). Demand for full-time undergraduate higher education (2013 cycle, March deadline), UCAS analysis and research. http://www.ucas.com/sites/default/files/ucas-demand-report-2013.pdf.

Weller, S. (2009). The different forms of flowers – what have we learned since Darwin? *Botanical Journal of the Linnean Society*, 160(3), 249–261.

Young, M. (1961). *The rise of the meritocracy*. Harmonsworth:Penguin.

Carolyn J. Boulter
Charles Darwin Trust,
Institute of Education,
University of London,
UK

Emma Newall
Charles Darwin Trust,
UK

SUSAN JOHNSON

27. TRANSFORMATION OF THE SCHOOL GROUNDS FOR DARWIN-INSPIRED LEARNING

INTRODUCTION

Darwin retained from childhood an eager curiosity about the world, coupled with an exceptional ability to pay attention; he noticed everything. He always carried a hand lens, and got down on his knees to use it, so that almost nothing, however small and seemingly insignificant, escaped attention. He recorded observations and thoughts in his notebooks for future reference. We know from frequent jottings in these notebooks that the quality of each encounter with the natural world aided the development of his intellect and creativity.

Drawing on these childhood experiences, Charles Darwin explained that a child could come to understand the world:

... by acquiring the habit of patiently seeking the cause of everything which meets his eye, and by comparing it with all that he has himself seen or read. (Darwin, 1851, p.204)

He also recalled that, at the age of 13:

... a vivid delight in scenery was first awakened in my mind, during a riding tour on the borders of Wales, and which has lasted longer than any other aesthetic pleasure. (Darwin, 1958, p.7)

After the *Beagle* voyage Charles Darwin drew together countless ideas he formed from his observations and later he set up experiments in the grounds of Down House, Kent, to refine his thinking and test his flashes of inspiration (see Chapters 1, 2 and 10). He used the understanding he distilled, to question prevailing theories about the variation amongst life forms. Finally, in 1859, his big ideas and radical theories were published as *On the origin of species*.

Darwin acquired a rich sense of place, as he walked daily in his kitchen garden, orchard, flower garden and the countryside nearby, and recognised organisms and patterns of change in the local environment. In the species-rich meadows and heaths of Kent he observed a great range of wildlife.

The thinking path he constructed, his Sandwalk, was bordered by a hedgerow that he passed several times daily, in all seasons and all weathers. He studied its intricate structure and growth which, together with evidence from others hedges locally, alerted him to the ceaseless pressure of competition for survival that ensures any fresh opportunity for maintaining life is seized by species able to evolve special adaptations for the purpose. He named this process the Principle of Divergence and showed that, applied on a larger scale, is the key to global biological diversity.

He recorded encounters between plants and animals that signified interdependence and co-evolution. His mind map, illustrating a tree of life, implies a long history of transmutation of species (Darwin, 1869, p.165). First-hand observations across a range of environments gave Darwin the evidence to draw out salient patterns from diurnal and seasonal changes to those protracted, slow processes, like soil creep, that brought about landscape change. He realised the significance of fossils in measuring the time available for change.

Darwin tested questions, he formulated and designed experiments to investigate his ideas using an assortment of simple household or garden paraphernalia. To verify his suppositions he also wrote more than 15,000 letters, not only to scientific peers but also to ask for information from fellow gardeners, nurserymen or experts in a relevant field, pigeon breeders, for example. In Darwin's letter to T. C. Eyton, in 1855:

> 3rd December. Very many thanks for the information which will be of the greatest use to me.— I am well in my subject & have got several Pigeons already in water & very many alive & flourishing, & I mean to try to get *Domestic* Pigeons from all parts of the world.[1]

He reasoned to and fro with collaborators until innumerable small facts offered a foundation from which to theorise. From his entire accumulation of evidence he originated a synthesis of evolutionary change, geological timescales and extinction, variability within species, the struggle for life and the inheritance of traits that influenced the survival prospects of plants and animals, all linked with knowledge and understanding gleaned from familiar places.

The details Darwin noted indicate his ways of working and the painstaking development of his overarching ideas. Teachers can inspire pupils by transforming his methods into learning activities. Secondary schools (pupils aged 11-16 years) might use their school grounds to encourage the sorts of organisms that inspired Darwin and maintain them in ways that maximise exemplary habitats to enrich science lessons. Primary schools (pupils aged 5-11 years) could emulate Darwin's daily walks, in their school grounds or local park, so that all in this age group observe daily and seasonal change. Observations and recordings of the familiar and commonplace made regularly are a starting point for engaging pupils in discussions about Darwin's findings and how their own data shed light on biological change today.

Jacobson et al. (2006) found that school grounds vary worldwide but the best provide a rich resource to investigate living and non-living elements of biodiversity, plant and animal life cycles, the interdependence of organisms, food webs, and food growing, as exemplified by *Growing minds* in the United States and *Growing schools* in England and Wales, and investigating continent-wide environmental issues (Science for Environment Policy, 2012). Adopting Darwin-inspired learning

(DIL) would provide an holistic approach to teaching in the school grounds and ensures that all pupils can add to a scientific data set over a prolonged period.

GATEKEEPERS

Gatekeepers, who manage pupils' study of the familiar and commonplace, may present more barriers to learning than opportunities:

- Commonly, teachers lack confidence in their knowledge and understanding of the outdoor environment and teaching in the school grounds (Johnson, 2001).
- Local concerns about health and safety when working out-of-doors may also intervene.
- Long-established external forces may also preclude pupils from discovering anything about science at first hand.
- Government is a gatekeeper in terms of a nationally-prescribed curriculum and tests. Teachers may perceive a conflict and compromise the value they place on practical work out-of-doors because they are under pressure to complete all aspects of a curriculum and, via national testing, are accountable for pupils' attainment (Waite, 2009).
- Teacher-trainers influence pedagogical knowledge, understanding and communication skills. The number of days a trainee teacher spends on planning and teaching lessons out-of-doors will vary, thereby affecting their confidence and competence. 'Experience is key to eco-literacy ... factors that affect level of environmental experience have the ability to subsequently affect ecological knowledge.' (Pilgrim, 2006, p.148). Regrettably, lack of environmental or ecological knowledge has the potential to reduce confident use of creative pedagogy.
- In a study of teaching out-of-doors in four European countries, Kapelari et al. (2007) found the teachers thought that bringing plants into class was sufficient and considered going outside 'unnecessary for understanding'. Comments like 'easier to teach indoors' and 'not a priority' indicate ambivalence. The weather and a lack of outdoor resources were obstacles for some.
- Neither can it be assumed that subject-based teaching will promote thinking skills. Freeman (1999) points out that, without high quality learning, the 'potential for excellence' (p.187) is unlikely to be achieved.
- Teachers and parents may differ in their fascination for science and in their belief that their child needs to have outdoor experiences at school. The pressure parents exert diverts attention from teachers' choice of pedagogy and affects the potential for pupils to develop skills and capabilities that encourage co-operation and collaboration (Eames et al., 2006).
- Landscape architects design planting schemes and hard-landscape features in the school grounds that reflect the funds available as much as educational requirements. Pupils' participation, in either the design process or execution

of projects, is not guaranteed. Funding may inhibit long-term maintenance of experiments or planting but equally, unless teachers become personally committed to holistic teaching approaches, a context-driven curriculum is unlikely to succeed (Johnson, 2001).
- The media have huge potential to make pupils aware of environmental issues, but even citizen science programmes cannot represent all points of local reference from which to make specific ecological judgements.
- Visual media representation of the natural world often focuses on the photogenic or exotic rather than the familiar and commonplace. Direct, personal contact with living organisms affects pupils in ways that vicarious experiences cannot.

The potential of gatekeepers to preclude new pedagogical approaches to learning based on Darwin's work is shown to an extent in research funded by the Wellcome Trust to inform educational resources produced during Darwin's bicentenary year. (Grace, Hanley & Johnson, 2008)

From 10 focus groups in the south of England, it was possible to summarise primary and secondary teachers' knowledge of Darwin's ways of working, their current Darwin-related teaching, school resources available and the training teachers wanted to further their knowledge and improve practice. Expansion of the research to investigate teaching and learning in Northern Ireland, Scotland and Wales involved a survey of teachers via post and email. The following major points emerged:

Level of Interest

The low response to the questionnaire survey was underlined by difficulties researchers experienced when recruiting primary school teachers of pupils aged 4–7 years and 8–11 years for focus groups in England. Face-to-face contact indicated that teachers did not regard Darwin-related topics as a priority in primary schools.

The topics seen as most strongly linked to Darwin – evolution, natural selection, adaptation, extinction, variation, inheritance, genetics and biodiversity – they regarded mainly as secondary and post-16 topics. Shortage of time in the primary school curriculum was a key consideration because teachers felt constrained by curriculum pressures and Darwin-related topics were not regarded as important or relevant to their pupils.

Knowledge of Darwin

2009 was also the 150th anniversary of the publication of *On the origin of species*, but across all countries and all ages, teachers lacked detailed knowledge about Darwin. Focus-group attendees admitted having insufficient confidence to teach details of his life, his experiments and their impact on current science. Cost was the main barrier to attending Continuing Professional Development (CPD) courses to overcome these shortcomings.

Ideas for Activities or Experiments

Some focus-group attendees recognised that Darwin's scientific methodology could support science lessons but cited time constraints, imposed by the curriculum, as preventing such inclusion. For pupils aged 4–11 years, the potential for experiments and work out-of-doors was greater than for pupils from 11–18 years. Some participants contributed ideas for activities or experiments during the focus-group workshops which motivated others to consider developing cross-curricular programmes. Asked whether colleagues teaching other subjects might be interested in Darwin-related topics, survey respondents anticipated little interest.

In terms of resources and facilities in school, access to online resources was widely available and used in lessons. Most of these teachers had access to, but admitted that they seldom used weeds, flowers, trees and hedges on their school sites.

OVERCOMING GATEKEEPER ISSUES TO BRING DARWIN-INSPIRED LEARNING INTO SCHOOLS

To study the commonplace and familiar is under-rated. Heyd (2007) advocated a value system that does not separate humans from nature. Åhlberg (1998) hoped that schools, as common denominators, could both raise environmental awareness and increase scientific and technological literacy but Stark & Gray (1999) found that Scottish children were more likely to see a mixture of habitats by way of a television or computer screen than from first-hand experience. Dasberg (1991) concluded that pupils are likely to have a 'scattered image of the world' (p.102), which ultimately dissipates their ability to take action to protect their local environment. The value of long-term projects in local, familiar places comes from pupils seeing their impact on this known environment (Johnson, 2012).

For pupils to learn more about Darwin, teachers need to understand new pedagogical approaches that include his methodology. Darwin-inspired learning (DIL) publications for science lessons are needed across the school age range. Shortage of time requires that new teaching approaches advocated to promote DIL are associated with CPD in ways that links them explicitly to the prevailing curriculum. Survey (Grace, Hanley & Johnson, 2008) respondents were interested in CPD to enrich their teaching of ideas and evidence and science enquiry.

Involvement in focus groups created an enthusiasm amongst teachers of all age groups for celebrating Darwin's life and work in 2009. The challenge was to stimulate this interest more widely and consistently. About half of those completing questionnaires wanted to know more about Darwin, especially his life and experiments and there was general agreement that electronic access to Darwin-related information was important; time-lapse videos, lesson plans and interactive whiteboard software were high on teacher wish-lists.

CPD that addresses teachers' lack of knowledge and confidence to study life cycles of animals and plants in a place well known to pupils is the starting point for developing Darwin-inspired learning. Senior managers must be convinced that commitment to such CPD is justified, so their involvement in promoting it and motivating teachers to participate would be essential. As experienced staff move on, new teachers will need similar induction to understand those processes in the natural world that Darwin observed and to conceptualise the implications of such observations.

A learning experience that embeds a sense of place is essential. It entails preparation that instils an understanding of why, for instance, pupils have to walk the same route within the school grounds daily. Such activities can be delegated to teaching assistants (TAs) or parents who work regularly with small groups of children. The advantage of doing the activity in small groups is outweighed by the findings of Blatchford et al. (2009); the more time pupils spend with TAs, the less time they spend learning with a teacher. Teachers, support staff and parents all need the confidence and competence to facilitate DIL lessons out-of-doors.

Insufficient time to deviate significantly from the prescribed curriculum and teaching to the tests that follow are persistent arguments and lead to pressurised teaching that masks the interconnectedness of subject domains (Johnson, 2004). If pupils are offered a wide range of experiences from which to accumulate knowledge, their scientific understanding can be enhanced. Research by Duschl and Grady (2008) suggests that changes to teaching approaches should be based on activities that are similar to the work of professional scientists (see Chapter 4). Darwin's experiments demonstrate the tentative nature of science as each inference from an experiment or observation added to or changed his thinking. Pupils also need opportunities to connect science to everyday existence.

The cost of employing a landscape architect might be saved if schools planted wildflowers and meadow grasses and reduced pointless and costly lawn mowing. The value of school ground's development in terms of the 'ecosystem services' it provides for example to teach biodiversity and health (Science for Environment Policy, 2011) and the potential for inclusive education, should not be underestimated. Decision-making and engagement in environmentally significant action may flow from a better understanding of the myriad of interactions within a place familiar to all pupils (Johnson, 2012).

Cross-curricular activities enhance outdoor interactions as pupils write well-argued letters or e-mails to experts, gather ecological evidence from the internet to support their arguments, engage in related role-play or research sustainable practices. Pupils may also be motivated to acquire a baseline of skills, attitudes and values from learning in a known context. Economic growth may stand in the way of conservation in their future, so an understanding of the interconnectedness of humans, plants and animals is vital.

Darwin built his scientific understanding from common knowledge and experience. He noticed everything and raised questions of his own. He set up simple experiments in his garden (see Chapters 1, 2, 10 for examples) rather than rely on dubious garden folklore or books of uncertain veracity. His experiments can be replicated in school grounds with a minimum of resources.

DARWIN-INSPIRED PROJECTS IN THE SCHOOL GROUNDS

Vegetables and Flowers

Cabbages, peas, beans, carrots, fruit trees and soft fruit in the school grounds offer Darwin-inspired resources for observations and experiments. It was Darwin's garden at Down House that alerted him to the process of selection:

> Every one can appreciate the difference between green or red cabbages with great single heads; Brussel-sprouts with numerous little heads; broccolis and cauliflowers with the greater number of their flowers in an aborted condition, ... savoys with their blistered and wrinkled leaves; and borecoles and kails, which come nearest to the wild parent-form. (Darwin, 1875, p.341)

To complete their life cycle, some cabbage varieties should be left to produce flowers in the summer of their second year of growth. Everyone who has responsibility for maintenance should understand that keeping a garden neat and tidy is not the objective of a Darwin experiment. It is essential that pupils see the yellow flowers, pollination by bees, the resulting green seed pods and brown, dried seed. As Darwin noted, it is unlikely these seed will come true to type if many cabbage varieties are grown in close proximity but pupils can find out for themselves with their dried seeds.

For older pupils more challenging cabbage-related experiments may be inspired by Darwin's observation that, while the large white butterfly takes advantage of abundant food grown in rows, so the tiny ichneumon fly also takes advantage of an abundant food source:

> ... natural selection can and does often produce structures for the direct injury of other animals, as ... in the ovipositor of the ichneumon, by which its eggs are deposited in the living bodies of other insects. (Darwin, 1869, p.247)

Here the living bodies are those of large white butterfly caterpillars. The life cycles of each organism coincides and pupae collected will either produce a butterfly or an ichneumon fly (Charles Darwin Trust, 2012).

Darwin wrote letters to popular gardening magazines to find out more about crop planting times and successful growing conditions for runner beans. He wanted to discover whether frost resistance in beans had increased over time through natural selection. Planting beans in the school grounds at weekly intervals from March onwards provides data on germination rates and the effect on growing plants of late frosts. Bean plants that survive to produce seed may be better adapted to the local environment and may be compared in future years with germination times and rates from saved and shop-bought seed.

Bean climbing methods could also be linked with Darwin's published work on plant adaptations. Pupils might use a range of supports to follow his experiment (substituting plastic for glass rods):

> I allowed kidney-beans to run up stretched string, and up smooth rods of iron and glass, one-third of an inch in diameter .... (Darwin, 1875a, p.9)

His ongoing experiments to understand the struggle between existing plants and newly arrived seed brought by various dispersal methods had Darwin sowing pea and bean seed in grassed area:

> It is good thus to try in our imagination to give any form some advantage over another. (Darwin, 1859, p.78)

Methods of dispersal he studied are discussed in the *Discover Darwin* series for the London Borough of Bromley (2010). The EU-funded Plant Scientists Investigate project (Kapelari et al., 2007) suggests, in its unit on conservation, model making to develop pupils' understanding of seed dispersal and a game to discover the factors that give some plants an advantage over others.

Research for older pupils could begin with Darwin's (1869) investigation of mistletoe, an epiphytic plant on apple trees, whose 'existence depends on birds' (p.74). Study of his work on pollination (Darwin, 1876) and co-evolution of orchid pollinators (Darwin, 1862) has the potential to make orchid growing a school enterprise (Writhlington school[2]).

A Hedgerow

In 1846 Charles Darwin planted a hedgerow and observed it for 20 years. Planting a school hedgerow is a cross-curricular project: planning a site, research to find appropriate local species, sourcing saplings and co-ordinating planting in autumn or spring. Within six months of observations, daily, weekly or monthly, aspects of plant and animal life cycles become apparent.

Within this habitat pupils observe life processes, the interconnectedness of plants and animals (Charles Darwin Trust, 2012a) and, as Darwin noted, the struggle for existence:

> ... that each [organic being] at some period of its life, during some season of the year, during each generation or at intervals, has to struggle for life, and to suffer great destruction. When we reflect on this struggle, we may console ourselves with the full belief, that the war of nature is not incessant, that no fear is felt, that death is generally prompt, and that the vigorous, the healthy, and the happy survive and multiply. (Darwin, 1859, p.80)

Pupils may find classification more interesting when organisms are identifiable by familiar features. Recording a broad baseline of hedgerow inhabitants will underpin future counts of individual species. Data added each year gains in value until it represents a vivid picture of the natural world locally (National Biodiversity Network, 2009).

Annual records of a secondary school hedgerow can assist in progression to an understanding of ecological concepts. Energy, initially from the Sun, flows through the hedgerow and through organisms that rely on it for food and shelter. Minerals and gases will cycle through the hedgerow diurnally and seasonally. It can be examined at the underground, field and shrub levels and hedgerows will, over time, experience death, decay and new arrivals, some influenced profoundly by human actions. Understanding this one environment in depth could influence pupils' perception of human reliance on the natural world.

The Sandwalk

A hedgerow planted as a border to a circular path around a wooded area of the school grounds, or perhaps around newly planted saplings (Woodland Trust, 2013) replicates Darwin's sandwalk at Down House. Here, whatever the weather, he mulled over his thoughts and findings; he questioned how individual organisms responded to their environment, their adaptive structures and behaviours.

Giving pupils time, and a place to think, is essential for Darwin-inspired learning. We learn daily and cyclically through our surroundings (Duncum, 1999) and everyday life brings with it unconscious learning. Such subliminal influences ultimately affect the way pupils think and act.

Darwin's Weed-Plot Experiment

From January to August 1857 Darwin investigated how natural selection drove evolution through the life cycles of every organism. He sought evidence of change taking place from day to night, from season to season, through all stages of individual life cycles and the intrusion of external forces for any organism. This is a cross-curricular activity but with an emphasis on mathematics.

Darwin devised an experiment to investigate why each plant produces a super-abundance of seed. In January he cleared perennial weeds from a patch of poor soil (above and below ground) and fenced it to deter animals. In effect he isolated a group of organisms (plants) at the seedling stage, free from the pressure of crowding by other plants but still subject to other destructive forces: insects, rain drought and frost. As plants were destroyed he considered which destructive force had caused the eradication.

From early March he visited the plot daily to mark each emerging seedling with a wire (use 10 cm lengths of galvanised wire). He noted any insect activity and weather conditions to explain loss or survival of seedlings.

On 31 March, 10 April, 20 April, 8 May, 1 June, 1 July and 1 August, he counted wires without a seedling, the plant having been destroyed, and removed those wires. 357 seedlings emerged but only 17% survived until August. In the school ground, data from this same experiment (ending late in the summer term) can be compared with Darwin's results for 1857 (Johnson, 2009).

Data collection leads to consideration and explanation of all of the experimental factors. Differences between Darwin's results in 1857 and pupils' data should raise questions. Investing time thinking through their ideas and engaging in dialogue with peers, teachers and experts, pupils construct new understanding for themselves.

A new school weed plot made each year enables long-term comparisons. If each weed-plot is left untouched, the process of succession begins, bringing new questions and provoking progression in reasoning.

Density, Distribution and Extinction

Darwin's garden-scale investigation encompassed the relationship between bees and flowering plants. Flower beds, borders, a wildflower meadow or flowering shrubs in the school grounds will attract many bee species. Their interactions with flowers can aid understanding of plant structure and co-evolution of species. Watching bees and other insects out-of-doors requires planning and discussion of how best to observe, record, present findings and interpret results. A visit from a beekeeper with a demonstration hive will stimulate pupils' curiosity. For older pupils the beekeeper can clarify Darwin's work on comb building in hives (Charles Darwin Trust, 2012b)

Darwin was fascinated by bees but, without making connections to his work, teaching may disconnect a vital environmental topic from early research that underpins current scientific understanding of their ecology. A Darwin experiment with direct relevance to the density, distribution and extinction of plants involves covering half a row of white clover heads and leaving the remainder uncovered:

> I have also found that the visits of bees are necessary for the fertilisation of some kinds of clover: for instance, 20 heads of Dutch clover (*Trifolium repens*) yielded 2,290 seeds, but 20 other heads protected from bees produced not one. (Darwin, 1876, p.378)

Today we might use horticultural fleece to cover plants and, in the time it takes for clover to produce seed, pupils may look for secondary data on the potential outcomes of this experiment. Science and Environment Policy (2012 & 2013) research digests from the European Commission are accessible for older primary-aged pupils. Other examples of Darwin's own work in *The effects of cross- and self-fertilisation* (Darwin, 1876) suggest experiments suitable for secondary and post-16 pupils.

Encouraged to watch bees as they take pollen from one fruit tree, or bean plant, to another, younger pupils may begin to appreciate human reliance on bees for food production. Establishing a long-term record of bee species and numbers over several months each year is critical for any secondary school creating an ecological profile of its grounds.

Habitat Range

Concrete slabs or the edge of asphalt paving can be investigation sites if shallow cracks between slabs are examined as if they were a rocky landscape where rocks heat up during the day and stay warm all night and from which any rainfall soon evaporates in summer. This is an inhospitable habitat but plants can grow there.

Darwin's work tells us that the plants we see around us are the ones that have survived in the struggle for life. The seed went unnoticed by birds, the slugs and snails missed them as they slimed around and the growing plants survived both heat and drought in the micro-climate between slabs or near asphalt. Identifying the plants and comparing them with the same species in other habitats is important to show the range each plant has and this can be compared with its geographical range or potential to colonise any new niche.

Small white or yellow patches of lichens, part fungus and part algae, grow on most hard landscaping. The algae photosynthesise and provide the fungus with sugars. The fungus protects the algae from high light intensity and from drying out. Lichen also survives all year on tree trunks and branches. Darwin visited some inhospitable habitats during the *Beagle* voyage but lichen was one of the few organisms that thrived almost everywhere. In the harsh, coastal mountain climate of Chile he noted:

> Friday 5th [June 1835] Mountains covered with tiny bushes encrusted with a gree[n] filamentous Lichen. (Chancellor & van Wyhe, 2009, p.12)

He realised too that lichens grow very slowly, taking hundreds of years to break down rock, enabling mosses and other small plants to colonise new sites. He theorised that it takes tens of thousands of years for some processes in nature to have a detectable effect. By photocopying fine gauge graph paper onto clear acetate, pupils may record the outline of a lichen patch on the same sheet annually.

DARWIN-INSPIRED TEACHING

As Darwin admitted, he was not an early genius:

> Looking back as well as I can at my character during my school life, the only qualities which at this period promised well for the future, were, that I had strong and diversified tastes, much zeal for whatever interested me, and a keen pleasure in understanding any complex subject or thing. (Darwin, 1958, p.45)

Nadelson et al. (2009) describe Darwin as a plodder, not particularly fast thinking nor mathematically gifted, facts which may encourage some pupils (Wilson, 2012). Nevertheless, he was patient, persistent and endlessly curious about the world around him. He was also knowledgeable about natural history, plants (Wycoff, 2009) and beetles and, later on, barnacles, worms and insectivorous plants, amongst other organisms discussed in his published works (Darwin, 1829 to 1882).

Essentially a Darwin-inspired lesson entails a teacher facilitating excitement, curiosity, questioning, fluent and articulate conversation and argumentation. Initial lessons indoors provide a background to Darwin's experiments and learners' own questions and thinking skills initiate investigations and discussion[3]. Time is devoted in Darwin-inspired learning lessons to individual and group activities, close observation and problem solving in a way that all pupils contribute questions, find evidence, make discoveries, describe the organisms they find, record in a range of ways, collaborate with others and begin to build theories of their own from their evidence.

FACILITATING DARWIN-INSPIRED LESSONS

Engaging, well-resourced, simple experiments outlined here increase the probability of learning because they encourage pupils to explore specific plants or animals that were important to Darwin's work. Designing experiments, data recording with a purpose, use of identification charts or internet resources, research to find images and the letters Darwin wrote all involve independent or group tasks.

When teaching Darwin-inspired lessons, teachers must be prepared to:

- stand back and let pupils ask questions.
- give pupils time to think of an answer, without any prompting with a further question or giving the answers. If no one knows or there is disagreement, suggest an investigation.
- let pupils design their own investigations (Mayer et al., 2008).
- let everyone look for their own evidence.
- give means of recording findings. Darwin, who did not fill in worksheets, wrote in different notebook for each of his research topics. A cognitive notebook or digital alternative, is essential to record observations and questions (Johnson, 2007).
- listen to everyone's ideas and do not dismiss them out-of-hand.

Pupils must become accustomed to:

- thinking about where they will look for answers.
- setting up experiments out-of-doors and making recordings daily.
- using their own data to theorise and draw inferences for the wider environment.
- considering what further research is necessary.
- understanding that their contributions to scientific understanding matter.
- thinking the unthinkable just as Charles Darwin did with his big idea of evolution.

Co-ordinating the use of school grounds to provide Darwin-inspired resources and to make them available to pupils of all ages involves management, from the head teacher and leadership team to grounds maintenance providers. Discussion involving governors, teachers, teaching assistants, pupils, parents and the local community could reduce anxiety about poor behaviour, risk and wasting teaching time (Pether, 2012).

Where habitats used are in a nearby park or community garden, site managers and gardeners need to be included in any discussion and negotiation to use specific experimental sites.

With the help of a local beekeeper, Darwin kept beehives at Down House to learn more about the relationship between bees and plants. The pigeons and rabbits he bred helped him to understand their wild origins and behaviour, their boiled bones indicated anatomical structure. He consulted experts in all of these fields and the same opportunities to engage in dialogue with experts should be open to pupils. Today, wildlife and wild plant organisations are all relevant to Darwin's experiments and concepts (National Biodiversity Network, 2009). He too verified his findings with others and reflected on his inferences before he could apply his theories to the natural world as a whole. Involving external collaborators locally gives teachers links for a contextual framework that underpins and enriches Darwin-inspired lessons out-of-doors.

A Darwin-inspired lesson does not rely on pupils being given sufficient equipment and information to reach the conclusions he reached. Working in this way denies pupils the opportunity to develop their own understandings, formulate their own questions, create the experiment, record results for a reason and engage in scientific thinking that aids dialogue and deep reflection.

The theory of natural selection remains *the* central idea in biology and we still need to recognise the struggle for existence. Research undertaken in 2008 for the Darwin bicentenary (Grace, Hanley & Johnson, 2009) indicates that the link between Darwin's scientific experimentation and observations out-of-doors, as ways of detecting and showing what is happening in the natural world, is largely absent in schools. The potential for pupils to develop a good knowledge of life cycles and interconnectedness within the environment that ensues is limited.

Darwin's theory of evolution by natural selection appeared in print in 1859 but its relevance to current science is undiminished. If we continue to observe an individual species of plant, bird or insect we may fail to realise that the struggle for existence and interdependence are still going on '... in so complex a manner' (Darwin, 1859, p. 489).

Being out-of-doors and having time to think were pivotal to Darwin's work as these situations stimulated his scientific questioning and reasoning. By working like him, pupils of all ages can experience scientific understanding through a continuum of enquiry gained in their school grounds.

NOTES

[1] Charles Darwin to T. C. Eyton. 26 November, 1855. Darwin Correspondence Database, http://www.darwinproject.ac.uk/entry-1784 accessed on 13 August 2013.
[2] Writhlington school (http://wsbeorchids.org/).
[3] Resources for teachers for Key Stage 3: http://www.charlesdarwintrust.org/content/58/resources-for-teachers/ks3 and for Key Stage 2: http://www.charlesdarwintrust.org/content/22/resources-for-teachers/ks2

REFERENCES

Åhlberg, M. (1998). Ecopedagogy and Ecodidatics: Education for sustainable development, good environment and good life. *University of Joensuu Bulletins of the Faculty of Education,* 69.

Blatchford, P., A. Russell, P. Bassett, P. Brown, & C. Martin (2009). The role and effects of teaching assistants in English Primary Schools (Years 4 to 6) 2000-2003. *British Educational Research Journal,* 33(1), 5-26.

Chancellor, G & van Wyhe, J. (Eds). (2009). Charles Darwin's notebook from the voyage of the Beagle. Cambridge: Cambridge University Press.

Charles Darwin Trust, (2012) *Enquire with Darwin: life cycles* accessed on 23 October 2013. http://www.charlesdarwintrust.org/content/23/resources-for-teachers/ks2-7-11/module-1.

Charles Darwin Trust, (2012 a). *Enquire with Darwin: hedgerows.* http://www.charlesdarwintrust.org/content/73/resources-for-teachers/ks3/hedgerows.

Charles Darwin Trust, (2012b). *Enquire with Darwin: bees.* http://www.charlesdarwintrust.org/content/71/.

Darwin, C.R. (1829-1882). Accessed on 13 August.2013 from http://darwin-online.org.uk/contents.html.

Darwin, C. R. (1851). Section VI: Geology. In J. F. W. Herschel, (Ed.). *A manual of scientific enquiry; prepared for the use of Her Majesty's Navy: and adapted for travellers in general.* London: John Murray.

Darwin, C. R. (1859). *On the origin of species by means of natural selection, or the preservation of favoured races in the struggle for life.* (1st edn). London: John Murray.

Darwin, C. R. (1862). *On the various contrivances by which British and foreign orchids are fertilised by insects, and on the good effects of intercrossing.* London: John Murray.

Darwin, C. R. (1869). *On the origin of species by means of natural selection, or the preservation of favoured races in the struggle for life.* (5th edn). London: John Murray.

Darwin, C. R. (1875). *The variation of animals and plants under domestication.* (2nd edn. Vol. 1). London: John Murray.

Darwin, C. R. (1875a). *The movements and habits of climbing plants.* (2nd edn). London: John Murray.

Darwin, C. R. (1876). *The effects of cross and self fertilisation in the vegetable kingdom.* London: John Murray.

Darwin, C. R. (1958). *The autobiography of Charles Darwin 1809-1882.* With the original omissions restored. Nora Barlow (Ed.). London: Collins.

Dasberg, L. (1991). The World as our home. In S. Keiny, S & U. Zoller, (Eds). *Conceptual Issues in Environmental Education,* pp. 101-108. New York: Peter Lang.

Duncum, P. A. (1999). A case for an art education of everyday aesthetics. *Studies in Art Education,* 40(4).

Duschl, R. & Grandy, R. (Eds). (2008). *Teaching scientific inquiry: recommendations for research and implementation.* Rotterdam, Netherlands: Sense Publishers.

Eames, C., B. Law, M. Barker, H. Iles, J. McKenzie, R. Patterson, P. Williams, F. Wilson-Hill, C.Carroll, M. Chaytor, T. Mills, N. Rolleston, & A. Wright. (2006). Investigating teachers' pedagogical approaches in environmental education that promote students' action competence. Waikato University: Teaching and Learning Research Initiative. http://www.tlri.org.nz/sites/default/files/projects/9224_finalreport.pdf accessed on 13 August 2013.

Freeman, C. (1999). Children's participation in environmental decision making. In S. Buckingham-Hatfield & S. Percy, (Eds). *Constructing local environmental agendas: people places and participation.* London: Routledge.

Grace, M., Hanley, P. & Johnson, S. (2008). 'Darwin-inspired' science: teachers' views, approaches and needs. *School Science Review,* 90(331).

Kapelari, S., Johnson, S., Bonomi, C., Bromley, G. & Kossov, K. (2007). Plant scientists investigate at school and at a botanic garden: conservation. A Cordis EU 6th Framework project. http://www.plantscafe.net/index.htm accessed on 13 August 2013.

Jacobson, S.K., M.D. McDuff, and M.C. Monroe. (2006). *Conservation education and outreach techniques.* Oxford: Oxford University Press.

Johnson, S. (2001). Models of gardening in education. PhD thesis, Department of Science Education, University of Reading.

Johnson, S. (2004). Learning science in a botanic garden. In M. Braund & M. Reiss, (Eds). *Learning science outside the classroom,* pp. 75-93. London: Routledge Falmer.

Johnson, S. (2007). Mobile phone technology use in school science enquiry indoors and out-of-doors; implications for pedagogy. Research Methods in Informal and Mobile Learning: How to get the data we really want. WLE Centre, Institute of Education, London, UK. 14 December.

Johnson, S. (2009). Teaching science out-of-doors. *School Science Review*, 90, 331.

Johnson, S. (2012). Reconceptualising gardening to promote inclusive education for sustainable development. *International Journal of Inclusive Education,* 16, 5-6.

London Borough of Bromley (2010). (http://www.darwinslandscape.co.uk/topic.asp?navid=62&tid=234)

Mayer, B, Haywood, N., Sachdev, D. & Faraday, S. (2008). Independent learning literature review. Research Report DCSF-RR051. London: DCSF.

Nadelson, L., Culp, R., Bunn, S., Burkhart, R., Shetlar, R, Nixon, R., Nixon, K. & Waldron, J. (2009). Teaching Evolution Concepts to Early Elementary School Students. *Evolution Education Outreach,* 2.

National Biodiversity Network. (2009). *The Darwin guide to recording wildlife.* Nottingham: NBN Trust. http://www.nbn.org.uk/ accessed on 24 October 2013.

Pether, T. (2012). Leadership for embedding outdoor learning within the primary curriculum. Nottingham: National College of School Leadership.

Pilgrim, S.E. (2006). A cross-cultural study into local ecological knowledge. PhD thesis, Department of biological Sciences, University of Essex.

Science for Environmental Policy. (2012). European Commission DG Environment News Alert Service, edited by SCU, The University of the West of England, Bristol. http://ec.europa.eu/environment/integration/research/newsalert/ accessed on 13 August 2013.

Science for Environment Policy. (2012 and 2013). http://ec.europa.eu/environment/integration/research/newsalert/, Issue 275 Garden bees. 2013: Issue 319 Bee monitoring; Issue 324 Wild and honey bee pollination.

Science for Environment Policy, (2011). Future Briefs; Biodiversity and Health http://ec.europa.eu/environment/integration/research/newsalert/pdf/FB2.pdf

Stark, R. & Gray, D. (1999). Scientific knowledge and its sources: the view of Scottish children. *The Curriculum Journal,* 10(1), 71-83.

Waite, S. (2009). Outdoor learning for children aged 2-11: perceived barriers, potential solutions. Fourth International Outdoor Education Research Conference, La Trobe University, Beechworth, Victoria, Australia, 15-18 April 2009. www.latrobe.edu.au/education/downloads/2009_conference_waite.pdf

Wilson, E.O. (2012). Advice to young scientists. http://www.ted.com/talks/e_o_wilson_advice_to_young_scientists.html?quote=1704 accessed on 13 August 2013.

Woodland Trust, (2013). http://www.woodlandtrust.org.uk/en/planting-woodland/Pages/default.aspx#.UgevGz_uojU

Wycoff, M. (2009). Scholar's Dilemma: 'Green Darwin' vs. 'Paper Darwin'. An interview with David Kohn. *Evolution Education Outreach,* 2.

Susan Johnson
Research Associate, Institute of Education,
University of London,
UK

SUSAN JOHNSON

28. TRANSITION

Darwin-Inspired Learning Approaches at Crucial Junctures in Science Education

INTRODUCTION

Transition from one school to another may be a stressful time for pupils, especially when it also involves a perceived lack of continuity of curriculum and teaching approaches. Many schools are using 'bridging units' (DfES, 2006, p.4) which are taught at the end of primary school (10–11 age range), continued through summer schools or independent learning packages and then re-visited by teachers in the first year of secondary school (11–14 age range) to provide continuity and progression.

The link between observations made out-of-doors and scientific understanding has not been strong; time pressures, poor school grounds and management of classes are amongst the impediments that cause sporadic education out-of-doors even on easily accessible school sites (DfEE, 2000). From infrequent experiences, one might argue that pupils can only be expected to learn *about* the immediate environment. Appreciation of wider environmental *contexts* or environmental *change* is unrealistic under these circumstances (Johnson, 2001).

Charles Darwin built his understanding from common knowledge and experience, rather than obscure or abstract sources. Observing the local environment is essential to Darwin-inspired learning because he observed and thought deeply about the continually active natural processes all around. He used hand lenses and other methods to focus attention on the seemingly insignificant and kept a field notebook of his observations, thoughts and feelings about what he saw. Pupils need to learn how to look, where to look and how to interpret what they see. Darwin's evidence came from collecting and pressing plants, finding fossils, collecting dead butterflies, beetles, bird wings and bird and mammal bones to help him in his research and to advance his ideas. Darwin also worked on many small-scale experiments, including soaking seeds in brine, recording the movement of climbing plants, determining why and how the insectivorous sundew kills insects (see Chapter 18) and comparing seed production in pollinated and covered clover plants, then linking his findings to his large-scale scientific ideas. These small-scale experiments can be integrated into Darwin-inspired lessons and the links Darwin made investigated.

The 2014 introduction of evolution and inheritance to the Key Stage 2 (age 7–11) science curriculum in England (DfE, 2013, p.168) may present challenges for primary school teachers. Support from secondary colleagues might be forthcoming during preparations for Darwin-inspired learning activities for a transition project. There may be opportunities for joint Continuing Professional Development when the depth and breadth of knowledge based on Darwin's work may be reviewed. Discussion in the classroom of early work on evolution or genetics may otherwise be incomplete where a teacher's knowledge of Darwin's work is inadequate to answer pupils' questions. Intelligent Design or Creationism may seem acceptable, especially when discussed by non-scientists teaching other subjects (Jones & Reiss, 2007).

As the pace of teaching increases in secondary school science lessons, corresponding curriculum flexibility is essential to engage pupils and motivate them to learn quickly and successfully. A transition programme of Darwin-inspired learning can be tailored for a whole year intake, subdivided into small groups, for intensive activity on one or two days. Transition activities are continued during the summer term in primary schools or used as independent learning packages over the school holidays before being revisited in science and related subjects at the start of secondary school. Shared experiences by those primary-aged pupils who engage in transition activities ease their transition to new ways of interacting with scientific data and the analysis of evidence through argumentation. The potential for continuity and progression (DfES, 2006) is offered in the projects suggested here.

DEVELOPING EFFECTIVE DARWIN-INSPIRED TRANSITION PROJECTS

Outlined in this chapter are elements of best practice identified by education consultants for the Charles Darwin Trust when working with secondary school science co-ordinators to develop Darwin-inspired transition projects. Teachers from both primary and secondary schools were involved in planning the projects and it was not inevitable that secondary-dominated approaches were the most effective models. All teachers involved became familiar with Darwin's ways of working by studying resources available online, *Discover Darwin* (2010) and *Enquire with Darwin* (2012).

Enabling teachers to visit Down House, where Darwin lived and worked for 40 years, is helpful. Those who have seen his experimental garden, and some other experiments on display, have been inspired and motivated to develop their own well-researched activities for transition projects.

The intention of Darwin-inspired transition days is to make full use of the outdoor environment to explore those principles underpinning Darwin's work. Even seemingly unpromising school grounds or public parks have a small grassed area, thickets of thorny plants, weeds, trees and climbing plants. In urban school playgrounds, tiny habitats are found between paving stones, on brick walls and the weedy edges of asphalt. Understanding plant life cycles, habitats locally and the wildlife that may be attracted are crucial to illustrate Darwin's big ideas and skills as a scientist.

Teachers must decide what outcomes they expect from a pupil-centred programme of transition activities. Setting up long-term investigations that pupils work on during transition days is one option, and potential experiments are discussed in Chapter 27. Short-term experiments and research may be an easier alternative, in terms of organisation, for a transition programme that introduces pupils to Darwin's ways of working. Nevertheless, experiments initiated will need to be sustainable and available to work on in primary schools immediately after the event and at secondary school in the new school year.

Observations made out-of-doors have the potential to achieve cross-curricular objectives if planning includes teachers from a range of secondary subjects. Cognitive, communication, argumentation and literacy skills together with internet research, electronic data collection, music, art, drama, dance and presentation skills can be accommodated as avenues to scientific understanding. All pupils should be expected to engage in presenting group findings in a way that focuses on *how* they worked like Darwin rather than just stating facts they have encountered.

ORGANISATION

Accommodation, room or laboratory size and the outdoor space available, are initial considerations that limit group size. Room and staff allocation must be fixed in the timetable for the dates scheduled before detailed organisation can begin.

Primary and secondary teachers will need to meet to finalise the topics that will be included and the time allocation for each topic session. Within a two-day transition programme for an intake of 120 pupils, six topic sessions are sufficient for groups of 20 pupils to move on approximately every hour. A risk assessment must be completed by the teacher responsible for a topic session before the event.

To make the transition day more primary school orientated, the six rooms used can be named; places where the *Beagle* stopped on its voyage serve this purpose (Natural History Museum, 2013) and introduce pupils to Darwin's travels. Each group of 20 or so pupils also needs a name; the Christ's College Cambridge website (2009) presents a list of Darwin's children and a map of the Galapagos Islands (2009a) from which to choose group names.

Many pupils will be working in a new way and need support in order for them to generate their own questions and find the answers for themselves. An appropriate level of support from primary school teachers and adult learning support assistants (LSAs) will be important but must not compromise the intention that pupils think for themselves. Each pupil also needs a Darwin notebook to write thoughts and questions as they arise because:

> [A naturalist] ... ought to acquire the habit of writing very copious notes ... and no follower of science has greater need of taking precautions to attain accuracy; for the imagination is apt to run riot when dealing with masses of vast dimensions and with time during almost infinity. (Darwin, 1851, p.173)

It is helpful on transition days if 'pupil assistants', in their first year of secondary school, work with primary school pupils. Pupil assistants, about three per topic session, need to apply for their 'post' as the recruitment process helps to ignite their enthusiasm. Successful applicants can receive coaching to help them emphasise Darwin's ways of working and talk about his big ideas in a way that primary age pupils can grasp. Secondary LSAs may work with individual pupils they will support in the following term.

Contacting a pigeon breeder has the potential to contribute birds that pupils can handle during a transition session. A local beekeeper can offer reliable background information and probably an exhibition hive to bring a degree of wonder and excitement to an indoor task. Educators from botanic gardens or wildlife organisations are experts in outdoor learning that fires the imagination of pupils more used to sitting in a classroom all day. For sustaining pupils' interest post-event, e-mailing experts for help with further research can be invaluable.

Depending on the funding available it is useful for each pupil to have: a letter of introduction about or even *from* Darwin; a postcard to send to parents; and a bag to carry these and any specimens they collect. A Darwin expert, engaged to set the event in motion and comment on final representations of Darwin's ways of working, adds to the overall impact of the event.

TEACHING PRACTICES

> Practical work is always going to have a key role in science teaching. The challenge is to continue to find ways to make it as effective a teaching and learning strategy as possible, whilst retaining its clear, and refreshingly evident, affective value. (Abrahams & Reiss, 2010)

Darwin-inspired learning transition days have had the effect of making teachers think about their pedagogy, how they teach secondary science in particular. Each year different science teachers can engage with Darwin-inspired learning in order to develop their pedagogy to support one or more of the topics. In time the underlying concepts can permeate a whole department. Staff turn-over, at both primary and secondary schools, affects the demands on teachers and increases pressures of work but planning for transition days presents an opportunity to reflect on and revitalise practice.

Darwin's experiments demonstrate that each inference he drew or observation he made added to or changed his thinking; the tentative nature of science is evident. Like Darwin, pupils need opportunities to relate to a familiar place to find their own tentative evidence and connect science to everyday life. Well coordinated and resourced sessions provide an inclusive environment that encourages pupils to ask questions. The answers will come mostly from individual observations out-of-doors and group interpretation of data from their notebooks.

Scientific investigation protocols are introduced, pupils engage in hands-on, practical tasks, use easily available resources and access records from their experiment at a later date to make comparisons. Teachers can gauge pupils' understanding of the processes and concepts relevant to Darwin's work on each of the topics during pupil-centred scientific discussion (Newton, Driver & Osborne, 1999). Postcards written to parents provide evidence of engagement, learning and enjoyment associated with the event and gives teachers a degree of formative assessment, when they collect them to post.

TRANSITION SESSIONS FOR DARWIN-INSPIRED LEARNING

Worms Mix Soil

Darwin observed the trivial, usually overlooked, things around him. Worm casts are just one small marvel he went on to investigate, revealing the hidden aspects of their crucial role in landscape change.

> Worms live chiefly in the superficial mould [soil], which is usually from 4 or 5 to 10 and even 12 inches in thickness; and it is this mould which passes over and over again through their bodies and is brought to the surface. But worms occasionally burrow into the subsoil to a much greater depth, and on such occasions they bring up earth from this greater depth; and this process has gone on for countless ages. (Darwin, 1881, p. 174)

The teacher responsible for this session will become familiar with the *Discover Darwin* (2010) resource pack with its downloadable powerpoint presentation and explanation of Darwin's worm-stone experiment in his garden. A soil pit (60 cm dimensions) in the school grounds is needed to show the soil profile under grass or a flowerbed.

Learning out-of-doors begins with pupils searching for wormcasts, drawing or photographing them, followed by discussion of what they can see in the soil pit. Progression is made from observations and description to the causes of what they see. The implications for slow landscape change can be discussed in the field.

Indoors, each small group makes a small-scale soil pit, using a 2-litre plastic bottle, compost, natural and coloured sands, wet newspaper and four earthworms per group. Wet newspaper strips are added to the top of the soil column; then the worms are introduced, allowed to take cover and acclimatise before starting to burrow. Each wormery is covered with a box or envelope to reduce light levels which encourages the earthworms to work at the soil/plastic interface rather than within the column of soil.

As baseline references, digital images are taken of each wormery (Figure 1) and everyone draws a labelled diagram of the wormery in their Darwin notebook. They add notes describing how the wormeries were made and what they expect to happen to the layers by the beginning of secondary school.

Figure 1. Composition of the initial soil columns. (© Susan Johnson)

Pupils explain their observation of the soil pit and make links to the layers of sand and compost in the soil columns.

Taken back to the primary schools, the columns encourage pupils to take responsibility for living organisms, and feed the worms with vegetable waste. Wormeries could be returned to the secondary school for the summer holiday, where science technicians continue the feeding and maintain low light and temperature levels.

At the beginning of the new school year pupils who participated in the transition event recall the experiment and explain what was involved to any pupils who did not attend. A search for wormcasts and a soil pit visit are possible because they are in the school grounds. Digital images and diagrams of the original layering in the column are compared with the new landscape created as earthworms moved through and mixed the layers (Figure 2). Potential plenary discussions could be about the importance of earthworms for farmers and gardeners.

One teacher commenting on this experiment said:

> They loved having a look at [the wormeries] again and were surprised at the amount of soil that had been moved. The start pictures were invaluable for this part. They were asked to work out in groups how the worms moving of soil

would impact on soils in fields – they had loads of ideas. I then reintroduced the [Worm]stone from Darwin's garden and tried to link the ideas from the class with the experiment he used in his garden.

Figure 2. Several soil columns eight weeks after a Darwin-inspired transition event. (© Susan Johnson)

Pupils might discuss individual earthworm behaviour and the effect of earthworm populations on the soil of Darwin's 'entangled bank' (Darwin, 1869, p.579). Discussion could also highlight the conclusion Darwin drew, that miniscule additions to the surface will, in the long term, create landscape change.

Darwin's Bees

In this session pupils look at a simple food chain and progress to an understanding of the interdependence of life cycles. Darwin kept beehives for honeybees but he also observed bumblebees and noted: 'Humble-bees [bumblebees] alone visit red clover, as other bees cannot reach the nectar' (Darwin, 1866, p.85). The teacher leading this session liaises closely with a beekeeper. The expert must understand that a lecture on bee behaviour is not required.

If the school grounds have flower beds, the pupils can be divided into two groups. The first group observes bees working, their body structure and colour, their interactions with plants, pollen brushed onto them from anthers and pollen sacks on their legs. Pupils note down exactly what they see and their questions.

Inside, the second group can watch bee activity in an exhibition hive via a camera linked to a whiteboard. It is helpful if the beekeeper talks with three to four pupils about this activity at any one time while others move around a circus of displays, such as honeycomb, wax bars, honey from different flowers, a microscope (Jardine, 2013) to view the anatomy of a dead bee and tablets set up to view pollen from a range of plants from the Science and Plants for Schools website (2013). The half groups change over so that everyone makes similar observations. A plenary is essential, as both groups come together to put their questions to the expert.

At primary school and in the holidays, pupils are encouraged to watch bees, identify them, photograph them and take notes on the flowers bees visit, including flower colour, patterns and scent. Counting the number of flowers a single bee visits before it flies away can also be helpful for later discussion.

Darwin did not just work with beekeepers to obtain their knowledge of bees *per se* but to develop two of his big ideas: plants and animals are interdependent; and bees' instinct, not guidance from a deity, prompts them to use wax efficiently. The secondary school lesson can start with discussion of the notes pupils made on their observation of bees and the plants they visited. A video on YouTube[1] of pollen tube growth shows the implications for plant reproduction of flowers and the interdependence of insects and such plants. Darwin's big idea that bees' instinct to use wax efficiently affects their comb building prompted him to experiment with a source of coloured wax in a hive. The experiment features in the Charles Darwin Trust's web resources for teachers, *Enquire with Darwin* (2012a), with a video of the beekeeper at Down House explaining how bees create hexagonal comb (*Enquire with Darwin*, 2012b).

As a resource for further research, primary schools could increase the number of pollinating insect visits by creating a wildlife garden (Baines, 2000). With future transition events in mind, secondary schools could create a bee garden (BBC, 2013).

Seeds in Brine

Scientists in Darwin's day thought similar plants on either sides of an ocean resulted from land between them sinking, resulting in sea water inundating the sunken land. Islands in the ocean were thought to be tops of sunken mountains. In June 1855 Darwin wrote in a letter to Joseph Hooker: '... it shocks my philosophy to create land, without some other & independent evidence'[4] and set about disproving this widespread misconception (see Chapter 10).

Pupils could start this session by looking for different dispersal methods amongst plants in the school grounds and discuss how far their seed might travel (*Discover Darwin*, 2010). To cross oceans, seeds would need to float or be carried in ways which would result in them being splashed or soaked with brine. Pupils can think about how they could set up an experiment to answer Darwin's question; does sea water kill seeds? (Darwin, 1855) and compare their ideas with Darwin's own experiment. To reconstruct Darwin's experiment requires a solution of tap water and sea salt in the ratio 35 g salt per litre (Dockery & Tomkins, 2000). Darwin used glass bottles and jars he had to hand rather than specialised equipment; today a range of plastic containers will suffice. For five groups in each topic session five different kinds of seeds are needed. Darwin used these easily obtainable seeds: broccoli, radish, flax, spinach, common peas, capsicum (peppers) and lettuce.

On the transition day each small group puts five seeds of one seed type into a container and just enough water to cover them. They label the container, cover it and take it back to school with them. In their Darwin notebooks pupils record how they carry out the experiment, explain what they think the outcome might be and speculate on why similar plants are found on either side of an ocean.

As Darwin's friends noted, open jar experiments began to smell after a couple of days; the brine has to be changed every two days as the containers must be left open. The seeds soak for three days before one is removed from each container, sown in compost and labelled. Pupils do the same on the next five days. The time taken for each seedling to emerge is noted and digital images taken daily thereafter.

Pupils can begin to answer Darwin's question in their own words. The experiment runs until the end of term when results, notes and images must be retained for later use and germinated plants taken to the secondary school until required.

In the new term pupils recount the process they followed and use the images and notes to make a presentation. Pupils can discuss how well Darwin's experiment worked and are then given this quotation showing how his initial ideas changed:

> The bore is, if the confounded seeds will sink, I have been taking all this trouble in salting the ungrateful rascals for nothing ... the fish at the Zoolog. Soc. ate up lots of soaked seeds, [and regurgitated them] ... But I am not going to give up the floating yet: in first place I must try fresh seeds ... and secondly ... I must believe in the pod or even whole plant or branch being washed into the sea. (Darwin, 1887, p.56)

The conclusions pupils draw from the experiment provide insights into their understanding of experimental design, the question Darwin struggled to answer and why he needed to be so painstaking and persistent. They might also consider the theories that replaced the one of the land sinking – continental drift and plate tectonics (2013) – and whether Darwin's experiments are still valid.

Adaptations

The intention of this session is that pupils progress along a continuum from appreciating the environment as a habitat to understanding competition and survival. Pupils split into two groups; one group looks for local bird species outside. The Field Studies Council fold-out chart of common birds (Jackson, Sims & Shields, 2010) is helpful for their investigation. An expert from a wildlife organisation could assist here, particularly with bird identification. Pupils note the species they see and their characteristics: colours, flight pattern, feeding preferences and potential habitats. This half of the session aims to raise interest in birds for future research and investigation either at primary school or during the holidays.

The other half-session relates to March 1855, when Charles Darwin set up a pigeon breeding loft at his home in Kent. Darwin's ideas and the steps in his thinking towards species change – mutation (variation), selection and heritability – are all discussed in *Discover Darwin: Darwin's pigeons* (2010).

> The man who first selected a pigeon with a slightly larger tail, never dreamed what the descendants of that pigeon would become through long-continued, partly unconscious and partly methodical, selection. (Darwin, 1866, p. 40)

Darwin's collaboration with pigeon breeders was fundamental to his understanding of a process of artificial selection (Darwin, 1886) that changed several characteristics of the wild rock dove *Columba livia*. Pigeon breeder, John Ross (2009) provides examples of how selection and breeding over time can change pigeon anatomy[2] and Randal Keynes describes the pigeons Charles Darwin kept, in a YouTube video[3].

Darwin chose six breeds to work with: Almond Tumbler, Barb, English Carrier, Exhibition Fantail, English Pouter and Scanderoon. Indoors, a breeder can introduce this range of pigeons and, by handling birds and noting their different characteristics, pupils should be engaged and motivated to find out more about the processes of artificial selection. The half groups change over so that everyone makes similar observations. A plenary, when the groups come together, allows time for the expert to answer questions.

In the new school year, recounting experiences of handling pigeons and revisiting their notes, pupils might put into their own words Darwin's 1866 theory that humans can, by artificial selection, change a bird's characteristics within a few years. A discussion of the outdoor element of this session could follow to explore pupil's ideas about whether wild birds might be changed by environmental pressures in ways similar to changes created by breeders in the rock dove.

Teachers might model structural descriptions of beak change within a species (e.g. Darwin's finches) by offering a range of implements, including tweezers, sugar tongs, linked chopsticks and nut crackers, for pupils to pick up assorted bird food. Such an investigation takes structural descriptions of birds' beaks to an understanding of functional adaptations. A summary of Peter and Rosemary Grants' work shows that beak size is crucial to the survival of finches in the Galapagos Islands (Montgomery, 2009). A simple food chain of a common local bird can lead to a life-cycle study in which variation in feeding and interactions with other organisms seasonally is likely (*Enquire with Darwin*, 2012c). Pupils progress from linear explanations, like food chains, to an understanding of interconnected life cycles, food webs and interdependence. Human influence on bird survival, such as putting out winter feed could be investigated (RSPB, 2009) to gain insights into Darwin's note on the seasonal decline in numbers of small birds:

> I estimated (chiefly from the greatly reduced numbers of nests in the spring) that the winter of 1854–5 destroyed four-fifths of the birds in my own grounds ... The action of climate seems at first sight to be quite independent of the struggle for existence; but in so far as climate chiefly acts in reducing food, it brings on the most severe struggle between the individuals, whether of the

same or of distinct species, which subsist on the same kind of food. Even when climate, for instance, extreme cold, acts directly, it will be the least vigorous individuals, or those which have got least food through the advancing winter, which will suffer most. (Darwin, 1859, p.69)

In terms of environmental implications of this work, it is important for pupils to understand that an environment is not an abstract concept but a constantly changing place where plants and animals live in non-stop competition. Pupils need to understand that survival is only a first step; after germination in a new place, a plant competes with established plants and, if it survives to produce seed, it competes with its progeny too. Animals too compete, for food shelter and mates, in their struggle to survive and any slight advantage is crucial.

Entangled bank

This session begins with a reading the last paragraph of *On the origin of species*:

It is interesting to contemplate a tangled bank, clothed with many plants of many kinds, with birds singing on the bushes, with various insects flitting about, and with worms crawling through the damp earth, and to reflect that these elaborately constructed forms, so different from each other, and dependent upon each other in so complex a manner, have all been produced by laws acting around us. (Darwin, 1869, p.579)

Darwin collected all the plants in a field which had run to waste for 15 years; even in an urban area, the school grounds or local park hold the potential for pupils to find wild plants. Thirty plant species were found on a transition day at a newly built Swindon school: common grasses, weeds, flowering shrubs, trees and saplings, evergreen and deciduous plants and climbers sprawling over fences.

The aim of this session is for pupils to make the same small circuit of part of the grounds two or three times. It seems that Darwin simply walked the fields and collected as many different plants as he spotted. Initial discussion with the group might be about how they will do something similar without picking plants. A digital camera is needed for each small group.

Pupils in single file walk as quietly as possible around a specific route, recording the plants and other wildlife they find. Even Darwin needed help to name plants and wrote to Joseph Hooker to ask for his help in identification and naming. exclaiming: 'How dreadfully difficult it is to name plants'[4]. Pupils are encouraged to look at the external features of the plants they encounter and to use a range of Field Studies Council (2013) fold-out charts to help in identification. They record the plants they find and make a count of all plants found on the first circuit. Subsequent circuits should be more productive as pupils begin to see plant patterns and anomalies. Similarly, more animals may be spotted.

A plenary begins with pupils looking at their lists of descriptions and progresses to considering causal factors; why these plants in particular and why in the places they found them? The interaction between the plants and wildlife observed can be discussed in terms of one of Darwin's early observation:

> March 12th It is difficult to believe in the dreadful but quiet war of organic beings going on in the peaceful woods & smiling fields. (Darwin, 1838/9, p.114)

Remind pupils that Darwin added to his knowledge daily with observations at different times from early morning until night time and walked the same route at least once a day whatever the weather. After the transition day, pupils continue to look for plants and wildlife at primary school and in their own garden or local park and think about the complex relationships happening around them. Continued note and image taking will be essential for lessons in the new school term.

In a secondary science lesson, some pupils' research data may show a deep knowledge of a place and of the links between its plant and animal inhabitants. Introduction of tools for simple scientific fieldwork is worthwhile as is some time spent training pupils to use hand lenses, to frame and focus their observations and to make effective records with their improved skills. Notes for teachers in the module Understanding the Environment may be helpful for those pupils who have limited experience of fieldwork in their previous schools (*Enquire with Darwin*, 2012d).

A series of visits to the same locations in the school grounds will allow pupils to practise their field competence and begin to make seasonal profiles of local plants and animals. Once they can name the external features of the plants they find, pupils go on to sort them into major plant groups. Doing so could be part of the process towards making a presentation of plant and animal images that interpret the last paragraph of *On the origin of species*. Data from this session could, when linked with the Adaptation session, make the case for introducing a greater range of plants to attract wildlife into the secondary school grounds.

Communication

A communication session gives pupils the opportunity to find primary or secondary data that will increase their understanding of the ways in which Charles Darwin worked. Many of the references mentioned in the previous five session outlines in this chapter may be differentiated for individual pupil needs. An interactive list on a computer file created by the teacher responsible for this session allows ease of access and time is used effectively.

In addition to references in the other sessions, ARKive (2013) image resources include Darwin's finches and a scrapbook of 13 finch species to emphasise the differences in their beaks. The Charles Darwin Trust website offers image galleries of Darwin-related topics relevant to the Bees, Pigeons and Artificial Selection sessions. Darwin's letters on specific topics, for example, Darwin's childhood, the

Beagle voyage, family life, Darwin's health and evolution have been collected as specific 'packs' for the Darwin Correspondence Project and show his collaboration with peers and something of his daily life (see Chapter 3). The letters also indicate the extent to which Darwin explained his ideas, asked for assistance or invited comment on his work.

CELEBRATION

A final celebration session motivates pupils to share and demonstrate their learning. Time and guidance on how to make a presentation, about the last unit each group works on, can be introduced by a teacher so that pupils understand that their objective is to explain how they worked like Darwin and which of his big ideas they encountered. Secondary pupil assistants are then left to encourage all pupils to engage fully and ensure a gender mix and inclusivity.

Individual talent for music, dance, rap, ICT, poetry, drama and art can be accommodated although each group will have only about 10 minutes to make its point. A Darwin expert or the secondary science co-ordinator of the event comments on the presentations with brief elaborations on how each aspect of pupils' learning over the transition event was relevant to Darwin's skill as a scientist. Drawing on the seemingly simple activities they have experienced and other examples of huge scientific leaps of insight from Darwin's copious letters and books, the specialist can motivate pupils to continue their research and invite them to be curious about everything in the natural world and work painstakingly in those areas of science that others have overlooked.

NOTES

[1] Pollination, YouTube. http://www.youtube.com/watch?v = pVhH2GPlckE accessed on 24 October13.
[2] John Ross (2009). Darwin's pigeons, http://darwinspigeons.com/ accessed on 24 October 2013.
[3] Randal Keynes on Darwin's pigeons (2009), You Tube http://www.youtube.com/watch?v = VFVueCs3gFI accessed on 6 February 2014.
[4] Charles Darwin to Joseph Hooker, 5 June, 1855. Darwin Correspondence Database, http://www.darwinproject.ac.uk/entry-1693 accessed on 24 October 2013.

REFERENCES

Abrahams, I. & Reiss, M. (2010). Effective practical work in primary science: the role of empathy, *Primary Science*, *113*, 26-27.
ARKive. (2013). *Darwin's finches*. http://www.arkive.org/ accessed on 24 October 2013.
Baines, C. (2000). *How to make a wildlife garden*. London: Frances Lincoln.
BBC (2013). Plants for bees. http://www.bbc.co.uk/gardening/basics/techniques/organic_bees1.shtml. accessed on 24 October 2013.
Charles Darwin Trust. (2012). Image galleries. http://www.charlesdarwintrust.org/content/67/galleries. accessed on 24 October 2013.
Christ's College Cambridge. (2009). http://darwin2009.christs.cam.ac.uk/FamilyTrees.html) accessed on 24 October 2013.

Christ's College Cambridge. (2009a). http://darwin2009.christs.cam.ac.uk/Galapagos.html accessed on 24 October 2013.
Continental drift and plate tectonics. (2013). http://www.ucmp.berkeley.edu/geology/techist.html accessed on 24 October 2013.
Darwin, C. R. (1838-1839). *Notebook E*: (Transmutation of species [10.1838-07.1839]) Transcribed by Kees Rookmaaker. http://darwin-online.org.uk/ accessed on 13 August 2013.
Darwin, C. R. (1851). Section VI: Geology. In Herschel, J. F. W. (Ed.). *A manual of scientific enquiry; prepared for the use of Her Majesty's Navy: and adapted for travellers in general.* London: John Murray.
Darwin, C. R. (1855). Does sea-water kill seeds? *Gardeners' Chronicle and Agricultural Gazette*, 15(14 April), 242.
Darwin, C. R. (1859). *On the origin of species by means of natural selection, or the preservation of favoured races in the struggle for life.* (1st edn). London: John Murray.
Darwin, C. R. (1866). *On the origin of species by means of natural selection, or the preservation of favoured races in the struggle for life.* (4th edn). London: John Murray.
Darwin, C. R. (1868). *The variation of animals and plants under domestication.* Vol 1. (1st edn). London: John Murray.
Darwin, C. R. (1869). *On the origin of species by means of natural selection, or the preservation of favoured races in the struggle for life.* (5th edn). *London: John Murray.*
Darwin, C. R. (1881). *The formation of vegetable mould, through the action of worms, with observations on their habits.* London: John Murray.
Darwin, F. (1887). (Ed.). *The life and letters of Charles Darwin, including an autobiographical chapter.* Vol 2. London: John Murray.
Darwin Correspondence Database. (2013). Explore the letters. https://www.darwinproject.ac.uk/ accessed on 24 October 2013.
DfES. (2006). *Secondary national strategy. A condensed Key Stage 3: Improving Key Stage 2 to Key Stage 3 transfer.* London: DfES.
DES. (2013). *The National Curriculum in England and Wales. Framework document.* London: Department for Education.
Discover Darwin. (2010). http://www.darwinslandscape.co.uk/topic.asp?navid=62&tid=234 accessed on 24 October 2013.
Dockery, M. & Tomkins, S. (2000). *Brine shrimp ecology.* London: British Ecological Society. http://www.britishecologicalsociety.org/wp-content/uploads/Brine-Shrimp-Ecology.pdf accessed on 13 August 2013.
Enquire with Darwin. (2012). http://www.charlesdarwintrust.org/content/20/resources-for-teachers accessed on 24 October 2013.
Enquire with Darwin. (2012a). http://www.charlesdarwintrust.org/content/71/ accessed on 24 October 2013.
Enquire with Darwin. (2012b). http://www.charlesdarwintrust.org/content/96/ accessed on 24 October 2013.
Enquire with Darwin.(2012c http://www.charlesdarwintrust.org/content/73 accessed on 24 October 2013.
Enquire with Darwin. (2012d). http://www.charlesdarwintrust.org/content/24/resources-for-teachers/ks2-7-11/module-2 accessed on 24 October 2013.
Field Studies Council (2013). Fold-out charts. http://www.field-studies-council.org/publications/fold-out-charts.aspx accessed on 13 August 2013.
Jackson, E., Sims, A. & Shields, C. (2010). *Guide to the top 50 garden birds* (OP52). Shrewsbury: Field Studies Council.
Johnson, S. (2001). Models of gardening in education. PhD thesis, Department of Science Education, University of Reading.
Johnson, S. (2004). Learning science in a botanic garden. In M. Braund & M. Reiss (Eds.), *Learning science outside the classroom* (pp. 75–93). London: Routledge Falmer.
Jardine, B. (2013). *Darwin's microscopes.* http://www.hps.cam.ac.uk/whipple/explore/microscopes/darwinsmicroscopes/ accessed on 13 August 2013.

Jones, L.S. & Reiss, M.J. (Eds). (2007). *Teaching about scientific origins: taking account of creationism?* London: Peter Lang.

Montgomery, S. (2009) *Darwin's Finches.* http://darwin200.christs.cam.ac.uk/pages/index.php?page_id=g7 accessed on 24 October 2013.

Natural History Museum. (2013). http://www.nhm.ac.uk/nature-online/science-of-natural-history/expeditions-collecting/beagle-voyage/ accessed on 24 October 2013.

Newton, P., Driver, R. & Osborne, J. (1999). The place of argumentation in the pedagogy of school science. *International journal of Science Education*, 21, 553-576.

RSPB. (2009). *When to feed wild birds.* http://www.rspb.org.uk/advice/helpingbirds/feeding/whentofeed.aspx accessed on 24 October 2013.

Science and Plants for Schools. (2013). http://www-saps.plantsci.cam.ac.uk/pollen/ accessed on 24 October 2013.

Susan Johnson
Research Associate, Institute of Education,
University of London,
UK

DAWN L. SANDERS

29. STAGING DARWIN'S SCIENCE THROUGH BIOGRAPHICAL NARRATIVES

INTRODUCTION

Darwin has been the subject of many published biographies (e.g. Desmond & Moore, 1991; Browne, 1995, 2003) and, as a prolific correspondent (see Chapter 3), offers extensive personal material with which to build a biographical reading of his life, his science and the landscapes in which he developed his ideas. It has been suggested that Charles Darwin's story is 'the story of an era' (Browne, 1995, p.xiii) and as such offers educators a platform for learners to engage with scientific ideas throughout his life, and to appreciate the 'power of place' (Browne, 2003) written into his scientific identity. This chapter proposes a biographical model for using the work of scientists in teaching science. It will draw on the writings of Hustak and Myers (2013), Avraamidou and Osborne (2009), Browne (2005), Szybek (1999) and Bruner (1986, 2004) in developing a narrative-based approach through which to stage Darwin's science. In so doing it will build on Browne's assertion that, 'the material grounds of lived experience provide an avenue of historical access extending beyond the reaches of textual evidence' (Browne, 2005, p. 273).

SCIENTIFIC BIOGRAPHY

Söderqvist (2007, p. 2) laments the lack of research attention given to the cultural impact of scientific biography, and poses two critical questions for science education: how has scientific biography contributed to (1) 'the recruitment and socialisation of young scientists' and (2) 'the self-understanding and formation of scientists, engineers and clinicians'? If biographical narratives are to be used in ways that inspire young scientists, or at the very least engender greater interest in school science, then it is necessary to reflect on how these life-stories are constructed, in order to avoid scenarios in which the narrative is 'not a biography, but a laboratory report on a specimen that seems never to have been alive' (Shalin, 1963, p. 27). Lemke situates these issues of relevance in a wider culture of what he terms the 'mystique of science':

> In teaching the content of the science curriculum, and the values that often go with it, science education, sometimes unwittingly, also perpetuates a certain harmful 'mystique of science'. That mystique tends to make science seem

dogmatic, authoritarian, impersonal and even inhuman to many students. It also portrays science as being much more difficult than it is, and scientists as being geniuses that students cannot identify with. It alienates students from science. (Lemke, 1990, p. xi)

Building on Lemke's work, Avraamidou and Osborne (2009) present the case for the use of narratives in science education 'as a way of making it meaningful, relevant, and accessible' (p. 1704). In this chapter, I will frame two biographical narrative-based approaches to Darwin-inspired learning:

– Using Boehm's statue of Darwin in the Natural History Museum, London to stage his science as one which bridged 'the lab-field border'. (Kohler, 2002, p. 1)
– Bringing Darwin, the kinaesthetic scientist, alive through his personal correspondence.

Visual Representation and Scientific Biography

Fara has eloquently critiqued the privileging of textual over visual evidence in biographical contexts; in so doing she asserts the value of portraiture:

Despite being unable to offer the unmediated insights into character that some authors would like to derive, portraits can – like texts and other sources – yield unique information about a sitter. They are instructive not because of what they *do* show, but also because they are imbued with assumptions of what *should* be shown or concealed. (Fara, 2007, p. 73)

In the case of Darwin, Fara notes that his personal responses to commissioned portraiture have survived (Fara, 2000) and thus we know that Darwin disliked the portrait he received as a present on his 64th birthday because he felt the image presented him 'as a very venerable, acute, melancholy old dog' (Fara, 2000, p. 143). Likewise, Darwin considered a photographic *'cartes de visite'* to portray him as 'atrociously wicked' (Fara, 2007, p.76). Browne (2003) points out he did, however, feel more positive about another portrait, for use with family and friends, in which he was dressed in fashionable 'Great Exhibition' check trousers, albeit both portrait and response were as a younger man. In this chapter I will focus mainly on one representational portrait of Darwin – the seated, full body statue in the central hall of the Natural History Museum, London (see Figure 1).

I have chosen this statue for three reasons: it is in a public museum and therefore accessible to regular viewings by a broad range of visitors; it is extensively used in the museum-learning programme[1]; and specific elements of this statue can be interpreted as representations of Darwin's science out-of-doors[2].

In her discussion of scientific biography and portraiture, Fara (2007) focuses our attention on Collier's painting of 1881 (see Figure 2) with its large swathes of dark clothes, in a setting devoid of books and scientific instruments, as a 'reflective and intimate' (p. 87) study of Darwin. In contrast, the statue by Joseph Boehm,

Figure 1. Boehm's statue of Darwin. (© The Trustees of the Natural History Museum, London)

Figure 2. Collier's portrait of Darwin. (© The National Portrait Gallery, London)

unveiled in 1885 (Figure 1), is replete with symbols of Darwin's active scientific self: the overcoat lain across his lap, the creased walking shoes, the possibilities that his notebook, a magnifying lens and other scientific accoutrement could be in one of his pockets. Darwin's chair, in this representation, with its cushion behind his back, embodies both the domestic intimacy of Down House and, at the same time, symbolises the study in which he theorised from his outdoor experiences. His eyes are contemplating distant horizons and his hands intertwined. Thus, this three dimensional portrait presents Darwin in a different light, one in which scientific knowledge is staged as 'rooted in the soil of individual experiences of, and in, the world ... and preceded by bodily experiences in particular situations' (Szybek, 1999, p. 28). In using such a representation of Darwin the man and Darwin the scientist, students' 'horizon of expectations' (Szybek, 1999, p. 157)[3] regarding his biography can be enlarged by 'looking at the modalities and relationships which are there, as well as by looking at what is absent' (Szybek, 1999, p. 140). In this, Darwin's statue both shows an individual and 'yet simultaneously' reveals 'the face of science itself' (Fara, 2007, p. 79). In terms of portraiture, however, there is an interesting twist to this narrative – Collier's original painting, commissioned by The Linnean Society and completed in 1881, was observed from the living man, whereas Boehm's sculpture is a posthumous commission possibly inspired by a photograph taken by Leonard of his father at Down House in 1874 (Browne, 2005). Both representations focus on ordinary day clothes, potential walks and thus opportunities for science out-of-doors, and both position Darwin's eyes contemplating middle to far distant views – inferring outdoor landscapes as the inspirational source of his science.

A Sensory and Tactile Science

Darwin's letters and many of his books are filled with sensory and tactile language, orientating his scientific life around verbs and adjectives, rather than solely, as is often the case with scientific texts, a noun-based 'arrested universe' (Martin, 1993). He was, as has been stated by several authors, aware of the need to use the tools of communication used by novelists and poets to bring his scientific ideas to a readership subscribing to such literary resources as Mudie's travelling library (Otis, 2002; Browne, 2003). This is especially the case for *On the origin of species*, which uses analogy and metaphor to engage his popular audience with his 'big idea'. As a nineteenth-century scientist, Darwin occupies a specific place in the cultural milieu of his time and the history of science. Boehm's statue holds many narrative possibilities with which to imagine Darwin's scientific life. The scale of the statue and its prominent position – at the top of a staircase overlooking the central hall of the museum – provides opportunities to look in detail at the 'small stories' (Bamberg & Georgakopulou 2008) often obscured by the 'grand narrative' (Lyotard, 1984) of Darwin as the 'father of evolution'. For example, we can look closely at his hands and consider his letter to Hooker: 'After having been so many years employed in writing my old geological observations it is delightful to use one's eyes and fingers again'[4]. His shoes, in Boehm's statue, are creased and worn – the shoes of a man who walked regularly, indeed Browne, (2005) observes the 'lovingly wrought' shoelaces as those of a 'naturalist waiting to go for a walk' (p. 265). In Collier's painting too we have an image of Darwin in which 'ordinary-ness' is exemplified –'No scholarly gown, no classical toga, the usual symbols of intellect and wisdom' (Browne, 2005, p. 265) a man in his overcoat, fingers wrapped round the brim of his hat; 'ready to go for a walk' (Browne, 2005, p. 265). We see recognition of the walking scientist in Moore's chapter in which he states, for Darwin 'to walk, however, was to think' (see Chapter 7, p. 94). Selles observes that students walking in the same places in Brazil as young Darwin were motivated to 'search for their own stories, to deal with their memories, and to discover themselves as part of history' (see Chapter 6, p. 75). We can imagine Darwin and Miss Thorley on their hands and knees counting and identifying plants in Great Pucklands meadow while we read the report of scientists attempting a similar survey in the twenty-first century. Through these narratives students can reflect on the situational science embodied in such everyday clothing.

Darwin's overcoat, as depicted in Boehm's statue and in Collier's painting, suggests a man for whom science was not practised solely indoors, a man whose garden was part of his life and science: 'Darwin became at the end what he had always been in his heart, almost part of nature himself, a man with time to lean on a spade and think, a gardener' (Browne, 2003, p. 480). In our book, Chapters 2 (The World of Downe), 27 (Transformation of the School grounds) and 10 (Sailing the Backyard *Beagle*) situate Darwin's science at Downe. This overcoat represents a scientific life lived out-of-doors, a creative doorway through which students can begin to build an understanding of Darwin's experience of *being* a scientist (see Chapter 4). The many pockets of possibilities in his waistcoat, jacket and overcoat in Boehm's rendition, although not visibly explicit, allow students to imagine their contents, as Darwin metaphorically sailed his 'scientific ship' (Browne, 1995, p. 530) across the grounds at Down House and beyond. What 'random odds and ends were creatively assembled into problem-solving tools' (see Chapter 10) for his science. Might a strand of Emma's hair or even a bit of old toenail reside in these temporary stores of everyday objects awaiting a scientific task? Moreover, we can ask students to imagine how Darwin used these objects in his 'multisensory experiments' (Hustak and Myers, 2013 p. 94) as discussed by Costa (see Chapter 10).

Staging Darwin's life and science through portraiture challenges educators to consider the possibilities of experiencing scientists beyond 'life as a noun' (Martin, 1993, p. 221), perhaps enabling science educators, as Avraamidou and Osborne (2009) suggest, to 'forge a stable plane between scientific and non-scientific speech' (Montgomery, 1996, p. 52), embodied in the 'small stories' (Bamberg & Georgakopulou, 2008, p. 377) of diverse scientific lives, both historic and modern. Portraiture, whether it be in paint, print or carved stone, offers students a setting which 'makes us see the person in a specific way, it makes the person specific' (Szybek, 1999, p. 60) and, in the case of Boehm's portrayal of Darwin, represents science as 'enacted' (Szybek, 1999, p. 208) in an 'affective ecology that also includes the scientist' (Hustak & Myers, 2013, p. 94); thus, science is represented as an essentially human endeavour rather than the actions of seemingly distant geniuses from which students can, and often do, feel alienated.

DARWIN'S HANDS

Darwin's hands have received somewhat prejudicial attention from a range of interested spectators, both within and beyond familial contexts. For example, in his book *Celebrated Hands,* Claude Warren writes, next to a traced sketch of Darwin's hands:

> Darwin is rather a large man, and his hand is not a large one in proportion. It is hard and rough, (the right one most so), very spatulous, and rather hairy, with knotty fingers; the lines are numerous and confused. It is a very interesting hand to those studying 'fingerology', for instance compare it with that of an artist, or, of a man devoid of reasoning power. (Warren, 1881)

Although Boehm's sculpture was, in general, well-received, the hands were much critiqued:

> Concerning the statue itself, we have only to speak in terms of almost unqualified praise. It is, in the truest sense of the phrase, a noble work of art. The attitude is not only easy and dignified, but also natural and characteristic; the modelling of the head and face is unexceptionable, and the portrait is admirable. The only criticism we have to advance has reference to the hands, which not only do not bear the smallest resemblance to those of Mr. Darwin, but are of a kind which, had they been possessed by him, would have rendered impossible the accomplishment of much of his work. Although this misrepresentation is a matter to be deplored, it is not one for which the artist can be justly held responsible. Never having had the advantage of seeing Mr. Darwin, Mr. Boehm has only to be congratulated upon the wonderful success which has attended his portraiture of the face and figure; the hands were no doubt supplied by guess-work, and therefore we have only to regret that the guess did not happen to be more fortunate. (*Popular Science Monthly*, 1885, p. 533)

Family memories have inscribed Darwin's hands as 'large, long and pointed' (Keynes, personal communication) suggesting that the Tissot cartoon from *Vanity Fair* (see Figure 3) best fits that view (Keynes, personal communication). Perhaps, the aforementioned criticism of Boehm's rendition of Darwin's hands is not simply a question of scale but an aesthetic consciousness imbued with associations of profession, and thereby social class, commonplace amongst affluent Victorians. Such distinctions could produce rich debate between students studying Darwin in their science lessons and Victorian Britain in history.

Figure 3. 'Natural Selection'-a caricature of Darwin in the magazine Vanity Fair, *30 September 1871 by James Tissot.*

SCIENTIFIC OBSERVATION

The essence of Darwin's scientific 'persona' (Daston & Sibum, 2003) was his use of continuous and critical observation using simple microscopes and lenses in combination with asking timely questions as a 'powerful heuristic' (Eberbach & Crowley, 2009 p. 43). In two letters to Hooker in November 1846[5] and 1 May 1847[6], Darwin describes how delighted he is with his 'splendid plaything' – his new microscope. In a long and detailed letter to Richard Owen in March 1848, Darwin eulogises on the effectiveness of his new microscope made by Smith and Beck and asks Owen to recommend such a 'simple microscope' if he is 'consulted by any young naturalist'. Darwin is forthright in his feelings for his new microscope, for which he feels 'quite a personal gratitude', and his old one, for which he holds 'quite a hatred'[7]. This same microscope, as described in the letter to Owen, allows him to observe in detail colour changes in the valves of a barnacle (see further discussion in Chapter 20). In writing to John Herschel, Darwin notes:

> The borders of the valves when a slice is scaled off are of a very fine blue colour, but which colour, (& this is the point) on slight pressure instantly changes into a translucent red like the clouds of sunset. It is curious under the microscope to press it with a needle & see spot after spot assume this fine permanent glow of red.[8]

Thomashow reflects on 'the learning pathways of the naturalist sensibility' (2002, p. 83). He suggests the following pathways are implicit to the naturalist practice:

– Collecting and systematising as a means of organising knowledge of the natural world.
– Striving to ascertain patterns in nature.
– Being a passionate explorer.

In addition to these 'learning pathways', Thomashow characterises what he defines as 'the deliberate gaze' in which 'wonder, intent and consideration' are combined using sensory awareness, detailed scientific observation and imagination – 'interconnected approaches' which he considers 'crucial for observing the natural world' (Thomashow, 2002, pp. 82-83). In defining these learning pathways and approaches, Thomashow (2002) argues for 'a place-based perceptual ecology' (p. 73) in which 'proximity and attentiveness' (p. 75) thrive. Darwin's letters, concerning the joy of using his 'simple microscope' and the sensory mapping of his observations in the example of the barnacle valve, present an attentive and proximal view of the natural world. Moreover, Darwin's detailed descriptions of his experiments with weeds, orchids, insectivorous plants, barnacles and pigeons demonstrate his 'kinaesthetic dexterities' and 'an experimental form of life contoured by both love and violence' (Hustak & Myers, 2013, p. 93).

These life contours are exemplified by his letter to Hooker, concerning his 'Pigeon Fancy', in which Darwin says he now has 'pairs of nine very distinct varieties, & I love them to the extent I cannot bear to kill and skeletonise them'[9], although, in reality, he did just that; 'The most tangible relic of Darwin's time as a pigeon-fancier was his set of dismembered skeletons and the dried skins of representative specimens. His pets had become data ready to be turned into ammunition' (Browne, 2003, p. 205) and see Figure 4.

Jerome Bruner (2004) suggests that, 'narrative, even at its most primitive, is played out on a dual landscape'. These two landscapes he describes as one of action 'on which events unfold' and a second landscape 'of consciousness, the inner worlds of the protagonists involved in the action' (p. 698). The extensive archive of Darwin's letters, books and notebooks (see Chapters 3 and 8), along with the preservation of his house and garden at Downe, allow access to these dual narratives. An intensely documented history in which we find a man whose

Figure 4. A selection of Darwin's pigeons. (© The Trustees of the Natural History Museum, London)

scientific method 'refuses to emulate the idealized model of a disengaged, impartial, scientific observer. He participated actively with his experimental subjects, to such an extent that he moved with and was moved by them' (Hustack & Myers, 2013, p. 85). Using a range of artefacts, spaces and places through which to imagine Darwin's life separates 'learning to be a scientist' from 'learning science' (Bruner, 1986, p. 132). Thus, it becomes 'learning a culture, with all the attendant non-rational meaning-making that goes with it' (Bruner, 1986, p. 132). Such acts of imagination (Bruner, 1986) can create 'epiphanies of the ordinary' (Bruner, 2004; Joyce, 1914) rather than the 'mythic and allegorical' (Daston & Sibum, 2003, p. 7) lives so often characterised by school science. Furthermore, the multi-vocal language with which he voices the first edition of *On the origin of species* is, in Beer's words 'expressive rather than rigorous':

> He accepts the variability within words, their tendency to dilate and contract across related senses, or to oscillate between significations. He is less interested in singleness than in mobility. In his use of words he is more preoccupied with relations and transformations than with limits. (Beer, 2009, p. 33)

Thus, through Darwin's words, we have a richly *sensed* scientific life from which to develop a narrative-based approach to learning science.

ACKNOWLEDGEMENTS

I wish to acknowledge and thank Randal Keynes and Joe Cain for our animated discussions on Darwin's hands on a winter's night in London town the content of which has added to this chapter.

NOTES

[1] 'The Great Debate Workshop (KS4 14-16-year-olds) at The Natural History Museum plunges students into the heated debate surrounding the publication of Darwin's *On the origin of species*. With the main galleries as their stage, watch as your students become animated proponents of the historic protaganists' views' (Sally Collins, pers. Comm. Natural History Museum, London).

[2] On May 6, 2009 Janet Browne gave a Burlington House Lecture entitled 'Two hundred Years of Evolution: Celebrating Charles Darwin in 2009'. During her lecture she suggested elements of Boehm's statue, such as the inclusion of an overcoat, could be taken as representations of Darwin's science out-of-doors. Since attending this lecture I have accessed her 2005 presidential address 'Commemorating Darwin' for the British Society for the History of Science.

[3] Szybek draws on the theoretical works of Husserl and Merleau-Ponty to inform his work on 'Staging Science'.

[4] Charles Darwin to J. D. Hooker, 6 November, 1846. Darwin Correspondence Database, http://www.darwinproject.ac.uk/entry-1018 accessed on 24 November 2013.

[5] Charles Darwin to J. D. Hooker, 14 November, 1846. Darwin Correspondence Database, http://www.darwinproject.ac.uk/entry-1024 accessed on 24 November 2013.

[6] Charles Darwin to J. D. Hooker, 1 May, 1847. Darwin Correspondence Database, http://www.darwinproject.ac.uk/entry-1085 accessed on 24 November 2013.

[7] Charles Darwin to Richard Owen, 26 March, 1848. Darwin Correspondence Database, http://www.darwinproject.ac.uk/entry-1166 accessed on 14 October 2013.

[8] Charles Darwin to John Herschel, 11 May, 1848. Darwin Correspondence Database, http://www.darwinproject.ac.uk/entry-1175 accessed on 14 October 2013.

[9] Charles Darwin to J. D. Hooker, 8 November, 1855. Darwin Correspondence Database, http://www.darwinproject.ac.uk/entry-1774 accessed on 24 November 2013.

REFERENCES

Avraamidou, L., & Osborne, J. (2009). The role of narrative in communicating science. *International Journal of Science Education, 31*(12), 1683–1707.

Bamberg, M., & Georgakopulou, A. (2008). Small stories as a new perspective in narrative and identity analysis. *Text and Talk, 28*, 377–396.

Beer, G. (2009). *Darwin's plots: Evolutionary narrative in Darwin, George Eliot and nineteenth- century fiction*. Cambridge, UK: Cambridge University Press.

Bruner, J. (1986). *The culture of education*. Cambridge, MA: Harvard University Press.

Bruner, J. (2004). Life as Narrative. *Social Research, 71*(3), 691–710.

Browne, E. J. (1995). *Charles Darwin: Voyaging*. New York, NY: Alfred Knopf.

Browne, E. J. (2003). *Charles Darwin: The power of place*. London: Jonathan Cape.

Browne, E. J. (2005). Presidential address commemorating Darwin. *The British Journal for the History of Science, 38*(3), 251–274.

Daston, L. & Sibum, H. O. (2003). Introduction: Scientific personae and their histories. In Scientific personae: Special issue of *Science in Context, 16*(1/2), 1–8.

Desmond, A. J., & Moore, J. (1991). *Darwin*. London: Michael Joseph.

Eberbach, C., & Crowley, K. (2009). From everyday to scientific observation: How children learn to observe the biologist's world. *Review of Educational Research, 79*, 39–68.

Fara, P. (2000). Images of Charles Darwin. *Endeavour, 24*, 143.
Fara, P. (2007). Framing the evidence: Scientific biography and portraiture. In T. Söderqvist (Ed.), *The history and poetics of scientific biography*. Hampshire: Ashgate.
Hustak, C., & Myers, N. (2013). Involutionary momentum: Affective ecologies and the sciences of plant/insect encounters. *Differences: A Journal of Feminist Cultural Studies, 25*(5), 74–118.
Joyce, J. (1914/1996). *Dubliners*. London: Penguin Popular Classics.
Kohler, R. (2002). *Landscapes and labscapes: Exploring the lab-field border in biology*. Chicago and London: The University of Chicago Press.
Lemke, J. L. (1990). *Talking science: Language, learning and values*. Norwood, NJ: Ablex Publishing Corporation.
Lyotard, J. F. (1984). *The post-modern condition: A report on knowledge*. Minnesota, MN: University of Minnesota Press.
Martin, J. R. (1993). Life as a noun: Arresting the universe in science and humanities. In M. A. K. Halliday & J. R. Martin (Eds.), *Writing science*. London and New York: Routledge.
Montgomery, S. L. (1996). *The scientific voice*. New York, NY: Guilford Press.
Otis, L. (2000). *Literature and science in the nineteenth century*. Oxford: Oxford University Press.
Popular Science Monthly, (1885, August). The Darwin Memorial (Vol. 27), pp.533–536.
Shalin, H. (1963, November). The scientist in biography. *Bulletin of the Atomic Scientists, 19*, 27–28.
Söderqvist, T. (2007). *The history and poetics of scientific biography*. Hampshire: Ashgate.
Szybek, P. (1999). Staging science: Some aspects of the production and distribution of science knowledge (Doctoral Dissertation) Lund University, Department of Education, Sweden.
Thomashow, M. (2002). *Bringing the biosphere home: Learning to perceive global environmental change*. Cambridge, MA: MIT Press.
Warren, C. (1881). *The life-size outlines of the hands of twenty-four celebrated persons* (No. 20). London: The Modern Press.

Dawn L. Sanders
Institute of Pedagogical, Curricular and Professional Studies,
Gothenburg University,
Sweden

DAWN L. SANDERS, CAROLYN J. BOULTER & MICHAEL J. REISS

EPILOGUE

Transforming the Ordinary

INTRODUCTION

A wild bird but an ordinary one. I looked up the definition of 'ordinary' – with no special or distinctive features, common, of ordinary rank, undistinguished, commonplace. Which of us is any more or less? Whatever he was, this bird was beautiful. His new fresh feathers were lavender and navy, shading to a fine line of black towards the tips of his wings, his eyes bright and watching. (Woolfson, 2013, pp. 6-7)

Thus, a young injured bird is described in Woolfson's *Field notes from a hidden city: an urban nature diary*. The city is Aberdeen, the bird a blue rock pigeon *Columba livia*. The species encapsulated in textbook narratives on Darwin are often from the Galapagos and yet, for much of his life, it was the ordinary plants and animals close to Darwin's home (Jones, 2009) that inspired and transfigured his ideas; pigeons, everyday weeds, garden cabbages, the common sundew *Drosera rotundifolia* and the twining hops of the Kent countryside (Chapters 1, 2, 10, 14, 17 and 18). As a writer, Darwin is a master at transforming the ordinary into a richly 'tangled bank' of crawling worms, singing birds and flitting insects (Darwin, 1859) in order to create a metaphorical picture of his *Origin* theory. Indeed, Darwin creates multiple narratives with which to render his life and science. In his *Autobiography* he reflects on his experiences of education, creating both a narrative of enquiry and one of disillusionment. Remembering, at age eight and a half, his passion for natural history Darwin notes:

> I remember I took great delight at school in fishing for newts in the quary pool – I had thus formed a strong taste for collecting, chiefly seals, franks & but also pebbles and minerals, – one which was given me by some boy, decided this taste. – I believe shortly after this or before I had smattered in botany. (Darwin, 2002, p. 3)

However, his overall impression of school is perceived to be less experientially rich: 'Nothing could be worse for the development of my mind … the school as a means of education to me was simply a blank'. (Barlow, 1958, p. 9)

Writing to his wife, Emma, on the deteriorating health and subsequent death of their ten-year-old daughter, Annie, we witness a father's love, loss and grief; in essence a narrative of what it is to be human. In expressing such tangible emotions Darwin becomes a public proxy for the ordinary person[1]:

> A letter had come from Emma, and Charles replied: 'Your note made me cry much, but I must not give way, and can avoid doing so by not thinking about her. It is now from hour to hour a struggle between life and death'. (Keynes, 2002, p. 205)

Whether at home, or travelling on the *Beagle*, Charles Darwin converts seemingly simple cameos of natural history into sublime poetic expression, as Keynes demonstrates:

> Charles had long had a special interest in plant shoots. In the Brazilian forests in 1832 he had seen them growing, and had watched entranced. One day he wrote in his pocket notebook: 'Twiners entwining twiners – tresses like hair – beautiful Lepidoptera – silence'. Now looking at the plant in his study from hour to hour, Charles spotted the circular sweeping of the tendrils, now clockwise and now anti-clockwise, as they searched for an object to attach themselves to. (Keynes, 2002, p.299)

Furthermore, poetic metaphors, such as the aforementioned 'tangled bank' in *On the origin of species* (Darwin, 1859), are harnessed by Darwin to scientific evidence in order to bring the theory of evolution alive in the mind of the general reader, an authorial approach replicated in the twentieth-century work of marine biologist Rachel Carson (Lear, 1998) in her sea-life trilogy, in particular her middle volume *The edge of the sea* (Carson, 1955). Carson is not alone in producing such poetic science writing:

> The last fallen mahogany would lie perceptibly on the landscape, and the last black rhino would be obvious in its loneliness, but a marine species may disappear beneath the waves unobserved and the sea would seem to roll on the same as always. (Ray, G. C. 1988, p.45)

Beyond the poetic science genre, poetry itself, as Holmes suggests, 'addresses most directly the question of what it is to be a human being in a Darwinian universe' (2013, p.4). Tina Gianquitto (Chapter 22) explores this same question, albeit from the view of what it is to be a carnivorous plant, as perceived by nineteenth-century humans, in a Darwinian universe. Ruth Padel, in her poem written for this volume, speaks for Darwin the loving husband, as he watches Emma open the window and 'is glad that she is glad. He has not publicly rejected the idea of a Creator' (p. xiii).

The traditional hypothetico-deductive experimental narrative of school science is known to restrict young people and can turn young minds away from the further study of science, as described in Chapter 26. So, how then, can we find ways to use the multiple narratives about Darwin, and within his own documentation, to enrich pupils' experience of learning science? Many chapters in this volume make encouraging suggestions, for teachers struggling against restrictive curricula, to produce teaching materials that enable students to express their developing relationship with science through story and letters (Chapter 3), poetry, drama (Chapter 21), argumentation (Chapters 12 and 15), exploring collections (Chapter 8 and 20) and artistic forms. Central to these 'multiple narratives' is the 'tonal mix of the poetic and the scientific and analytical' (Macfarlane, 2013, p.167) that Charles Darwin models for learners through his personal letters, notebooks and published works. In many respects, his writing allows us to see the landscape with 'new eyes', as Costa, drawing on Proust, suggests in Chapter 10 enabling us to transform ordinary experiences into extraordinary ones.

SEEING WITH 'NEW EYES'

When interactions with 'wild nature' are increasingly limited, 'when grey is more common than green' (Sanders, 2010, p. 6) where can children see 'endless forms most beautiful and most wonderful' (Charles Darwin, 1859, p. 360)? In these situations 'ordinary, everyday' organisms take on a new role. It is fitting then that, as his final study, Darwin himself offers us deep insights into the life of the common earthworm *Lumbricus terrestris* (Darwin, 1881). Likewise, the North American naturalist, John James Audubon (1785-1851), known for his extensive work on birds, 'researched rats for months' in the latter years of his life (Sullivan, 2004, p. 4).

Modern cities have become a 'complex web of connection' (Woolfson, 2013, p. 8) between humans and numerous organisms; some species, such as the aforementioned pigeon, have become familiar, whether loved or loathed (Tunnicliffe, Boulter & Reiss, 2007). Many remain hidden and invisible. Others have become increasingly purged, and a few, such as the brown rat *Rattus norvegicus*, reviled as the 'most unwanted inhabitants' (Sullivan, 2004) of the contemporary conurbation. 'Edgelands' (Shoard, 2002; Farley & Symmons Roberts, 2012), strips of land caught between city and countryside, now provide temporary refugia for plants and animals, either estranged from their natural habitats or 'blow-ins', resulting from global travel networks, as was once the case for the brown rat. These transitory spaces are often the notional wilderness for the modern urban imagination. Do we pay attention to these pockets of natural history in our midst? How might we develop students' abilities to transform the ordinary into the extraordinary in their ability to 'read nature' (Chapter 5) in our cities, edgelands and the diminishing countryside? What role might school gardens (Chapter 27) play in these hinterlands of biodiversity? Could 'having a nice little definite world to work on',[2] as Darwin did in Great Pucklands (Chapter 19), instead of the 'awful abyss and immensity of all British Plants'[3] make a difference to students' perceptions of local plants and animals, as Tompkins and Tunnicliffe discuss in Chapter 11?

Paying Attention

Susan Johnson, the first academic to join the Charles Darwin Trust, notes in Chapter 27, that Darwin 'always carried a hand lens, and got down on his knees to use it, so that almost nothing, however small and seemingly insignificant escaped his attention' thus, she claims, 'paying attention' and 'close observation' are essential characteristics of Darwin-inspired learning. Bachelard (1994) suggests such activities are intertwined:

> To use a magnifying glass is to pay attention, but isn't paying attention already having a magnifying glass? Attention by itself is an enlarging glass. (Bachelard, 1994, p. 158)

In her paper, 'Voices inside schools – notes from a marine biologist's daughter: on the art and science of attention,' McCrary-Sullivan re-presents an 'autobiography of attention' (2000, p. 212):

> My mother the scientist, taught me to see. She taught me attention to the complexities of surface detail and also attention to what lies beneath those surfaces. She taught me the rhythms of tide and regeneration, and the syllables of the natural world rubbing against each other. In doing so she made me a poet.
>
> My mother, the teacher, held classes in mud and water and light. She taught with buckets and shovels and nets. Her students' tennis shoes, and hers squished loudly as they worked, discovered, learned. I observed that my mother and her students were happy. I became a teacher.
>
> My mother, the researcher, went into the field twice a day whatever the weather for years, methodically, with her plankton nets. Then she sat patiently at the microscope on the kitchen table, observing, noticing, discovering patterns, making sense. In that kitchen, I learned the patience of research. (McCrary-Sullivan, 2000, p. 221)

The notion of students 'paying attention' is much discussed in educational settings. McCrary-Sullivan (2000) recognises that 'the issue of attention is critical'; however, she suggests that despite a consistent concern with 'engaging and maintaining student attention ... our investigations of the nature of attention and its development have been rather weak' (p. 211). Critically, in relation to our discussions of Darwin-inspired learning, she asks, 'How do we learn to attend with keen eyes and fine sensibilities?' and 'how do we teach others to do it?' (McCrary-Sullivan, 2000, p. 212).

McCrary-Sullivan's work has resonances for the complexities of 'paying attention' in relation to observing, experiencing and understanding living organisms, as an intrinsic part of contemporary science education and wider sensibilities of the natural world. Furthermore, within this autobiography, she recognises the complex layers involved in learning experiences, particularly those that appear to take place without explicit instruction:

> There is another layer to this, because years later I remember with a vividness and intensity that compel me to poetry. On some level, in some hidden and inarticulate way, I must have been attending and recording extremely well. I was learning, internalizing without any direct instruction. (McCrary-Sullivan, 2000, p. 222)

Moore, in Chapter 7, mirrors these complex layers of learning, by offering stories from Darwin's family life at Down House; informal vignettes, in which close observation, such as watching male bumble bees to determine the routes they took, plays a central role. Darwin was fascinated by behaviour and in *The expression of emotions in man and animals*, published in 1872, he analyses the similarities in the expression of emotions in human beings and animals, suggesting this as evidence of evolutionary links. Today, emergent scanning technologies have enabled us to probe and visualise the behaviour of the brain during emotion, memorising and attention (Sylwester & Cho, 1993). Can we use these new insights into the processes of attention in teaching and learning? A Darwin-inspired approach to attention using framing and focusing can be found in the Charles Darwin Trust unit 'Understanding the environment'.[4]

Close Observation

> A lily is more real to a naturalist than it is to an ordinary person. But it is still more real to a botanist. And yet another stage of reality is reached with that botanist who is a specialist in lilies. (Nabokov, 1962)

How we view the material world is, as Nabokov states, influenced by our cultural framing of what we see. Eberbach and Crowley (2009), in their critique of teaching children to move from 'everyday noticing' to 'scientific observation', assert the importance of disciplinary frameworks in aiding such transitions. However, beneath these perceptual changes lies a more complex hegemonic web of scientific literacy, as demonstrated by several chapters in Roth & Calabrese-Barton's book (2004, p. 109), informed by 'multiplicities of identities and borderlands':

> Any sort of scientific literacy exists within critical reflections around margin and center, including such reflections as: How are margin and center constructed in classrooms, and how is their existence used to hinder or promote education for particular groups or people in particular contexts? What does it mean to be positioned in the margin or center, and what are the implications this has for ways of knowing, talking and acting? What happens when the center or margin is used to understand, challenge and collapse the other? (Roth & Calabrese-Barton, 2004, p. 110)

Twentieth-century fiction provides us with examples of complex transitions between social margins and the solace that elements of the natural world can bring to isolated individuals. Barry Hines, in the novel *Kestrel for a knave* (1969), presents Billy Casper, a fifteen-year-old from a poor mining town in Yorkshire, as he develops a relationship with a kestrel he takes from a nest and trains in falconry, using a stolen book, after failing to gain access to the local library:

'Got any books on hawks, missis?'

The girl behind the counter looked up from sorting coloured tickets in a tray. 'Hawks?'
'I want a book on falconry.'
'I'm not sure, you'd better try ornithology.'
'What's that?'
'Under zoology.'
She leaned over the desk and pointed down a corridor of shelves, then stopped and looked Billy over.
'Are you a member?'
'What do you mean, a member?'
'A member of the library.'
Billy pressed a finger into the ink pad on the desk and inspected the purple graining on the tip.
'I don't know'owt about that. I just want to lend a book on falconry, that's all.'
'You can't borrow books unless you are a member.'
'I only want one.'
'Have you filled one of these forms in?'
She licked a forefinger and flicked a blue form up on her thumb. Billy shook his head. (Hines, 1969, p. 32)

In William Golding's unsettling exploration of survival and competition among a group of children, *Lord of the flies* (1964), Simon finds temporary respite in an aromatic cave:

He came at last to a place where more sunshine fell. Since they had not so far to go for light, the creepers had woven a great mat that hung at the side of an open space in the jungle; for here a patch of rock came close to the surface and would not allow more than little plants to grow. The whole space was walled with dark aromatic bushes, and was a bowl of heat and light. A great tree, fallen across one corner, leaned against the trees that still stood and a rapid climber flaunted red and yellow sprays right to the top. Simon paused. He looked over his shoulder as Jack had done at the close ways behind him and glanced swiftly to confirm he was utterly alone. For a moment his movements were almost furtive. Then he bent down and wormed his way into the centre of the mat. The creepers and bushes were so close he left his sweat on them and they pulled together behind him. When he was secure in the middle he was in a little cabin screened off from the open space by a few leaves. (Golding, 1964, p. 54)

Such stories of 'margin and center' are limited neither to the school classroom nor to literary contexts, as Keller's biography of Barbara McClintock (Keller, 1983) reveals; life as a scientist is socially complex:

> Scientific knowledge as a whole grows out of the interaction – sometimes complex, always subtle – between individual creativity and communal validation. But sometimes that interaction miscarries, and an estrangement occurs between individual and community. Usually, in such a case, the scientist loses credibility. But should that not happen, or, even better, should it happen and then be reversed, we have a special opportunity to understand the meaning of dissent in science. (Keller, 1983, p. *xx*)

The same will perhaps be true for the exploration of science in school, where there needs to be interaction between the individual learner and the community of school science, along with the professional science community. How can schools both provide for this triad of interaction and, at the same time, support students to materialise 'everyday noticing' into 'scientific observation' (Eberbach & Crowley, 2009)? What might the implications of such transitions have for potential learning spaces in, and beyond, the classroom?

SCIENTIFIC INVESTIGATION

Recent commentaries have examined the ways in which biological investigation is conducted, expressed and communicated (see for example, Cohen, 2004; Greene, 2005; Canfield, 2011). Underpinning such debates are deeper discussions pertaining to scientific methodologies, praxes and identities (Greene, 2005; Wilson in Canfield, 2011). Wilson (2011) has argued for communities of 'scientific naturalists' in which there is a consilience of knowledge between molecular biology and 'higher levels of biological organization, from organism to population, ecosystem and society' (Wilson, 2011, p. ix). He suggests biological science should aspire to 'understand the full diversity of life from molecule to ecosystem' (Wilson, 2011, p. ix). Furthermore, mathematical modelling appears to be 'biology's next microscope' (Cohen, 2004, p. 2017).

I Think

Where might Darwin fit into this emerging picture of scientific endeavour and how might his multi-modal representations inspire twenty-first-century biological learning? As noted by Prain in Chapter 24, *On the origin of species* has only one illustration –the iconic 'tree of life' sketch of a generalised phylogenetic tree (see Figure 1). The original drawing, as shown in Darwin's Notebook B, has the annotation 'I think' (see Figure 2). Richard Fortey (2009) describes this brief note as a 'wonderfully ambiguous statement' suggesting that its appeal, in contrast to statements such as 'I know' or 'I understand' is, in its 'modest approach to originality, a tentative prod towards W*eltanschauung*' (Fortey, 2009, p. 184). Johnson (Chapter 27) advocates the use of this diagrammatic sketch as an example of an early 'mind-map', and, as such, could be used as an inspirational model for contemporary learners. Indeed, in Chapter 24, Prain argues for multi-modal ways of writing science, an argument reflected in Canfield's anthology on the role of field notes in modern science (Canfield, 2011).

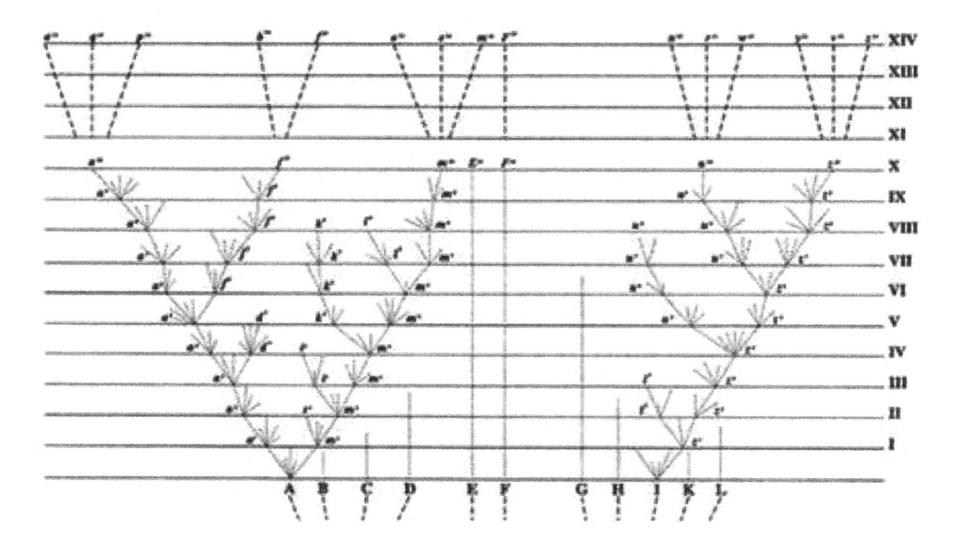

Figure 1. Darwin's generalised phylogenetic tree diagram from
On the origin of species *(1859).*

The Red Notebook

Pivotal to the ideas expressed in Darwin's Notebook B was his transitional, and preceding, Red Notebook (Herbert, 1980). Darwin needed to move from observing and questioning, through investigation and experimentation, to theory-building. His notebooks provide critical evidence of epistemological shifts from the *Beagle* voyage onwards. As Herbert observes, of his Red Notebook, 'the tentative and empirical nature of Darwin's inquiries is paramount' (Herbert, 1980, p. 8). Art education researchers have conceptualised the notion of 'rigorous doubt' (Pringle, 2008, p. 42) in relation to knowledge-building in teaching and learning visual arts,

EPILOGUE

a phrase which is equally pertinent to Darwin's notebooks, throughout which a tension is revealed 'between fact and theory, data and narrative' (Canfield, 2011, p.11). Herein lies an essential element of Darwin-inspired learning – tentative exploratory questioning and theorising combined with rigorous use of empirical data; students and teachers are encouraged to get 'under Darwin's skin' and experience his ways of working outdoors using close observation, simple data-gathering tools along with critical quotes from his journals, correspondence and books to question what they observe, and to 'think like Darwin' (Maloney, Johnson & Goldie-Morrison, 2011).

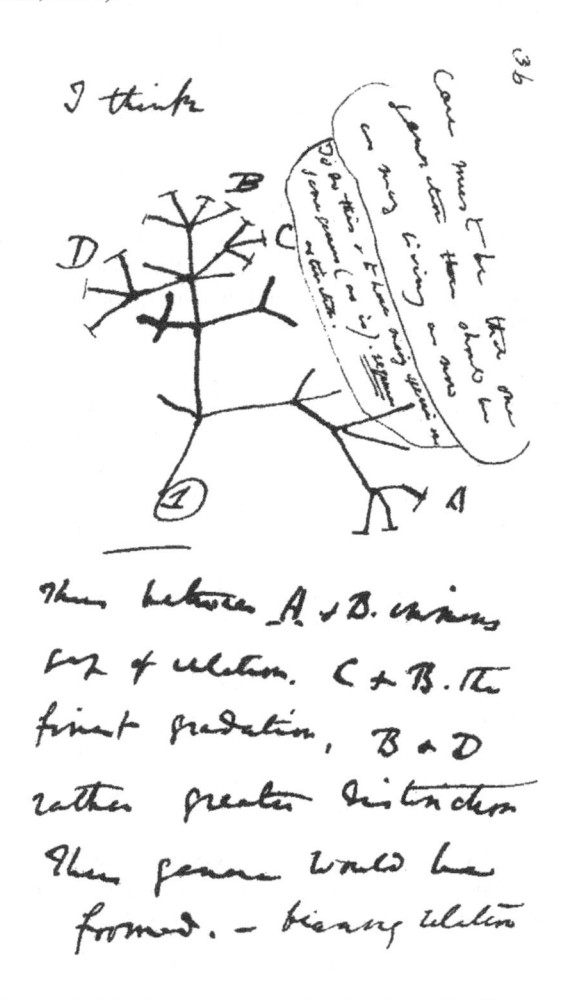

Figure 2. Darwin's 'I think' diagram from his Notebook B. (Classmark: DAR121. Reproduced by kind permission of the Syndics of Cambridge University Library.)

READING NATURE

The work of Johnson (Chapters 27 & 28), Corbishley (Chapter 9), Selles (Chapter 6) and Costa (Chapter 10) in creating Darwin-inspired approaches with teacher communities in the UK, Brazil and USA respectively has been significant in defining what it means to be 'Darwin-inspired' teachers and learners in authentic science contexts (Braund & Reiss, 2006). Moreover, in Sweden, Ola Magntorn and Gustav Helldén's work on 'reading nature' (Chapter 5) is important in relation to how students perceive individuals, populations and communities in ecological learning contexts, and what it means to a student to 'speak ecologish' (see Chapter 5). One of the teachers using the method of 'reading nature' commented during Magntorn and Helldén's research:

> From being restricted to the school book and teacher's desk it has changed. I work very differently today. For example, the lapwing, and how we now concentrate on one bird and look at it and draw it and find it in its habitat. This gives you other knowledge – more knowledge but you have to be much more alert. Knowledge is important but the key to it is to listen to the children and work with their questions. The knowledge of the method is most important. I am not a nature expert but I feel confident in doing these type of studies. (Magntorn & Helldén, 2006, p. 73)

Within educational research with young children there has been much work on how children learn to read text, leading to the development of a whole field of emergent literacy (Raban, 1997). We might consider the capacity of this work to enhance our understanding of how young children can learn to read nature, for the natural world has multiple ways in which, and through which, to be read (Berger, 1980; Reiss, 2002). Richard Mabey has suggested,[5] that curiosity cabinets, or *Wunderkammer*, have a role to play in such nature narratives, as they can be perceived diversely: as a mausoleum, a collection of ecological biographies or a work of art in which the objects can mediate between feelings and the natural world. In making this statement, Mabey takes us back to examine encounters between art and science; to explore the interstices of curiosity, exploration and representation played out repeatedly across time and discipline; a space in which interrogation, disruption, witness and documentation play lead roles. In the following commentaries, extracted from a scientist, a visual-arts essayist and a fiction-writer, these interstices are made explicit:

> I have meticulously documented my observations, and this has made the difference between simply being a witness to nature and being one who identifies themes and questions. (Heinrich, 2011, p.38)

> Vera Möller's drawings, photographs and sculptures draw us into a fascinating world ... Her work forces us to re-consider the role of 'canonical images',

those seemingly authoritative scientific representations of nature, in our understanding of life. (Vujakovic, 2011, p.33) See Figure 3.

My own painfully slow progress from the sick days of my own little schoolboy *Wunderkammer* during the *entre-deux-guerres* has shown me that nature is in fact not about collecting at all, but something infinitely more complex and difficult: being. (Fowles in Salway, 1996, pp. 8-9)

Figure 3. Spotted Leatherlings (2009), a Vera Möller sculpture. (© Vera Möller)

As noted by Tina Gianquitto (Chapter 22):

Darwin's re-mapping of the natural world placed many in the nineteenth century in a profoundly disturbing position, facing a paradigm shift that necessitated an entirely new way at looking at the world and its natural systems.

This 're-mapping of the natural world' is no less important today. The development of Darwin's scientific praxis, and its far-reaching effects, can, we believe, challenge and provoke teachers and learners to reflect on the numerous ways in which scientists work and how individuals 'read', and interact with, nature in all its cultural complexity. More specifically, there remains the critical role of creating learning experiences in which, as Rosemary and Peter Grant suggest (see Foreword, p. *ix*), both the scientific and the creative imagination are given opportunities to flourish. In response to their suggestion, we consider Darwin-inspired learning to be, as Johnson writes in Chapter 27, 'a continuum of enquiry' along which curiosity and imagination make border crossings between the arts and sciences. The inter-disciplinary nature of our book reflects such a pedagogical milieu, one in which imagination and the material world coalesce through 'curiosity, fascination and mobility of thought' (Brice-Heath & Wolf, 2004, p. 13).

NOTES

[1] Professor Joe Cain presented Darwin as both role-model and proxy at a meeting of the Science and Technology Education Group at the Institute of Education, London, UK in December, 2013.
[2] Charles Darwin to J. D. Hooker, 15 June, 1855, Darwin Correspondence Database, http://www.darwinproject.ac.uk/letter/entry-1700 accessed on 12 February 2014.
[3] Charles Darwin to J. D. Hooker, 15 June, 1855, Darwin Correspondence Database, http://www.darwinproject.ac.uk/letter/entry-1700 accessed on 12 February 2014.
[4] Charles Darwin Trust Enquire with Darwin resources for teachers. Module 2, Understanding the Environment, http://www.charlesdarwintrust.org/content/24/resources-for-teachers/ks2-7-11/module-2 accessed on 20 February 2014.
[5] Ways with words. Southwold Literature Festival, Suffolk. 8-12 November 2012. Richard Mabey, 9 November, 'Cabinet of curiosities' lecture.

REFERENCES

Bachelard, G. (1994). *The poetics of space: a look at how we experience intimate spaces*. Boston, Massachusetts: Beacon.
Barlow, N. (Ed.). (1958). *The autobiography of Charles Darwin*. London: Collins.
Berger, J. (1980). *About looking*. London: Writers and Readers.
Braund, M. & Reiss, M. (2006). Towards a more authentic science curriculum: the contribution of out-of-school learning. *International Journal of Science Education*, 28(12), 1373-1388.
Brice-Heath, S. & Wolf, S. (2004).Visual Learning in the Community School-Hoping for accidents: media and technique available at: http://www.colorado.edu/education/sites/default/files/attached-files/Visual%20learning_Hoping%20for%20accidents.pdf accessed on 20 February 2014.
Canfield, M. (Ed.). (2011). *Field notes on science and nature*. Cambridge Massachusetts: Harvard University Press.
Carson, R. (1955). *The edge of the sea*. London: Staples.
Cohen, J. (2004). Mathematics is biology's next microscope, only better; biology is mathematics' next physics, only better. *PLOS Biology*, 2(12), 2017-2023.
Darwin, C. (1859) *On the origin of species*. G. Beer (Ed). (2008). Oxford: Oxford University Press.
Darwin, C. (1872). *The expression of emotions in man and animals*. London: John Murray.
Darwin, C. (1881). *The formation of vegetable mould, through the action of worms*. London: John Murray.
Darwin, C., Neve, M. & Messenger, S. (Eds.). (2002). *Autobiographies*. London: Penguin.
Eberbach, C. E. & Crowley, K. (2009). From everyday to scientific observation: how children learn to observe the biologist's world. *Review of Educational Research*, 79(1), 39-69.
Farley, P. & Symmons Roberts, M., (2012). *Edgelands: journey into England's true wilderness*. London: Vintage.
Fortey, R. (2009). Charles Darwin: The Scientist as Hero. *Contributions to Science*, 5(2), 183-191.
Fowles, J. (1996). Introduction. In K. Salway *Collector's Items*. London: Wilderness Editions.
Golding, W. (1954). *Lord of the flies*. London: Faber & Faber.
Green, H. (2005). Organisms in nature as a central focus for biology. *TRENDS in Ecology and Evolution*, 20(1), 23 - 27.
Heinrich, B. (2011). Untangling the bank. In M. Canfield (Ed.) *Field notes on science and nature*. Cambridge, Massachusetts: Harvard University Press.

Herbert, S. (Ed.). (1980). The red notebook of Charles Darwin. *Bulletin of the British Museum (Natural History), Historical Series* 7 (24 April), 1-164.
Hines, B. (1969). *A kestrel for a knave.* London: Penguin.
Holmes, J. (2013). *Darwin's bards: British and American poetry in the age of evolution.* Edinburgh: Edinburgh University Press.
Jones, S. (2009). *Darwin's island: The Galapagos in the garden of England.* London: Little Brown.
Keller, F.E. (1983). *A feeling for the organism: The life and work of Barbara McClintock.* San Francisco: W. H. Freeman.
Keynes, R. (2002). *Darwin, his daughter and human evolution.* New York: Riverhead.
Lear, L. (2009). *Rachel Carson: witness for nature.* New York: Henry Holt.
McCrary Sullivan, A. (2000). Voices inside schools - notes from a marine biologist's daughter: on the art and science of attention. *Harvard Educational Review,* 70(2), 211-227.
Macfarlane, R. (2013). New words on the wild. *Nature,* 498, 166-167.
Magntorn, O. & Helldén, G. (2006). Reading nature - experienced teachers' reflections on a teaching sequence in ecology: implications for future teacher training. *NORDINA,* 5, 67-81.
Maloney, J., Johnson, S. & Goldie-Morrison, K. (2011). A memorable day out. *Primary Science,* 119, 30-32.
Nabokov, V. (1962). In *The Listener* (London), 68 (1756), November 22, 1962, pp. 856-858. Reprinted as 'What Vladimir Nabokov thinks of his work, his life'. *Vogue,* New York, March 1, 1963, pp. 152-155.
Pringle, E. (2008). Artists' perspectives on art practice and pedagogy. In J. Sefton-Green (Ed.) *Creative learning.* London: Creative Partnerships. Available from www.creative-partnerships.com.
Raban, B. (1997). Reading skills: emergent literacy. Encyclopedia of Language and Education, 2, 19-26.
Ray, G. C. (1988). Ecological diversity in coastal zones and oceans. In E.O. Wilson & F.M. Peter (Eds) *Biodiversity,* (pp. 36-50). Washington DC: National Academy Press.
Reiss, M. (2002). Representing science. Professorial Inaugural Lecture. Institute of Education, University of London.
Roth, W-M, & Calabrese-Barton, A. (2004). *Rethinking scientific literacies.* New York: Routledge Farmer.
Sanders, D. (2010). Invertebrates: revealing a hidden world in the year of biodiversity. *Primary Science,* 113, 5-10.
Shoard, M. (2002). Edgelands. In J. Jenkins (Ed.) *Remaking the landscape.* London: Profile Books.
Sullivan, R. (2004). *Rats: observations on the history and habitat of the city's most unwanted inhabitants.* New York: Bloomsbury.
Sywester, R. & Cho, J. (1993). Students at risk: what brain research says about paying attention. *Educational Leadership,* 50(4), 71-75.
Tunnicliffe, S., Boulter, C, & Reiss, M. (2007). Pigeon - friend or foe? Children's understanding of an everyday animal. Paper presented at the British Educational Research Association Annual Conference, Institute of Education, University of London, 5-8 September 2007.
Vujakovic, P. (2011). Animal? Vegetable? Mineral? In Vera Möller *Fictional Hybrids.* Ashford: Stour Valley Arts.
Woolfson, E. (2013). *Field notes from a hidden city: an urban nature diary.* London: Granta.

Dawn L. Sanders
Institute of Pedagogical, Curricular and Professional Studies,
Gothenburg University,
Sweden

Carolyn J. Boulter
Charles Darwin Trust,
Institute of Education,
University of London,
UK

D. L. SANDERS, C. J. BOULTER & M. J. REISS

Michael J. Reiss
Institute of Education,
University of London,
UK

ABOUT THE CONTRIBUTORS

Ruth Amos is a lecturer in science education at the Institute of Education, University of London where she has for many years been undertaking research into the opportunities presented by outdoor learning. She graduated with a degree in chemistry from the University of Bristol and worked as an environmental researcher in the field of degradation and persistence of pesticides. She is committed to education for sustainability.

Ruth Barlow studied philosophy and mathematics at Lancaster University, before completing a research degree in the history of philosophy. She has worked as a policy consultant in local and central government and a number of national charities. In 2011 she became a member of the Darwin clan by marrying Charles' great-great-grandson Jeremy Barlow. She is the company secretary of the Charles Darwin Trust, responsible for the management of the Trust's collections.

Carolyn J. Boulter taught science in secondary schools after taking a BSc in biological Sciences. Her PhD in the speech of collaborative learning in primary science was followed by initial teacher training and research in science education at the University of Reading. Latterly, at the Institute of Education, University of London, she researched children's understandings of the natural world. She is a Fellow of the Linnean Society. She was a consultant to the Charles Darwin Trust from 2006-2012.

Martin Braund is Adjunct Professor at Cape Peninsula University of Technology in Cape Town, South Africa and Honorary Fellow in the Department of Education at the University of York. After graduating in zoology and geology from Exeter University he taught science in secondary schools in Cardiff, York and Boroughbridge for 18 years. His research interests are in teacher and biology education, particularly the use of drama.

Mike Corbishley has spent his working life promoting heritage education in a variety of ways. He was appointed the first education officer at the Council for British Archaeology in 1977 and was later Head of Education at English Heritage where he was responsible for commissioning the interpretation scheme at Down House. He now teaches postgraduate courses in archaeology and education at the Institute of Archaeology, UCL and at Eleusis in Greece for the University of Kent.

ABOUT THE CONTRIBUTORS

James T. Costa is Executive Director of the Highlands Biological Station and Professor of Biology at Western Carolina University, where he teaches biogeography, Darwin's *Origin* and a field course on teaching evolution. He also co-teaches Harvard's Darwin course in the UK. His research ranges from social evolution to the history of evolutionary biology. He authored *The Other Insect Societies* (2006), *The Annotated Origin* (2009) and *On the Organic Law of Change* (2013), all from Harvard University Press.

Paul Davies is Lecturer in Science Education at the Institute of Education, University of London. Before training to be a science teacher he gained a PhD in evolutionary biology. He has particular research interests in the role that out of classroom experiences play in biology education and the use of technology in supporting learning in science. He taught for 10 years in London schools before moving to work in teacher education.

Aaron M. Ellison is the Senior Research Fellow in Ecology at the Harvard Forest, and an adjunct research professor in the Departments of Biology and Environmental Conservation at the University of Massachusetts at Amherst. He received his BA in East Asian philosophy from Yale University in 1982 and his PhD in evolutionary ecology from Brown University in 1986. In 2012, he was elected a Fellow of the Ecological Society of America.

Tina Gianquitto is Associate Professor of Literature at the Colorado School of Mines. She has authored *Good observers of nature: American women and the scientific study of the natural world, 1820-1885* (2007), as well as articles and book chapters on women naturalists and, in a different vein, on Jack London and evolutionary theory. She has received fellowships from The Huntington Library, the National Endowment for the Humanities and the American Council of Learned Societies.

Peter & Rosemary Grant have been studying Darwin's finches on the Galápagos islands since 1973. Rosemary was initially trained at the University of Edinburgh, received a PhD degree from Uppsala University, and was a Research scholar and lecturer with the rank of Professor in the Department of Ecology and Evolutionary Biology at Princeton University until she retired from teaching in 2008. Peter is the Class of 1877 Professor Emeritus in the same Department, having trained at Cambridge University and the University of British Columbia. Before joining Princeton in 1986 he taught at McGill University and the University of Michigan. Their books include Grant, P. R. & Grant, B. R. (2008) *How and Why Species Multiply*, Princeton University Press, and Grant, P. R. & Grant, B. R. (2014) *40 Years of Evolution. Darwin's Finches of Daphne Major Island*, Princeton University Press.

ABOUT THE CONTRIBUTORS

Margarita Hernández-Laille is Doctor *cum laude* on Sciences of Education with Extraordinary Prize, has a degree in philosophy and sciences of education, and has an MSc in advanced studies on theory and history of education. She is a researcher at the Manes Centre (UNED). Her research and books focus on the teaching of Darwinism in England and Spain. She is a Fellow of the Linnean Society of London and representative for Spain of the Society for the History of Natural History.

Neil Ingram taught biology in English secondary schools for over 20 years. Since this time, he has been involved in A-level biology assessment and is a co-author of a popular GCSE biology textbook for schools. He has a PhD in plant genetics and now trains secondary science teachers on an initial teacher training course in the University of Bristol, where he also teaches a master's course on the ethical issues of teaching evolution in schools.

Karen E. James is a staff scientist at Mount Desert Island Biological Laboratory in Maine, USA. She works at the intersection of research, education and outreach to adapt DNA-assisted species identification (DNA barcoding) for use in projects involving public participation in scientific research (citizen science). She is also co-founder and director of the HMS Beagle Trust, a UK-based charity working together with its sister charity in Chile, La Fundación Beagle, to rebuild *HMS Beagle*.

Susan Johnson had a teaching career of 17 years and then became Senior Education Officer for the Royal Horticultural Society, during which time she won a silver gilt medal for the exhibit 'Gardening education and science' at the Chelsea Flower Show and completed a PhD on models of gardening in education. She was the first educational consultant for the Charles Darwin Trust and initiated the transposition of Darwin's works into lessons that could be incorporated within school science.

Peter Kennett has a BSc (Hons) in geology from University College London and an MSc in applied geophysics at Durham University. He worked with the British Antarctic Survey as a field geophysicist for five years and then received his teaching certificate (PGCE) from Birmingham University after which he taught in state schools. He is a founder member and past Chairman of the Earth Science Teachers' Association in the UK (ESTA) and co-founded the Earth Science Education Unit (ESEU).

Randal Keynes, OBE, FLS is a British conservationist, author and great-great-grandson of Charles Darwin. He is the author of the intimate exploration of his famous ancestry, *Annie's Box*, subtitled *Darwin, his daughter, and human evolution* (2001), a book about the relationship between Darwin and his daughter Annie, whose early death deeply affected him. He has taken a leading role in the campaign to have Down House, Darwin's former home, designated a World Heritage Site.

ABOUT THE CONTRIBUTORS

Chris King studied BSc (Hons) in geology at Bristol University and worked as a diamond prospector for De Beers in southern Africa and Australia for five years. He has an MSc in sedimentology from Reading University and a teaching certificate (PGCE) from Keele University. He is Professor of Earth Science Education at Keele University and Director of the Earth Science Education Unit (ESEU). He is a past Chairman of the Earth Science Teachers' Association in the UK (ESTA).

Ralph Levinson is Reader in Education at the Institute of Education, University of London. He was the author of *Valuable lessons* on the teaching of controversial biological topics in schools. He has since written widely on the topic and given many seminars and talks. He taught for 14 years in comprehensive schools in London before teaching in higher education.

Miranda Lowe is the Collections Manager of the Aquatic Invertebrates Division, Life Sciences Department, the Natural History Museum (NHM), London. She is a scientific expert in pericardia crustacea and she specifically cares for and maintains the Museum's preserved crustacea collections which are also aligned with her marine biodiversity research. Darwin's barnacles are amongst some of the historical treasures under her curatorial care.

Ola Magntorn is a senior lecturer in science education at Kristianstad University, Sweden. His PhD thesis was about students' understanding of ecosystems and cycles in nature. His research is mainly based on student learning and activities in outdoor environments. Prior to his position as a researcher at the university, Ola had a long teaching experience in biology ranging from primary school to upper secondary school students.

James Moore is co-author with Adrian Desmond of the best-selling biography *Darwin* (1991), now published in 10 languages, and *Darwin's sacred cause: race, slavery and the quest for human origins* (2009). His other books include *The Darwin legend* (1994) and *The post-Darwinian controversies* (1979). With degrees in science, divinity and history, and a PhD from Manchester University, he is Professor of the History of Science at the Open University.

Emma Newall is a freelance science communication consultant experienced in interpreting topics in biological science for a variety of audiences. She worked for a number of years as a medical researcher, studying the control of gene expression, and then as a genetic counsellor. She has worked with the Charles Darwin Trust since 2008, supporting the Trust's programmes for schools and developing relationships with the science education community.

ABOUT THE CONTRIBUTORS

Ruth Padel FRSL, FZS is a British poet, an author known also for her poetry criticism, nature writing and connections with science, music and conservation and a novelist. She has a PhD on Greek poetry and is a great-great-grand-daughter of Charles Darwin. She broadcasts for BBC Radio 3 and 4, especially on poetry, literature, music and wildlife. She is on the board of the Zoological Society of London and is active in promoting its global conservation through literary programmes.

Vaughan Prain is Professor in the Faculty of Education, La Trobe University, Bendigo. He has over 30 years of teaching experience in undergraduate and postgraduate programmes at La Trobe, and in Canada, the UK, the USA and Spain. His main research focus addresses learning the literacies of science, defined broadly as learning how to interpret and construct the multi-modal representational practices of this subject area. He has also won awards for papers in *Teaching Science*.

Michael J. Reiss is Professor of Science Education at the Institute of Education, University of London. After a PhD and post-doctoral research in evolutionary biology and population genetics, he trained as a teacher and taught in the secondary school sector. Books of his include Reiss, M. J. & White, J. (2013) *An aims-based curriculum*, IOE Press and Jones, L. & Reiss, M. J. (Eds) (2007) *Teaching about scientific origins: taking account of creationism*.

Dawn L. Sanders is an Associate Professor at Göteborgs Universitet, Sweden and a Fellow of the Linnean Society. Her doctoral study (Sussex University, 2004) examined the educational role of botanic gardens, a study inspired by her ten years as an educator in the Chelsea Physic Garden, London. She trained as an artist before completing her botanical education and draws on both in her academic work. Dawn is a scientific associate of the Natural History Museum, London.

Sandra Escovedo Selles has a first degree in biology and after working as a secondary biology teacher, since 1992 she has worked as Associated Professor at the Universidade Federal Fluminense, Brazil. She was the President of the Brazilian Association for Biology Education from 2007 to 2011 and was recently elected as President of the Brazilian Association for Science Education. Her research interests involve curriculum studies, teacher education and public understanding of science.

Shirley Simon is Professor of Education at the Institute of Education, University of London. She began her career as a chemistry and biology teacher in secondary schools in Sussex and London. She developed an interest in enquiry and assessment, which led to her doctoral study that featured curriculum innovation in enquiry. She has also worked on funded research projects focusing on progression in learning and children's perceptions of learning in mathematics and science.

ABOUT THE CONTRIBUTORS

Sally Stafford is an experienced researcher and education consultant creating bespoke resources for informal and formal learning audiences for the heritage and museums sector. She currently works as Education and Outreach Officer for the Darwin Correspondence Project at the University of Cambridge.

John L. Taylor is Head of Philosophy and Director of Critical Skills at Rugby School. He studied physics and philosophy at Balliol College, Oxford before going on to do a PhD in philosophy and to teach philosophy of science at the university. In 1999 he moved to Rugby School to teach physics. He directed the Perspectives on Science Project. He is a Chief Examiner for the Extended Project and has been a Visiting Fellow of the Institute of Education, University of London.

Stephen P. Tomkins graduated from Cambridge University in natural sciences, trained as a teacher and taught in East Africa for seven years. He returned to England where he taught, as Head of Biology, in secondary community colleges and at Hills Road Sixth Form College in Cambridge before becoming Head of Science at Homerton College, Cambridge. At Homerton he pioneered fast-plants, was a brine-shrimp bottle-ecology devotee and researched into children's observations of living things.

Sue Dale Tunnicliffe graduated in zoology from Westfield College, London, then took a teaching qualification at the London Institute of Education. She holds a PhD from King's College, entitled *Talking about animals: studies of young children visiting zoos, a museum and a farm*. Previously Head of Education at the Zoological Society of London, she is the co-author of Patrick and Tunnicliffe (2013) *Zoo Talk*, Springer, a researcher and Reader at the Institute of Education, University of London.

James D. Williams is a lecturer in science education at the University of Sussex. He graduated in geology and, after training as a secondary science teacher, taught biology and science in a variety of secondary schools. He has extensive experience in teaching and teacher education, working in a variety of state schools as a head of department, head of year and assistant head-teacher. He has written a number of single-authored books and co-authored a major key stage 3 science textbook series.

INDEX

A

Adam Sedgwick, 16, 40, 44n6, 202
Adaptation, 8, 9, 61, 66, 149, 157, 216, 252, 303–305, 315, 320, 327, 341, 342, 346, 356, 359, 368, 370, 374, 391, 392, 394
Alfred Russel Wallace, 7, 49, 60, 73, 168, 199, 201, 205, 207, 209n1, 238, 239, 257, 269n7, 315
Annie Darwin, 91, 94, 295, 296, 411
Apes-orangutan, 17
Argumentation, 1, 5, 167, 168, 170–173, 289, 297, 343, 378, 384, 385, 413
Art, 36, 74, 120, 340, 385, 395, 405, 414, 418, 420
Artificial selection, 111, 112n7, 244, 392, 394

B

Barbara McClintock, 417
Barnacles, 2, 3, 7, 8, 10, 18, 92, 98, 117, 203, 206, 273–283, 283n9, 283n11, 336, 359, 377, 407
Beagle, 1, 2, 8, 16–20, 25, 27, 35, 37, 60, 74, 75, 77, 79, 82, 86n1, 86n9, 86n15, 90, 93, 98, 119, 131–145, 160, 167, 169, 179, 180, 183, 184, 186, 187, 189, 190, 199, 202, 203, 205, 233, 274, 280, 283n8, 286, 294, 321n10, 327, 345, 354, 367, 377, 385, 395, 404, 412, 418
Beetles, 4, 15, 20, 47, 94–98, 107, 159, 202, 354, 377, 383
Behaviour, 9, 27, 42, 51, 52, 63, 65, 132–134, 144, 148, 151, 157, 170, 225, 254n7, 290, 292, 302, 303, 331, 332, 344, 346, 347, 355, 375, 378, 379, 389, 415

Brazil, 37, 73, 74, 80, 85, 86n11, 181, 188, 286, 404, 420
Brine shrimps, 153, 154
Broad bean, 21
Bruner, 50, 150, 399, 407
Bumblebees, 20, 389

C

Cambridge University, 2, 22n2, 33n2, 35, 41, 93, 107, 321n11, 363n4, 419
Carnivorous plants, 7, 8, 27, 28, 134, 243–255, 299, 300, 302–307, 308n2, 315, 357, 359
Charles Lyell, 7, 16, 27, 136, 167, 188, 194, 238, 253n3, 308n3, 314
Cirripedes, 18, 273, 274, 278
Classifying, 147, 153, 171, 360
Climbing plants, 9, 10, 31, 206, 301, 328, 346, 353, 359, 383, 384
Collecting, 15, 18, 36, 39, 47, 49, 94, 95, 101, 150, 157, 159–161, 201, 202, 259, 274, 275, 280, 286, 348, 360, 383, 407, 411, 421
Common ancestry, 360
Corals, 194
Correspondence networks, 27
Countryside, 15, 17, 19, 22, 25, 28, 53, 93, 131, 159, 160, 243, 258, 345, 353, 354, 357, 367, 411, 413
Creationism, 6, 211, 214–218, 231, 232, 240, 241, 384
Critical thinking, 5–7, 127, 195, 213, 297, 345, 360
Curiosity, x, 15, 35, 36, 43, 47, 48, 55, 60, 64, 69, 84, 96, 135, 161, 339, 340, 345–348, 359, 367, 376, 378, 420, 422

431

Curriculum, 1, 2, 6, 10, 37, 38, 44, 48, 50, 51, 55, 62, 75, 80, 81, 85, 95, 118, 121, 148, 169, 171, 179, 184, 237, 293, 297, 340, 353, 355, 356, 358, 363, 369–372, 383, 384, 399

D

Darwin children, 89
Darwin Correspondence Project, 2, 35–44, 49, 128n1, 128n3–5, 282n2, 395
Deductive, 11, 132, 147, 202–205, 208, 244, 412
Dewey, 47, 134, 216
Diversity, 2, 4, 6, 7, 9, 28, 33, 60, 70, 74, 79, 85, 118, 131, 134, 137, 144, 147, 159, 161, 201, 207, 211, 214, 215, 224, 257, 258, 266, 279, 280, 331, 332, 353, 368, 370, 372, 413, 417
DNA, 7, 112, 225, 252, 257–269, 336, 337, 343, 344, 357, 358, 363n1
Domestication, 132
Down House, 2, 4, 7, 10, 15, 17, 19, 20, 22n1, 25, 26, 28, 29, 32, 33n1, 35, 47, 52, 53, 89–93, 98–100, 103n1, 107, 109, 111, 112n4, 118, 131, 133, 145, 145n1, 171, 257–269, 275, 345, 353, 361, 367, 373, 375, 379, 384, 390, 403, 404, 415
Downe village, 33, 90, 258
Drama, 8, 29, 285–297, 340, 385, 395, 413
Drawings, 98, 172, 278, 332, 334, 420

E

Earth, age of, 241
Earthworms, 22, 26, 29, 30, 60, 64, 69, 100, 110, 118, 128n3, 134, 144, 233, 387, 388
Ecological Literacy, 3, 59, 61, 66, 68
Ecosystems, 62, 65, 66–68, 70, 252, 253, 255n13

Edinburgh University, 201, 354
Elizabeth Darwin, 90
Embryology, 17, 277
Emma Darwin, 17, 21, 36, 44n4, 81, 89–91, 95, 100, 103n4, 117, 123, 131, 161, 411, 412
Enquiry, 4, 5, 9, 16, 48, 53, 55, 117, 122, 128n7, 133–135, 140, 144, 165–173, 240–242, 252, 327, 328, 330, 332, 336, 337, 340, 371, 379, 411, 422
Entangled Bank, 25, 33, 55, 328, 389, 393
Erasmus Darwin – brother and grandfather, 158, 159, 201, 207
Ernest Mayr, 84, 214, 222, 358
Ernst Haeckel, 59, 60, 318
Everyday materials, 360
Experimentation, 2, 21, 25, 27, 134, 167, 244, 311, 328, 347, 349, 379, 418
Experiments, ix, 2, 4, 5, 7, 15, 17–19, 21, 25–29, 31, 41, 42, 101, 110, 117, 118, 131, 133–135, 137–141, 144, 145, 159, 166, 167, 200, 207, 208, 228, 243–255, 297, 353, 357, 367, 368, 370–374, 376, 378, 379, 383–386, 391, 404, 407
Expression of emotion, 415
Extinction, 26, 153, 155, 181, 368, 370, 376

F

Fertilisation in plants, 32, 315
Finches, 16, 169, 170, 192, 202, 203, 233, 353, 360, 392, 394
Fools experiments, 21
Fossil cirripedes, 278
Fossils, 47, 132, 173, 181, 187, 188, 202, 204, 224, 229, 286, 316, 319, 368, 383
Francis Darwin, 32, 92, 96, 99, 101, 102, 103n19, 139, 140, 207, 208, 249, 254n5–7, 314,

Freshwater shrimp, 3, 62, 63, 69, 70
Froebal, 47

G

Galapagos, ix, 16, 17, 22, 25, 37, 69, 169, 181, 192, 202, 203, 233, 327, 353, 360, 385, 392, 411
Genes, 112, 214, 224, 226, 227, 231, 232, 292, 343, 344, 358
Geological time, 136, 214, 368
Geology, 40, 86n15, 101, 119, 167, 194, 199, 201–204, 207, 313–317, 321n4–5, 321n13, 321n19
George Darwin, 90, 95, 97, 99, 100, 101, 117, 118
Georges Cuvier, 7, 8, 26, 238, 275
Gilbert White, 18, 31
Great Pucklands, 7, 257–259, 264–266, 268, 269, 404, 413
Greenhouses, 52, 253, 282n3

H

Habitats, 2, 10, 17, 28, 55, 59, 167, 254n5, 279, 304, 368, 371, 377, 379, 384, 391, 413
Hand Lens, 20, 135, 367, 383, 394, 414
Hands-on, 4, 5, 19, 134, 161, 177, 340, 360, 387
Henrietta Darwin, 4, 90, 99, 100, 102, 302
Herbert Spencer, 180, 314
Honeybees, 328, 389
Hops, 411
Horace Darwin, 29, 92, 95, 96, 100, 101, 103n16, 109, 110, 112n5
Hypothesis, ix, 11, 16, 26, 53, 122, 132, 138, 140, 153, 160, 194, 202, 203, 205, 206, 209, 244, 247, 250, 253, 266, 341

I

Imagination, ix, 11, 29, 51, 84, 93, 287, 301–303, 337, 339, 340, 347, 374, 385, 386, 407, 408, 413, 421, 422

Inductive, 16, 132, 203, 205, 208, 222, 226, 278
Inheritance, 19, 30, 31, 98, 100, 108, 113n10, 244, 251, 295, 315, 319, 342–345, 359, 363, 368, 370, 383
Insectivorous plants, 27, 31, 41, 42, 47, 245, 246, 249–252, 254n4–5, 254n7, 300–303, 305, 308n11, 328, 377, 407
Intelligent design, 207, 217, 231, 232, 240, 241, 341, 384
Investigations, 4, 5, 18, 19, 21, 27, 28, 50, 120, 134, 135, 144, 166, 177, 209, 230, 242n1, 280, 345, 359, 378, 385, 414

J

James Audubon, 413
Jean-Baptise Lamarck, 160, 201, 232, 294
John Henslow, 16, 257
Joseph Hooker, 49, 91, 141, 168, 257, 275, 278, 283n4, 283n10, 286, 306, 390, 393, 395n4
Joseph Sowerby, 278, 283n11

K

Karl Popper, 203
Kent, 17, 25, 28, 30, 32, 35, 52, 53, 97, 109, 131, 181, 257, 258, 345, 353, 357, 367, 391, 411
Kew Gardens, 19, 92, 141, 155

L

Laboratory, 2, 4, 15, 19, 21, 25–33, 36, 74, 131, 133, 179, 200, 201, 207–209, 248, 264, 275, 282n3, 297, 302, 339, 345, 357, 360, 385, 399
Leonard Darwin, 29, 90, 95, 96, 100–102, 103n18, 403
Letters, ix, 2, 16, 19, 25, 29, 35–44, 49, 60, 74, 89, 94, 99, 100, 101, 132, 275, 282n2, 368, 372, 373, 378, 394, 395, 403, 406, 407, 413

INDEX

Life cycles, 10, 64, 155, 368, 371, 373–375, 379, 384, 389, 392
London Zoological Gardens, 19

M

Mary Treat, 8, 27, 28, 41, 44n7, 302
Mathematics, 66, 127, 297, 346, 356, 375
Microscope, 3, 8, 92–94, 97, 98, 102, 203, 273, 274, 276, 281, 357, 358, 389, 406, 407, 414, 417
Miss Thorley, 7, 67, 90, 257, 259, 404
Mockingbird, 16, 17
Montessori, 47
Movement in Plants, 134, 254n10
Multi-Modal, 328, 330, 417, 418

N

Narrative, 8, 10, 11, 32, 37, 119, 149, 157, 159, 223, 231, 257, 275, 281, 294, 299–308, 345–349, 399–409, 411–413, 419, 420
Natural History museum, 7, 10, 20, 107, 108, 111, 112, 172, 258, 268, 269, 273, 279, 282, 283n8, 311, 385, 400, 401, 408, 409n1
North America, 151, 153, 413
Notebooks, ix, 17, 25, 29, 74, 107, 117, 179, 188, 199, 205, 328, 360, 367, 386, 391, 407, 413, 418, 419

O

On the Origin of species, 1, 4, 9, 16, 18, 25, 28–30, 32, 40, 89, 96, 99, 100, 108, 109, 113n10, 131, 140, 168, 207, 211, 218, 222, 223, 227, 244, 250, 253n3, 258, 275, 278, 280, 283n16, 294, 299, 300, 314, 315, 317, 320, 328, 330, 367, 370, 393, 394, 403, 408, 409n1, 412, 417, 418
Orchids, 31, 93, 301, 359, 407
Outdoors, 60, 93, 419

P

Paying attention, 11, 75, 360, 414
Pestalozzi, 47, 117, 123, 128n2
Peter Grant, ix, x, 392, 421
Philosophy, 6, 134, 150, 200, 206, 218, 230, 237–242, 319, 390
Photography, 95, 357
Phylogeny, 8, 267, 281, 282, 336, 356, 363
Piaget, 148
Piagetian, 153
Pigeons, 3, 25, 91, 92, 111, 112n9, 359, 368, 379, 392, 394, 395n2–3, 407, 408, 411
Poetry, 97, 285, 286, 395, 412, 413, 415
Pollen, 36, 161, 314, 376, 389, 390
Psychology/child development, 5, 22, 147, 150, 152, 212, 297

Q

Questioning, 20, 25, 122, 125, 127, 134, 157, 170, 242, 280, 339, 356, 360, 378, 379, 418, 419

R

Reading nature, 3, 59–63, 66, 67, 69, 70, 420–422
Reductionism, 214
Religion, 1, 6, 40, 223, 227, 230, 233, 237, 241, 242n3, 253n1, 311, 313, 316, 317
Representation, 9, 68, 152, 281, 327, 328, 330–335, 370, 386, 400, 403, 409n2, 417, 420, 421
Richard Owen, 168, 172, 283n8, 406, 409n7
Robert Grant, 16, 160
Role-play, 8, 289, 290, 334, 372
Rosemary Grant, ix, x, 392, 421

S

Sandwalk, 20, 90, 96, 353, 367, 375
School Gardens, 47, 311, 413

434

Seeds, 29, 95, 121, 134, 135, 137–144, 151, 155, 169, 170, 249, 268, 373, 376, 383, 390, 391
Selective breeding, 9, 244, 346
Simulations, 8, 285, 288–290, 292, 293, 331, 336
Slavery, 1, 3, 37, 79, 80, 84, 85, 300
South America, 16, 17, 86n1, 187, 274
Species change, 17, 131, 132, 277, 278, 341, 342, 359, 392
Species counts, 7, 257
Species theory, 16, 18, 274, 277, 278
Struggle for survival, 29, 306, 393
Student-centred, 55
Survival of the Fittest, 299

T

Taxonomy, 8, 16–18, 61, 62, 70, 153, 154, 265, 266, 276, 279–282, 360
Theodosius Dobzhansky, 199
Thomas Huxley, 49, 92, 168, 172
Thomas Kuhn, 213, 238
Thomas Malthus, 17
Transition, 10, 133, 287, 312, 383–395, 415–417

V

Variation, ix, 9, 16, 21, 38, 85, 111, 113n10, 123, 168, 171, 214, 217, 221, 222, 232, 244, 253, 277, 278, 290, 294, 314, 315, 317, 321n10, 336, 341, 342, 346, 347, 353, 360, 367, 370, 392
Victorian Society, 40
Vygotsky, 50

W

Wedgwood, 44, 70, 160, 182, 357
Weeds, 10, 25, 29, 141, 371, 375, 384, 393, 407, 411
Wilberforce, S., 7, 81, 83, 223, 227, 228, 233, 238, 294
William Whewell, 132, 200
William Wilberforce, 7, 81, 83, 223, 227, 228, 233, 238, 294
Wilson, E.O., 4, 144, 153
Worms, 25, 29, 36, 55, 60, 99, 109, 110, 121, 274, 359, 377, 387, 388, 393, 411
Writing, ix, x, 8, 9, 15, 22, 25, 29, 31, 36, 38, 39, 59, 64, 73, 75, 77, 86n6, 91, 118, 122, 144, 148, 149, 159, 160, 172, 173, 179, 180, 211, 233, 239, 257, 275, 275, 299, 322n31, 327–337, 340, 342, 345, 349, 353, 385, 399, 403, 407, 411–413, 418

Z

Zone of Proximal Development, 50